SHELLEY

WATER–COLOR PORTRAIT BELIEVED TO BE THE
LOST MINIATURE OF SHELLEY
BY EDWARD ELLERKER WILLIAMS

Here first published through the generosity of the owner, Mrs. W. Murray Crane

SHELLEY

BY

NEWMAN IVEY WHITE

VOLUME
I

ALFRED A KNOPF : NEW YORK
1940

PREFACE

In the hundred and eighteen years since Shelley's death he has
been the subject of more than a dozen biographies, exclusive of
the reminiscences and memoirs of his wife and three of his
friends. Two biographies, those of Professor Dowden and Professor Peck, have been " full-length " ones.

And yet no biographer of Shelley except Dowden has had access to two of the most important primary sources, the joint
journals of Shelley and Mary and the journals of Jane, or Claire,
Clairmont. This lack alone was sufficient to render Professor
Peck's biography inconclusive, whatever its other faults and virtues may be. But in the more than a half-century since Professor Dowden wrote, and even in the twelve years since Professor
Peck's work was published, much additional material has appeared. The diary of Harriet Grove, most of Shelley's correspondence with his first wife, the true text of the many letters
to Hogg which have previously been published in a garbled
form intended to conceal certain facts, the important letter of
William Godwin on Shelley's elopement with Mary, the surprising letters of Mary Shelley to Hogg in 1815, and numerous other
smaller items were unknown to both Dowden and Peck. The
amount and quality of the attention Shelley received from the
reviewers were considerably underestimated. In the one item
of letters, the most important single source in Shelley's case,
Professor Dowden had access to not more than a hundred and
fifty of Shelley's letters as compared with more than six hundred now available. The extensive body of scholarly and critical literature generated by the growing recognition of Shelley's
importance since 1886 has made contributions to knowledge
that were only partly integrated by Professor Peck with the
full-length biography of the poet. Shelley is now generally recognized as one of the four or five greatest English poets since

Shakespeare. If another full-length biography could be based on all the important basic materials accessible only to Professor Dowden and also upon the mass of new materials that has since accumulated, and if the additional perspective of time has any critical value, surely a new full-length biography of such an important poet as Shelley is needed. The present work claims all these advantages, whether or not it has used them well.

So much for the formal justification which writers on well-worn subjects always feel bullied into advancing. Actually I wrote this book because twenty-four years of studying, teaching, and writing about Shelley made me think that in some respects I could add to and refine the body of truth which is necessary to the understanding of so great a poet and personality.

The responsibilities of a biographer are so intensely serious that it is hard not to appear a little pompous in adverting to them. Nevertheless I should like to state as briefly as possible the principles according to which I have tried to write. Fidelity to fact, the primary principle, which in a sense includes all the others, is never fully attained because of limitations of both data and personality. It involves the duty of suppressing nothing of possible importance and of proportioning the treatment so as to magnify or minimize nothing beyond its true significance.

Only less important than the abstract truth is justice to personality, which is also impossible of complete attainment, since both the biographer and his subject have probably several personalities, according to different points of view. No subject of a biography ever lived primarily for the purpose of allowing someone to write cleverly about him, as some biographers have assumed. His world was never the two-dimensional one of the printed page to which biographer and reader both tend to reduce it. He was once much more alive upon the three-dimensional earth than the biographer himself. As living persons he and his friends may have had facts to conceal, facts which the biographer is compelled to seek for if his work is to be genuinely truthful, though he may at times feel uncomfortably intrusive in doing so. Then, as always, he must remember that though the subject of a biography may be dead and beyond the possibility of writhing, his personality is still alive (else why write about him?), and still sensitive to injustice against which the biographer alone may be capable of offering a defence.

Attempts to be witty or profound commonly warp the straight grain of truth and justice. Cleverness and brilliance usually score their points *for* the biographer and *against* his subject. The " style " may indeed be the man, but it is too often not the man for whom the reader's interest has been engaged. No style can disguise the fact that certain passages in the life of any person are dull except in their relation (present or future) to a larger, comprehensive truth. The best the biographer can do is to keep himself as far as possible in the background and try as unobtrusively as he can to provide his readers with every opportunity of forming just judgments of their own.

Having thus ventured to suggest a biographical creed, I may be pardoned a few supplementary remarks on how I have attempted to apply it.

According to these views, I may have worked such expressions as " apparently," " perhaps," " probably," " it seems," etc., somewhat beyond the tolerance of rapid readers of rapid biography. In such cases I confess candidly that the fault was intentional, against my own inclination to be more positive, and due to my own " sheer ignorance " of the absolute truth. I have invented no conversations, though I have repeated some upon authority; and I have imputed no thoughts to any person without clearly stating or implying good authority. Feeling that any reader so inclined should be able to probe any statement of fact, I have given references for practically all such statements that are not self-evident or trivial; and in all or most cases of testimony I have offered materials for judging the reliability of the witness. This has produced a multiplicity of notes and comments which for many it would be intolerable to read entire. I have therefore offered what relief I could by distinguishing between notes that are mere citations of authority and notes that contain additional information or opinion. The index-numbers for the latter are printed in italics.

It should be evident that certain peculiarities in the subject result in what may seem to be peculiarities in the treatment. The extraordinary extent to which the mature Shelley seems to be an expression of his boyhood and youth results in a rather closer analysis of these periods, I believe, than other biographers have thought necessary. The evident great influence of Shelley's reading upon his thought and conduct, the importance of his strong sense of mission, the frequent close interrelation of health and mental peculiarities with each other and with conduct, have prompted a rather special attention to these subjects. Though I speak of these peculiarities as evident, I believe that hitherto they have not been evident enough.

Some readers may think that Shelley's mental peculiarities should have been pursued to the point of Freudian analysis. It will seem obvious to them, as it sometimes seems to me, that Shelley was a bundle of complexes. Lacking the requirements laid down by Professor Freud — experience as both a practitioner and a subject of psychoanalysis — I am unqualified for such an undertaking. Lack of proper qualifications, however, might have deterred me no more than others, except that I do not believe such an approach yet consistent with the larger purposes of biography. To catalogue a genius according to the terminology of a science or art — and a new one at that — is to ticket him according to certain common denominators and to obscure the very genius which rebelled against being ticketed. It is a fair inference from Professor Freud himself that the average mind may never be able to interpret correctly the proper boundaries between the conscious and the unconscious. Thus the only psychology yet proper for general biography has seemed to me to be the psychology whose most distinguished practitioners died long before the gods of psychology were born — the common-sense judgment of actions and motives that does not require special techniques and terminologies to make them fairly comprehensible.

Rather than risk falling unconsciously into any rut of previous thought, I have written as nearly as possible *de novo,* basing my statements almost entirely upon the original sources. In general, I have used previous biographies, except personal reminiscences, only for purposes of correction, after the individual chapters were written from the primary sources.

For my use of the most important primary sources previously

available only to Professor Dowden, I am indebted to the interest and generosity of the late Mr. T. J. Wise, who allowed me to make photostats of *Shelley and Mary,* the manuscript journals of Maria and John Gisborne, various unpublished letters, and the manuscript journals of Claire Clairmont, except for a missing section very kindly supplied by Mr. Carl Pforzheimer. I have also received useful suggestions from discussions with my colleagues. To list here the scores of people — librarians, booksellers, manuscript dealers, scholars, personal connections or descendants of characters about whom information was needed, students, clerical assistants, readers, furnishers of technical information, granters of necessary permissions, useful conversational victims — who have been helpful to me would be impossible and might seem ostentatious. One of the happiest feelings about completing a book is the renewed confidence of the author in the mutual goodwill and helpfulness of hundreds of scholars the world over. Of the many to whom I feel indebted I have endeavoured to mention specifically in particular notes most of those whose contributions were positive; but many equally useful negative contributions have had to go unrecorded, though they have not been received without both profit and gratitude. For several grants which were a very valuable help in obtaining materials and clerical aid I am indebted to the Research Council of Duke University.

A very special acknowledgment is due Henry Holt and Company, of New York, for their generosity in allowing me to retain in my text the summaries and other statements drawn from Professor George Stuart Gordon's *Shelley Letters,* the publication of which has been unavoidably delayed by the war in Europe and by other circumstances beyond Professor Gordon's control. While it was yet hoped that this valuable contribution would precede the present work I was allowed to make use of the galley proofs. Afterwards I was generously given permission to retain these materials.

N. I. W.

CONTENTS

VOLUME I

ILLUSTRATIONS

VOLUME I

SHELLEY

VOLUME I

Chapter I

THE BACKGROUND

SHELLEY'S BIRTHPLACE; HIS ANCESTRY
AND PARENTAGE; THE TIMES

IN the late eighteenth century the pleasant southeastern county of Sussex had almost forgotten some of its former glories. The puissant Cinque Ports of Plantaganet times had degenerated into towns of secondary importance or mere watering-places. The remains of feudal grandeur that caused Horace Walpole to regard eastern Sussex as "the Holy Land of Gothic abbeys and castles" were of antiquarian interest only. A once flourishing iron industry had moved nearer the northern coal-fields, leaving only shallow pits to be utilized occasionally as fish ponds. Only about a third of the land was arable, and much of this was of poor quality. The principal products — potatoes, grain, and hops — were hardly more than enough to supply local markets. The domestic manufacture of woollen fabrics was expiring under the new competition in the north.

Sussex oak, however, retained its former eminence in providing timber for English ships and English homes. The Sussex downs still kept their ancient importance as grazing land. Southdown cattle supplied many a cattle-market with its best breed. Yoked in teams of eight, in order to conserve their weight for the cattle-market, they ploughed the rather stubborn clayey soil. During Shelley's boyhood the county supported about three hundred thousand of the best sheep in England. In the guide-books and local histories of the day there is scarcely a landscape depicted without at least a few sheep in the background.

3

Such was the region in which Percy Bysshe Shelley was born on August 4, 1792. In all its recorded history since the thirteenth century, the county of Sussex had given to literary fame only five names, those of Henry Howard, Earl of Surrey, who had an occasional residence in Horsham, Thomas Sackville, Thomas Otway, William Collins, and Bernard Lintot, the eighteenth-century publisher. The first and last of these were from Horsham. There were no particular traits of the region to mark it as an especially appropriate birthplace — unless by the rule of opposites — for England's greatest poet of radicalism. It had been the last Saxon kingdom to embrace Christianity and the slowest part of England to be affected by the Reformation. The town of Horsham furnished the last example in England, in 1735, of the old barbarous execution by pressing, and clung tenaciously to its ancient sport of bull-baiting, which was quite common there until 1814 and was not finally suppressed until Parliament abolished the sport throughout the Kingdom in 1835. If the young poet did not actually witness this sport, he certainly knew of it from eyewitnesses. "We won't be druv" was a favourite saying with which the young Shelley might have been impressed, but in Sussex, Hilaire Belloc's "the resistant county," it signified mainly a determined conservatism. As late as 1865 Sussex was still very doubtful about its greatest poet. A Sussex historian of that date approaches the subject with considerable hesitation, "knowing with what abhorrence the very name of Shelley is generally regarded among our Christian community." [1]

The towns of Warnham and Horsham, and the Shelley family seat of Field Place, lie in the northwest section of the county, from two to five miles from the Surrey line. Horsham, with a population in 1811 of 3,839, and 4,575 in 1821, was the most important town in that section of the county. It was then an assize town and was entitled to two members in the House of Commons. Its houses, between 500 and 800 in number, were of irregular dates and architecture, and were grouped mainly around the four streets called East, West, North, and South. A fine parish church (since "re-decorated") stood at the extreme south, on the banks of the Arun River. The streets were paved with local stone, cut and set irregularly, and were lined with old trees. The houses were commonly roofed with slabs of local stone that weathered in picturesque dull tones.

The town held two regular weekly markets, a corn-market on Saturday, and a poultry-market on Monday. There were cattle-markets on the last Tuesday of each month, and several fairs each year for cattle and sheep. Since the middle of the eighteenth century Horsham had been on a good highway to London, thirty-five miles to the northwest. Shortly before the coming of the railway, in 1847, the stagecoach made the journey in four hours. In general, however, most Sussex roads of the times were described by contemporaries as rather bad, because of either too much sand or too much clay in the soil.

Three miles north of Horsham is the hamlet of Warnham, with a population, in 1811, of 774. It is a place of no particular interest to the Sussex historians and topographers. Field Place, one of the three homes of country gentry then in the parish, is about a mile southeast, on the road to Horsham. It is listed by several contemporary writers as the seat of Timothy Shelley, Esq., but was never deemed worthy of any particular description in the literature of the region until it became famous as the birthplace of Percy Bysshe Shelley.

Field Place is a comfortable, undistinguished country home that had been in the possession of the Michell family for several generations. It came into the Shelley family when it was purchased in 1729 by Edward Shelley, uncle of the poet's great-grandfather Timothy, who inherited it in 1748. The house is situated in a slight depression, but commands some view of the downs and hills in the distance. It is a two-storey structure, with slightly projecting ells at either end. In Shelley's lifetime the entrance was in the centre, giving access to a central hall, which is faced by the stairway. On the left of the hall is the drawing-room; on the right, the dining-room. The room in which Shelley was born is a small, upstairs bedroom, in an angle formed by a westward projection of the northern ell from the main north-and-south lines of the building. Since the poet's death the front entrance has been changed and a pillared veranda has been added connecting the two ells. The interior of the building has

5

been changed little, if at all, since Shelley's birth, and the roof is still of the weathered grey stone known as Horsham slate that was the most individual trait of local architecture in Shelley's day.

As FAR as it can be traced back in unbroken lineal descent, the poet's ancestry is fully established by a pedigree attested by Sir Timothy Shelley and Mr. John Shelley Sidney in 1816, and deposited with the College of Heralds.[2] This pedigree stems from Henry Shelley, of Worminghurst, Esquire, who died in 1623. Shelley's eight male ancestors in the direct line are all described as squires or gentlemen. At the time of Shelley's birth no one of them had won national or even local distinction as a public servant or in any profession. Their wives were all members of good, undistinguished county families. One of them was the daughter of a knight, the others were daughters of squires, clergymen, or country gentlemen. No more than two generations of the family had maintained its seat at the same place. They are not mentioned by local historians until after the poet had attracted attention, and when they are occasionally mentioned in the early years of the Victorian era it is as likely as not to record the peculiar actions of old Sir Bysshe, with a hint of insanity, or to mention that Field Place was for generations a Michell possession and to suggest that Shelley's genius might be more easily traceable on the distaff side than in the male line.

It is probable, but not absolutely established, that this family of Shelleys was a younger branch of the Michelgrove Shelleys, an old Sussex family of real distinction.[3] They were landholders in Kent under the first Edward, and one of the family sat in Parliament from 1415 to 1428. Their family history is traceable in unbroken sequence from John Shelley, who married the heiress of Michelgrove. Of his six sons one was a Knight of Rhodes, slain when the Turks captured the island. His second son, William Shelley, attained several high distinctions under Henry VIII and was the Judge of Common Pleas whom Henry

6

FIELD PLACE, HORSHAM

Etching by A. Evershed, 1877. From the H. B. Forman edition of Shelley's Works, by permission of Mr. M. B. Forman

sent to Wolsey to demand the surrender of York House. From William Shelley's time the Michelgrove Shelleys were knights. They were baronets from the time the order was created by James I in 1611. They intermarried with a number of knightly and noble houses. The head of the Michelgrove Shelleys during most of the poet's lifetime was Sir John Shelley, M.P. for Lewes, who was fairly well known in racing and sporting circles and who furnished brief anecdotes, of somewhat lively significance, for the memoirs of several of his contemporaries.

The family fortunes of the poet's branch of the Shelleys were apparently quite modest until augmented by his grandfather. In 1692 Fen Place became the family seat through the marriage of John Shelley [4] with Hellen Bysshe, one of the heirs of that property. His third son, Timothy, succeeded to the property at the age of forty-three, having first spent some years in America. Here he had married and had become the father of two sons, the second of whom, Bysshe, was the poet's grandfather and the real founder of the family fortunes. The American home of the Shelleys was Newark, New Jersey. [5] Legal records of the family in America are with one exception too slight to have any biographical value, and the church records were destroyed by the Hessians during the War of Independence. There is no American verification of the family tradition handed on by Medwin that the poet's grandfather (meaning his great-grandfather) was a "quack doctor" in Newark. In the only significant document discovered, [6] Timothy Shelley describes himself as a merchant of Newark. The document, dated December 6, 1735, is a post-obit for £200, to be voided, however, on the payment of £100, as soon as he should have inherited Fen Place in Sussex. A post-obit depending for its validity on the prior death both of the present holder and of an intermediate heir must have realized for the borrower only a small fraction of the £100 that was to be repaid under such distant and uncertain conditions. From this one may infer that the Shelley fortunes in America were rather modest. The same document furnishes a clearer hint of the family fortunes in England when it describes Fen Place as having a value of £200 a year. [7]

7

In 1743, when his older brother John (the poet's great-great-uncle) was declared insane, Timothy Shelley probably came into control of all the estate of his father not otherwise disposed of by will. The holder of Timothy's American post-obit, executed seven years earlier, considered that document worth recording, and recorded it on May 30. Five years later, on the death of an uncle, Timothy inherited Field Place also.

A part of John Shelley's estate had been devised to the younger of Timothy's sons, Bysshe. Likewise John Shelley's widow, on her decease, left her favourite grandson much of her personal property and made provision for his education as a gentleman. He did not inherit the principal estates of the family until the death of his older brother, John, in 1790, but long before that he had acquired a considerably greater estate of his own.

Bysshe Shelley, as a youth, was tall and straight, with regular features, large brown eyes, well-marked eyebrows, and wavy brown hair. Apparently he had manners; he had probably travelled abroad as a part of the education provided for by his grandmother. He had a small inheritance of his own and an ambition to found a Shelley family of more consequence than the local squires and gentlemen who had preceded him.

His first step was his marriage with Miss Mary Catherine Michell, the sixteen-year-old orphan and heir of the Reverend Theobald Michell, of Horsham. Her guardians disapproved his courtship, so he eloped with her to London to be married at the uncritical chapel of Alexander Keith. Her family had long held an honourable position among the Sussex gentry, and her inheritance is said to have been considerable. She died at the age of twenty-five, leaving two daughters and a son, Timothy, the father of the poet.

The handsome Bysshe waited nine years before he again approached the altar. This fact hardly sorts with the view of him as a fortune-hunter purely and simply by matrimonial means. An acquisitive-minded man of his address and determination doubtless found other means of increasing his fortune. All that seems to be known, however, is the doubtful rumour [8] that he

had some financial interest in the establishment of a rather notorious medical charlatan, Dr. James Graham, in whose employ
Lord Nelson's " Emma " first attracted attention before she became Lady Hamilton.

Bysshe Shelley's second marriage was a really astonishing
one. At the age of thirty-eight, with a family of three children,
he married Miss Elizabeth Jane Sidney Perry, who from her
birth and fortune might have been expected to marry within
the higher nobility. According to Medwin this marriage, like
the first, was an elopement. On her mother's side Miss Perry
was descended from Sir Philip Sidney's younger brother and
the Earls of Leicester; from her father she inherited extensive
estates in Buckinghamshire, Gloucestershire, and Kent.

Seven children were the fruit of this marriage. The eldest
son, John, was made a baronet in 1818; the second baronet became Baron De L'Isle and Dudley in 1835. The present head
of the family is Algernon Sidney, fourth Baron De L'Isle and
Dudley.

From the death of his second wife in 1781, Bysshe Shelley
seems to have devoted himself entirely to the increasing of his
estates. In 1790 the Fen Place and Field Place estates of the
Shelleys came into his hands through the death of his older
brother, without issue. He was now one of the wealthiest landholders in the county. The Duke of Norfolk, one of the Whig
leaders who possessed considerable holdings in the district, became alive to his possibilities of political usefulness. Such a
man as Bysshe, no doubt, was also alert to the advantages of
benefiting from the Duke's interests. In 1806, therefore, Mr.
Bysshe Shelley was made a baronet, apparently in anticipation
of services still to be performed for the Whigs.

Thus Sir Bysshe brilliantly accomplished rather more than his
early ambition to found a house. He had raised his own branch
of the Shelley family from an obscure, modestly endowed line
of country gentlemen to a wealthy family with a baronetcy. He
had also begun another Shelley family who were to be baronets
and barons in his son's lifetime. Incidentally, this " gentleman
of the old school," as Dowden calls him, had interpreted his mis-

9

sion rather generously and had founded several other families not of the Shelley name. His will duly provides for his bastard offspring.

In his later years Sir Bysshe lived meanly in a small house in Horsham, convenient to the tavern tap-room he loved to frequent, not for the drinking, but for the conversation to be absorbed. His family ambition he ministered to by undertaking the building of a magnificent country-seat, known as Castle Goring. This he never completed, though he is said to have spent over £80,000 on it. It was eventually sold, thirty years after his death, for less than £12,000. He allowed his son Timothy the use of Field Place, but he disliked him heartily and used to curse him, even in the presence of young Percy Bysshe, his grandson. The young poet later told Hogg at Oxford that this was the origin of his own habit of cursing his absent father. Sir Bysshe's two daughters were treated so badly at home, says Medwin, that they both eloped and so went without dowries and without benefit in their father's will. In this, however, Medwin exaggerated, for Mr. Roger Ingpen notes some " scanty provision for his errant daughters " in his will.[9]

After this Sir Bysshe lived alone with his steward.[10] In his last days he was very careless of his personal appearance, but was still distinguished by a fine, impressive manner. He seems to have had some slight interest in his young grandson, the poet, making him occasional small presents of money and paying the local printers who printed some of Shelley's boyish verse. Neither the poet, however, nor his cousin Tom Medwin spoke very well of the old man as they remembered him. Shelley wrote in a letter in 1812 that he had acted very ill to three wives — though no biographer has been able to account for more than two — and that he was a complete atheist; while Medwin describes him in his old age as a cynical materialist, a miser whose fine presence in no way palliated his mean habits and avaricious dealings. A young man who met him in his old age thought that his eccentricity was tinged with insanity.[11]

Unkempt and odd, still dominating in his old age a son whose commonplace virtues he despised, old Sir Bysshe sat for hours at a time in a smelly little inn tap-room while farmers attending the markets talked materialistically of lands and profits. These were the objects to which he had successfully devoted the finest talents his family had yet produced. Behind the impressive manners which still lent a shadow of dignity to his mean habits he was projecting his success into the future. Young Bysshe already gave signs of the imagination, daring, and persuasive, compelling personality that had characterized his own youth. In addition he seemed likely to add to the family name a literary distinction hitherto missing. But wealth and influence were the main desiderata. Leaving as little as possible to chance, Sir Bysshe framed his will in a way calculated to compel his grandson to serve the interests of the family estate.

The poet's father, Timothy Shelley, was a man of better principles but of much less energy and resourcefulness than the dominating founder of the family fortunes. Until the death of Sir Bysshe he was little more than the country squire his ancestors had been, except that he was the first of his line to sit in Parliament and was better educated than most of the preceding Shelleys. Medwin, who knew him well, speaks scornfully of his " parts." He attended University College, Oxford, made the " grand tour " (bringing back a poor knowledge of French and a bad painting of Mount Vesuvius), and sometimes displayed a Chesterfieldian manner; but he really knew no more of Europe than the luggage that accompanied him. This is to say no more of Timothy Shelley's education than might have been said of nine-tenths of the other gentry of the eighteenth century who had the same training. In fact, something very like this was said by such men as Addison, Chesterfield, Gibbon, and Francis Jeffrey. The poet's intemperate youthful letters characterize his father as a clod, but they also furnish some evidence of intellectual interests in which the father was included. It seems fair to describe his interests simply as practical and non-cultural, like those of most of the country gentry with whom he associated. About twelve years after the poet's death this is precisely the impression made upon one who had become intimate with the family at Field Place:

Both Sir Timothy and his wife — excellent persons both — were, of all imaginable parents, the very last from whose union a looker-on would

11

suppose it possible that a " child of fancy," such as was the youthful author of " Queen Mab," would be likely to spring. The former, clad in his yeoman-like garb and his tanned leather gaiters, was, like the rest of his family (with the exception of Percy) thoroughly practical and prosaic; all were endowed with a fair amount of good sense.[12]

Some years later, Timothy's younger son, John, told Lady Shelley, daughter-in-law of the poet, that Sir Timothy had impressed upon him: " Never read a book, Johnnie, and you will be a rich man " — advice which, according to Lady Shelley, both Johnnie and his children minded well.[13]

In his politics Timothy Shelley was consistently a supporter of the Whig policies, serving the interests of the Duke of Norfolk. In 1790 he was elected M.P. for Horsham, but the Irvine interests (which continued till 1811 to contest the Norfolk supremacy in Horsham) protested the election as irregular and succeeded in unseating him in favour of their candidate. Afterwards he was for many years M.P. for New Shoreham, in the Rape of Bramber, in which district Horsham was included. During his long service in Parliament he was entirely undistinguished, and seemed content to limit his services by voting consistently as the Whig interests of the Duke of Norfolk required. He enjoyed referring to committee engagements, but nowhere in the records of Parliamentary debates have I been able to find mention of any speech by the member for New Shoreham.

Timothy Shelley was not entirely lacking in some of the liberal principles by which the Whigs were distinguished from the Tories. As " a friend of religious liberty " he once subscribed for two copies of the Unitarian sermons of the Reverend Mr. Sadler and even said he would like Mr. Sadler for his own clergyman. References to religious questions in the early letters of the poet to his father suggest more elasticity on this subject than belonged to the average country squire of his generation. He had slight appreciation of the spiritual values of religion, but in Christianity as an institution he saw the bulwark of the state and the home. He even claimed, in his cups, to have originated most of the arguments employed in Paley's *Evidences of Christianity*.[14] His attitude toward morals was somewhat similar, if we are to credit Medwin's statement that Timothy told his

12

youthful son he would provide for illegitimate children but would not tolerate a mésalliance.

It was the practical effect of his son's heterodoxy in his own family that first enraged Mr. Timothy Shelley. Some twelve years after the poet's death his sister Hellen told a friend:

My father . . . one day made the discovery that Bysshe was endeavouring to inoculate me with his peculiar tenets and opinions, and he then and there ejected my brother from the house, ordering us, on pain of his severest displeasure, never to mention Bysshe's name to him again.[15]

No doubt the miscreant's consequent notoriety was deeply felt as an affront to the family respectability and hardened his father's attitude into inflexibility. When Mrs. Houstoun first met Hellen Shelley, she was warned never to utter the poet's name in Sir Timothy's hearing.[16] After the poet's death Sir Timothy made his financial provisions for Mary Shelley and her son contingent upon Mary's not bringing Shelley's name before the public. He relaxed this attitude sufficiently in 1839 to allow her to edit Shelley's works *without* a life; [17] but he had previously suspended her allowance because of her publication of *Posthumous Poems* in 1824. When the poet's first son, Charles, died in 1826, Sir Timothy buried him in the Warnham parish church with the other Shelleys there, but the tablet mentions him as the grandson of Sir Timothy and pointedly omits the names of his parents.

These facts, together with the details of his treatment of Percy Bysshe, form the chief basis for the current characterization of the poet's father as wrong-headed and stubborn. According to later standards the characterization seems just, but only as applied to the treatment of one of his children who would have been similarly treated by most orthodox English parents of his class and generation. Shelley's daughter Ianthe was brought up in a similar attitude by her guardians. Several years after Sir Timothy's death she expressed unwillingness to visit Lady Jane Shelley without the assurance that her father would not be discussed.[18]

In his dealings with others Sir Timothy seems to have been kindly and well-meaning. He had the love and respect of his wife and his other children besides Percy, all of whom seemed to regard his treatment of Percy as not exactly unjust. Over thirty years after his death the old sexton of Warnham parish church remembered him kindly as a tall man whose piercing blue eyes had never needed spectacles even at the age of ninety. Before judging his character too exclusively from his treatment of his son, we should consider also the point of view more general to those who knew him other than as the poet's father. Obituary characterizations are conventionally kindly, but there seems to be genuine truth in his obituary notice in the *Gentleman's Magazine,* which concludes:

> Sir Timothy Shelley was sincerely respected. As a landlord, and as a practical agriculturalist, he enjoyed a high reputation. In him the agricultural labourer has lost a kind benefactor and a constant rewarder of honest industry; in short, he possessed, in a high degree, the best qualities of the English country gentleman.[19]

The poet's mother was before her marriage Elizabeth Pilfold, of Effingham, Sussex. The Pilfolds were country gentry of local importance somewhat less than that of the Shelleys before Sir Bysshe elevated the family. Timothy Shelley's wife was a woman of unusual beauty, and of strong good sense. She is described as an excellent letter-writer, but not interested in literature. Her son regarded her in 1811 as " mild and tolerant, yet narrow-minded." [20] Her idea of the son's early training was to fit him for the position of country gentleman held by his ancestors. Accordingly she was disappointed when he preferred reading to the fishing and hunting she thought more appropriate. She tried hard, and more sensibly than the others, to reconcile father and son, but after a reconciliation seemed impossible she concurred in her husband's attitude toward the poet. Mark Antony Lower remarks in his *The Worthies of Sussex* [21] that Shelley's grandfather was evidently slightly mad and that whatever genius the poet inherited must have come from his mother's side of the family.

There is, indeed, very little in the poet Shelley that can be

WARNHAM CHURCH, SUSSEX

From the Illustrated London News, *August 6, 1892, by permission*

HORSHAM IN THE EARLY NINETEENTH CENTURY

Engraved by J. Rogers from a drawing by N. Whitlock

plainly attributed either to family heritage or to the influence of
" resistant " Sussex, probably the most conservative county in
England. One finds in Shelley's ancestry the post-obit, the read-
iness to elope, the unconventionality of dress, religious opinion,
and conduct, the whisper of insanity, that are a part of Shelley's own early history. The similarity to his paternal grandfather is especially noticeable. One ancestor, John Shelley,
was particularly praised for a quality — forgiveness of injury —
that the poet especially enjoins as one of the most important
principles of life. But these traits are distinctly sporadic rather
than characteristic, and it might easily be maintained that they
are no more than accidental. If one must look for an exterior
explanation of the poet's character one will find it more in the
times than in any discernible heredity or environment.

PERHAPS the boyish Shelley did not feel any direct impact from
the times until he went to Eton. But not even conservative Sussex could be totally oblivious or unaffected. On the very day
the poet was born the National Assembly of France decreed the
sale of all religious houses, and the King's grenadiers were protesting and revolting at the indignity of having to guard the
King. It was the very day that the allied monarchs threatened
dire vengeance on Paris if the King were harmed or insulted —
and five days later the Swiss Guard were slaughtered. In England the Whigs were split violently into the Old and the New.
Burke trained the heavy artillery of his eloquence against the
Revolution. Paine and Godwin were encouraging its English
supporters. Mary Wollstonecraft was publishing her *Vindication of the Rights of Woman*. The government was becoming
alarmed about seditious writings and beginning a repressive attitude toward them that lasted through the poet's life and
caused him some danger and inconvenience. Henceforth for a
generation there were to be more government spies and less of
the right of habeas corpus than England had known for centuries. Sussex, perhaps, or at least the Shelleys of Field Place,
may have been rather apathetic to the excitement of the larger
centres. But it could not fail to realize that important events

were afoot when the French refugees began arriving on the coast in smugglers' packets, open boats, or anything that would get them across the Channel. They left France in various disguises, arrived in various states of distress and destitution, and set out inland afoot or in any conveyance — a coach, a wagon, or even a fish-cart. From several of the Sussex ports at which they landed — Brighton, Worthing, and Bognor — the road to London, Oxford, and Winchester ran through the town of Horsham.

During the next ten years fear of revolution gradually yielded precedence to fear of Napoleon. Wordsworth made the common discovery that the coast of France was " drawn almost into frightful neighborhood "; Napoleon waited at Boulogne for only a few hours' mastery of the Channel to make him master of the world. As Shelley scanned his first lessons at Eton the inhabitants of the coastwise towns received their detailed instructions for burning supplies that might have to be abandoned and breaking the axles of all conveyances before letting them fall into the hands of invaders. Militia companies were formed for home defence, mothers silenced their children with threats of " Boney." Press-gangs were active in the seaports, and disabled returned soldiers became a common sight in Sussex as well as in the rest of England.

Chapter II

THE EARLY YEARS

FIELD PLACE; SYON HOUSE ACADEMY;
DEVELOPING INTERESTS AND PERSONALITY

THE DAY on which Percy Bysshe Shelley was born, August 4, 1792, has been recorded as calm and pleasant, with a light wind. The storm and strife of opinion, already blowing from France and driving its " dead leaves " of royalist refugees westward through the Sussex ports past Horsham, was of no very vital concern in the household or neighbourhood of Field Place. The even tenor of stubborn local ways was hardly disturbed as yet. More important, probably, was the big cattle and sheep fair that had been concluded in Horsham only about a fortnight before, or the bustling weekly corn and poultry market toward which the local countrymen were carrying their produce on that very Saturday, probably passing French refugees on the way. Most important to Field Place and its forty-year-old squire was the birth of a son and heir in a small, upstairs bedroom.

No one who saw the infant thought it necessary to record its appearance for posterity. Later an authorized biographer described this " pretty fledgeling " as " already distinguished by his delicate hands and feet, his bright down of baby hair (afterwards curling in ringlets), and his great blue, luminous eyes." [1] These details are all fairly deducible from authentic descriptions of his appearance a few years later and are consistent with the authentic portrait of Shelley as a boy (now in the Morgan Library) and with the supposed miniature of Shelley as a boy, by the Duc de Montpensier. In both these angelicized early portraits we look in vain for the small, turned-back nose, receding chin, and general irregularity of features which Shel-

17

ley's own testimony and that of later friends establish as genuine.[2]

The child's nurse seems to have recorded no descriptions or impressions, although she lived in the neighbourhood for thirty years after the poet's death and continued to appear annually at Field Place for her regular Christmas remembrance. Practically everything we know of the poet's boyhood at Field Place depends upon the recollection of his sister Hellen, in a series of ten letters beginning November 26, 1856, printed in Hogg's unfinished biography of the poet.[3]

At the age of six Bysshe was sent daily to the Reverend Mr. Edwards, an elderly Welsh parson at Warnham, to be taught Latin. Mr. Edwards may have been " a good old man of very limited intellects," [4] but he seems to have given his pupil an excellent start in Latin, as Shelley's later record at Syon House and Eton testifies. The boy had a remarkable memory and quoted Gray's poem " On the Death of a Favourite Cat " entire after hearing it read. He also recited long Latin passages to his father, which his little sisters supposed to be drama, from the emphasis of their delivery.

There is no record of Shelley's association with boys of his own age before he entered Syon House Academy at the age of ten. Warnham and Horsham were certainly not without small boys with whom young Percy Bysshe had casual contacts, but his most frequent associations were with girls, and girls younger than himself. He was their natural protector and leader. " His good temper was a pleasant memory always," wrote Hellen, " and I do not recollect an instance of the reverse toward any of us." One reads between the lines of her memoranda, however, that he was nevertheless a pretty complete dictator to his sisters.

SHELLEY entered Syon House Academy in 1802 and remained there for two years. This school, located at Isleworth, near Brentford, six or seven miles from London, was patronized by the sons of well-to-do tradesmen, doctors, lawyers, and country squires. Bysshe, as he was called in the family, was not yet heir

to a baronetcy. Shelley's cousin, Tom Medwin, son of a Sussex
lawyer, was already a student at Syon House. It is to his account, eked out by the recollections set down many years later
by two schoolfellows, that we owe our knowledge of Shelley at
his first school.

The house is a substantial brick house that was about two
hundred years old in Shelley's day and still stands, though no
longer used as a school and so changed by external alterations
that Professor Dowden was unable to locate it exactly.[5] It
stands on the London Road, nearly opposite the lane that leads
to Syon Park. In Shelley's day it was surrounded by high walls,
and adjoined excellent gardens and a playground, which was
also enclosed.

There were about sixty boys in the school, between the ages
of eight and sixteen. The subjects taught were reading and
writing, arithmetic, Latin, French, geography, and astronomy.
Dr. Greenlaw, the master, is described somewhat unfavourably
by Medwin as being irritable and capricious, but he seems to
have been a tolerable scholar in the classics and to have conducted a fairly good school. Shelley described him to Hogg with
some respect as having rather liberal opinions. Medwin's testimony about Syon House has the appearance of being over-
coloured. He speaks quite disparagingly about the quality and
quantity of the food provided by Mrs. Greenlaw, which Sir John
Rennie speaks of as good.[6]

The sensitive and slightly-built boy of ten had been poorly
prepared by his previous experience for the world he was now
entering. He did not even know enough to laugh with counter-
feited glee when Dr. Greenlaw occasionally offended his sensi-
bilities with a coarse story at which the other small boys cackled
manfully. His girlish looks were alone a sufficient handicap, but
his girlish associations were fatal to any chance of happiness
with his fellows. He had no knowledge of or interest in the
usual boyish sports. He knew nothing whatever of either the
technique or the ethics of giving or taking punishment. After
a lapse of eighty years one of his schoolmates clearly remembered that he was " like a girl in boy's clothes, fighting with open

hands and rolling on the floor when flogged, not from the pain, but from a sense of the indignity." [7] He had been used to dominating his sisters at home. But at Syon House, where there was no fagging system to allot one a principal bully, all the older and stronger boys bullied all the younger ones. Shelley had to chase hoops and balls for them until he was utterly exhausted. He also suffered punishment more than once for breaking bounds or rules in executing their commands.

No doubt the child in this environment was, as Medwin says, a strange, unsociable creature, to whom the place was "a perfect Hell." [8] Occasionally Medwin, playing with the older boys and noticing the wretched loneliness of Shelley, would leave his play to walk and talk with him. The talk, he records, was sometimes far beyond the boy's years. Medwin also speaks of playing truant with his young cousin and going in a boat on the Thames to Richmond to see a play.

It is very likely that some of the boy's half-holidays were employed in walks about the neighbourhood. He could hardly have found it very inspiriting, if they were. Brentford, beyond the school walls, was a dirty, noisy little suburb with far more low-grade public-houses than it needed. It had been a byword with the eighteenth-century writers for dingy unattractiveness. Goldsmith had suggested it as the proper terminus for "a race between a turnip-cart, a dust-cart, and a dung-cart." A generation earlier it had rioted most enthusiastically for John Wilkes and Liberty, but this fact could hardly have been of any inspiration to the young schoolboy.

Just across the Thames from Brentford were Kew Gardens, with whose loveliness he must have been acquainted. He visited Richmond with Tom Medwin, and he probably walked to Twickenham, near by, and saw Pope's famous grotto. Equally near also was Orleans House, the home for many years of the exiled royal family of France. Its location must certainly have been known to Dr. Greenlaw's boys, among them the future uncompromising foe of all kingship.

Such a schoolboy as young Bysshe Shelley was certain to be remembered by his mates. "His imagination was always roving upon something romantic and extraordinary," Sir John Rennie

SHELLEY AS A BOY

Artist unknown. By permission of the Pierpont Morgan Library

recalled,[9] " such as spirits, fairies, fighting, volcanoes, etc., and he not unfrequently astonished his schoolfellows by blowing up the boundary palings of the playground with gunpowder, also the lid of his desk in the middle of schooltime, to the great surprise of Dr. Greenlaw himself and the whole school. In fact, at times he was considered to be almost on the borders of insanity." Once, according to a story long current in Dr. Greenlaw's family, he poisoned the doctor's pigs as the accidental result of a wild experiment and escaped detection through the kindly silence of Dr. Greenlaw's son, who knew the truth.[10] Once, at least, he handed Dr. Greenlaw as his own two verses that came straight from Ovid.[11] He also imposed a Latin verse upon a schoolmate, the W. C. Gellibrand whose description of Shelley's fighting technique has already been quoted. Gellibrand being unable to write a required Latin verse, Shelley voluntarily supplied him with the following:

> *Hos ego versiculos scripsi,*
> *Sed non ego feci.*

These verses resulted in exposure and punishment for Gellibrand and a pummelling for Shelley at the hands of his victim. Shortly before he left Syon House Academy, Shelley spent his Easter vacation on a visit to his Grove relations, where he induced his two young cousins to turn woodsmen with him and cut down their father's young fir trees.[12]

The boy found class-work so easy that it was sometimes rather a bore. Tom Medwin observed that he often sat idly at his desk gazing out of the window or sketching pine trees on his papers, ancestors of that trim procession of pines or firs that marches across the borders of Shelley's later manuscripts. Nevertheless, he entered Eton well prepared, and was remembered by Sir John Rennie as a good scholar: " He used to write verse, English and Latin, with considerable facility, and attained a high position in the school before he left for Eton." [13] Dr. Greenlaw was in the end more successful than the dancing-master whose classes Shelley attended. The boy positively hated his dancing-lessons and did his best to avoid them, with the result that his master soon pronounced him impossibly awkward.

The very qualities that made Bysshe miserable at Syon House also provided recompenses. Adam Walker, a self-taught natural philosopher and inventor of scientific toys who occasionally lectured near by at Eton, was engaged by Dr. Greenlaw to lecture to the Syon House boys on some of the wonders of science by which Herschel and others were thrilling the imagination of the age. Adam Walker was no Huxley, but his scientific apparatus, his experience as a teacher of boys, and his wide scope of scientific and pseudo-scientific information made him the ideal herald of a new wonderland. Young Bysshe heard and was entranced. Various experiments at Field Place, Syon House Academy, and later at Eton with gunpowder and fire may have originated from other sources, non-scientific in nature; but it is very probable that Adam Walker was the starting-point for the electrical experiments, burning-glasses, microscopes, Leyden jars, and chemical mixtures that Shelley toyed with for about ten years thereafter.

Tom Medwin, who had a far less impressionable and retentive mind than Shelley, recalled Adam Walker's lectures at Syon House with considerable fidelity. They occurred during Shelley's second year [14] and "opened to Shelley a new universe of speculations," [15] especially in astronomy and chemistry. Walker demonstrated the wonders of telescope and microscope and performed some simple scientific experiments. Fortunately his own description of his offerings are at hand, to substantiate and elaborate Medwin's memory. Either at Syon House or Eton (where he heard Walker again) Bysshe must have paid his eighteen pence for a pamphlet of eighty-six pages entitled " *Analysis of a Course of Lectures on Natural and Experimental Philosophy, viz. Magnetism, Mechanics, Chemistry, Pneumatics, Fortification, Optics, Use of the Globes, etc., Astronomy,* by A. Walker, Lecturer to his Royal Highness the Duke of Gloucester, to Eton and Westminster Colleges, and Member of the Dublin Society." There was also an eight-page syllabus, listing the lectures, each of which was of two hours' duration.[16] They covered every branch of science in which Shelley later showed any interest. There were two lectures on pneumatics, or " principles of the air," two on electricity, three on astronomy, and one on chem-

istry. Immediately after these lectures were delivered we begin
to hear of chemical and electrical experiments at Field Place
and Syon House and of excited speculations inspired in the
schoolboy by the possibilities of telescope and microscope.

Adam Walker was no dryasdust; he consciously gave his lectures an imaginative appeal. "We find the worlds of our system," he concluded,

covered with continents, seas, hills, etc. Who can doubt, therefore,
but they are inhabited, as well as all the worlds of the other systems?
How much too big is this idea for the human imagination! By the
lately improved telescopes 30,000 of these suns have been found more
than the naked eye can perceive! Were our glasses still better we
should, no doubt, find more. — 'Tis not improbable that many be stars
so distant that their light has not reached the earth since creation.
Many of these stars appear double, and coloured green, blue, red,
violet, etc.

Let us on the wings of imagination then launch into the immensity
of space, and behold *system* beyond *system, above us, below us,* to
the *east,* the *west,* the *north,* and the *south!* Let us go so far as to see
our sun but a star among the rest, and our system itself as a point,
and we shall but even then find ourselves on the *confines of creation!*
How inadequate then must be the utmost stretch of human faculties,
to a conception of that amazing *Deity* who made and governs the
whole! Should not the narrow prejudices, the littleness of human
pride, soften into humility at this thought? [17]

The imaginative boy quickly adopted Adam Walker's convictions that these numerous worlds were inhabited. Excitedly
he urged upon Medwin the possibility that some of the celestial
inhabitants were a higher race than ours and that in future
existences mere mortals might be destined to pass through a
series of stages on various planets that would ultimately make
them more gods than men.[18] It was eight years before he was
to write *Queen Mab,* his first important poem; but Shelley's
prose notes to that poem, on the plurality of worlds, and Ianthe's
view of a million variously coloured constellations, among
which the earth was only the " smallest light that twinkles in
the heavens," might almost have been written with Adam
Walker's peroration before him. Clearer evidence of a still

longer memory may be found in "The Cloud," written in 1819. Here Shelley describes quite scientifically the operation of clouds under the influence of wind and electricity as an unending cycle:

> I pass through the pores of the ocean and shores,
> I change, but I cannot die.

Fifteen years earlier he had heard Adam Walker explain the interrelation of air and water, how thunder and lightning and electricity and clouds are related, how clouds are formed by wind, water, and air and precipitate themselves in rain, hail, snow, and fog, and how air "is so subtil that it pervades the pores of all bodies." [19]

But though Adam Walker's revelations were vastly stimulating, his actual presence was a comfort and relief of only short duration. A much more lasting comfort was that of reading. The habit probably started at Field Place, where, according to Medwin (and somewhat inconsistently with Squire Timothy's reported attitude toward books), there was a tolerable library. Bysshe had not been long at the school before the older boys, among other exactions, required him to fetch them books from the circulating library maintained at Brentford by Mr. P. Norbury. Most of the books so obtained were trashy thrillers of a very extravagant type. Norbury himself published some of them. They were generally known as "blue books" and were published principally at the Minerva Press by Lane, who made a fortune from them at sixpence a copy. Medwin describes them as "stories of haunted castles, bandits, murderers, and other grim personages." This is amply supported by the titles of several such books published during the two years Shelley was at Syon House; for example, *Don Algonah, or the Sorceress of Montillo*; *The Black Forest, or The Cavern of Horrors*; *The Subterraneous Passage, or Gothic Cell*; *The Cavern of Horrors, or Miseries of Miranda, a Neapolitan Tale*. Such books as these were greedily devoured by the Brentford schoolboys. On returning from holidays they brought in fresh titles, which circulated till worn out or discarded.

Though Shelley read scores of novels of this type, there are

24

no particular titles that he is known definitely to have read.[20]
Several books of a more lasting quality known to have been
read by him at this time are the novels of Mrs. Ann Radcliffe
and " Monk " Lewis and Robert Paltock's *Life and Adventures
of Peter Wilkins*.

If Syon House, with its brutal world of fact and over-exciting
world of imagination, furnished the young schoolboy with an
inharmonious introduction to social life, Field Place in vacation
was fortunately a partial corrective. As a leader and entertainer
of his younger sisters Bysshe fancied himself tremendously. He
told them tales of the legendary Great Tortoise that haunted
Warnham Pond, where the family sometimes went for a picnic
dinner; and of the Old Snake that had led a peaceful existence
for many years in the Field Place grounds until accidentally
slain by a gardener. Very probably he told also of that much less
respectable reptile that had infested St. Leonard's Wood, only
two miles away, some two hundred years before — " a strange
and monstrous Serpent or Dragon," to quote the old account,[21]
" nine feete, or rather more, in length, and shaped almost in the
forme of an axeltree," black above, red underneath, and with a
white ring round its neck, leaving a foul-smelling, glutinous,
and slimy track. Another denizen of the Wood about whom he
probably thrilled his sisters was the Headless Horseman who
vaulted to the back of any horse being ridden within the Wood.

There were other mysteries closer at hand. He tapped the
ceiling with a stick to discover to them a secret passage which
must certainly be beyond; he drew graphic pictures of an old
grey alchemist who dwelt in a garret that was closed against
their explorations.

He developed other devices for improving upon humdrum
reality. Fantastic costumes were devised in which to personate
spirits or fiends while Bysshe, as the arch-fiend, rushed through
a passage with a flaming liquid in a portable stove. According
to neighbourhood tradition he once set fire to a faggot-stack
so that he might have " a little hell of his own." [22] And when
he was about fifteen one of the first words he taught his brother
John to say was " debbee," for devil.[23]

There were also chemical and electrical experiments with

shocks, and electrical cures for chilblains, which Hellen
dreaded and was finally excused from participating in. Like
Franklin, he flew kites to catch electricity.[24] When he left home
to enter Eton the wash-room reeked with smoke from some
experiment gone awry.

All this was not much more than a boyish effort to turn the
vivid imaginative world in which he withdrew himself at Syon
House into actual experience in the more friendly environment
of Field Place. The device for conveying electric shocks and
the flying of kites for electricity had both been described in
detail in Adam Walker's lectures. No longer a slave in a world
of tyrants, but a benevolent despot among adoring subjects, he
could make the occasional innovations from the wilder world
of his reading that Hellen's recollections show he did make.
Mystification, sudden surprise, and extreme benevolence and
diabolism characterize both his reading and the exploits related
of him at Field Place.

It happens that Medwin comments particularly on Shelley's
delight in Robert Paltock's *Peter Wilkins*. Peter shaped first a
family and then a kingdom to his benevolent wishes; two of
his winged children were adopted by royalty. Medwin remembered " how much Shelley wished for a winged wife and little
winged cherubs for children." [25] Hellen, without mentioning
the book, recalled how the benevolent king of the Field Place
nursery first contemplated adopting a vagrant child who occasionally came to the back door as a tumbler, and later scoured
the near neighbourhood on his pony seeking whom he could
adopt.

At Syon House there was no such natural outlet for his highly
excited imagination. Driven in upon himself, he walked in his
sleep and experienced severe nervous shocks when awakened.
He was given to waking dreams in which he appeared unconscious of his surroundings. Afterwards " his eyes flashed, his
lips quivered . . . his voice was tremulous with emotion, and
he talked more like a spirit or an angel than a human being." [26]
Nothing like this seems to have happened at Field Place. His
willing subjects there remembered him as unvaryingly sweet-
tempered and kind. At Syon House, however, John Rennie was

particularly impressed with his " violent and extremely excitable
temper, which manifested itself in all kinds of eccentricities.
. . . The least circumstance that thwarted him produced the
most violent paroxysms of rage; and when irritated by other
boys, which they, knowing his infirmity, frequently did by way
of teasing him, he would take up anything, or even any little
boy near him, to throw at his tormentors." [27] Similar testimony
was to come later from Eton. " Yet with all this," Sir John
added, " when treated with kindness, he was very amiable,
noble, high-spirited and generous." [28]

He was really living in three very vivid worlds: an actual,
predominantly hostile world of schoolroom and playground;
an actual, friendly world of Field Place; and an ideal world of
romantic and pseudo-scientific imagination. These worlds constantly overlapped, with results that careful parents should have
noticed with some anxiety. Since there is no evidence that Mr.
Timothy Shelley and his wife noticed, it may be that Shelley
was still more a normal boy than the recollections of his contemporaries represent. Once, at least, his own voice emerges
to assure us that his overwrought boyhood was not altogether
abnormal.

" Dear Kate," he wrote from Field Place during his first summer vacation,

We have proposed a day at the pond next Wednesday; and, if you
will come to-morrow morning, I would be much obliged to you; and,
if you could any how bring Tom over to stay all the night, I would
thank you. We are to have a cold dinner over at the pond, and come
home to eat a bit of roast chicken and peas at about nine o'clock.
Mama depends upon your bringing Tom over to-morrow, and, if you
don't, we shall be very much disappointed. Tell the bearer not to
forget to bring me a fairing, — which is some ginger-bread, sweet-
meat, hunting-nuts, and a pocket-book. Now I end.

> I am not
> Your obedient servant,
> P. B. SHELLEY.[29]

Another and more touching friendship than that with Tom
Medwin was formed at school at almost this same time. Shelley's first close friend remains anonymous; he vanished from

Shelley's life in a year or two, but he was long remembered as " generous, brave and gentle " with " a delicacy and a simplicity in his manners, inexpressibly attractive." " I remember we used to walk the whole play-hours up and down by some moss-covered palings, pouring out our hearts in youthful talk. We used to speak of the ladies with whom we were in love, and I remember that our usual practice was to confirm each other in the everlasting fidelity, in which we had bound ourselves towards them, and towards each other. I recollect thinking my friendship exquisitely beautiful. Every night, when we parted to go to bed, I remember we kissed each other." [30] This boy may have been Henry Tredcroft, of Horsham, whom Shelley would almost certainly have known at home if not at school.[31]

Whoever he was, this friend was probably the only one to whom Shelley confided a precocious decision that was to shape the whole subsequent course of his life. One fresh May morning, which he clearly remembered for years afterwards, young Bysshe walked forth upon the glittering grass, listening to the voices from the near-by schoolroom as " The harsh and grating strife of tyrants and of foes." With a sense of intolerable outrage he took his resolution:

> I will be wise
> And just, and free, and mild, if in me lies
> Such power, for I grow weary to behold
> The selfish and the strong still tyrannise
> Without reproach or check.

The resolution tranquillized him, and from that hour he began consciously to prepare himself for the warfare he had undertaken, fortifying his soul with " knowledge from forbidden mines of lore." This knowledge, somewhat absurdly, he thought of as more likely to be gained through ghosts and incantations, and possibly the no less supernatural powers of science, than through the stale and tainted instruction of schoolmasters.[32]

Such was Shelley's later account of a scene which he claimed to remember well even to the day and hour. It sounds a little odd for a boy of eleven or twelve, but it is hardly more ex-

28

traordinary than the boy himself. Very likely he had several such experiences at Syon House and Eton, and in describing the first of them he gave a composite account, somewhat coloured by the comparative maturity he had attained by the time he recorded it. Certainly the boy became conscious at Syon House of the disparity between an actual miserable world and a possible happy one at the same time that he perceived his own unusual mental capacities and his own partly frustrated thirst for high adventure. Shelley's claim in 1816 that he had kept his vow is supported by the record of his life from the moment that consistent and trustworthy records become available.

More than is commonly realized, the small boy driven in upon himself was laying up impressions for more mature use. This may be traced particularly in his reading. Of the few books whose titles are definitely known two are mentioned rather particularly — the novel *Peter Wilkins* and the ballads and novel of " Monk " Lewis, though Hellen Shelley does not mention *The Monk* specifically. We have already noted the probable influence of *Peter Wilkins* on the poet's immediate conduct. If it did not also influence some of his most characteristic later beliefs it certainly helped prepare the mental attitude in which they grew. Peter was the first Prometheus Shelley knew, the giver of arts and laws to the winged race of glumms and glowries. He purified their religion, which had degenerated through the selfishness of the priests. He, too, found priests the chief obstacles to progress, though he proceeded against them much more tactfully than the poet did. He was particularly a foe of slavery and abolished it everywhere he went. Incidentally, the rocky whirlpool through which Peter descended into his strange new regions is somewhat suggestive of the later progress of the young poet in *Alastor*. It is not surprising, therefore, that we find Shelley re-reading this book only a few months before *Alastor* was written. The violent extravagances of Lewis's *The Monk*, which he also re-read later, would be hard to isolate from those of numerous nameless shockers that helped form the background of Shelley's prose romances a few years later. It should be remembered, however, that the novel

29

is a continuous record of priestly depravity. Lewis's Ambrosio and Mrs. Radcliffe's Schedoni were the first patterns on which Shelley formed his notions of priests, some time before he became antagonistic to their religion. If we pause to recall that the tyrannical father or guardian was a stock character in the books from which the boy's ideas and conduct were taking such a perceptible colour, is it so strange that the respectable Mr. Timothy Shelley soon fitted into the pattern, or that he later felt that his son had been ruined by books?

EVEN our own memories hardly enable us to reconstruct childhood as it was. The recollections of others, from twenty to sixty years after the events, are more doubtful still. In Shelley's case they show a striking concurrence and consistency. This may be due partly to an accepted tradition that had grown up in the interval, with which their independent memories sought unconsciously to harmonize. But the books he read were subject to no such variability, and as far as they can be traced they offer striking support to the picture based upon memories alone. With some allowance for error in detail, we may " see Shelley plain " as he entered Eton at the age of twelve. He was entirely lacking in the appearance of normal boyishness, but not entirely lacking in its spirit, if his one letter of the period means anything at all. He was a good student through natural quickness of mind rather than industry and self-discipline. He possessed an extremely good memory and an imaginative and intellectual energy far beyond his years and physical strength. He was extraordinarily sensitive, normally sweet-tempered and generous, but capable of distressingly intemperate, helpless rage. Already he was living the vivid part of his life in a world of his own, so different from that of his fellows that a reconciliation was almost impossible. He realized clearly — though not so clearly perhaps as he later remembered — that between his benevolent world of imagination and his tyrannical world of reality continual warfare was inevitable. At the age of twelve he had dedicated himself to a Messianic mission.

30

Chapter III

AT ETON: THE SCHOOLBOY

ETON COLLEGE; MISFORTUNES AND GENERAL
REPUTATION; INTERESTS, FRIENDS, AND
INTELLECTUAL PROGRESS

On July 29, 1804 Percy Bysshe Shelley, not yet quite twelve years of age, signed his name in the entrance book of the headmaster of Eton College. It was in some respects a new world he was entering. The venerable fifteenth-century brick structures just across the Thames from Windsor Castle represented a vast improvement in atmosphere and tradition over the respectable but gloomy-looking structure of Syon House Academy, on the edge of dirty, brawling Brentford. A similar change shortly took place in the worldly prospects of the young scholar. For whereas at the academy he had been merely the son of a local squire who would eventually inherit a considerable fortune, he was from the year 1806 heir to a baronetcy, his grandfather having been made a baronet in that year.

At no other time in his life was Shelley to live even half as long in any one environment as at Eton. It behoves us, therefore, to take a rather careful view of the life of which he now became a part. Eton was at that time very much what it had been when Horace Walpole gave glimpses of it in his letters and Gray wrote his affectionate "Ode on a Distant Prospect of Eton College." Dr. Goodall, the headmaster in 1804, had improved the general tone and quality of the school, which had lapsed under his immediate predecessors, but had rather neglected discipline. His successor, Dr. John Keate, was advanced from the mastership of the Lower School to become headmaster on December 28, 1809.[1] Dr. Keate continued to improve the

31

general standards and became probably the most famous of all Eton headmasters for his enforcement of discipline. His floggings were proverbial and have given rise to many doubtless exaggerated stories. "'Blessed are the pure in heart,'" he quoted — "If you are not pure in heart I'll flog you"; or "Read your Bible, boy, or I'll flog you." [2] The more sober historical truth seems to be that there were many boys at Eton who were never flogged at all and that the victims were mostly habitual offenders from the fourth form and remove. Keate was in fact one of the ablest of Eton headmasters, described by those who knew him best as generally kind-hearted and just. The brilliant sketch of him by Kinglake [3] was humorously intended and hardly does him justice. Though Shelley was in his classes and was otherwise liable to unfavourable notice from him, there is no record of his having been flogged by the redoubtable, bushy-browed headmaster. It was only during Shelley's short period in the lower part of the school, where Keate was then master, and during the last seven months, when Keate was headmaster, that Keate *could* have flogged him. [4]

The schedule of work at Eton for a normal school day was from 8.00 to 9.00 a.m., 11.00 to 12.00, 3.00 to 4.00 p.m., and 5.00 to 6.00. Religious services were held at 11.00 and 3.00. On Fridays the first afternoon lesson was from 2.00 to 3.30. The boys prepared their lessons in their own rooms, between recitations and in the evening. Fourth-form and lower-form boys also had to rise early for a "six-o'clock lesson" four or five times a week — the lower form, however, only in summer. This regular schedule was constantly interfered with by holidays, half-holidays, and the Saturday "play-at-four." Tuesdays were regularly whole holidays and Thursdays half-holidays. In addition there were numerous red-letter days, or saints' days, that were observed as holidays, as well as royal birthdays and special holidays to celebrate British victories.

Young Shelley and his fellow Etonians were not so free on their holidays, however, as might be supposed. Always there were bounds to be kept, with a penalty of flogging for being caught out of bounds. Wide wandering was also made more difficult by a nine-o'clock roll-call in the morning. Further requirements saw to it (since there was a seven-o'clock roll-call) that the hours of consecutive freedom were at most three or four in the afternoon. On Sunday mornings attendance was required at a ten-o'clock church service. There were two required services on Sunday afternoon — a short reading between two and three from *The Whole Duty of Man* by one of the fifth-form boys, and regular services at three o'clock.

It was only during vacation that the young Etonians enjoyed unrestricted freedom. Vacations totalled about two and a half months out of the year — a month at Christmas, the month of August (approximately), and two weeks at Easter.

Students were divided into two classes: "oppidans" and "collegers." The collegers, or "King's scholars," were limited by statute to seventy, but in Shelley's time the number was only twenty-five or thirty. They held scholarships and ancient statutory rights and lived in the college. The oppidans numbered about 350 when Shelley entered Eton and about 470 when he left. They lived in boarding houses, some of which were kept by women called "dames," others by men called "domines," and others by classical masters who were called "tutors." Shelley lodged first with Mr. Hexter, master of writing, and later with his tutor, George Bethell, an assistant master.

The rules under which the boys lived were enforced by the various masters and several monitors, or præpostors, from the upper forms. Sixth-form boys could report students from lower forms for certain infractions of rules. Only the headmaster and the lower master could flog. This was an affair of some ceremony, performed (unless originating with the headmaster) upon a kind of warrant sent up by one of the masters. The culprit knelt on a whipping-block in the headmaster's room and was attended on either side by a præpostor. He could, and infrequently did, refuse his flogging and accept expulsion.

The conduct of the boys toward each other was a matter of tradition and brute force. Under the fagging system upper-form boys could have from one to three "fags," who performed for them such personal services as preparing breakfast, brushing clothes, stopping balls at cricket, and running errands. It has been argued by Etonians that this was really a benefit for the

33

younger boy, who generally considered the service and the association with an older boy an honour and who was protected thereby from indiscriminate bullying.

As in all boys' schools, bullying and fighting were not unusual. On one occasion two boys fought for three hours, until stopped by the redoubtable Keate himself. One small boy was killed by fighting to exhaustion and then swallowing the brandy with which his second had told him to rinse his mouth. Students who were sensitive or peculiar might expect to be treated intolerantly. The Reverend Dr. Edward Craven Hawtrey, Provost of Eton after Shelley's time, called attention to this in a sermon [5] as one of the principal weaknesses of the school and described two cases of its ill effects that are almost certainly those of Shelley and his immediate successor at Eton, W. S. Walker.

The life of the average Etonian in the early nineteenth century was very largely play. According to a critic in the *Edinburgh Review*,[6] a boy about half-way through the school had about eleven hours a week of " school-time " without allowing for extra holidays. Except for preparation, which was rather a light matter, the rest of the time was largely for play. A list of games in vogue at Eton in 1766 [7] includes upwards of thirty. Cricket, fives, hoops, marbles, several top games, several ball games, several hunting games, football, leaping pole, and kites were among the best-known. Swimming and boating were quite popular in Shelley's day. Some of the more daring broke rules by driving, riding, hunting, coursing with beagles, attending races or fairs, or even poaching in the royal forest of Windsor. Boyish pranks, such as one or two related of Shelley, were not uncommon.

Studies were limited in scope and poorly directed. Greek and Latin and a smattering of divinity and geography were the only subjects taught regularly, though French, drawing, dancing, and fencing could be had outside of regular school hours, as extras. The two anthologies used, *Poetæ Græci* and *Scriptores Græci et Romani*, contained much ill-chosen matter, and the Eton Greek and Latin grammars, according to the *Edinburgh Review*,[8] were inaccurate, ill-arranged, and bur- .

dened with useless and perplexing distinctions. The same censorious writer says

The Etonian who goes either to Cambridge or Oxford has not read a single book of Herodotus, Thucydides, Xenophon, Livy, Polybius, or Tacitus. He has not read a single Greek tragedy or comedy; [9] he is utterly ignorant of mathematical or physical science, and even of arithmetic. Modern history and modern languages are, of course, out of the question.

There was a considerable amount of memory work and of Latin composition in both prose and verse. According to the *Edinburgh Review*, most boys who remained in a public school to the age of eighteen or nineteen had written " above 10,000 Latin verses, a greater number than is contained in the Æneid." [10] The exercises were seldom adequately read, with the result that many of them were not the work of their supposed authors. Hence a good many floggings, and a continued dearth of English poets in Latin. The proportion of masters to boys — about one to fifty or sixty in Shelley's day — made the instruction largely mechanical and superficial, though this was less true for the boys who had private tutors. Even the invincible Keate, who taught the sixth and upper-fifth forms, could hardly have done more than preserve discipline and a decent show of instruction among his 150 to 190 boys. Until about thirty years after Shelley left Eton, progress of the boys from form to form was based upon length of attendance rather than examinations.

Fifth- and sixth-form boys " were supposed " to read in their leisure [11] " Dr. Middleton's Cicero," Tully's *Offices*, Ovid's long and short poems, the *Spectator*, Milton, Pope, Roman history, Greek history, Potter's *Antiquities*, " and Kennet's and all other books necessary toward making a compleat scholar." In the upper forms boys were expected to be able to furnish ancient and modern parallels for some of their reading.

From 1766 to 1834 there was almost no change in the curriculum. Thus the weekly course of studies prevalent in 1766 [12] will furnish a fairly reliable index to what Shelley may be supposed to have been taught between 1804 and 1810, in his progress through the fourth form, the remove, the fifth, and the sixth. Construing lessons included from sixteen to sixty lines a time, depending upon the form and the difficulty of the material. Making some allowance for holidays, a rough calculation indicates that Shelley got through 75,000 lines of Greek and Latin prose and poetry during six years at Eton, much of it being done over and over again. He memorized much of this and based a considerable number of prose and verse exercises on it, and this was practically all he got from his Eton classes. The authors and books studied were mainly Homer, Vergil, Horace, and Ovid and the Greek Testament, with a touch of Greek drama, Cornelius Nepos, Cæsar, Terence, Æsop, Lucian, and various authors contained in the two Eton anthologies. During Keate's time as headmaster (1810–34) [13] a boy who had been at Eton eight or ten years was sure to have been through the *Iliad* once and a half, the *Æneid* twice, several hundred lines of the *Odyssey*, and all Horace's *Odes*.

Such was the situation into which Field Place's young Master of the Revels and Dr. Greenlaw's sensitive young schoolboy was introduced on July 29, 1804. It was a rather unsympathetic discipline imposed from above, a scheme of life that he was ill fitted for and had already learned to resent, yet it was the longest and probably the strongest single environmental influence of his life. But it was not radically different from what he would have encountered at any of the other public schools, and was practically the best school environment available.

Shelley entered Eton in the upper fourth form; next year he was in the remove; in 1808 he was in the upper fifth, and in 1810 he was in the sixth. Living in succession with two masters, one a domine and the other a tutor, he received better food and lodging and was thrown into less crowded contact with his fellow lodgers than the majority of oppidans who lodged at the houses kept by dames. Hexter, with whom he first lodged, taught writing in the lower forms and was also a major in the militia; George Bethell, his tutor and second house master, was a genial, kind-hearted gentleman, notoriously dull and inept as a teacher of the classics.

Out of more than a thousand boys who were at Eton during

Shelley's six years there, probably a majority knew of and remembered him as one of the most extraordinary boys in the school. Some eight or ten of these have left slight accounts, anecdotes, or impressions of him, all recollected and stated many years after his death.[14]

At Eton young Shelley's habits and associations were not very different from what they had been at Syon House Academy. It has even been stated that he led a revolt against the fagging system,[15] but this is very improbable and was denied by a number of Etonians whom Medwin questioned on the point. Any revolt once started would have created a disturbance sufficient at least to be remembered and chronicled. Most of the boys thought him mad. He became known as " Mad Shelley," also as " Shelley the atheist," although " atheist " in this sense may have meant merely an opposer of the local powers, rather than one who denies the existence of a God.[16] His dress was careless — he was conspicuous for wearing his shoes without strings and dispensing with his hat entirely — and his lack of skill and interest in most of the popular games was obvious. Such facts as these, the basis on which all but a few of his schoolmates judged and remembered him, gave him no recommendation to either their favour or that of the masters. Mrs. Shelley, who got her impressions from the poet, says that he was rather generally unpopular with both.[17]

There are certain bits of evidence indicating the truth of this reputation. "We know the author's disgraceful and flagitious history well," wrote the first schoolmate who recorded any impression of the poet, " and could put down some of the vain boasting of his preface [to *The Revolt of Islam*]. At Eton we remember him notorious for setting fire to old trees with burning glasses." [18] A kindlier critic, Dr. Hawtrey, who succeeded Keate as headmaster and deplored the treatment Shelley received at Eton, believed that " what Shelley had to endure at Eton made him a perfect devil." [19]

Bysshe's inability to fight was early recognized and was well remembered by his schoolmates. It must have made him a

convenient stepping-stone for younger boys desirous of rising
by their fists. Thomas Style,[20] a smaller and younger boy, thus
achieved a place in Eton tradition. Challenging the future poet
to a fight, he seemed during the two opening rounds to have
undertaken too much. During the rest-periods the over-confident Bysshe is said to have spent his time striding about the
ring spouting defiant speeches from Homer. Young Style improved his rest-periods and completely defeated his antagonist
in the later rounds. Like Falstaff, Bysshe did not care to fight
longer than he saw reason in it. To the scandal of his backers,
he broke through the ring and fled swiftly from the scene.[21]
Nor was this the only fight in which he preferred declaiming
Homer to resting on the knee of his second.[22] Owning so in-
glorious a pugilistic reputation as this, it is peculiarly unjust
that young Shelley should have been cheated by all biographers
of one victory at least as well authenticated as his defeats. One
George Lyne, apparently a younger boy (he was two forms below Shelley in 1805 and half a form below him in 1808), thirsted
to build a reputation for prowess on Shelley's lack of it. His
only record runs: " Son of a tailor in the Strand. He fought
Shelley at school and was soundly beaten." [23]

The nagging and teasing that had contributed to Shelley's
misery at the academy continued, but on a larger scale. The
helpless, frustrated rage to which he had sometimes given utterance at Syon House seemed to many of his schoolmates a
show well worth promoting. " I have seen him surrounded,"
wrote one of them, " hooted, baited like a maddened bull, and
at this distance of time I seem to hear ringing within my ears
the cry which Shelley was wont to utter in his paroxysm of
revengeful anger." [24] Sometimes Shelley would find himself
surrounded and " nailed " with a muddy ball, at other times
his tormentors would beset him and yell his name, or point,
or push his books from his arm, or pluck at his garments — anything to produce the rage which " made his eyes flash like a
tiger's, his cheeks grow pale as death, his limbs quiver." Occasionally, according to his schoolmate Packe,[25] Shelley could
succeed in practically ignoring his tormentors. Once, however,

he was so maddened that he seized a fork and stabbed another boy in the hand with it.[26] These " Shelley-baits " were of almost daily occurrence,[27] at least during Shelley's early years at Eton.

FROM all this he escaped in vacations to the warm, friendly society of Field Place, where his two worlds of imagination and of fact could be harmoniously blended. One of his principal pleasures among his sisters was disguise, a pleasure he had many times enjoyed vicariously in his reading. Sometimes he pretended to be a fiend. Once he dressed himself as a countryman and paraded past the nursery windows carrying a truss of hay to a lady in the village so that she might make hay-tea to relieve her chilblains. In the guise of a country boy with a broad Sussex dialect he succeeded in engaging himself to a Horsham lawyer as gamekeeper's boy. Riding with a gentleman toward Horsham and concealing his own identity, he brought the conversation round to Squire Shelley's son, at Field Place, only to learn that there were some who considered him a trifle insane.[28]

Some of his boyish adventures took place solely in his own imagination. This common fact of childhood would scarcely be worth recording except for the fact that with Shelley it persisted into his maturer years. Hellen relates how Bysshe described with particular and elaborate detail a wholly fictitious visit to some ladies in Warnham.

These boyhood exploits, as Hellen looked back upon them, seemed definitely " eccentric." Her brother's mind appeared to have been " almost alone in its peculiar nature." The tricks and wild experiments that had already impressed those who knew Shelley at Field Place and Syon House Academy continued at Eton. There were a few tricks of a purely mischievous nature such as are always recollected by former schoolmates, though not always accurately. One schoolmate, Edward Leslie,[29] remembered that he and Shelley were generally given credit for putting a bulldog in Keate's desk — but the real culprit re-

39

vealed his identity in 1844. Another story [30] is that one night Shelley stole the huge gilded bunch of grapes that hung in front of the Christopher Inn and suspended them over Dr. Keate's door, where the doughty doctor collided with them on rushing forth next morning. Most probable of all these doubtful legends is the story that Shelley set fire to an old tree by the use of gunpowder and a burning-glass. Many years later the tree itself was exhibited, which shows that if the youth did accomplish this difficult feat he did it rather incompletely.

Shelley's scientific exploits at Eton, which must have seemed to some to be mere wilful pranks, are better authenticated and were much more numerous. He sent up fire-balloons, as other Eton boys were doing also. One Etonian [31] represents Shelley's interest in explosives as extending to the purchase at auction of a brass cannon, which was captured by the tutors before it went into action. The lack of singularity in Shelley's Eton experience with fireworks, as well as some official antagonism to the practice, may be deduced from the fact that within a few months after Shelley entered Eton one boy was killed when a pocket full of fireworks was ignited by another boy.[32]

Shelley experimented with chemical brews and nearly blew himself up; he poisoned himself once. In confederation with Edward Leslie, he electrified a tom-cat. Striking higher, he even electrified " Butch " Bethell when that blundering tutor and landlord too hastily investigated a galvanic battery. At Field Place during vacations he was also demonstrating certain effects of powders and acids to his young sisters. He bought small electrical machines that were vended among the students by Adam Walker's assistant [33] and with the aid of a travelling tinker he constructed a steam engine that duly exploded.[34]

Up to this point Shelley's scientific interests simply continued the enthusiasm for the mysteries and possibilities of natural science first aroused by Adam Walker. Two or three times, at least, the stimulus was renewed, for every other year Walker gave his lectures and demonstrations at Eton. But young Shelley would not be confined within the very generous bounds of Walker's interests. Ranging from the physical to the metaphysical, he absorbed the scientific reveries

of Albertus Magnus and Paracelsus with eager enthusiasm for
new sensation. He sought out the lore of magic and witchcraft
and learned incantations for raising ghosts and devils. He
watched all night for ghosts. At Field Place he planned to gain
entrance to the charnel house at Warnham Church and watch
beside the bones of the dead. Once at Eton he stole forth at
midnight fearfully intent on raising a ghost. Afraid to look
back lest he should see the devil, he crossed the fields to a spot
where he could bestride a small stream of running water. Here
he repeated his incantation, drinking three times from a skull,
and when no ghost appeared he concluded that the fault lay in
his magic formula.[35] Well might Tom Medwin remember that
Shelley's mind at this time " ran on bandits, castles, ruined
towers, wild mountains, storms and apparitions — the terrific." [36]

These incidents are corroborated by Shelley himself in his
" Hymn to Intellectual Beauty ":

> While yet a boy I sought for ghosts, and sped
>   Through many a listening chamber, cave, and ruin,
> And starlight wood, with fearful steps pursuing
> Hopes of high talk with the departed dead.
> I called on poisonous names with which our youth is fed:
>   I was not heard: I saw them not.[37]

As he looked back on them in 1816, they appeared to him to
have been the prelude to his awakening to the unseen presence
of " Intellectual Beauty." They could hardly have seemed so
at the time, but they are at least evidence of a keen intellectual
curiosity and thirst for sensation.[38] Bizarre as such adventures
seem today, they were probably not so unusual for a generation
of children fed on horror-stories. Many other boys who later became staid citizens sought the same thrills. Shelley's ghost-
raising efforts reminded his friend Thomas Jefferson Hogg of
an even more elaborate undertaking of the same sort by his
own early schoolmates in Yorkshire.[39]

Shelley was never quite so abnormal at Eton as he later became in the memories of those who had known him there. He
did not lose or flee from every fight, nor did he abstain en-

41

tirely from boating and other boyish sports, as asserted in the recollections of Walter Halliday to be quoted later. Even at Syon House he had learned to enjoy boating; he told Medwin that boating was one of his principal pleasures at Eton; and Medwin saw him take part in a regatta there in 1809.[40] The pleasures of boating in Italy reminded him most comfortably of picnics at Eton, when the boys would cram their pockets with hard-boiled eggs, rolls, and radishes and feast until eight in some green nook made dry and comfortable with stolen hay.[41]

Another sport of the Eton boys was duck-spearing. Shelley was no stranger to this sport either. A boy named Seymour [42] recalled finding Shelley disabled on the river bank, having speared himself instead of the duck. Since he went abroad at Field Place with his gun during vacations and became a very good shot, it is not at all unlikely that at Eton he occasionally borrowed a gun from one of the " cads " hanging around outside the gates and went shooting as other Etonians did. He certainly shot ducks at Field Place in vacation. " Here are thousands of wild Ducks & Geese in our River & Lake," he wrote to a fellow Etonian. " I have shot at numbers, but killed only one." [43] When Hogg first met him he was tanned and freckled from out-door exercise.[44]

Shelley also took part in the two " Montem " celebrations that occurred while he was at Eton. These ceremonies were Eton's most picturesque inheritance from earlier centuries. Having sent out " salt-bearers " to collect forced tribute from all pas-sengers on near-by roads, the students would dress themselves in picturesque costumes and march in semi-military style to Salt Hill (" *ad montem* "), where certain more or less vague rites and horseplay were indulged in. George III, when his health permitted, always saw the spectacle, and it is probable that he saw Shelley, just as that young rebel probably saw George III in 1804 when he visited the school and was lustily cheered by the boys. In the 1805 procession Shelley was uniformed as a midshipman; in the 1808 event he " walked as full corporal." [45] Shelley's only other public appearance at Eton was when he delivered an oration of Cicero against Catiline, on Election Day, shortly before entering Oxford.

Young Shelley was certainly not as friendless at Eton as he had been at Brentford, though he was too unusual ever to be popular. One schoolmate [46] remembered that most of the boys avoided Shelley, and two of his best friends, Andrew Amos and Walter Halliday, agree that Shelley rather avoided the other boys. "Shelley was too peculiar in his genius to be the 'hare with many friends,'" said Charles Packe, "but the few who knew him loved him, and, if I may judge from myself, remember with affectionate regret that his schooldays were more adventurous than happy." [47] Hogg noticed at Oxford that Shelley's room contained a considerable number of books given him by Eton schoolmates and that some of these boys continued to call on him.

Most of these friendships belong to Shelley's later years at Eton. His first friend, apparently, was Andrew Amos, who was one of the two other lower-form boys living at Hexter's. Amos used to enjoy composing and acting plays with Shelley for the benefit of the other boy.[48] A little later Shelley possessed the esteem of Charles William Packe, who sat near him in Bethell's class and "always liked him; he was such a good, generous, open-hearted fellow." [49]

Captain Rees Howell Gronow, who speaks of Shelley in his *Reminiscences and Recollections,* must have known him about midway in Shelley's Eton career, or even later, since he was two years Shelley's junior. Gronow remembered him as studious and meditative, with a distaste for sports and games and a great interest in novels and romances. By inference, at least, he also remembered Shelley's fondness for " the excellent brown bread and butter we used to get at Spires " — one of the shops famous in Eton tradition. Gronow mentions that Shelley's best friend was Price, an excellent classicist.[50]

Another good friend was Edward (or Edmund) Leslie, who roomed in the same house with Shelley (probably Bethell's) along with Ball — later a well-known dandy — and Lord Howe. Leslie was the recipient of several copies of Scott's poems " from his affectionate friend, Percy Bysshe Shelley." His son told Professor Dowden that he was Shelley's best and dearest friend at Eton, and that he lived in the same house with Shelley,

Lord Howe, and Charles Ball, who appreciated Shelley's genius more than any other boy.[51]

The most glowing memory of Shelley at Eton comes from Walter Halliday, later a clergyman, who was in the upper fifth form with Shelley in 1808. In 1857 he wrote Lady Shelley as follows:

Glenthorne, February 27th, 1857

My Dear Madam,

Your letter has taken me back to the sunny time of boyhood, ' when thought is speech, and speech is truth; ' when I was the friend and companion of Shelley at Eton. What brought us together in that small world was, I suppose, kindred feelings, and the predominance of fancy and imagination. Many a long and happy walk have I had with him in the beautiful neighbourhood of dear old Eton. We used to wander for hours about Clewer, Frogmore, the Park at Windsor, the Terrace; and I was a delighted and willing listener to his marvellous stories of fairyland, and apparitions, and spirits, and haunted ground; and his speculations were then (for his mind was far more developed than mine) of the world beyond the grave. Another of his favourite rambles was Stoke Park, and the picturesque churchyard, where Gray is said to have written his *Elegy*, of which he was very fond. I was myself far too young to form any estimate of character, but I loved Shelley for his kindliness and affectionate ways: he was not made to endure the rough and boisterous pastime at Eton, and his shy and gentle nature was glad to escape far away to muse over strange fancies, for his mind was reflective and teeming with deep thought. His lessons were child's play to him, and his power of Latin versification marvellous. I think I remember some long work he had even then commenced, but I never saw it. His love of nature was intense, and the sparkling poetry of his mind shone out of his speaking eye, when he was dwelling on anything good or great. He certainly was not happy at Eton, for his was a disposition that needed especial personal superintendence, to watch, and cherish, and direct all his noble aspirations, and the remarkable tenderness of his heart. He had great moral courage, and feared nothing, but what was base, and false, and low. He never joined in the usual sports of the boys, and, what is remarkable, never went out in a boat on the river. What I have here set down will be of little use to you, but will please you as a sincere, and truthful, and humble tribute to one whose good name was sadly whispered away. Shelley said to me, when leaving Oxford

44

under a cloud: 'Halliday, I am come to say good-bye to you, if you are not afraid to be seen with me!' I saw him once again in the autumn of 1814, in London, when he was glad to introduce me to his wife. I think he said he was just come from Ireland. You have done quite right in applying to me direct, and I am only sorry that I have no anecdotes, or letters, of that period to furnish.

I am yours truly,

WALTER S. HALLIDAY.[52]

The Shelley of Walter Halliday's remembrance is very similar to the older brother that Hellen Shelley recalled, as she remembered his later vacations at Field Place. He enjoyed taking his sisters for walks through the country lanes or across the open fields. On one such occasion Hellen remembered that he "gently" threw his youngest sister, Margaret, across a sunk fence to the turf beyond, because she was too young to be pulled across, like Hellen. Sometimes he walked forth alone, at night. Possibly these walks lay in the background of one of the first passages in his poems to excite the admiration of his countrymen — the passage in *Queen Mab* beginning "How beautiful this night"; possibly they were connected with that search for hidden mysteries that he refers to in *Alastor* as a part of his early experience. The servant who followed him reported merely that Master Bysshe had taken a walk and come back again.

Like any other son of a country squire, he learned the use of fire-arms. Years later, in Italy, Byron found him a tolerable shot with a pistol. This was a side of his life in which the younger sisters could hardly be partners or subjects. He also rode frequently about the country lanes on his pony. His mother, whether because she had grown up among horse-lovers herself or because she was disquieted by his hectic imaginative energy, did what she could to encourage this side of his development. She sent him abroad with the gamekeeper or went fishing with him herself. Medwin tells us that Shelley read a book while the gamekeeper hunted, from which it has been inferred that these expeditions were wholly distasteful to the boy. This makes it rather odd that Shelley should also have had the habit of going forth alone with dog and gun. There can be little doubt, though

45

no one has recollected it, that the Squire Shelley who was a good husbandman and a conscientious father had occasional walks and talks with Bysshe in which he saw to it that his son and heir knew something of Field Place, its crops, its livestock, and its tenants.

The author in Shelley began stirring at an early age, probably before he entered Eton, but his first recorded poem belongs apparently to his later vacations at Field Place. It consisted of five six-line stanzas on a cat — ending with somewhat heavy-footed ferocity:

> But this poor little cat
> Only wanted a rat,
> To stuff out its own little maw;
> And it were as good
> *Some* people had such food,
> To make them *hold their jaw.*

With his oldest sister, Elizabeth, he wrote a play which they seriously submitted to a producer and which was returned with equal seriousness.[53] Hellen displayed budding genius as a poet, and Bysshe forthwith became her mentor and publisher. Certain verses of his own were printed at Horsham, and old Sir Bysshe is said to have paid the bills, but no trace of these verses remains.

Shelley was probably miserable a good part of the time at Eton, but at home he was " full of cheerful fun and had all the comic vein so agreeable in a household." [54] The cat poem was a successful effort at juvenile humour. For the delight of his sisters he next wrote verses ridiculing their French teacher — verses so excitedly circulated that they eventually fell into the hands of the enemy. Once while calling on the rector's daughter he made a sudden dive under the table when fresh callers appeared, a trick which he twice repeated, with variations, years after he had reached manhood.[55]

During these vacations reading continued, and we have the father's word for it that he made a habit of reading with his son.[56] Relations between the two were as yet affectionate and unstrained. Shelley's sisters remembered very well his constant solicitude about his father when Mr. Timothy Shelley was ill during the boy's second year at Eton.[57] There is no record of the boy's own illness during the six years he was at Eton except once when he was sent home to recover [58] and again during a vacation.[59]

As Walter Halliday looked back upon his association with Shelley at Eton he could see that what Shelley needed and never received was personal, sympathetic interest from one of his masters. Not long before he left Eton the boy found such a friend across the Thames at Windsor. In *The Revolt of Islam* Shelley describes a stately and beautiful old man who had spent his life storing up knowledge and good deeds, who frees Laon from imprisonment and restores him to sanity and health. Again, in "Prince Athanase" he describes the Prince's instructor, Zonoras, as an old, white-haired man of great wisdom and benevolence, almost the only man still free from superstition, who fills the young Prince's mind

> With soul-sustaining songs of ancient lore,
> And philosophic wisdom, clear and mild.

Both these benevolent old men have their original in Dr. James Lind, physician to the royal household at Windsor.[60] Dr. Lind was an eccentric old man of over seventy, white-haired, tall and thin, yet lively and energetic, full of odd bits of wisdom and experience from his early life on an East Indiaman. He was given to all sorts of curiosities and speculations and welcomed the same interests in others. Young Shelley often crossed over to Windsor to browse among his books, witness his little tricks of Eastern conjury, and hear exciting talk about the possibilities and bounds of knowledge and experience.

"This man," Shelley told Mary Shelley some years afterwards,

is exactly what an old man ought to be. Free, calm-spirited, full of benevolence and even of youthful ardour; his eye seemed to burn with supernatural spirit beneath his brow, shaded by his venerable white locks; he was tall, vigorous, and healthy in his body; tempered, as it had ever been, by his amiable mind. I owe to that man far, ah! far more than I owe to my father; he loved me, and I shall never for-

get our long talks, where he breathed the spirit of the kindest tolerance and the purest wisdom. Once, when I was very ill during the
holidays, as I was recovering from a fever which had attacked my
brain, a servant overheard my father consult about sending me to a
private madhouse. I was a favourite among all our servants, so this
fellow came and told me as I lay sick in bed. My horror was beyond
words, and I might soon have been mad indeed, if they had proceeded in their iniquitous plan. I had one hope. I was master of
three pounds in money, and with the servant's help, I contrived to
send an express to Dr. Lind. He came, and I shall never forget his
manner on that occasion. His profession gave him authority, his love
for me, ardour. He dared my father to execute his purpose, and his
menaces had the desired effect.[61]

Perhaps the madhouse story is no more to be taken literally
than some other imaginary or half-imaginary episodes before
and after it, but the probability that it seemed true to Shelley
indicates the time at which he began to consider his father
an enemy.

One of Shelley's most intimate friends during his last years
at Eton was Edward Fergus Graham, whom he saw, not at
Eton, but at Field Place and in London. Young Graham was
a protégé of Shelley's father, who was paying the expenses of
his musical education in London. When he entered the family
circle at Field Place is uncertain, but he appears to have spent
his vacations there at least. He was about five years Shelley's
senior. Shelley's letters from Eton and Oxford in 1810 and 1811
show that he considered Graham's London lodgings his home
while in town. Graham was his agent and confidant in matters
of all sorts, from receiving and holding correspondence and
acting as London shopping agent, to seeing that the press took
proper notice of his first publications. He had a secret to tell
Graham, Shelley wrote once,[62] that he would tell no one else.
He and his sister Elizabeth seem to have made Edward a
partner in some of the Gothic nonsense that passed between
them.[63]

Through Graham Shelley met in London a young man who
became for a while one of his intimate friends. Joseph Gibbons
Merle [64] was the son of a French émigré who had married —

48

according to the son's erroneous belief — a descendant of
Shakespeare. In 1809 young Merle became a clerk at Ackerman's art and music store, where he was employed partly in
connection with Ackerman's *Poetical Magazine,* a magazine in
which Merle actually published a poem.[65] Merle was a pupil
of Graham's music master, the rather well-known Joseph Woelff.
When Graham was shown Merle's poem he remarked that his
young friend Bysshe Shelley was also a poet, and undertook
to make the two acquainted. Since Graham was arranging at
about this time for Woelff to set some of Shelley's verse to
music,[66] it may be that he saw in Merle an opportunity to introduce Shelley to Ackerman's *Poetical Magazine.* The meeting occurred in Graham's rooms in April or May 1810.[67] Merle
was nervous and self-conscious. Though he considered his own
family as good as Shelley's he realized acutely the difference
between their positions in life and expected his new acquaintance to be stiff or patronizing. Instead he found a somewhat
slightly-built youth, with a look of health and vigour, who
talked affably and enthusiastically about their common interest
in poetry and about his own ideals. Afterwards (or possibly
before they met, during a correspondence instigated by Graham) Shelley did regard him briefly with something of the
suspicious aloofness that he had feared. " It is never my custom," Shelley wrote Graham, " to make new friends whom I cannot own to my old ones . . . I have knowledge enough of the
world, to perceive that no disinterested motive can lead a man
to enter into a friendship with another with whose temper,
capacity and talents he is most certainly ignorant . . . in short,
I am resolved to have no more to do with him, not even for
drawing utensils, as I fear the man has some deep scheme.
Where does he come from, and who is he? " [68]

Nevertheless a rather close friendship developed between the
two.[69] Shelley visited Merle several times in London, and the
two exchanged letters frequently. Within a few months Merle
was visiting Shelley at Field Place and making the acquaintance
of Sir Bysshe. Already Shelley was beginning to feel that his
father misunderstood him and treated him stingily in the matter
of pocket money. Young Merle admired Shelley greatly for his

intelligence, generosity and sympathy, but he was disturbed by his antagonism to Christianity and felt obliged to remonstrate against his efforts to " convert " him.

Dr. Lind was almost the only person sure to sympathize with and encourage the extraordinary thirst for intellectual excitement that had characterized Shelley before he entered Eton and that was increasing steadily. The classroom and his various masters fell far short of doing so, though even the dull and limited fare of Eton was not utterly devoid of stimulation. Captain Gronow remembered him as " studious and meditative." He was constantly helping other boys with their lessons, according to Charles Packe, and composed Latin verse with wonderful ease.[70] Walter Halliday says Shelley's lessons were " child's play " to him. It must have been in the Latin class that he got the inspiration to translate Pliny's *Natural History,* on which he made considerable progress in his leisure hours,[71] and perhaps also the impulse which led him to read Plato's *Symposium* with Dr. Lind — if Medwin's assertion that he read it is correct.[72] Outside the regular courses, Shelley was also becoming a tolerable French scholar [73] and, in his last year, working hard at German.

THE MEN who taught Shelley at Eton must have furnished him with considerably more stimulation than either the poet or his biographers supposed. Dowden mentions Bethell, a good-humoured, blundering teacher whose dullness was proverbial among Etonians, and also Ben Drury, Shelley's first master, who was an admirable scholar quite likely to do justice to the young poet's Latin verses on a basis much broader than that of true or false quantities. No one mentions either Keate or Goodall as Shelley's instructor. At Eton the headmaster always taught the sixth form and the upper fifth. This means that Keate taught Shelley during the last seven months he was at Eton and that Goodall taught him for at least a year or two previously. Whatever Keate's ferocity as a disciplinarian, he was universally admitted to be an excellent teacher and scholar. As for Goodall, under whom Shelley probably sat longer than under anyone else, he has been described in terms that make him the ideal teacher for a youth such as Shelley must have been. Edward C. Hawtrey, a great teacher himself, who was three years Shelley's senior at Eton, gives an impressive account of Goodall's particular merit in discovering and encouraging talent among his students.[74]

Nevertheless, Shelley's most active intellectual life had slight connection with the classroom. His own account of his early life, written to interest Godwin, is not altogether trustworthy in detail and is somewhat exaggerated in tone, yet there must be considerable truth in his statement to Godwin: " I have known no tutor or adviser (*not excepting my father*) from whose lessons and suggestions I have not recoiled with disgust. The knowledge which I have . . . has been acquired by my unassisted efforts." [75]

The books that had been both a refuge and a secret stimulus at Syon House Academy continued their important rôle in his life at Eton. His pocket-money went largely for books and scientific toys. Most of those who remembered him at all well made note of his reading. Captain Gronow spoke of him as " a great reader of novels and romances," and Edward Leslie said " he wandered alone, generally with a book, for hours together, day after day, learning verses or composing them." [76]

An active mind devoted to reading can absorb a great many volumes in six years. For Shelley's six years at Eton we possess less than a dozen titles of the many books that he read. The numerous Gothic romances and thrillers of other sorts are represented by one title only, Charlotte Dacre's *Zeluco, or the Moor,* which Medwin says Shelley read at Syon House Academy, but which was not published until he was at Eton. It had a considerable effect on *Zastrozzi,* which Shelley wrote and published while he was at Eton.[77] He had made his fateful acquaintance with the works of William Godwin, but as yet knew only his *St. Leon,* which he read as a novel without much cognizance of underlying revolutionary doctrine.[78]

Medwin fails to specify the books of chemistry that were bor-

51

rowed from Medwin's father and returned because chemistry was "a forbidden thing" at Eton,[79] but among the "ancient books of Chemistry and Magic" which were perused at Eton "with an enthusiasm of wonder, almost amounting to belief"[80] were the works of Albertus Magnus and Paracelsus, the former of which he read in Latin.[81] Among more modern writers who emphasized the scope of the human mind and human experience he read Franklin and Condorcet. Franklin he "swore by," as he quoted both writers to Medwin in support of his belief in the ultimate complete triumph of mind over matter.[82] By the time he entered his last year at Eton Shelley was already an enthusiastic reader of poetry, though his taste was somewhat limited. Southey was his favourite. He read *Thalaba* so constantly that he almost knew it by heart. *The Curse of Kehama* was even more a favourite with him; he went about declaiming it among his intimates. He read and imitated Scott, but did not greatly admire *The Lady of the Lake,* and he disliked Wordsworth's poems as too simple.[83]

The two remaining books to be mentioned, Pliny's *Natural History* and the *De Rerum Natura* of Lucretius, both left an undoubted impression upon his mind. According to Medwin,[84] Shelley was deeply impressed with Pliny's chapter "*De Deo,*" which was "the first germ of his ideas respecting the nature of God," and he "studied deeply Lucretius, whom he considered the best of the Latin poets." Pliny's famous chapter told him that to conceive of God under any definite form or image was ridiculous. Lucretius told him that there was no God other than blind chance, and that revealed religions were nothing but superstition encouraged by priests for selfish purposes. A few years later these ideas, reinforced by the doctrines of eighteenth-century rationalism, were to find striking expression in *Queen Mab.* Still earlier their traces may be seen in his novel *St. Irvyne,* where the Rosicrucian expresses his doubt of a first cause and asserts his belief that human religions are mere priestcraft and superstition.[85] In the same work, transmuted into the Rosicrucian's secret of immortal life, also may be found echoes of Franklin and Condorcet on the possibility of abolishing disease and death by human development.

It was not only in his reading and speculations, however, that
young Shelley passed beyond the traditional bounds of Eton.
Before he left school he was a full-fledged author. He was also
very much in love.

Chapter IV

AT ETON:

THE BUDDING AUTHOR AND LOVER

BOYHOOD POEMS; *ZASTROZZI; ORIGINAL POETRY;*
THE WANDERING JEW; LETTER–WRITING;
LOVE FOR HARRIET GROVE

FROM the earliest recollections of Hellen Shelley her brother
had been the narrator of fanciful stories, sometimes traditional
and sometimes fictitious. Nothing is clearer about his early boyhood than the fact that he craved an audience. At Eton the
same trait was constantly in evidence. It was with " great vivacity " that he composed and produced with the help of Andrew Amos little impromptu plays for the one other little boy in
his first lodging-house. Later he composed poems and plays
which he delighted to rehearse to his schoolmates, and continued to rehearse in spite of the fact that they encouraged him
only to make boisterous fun of his efforts. Certain printing bills
that his grandfather is said to have paid in Horsham [1] were the
result of his desire for a larger or more favourable audience.

During the winter of his last year at Eton Shelley was almost
feverishly eager to write and publish. When he was at Field
Place for the winter vacation Medwin took long walks with him
through the fields and in St. Leonard's Wood — walks that were
filled with much high speculation and with a great yearning for
authorship.[2] Before he had left Eton for Oxford he was the author or co-author of no less than five separate volumes, one of
which was published while he was still at Eton, one during the

54

summer vacation, and one shortly after he entered Oxford. Three of the five were more or less collaborative, and one was left unfinished.

The unfinished work was the first one, written in collaboration with Medwin, whose account of it is all that remains to prove its existence. " We that winter wrote, in alternate chapters," says Medwin,[3] " the commencement of a wild and extravagant romance, where a hideous witch played the principal part." This novel was called " The Nightmare " and failed to reach completion, but a part of it — the character of an awful witch, was versified in *The Wandering Jew.*

Zastrozzi, the young author's next attempt, reached a triumphant conclusion. By May 7, 1809, even before " The Nightmare," a considerable part of *Zastrozzi* may have been written, for on that date we find Shelley writing to Longman and Company offering them a partly finished romance and describing himself a trifle grandly as the author.[4] It was finished during the next year and was published late in March 1810.[5] On the first day of that month Shelley wrote to Edward Graham, in London, proposing plans for launching the book successfully. At Easter he and Graham would visit the bookseller's in a barouche and four to " shew them " — as he had already hinted to Longman and Company — " that we are no Grub Street garretteers." [6] And because it was " of consequence . . . to establish your name . . . high," Graham was instructed that he must " *pouch* " those venal rascals, the reviewers, and especially the *British Review.*

Since *Zastrozzi* is one of the poorest examples of one of the poorest types of fiction ever published in England, it could easily benefit by a little pouching of reviewers. Zastrozzi, the hero, is a fiery, terrible person who turns out in the end to be a self-elected minister of justice inspired by the memory of his mother's wrongs. His foil is a benevolent, mysterious character named Verezzi, an object of revenge. One heroine, Matilda, is beautiful and passionate; the other, Julia, is ethereally virtuous. These characters interact upon each other as if hypnotized by

a nervous practitioner whose intent is only hazily perceptible
through a thick murk of Gothic-novel passions.

One wonders how such a novel could have been seriously reviewed, until one sees its competitors. The *Monthly Magazine*,
which claimed that its list of new publications was the only complete one, listed five other novels in the same month, to wit: *The
Novice of St. Ursula*, 4 vols., £1. 15; *The Prince of Montauban,
or Times of Terror*, 6s.; *The Maid of Sensibility, or The History
of Edward and Matilda*, 2 vols., 8s.; *The Castle of Vivaldi, or
The Mysterious Injunction*, by Caroline Horwood, 4 vols., £1;
Lindamira, or An Old Maid in Search of a Husband, 3 vols., 15s.
Zastrozzi, a Romance, at five shillings was the shortest, least expensive, and one of the most soberly entitled of the lot; moreover it fulfilled the principal test by which two of Jane Austen's
characters judged a list of books, in the sixth chapter of *Nor-
thanger Abbey* — "but are they all horrid? Are you sure they
are all horrid?" "Yes, they are all horrid."

Zastrozzi was not only noticed, it was even revived. As late
as 1839 it appeared in a series known as The Romancist and
Novelist's Library. The staid and austere *British Review* resisted Graham's blandishments, if they were exerted, and ignored the volume, but the short respectful notice carried by
the *Gentleman's Magazine* suggests that Shelley's authorized
"poucher" may not altogether have disappointed his principal.
Since it has previously been unnoticed by the poet's biographers, it may be quoted in full:

> A short, but well-told tale of horror, and, if we do not mistake, not
> from an ordinary pen. The story is so artfully conducted that the
> reader cannot easily anticipate the denoument, which is conducted
> on the principles of moral justice; and, by placing the scene on the
> Continent, the Author has availed himself of characters and vices,
> which, however useful in narratives of this description, thank God,
> are not to be found in this country.[7]

But though the *Gentleman's Magazine* compounded for vicious traits in Shelley's characters as belonging only to lesser
breeds without the law, the *Critical Review* scourged them with
Draconian severity.[8] "Zastrozzi is one of the most savage and

improbable demons that ever issued from a diseased brain," it began. Proceeding thence to a long and outraged summary, embellished with excerpts, it pronounced the work too contemptible for review, except that such " open and barefaced immorality " required castigation. Did the author think a modest young woman could read such " gross and wanton pages "? [9] The review concludes that the author " cannot be too severely reprobated " and that " Not all his ' scintillated eyes,' his ' battling emotions,' his ' frigorific torpidity of despair,' nor his ' Lethean torpor,' with the rest of his nonsensical and stupid jargon, ought to save him from infamy, and his volume from the flames."

The anonymous young author, however, took his infamy in high spirits. Before either of these reviews appeared he had given a celebration dinner to eight of his fellow Etonians. According to one of the guests, it was " a most magnificent banquet," and was paid for out of the price received for the book, which the same informant thought was forty pounds. [10]

DURING the same period in which *Zastrozzi* was being written the active young author had two other volumes nearing completion, each with a different collaborator. The first of these was finished by September 6, 1810, on which date Shelley received the last proof impression from the printer. [11] The volume was entitled *Original Poetry by Victor and Cazire,* and was the work of Shelley and his oldest sister, Elizabeth. The publisher was John Joseph Stockdale.

In the early autumn of 1810 Shelley sought the publisher, Stockdale, and asked him to take over for publication a quantity of volumes then being printed for him. [12] The volumes were nearly ready, but the money to pay the printer in Worthing was not at hand. Could Stockdale, who was a dealer in remainders, handle the matter? Stockdale undertook to do so, and on the 17th of September received 1,480 copies of *Original Poetry,* which he immediately advertised for sale in the *Morning Chronicle* of September 18 and the *Morning Post* of the 19th. Harriet Grove's journal notes receipt of her copy on September 17. [13] After some copies had been sold, Stockdale discovered that one of the poems was a plagiarism from "Monk" Lewis. He apprised Shelley of the fact, whereupon "With all the ardour natural to his character he expressed the warmest resentment at the imposition practised upon him by his coadjutor," [14] and entreated Stockdale to destroy all the copies.

Stockdale's discovery must have been made at least three weeks after publication, since he advertised the book again in *The Times* of October 12. Three monthly magazines listed it among the new books: the *British Critic* for September, the *Literary Panorama* for October, and the *Monthly Magazine* for November. It received three reviews: in the *Literary Panorama* for October 1810; the *British Critic* for April 1811; and the *Poetical Register* for 1810–11.

It is rather a pity that Shelley's biographers have failed to note the first of these reviews, which exposes the flimsiness of the volume with a sympathetic, patronizing humour that is both amused and amusing. Either the reviewer guessed the true status of the authors from the first two poems (no difficult feat) or had gleaned information from Edward Graham, the official poucher. Limiting himself to the Gothicism which forms a large part of the volume, the reviewer began by deploring the unhappiness of modern poets. "In the evening 'black whirlwinds' and 'yelling fiends' beset them on every side . . . at night, — ghosts, hobgoblins, — shadowy forms, death, devils, disaster, and damnation dance around them, in dire dismay, till their 'souls are chilled,' — their 'blood is frozen,' — their 'heart sinks within them,' and miserable they are, to be sure!" How much better the blithe gayety of old-fashioned elves and fairies than the "full range of fine compound epithets, intermingled with blue lightning, chilling blasts, howling storms, sulphurous clouds. . . . Could anything possibly be finer — that is, more terrific — that is — ahem! — than the following?" — quoting the last nine stanzas of "Revenge." The *British Critic* spoke out much more sharply, with nasty aspersions on the grammar and metre of Elizabeth's introductory poem. Quoting a short passage from this poem through the line "What a tiresome girl! — pray soon make an end," the reviewer underscores the first half, and comments: "This last line, if not measure, contains at least

truth in the first part, and a reasonable wish in the second."
The other poems are characterized as "songs of sentimental
nonsense and very absurd tales of horror."

The *Poetical Register* for 1810–11 (which did not appear until 1814) bestowed an unnecessary *coup de grâce* in four crisp,
impatient sentences beginning: "There is no 'original *poetry*'
in this volume; there is nothing in it but downright scribble."

By 1814 Shelley himself would probably have endorsed this
drastic obituary. Even the charitable Professor Dowden, who
wrote before the volume was recovered, would have found difficulty in discovering its literary merits. The book contains seventeen poems, all dated from October 1809 to August 1810. The
first two are familiar verse epistles, assignable on internal evidence to Elizabeth Shelley. Five or six of the sentimental
poems seem quite clearly to be by Shelley. At least three of the
latter deal with his love for Harriet Grove. Most or all of the
ballads of terror are believed by Mr. Garnett to be by Shelley,
except the plagiarism. This plagiarism, which oddly enough no
reviewer detected, consists in printing "Monk" Lewis's "The
Black Canon of Elmham, or Saint Edmund's Eve," as "Saint
Edmond's Eve." It was lifted unchanged from Lewis's *Tales of
Terror*, a copy of which reposed in the Field Place library and
bears evidence of hard usage.[15] There are other signs of literary
"influence" bordering upon plagiarism, particularly a stanza of
"Ghasta" paraphrased from Chatterton's "Ælla."[16] The volume, like all Shelley's poetry before *Queen Mab*, is without literary value, but it is not therefore without significance, since it
helps present the picture of an active, unstable mind and the
food it fed upon. Certainly there was nothing original or impressive about the young author's Gothicism. James Beattie, in
his *The Minstrel*, written nearly twenty years before Shelley's
birth, might almost be thought prophetic of Shelley's youthful
compositions in the following lines (lines 284–8):

> There would he dream of graves and corpses pale;
>   And ghosts that to the charnel dungeon throng,
> And drag a length of clanking chain, and wail,
>   Till silenced by the owl's terrific song
> Or blast that shrieks by fits the shuddering isles along.

Shelley was in all probability writing his part of *The Wandering Jew* at the same time that he was functioning as the Victor of Victor and Cazire.[17] Tom Medwin was the supposed collaborator. Unfortunately Medwin's two accounts of the poem [18] are contradictory in detail, but they agree that Medwin wrote part of the poem, that it was a youthful cento containing a description versified from their novel, " The Nightmare," with materials from Lewis's *The Monk*, and a crucifixion scene lifted almost bodily from a volume of Cambridge Prize Poems.[19] Thomas Campbell, to whom the poem was sent for an opinion, pronounced that there were only two good lines in it. Medwin seems to have thought the idea of publication abandoned after this, but, as a matter of fact, Shelley sent it to two publishers. The first, Ballantyne and Company of Edinburgh, declined it on the ground that it was " perhaps better suited to the character and liberal feelings of the English than the bigoted spirit which yet pervades many cultivated minds in this country." The second was Stockdale, who had just published *Original Poetry by Victor and Cazire*. Stockdale could not remember what happened thereafter, except that he did not publish it.[20]

Like *Poems by Victor and Cazire*, the poem offers no indication of great latent abilities. Its verse is badly imitated from Scott, its narrative technique is bad, and its Gothic love-story element and Wandering Jew element war with each other for supremacy. The Wandering Jew himself seems compounded about equally from the one whom Shelley first met in Chapter iv of Lewis's *The Monk* and the tragic sufferer of Schubart's poem, a translation of which had accidentally come into Shelley's hands in 1809.[21] Shelley's first Wandering Jew is a rather orthodox creation. He is not yet the scorner of Divine judgment he later became in Shelley's imagination and is thus a witness to the fact that Shelley's religious opinions were still largely orthodox.

Shelley was engaged in still other literary activities at this time. In a letter to Edward Graham dated April 1, 1810, he mentioned a " new romance " on which he was at work. This may have been an uncompleted work that has been lost, or it may be *St. Irvyne*, which was largely completed before he took up residence at Oxford. His letters to Edward Graham in 1810 enclose several poems which he hoped Graham or Graham's music teacher, Woelff, would set to music. This practice of sending occasional poems to Graham he kept up after his expulsion from Oxford until shortly before his elopement with Harriet Westbrook. He also told Edward Graham [22] that he was working on a tragedy to be offered to Covent Garden when completed, and that he hoped for some notice in *Ackerman's Poetical Magazine.*

WITH all this literary activity went another activity closely allied to it. Shelley was becoming quite a voluminous letter-writer. He had learned from the unconventional Dr. Lind not to regard lack of personal acquaintance as a bar to opening a correspondence. Thus, after hearing Rowland Hill preach in Surrey Chapel in Blackfriar's Road, he did not hesitate to write a letter offering to fill the pulpit once himself. [23]

Tom Medwin returned from a visit to Wales in 1807 or 1808, bringing with him a volume of poems published by Felicia Dorothea Browne, later Hemans, a promising young poetess of thirteen or fourteen. Shelley's delight in this volume was heightened by Medwin's enthusiasm over "the beauty . . . the grace, the charm, the simplicity, the naiveté of this interesting girl." Why not write to this young goddess? A correspondence developed. [24] Hellen Shelley remembered it, but thought that it terminated with Shelley's receiving a discouraging reply to his first letter. [25] But, according to Medwin, it throve temporarily and was only terminated when Miss Browne's mother became alarmed at the boldness of the opinions expressed in Shelley's letters. Years later she wrote a poem, "The Sceptic," which was suggested by Shelley's tragic death, but which contains no trace of remembered acquaintance. Shelley's disillusion was fairly well advanced by July 28, 1811, when he referred to her parenthetically as "certainly a tigress." [26]

Shelley wrote to the poet Campbell also, as we have seen, asking literary criticism. He planned, at least, to open a correspondence with the painter Fuseli. [27] A little later he was to extend this practice widely and write to Scott, Godwin, Moore, and Byron, with some results from the two first. Numerous letters went out from Eton signed with Shelley's name, addressed to all sorts of unknown persons and initiating embarrassing scientific discussions. When one irate correspondent threatened to write to his master and have him caned, he adopted a pseudonym.[28]

Various publishers received letters from him about literary ventures either completed or planned. Such of these letters as have been preserved are excellently written and show a surprising aptness at business affairs. His friend and general London factotum, Edward Graham, was no doubt the recipient of many more letters than have been recovered. When Shelley wrote to Graham on business matters he was crisp and almost ludicrously worldly-wise, as in his high and mighty attitude toward reviewers and publishers. In commenting on the proffered friendship of Joseph G. Merle he was quite as haughty and disdainful as any other young aristocrat.

In the midst of flourishing activities as author and letter-writer Shelley's first love-affair was developing. His cousin, Harriet Grove,[29] was in 1810 a strikingly beautiful girl of nineteen, one year older than Shelley. "When I call to mind all the women I have ever seen," wrote Tom Medwin nearly forty years later, "I know of none that surpassed, or that could compete with her. She was like one of Shakespeare's women — like some Madonna of Raphael." [30] Naturally one does not find this enthusiastic picture substantiated by Harriet's journal for the years 1809–10, which has only recently come to light.[31] Her brief daily records of events provide an unconscious revelation of a naturally good-tempered and somewhat naïve girl, fond of her family, her "Aunt Shelley," and her cousins, a moderate reader, and a fairly regular member of the Church of England — not unusually intellectual or sensitive, but well balanced both mentally and emotionally.

Shelley's visit with his Grove cousins during the Easter vacation of 1804 was only one of many visits exchanged by the children of the Grove and Shelley families. An unpublished poem of Shelley's headed " February 28, 1805. To St. Irvyne " pictures the writer as viewing a romantic scene near Field Place with " his Harriet." [32] A line in one of Shelley's poems of 1810 that is clearly devoted to Harriet states that " Two years of speechless bliss are gone " since their love began.[33] Harriet herself seems hardly to have regarded these years so warmly, even at the time, unless several entries that have been carefully crossed out contradict the general tenor of her journal. Bysshe is often " Dear Bysshe," several times " Dearest Bysshe," but the same adjectives are applied to her brothers, her Aunt Shelley, Elizabeth, and Field Place. During the first nine months of 1809 she recorded the receipt of forty-four letters from Bysshe and the writing of twenty letters to him. He was almost her only correspondent, except for his mother and his sister Elizabeth.

When Harriet went up to London in the spring of 1809 to visit her brother, Bysshe arrived four days later with his father. " The former I am very glad to see," Harriet recorded on April 16, 1809; " I think Mr. Shelley appears cross." For four days Bysshe squired her about town, to the theatre, to an exhibition of worsteds, to the Panorama of Grand Cairo, and to Clapham to see Shelley's younger sisters at school there. Harriet thought them " the Nicest Girls I ever saw." One of them preserved a glowing memory of the same visit. " How fresh and pretty she was," wrote Hellen Shelley many years later. " Her assistance was invoked to keep the wild boy quiet, for he was full of pranks, and upset the port wine on the tray cloth . . . then we all walked in the garden, and there was much ado to calm the spirits of the wild boy."

In September of 1809, however, the correspondence between Bysshe and Harriet practically ceased. For fifteen months Harriet recorded only one letter from Shelley and two letters to him. It would look as though someone had decided already that it would be as well not to allow matters to proceed too far. Yet Harriet's less frequent references to Bysshe continued as affectionate as ever. She longed to be invited to Field Place, but her brother John was invited instead. Later, in April 1810, the

Grove family spent a week in Field Place and its neighbour-hood. Harriet had been looking forward to this visit with great pleasure. A mysterious something at Field Place puzzled her greatly from the moment of their arrival; but it did not prevent her enjoyment of a moonlight walk to Strood and of " the pleas-antest party in the world."

Whatever the circumstances were that puzzled Harriet, they made no impression on the memory of her brother. " Bysshe was at that time more attached to my sister Harriet than I can express," wrote Charles Grove,[34] who recollected well the moon-light walks of the four cousins (he and Elizabeth being the other couple). " Bysshe was thoroughly happy and his spirits were high." When the quartet visited the Duke of Norfolk's house at Horsham, Shelley improvised a typical piece of dra-matic humour by dressing as a workingman and starting off to-ward Field Place " with one of those very little chests of drawers peculiar to old houses like Hills." [35] It made Elizabeth nervous, " but Bysshe had the power of entering so thoroughly into the spirit of his own humour that nothing could stop him when once his spirits were up, and he carried you along with him in his hilarious flight and made you a sharer in his mirth, in a man-ner quite irresistible." [36]

Bysshe's high spirits took a rather odd form of expression. A letter to Edward Graham, dated April 22, enclosed a poem which must have been written when Harriet was still at Field Place, picturing a conventionally despondent lover in the moon-light of " St. Irvynes glade ":

> For there a youth with dark'nd brow
> His long-lost love is heard to mourn
> He vents his swelling bosom's woe
> Ah! when will hours like these return
>
> O'er this torn soul, o'er this frail form
> Let feast the fiends of tortured love
> Let hover dire fate's terrific storm
> I would the pangs of death to prove.

. . . .

> No power of Earth, of Hell or Heaven
> Can still the tumults of my brain
> The power of none save ——'s given
> To calm my bosom's frantic pain.[37]

In the second of these stanzas we have the original mould from which the later Shelley poured so many descriptions of himself as a frail form and a storm-tossed spirit almost in love with death. Yet the same pen, at almost the same time, furnished evidence of the high wild spirits that Charles Grove remembered.

Three days later, on April 25, Shelley, his mother, and Elizabeth visited the Groves at Lincoln's Inn Fields, stopping at the school in Clapham Common to see the two younger sisters, Mary and Hellen. Graham was to accompany them, assuming for some fell mysterious purpose the name of William Grove. The letter in which Graham received his instructions to this effect is Gothically ebullient:

. . . My Mother brings a blood-stained stiletto which she purposes to make you bathe in the life-blood of her enemy.

Never mind the Death-demons, and skeletons dripping with the putrefaction of the grave, that occasionally may blast your straining eyeball . . . the fiend of the Sussex solitudes shrieked in the wilderness at midnight. . . . DEATH + HELL + DESTRUCTION if you fail.[38]

Charles Grove recorded of this visit that " Bysshe was full of life and spirits, and was well pleased with his successful devotion to my sister." [39] Harriet's journal shows that she was at least comfortably happy in the attentions of Bysshe and in the congenial society of " dear Aunt Shelley " and the lively Elizabeth. (The brackets represent passages later crossed out by Harriet.)

Wednesday 25. We made morning visits on Miss Packington & Dear Mrs. Portman. Dear Aunt Shelley & My Cousins came. Mr. Wm. Fraser dined with us & we spent a most pleasant day.

Thursday 26. Walked in the Fields [with dear Bysshe] then went shopping & had great fun. Left Aunt & Mama at Mrs. Bartons & they came home in a Hackney Coach a shocking dirty one. Aunt S— says she shall send for a chain & chain us to her. Went to the Play, Mr. W. Fraser with us.

Friday 27. Walked out [with dear Percy] then went shopping. Went to the Play. C. my Father & Mother came home directly as the play was over. P[ercy] Mama & myself sat up till the rest of the party came home & had a most delightful conversation.

Saturday 28. Went shopping with the Shelleys in a Hackney Coach. [   ] We staid at home. Elizabeth as noisy as ever.

Sunday 29. Went to St. Paul's in time to meet everybody coming out. Two Jack Tars said I was painted so Aunt S— said. Went afterwards to Ken— Gardens & saw the Persian Ambassador there. Hurt my foot. A dinner party.

Monday 30. Staid at home all day on account of my Foot. The rest of the party went to the Play all but Mama & Percy.

Tuesday 1. [Percy &] I staid in doors, the rest went out. We all staid at home in the Evening. I played & they all danced. Elizth. talks & is in as great spirits as ever.

Wednesday 2. [   ] I staid at home. [   ] my foot still being bad, however I went to the Play in the Evening & liked it well enough.

Thursday 3. All the Party went out but me [and Dearest P.]. Tom Medwin dined here. Went to the Opera I hate it more than ever [so does Percy]

Friday 4. Staid in again [   ] Dined at Mr. Long's, a most stupid. E. S. has told me something that kills me with amazement but which hinders her from coming to Tollard, I am sorry to say.

Saturday 5. [   ] The Shelleys left us, very sorry. [   ] [40]

Since Harriet and Shelley were never together again in 1810, it must have been the walk in Lincoln's Inn Fields that inspired Bysshe to a poem, dated April 1810, which he later published in *Original Poetry by Victor and Cazire:*

> Come ——! sweet is the hour,
>   Soft Zephyrs breathe gently around,
> The anemone's night-boding flower,
>   Has sunk its pale head on the ground.
>
> .   .   .   .   .   .
>
> The world, with its keenness and woe,
>   Has no charm or attraction for me
> Its unkindness with grief has laid low,
>   The heart which is faithful to thee.

> The high trees that wave past the moon,
>   As I walk in their umbrage with you,
> All declare I must part with you soon,
>   All bid you a tender adieu! —
>
> Then ——! dearest farewell,
>   You and I love, may ne'er meet again;
> These woods and these meadows can tell
>   How soft and how sweet was the strain.[41]

It seems unlikely that any further evidence will ever be adduced to throw an additional light upon Shelley's first love. Strongly as it survived in his later poetry, its most unclouded period seems to belong to the years immediately preceding 1810, and to be wrapped in almost complete obscurity. In the spring of 1810 a decision seems to have been reached by one or both of the families that the idea of a marriage must be abandoned. Shelley seems to have understood this clearly enough, as shown by the two poems of April 1810. One may suppose that her previous ignorance of a family decision was the reason why Harriet was so puzzled at the atmosphere of Field Place in that same April. Perhaps she had not yet distinguished friendship from love and relapsed more easily into the former than Shelley was able to do.

The Shelleys returned to Field Place and the Grove family to their estate at Fern, in Wiltshire. Like a character in Jane Austen's novels, Harriet took up a leisurely round of occasional family dinners, county or regimental dances, and small neighbourhood affairs. An occasional caller in whom her journal displays no special interest was Mr. William Helyar, scion of a near-by county family, whom Harriet had known since the previous October. Bysshe and Harriet exchanged few letters, but her rather infrequent references to him continued as affectionate as ever. Bysshe continued to hope and to send her presents of art crayons, books, and his own compositions, published and unpublished.[42]

All the exuberant interests of young Shelley must have found a place in his conversations with Harriet and in the letters he wrote to her. Was she vaguely disquieted, after she returned home, by a reflection that there was something a little odd and reckless in his high spirits? The religious and political radicalism that began to appear in his writing in the autumn of 1810 must have been plain enough in his conversation during the spring. Did Harriet's calm sanity tell her that she was meant to marry a country gentleman like William Helyar rather than a favourite cousin for whom she had a warm affection but with whom she could never feel complete sympathy? On this point her journal is silent, though there may be some significance in an entry for September 25: " My father has a letter from Mr. S. which I am sorry for, as it gives more trouble."

On July 30, 1810 Shelley delivered at Eton his oration of Cicero against Catiline and returned to Field Place to await the opening of Michaelmas term at Oxford on October 10. When he went up to Oxford in October, his prospects were bright. The six years at Eton had done much for the twelve-year-old boy who had left Syon House Academy in 1804. The old character remained, but he was no longer to the same extent the fragile, self-conscious youngster, full of romantic ideas and living largely in an imaginary world, driven in upon himself everywhere except at Field Place. With all its faults, Eton had proved, as Medwin said, " a new and better world." [43] The strangeness and brutality of the external world still made him suffer, but gradually he was learning enough of its ways to feel at home in it. He considered his financial allowance cramped and had not learned to stay within it, but Oxford would no doubt bring an increased allowance.

The old wild spirit of prankish self-assertion persisted in diminished form, perhaps as a defence mechanism. His health was better; he enjoyed several forms of physical exercise; he had learned how to make friends. He was definitely beginning to realize his superior mental and imaginative qualities. Already he was a great reader and a voluminous writer of letters, poems, and novels — all of which reflected an amazing mental life with an insufficient basis in human experience. Tom Medwin, several years older, had noticed in the vacations that each succeeding half-year produced a rapid mental development in him; [44] some of his talk must have been over Tom's head

ETON COLLEGE

Artist unknown

OXFORD FROM THE RIVER ISIS

Engraved by J. Lewes from a painting by W. Westal

already. Squire Timothy Shelley, still reading with his son in
vacations,[45] was already falling behind and was soon to be bewildered and distracted by a widening gap of which he was
quite unconscious. Some of the " wild notions " that were to occasion later disasters were already present in the manuscript of
St. Irvyne.

Together Bysshe and his father went up to Oxford, Mr. Timothy Shelley obviously proud of his " young man," who had
come through Eton with credit and who was such an extensive
reader and writer.

Chapter V

OXFORD

OXFORD IN 1810; FRIENDSHIP WITH T. J. HOGG;
HABITS OF STUDY AND AMUSEMENT; *ST. IRVYNE*
AND OTHER LITERARY INTERESTS;
VACATION AT FIELD PLACE; EXPULSION

In 1810 the city of Oxford was a town of about ten thousand inhabitants, not more than three miles in circumference, even including the suburbs. It was by this time connected with London by the marvellous new turnpike roads, reducing the stage journey to London from two days to one in duration. Oxford University in 1810 was a collection of twenty colleges and five " halls " with a total membership, including officials as well as students, of slightly more than two thousand people. Throughout most of the preceding century the university had established a pretty general reputation as a centre of " port and prejudice," the " Jacobite capital of England." Some of its students had rioted in the streets for Prince Charlie at the time of the '45, and even Thomas Warton, one of its few literary ornaments of the century, had attracted some government notice for Jacobite utterances.

When the Jacobite cause sank into unimportance after 1745, there were still numerous questions of Whig and Tory, High and Low Church, and of college and university policy to be discussed over the pipes and ale that the satirists invariably associated with dons. No regulations required the professors to lecture. The minority who troubled to lecture at all did so but seldom and were not encouraged by the size of the audience. For many years, said Adam Smith, the greater part of the pro-

70

fessors had given up even the pretence of teaching — an indictment which another Oxonian, Jeremy Bentham, intensified by
saying that he found most of the tutors and professors morose,
insipid, or profligate.

Such examinations as were then held were not public and
were generally farcical. Students named their own examiners
and prepared for the examination by memorizing the answers
to a body of questions that through many years had become so
customary that they had acquired the status almost of common
law. It was very seldom that a student failed to pass such an
examination. Degrees depended, by general consent, not upon
ability, but on length of residence.

When the professors were criticized they replied, not unrea-
sonably, that such lectures as they gave were practically unattended, and that the audience were not equipped to understand
them. Even so, it was during this time that Blackstone delivered the lectures on law that formed the basis of his *Commentaries.* In general, however, there was an intellectual torpor at
Oxford during the eighteenth century with which the university, the students, and the English public were fairly well
content.

It must not be forgotten, as various Oxford historians have
pointed out, that from time to time during this period certain
colleges had brief " golden periods " of intellectual activity, nor
that at all times there were some tutors who furnished intellectual guidance to such students as really desired it. University
College was reaching the close of such a period in 1779, when
Shelley's father entered there. Dr. Johnson was an occasional
guest in the Common Room and the great Orientalist Sir William Jones was one of its fellows.

Visiting Continental scholars were shocked to observe that
the Bodleian was little used by the students and seemed almost
to relish its desuetude. In such an easy-going atmosphere,
when the morning began late and the Bodleian Library, then
the greatest in Europe except the Vatican, closed at three in the
afternoon, the scholastic standard of Magdalen College appears
to be fairly typical. Here the curriculum, as described by a late
eighteenth-century " vindicator," [1] consisted of Greek, Latin,

logic, and divinity, to which were added a limited list of required reading, a weekly theme, and declamations in the third year. In his first year the student studied Virgil, and in his fourth year he studied Virgil. He was "required" to attend his tutor's lecture once a day. The ease with which Johnson and Gibbon, in other colleges, ignored their tutors suggests that such requirements were probably not stringent. The literature of England received no more attention than in the curriculum of Eton. De Quincey, entering Oxford only a few years before Shelley, noted that "few or none of the Oxford undergraduates . . . knew anything at all of English literature. The Spectator seemed to me the only book of classical rank which they had read. . . ." [2]

When not engrossed in study, the undergraduate took a leisurely part in the amusements of the day. These were principally boating, hunting, shooting, and fishing, with occasional excursions within the neighbourhood or even to London. The old game of tennis still survived; cricket was beginning to attract some notice by the end of the century; football and organized rowing were still in the future. Quite a considerable outdoor interest, if the satirists do not exaggerate, was walking in the various gardens with "Oxford toasts" — the sprightly and aspiring young daughters of local tradesmen who occasioned a large proportion of the undergraduate verse of the day. The most popular pastime indoors was billiards.

Discipline at Oxford was decidedly lax. Expulsions were extremely rare. Penalties in the form of imposed tasks were unsatisfactory because the tasks were easily performed by deputy. The most common penalty was "crossing" — deprivation of certain privileges for a week or a month. These were imposed without much distinction between offences, for slipping off to London, creating an uproar, drunkenness in chapel, and even gross immorality. Such requirements as chapel attendance, sleeping and eating within the college, etc., were easily avoided by the gentleman commoners by the payment of certain trivial fines. Only the regulations about the wearing of gowns seem to have been well observed. The social distinctions between

noblemen, gentleman commoners, and servitors made it difficult to impose and maintain uniform regulations.[3]

The general temper of the university during the eighteenth
century was still dominant when Shelley entered University
College in 1810. The effect of the French Revolution had been
rather slightly felt at Oxford and seems to have shown itself
mainly in a laudable effort to succour the refugee clergymen
of the old régime. In June 1792 the Corporation sent in one of
the loyal addresses of confidence which from all sides were
pouring in on the Crown. " Kingly power," said the Corporation, in the year of Shelley's birth, " wisely limited, is the surest
safeguard of the rights and liberties of a great nation." The next
year an effigy of Tom Paine, clutching a copy of the *Rights of
Man,* was paraded through the streets by the Oxford rabble and
burned on the top of Carfax.

In the year 1810 Oxford was rather unusually in the public
eye. The pages of the London *Times* were full of the installa-
tion of the new Chancellor, Lord Grenville, whose election by
a narrow margin over Lord Eldon had created considerable
feeling among rival partisans, largely over Grenville's unorthodox support of Catholic emancipation.

The *Edinburgh Review,* with its enormous prestige and its
impatience of mere tradition, was in mid-career of a series of
attacks upon Oxford. Its principal charges were that the university's curriculum ignored the advance of science and that it
did not cultivate a spirit of free inquiry. Oxford was a place
where " the dictates of Aristotle are still listened to as infallible
decrees, and where the infancy of science is mistaken for its
maturity." [4] Admitting the great advantage to be derived from
a knowledge of the classics, the *Edinburgh* contended that these
were largely lost by the manner of the teaching.

There never was a more complete instance in any country of such
extravagant and overacted attachment to any branch of knowledge.
A young Englishman goes to school at six or seven years old; and
he remains in a course of education till 23 or 24 years of age. In all
that time, his sole and exclusive occupation is learning Latin and
Greek.[5]

73

"Had all the scientific acquirements of the last three hundred years been annihilated," the review asserted again in April 1810, "it would have produced very little effect on the course of study at Oxford." [6] One passage is particularly interesting in view of the experiences awaiting Shelley:

The English clergy, in whose hands education entirely rests, bring up the first young men of the country as if they were all to teach grammar schools in little country towns. . . . There is a timid and absurd apprehension on the part of ecclesiastical tutors of letting out the minds of youth upon difficult and important subjects. They fancy that mental exertion must end in religious scepticism; and to preserve the principles of their students they confine them to the safe and elegant imbecility of classical learning. A genuine Oxford tutor would shudder to hear his young men disputing upon moral and political truth, forming and pulling down theories, and indulging in all the boldness of youthful discussion. He would augur nothing from it but impiety to God and treason to kings. And yet, who vilifies both more than the holy poltroon who carefully averts from them the searching eye of reason, and who knows no better method of teaching the highest duties than by extirpating the finest qualities and habits of the mind? If our religion is a fable, the sooner it is exploded, the better. If our government is bad, it should be amended.[7]

The *Edinburgh Review* was very ably answered by Edward Copleston in several pamphlets,[8] for which a grateful university rewarded him with an honorary degree. Copleston, then a vigorous young Professor of Poetry in his middle thirties, thought no more of bearding the reviewers than of walking from Oxford up to London. Let critics first understand what they meant by utility, he challenged, before setting up such a standard for Oxford. Not utility and not the interests of the individual were Oxford's primary concerns; her principal duty was "to execute an established system, to teach and to recommend what is thoroughly approved." Let individuals make discoveries if they wished, without troubling Oxford "with every crude opinion or untried theory." But let them beware of one field of "discovery," he warned, in words that were not sufficiently heeded by the young freshman Shelley, who probably read them: "The scheme of Revelation, we think, is closed, and we expect no new light on earth to break in upon us. Oxford must guard that sacred citadel." [9]

Oxford had already laid a foundation for improvement by instituting some changes in 1800 and 1807, but they were as yet rather slight, and hardly noticeable in their effects. Miss Elizabeth Grant, a niece of the Master of University College, who was a visitor there in 1810 and 1811, failed to notice them. In her memoirs [10] she pictured a dull, pompous, indolent set of dons, avoiding as much as they could any contact with undergraduates — who were none too eager themselves. " The very meaning of the word education did not seem to be understood."

Both the election of Lord Grenville as Chancellor and the criticisms of the *Edinburgh Review* were common topics of conversation among Oxonians everywhere. It was a battle of conservatism and liberalism. At Field Place in the summer of 1810 there was much dinner talk on politics, Sir Francis Burdett, and the state of the nation [11] — talk that seems to have been entirely to Bysshe's taste, as he indicated a few months later by dedicating *The Wandering Jew* to Sir Francis.[12] On the point of Catholic disability also, Shelley and his father were in agreement. This point was involved in the Oxford election contest between Lord Grenville and Lord Eldon. Undoubtedly the contest was watched with keen interest from Field Place. University College was for Lord Eldon, who was a member of the college and a friend of its Master; but the Duke of Norfolk, Mr. Timothy Shelley's political patron, was for Lord Grenville.

Bysshe was " by his family and connections, as well as by disposition " of the Grenville faction, and was " plain and loud " in avowing his sentiments.[13] He even published a letter on the subject in one of the London papers, which Medwin recollected as the *Morning Chronicle,* signed " A Master of Arts of Oxford." [14]

Thus when Shelley took up his residence at Oxford in October 1810, he was far from being an utter stranger. Since April 10 he had been a member of the University, passing his " grace term," as it was called, at Eton and Field Place. His father was a Bachelor of Arts and Master of Arts of University College and had been a Lord Leicester scholar, as Bysshe now was.[15] Bysshe was opposed to the feeling of University College in the recent Chancellor's election, and he was in hearty concurrence with the view of university education which the *Edinburgh Review* was opposing to the traditional one. Though the new Chancellor had been installed on June 30, so hotly contested an election was a subject for frequent conversation during the next term, especially at University College. The contest with the *Edinburgh Review* was still in progress and was sure to be a subject of conversation. On both these matters Shelley was pretty certain to have talked and to have disputed the opinions in vogue at his college.

WHEN Shelley went up to Oxford in October 1810, he was accompanied by his father, who wished to see his " young man " well started.[16] Together, no doubt, they talked with the dreamy, seclusive Master, Dr. James Griffith, who was much more interested in executing his portraits in burnt wood than in the life of his college; and with the bustling, repressive Dean, George Rowley.[17] The latter may have recalled that the estimable M.P. for New Shoreham had most regrettably voted for the wrong Chancellor.

Excellent rooms were assigned Bysshe on the first floor, next to the hall. During the several days that Mr. Timothy Shelley lingered, savouring his own undergraduate days anew, anticipating a more brilliant scholastic career for his son, these rooms were newly fitted up with excellent furnishings. One thing only remained. In renewing his old associations at Oxford Mr. Timothy Shelley found that Henry Slatter, the son of his former landlord, had just established a partnership with the Oxford bookseller and printer Munday. He took young Bysshe to their shop, introduced him, and advised him to buy his books and stationery there. Then, with a pride that was soon to be shattered, he instructed the printers: " My son here has a literary turn; he is already an author, and do pray indulge him in his printing freaks." [18] The youth was well launched, and the squire could return to his acres.

76

HALL AND CHAPEL OF UNIVERSITY COLLEGE

Engraved by J. Le Keux from a drawing by F. Mackenzie

Ego Percy Bysshe Shelley filius natu
maximus Timothei de Field Place in Co-
-mitatu Sussex Armigeri lubens subscribo
sub tutamine Magistri Rowley et Dom-
-ini Davison annos natus septemdecem.

SHELLEY'S REGISTRATION IN THE UNIVERSITY COLLEGE
REGISTER OF ADMISSIONS

By permission of the Master and Fellows of University College

Among Bysshe's first actions when left to himself was the
unpacking and setting up of the various scientific accoutre-
ments he had sent up from Eton and Field Place. Soon he
visited the Bodleian Library in a vain effort to discover the
German author of his precious magazine fragment on the Wandering Jew. In the various colleges there were a good many
of his fellow Etonians, including his very good friend Walter
Halliday. Some of these boys he doubtless looked up at once.
A little later Hogg met them more than once in Shelley's
rooms.

The all-important acquaintance with Thomas Jefferson Hogg
which was to affect the whole course of Shelley's life began
early in the Michaelmas term, probably within a week of the
20th of October.[19] Thomas Jefferson Hogg, two months Shelley's senior, had entered University College in the preceding
January. The son of a well-to-do barrister of Stockton-upon-
Tees, near York, he was a healthy youth, considerably more
vigorous in mind and body than most undergraduates. Oxford
was to prepare him to enter the law, and he was generously
eager to provide himself with the most liberal background for
his legal studies. Cool, practical, and perhaps already a trifle
sardonic on occasion, he was far from being the materialistic
egotist he was later accused of becoming. Already he perceived that his college lacked intellectual stimulus, though his
condemnation was probably not quite so sweeping as when
he wrote in retrospect of its complacence toward " a total neglect of all learning, an unseemly turbulence, the most monstrous
irregularities, open and habitual drunkenness " and " universal
laziness." [20]

SHELLEY was eating his first dinner in hall. To young Hogg,
a stranger seated next to him, he seemed thoughtful and absent-
minded; he ate little and seemed to have no acquaintance with
his neighbours. A conversation opened so casually that neither
could recall later how it began. The early phases were quite
typical of the usual freshman " getting acquainted " conversation, but it soon became apparent that neither of these young

men was quite a usual freshman. They argued earnestly over the comparative originality and imaginative qualities of German literature versus Italian. The dons and dignitaries of the high table filed out; the uproar of undergraduate talk increased with the withdrawal of Dignity. Still they argued and discussed. The undergraduates gradually left the hall, and the servants began clearing off the table. The rattle of dishes, as usual, prevailed against mere conversation, but in this case only momentarily. The young disputants adjourned to Hogg's rooms, where they calmly confessed to each other that they knew almost nothing of the languages and literatures they had respectively championed.

What did it matter, anyhow, said Shelley. Languages were nothing but words and phrases standing for things; the really important point was to understand *things* — whereupon, with increased ardour, he launched upon a eulogy of chemistry. Hogg kept him going with occasional questions and doubts. He was greatly impressed, but at the same time he was coolly appraising this slender boy with the stooped shoulders and the delicate red-and-white complexion, whose small, animated features, tousled hair, odd gestures, and lively enthusiasm were so out of the ordinary. It seemed to him a pity that such a fine clever fellow had to express himself in a voice " intolerably shrill, harsh and discordant "; otherwise he would be a most desirable acquaintance. At a quarter to seven Shelley suddenly remembered that he must go to a lecture on mineralogy. Hogg invited him to come back later for tea.

But all the lecturer would talk about was " stones! stones, stones, stones! nothing but stones! " How different it was from old Adam Walker's all-inclusive scientific magic at Eton! The outraged listener soon made an awkward escape and returned to conclude his own lecture in Hogg's rooms. Tea was consumed, and afterwards supper.

After supper Shelley proved himself a true disciple of Adam Walker in a glowing account of the blessings humanity would shortly inherit from sciences as yet only in their infancy. Synthetic foods and fertilizers, the discovery of new principles of heating and irrigation, the control of electricity, would render human life infinitely less toilsome and uncomfortable. Man had only just learned to lift himself from the earth in balloons, but eventually unexplored regions would be charted from the air. The shadow of the first balloons falling upon Africa would end slavery there and elsewhere, " for ever." It is a remarkable fact that, though Hogg was careful nearly fifty years later to call these speculations " wild," they have practically all been verified — except the belief that scientific advancement would necessarily bring freedom. Neither Shelley nor Hogg was to know the story of King Leopold and the Belgian Congo.

The talk swung to the moral sciences, in which Hogg, as a future lawyer, was more interested; then to mathematics, which Shelley scornfully dismissed. Metaphysics, proclaimed Shelley in the end, was the noblest of all studies, because it was the key to the mind itself, and not to mere matter. By this time the fire was out, and there was just enough virtue in the guttering candles to light the visitor downstairs.

The meeting, in its various phases, had lasted seven or eight hours. The two boys now learned each other's names, and Hogg promised to visit Shelley's rooms next day to see his scientific instruments. Already the irritating harsh voice seemed to him of little consequence. Thus began a friendship to which we are indebted for most of the information which vivifies, and perhaps slightly distorts, our picture of Shelley at Oxford.[21]

The next afternoon, at two, Hogg kept his engagement. He found Shelley in rooms that had been freshly papered and painted, with carpets, curtains, and furniture all quite new, instead of the more usual second-hand furniture purchased from the preceding occupant. The general impression, however, was a characteristically mixed one:

Books, boots, papers, shoes, philosophical instruments, clothes, pistols, linen, crockery, ammunition, and phials innumerable, with money, stockings, prints, crucibles, bags and boxes, were scattered on the floor and in every place; as if the young chemist, in order to analyse the mystery of creations, had endeavoured first to reconstruct the primeval chaos. The tables, and especially the carpet, were already stained with large spots of various hues, which frequently proclaimed the agency of fire. An electrical machine, an air-pump, the

galvanic trough, a solar microscope, and large glass jars and re-
ceivers, were conspicuous amidst the mass of matter. Upon the
table by his side were some books lying open, several letters, a
bundle of new pens, and a bottle of japan ink that served as an inkstand; a piece of deal, lately part of the lid of a box, with many
chips, and a handsome razor that had been used as a knife. There
were bottles of soda water, sugar, pieces of lemon, and the traces
of an effervescent beverage. Two piles of books supported the tongs,
and these upheld a small glass retort above an argand lamp. I had
not been seated many minutes before the liquor in the vessel boiled
over, adding fresh stains to the table and rising in fumes with a most
disagreeable odour. Shelley snatched the glass quickly, and dashing
it in pieces among the ashes under the grate increased the unpleasant
and penetrating effluvium.[22]

While listening to another enthusiastic discourse on the possibilities of science, Hogg saw Shelley demonstrate his electrical
machine, his galvanic battery, and other contrivances. After
dinner the conversation was resumed and lasted until a late
hour. This time there was much ardent discourse of poetry.
Each had discovered in the other an intellectual liveliness and
curiosity quite at variance with the general tone of the place.
They were, in a sense, universities to each other. Hogg found
the intellectual and moral ardour he had previously missed,
and Shelley, for his part, probably profited almost as much from
the greater coolness, calmer judgment, and more methodical
habits of his friend. From this time on, the two passed most
of their time together, more often in Shelley's rooms than in
Hogg's.

SHELLEY's interest in the physical sciences waned perceptibly
after the first early meetings. Hogg had no enthusiasm for experiments with which to reinforce Shelley's. In fact, they made
Hogg nervous, both for himself and for his friend. He had almost imbibed aqua regia in Shelley's rooms out of a cup that
should have contained only tea. He was informed by the young
wizard himself that Shelley had already taken poison by mistake
at Eton, and fancied his health permanently injured thereby.

Contemplating various acid burns in the carpet and on the furniture, Hogg feared the "rash ardour" of his friend might some day set the whole college on fire. Shelley continued for a while spending his hours and his money on chemistry, but his interest was feverish, energetic, sporadic; he was disorderly and impatient in his experiments; he lacked manual dexterity — and Hogg's calm failure to take him very seriously as a practical scientist gradually diminished his energies. His scout's persistent efforts to put the rooms in order further discouraged him by making it difficult to lay hands on a particular ingredient or piece of apparatus in any of the minor crises by which experiment seemed to proceed. The scout's son, a gawky boy who had unwittingly helped demonstrate the wonders of charged doorknobs, soon grew so wary that he yelled with alarm if Shelley approached him with apparatus in his hand.

The daily life of the two young men soon settled down to a fairly regular routine. Hogg rose early, at six or seven, attended college "lectures," read in private for several hours, and joined Shelley nearly every day at one o'clock. As the tutors' "lectures" at Oxford generally required about two hours at this time [23] and as University College, according to Hogg, required much less than the average, we may take it that Hogg generally read four or five hours every morning before meeting Shelley. It is probable that Shelley did not rise regularly as early as Hogg or visit his tutor as regularly. Very likely he spent part of the four or five free hours of the morning in "scientific" tinkering and in attending to a correspondence that was at times considerable. If, however, he read as much as Hogg supposed, he too must have spent the larger part of this period in reading.

From one o'clock till six they were generally together in Shelley's rooms, sometimes reading together, sometimes studying separately, eternally discussing, arguing, and speculating. At six their paths suddenly diverged for a while. With reasonable punctuality the scandalously unpunctual Shelley regularly went to sleep at that hour, either on the couch or curled up on the rug before the fire, with his head always in the hottest position. Hogg made tea, read, and wrote by himself until eight or ten o'clock, meanwhile keeping an eye on the sleeper, who sometimes rolled over and sometimes talked excitedly in his sleep. At eight or ten Shelley awoke. At ten they had supper together, after which they remained together, generally reading and discussing, until one o'clock.

This program was occasionally interrupted by callers. More than once Hogg met Etonians in Shelley's rooms. But though Shelley always spoke of them kindly, he did not encourage their visits and they seem not to have entered very largely into his life at Oxford. One of these was young Walter Halliday who later remembered him so kindly. Another friend, not an Etonian, was James Roe, of Trinity College, who seems to have had poetic interests, for he was the recipient of two undated notes from Shelley, one asking for the return of a " poetical scrap " he had been criticizing, and the other inviting him to an afternoon of " wine and Poetry." [24]

Shelley also had an older friend at Wadham College whose name Hogg could not recall — a gentleman whose acquaintance he made by engaging in philosophical discussion while taking shelter from a windstorm. There were later meetings which Hogg mentions as an example of what Oxford dons could do, and didn't, to engage the confidence of their students. [25] If Shelley had not met him before, he must have quickly discovered another basis of interest, for the young man's name was George Marshall and his father was rector of Horsham from 1784 until his death in 1819. In 1811 George Marshall was twenty-three years of age, a B.A. and M.A. of Wadham College. He held the Wills Law Exhibition as fellow and was next year elected Moderator of Philosophy. [26] A friend of George Marshall who visited him for a few days at this time was Thomas Barnes, who was later to edit *The Times* from 1817 to 1841. Shelley was by now on very intimate terms with Marshall and spent a long evening with him during Barnes's visit. This one conversation left upon Barnes an indelible impression of the " frankness and uprightness " of Shelley's character. " He was then," Barnes recalled, " a fine looking youth — with one of those ingenuous countenances which ought never to look old." [27]

Another native of Horsham, John Thornton (1778–1866), was

also a member of Wadham College, but his list of degrees and appointments in the college register does not make it certain that he was in residence while Shelley was at Oxford.[28]

When the weather was suitable, Shelley and Hogg often sallied forth for long afternoon walks in the country around Oxford. These were no interruptions to the conversation, of course, nor did the walking entirely exclude reading. Shelley generally had a book in his hand or in his pocket. Only considerable experience could have developed the awkward agility that seemed so surprising to Hogg, by which with his attention fixed on anything except the course of travel Shelley dextrously and unconsciously avoided collisions and mis-steps.

Out they would sally, past the old porter and into the High Street (proudly called by the current guide-book one of the widest and handsomest streets in the Kingdom), past the imposing fronts of colleges, past townsmen and gownsmen — the latter still scrupulously designated by their insignia according to their various social ranks — out along the highways for several miles, and then across open country, sportsman style, crossing roads and lanes, skirting woods and enclosures or boldly walking through, until it was time to return to the college. It was Shelley's favourite recreation. They probably covered most of the country within moderate walking distance, but the region around Shotover Hill pleased Shelley most, because of a pond into which he loved to toss pebbles or on whose surface he skimmed flat stones, gleefully counting the number of skips. The earlier excursions were somewhat warlike in appearance, from Shelley's habit of carrying two duelling pistols, with which he demonstrated great accuracy at target shooting. But he handled his firearms so recklessly that Hogg, by a combination of trickery and persuasion, soon succeeded in having the pistols left at home.

On one occasion, at least, it was well that the pistols were not at hand, for in crossing a barnyard they were injuriously set upon by an over-officious watchdog. Shelley, usually careless about his clothes, was wearing a new coat of which he was for the moment quite enamoured. The dog was beaten off, but not without the demolition of Shelley's coat-tails, which had borne the burden of his onset. On this occasion Shelley's habitual mildness gave way to rage, and Hogg had much ado to prevent his securing the pistols and killing the dog forthwith.[29]

Hogg mentions interesting characterizing details of various other rambles. Once Shelley became very angry at seeing a boy mistreat an ass — only Hogg was the real hero of this incident, unless of course it was Laurence Sterne. On another ramble Shelley made generous efforts to relieve the distress of a small girl whom they found hungry and apparently deserted; and on another Shelley stopped to engage in odd friendly pranks with some gypsy children whom they encountered. One of their excursions brought them suddenly upon a secluded garden whose desolate quiet stimulated Shelley's imagination wonderfully for the rest of the walk, and may in fact be an ingredient of " The Sensitive Plant," written nine years later in Italy.

These adventures were often accompanied by philosophic reflection, as in the case of Shelley's famous inquiry into pre-existence. This story, at least, the inimitable Hogg must be allowed to tell for himself:

One Sunday we had been reading Plato together so diligently, that the usual hour of exercise passed away unperceived: we sallied forth hastily to take the air for half an hour before dinner. In the middle of Magdalen Bridge we met a woman with a child in her arms. Shelley was more attentive at that instant to our conduct in a life that was past, or to come, than to a decorous regulation of the present, according to the established usages of society, in that fleeting moment of eternal duration, styled the nineteenth century. With abrupt dexterity he caught hold of the child. The mother, who might well fear that it was about to be thrown over the parapet of the bridge into the sedgy waters below, held it fast by its long train.

" Will your baby tell us anything about pre-existence, Madam? " he asked, in a piercing voice, and a wistful look.

The mother made no answer, but perceiving that Shelley's object was not murderous, but altogether harmless, she dismissed her apprehension, and relaxed her hold.

" Will your baby tell us anything about pre-existence, Madam? " he repeated, with unabated earnestness.

" He cannot speak, Sir," said the mother seriously.

"Worse and worse," cried Shelley, with an air of deep disappointment, shaking his long hair most pathetically about his young face; "but surely the babe can speak if he will, for he is only a few weeks old. He may fancy perhaps that he cannot, but it is only a silly whim; he cannot have forgotten entirely the use of speech in so short a time; the thing is absolutely impossible."

"It is not for me to dispute with you, Gentlemen," the woman meekly replied, her eye glancing at our academical garb; "but I can safely declare that I never heard him speak, nor any child, indeed, of his age."

It was a fine placid boy; so far from being disturbed by the interruption, he looked up and smiled. Shelley pressed his fat cheeks with his fingers, we commended his healthy appearance and his equanimity, and the mother was permitted to proceed, probably to her satisfaction, for she would doubtless prefer a less speculative nurse. Shelley sighed deeply as we walked on.

"How provokingly close are those new-born babes!" he ejaculated; "but it is not the less certain, notwithstanding the cunning attempts to conceal the truth, that all knowledge is reminiscence: the doctrine is far more ancient than the times of Plato, and as old as the venerable allegory that the Muses are the daughters of Memory; not one of the nine was ever said to be the child of Invention!"[30]

Possibly Hogg did not swim, and, unlike Shelley, objected to boating on that score; possibly the boating would have been mentioned with the advent of warmer weather had the young friends remained longer at Oxford; but at any rate Hogg does not mention boating as one of Shelley's amusements at Oxford. Individual boating (as distinguished from organized races) was already popular there, however, and Shelley was already fond of it.

Hogg, whose memory is likely to be quite trustworthy on matters of food, was impressed with Shelley's carelessness in such matters, and perhaps overemphasized it. Shelley had not yet become a vegetarian, but he liked his food plain and simple. He was particularly fond of bread, which could be munched very conveniently while engaged in reading or experimenting, or even while walking along the street. He also liked raisins, oranges and apples, vegetables, salads, pies and puddings.[31] He had a decided sweet tooth and loved cakes, gingerbread, sugar, and honey. Cold water was his usual beverage, but he liked tea and coffee and at intervals drank diluted wine. After supper he often drank two tumblers of hot negus, each containing two glasses of sherry.[32] This adds up to a moderately inclusive diet list and suggests that it was only when he was intensely absorbed in something else that Shelley was particularly Spartan in his diet. He was generally restless at set dinners, not so much from dislike of his food as from an impatience of it.

Naturally young Shelley had interests and personal relations at Oxford other than those connected with the bland and self-confident Hogg. Such easy demands as his college made upon its students he probably met much more punctiliously than the average freshman. At the very outset of his career he broke off an absorbing conversation with Hogg to attend a university lecture that students were not required to attend, the unfortunate mineralogical disquisition on "stones, stones." If he attended no more he had a better record than most undergraduates and even dons. He duly visited his tutor and was told somewhat drearily that he must "read, read" — not the books that Shelley then and there produced to demonstrate his reading, but Æschylus, Demosthenes, Euclid, and Aristotle. All except possibly Euclid he did read, though perhaps not all at Oxford. The Aristotelian logic so dear to Oxford he took to with a real relish that was eventually disastrous. Apparently he complied with the modest requirements for weekly written exercises; Hogg happens to mention reading one of them in which Shelley had mischievously inserted Latin verses into a prose context, to see if his tutor would be as alert as Keate had been at Eton. He wrote a number of voluntary argumentative essays which he may or may not have shown to his tutor. At the time they were expelled Shelley and Hogg were complying with the college requirements by making abstracts of certain books they had read.

For some time Shelley seems to have avoided major collisions with college discipline. Absences from chapel and from dinner in hall probably occurred, but they could be taken care of by paying small fees or by "pricking aeger" — reporting oneself officially ill — which Shelley did on the first day Hogg called on him. Dean Rowley was a petty disciplinarian who did not balk at cutting down Mrs. Griffith's favourite pear tree to prevent boys who were out late from returning over the college wall by its aid; but though Shelley still retained some of " the monkey tricks of the schoolboy," he was apparently never caught in any specific dereliction that could not be passed off either by a fine or by one of his ludicrously humble apologies.

There are certain indications, however, that his college authorities regarded him with some misgiving. In a college with a total membership of only seventy persons he was much too fond of arguing his opinions for such a person as Dean Rowley not to have an inkling of what they were. Quite possibly some of his numerous correspondents may have known he was a student at University College and have informed the college authorities of the nature of his letters, as one offended correspondent threatened to do when he was at Eton. The Eton boys at Oxford who called and induced him to repeat his famous curse on father and King very probably happened to drop a few words to other Oxonians on Shelley's Eton career. The anonymous publications in which he was already engaging were not so secret as he imagined. Charles Kirkpatrick Sharpe,[33] a member of another college, was discussing them freely in his letters as matters of common gossip at Oxford. Both Medwin and Hogg believed that the Shelley championship of Lord Grenville in the election for chancellor had seriously offended the authorities of University College, who had actively supported Lord Eldon. Hogg even goes so far as to say that from the beginning Shelley was on this account " regarded with a jealous eye " and that it was the main cause of Shelley's misfortunes at Oxford.[34] One may well doubt that the college authorities were so seriously resentful of an undergraduate's views on a question already settled, but it is likely that they knew these views and were not thereby inclined more favourably in judging other matters. Certainly both Shelley and Hogg were generally unpopular in the college for some time before their departure.

Yet despite his unconcealed disapproval of prevailing standards, Shelley was happy at Oxford. He wished to spend his whole time in reading, writing, and talking, with a dash of " scientific " experiment; and the university made it possible for him to do this with practically no interference. He and Hogg often congratulated themselves on their opportunities. He particularly enjoyed the ease with which he could at any time deny himself to visitors by closing his outer door, known in Oxford parlance as " sporting his oak." [35]

His Oxford life, however, was much less confined than his enthusiasm for " sporting his oak " suggests. Though there is no definite record of it, he must occasionally have followed the common custom of running up to London for a day or two. Usually he must have stopped with Edward Graham in his Vine Street lodgings or with his Grove relations in Lincoln's Inn Fields. Gibbons Merle, who wrote anonymously as " A Newspaper Editor," records that during the year after their meeting — which would include Shelley's months at Oxford — Shelley visited him several times in London.[36]

There was also a rather voluminous correspondence to be maintained. A part of Shelley's correspondence which has been almost entirely lost was with his family at Field Place. Mr. Timothy Shelley wrote letters that amused the two boys by their rambling haphazard character. Bysshe's answers, sometimes innocently and sometimes by intention, occasionally provoked his somewhat irritable parent into an angry outburst.[37] His letters from his mother and sisters were always received with pleasure. Elizabeth, who was his advocate with Harriet Grove, was his favourite. How fine it would be to bring about a union between this sister, a promising candidate for enlightenment, and the wonderful Jefferson, already enlightened! Jefferson must visit him at Field Place and face his displeasure if he failed to fall in love with Elizabeth. Shelley was also in correspondence with Harriet Grove, who was growing farther and farther away from him, but of this he seems to have told Hogg little or nothing.

The bulk of his correspondence, however, was of the sort learned from Dr. Lind. His passionate fondness for arguing, and also for genuine enlightenment, could hardly be confined within oral bounds. Profiting eagerly by the university's empha-

sis on logic, he prepared analyses and briefs from his reading
and solicited the opinions of others on the matter by correspondence. He used several assumed names and took the further precaution of giving a London address — that of Edward Graham,
his patient London factotum. " If any letter comes directed to
the Revd. Charles Peyton," he wrote Graham,[38] " it is mine."
Another of his pseudonyms was Jeremiah Stukely.

At times his correspondence of this sort was considerable. In
the beginning the subjects were largely scientific, but science
was soon entirely superseded by ethical and moral questions.
In time he found that by printing his abstract he could more
readily elicit an answer. This abstract he would enclose as
something he had found that unfortunately seemed unanswer-
able, and solicit his victim's comment. Then, as Hogg expressed
it, " Unless the fish was too sluggish to take the bait, an answer
of refutation was forwarded to an appointed address in London, and then in a vigorous reply he [Shelley] would fall upon
the unwary disputant, and break his bones. The strenuous attack sometimes provoked a rejoinder more carefully prepared
and an animated and protracted debate ensued." [39] He was so
fond of the debate that he sometimes argued more for " the
shock of contending minds " [40] than from immediate conviction
of his own. The truth is that his motives were curiously mixed.
He sincerely desired to get at the truth. He also loved intellectual activity and adventure as a form of excitement, and he was
fascinated by the exercise of logic.

THE business of becoming an author, which had resulted in two
published volumes before he entered the university, continued
unabated. Shelley was still seeking to publish *The Wandering
Jew*. He had brought to the university his *St. Irvyne, or The
Rosicrucian*, almost if not entirely complete.[41] Stockdale, his
publisher, took some time in fitting it for the press, and was puzzled by the fact that one of the characters appears to die twice.
Shelley explained the plot somewhat lamely and Stockdale had
it printed and bound by December 10,[42] a few days before its
anonymous author returned to Field Place for the Christmas

vacation. It was somewhat brazenly advertised as "the University romance" in *The Times* for January 26 and February 2, 1811.[43]

Like the young author's preceding volumes, *St. Irvyne* is worthless from a literary point of view. Even a summary of its two hazily related plots makes decidedly listless reading.[44] It includes such standard Gothic ingredients as the elixir of life, a compact with the Devil, a band of brigands, free love, seduction, murder, suicide, beauty in distress, and a fatal duel to avenge an injured heroine. Where the sources are definitely attributable they are mainly Miss Byrne's *Zofloya, or the Moor,* Godwin's *St. Leon,* and Lewis's *The Monk* and *The Bravo of Venice.* The tinkering that both Stockdale and Shelley bestowed on them failed entirely to bring these elements into logical or even interesting relation to one another. Nevertheless they do possess an interest of another sort. They show Shelley's mind still dominated mainly by his Gothic interests, combining them for the first time (except for a brief passage near the end of *Zastrozzi* where one of the lovers defends free love) with revolutionary moral ideas. Even for this there is precedent in such novels as Godwin's *St. Leon,* which Shelley acknowledged as an influence, nor do the ideas suggest moral conviction so much as they do a rather conventional desire to shock.

With *St. Irvyne* the powerful stimulus given to Shelley's imagination by the terror school of literature reached its last full expression. At the same time that his passion for physical science was yielding primacy to a developing interest in ethical and moral questions, his love for physical sensationalism in writing was also giving way to an intellectual sensationalism which in turn was to be supplanted by moral fervour. But the literature of terror and wonder had already exerted a profound effect on the early thought and expression of a marvellously active and retentive mind, and it was never completely eradicated.

Another interesting feature of the novel is its autobiographical element, a prominent trait of Shelley's writing that had already appeared to a slight extent in *Original Poetry by Victor and Cazire.* In *St. Irvyne,* however, he makes his villain, Ginotti, relate the history of his early years to Wolfstein, who is to inherit his fatal secret of the *elixir vitæ*. The passage is easily recognizable as in part a penetrating self-analysis of the youthful Shelley, and was so characterized by Medwin, who best knew the original:

"From my earliest youth, before it was quenched by complete satiation, *curiosity,* and a desire of unveiling the latent mysteries of nature, was the passion by which all the other emotions of my mind were intellectually organized. This desire first led me to cultivate, and with success, the various branches of learning which led to the gates of wisdom. I then applied myself to the cultivation of philosophy, and the éclat with which I pursued it, exceeded my most sanguine expectations. *Love* I cared not for; and wondered why men perversely sought to ally themselves with weakness. Natural philosophy at last became the peculiar science to which I directed my eager inquiries; thence was I led into a train of labyrinthic meditations. I thought of *death* — I shuddered when I reflected, and shrank in horror from the idea, *selfish and self-interested* as I was, of entering a new existence to which I was a stranger. I must either dive into the recesses of futurity, or I must not, I cannot die. — 'Will not this nature — will not the *matter* of which it is composed, exist to all eternity? Ah! I know it will; and, by the exertions of the energies with which nature has gifted me, well I know it shall.' This was my opinion at that time: I then believed that there existed no God. Ah! at what an exorbitant price have I bought the conviction that there is one! ! ! Believing that priestcraft and superstition were all the religion which *man* ever practised, it could not be supposed that I thought there existed supernatural beings of any kind. I believed *nature* to be self-sufficient and excelling; I supposed not, therefore, that there could be anything beyond nature.

"I was about seventeen: I had dived into the depths of metaphysical calculations. With sophistical arguments had I convinced myself of the non-existence of a First Cause, and, by every combined modification of the essences of matter, had I apparently proved that no existences could possibly be, unseen by human vision." [45]

Shelley had thought that *St. Irvyne* would sell "mechanically" to circulating libraries,[46] but he was mistaken. Despite the advertisements, and despite more notice from reviewers than his biographers seem to have known,[47] the book sold badly. By 1827 Stockdale figured that he had lost three hundred

pounds on it, including interest.[48] The *British Critic* concluded
with suave sarcasm that the " Gentleman of the University of
Oxford " must be a very young gentleman indeed, to whom
better sense and taste would in due time be vouchsafed. The
Literary Panorama condemned the romance more subtly by limiting its comment to three captions placed over four lurid excerpts: " How to Begin a Romance, A.D. 1811 "; " How to End a
Romance, A.D. 1811 "; and " Conclusion." The *Anti-Jacobin Review*, however, matured its indignation for a year and then condemned the volume seriously and weightily, not merely as " en-
thusiastical and nonsensical," but as a reckless and dangerous
assault on all ideas of decency and morality — a comment
which elicited an approving letter from Oxford.[49]

In Oxford *St. Irvyne* was on sale at Slatter and Munday's and
was probably read by a number of people, since it was advertised as a university romance and might contain any amount of
veiled reference to Oxford toasts and dons. Charles Kirkpatrick
Sharpe, a brilliant young Tory who had been resident at Christ's
Church for some years after obtaining his degrees, was one
who had read it and knew a good bit about the author. He
sent a copy of the volume to his friend Lady Charlotte Campbell, with a sarcastic description, and received from her an
opinion not very different from his own.[50]

While *St. Irvyne* was still with the printers Shelley was engaged upon another volume which in fact preceded it from the
press,[51] as a rather handsome quarto containing twenty-two
pages, entitled *Posthumous Fragments of Margaret Nicholson*.

Hogg's interesting account of this volume [52] is in some details
misleading. One morning, Hogg relates, he found Shelley busily
correcting proofs. " I am going to publish some poems," he
informed his friend impressively. But the poems did not im-
press Hogg, who thought them rather badly finished. Finally
they agreed that with a little alteration the poems would
do very well as burlesque verse. They amused themselves
mightily with the alterations and even more with the fable
they devised, by which the poems were supposed to be the
work of a mad washerwoman, Margaret Nicholson, who had
attempted to assassinate George III, twenty-five years be-

fore. They were edited by "John Fitz-Victor," who was described as her nephew. It added to the joke that Fitz-Victor
meant also to the initiate " son of Victor," the co-author of *Original Poetry by Victor and Cazire*. The printer J. Munday, who
was indulging Shelley's printing freaks in accord with Squire
Shelley's directions, was so pleased with the new idea that he
asked and obtained permission to print the book on his own
account, instead of at Shelley's expense, as originally planned.

According to both Hogg and Shelley,[53] the book sold well at
Oxford, where grave gownsmen took it as the bona-fide expression of the poor washerwoman's unlettered muse. Mr. Slatter, who was a member of the publishing firm, stated later [54]
that it was " almost still-born."

It seems very doubtful that the poems were deliberately bur-
lesqued in the manner described by Hogg. They read no more
like burlesque than Shelley's previous poetry. One of them,
" Melody to a Scene of Former Times," was so far from being
burlesque that it expressed Shelley's keen despair at feeling that
his love for Harriet Grove had become almost hopeless. Two
of the others are lyrics of vague and generalized despair, one is
Gothic horror, and the two remaining are revolutionary attacks
upon despotism. Of these two, the " Epithalamium of Francis
Ravaillac and Charlotte Corday " contains a passage of love dialogue with echoes from odes v and vii of Catullus that is certainly excessive for modern taste. This passage Shelley wrote
Edward Graham,[55] who had evidently objected to it, would
make the volume " sell like wild-fire." He said that it had been
added as an afterthought, was " the production of a friend's *mistress* " (possibly a cloak for Hogg), and was omitted from some
copies, including the one sent to Shelley's mother. Moreover,
Graham was to publish some abuse of the volume to be sent by
Shelley, but whether the abuse was to be based on the passage
in question, in order to stimulate sales, is uncertain. Finally,
" Of course to my Father, Peg is a profound secret."

From this suggestive letter the suspicion arises that the real
point of the hoax was to provide a sure means by which the two
longest and most important poems would not redound to the
discomfort of " a Gentleman of the University of Oxford," son

of the M.P. for New Shoreham. Shelley had " a sly relish for a
practical joke," said Hogg in relating this episode, and " would
often exult in the successful forgeries of Chatterton and Ireland." Such sentiments as

> Oppressors of mankind, to *you* we owe
> The baleful streams from whence these miseries flow;

or

> Monarch of earth, thine is the baleful deed,
> Thine are the crimes from which thy subjects bleed;

and

> Yes, Francis! thine was the dear knife that tore
> A tyrant's heartstrings from his guilty breast;

could come with a secure grace only from such characters as
Margaret Nicholson or Charlotte Corday as imagined by a mad
washerwoman. Otherwise the printer might face trial for sedition. Perhaps the licentious passage added as an afterthought
was a red herring, in which case Hogg's elaborately scornful
condemnation of the first poem and attribution of it to " some
rhymester of the day " was possibly another safety device repeated after twenty years in deference to Mary Shelley. Such
a supposition would explain why Shelley was willing for his
mother to see the book with the love song omitted, but wished
to keep his father in entire ignorance. On such an assumption
Hogg's original objections would have been not to the crude-
ness of the verse, which is in fact superior to Shelley's previous
poetry, but to the rashness of the project.

In any event, Margaret Nicholson functioned efficiently as a
lightning-rod. " It was indeed a kind of fashion to be seen reading it in public . . . the thing passed off as the genuine production of the would-be regicide." [56] At least one Oxford
reader, however, was not so deluded. In his letter of March 15,
previously quoted, Charles Kirkpatrick Sharpe attributes the
volume directly to Shelley and remarks that it is " stuffed full
of treason," but is " extremely dull."

At about the same time that the Margaret Nicholson volume
appeared, Shelley was assisting Hogg with a novel called *Le-*

onora, which has never been recovered. It was being printed by Munday, says Mr. Slatter,

. . . but the printers refused to proceed with it, in consequence of discovering that he had interwoven his free notions throughout the work, and at the same time strongly endeavoured to dissuade him from its publication altogether; but this was disregarded, and he afterwards took the copy to Mr. King, the printer, at Abington, who had nearly completed the work, but was stopped in its further progress by the circumstance of Mr. Shelley's expulsion from Oxford, with his friend and associate, Mr. Hogg.[57]

In several of his letters [58] Shelley speaks of his plans for publishing an unnamed novel that is near completion. Its nature seemed somewhat similar to *Leonora,* as described by Slatter, and it encountered similar printing difficulties, so that it is generally assumed, perhaps mistakenly, to have been *Leonora.*

Shelley also appears to have printed occasional trifles at Horsham during his Oxford residence, for which his grandfather paid the bills.[59] One of these may have been an otherwise unknown poem which he later sent to William Godwin [60] as " the ' Essay on Love,' a little poem " which reflected the influence of Godwin's writings. It is possible, but hardly probable, that the poem on love is identical with another lost poem, " Poetical Essay on the Existing State of Things," to be discussed presently. Mr. D. F. MacCarthy [61] thinks it very likely that Shelley was also a contributor of anonymous trifles to the *Oxford University and City Herald.*

Probably these ventures in authorship occupied very little of Shelley's time. Published and unpublished, his entire literary output at Oxford, exclusive of letters, amounted in bulk to no more than half what he had written in the previous year. Much of it was written with extreme rapidity and carelessness. Mr. Slatter [62] marvelled at the rapid, offhand way in which he practically improvised some of his " copy."

There was plenty of energy and time for other publishing ventures besides his own. One of these was the publication of a volume of poems by Janetta Phillips, a young female genius whose volume was published by subscription at Oxford after

Shelley's expulsion. The names of Shelley and of his relatives and friends bulk large in the list of subscribers, but it appears that Shelley did not actually finance the publication.[63]

There was also at Oxford a former naval officer named Browne, passing under the assumed name of Bird, who was endeavouring to publish a comprehensive book on Sweden. From his last year at Eton Shelley had been interested in Bird as a victim of alleged " oppression " that had forced him out of the navy. Almost his last act at Oxford [64] was to sign a bond of six hundred pounds for the publication of Bird's book. The bond was ultimately paid by Shelley's publishers, who had gone security for it. The following note, herald of a long series that were to come later, was written during Shelley's Christmas vacation, and is probably connected with Shelley's activities as either patron or author:

I promise to pay to Wm. Sandham, Esq're the sum of 100£ which he lent me.

The note is signed by Shelley and dated January 14, 1811.[65]

By far the larger and most important part of Shelley's time at Oxford was spent in reading.

No student ever read more assiduously. He was to be found, book in hand, at all hours, reading in season and out of season, at table, in bed, and especially during a walk; not only in the quiet country and in retired paths; not only at Oxford in the public walks and High Street, but in the most crowded thoroughfares of London. . . . I never beheld eyes that devoured the pages more voraciously than his: I am convinced that two-thirds of the period of day and night were often employed in reading. It is no exaggeration to affirm that out of the twenty-four hours he frequently read sixteen. . . . Few were aware of the extent, and still fewer of the profundity of his reading.[66]

To this testimony of Hogg's may be added Medwin's amazement at the rapidity with which Shelley read:

He took in seven or eight lines at a glance, and his mind seized the sense with a velocity equal to the twinkling of an eye. Often would a single word enable him at once to comprehend the meaning of the sentence. His memory was prodigious.[67]

Even Charles Kirkpatrick Sharpe, who knew Shelley only slightly, observed with sarcastic exaggeration [68] that he lived upon " arsenic, aqua-fortis, and half an hour's sleep in the night." Hogg thought [69] that he read too assiduously and that the university might have done well to discourage this one student from reading.

Obviously no one could list more than a small fraction of the books that must have influenced the thoughts of so extensive a reader. Hogg remembered a number, and others are mentioned in Shelley's letters or definitely indicated by what he was writing at the time.[70]

Of mathematics he showed " marvellous impatience," and he was " quite cold " to botany.[71] If he still dipped into the muddy stream of contemporary romances, it must have been only occasionally, for we find no specific references to them while he was at Oxford, and not very many later. Though Hogg mentions no particular books on chemistry and physics and states that Shelley's earlier scientific interests were yielding to social and ethical ones, Shelley never entirely abandoned reading in this field.

Rather scorning the languages in which they were written, he read " with more than ordinary interest " [72] Eastern travels and translations of marvellous tales of the East. Though he found the theatre distasteful, he delighted in reading the Attic tragedians and the English dramatists, particularly Shakespeare.[73] His love of Plato showed itself in an enthusiastic reading with Hogg of several of the dialogues, including the *Phædo* and the *Republic.* At Oxford he read Greek literature mainly in translation,[74] but within a few years he read for hours on end in the original Greek — more, says Hogg, than many an aged pedant reads in a lifetime. One English poem, Walter Savage Landor's *Gebir,* he read both aloud and to himself with such " tiresome pertinacity " that Hogg completely lost patience with him and threw the book out of the window.[75] He also read Southey's *The Curse of Kehama* as soon as he could get hold of it,[76] quoted some lines from it as the motto for his lost poem on the " Existing State of Things," [77] and showed later in *Queen Mab* that it had greatly impressed him.

97

For Shelley, however, the most important single book that he read at Oxford — or at any other time — was William Godwin's *Political Justice*. With the possible exception of Tom Paine's *The Rights of Man,* which had a greater influence upon the popular mind, *Political Justice* was the most influential English expression of revolutionary ideas of government and morality. It had been published in 1793 and Shelley had undoubtedly heard of it at Eton; he may possibly have read it from the library of Dr. Lind, who, though loyal to his King, was sufficiently catholic to own and read such a book. He had been at Oxford only about a month when he asked Stockdale to send him a copy of the book.[78]

Shelley's letters to Hogg during the Christmas vacation [79] quote Godwin and show that Shelley was trying to ascertain his address. It seems odd, therefore, and rather suggestive of a desire to tone down Shelley's radicalism at the time, that Hogg does not mention Godwin in connection with Shelley's interests at Oxford.[80] Shelley himself considered the reading of *Political Justice* a landmark in his career. Writing to Godwin less than a year after leaving Oxford, he says: [81]

. . . it opened to my mind fresh and more extensive views; it materially influenced my character, and I rose from its perusal a wiser and a better man. I was no longer the votary of romance; till then I had existed in an ideal world — now I found that in this universe of ours was enough to excite the interest of the heart, enough to employ the discussions of reason; I beheld, in short, that I had duties to perform.

He concludes by calling Godwin "the regulator and former of my mind."

Such a stimulus as this might alone suffice for the changes in Shelley's interests that took place at Oxford. It was reinforced by the influence of Hogg himself,[82] who successfully preached the superiority of moral and ethical science to the merely physical. As a result, they "read several metaphysical works together, in whole or in part," including Locke, Hume, and "some productions of Scotch metaphysicians of inferior ability." [83]

Thus a combination of very dangerous ingredients was being

brought together that, under the conditions, must inevitably have produced an explosion as surprising as any of the less damaging purely chemical ones that Shelley had already fostered. A high-strung young man of extraordinary mental abilities, but so odd in his conduct that many people regarded him as half-mad,[84] had for the first time sufficient financial and physical scope for developing enthusiasms he had never learned to restrain. His whole previous career had shown a love of sensational ideas and conduct. Passionately fond of discussion and argument, he had learned to gratify both his love of the mysterious and sensational and his fondness for argument and intellectual activity by provoking controversial correspondence. He had also been used to reflecting his current enthusiasms in published works. So long as this combination was dominated merely by a love of the marvellous, with physical science gradually supplanting the literature of horror, no more damaging results need be expected than those Hogg observed on his first visit to Shelley's rooms. But when his university stimulated a love for exercises and experiments in logic, and *Political Justice* and Hogg turned his enthusiasm toward the political and moral sciences — always more dangerous than the purely physical — a considerable explosion was imminent.

Its imminence seems to have occurred to Timothy Shelley when his son returned to Field Place early in December for the Christmas vacation. Shelley's publisher, Stockdale, had become alarmed. Shelley had asked him to procure a Hebrew essay (in translation) attacking the truth of Christianity. His conversation and letters convinced Stockdale that the young author was cherishing dangerous opinions on the subject of religion.[85] He informed Mr. Timothy Shelley of his fears. Shelley's father called upon Stockdale, and left in a state of considerable alarm. In Stockdale's opinion the young man might best be saved through the effort of some tactful companion; but Thomas Jefferson Hogg was his only close friend, and a manuscript of Hogg's submitted to Stockdale for publication (*Leonora?*) made him think that Hogg might even be the chief cause of

Shelley's unorthodoxy. Mr. Shelley probably went into one of
the fits of anger to which he was subject. The rest of the story
is told best by Shelley himself.

As soon as he learned Hogg's London address, Shelley
wrote: [86]

My father called on S[tockdale] in London who converted him
to sanctity. He mentioned my name, as a supporter of sceptical principles. My father wrote me, and I am now surrounded, environed
by dangers, to which compared the devils who besieged St. Anthony
were all inefficient. They attack me for my detestable principles;
I am reckoned an outcast; yet I defy them, and laugh at their ineffectual efforts. . . . My father wished to withdraw me from college: I would not consent to it. There lowers a terrific tempest, but
I stand, as it were, on a pharos, and smile exultingly at the vain
beating of the billows below.

Shelley's manner of describing this rather ominous turn of
events suggests one of his favourite novels rather more than a
personal crisis. The situation, however, persisted. He had expected Hogg to spend a part of the vacation at Field Place, but
was now unable to invite him.[87] Mr. Timothy Shelley had not
been reassured by some inquiries about young Hogg made by
Stockdale's wife, who came from Hogg's native Yorkshire.[88]
" My mother imagines me to be in the high road to Pandemonium, she fancies I want to make a deistical coterie of all my little sisters: how laughable! " [89] It was indeed an exaggerated
fear, for Shelley maintained some caution in his talk even with
the oldest of his sisters, the admired and sympathetic Elizabeth,
with whom Hogg now imagined himself to be in love: " I do
not wish to awaken her intellect too powerfully." [90]

But " laughable " was hardly the word to apply to the alarm
of his parents. It was this same persistent conviction on the
part of his parents that ultimately barred him from his home.[91]
For the time being, however, events took a more favourable
turn when Mr. Timothy Shelley received better reports of young
Hogg. Shelley now wrote:

My father's prophetic prepossession in your favour is become as
high as before it was to your prejudice. . . . He came up from

100

London full of your praises; your family, that of Mr. Hogg of Norton House, near Stockton-upon-Tees. Your principles are now as divine as before they were diabolical . . . and, to sum up the whole, he has desired me to make his compliments to you and to invite you to make Field Place your headquarters for the Easter vacation. . . . I fancy he has been talking in town to some of the northern Members of Parliament who are acquainted with your family.[92]

Squire Shelley had evidently decided that Hogg could be turned into a useful ally in reclaiming his son from dangerous tendencies. Shelley was even then trying to argue his father into his own point of view. " He for a long time listened to my arguments; he allowed the impossibility (considered abstractly) of any preternatural interferences by Providence. He allowed the utter incredibility of witches, ghosts, legendary miracles. . . . But when I came to *apply* the truths on which we had agreed so harmoniously, he started at the bare idea of some facts generally believed never having existed, and silenced me with an Equine argument, in effect with these words: — ' I believe, because I do believe.' " [93] Shelley had sufficient respect for his father's stubbornness and determination in these beliefs to give out at home that he would publish no more, even though he was at the moment preparing for the press a novel, about which all that is known is that it apparently contained views similar to those which were already disturbing his parents.[94]

Mr. Timothy Shelley, for his part, did not wish to see his cherished schemes dissipated. He had expected that his son would make an advantageous marriage and succeed him as the brilliant Member of Parliament for New Shoreham.[95] He had taken Bysshe with him to the House of Commons and had paid little or no notice to the disgust with which Bysshe was inspired by the practical politicians he met there. His patron, the Duke of Norfolk, liked Bysshe and was willing to guarantee his political future. " Many times," said Shelley to Hogg, " the Duke advised me to turn my thoughts toward politics immediately . . . but he did not persuade me."

All this was endangered, according to Mr. Shelley's present beliefs, by the influence of bad companions on a nature that was generous, but innately flighty and reckless. He now exonerated Hogg, but there must be others. A few months later, when Gibbons Merle called at Field Place in Bysshe's absence, he met with a very frosty reception from the squire. This immediately turned to cordiality when Mr. Shelley learned that this friend, at least, disapproved of Bysshe's deistic tendencies.[96]

IF BYSSHE could stand " on a pharos " against parental pressure and disapprobation, there were other troubles at the same time against which he was less confident. News reached him that Harriet Grove was soon to be married; in his agitation he seems to have considered that she was in fact already married. The slender hopes that he had allowed himself to cherish since the previous summer were now completely dissipated. " She is gone! " Shelley wrote to Hogg on January 11. " She is lost to me for ever! She is married! Married to a clod of earth; she will become as insensible herself; all those fine capabilities will moulder." [97] Not even to Hogg would he write fully on the subject; with his family he did his best to conceal his feelings. " When you are compelled to live under the severest of all restraints, concealment of feelings poignant enough in themselves, how terrible is your lot," he confided to Hogg, and added: " My only ultimate wishes *now* are for your happiness and that of my sisters." [98] Again he wrote: " I am afraid there is selfishness in the passion of love, for I cannot avoid feeling every instant as if my soul were bursting. . . . Is suicide wrong? . . . I slept with a loaded pistol and some poison last night, but did not die." Suicide was constantly in his mind. " I never, never can feel peace again. What necessity is there for continuing in existence? Is she not gone? And yet I breathe, I live! " [99] Bysshe " wandered in the snow," was " cold, wet, and mad," and spent most of one night pacing Warnham churchyard. He suffered an attack of fever which prevented his going up to London to rejoin Hogg, whom he felt compelled to see because he could not " bear to suffer alone."

Elizabeth, who had been his abetter with Harriet in more hopeful days, knew something of his misery and was distressed on his account. She either heard or guessed his thoughts about

suicide. Hellen Shelley recalled many years later that during
this vacation whenever Bysshe took his gun and walked out in
the fields, Elizabeth always followed closely for fear that he
might shoot himself.[100] In another way, however, Elizabeth
only added to Bysshe's distress. Quite definitely she was beginning to slip out of the tight little world which he had imagined
she and Hogg shared only with him. One of his strongest desires was to see Jefferson and Elizabeth united in love, without
(in his opinion) malefit of clergy. Elizabeth had never seen
Hogg and only partly knew his beliefs and those of Shelley.
Evidently she did not yet know the nature of the union Shelley
desired. She was impressed by Bysshe's glowing account of his
friend, but her disapproval of Bysshe's religious scepticism
made her wary of Jefferson. She declined to enter into a correspondence with him: " What right have *I*, admitting that he is
so superior, to enter into a correspondence which must end in
delusive disappointment when he finds how really inferior I am
to the being which his heated imagination has pictured? " [101]

Jefferson's imagination was in fact very much heated. He had
never seen Elizabeth and knew nothing of her except from
Bysshe, but he was almost as despondent over Elizabeth as Shelley was over Harriet. He was also deeply troubled over the
" delicacy " of his courtship. Shelley argued fervidly against
both the despondency and the qualms, and Hogg sent Elizabeth a letter. She immediately redirected it and gave it to a
servant to post, nor could all Bysshe's arguments persuade her
to recall the servant and read the letter — " Reason, Justice,
Virtue forbade it . . . he would be disappointed in me —
most bitterly so." [102] Thereafter Bysshe urged Jefferson to write
to him the things he would say to Elizabeth, who might possibly
listen to them in that way. He showed her some of Jefferson's
letters and urged Jefferson to hurry the publication of his *Leonora,* that he might show her that also. He did not conceal
from Jefferson his fears that the case was desperate, that Elizabeth was " lost." His disappointment in Elizabeth was as great
as in Harriet. Nevertheless, he persisted for almost a year thereafter in his design to unite Jefferson and Elizabeth.

Wild and fevered as they were, self-confessedly " mad " and

strongly Gothic-novelized in their emotional passages, Shelley's thirteen letters to Hogg between December 20, 1810 and January 23, 1811 are the record of one of the great crises of his life. Like many another youth, he considered his life blasted, but unlike others, he did not blame Love. Even the emptiness of love, he assured Hogg, was better than the fullness of other states. "What, then, shall happiness arise from? Can we hesitate? Love, dear love, and though every mental faculty is bewildered by the agony which is in this life its too constant attendant, still is not that very agony to be preferred to the most thrilling sensations of epicurism? " [103] He wove this conception of love into the philosophic arguments that he was conducting with Hogg in the midst of their miseries. "Love, love, *infinite in extent,* eternal in duration, yet (allowing your theory in that point), perfectible, should be the reward; but can we suppose that this reward will arise spontaneously, as a necessary appendage to our nature, or that our nature itself could be without some cause — a first cause — God? " [104] Again: "Do I love the person, the embodied entity, if I may be allowed the expression? No! I love what is superior, what is excellent, or what I conceive to be so; and I wish, ardently wish, to be profoundly convinced of the existence of a Deity, that so superior a spirit might derive some degree of happiness from my exertions: for love is heaven, and heaven is love." "Even if the Universe were created by mere fortuitous concourse of atoms," he continued, "that fortuity must have had a cause, and that Cause must be Deity. O that this Deity were the soul of the Universe, the spirit of universal, imperishable love! Indeed, I believe it is. . . ." [105]

In the same letters Shelley accepted the imputation of sceptic, as he was to proclaim himself again in a few months and as Hogg now proclaimed himself. His normal state at the time seems to have been just short of belief in a deity; his emotions impelled him to belief, and his rationalism impelled him to hesitate. But in his moments of most intense feeling he believed in a God of Love. Christianity, however, he now hated as a system designed to frustrate Love. Long before this he had dedicated himself to warfare against oppression, but now for

the first time he saw clearly and intensely his Enemy. Hogg's
unhappiness, the defection of Elizabeth, his own deep dejection
over Harriet, even his relatively petty domestic discomforts of
the moment, all seemed to stem directly or indirectly from the
pernicious doctrines of Christianity. "My unhappiness is excessive. . . . But that which injured me shall perish! I even
now by anticipation hear the expiring yell of intolerance."
" I know the cause of all your disappointment — worldly prejudice; mine is the same, I know also its origin — bigotry." [106] On
two separate occasions he solemnly swore vengeance.

"O! I burn with impatience for the moment of the dissolution of Christianity; it has injured me. I swear on the altar of
perjured Love to revenge myself on the hated cause of the effect. . . . Indeed I think it to the benefit of society to destroy
the opinions which can annihilate the dearest of its ties." [107] This
was on December 20, immediately after he had returned to
Field Place. Two weeks later (January 3) he was even more
vehement: " Yet here I swear — and as I break my oaths, may
Infinity, Eternity blast me — here I swear that never will I forgive Christianity! It is the only point on which I allow myself
to encourage revenge; every moment shall be devoted to my object which I can spare; and let me hope that it will not be a blow
which spends itself and leaves the wretch at rest, but wasting,
long revenge! I am convinced, too, that it is of great disservice
to society — that it encourages prejudices which strike at the
root of the dearest, the tenderest of its ties. Oh! how I wish I
were the Antichrist! — that it were mine to crush the demon; to
hurl him to his native hell, never to rise again. I expect to gratify some of this insatiable feeling in poetry. You shall see —
you shall hear — how it has injured me. She is no longer mine!
She abhors me as a sceptic, as what *she* was before! Oh Christianity! When I pardon this last, this severest of thy persecutions, may God (if there be a God) blast me! Has vengeance,
in its armoury of wrath, a punishment more dreadful? " [108]

" This last, severest " of persecutions would seem to refer to
Elizabeth's defection rather than Harriet's, since no reader of
Harriet's journal could suspect that she had ever been a sceptic.
The last sentence is particularly interesting, in that it is a literal

quotation from the fragmentary translation of Schubart's *Wandering Jew* that Shelley had been treasuring for a year or two. Apparently without realizing it, Shelley identified himself with the greatest of all legendary victims of Christianity. Shelley's intense self-dedication to a warfare against Christianity was anything but the bit of Gothic fustian that a careless reader might suppose; it was more like Hannibal's vow against Rome. Two years later he was preparing its first powerful broadside, *Queen Mab,* prefaced by Voltaire's motto: " *Écrasez l'infâme,*" that is oddly reminiscent of the phrase: " crush the demon," above.

While Shelley's letters from Field Place were tense with personal emotion, they also continued calmly, though rather briefly, to discuss philosophical questions of common interest and to refer occasionally to the long, argumentative correspondence on philosophical and theological questions that the two youths were conducting with a gentleman named Wedgwood, who amused Shelley by assuming that he was a clergyman. Shelley sat up a whole night and wrote five sheets of argument, based upon the *existence* of a deity and revelation, to convince him that his system (presumably Christianity) was a mythology.

DURING the last week in January Shelley returned to Oxford, thwarted in his own love and in his design of uniting Hogg and Elizabeth. For the latter, however, he had hopes from Hogg's expected visit to Field Place at Easter; meanwhile he continued earnestly to sing their praises to each other. Unwittingly he had also taken the first step toward replacing the faithless Harriet. In the midst of his troubles he had visited his younger sisters' boarding-school with a present from his sister Mary to her friend, a beautiful, fair-haired girl named Harriet Westbrook. The meeting impressed him sufficiently to cause him to send her a copy of *St. Irvyne,* which came from the press on December 10. Charles Grove, who had been spending part of the vacation at Field Place, accompanied Shelley on the visit, which he says was in January.[109]

Once more in quiet Oxford after his unhappy vacation, Shelley addressed a very stiff letter to Stockdale, demanding a full and satisfactory explanation of his "scandalous" and "contemptible *attempts* at calumny," in his recent talks with Mr. Timothy Shelley.[110] Hogg had indited two similar letters to Stockdale less than a week before.

At Oxford the old pleasant life of reading, writing, arguing, and strolling began again. "It would be impossible," Hogg asserted, "faithfully to describe the course of a single day in the ordinary life of Shelley without showing, incidentally and unintentionally, that his nature was eminently benevolent." [111] He paints an attractive picture of Shelley's pawning his precious microscope in order to relieve the poverty of a man he had never seen before,[112] and gives several other instances of his benevolence that have been previously recorded in this chapter.[113] His grand views of the future to be perfected by science were strongly coloured by philanthropy. His sympathies were theoretically so extensive that he already questioned the right of humanity to take animal life merely for pleasure,[114] but he had not yet abjured hunting or the eating of flesh.

Hogg insists specifically that "the purity and sanctity of his life was most conspicuous" [115] and that he was offended by a coarse jest.[116] This point is worth emphasizing, since Thornton Hunt [117] seemed convinced by an unnamed informant that Shelley had injured his health through sexual immoralities at Oxford.[118]

In the matter of politics, "Shelley was entirely devoted to the lovely theory of freedom; but he was also eminently averse at that time from engaging in the far less beautiful practices wherein are found the actual and operative energies of liberty." [119] "His feelings and behaviour were in many respects highly aristocratic" and his fastidious spirit was offended by many of the crudenesses of democracy, even while he was "wholly republican" in theory.[120]

Two opportunities for practical political activity that was at the same time sufficiently patrician shortly presented themselves. Peter Finnerty, an Irish journalist, had recently been sentenced to eighteen months' imprisonment for speaking his mind to Lord Castlereagh in a letter published in the *Morning*

Chronicle. Liberals like Sir Francis Burdett and Leigh Hunt rushed to his defence, meetings were held, editorials written, and subscriptions taken. *The Oxford University and City Herald* opened a subscription for him. Shelley's subscription of one guinea, standing third on the published list (March 2, 1811), probably pained the Tory officials of University College. Shelley went further. He caused to be advertised in the same journal, for March 9, "A Poetical Essay on the Existing State of Things, By a Gentleman of the University of Oxford, for assisting to maintain in Prison Mr. Peter Finnerty, imprisoned for a libel." His tutors must have guessed the author's identity rather easily, in view of the published subscription list. Had they seen the poem, vigorous action might have been precipitated. Charles Kirkpatrick Sharpe mentioned it [121] and knew Shelley to be the author, but showed no knowledge of it that could not have been gained from the *Herald.* In fact, there is no evidence that anyone saw more than Sharpe, and it is quite possible that the poem was prudently withdrawn at the last minute, or even that it was never written, but was a fiction to support interest in Finnerty's case. [122]

At almost the same time Shelley became interested in Leigh Hunt, editor of the *Examiner,* as another victim of government persecution. Hunt had already been twice prosecuted by the government for his fearless editorials. He now emerged triumphant from a third prosecution. Shelley wrote to him on March 2, 1811, [123] to congratulate him on his victory and to suggest the formation of an association by which liberals could protect one another to some extent against government prosecution. He concluded: "My father is in parliament, and on attaining 21 I shall, in all probability, fill his vacant seat. On account of the responsibility to which my residence in the University subjects me, I of course, dare not publicly to avow all that I think, but the time will come when I hope that my every endeavour, insufficient as this may be, will be directed to the advancement of liberty."

Shelley was not so cautious in expressing his opinions in the shop of Munday and Slatter as he thought it necessary to be in public. These gentlemen, to whom he talked as boldly as formerly to Stockdale, became genuinely alarmed. They knew also that the printers of *Leonora* had refused to print it on account of its radical contents. Accordingly they remonstrated with their young patron most earnestly. They even called in a gentleman of their acquaintance, a Mr. Hobbes,[124] whose arguments they thought might succeed where theirs failed. Shelley remained unimpressed.

Shelley's father had also seen the drift and sought to change it. The consternation he had felt at Stockdale's revelations was only partly assuaged by his effort to understand his son's belief in religious matters and by Bysshe's pretence that he would print no more. About two weeks after Bysshe returned to Oxford he received a letter from his father arguing the reasonableness of Christianity. Perhaps a week later his father wrote (if we are to judge from Shelley's reply) to urge him to make the most of the college lectures and to encourage him to compete for the poetry prize, on the subject of the Parthenon. He had engaged the Reverend Edward Dallaway, a learned man, to furnish his son information on the subject.

Bysshe's replies [125] show that the young man was willing to be as reasonable and prudent as possible. On the religious issue he agreed at once that the thoughtless majority of mankind are best suited with a religion based on uncritical faith. But for the rational minority, among whom he classed himself, physical evidence is necessary to belief, and Christianity is not established by such evidence. These he called his " private " sentiments, to which he was willing to hear his father's objections. In his next letter he seemed to give his father to understand that he was working on the Parthenon poem, was attending lectures in logic, and was already sufficiently prepared for his examiners in divinity. On the religious question the following statement must have been very comforting to a father whose fears were much more worldly than spiritual:

It is needless to observe that in the Schools, Colleges, etc., which are all on the principle of Inquisitorial Orthodoxy, with respect to matters of belief, I shall perfectly coincide with the opinions of the learned Doctors, although by the very rules of reasoning which their own *systems* of logic teach me I *could* refute their errors. I shall not therefore publicly come under the act " De heretico comburendo."

At the actual moment of writing this letter, February 17, Shelley already had in his possession the printed document that was to bring this prudent resolve to naught. Some time earlier Shelley and Hogg had made synopses of much of their reading together, including Locke and Hume. From these synopses Shelley had prepared a brief abstract of arguments against revealed religion,[126] for use as a handy tool in the pseudonymous epistolary arguments carried on by the two youths. Soon it seemed desirable to have it printed, still apparently only with the idea of convenience in discussions with correspondents. It was printed at the shop of C. and W. Phillips in Worthing. This firm had already printed the *Original Poems by Victor and Cazire* and Shelley was on such familiar terms there (it was only nineteen miles from Horsham) that he is said to have learned there how to set up type himself.[127] But such an eager young author could hardly think of printing without soon feeling compelled to publish.

ON FEBRUARY 9 the *Oxford University and City Herald* carried an advertisement that *The Necessity of Atheism* " speedily will be published, to be had of all booksellers of London and Oxford." Four days later Shelley wrote to the ever useful Edward Graham, saying: " I send you a book, you must be particularly intent about it. Cut out the title-page, and advertise it in eight famous papers; and in the *Globe,* advertise the *advertisement* in the third page." [128] The short advertisement in the third page of *The Necessity of Atheism* would have been just the thing for arresting newspaper notice, but before Graham could advertise he received another note from Shelley, dated only 1811, telling him not to advertise — " it is not yet published, and we are afraid of the Legislature's power with respect to heretics."

These events actually preceded Shelley's letter to his father in which he gave that worried gentleman to understand that he purposed to be circumspect with regard to his real opinions. He probably considered that he was being circumspect by instructing Graham to cut out the title page, which contained the printers' names, and by printing and advertising the book anonymously instead of as "by a Gentleman of Oxford." As late as March 2 he was writing to Leigh Hunt the letter previously quoted,[129] indicating that he intended to be circumspect.

His next step, however, was one whose consequences he could hardly have hoped to escape, though it appears from Hogg's account that both were genuinely surprised at the result. Knowing from his former experience that Messrs. Munday and Slatter would probably refuse to handle the volume, he entered their shop in their absence and strewed the counters and windows with copies of the book, instructing the shopman to sell them quickly at sixpence each. In about twenty minutes a fellow of New College, the Reverend Mr. John Walker, strolling past the shop, was smitten with the alarming title, *The Necessity of Atheism.* He entered, examined the book, and straightway took counsel with the proprietors. All agreed that the copies should be burned. They were collected then and there, carried into the back kitchen, and burned in the presence of the Reverend Mr. Walker.

The victimized publishers also wrote at once to the printers, warning them of the danger of prosecution and advising the destruction of every vestige in their possession — books, manuscript, and type.[130] They then summoned to their support Councillor Clifford and held a conference with the author. Since they had already argued vainly with Shelley on the question of the general tendency of his beliefs, it may be guessed that at least part of the present argument turned on the proposed destruction of copies still in Shelley's possession. All three entreated and threatened, but "all seemed of no avail — he appeared to glory in the course he had adopted." [131]

There were in fact more grounds for Shelley's defending the pamphlet than might be supposed from those who have read it only by its deceptive title. Except for the title and the signature to the advertisement ("through deficiency of proof, an Atheist ")¹³² there was no atheism in it. In its seven pages of text it argued that belief can come only from three sources: physical experience, reason based on experience, and the experience of others, or testimony. None of these, it argued, establishes the existence of a deity, and belief, which is not subject to the will, is impossible until they do. Hence the existence of a God is not proved. The language was temperate and the conclusions were no more than agnostic. Shelley's desire for the truth (which he maintained in the document could not be harmful) was probably genuine. Only two months before in his letters to Hogg he had been advancing arguments for the existence of a deity. It was only " in the popular sense of the word 'God,'" as he later wrote to Godwin,¹³³ that he became an atheist at Oxford. His real inclination, as Hogg remarked,¹³⁴ " was toward instead of from the marvellous. The denial of the existence of gods and devils and spirits, if it was to be found in him at all, was only to be found in his words and arguments." Sceptical philosophy appealed to him largely because it seemed new and marvellous, and involved a temporary jeopardy delightful to " a soul living on excitement and change." ¹³⁵ Moreover, to argue on all questions was his dominant passion. *The Necessity of Atheism* was concerned less with Christian theology than with the right to argue, even about God.

From the time of the scenes in the shop of Munday and Slatter there could have been no hope of further concealment. It was on March 15 that Charles Kirkpatrick Sharpe informed Lady Charlotte Bury that Shelley had come out with " a prose pamphlet in praise of Atheism." ¹³⁶ The burning of the pamphlets must have occurred only two or three days before this. Shelley and Hogg were pursuing their usual routine and continuing to mail their pamphlets as if nothing had happened or could happen. Medwin, who received a copy, says ¹³⁷ it was circulated largely among professors, heads of colleges, and bishops. Henry Slatter ¹³⁸ said that Shelley even sent a copy to the head of his own college. " All the bishops have the Atheism," Shelley wrote to Edward Graham before it was published.¹³⁹ Even the sister university was not neglected. Dr. James Wood, Lady Margaret Professor at Cambridge, received a copy which later went into the library of St. John's College.[140]

Still University College took no action. James Griffith, the Master, absorbed in his avocation of burnt-wood portraits, may never have heard of the book-shop incident; but the officious Dean, George Rowley, must almost certainly have heard, and it is hard to imagine that what was considered good enough Oxford gossip for Charles Kirkpatrick Sharpe to pass on to Lady Charlotte Bury was not even mentioned at the high table of the culprit's own college. It is quite likely that the incident was known but was expected to blow over, now that the offending books had been burnt. There was no proof that Shelley was the author, and an expulsion for atheism might cause unfavourable talk about the college.

Perhaps the affair would have blown over if Shelley had not made the mistake of sending a copy of the pamphlet to the Reverend Edward Copleston, Professor of Poetry and Fellow of Oriel. Like all the others it was accompanied by a polite letter in the author's own handwriting signed Jeremiah Stukely and inviting criticism and discussion. So vigorous a personality as Edward Copleston would certainly see that some action was taken. It was not necessary to remember that in his own undergraduate days he had been a member of a discussion club, known as the Lunatics, which was discouraged by the authorities.[141] Necessity! — had he not written and published that " To make necessity the standard of what is praiseworthy or honourable is against the uniform judgement of mankind? "[142] Had he not publicly served notice against the *Edinburgh* reviewer's criticisms that Oxford would tolerate no new discoveries in the field of religion — that " the scheme of Revelation is closed, and we expect no new light to break in upon us "? Who was this new light-bringer?

Apparently it was easy to find out. Edward Copleston set out for University College with the pamphlet and the incriminating letter. Farewell now to any hope the peaceful Master of University College may have cherished of being left alone. He was forced into action, and his subsequent uncharacteristic display of temper may have been due in part to this fact. " Mr. Copleston, among others, had the pamphlet," Shelley informed

Godwin later; " he showed it to the Master and the Fellows of University College, and *I* was sent for." [143] Shelley told the same story to Southey, who repeated it in a letter to John Rickman on January 6, 1812.[144]

Shelley's summons occurred immediately after breakfast on the morning of March 25, 1811. Hogg, reporting at Shelley's room early for some reading they were doing together, found him absent. In a few minutes he returned, highly excited, and informed Hogg that he was expelled:

" I was sent for suddenly a few minutes ago: I went to the Common room, where I found our Master and two or three of the Fellows. The Master produced a copy of the little syllabus and asked if I were the author of it. He spoke in a rude, abrupt and insolent tone. I begged to be informed for what purpose he put the question. No answer was given, but the Master loudly and angrily repeated:

" ' Are you the author of this book? '

" ' If I can judge from your manner,' I said, ' you are resolved to punish me, if I should acknowledge that it is my work. If you can prove that it is, produce your evidence; it is neither just nor lawful to interrogate me in such a case and for such a purpose. Such proceedings would become a court of inquisitors, but not free men in a free country.'

" ' Do you choose to deny that this is your composition? ' the Master reiterated in the same rude and angry voice. . . . I told him calmly but firmly that I was determined not to answer any questions respecting the publication on the table. He immediately repeated his demand; I persisted in my refusal; and he said furiously:

" ' Then you are expelled; and I desire you will quit the College early to-morrow morning at the latest.'

" One of the Fellows took up two papers, and handed one of them to me; here it is." He produced a regular sentence of expulsion, drawn up in due form, under the seal of the College.[145]

Hogg immediately wrote a note to the Master and fellows, asking them to reconsider Shelley's expulsion. He was sent for at once, and the scene enacted with Shelley was repeated, with slight variations. He persistently refused to affirm or deny his authorship; but he did insist that if Shelley was guilty, he was equally so. He received the same sentence as Shelley.

The sentence of expulsion affixed to the hall door about noon was made out for both Shelley and Hogg and stated the grounds as "contumacy in refusing to answer certain questions put to them." The entry against Shelley's name in the College Register for March 25 reads:

At a meeting of the Masters and Fellows held this day it was determined that Thomas Jefferson Hogg and Percy Bysshe Shelley be publicly expelled for contumaciously refusing to answer questions proposed to them, and for also repeatedly declining to disavow a publication entitled "*The Necessity of Atheism.*" [146]

Shelley was greatly surprised and shocked by his expulsion. After he had finished his story to Hogg, he sat on the sofa "repeating with convulsive vehemence the words, 'Expelled, expelled!' his head shaking with emotion, his whole frame quivering." He was more deeply shocked and more cruelly agitated than Hogg ever saw him afterwards.

There can be no doubt, however, that Oxford was not grieved at his departure. Mrs. Smith (formerly Miss Elizabeth Grant) must have been expressing the official view of her uncle, the deeply withdrawn Master, when she described him as insubordinate, a ringleader in minor mischief, whose departure restored quiet within the College.[147] "I believe no one regretted their departure," wrote Mr. C. J. Ridley, a member of the university at the time of the expulsion and later a junior fellow. There were but few, if any, Mr. Ridley believed, who were not afraid of Shelley's strange and fantastic pranks and his still stranger opinions, "but all acknowledge him to [have] been very good humoured and of kind disposition. T. J. Hogg had intellectual powers to a great extent, but unfortunately misdirected. He was most unpopular." [148]

Matthew Rolleston, a fellow of University College from 1809 to 1817 and the winner of prizes for poetry in 1807 and 1808, may have had an early interest in young Shelley as a budding poet, but he was quite unsympathetic with him over his expulsion. Writing to his friend Edward Eden Mynors of Weatheroak Hall, Worcestershire, he stated that "On Monday we were obliged to expel Messers Shelley and Hogg for ' contumaciously refusing . . .'" quoting the decree. " They left us Tuesday. For Hogg I am sorry, not for Shelley." [149]

Charles Kirkpatrick Sharpe announced the expulsion to Lady Charlotte Bury [150] and added: " Was ever such bad taste and barbarity known? " Apparently this was irony, for he later wrote in the margin of Lady Charlotte's *Memoirs:* " Mr. S. was a strange tatterdemalion looking figure, dressed like a scarecrow; he had no credit for talent at Oxford, where he was thought to be insane." [151]

The " Oxford Collegian " who wrote to congratulate the *Antijacobin Review* on its stern treatment of *St. Irvyne* says that the author was expelled " in consequence of the freedom with which he avowed his singularly wicked tenets," and thinks it a good warning " that a vigilant eye is still kept in this University over improprieties of conduct." [152] Finally, when Hogg's father sought information on the matter he received the following letter from his London friend Mr. R. Clarke:

April 6, 1811.
B— J— came to me this morning from Oxford, I have had the whole history from him: and the reason of all this strange conduct in your son and Shelley is what I supposed, a desire to be singular. There is no striking impiety in the pamphlet: but it goes to show, that because a supreme power cannot be seen, such power may be doubted to exist. It is a foolish performance, so far as argument goes, but written in good language. These two young men gave up associating with anybody else some months since, never dined in College, dressed differently from all others, and did everything in their power to show singularity, as much as to say, " We are superior to everybody." They have been writing Novels. Shelley has published his and your son has not. Shelley is son to the member for Shoreham. He has always been odd, I find, and suspected of insanity: but of great acquirements: so is your son: I mean, as to the latter, he is of high repute in College.

C. R.[153]

The truth of the matter would seem to be that Shelley's many admirable qualities could not counterbalance his more unfortunate ones with those who did not know him well enough to real-

ize their value. It was so later, when Leigh Hunt vainly sought
to counteract the public impression of Shelley's private life.
Few people at Oxford knew him well enough to judge him with
entire justice. University College and the University of Oxford
as seen by Miss Grant were incapable even of the effort. Both
young men, but particularly Shelley, had deliberately set out
to be singular and had met with disastrous success.

The two friends had been requested to leave University College by the next morning. Before their departure they were informed that they might remain awhile longer if Shelley would
ask permission to do so, but he declined.[154] Certain appearances
had to be kept up, and probably the dons did see them strutting
about the quadrangle, as Mr. Ridley recorded,[155] or, in Charles
Kirkpatrick Sharpe's sarcastic version,[156] behaving like heroes
and talking of emigrating to America. A few days later Shelley
informed his father [157] that Oxford was a matter of perfect indifference to him. According to Medwin,[158] Shelley was little
affected by the expulsion, but Hogg was convinced that he
felt it keenly. Although there can be no doubt that he was
deeply moved by the indignity, it is by no means clear that
he felt any deep and lasting sorrow at leaving Oxford.

There were good-byes to be said, to his old friend Halliday,
for one. " Halliday, I am come to say goodbye to you, if you
are not afraid to be seen with me." [159] Very likely Shelley
looked up some other Etonians, and Roe, with whom he had
read verses and drunk wine. The matter of guaranteeing the
publication of Janetta Phillips's poetry had not yet been concluded; he must see Mr. Strong about the manuscript. As
Southey got the account of this farewell from Shelley shortly
afterwards:

Away goes Shelly [*sic*] to a graduate (a friend of Hannah More's)
whom he had been zealously helping to raise a subscription for
some protégée, to settle this business with him, tells him for what
he came, and that the reason was that he was about to leave Oxford,
having just been expelled for atheism, at which terrific word the
man absolutely fainted away! ! Poor Shelly, a little astonished at
finding himself possessed of this sort of basilisk property, used his
best efforts to recover him, lets him out into the garden, and had the

117

farther pleasure of hearing himself addressed, as soon as the Evangelist recovered his speech in these charitable words, I pray God, sir, that I may never set eyes on you again.[160]

There was still one more call to make, of a much more necessary nature. The sudden dismissal had found Shelley short of funds. He had to borrow twenty pounds from the brother of Henry Slatter for the expenses of the journey.[161] The next morning, March 26, 1811, Shelley and Hogg mounted to the top of the eight-o'clock stage and were soon on their way to London.

Chapter VI

FROM OXFORD TO MATRIMONY

LIFE IN LONDON; PROTRACTED NEGOTIATIONS;

FIELD PLACE; ELIZABETH HITCHENER;

HARRIET WESTBROOK; ELOPEMENT

WHEN Shelley and Hogg arrived in London after their expulsion, they went first to a coffee-house near Piccadilly, whence they sallied forth to take tea with the Grove family in Lincoln's Inn Fields. The remarkably meagre conversation there was imputed by Hogg to a Grove genius for stolid taciturnity, though it may well have owed something to the embarrassment of the situation. Back they went to their coffee-house, where Hogg, presumably, remained quietly for the night. Shelley was still restless and excited. Tom Medwin, lodging in Garden Court, in the Temple, had to be informed. So at four o'clock in the morning Tom was roused by an insistent knocking at his door. Shelley's well-known voice, cracked and high when excited, hailed him: "Medwin, let me in, I am expelled!" The suddenly awakened Medwin absorbed the news rather slowly; Shelley laughed loudly and half-hysterically and repeated: "I am expelled — for atheism." [1]

After breakfast at their coffee-house Shelley and Hogg set out to look for more congenial lodgings. In this matter Shelley proved obstructively fastidious. He was horrified and rushed wildly out of one pleasant parlour when he heard fishmongers in the street outside; at the next place he was startled by the noise of carters. One place he vetoed because of the maid's nose, another on account of the voice of the mistress. Then they reached Poland Street, a name that would always suggest freedom. Entranced by the name, they took two bedrooms and a sitting-room. Shelley was delighted with the sitting-room wallpaper — trellises and vine-leaves and huge clusters of green and purple grapes. "We must stay here," said the poet; "stay for ever." They moved in at once.

These more important matters having been concluded, it seemed desirable to apprise the squire of Field Place of the "late tyrannical violent proceedings of Oxford." On March 29, four days after the expulsion, Bysshe wrote his father a brief, indignant account, never doubting (except possibly between the lines) that his father would also resent the incident as an unjustifiable interference with intellectual freedom. But University College had anticipated him. Two days before Bysshe wrote, Timothy Shelley took the initiative by writing a brief note to Hogg saying that "the late occurrence at University College" obliged him to cancel the invitation that Hogg had already accepted to spend the Easter vacation at Field Place. This was the opening gun of a long, stiff battle between Shelley and his father, in which Hogg was to prove a more important issue than Oxford University.

The young liberty-lovers of Poland Street continued for a while to live as nearly as possible as they had done at Oxford. In the morning Shelley generally wrote, mostly letters, presumably. They took long walks, read and argued, dined generally at a coffee-house, and returned to have tea under their own brightly colored grapevines. They loved variety. Charles Grove, who was with them almost every day,[2] recollected dining with them at almost every coffee-house in London. One book, hot from the press, pleased Shelley immensely. It was Byron's *English Bards and Scotch Reviewers*, which Hogg erroneously considered to be Shelley's first acquaintance with Byron.[3]

Hogg describes a walk to Miss Fenning's school at Clapham Common to visit Shelley's younger sisters Mary and Hellen. Shelley made a great to-do over presenting Hellen with a pocketful of cakes. Almost certainly there were other visits to his sisters unaccompanied by Hogg. From Hellen Shelley's letters[4] we know of several undated visits to the Clapham

LONDON FROM THE RIVER

Engraved by James Redaway from a drawing by F. Robson

LONDON: CHEAPSIDE AND BOW CHURCH

Engraved by W. E. Albutt from a drawing by L. H. Shepherd

school. The sisters felt great sympathy for their brother and tried to help him with little contributions from their pocket-money.[5] In these dealings they sometimes used as an intermediary their friend Harriet Westbrook, an older girl, who lived in London, and who had been acquainted with Bysshe since the Christmas holidays.

There were also occasional teas and dinners with the Grove cousins, who continued as taciturn and matter-of-fact as Hogg had first thought them. John Grove introduced them to Kensington Gardens, whose quiet shady nooks became a favourite resort with them. He also took them to a bachelor dinner where there was port and much serious conversation on the subject of women.

JOHN GROVE was a surgeon and his younger brother Charles was a medical student. Despite Hogg's slurs on their conversational powers they talked interestingly enough of their profession for Shelley to become attracted to it. With Charles he attended a course of lectures on anatomy at St. Bartholomew's Hospital. Afterwards they would walk in St. James's Park, where the sight of soldiers provoked Shelley to comment on the evils of a standing army.

If all this was only a little less comfortable than Oxford, there was still an important matter to settle with Field Place. Timothy Shelley was an affectionate, stubborn father whose pride had been wounded. He had already come to regard Bysshe as odd, but he had built great hopes upon him. When Stockdale had first alarmed him a few months before, he had allowed himself to be reassured and had sent Bysshe back to Oxford and to Hogg. Considering himself somewhat on the liberal side in both religion and politics, he had sought to understand his son's views on religion. Apparently some understanding was reached, for one of Shelley's letters to him shortly before the expulsion expresses opinions [6] quite similar to those of the iniquitous pamphlet, as if they were already known to his father — as indeed they must have been, after the arguments

121

that had already occurred at Field Place. At that time Shelley quite clearly undertook to keep these opinions reasonably under cover. The conclusion is plain that Mr. Timothy Shelley's wound came not so much from the opinions as from their publication and the consequent disgrace.[7] Just as his son had previously sworn vengeance against Christianity because " it has injured *me*," so Mr. Timothy Shelley now hated his son's opinions that had wounded *him*.

Nevertheless he made a prompt effort to meet the situation. Two days after Shelley wrote his belated report we find Mr. Timothy Shelley at his regular London lodgings, Miller's Hotel, over Westminster Bridge. Since he could hardly have received Shelley's letter before March 30, he must have left Field Place at once in order to reach London, locate the boys through Graham (for Shelley's letter bore no address), and arrange an interview for March 31. After four days Mr. Shelley posted the following statement of his own position:

Miller's Hotel, April 5, 1811.
My dear Boy, — I am unwilling to receive and act on the information you gave me on Sunday, as the ultimate determination of your mind.

The disgrace which hangs over you is most serious, and though I have felt as a father, and sympathized in the misfortune which your criminal opinions and improper acts have begot: yet, you must know, that I have a duty to perform to my own character, as well as to your younger brother and sisters. Above all, my feelings as a Christian require from me a decided and firm conduct towards you.

If you shall require aid or assistance from me — or any protection — you must please yourself to me:

1st. To go immediately to Field Place, and to abstain from all communication with Mr. Hogg, for some considerable time.

2nd. That you shall place yourself under the care and society of such gentlemen as I shall appoint, and attend to his instructions and directions he shall give.

These terms are so necessary to your well-being, and to the value, which I cannot but entertain, that you may abandon your errors and present unjustifiable and wicked opinions, that I am resolved to withdraw myself from you, and leave you to the punishment and misery that belongs to the wicked pursuit of an opinion so diabolical and wicked as that which you have dared to declare, if you shall

not accept the proposals I shall go home on Thursday. — I am, your
affectionate and most afflicted Father,

T. SHELLEY [8]

Shelley's answer to his father's terms suggests the scornful
politeness of epistolary warfare rather than the abashed and
misunderstood son:

Poland Street,
[after *April* 5, 1811].

My dear Father,
    As you do me the honour of requesting to hear the determination
of my mind as the basis of your future actions, I feel it my duty,
although it gives me pain to wound " the sense of duty to your own
character, to that of your family, and your feelings as a Christian,"
decidedly to refuse my assent to both the proposals in your letter,
and to affirm that similar refusals will always be the fate of similar
requests. With many thanks for your great kindness,

I remain your affectionate dutiful son,
PERCY B. SHELLEY [9]

The sarcastic reference to his father's " sense of duty " and
so forth indicates that he completely underestimated the seriousness of the matter to his father.[10] Mr. Timothy Shelley
probably cared little about his son's opinions so long as they
were kept private, but he did care enormously about his own
reputation and that of his son. Bysshe cared nothing, apparently, for his father's point of view, but was resolved above
all things not to be forced away from the friend who had generously shared his expulsion, and not to compromise his favourite
axiom that the mind can accept opinions only upon conviction.
Mr. Timothy Shelley was as little capable of recognizing the
importance of these considerations to a highly idealistic nature
as Bysshe was of recognizing the importance of respectability
to his father.
    There was another interview at Mr. Shelley's hotel on Sun-
day, April 7. Hogg, who was present, has left an account of it
that few biographers of Shelley have been able to resist quoting.
It does full injustice to the obvious weaknesses of the squire
and also reveals a weakness of the two friends that apparently

123

did not occur to Hogg either at the time or many years later, when the scene still seemed to him primarily humorous. On the way to the meeting Shelley read aloud to Hogg from a violent criticism of the Old Testament, with much merriment at the expense of the ancient Jews and their tribal Jehovah. During the conference, when Mr. Shelley was out of earshot, Hogg compared him to Jehovah, which so amused Bysshe that he went into an uncontrollable paroxysm of laughter, to the great consternation of Timothy Shelley and Mr. Graham. The reckless humour with which they regarded the proceedings was much more ominous than Timothy Shelley's "odd, unconnected manner; scolding, crying, swearing, and then weeping again."

Willing to seek any port in a storm, Mr. Shelley seized upon a moment when Shelley was out of the room to ask Hogg's advice. Hogg suggested that marriage might temper the young man's wildness. The suggestion was endorsed by Mr. Graham,[11] who was present as a kind of factotum, and its possibilities were seriously discussed until Shelley's return.

From Hogg's amusing account of the end of the interview it is evident that Mr. Timothy Shelley was from the first convinced that his own feelings deserved far more consideration than they had received. He was also aware that he must be prepared to argue the original theological question, and he rather dreaded his son's prowess in that field.

"There is certainly a God," he then said; "there can be no doubt of the existence of a Deity; none whatever."

Nobody present expressed any doubt.

"You have no doubt on the subject, sir, have you?" he inquired, addressing himself particularly to me.

"None whatever."

"If you have, I can prove it to you in a moment."

"I have no doubt."

"But perhaps you would like to hear my argument?"

"Very much."

"I will read it to you, then."

He felt in several pockets, and at last drew out a sheet of letter-paper, and began to read.

Bysshe, leaning forward, listened with profound attention. "I

have heard this argument before," he said; and, by-and-by, turning
to me, he said again: " I have heard the argument before."

" They are Paley's arguments," I said.

" Yes! " the reader observed, with much complacency, turning
towards me, " you are right, sir," and he folded up the paper, and
put it into his pocket; " they are Palley's [*sic*] arguments: I copied
them out of Palley's book this morning myself: but Palley had them
originally from me; almost everything in Palley's book he had from
me.". . .

" Palley's arguments! Palley's books! " I said to my friend, as
we walked home.

" Yes; my father always will call him Palley; why does he call
him so? "

" I do not know, unless it be to rhyme with Sally." [12]

After referring to this meeting in a later letter to Mr. William
Whitton, Shelley's father remarked: " My son threw away the
chance he had of going to the Greek Islands because he would
not leave Hogg. Travelling would of course dispel the gloomy
ideas which he has too long fix'd on objects, tending to produce
Temporary Insanity. . . ." [13]

By this time Timothy Shelley was quite certain that the situation required that he should take a strong stand. The essence
of the problem was to separate the two boys. Immediately he
wrote to Hogg's father suggesting that they act together to this
end. Mr. John Hogg had already acted, having requested his
friend Mr. R. Clarke, in New Bond Street, to report to him on
the expulsion. [14]

Beginning to feel that the matter was beyond his own unaided
ability, Mr. Shelley consulted his legal adviser, Mr. William
Whitton, of Great James Street, Bedford Row. On April 8 [15]
he wrote to Whitton to say that the boys were determined and
that Shelley was beginning to cast off all duty, but " I shall and
will be firm." William Whitton undoubtedly supported this
attitude. He was one of those persons sometimes called men
of " strong sense," who know considerably more of rights and
duties than of sympathies and intuitions. Mr. Timothy Shelley,
with his erratic vacillations, impulsive outbreaks, and genuine
affection for his son, might have reached an understanding

125

by direct negotiation. Dealing through another person who sympathized with only one of the parties involved, he was soon to see the breach widened until eventually the very name of his son became intolerable to him.

Mr. Timothy Shelley's deep concern obliged him to seek help wherever he could get it. A friend and neighbour, a Mr. Hurst, undertook to influence Bysshe toward a proper attitude. The only result of his persuasions was a curt note from Bysshe to his father, saying that he was "astonished" that such a man should be employed to make "proposals"; he demanded that any change in his father's intentions should be communicated to him direct.[16] Mr. Shelley's interview with Mr. Clarke, who was handling Mr. John Hogg's interests, was hardly more fortunate. Clarke agreed that the two boys should be separated. Unfortunately, however, Mr. Shelley left the impression that he considered Hogg the original corrupter of his son's opinions, which caused Bysshe to write a letter to Mr. John Hogg assuring him that such a suggestion was totally false.[17]

Mr. Shelley immediately sought the influence of three other meditators — John Grove, Bysshe's cousin, and two uncles, Mr. Robert Parker and Captain John Pilfold.[18] John Grove, after several conversations with Bysshe, reported to Mr. Shelley [19] that there could be little doubt of Bysshe's desire for reconciliation, but not at the price of abandoning Hogg or giving up his beliefs until fairly persuaded they were false. He thought Bysshe would prove more tractable after Hogg's departure from London, which he understood to be impending. Mr. Parker had a long talk with Bysshe and made substantially the same report, only a day after John Grove's report. Bysshe certainly wished to be reconciled, he believed, but only on his own terms. Rather tactlessly he added that the young man expressed "*affection towards his mother and sister,*" upon which Mr. Shelley commented: "never to me." [20] Of Captain Pilfold's "very civil letter" [21] to Bysshe there were no apparent results except that it was taken in good part.

Spurred by Mr. Shelley's agitation, Mr. John Hogg was also not idle. Unluckily his choice as mediator fell upon the Reverend George Stanley Faber, vicar of Stockton-upon-Tees, where Mr. Hogg resided. The two boys already scorned him as a supporter of dogmatic theology.[22] Precisely how he mediated is unknown, but the results are fairly indicative. Soon Mr. Faber wrote a very long letter to Mr. John Hogg, which was duly shown to Mr. Timothy Shelley and which irritated him still further by the evident disrespect with which the vicar had been treated. Thereafter, for about a year, Mr. Faber appears from time to time in the Shelley-Hogg correspondence as F., an object of theological bear-baiting.

Thus after two weeks of negotiating there was no visible progress. On April 11 Mr. Shelley was convinced that he could do no more. Writing to William Whitton, he placed the affair in his hands, quite positively: " I will, my dear Sir, now leave this young Lunatic to your management, as I shall go home." [23] He went home on April 11 or 12 and shortly afterwards [24] wrote to Clarke, Mr. John Hogg's agent, that he had placed the whole affair in Mr. Whitton's hands " to guard my honour and character." But as the previous mediators had all interfered, as they thought, at Mr. Shelley's suggestion, though the latter protested to Mr. Whitton that it was really against his wish, the hardheaded lawyer evidently concluded that Mr. Shelley's resolution needed support. Writing on April 11 to old Sir Bysshe,[25] Whitton suggested that the grandfather co-operate in stiffening the father's attitude: " His impiety and effrontery in the avowal of it exceeds belief, and if anything can bring him to a sense of his duty it is the firm conduct in my opinion of Mr. Tim Shelley." Thereafter Mr. Shelley's letters to his lawyer contain frequent references to conferences with Sir Bysshe.

At this point the boy's mother also took a hand. Intercepting one of Bysshe's letters that she feared would irritate his father,[26] she sent him the money to come home. Had he done so, thus removing the matter from Whitton's hands to those of one who understood both parties better than they understood each other, the breach might have been healed. But Bysshe declined and returned the money, very possibly out of loyalty to Hogg.

At about the same time Mr. Shelley received a communication from the two boys, undated, but written probably on April 12 or 13, since it was sent on to Whitton on the 14th:

15 *Poland Street.*

My dear Father,

I enclose you a copy of the proposals which were submitted after the joint consideration of myself and my Friend to the latter's Father.

He has done us the honour of expressing his approbation of them with the consent of yours.

I do this with a real and sincere wish for coming to an accommodation which I respectfully hope will not now be refused. —

Your obt. affectionate Son,

P. B. SHELLEY

" The Parties will make to Mr. Faber any apologies that he or his friends may require.

" They will not obtrude Atheistical opinions upon any one whatever, they will refrain from publishing Atheistical Doctrines or even speculations.

" They will return immediately to their respective homes.

" The parties feel it their duty to demand an unrestrained correspondence.

" When Mr. T. J. Hogg enters at the Inns of Court or commences any other profession, that Mr. P. B. Shelley may be permitted to select that situation in life, which may be consonant with his intentions, to which he may judge his abilities adequate." [27]

To anyone less wounded and exasperated than Timothy Shelley this letter offered a real basis for agreement. Mr. John Hogg had concluded very sensibly that since there was no way actually to prevent a correspondence between the two youths it was useless to insist that they should not correspond. But Timothy Shelley had insisted on that point from the very first, and he was too stubborn and too offended to abandon it now for purely practical considerations. He endorsed the letter: " Fine fellows these, to presume to offer proposals," and wrote to Whitton:

They never think of their offended and injur'd Parents' situation, but endeavour to treat by a flag of Truce, like two contending armies, disagree in some point, and then go to Battle again — I am rous'd into energy and a determined resolution not to give way to his insolent demand of corresponding with Mr. Hogg, or his chusing for himself what would not be admitted with his monstrous opinions at the Inns of Court. Perhaps a correspondence could not be prevented

or the word of a person of such dreadful opinions could not be taken.
. . . This agitates me so that I cannot act for myself to my own
satisfaction.[28]

Old Sir Bysshe had been consulted and had given his opinion
that Mr. Timothy Shelley was right in leaving the matter entirely to Whitton's handling. Dreaming his dreams of family
grandeur in his inn tap-room, he scarcely imagined that they
were even then being frustrated by the stubbornness of a mere
youth. On the next day Sir Bysshe wrote to Whitton that
Bysshe's letter to his father showed him to be a complete rebel,
for whom no terms should be available but unconditional surrender. Since the two rebels could never be persuaded into
this, his opinion was that they would come to their senses more
quickly if left entirely alone.[29]

Mr. Timothy Shelley then wrote to Mr. Clarke, Mr. Hogg's
agent, to comment on the recent proposals. Clarke responded
with the welcome information that young Hogg had proved
amenable and was leaving London for the north on April 16.
Hogg's forthcoming departure seemed to offer grounds for
hope; Mr. Shelley immediately wrote Whitton that Bysshe was
now to be alone and expressed a wish that " something could
be done with the apostate."

Mr. William Whitton undertook to do something almost
immediately. First writing to confirm Mr. Timothy Shelley in
his unyielding attitude, he wrote to invite Bysshe to his house
to discuss matters with him. Now that Hogg was leaving London, the only points of difference were Bysshe's insistence that
he should choose his own profession and be free to correspond
with Hogg. Unluckily Whitton's note crossed a second proposal
from Bysshe. On April 17 he wrote Mr. Whitton offering to
resign all claim to the portion of Sir Bysshe's property entailed
upon him provided his father would divide the property in
question equally between Bysshe's mother and sisters and would
allow him an annuity of two hundred pounds. He was unaware
of the fact, soon pointed out by Whitton and Mr. Shelley, that
such an agreement could have no legal validity until Bysshe
reached his majority. To him his proposal was merely a pleas-

ant way of solving the present difficulties; it would give him all the income he wanted, would release him from all responsibilities of family and property (no light consideration to a young Godwinian), and would leave him entirely free.

The proposal shocked the family lawyer beyond anything that had yet happened. He wrote sternly refusing to transmit Bysshe's offer — " I am not a willing instrument by which insult may be offered to your father." [30] Bysshe, who resented Whitton's mediation and had apparently intended no insult, responded hotly:

> 15 *Poland Street,*
> [Postmark: 12 o'clock, *April* 19, 1811]
>
> Sir,
> I am not a likely person to submit to the imperious manner of address, of which this evening's letter is a specimen; nor *am* I inclined to withdraw, nor *ever will* I be inclined to withdraw the proposal which I sent you. As therefore you seem to have much to do in this business on the part of my father, it is your duty either to go through with it, or to give it up. I never *will* withdraw that proposal: It is for my father's or rather my family's interests which ought to be the same that I make it. *Here* is no appeal to mercy, leniency, or favour. I have *not* found nor do I care to find either: but an appeal to justice, reason, humanity if you, if he were deaf to that nothing can be done. — I will not listen to the suggestions of family pride, to interest to fortune I am indifferent and I desire that when I am addressed again, a less authoritative manner be used, or subsequent letters are returned unopened. — Yr. humbl. sert.
>
> P. B. SHELLEY [31]

Whitton's reply to this was quite stiff. He observed that he had intended no insult; he needed no instruction from Shelley as to his duties; it was not only silly but illegal for a minor like Shelley to dispose of property entailed to him; Shelley might well pay some regard to his own duty and to his manners; and until the latter improved there would be an interruption of all dealings between the two.

Thus all the good results anticipated from Hogg's departure were immediately cancelled. Whitton was so confirmed in his opinion of Bysshe that he explained to Mr. Shelley that he had

called off the personal interview lest the young man's insults
should necessitate turning him out of the house. Mr. Timothy
Shelley was much more deeply shocked than he had been at the
news of Bysshe's expulsion. This was not unnatural, for Bysshe's
proposal to renounce the entail completely reversed the situation. *He* was proposing to throw the family overboard, to accept a severing of all formal connections. It is evident from Mr.
Timothy Shelley's correspondence that up to this time he had
regarded the matter as one that could be settled by parental
discipline and threats he never anticipated having to carry out
to the end. When the boy himself coolly proposed to throw
away all the family hopes that were founded on him, Mr. Shelley realized for the first time something of the full gravity of the
situation. He wrote two letters to Whitton, and himself arrived
in London with the second, which he mailed from Miller's Hotel on April 23.

Certain passages from his letters to Whitton show how he regarded his son at this time. On April 14, after his return to Field
Place, he counselled Whitton: [32] " Don't spare my Apostate Son
though I know it is only obstinacy." On April 18 he wrote:

If he even now expresses the least goodness of Heart, he will be
very sorry that he has not seen that whatever a parent had requir'd
that he did not see it was sufficient, whose happyness has been so
wounded by his conduct and opinions, which to speak most mildly
of them, are not only extremely singular, but abhorent in a Christian
Society. He ought therefore to correct them, and not shut his mind
against conviction in favour of such abominable opinions merely
because he fancies his reasoning powers infallible. . . .[33]

A few days later, on April 22, he wrote:

To cast off all thoughts of his Maker, to abandon his Parents, to
wish to relinquish his Fortune and to court Persecution all seems to
arise from the same source [Diabolical Publications]. . . . Nothing
provokes him so much as civility, he wishes to become what he would
term a martyr to his sentiments — nor do I believe he would feel the
Horrors of being drawn upon a Hurdle, or the shame of being whirl'd
in the Pillory.[34]

THE LAST words that Timothy Shelley had written to Whitton, in a postscript added after his arrival in London, were: "I hear he is woefully melancholy." On the 16th or 17th Hogg, more amenable to parental control than his friend, had departed for a short vacation in Shropshire before beginning legal studies in York. The neo-Oxonian life in London undoubtedly became less attractive with his absence. Bysshe's first letter to Hogg, April 18, indicates that Mr. Timothy Shelley was not entirely misinformed:

> Certainly this place is a little solitary, but a person cannot be quite alone when he has even got himself with him, I get on pretty well. I have employed myself in writing poetry, and as I go to bed at eight o'clock, time passes quicker than it otherwise might.[35]

For a few days he had a slight fever that somewhat restricted his activities.

It was at this time that Shelley made the personal acquaintance of Leigh Hunt, to whom he had formerly addressed a letter from Oxford. Very graciously Hunt invited him to breakfast, where Shelley was delighted to learn that he was a man of "cultivated mind and certainly exalted notions" and his wife "a most sensible woman." A long argument between Hunt and some of his friends, in which Hunt defended deism, was duly reported by Shelley in his next letter to Hogg.[36] The meeting bore no immediate fruit, however, and Hunt later remembered only vaguely his first contact with the youth destined to become his greatest friend and benefactor.[37]

John and Charles Grove were still at hand, the latter almost daily. With Charles he attended a radical speech-making at the British Forum. Here he spoke and so skilfully mingled compliments and criticism that he was pressed for his name, but gave a false name and address.[38]

Once in a while Shelley appears to have seen Gibbons Merle. There was also Tom Medwin, who occasionally called at the Poland Street lodgings. They often walked together in Kensington Gardens, where Shelley delighted to sail paper boats on the Serpentine or the ponds and to skip flat stones over the water. On these walks a frequent subject of conversation was dreams.

Shelley kept a journal in which he noted his thoughts and experiences on the subject. His intense interest, aided probably
by the nervous strain of his situation, brought about a return of
his old sleep-walking habits. One morning, Medwin asserts, he
actually found the poet asleep in Leicester Square, after having
wandered there in a fit of somnambulism.[39] But Medwin was
unsympathetic with his cousin's most cherished opinions, and
Shelley had probably already formed the opinion he held later
that Medwin was a bore. There was the British Museum, where
he sometimes went for books, and there was still Mr. Faber, the
Yorkshire vicar, who for months to come seemed tied to the
stake of epistolary discussion. But the game seemed to be losing
its savour; even Faber's Christian forgiveness excited Shelley's
scorn.[40]

ONE SOLACE was already beginning to appear. In his first letter
Shelley informed Hogg that " Miss Westbrook has this moment
called on me, with her sister. It certainly was kind of them."
The next letter to Hogg (April 24) shows that six days had made
some progress in friendship:

My little friend Harriet W[estbrook] is gone to her prison-house.
She is quite well in health; at least so she says, though she looks
very much otherwise. I saw her yesterday. I went with her sister
to Miss H[awkes's?] and walked about Clapham Common with
them for two hours. The youngest is a most amiable girl; the eldest
is really conceited, but very condescending. I took the sacrament
with her on Sunday. You say I talk philosophically of her kindness in calling on me. She is very charitable and good. I shall
always think of it with gratitude, because I certainly did not deserve it, and she exposed herself to much possible odium. It is,
perhaps, scarcely doing her a kindness — it is, perhaps, inducing positive unhappiness — to point out to her a road which she is inclined
so nobly to follow; a road which leads to perfection, the attainment
of which, perhaps, does not repay the difficulties of the progress.
What do *you* think of this? If trains of thought, development of
mental energies influence in any degree a future state; if this is *even*
possible — if it stands on *at all* securer ground than mere hypothesis;
then is it not a service? Where am I gotten? perhaps into another

ridiculous argument. I will not proceed, for I shall forget all I have said, and cannot, in justice, animadvert upon any of your critiques.[41]

Here we may well pause for a brief comment on the family in which the young outcast was becoming more and more interested. Mr. John Westbrook, of 23 Chapel Street, Grosvenor Square, had formerly kept a tavern, the Mount Coffee House, near his present residence, but had accumulated sufficient money on which to retire from business. His nickname, " Jew Westbrook," may be an indication [42] that he was also a money-lender, or it may refer entirely to his swarthy complexion. His wife, though living in 1811, seems to have resigned the care of the household to her older daughter, Eliza, then thirty years of age. Eliza's appearance at this time may be conjectured by an imaginative fusion of Hogg's obviously libellous description and the favourable account left by her nephew. To Hogg, who saw her in her early thirties, she was thin, pasty-faced, pock-marked; she had long, coarse black hair and dull, dark eyes.[43] To her grand-nephew, several decades later, she was " a handsome, grand old lady, with a dark front of hair, piercing dark eyes, and with a kind manner to children." [44]

Harriet, who was sixteen years old at this time, has been favourably described by all who knew her.[45] Hellen Shelley testified that she was generally regarded as the most beautiful girl in the school, with a fine, brilliant pink-and-white complexion and " hair like a poet's dream, and Bysshe's peculiar admiration." Peacock admired her light, graceful figure, well-modelled features and beautifully transparent complexion, her good sense and manners, and her frank, pleasant cordiality. Bysshe's younger sisters had chosen a rather dangerous emissary for their little gifts of pocket-money.

MR. TIMOTHY SHELLEY soon reappeared in London, deeply alarmed and resentful over his son's proposal to renounce the entail to his property. The morning after his arrival he called on John Grove, his best source of information about Bysshe's state of mind. Bysshe happened to be calling at the same time. He met his father in the passage.

134

He looked as black as a thunder-cloud, and said, " Your most humble servant! " I made him a low bow, and wishing him a very good morning — passed on. He is very irate about my proposals.[46]

It must have been only a few days after this that the Duke of Norfolk stepped in as a friend of the family. For some time he had been urging a political career for Bysshe. He now arranged a dinner at which Bysshe and his father were present, and sought again to interest the young man in a political career. But practical politics under the ægis of a borough-monger did not appeal to Bysshe. He considered the suggestion an attempt to shackle his mind.[47]

Either from Captain Pilfold in Sussex, or more probably from the " reticent " John Grove, Bysshe learned that his father was set against his return to Field Place and was resolved to take Elizabeth away if he came. So Shelley changed his mind again and announced to Hogg [48] that he only awaited Captain Pilfold's arrival to go down to Field Place with him and that he should follow Elizabeth if his father removed her. Elizabeth's " conversion " and union with Hogg were still very important objects to Bysshe, a fact of which his father was at least partly aware.

John Grove persuaded Mr. Timothy Shelley to allow Bysshe two hundred pounds a year and his freedom, but within a day or two he wrote from Field Place to annul the agreement.[49] Shelley still planned to go to Field Place soon.

He is yet angry beyond all measure — pacification is remote; but I *will* be at peace, vi et armis. I will enter his dominions, preserving a Quaker-like carelessness of opposition. I shall manage à l'Amérique, and seat myself quietly in his mansion, turning a deaf ear to any declamatory objections.[50]

It was to be more than a fortnight, however, before Shelley re-entered Field Place.

EVER since Hogg had left London the two friends had been in close correspondence. Hogg's letters, like Shelley's letters to his Grove relations, have been lost, but Shelley's letters to Hogg form the real essence of any picture of the young man at this time. Philosophy — the old eager search for Truth — holds an important place there, somewhat incongruously tinged with the sheer love of argument. He argues (April 26?) that Christianity, by its insistence on faith as a moral duty, is fundamentally unamiable, since faith is not subject to the will. Though Christianity may still be best for the ignorant, the canaille, " the inquiring should reject it altogether." It is " an odious system " and " religion is the child of cold prejudice and selfish fear." " I once could tolerate Christ," he concludes, with unconscious self-revelation; " he then merely injured me once; he merely deprived *me* of all that I cared for, touching myself, on earth; but now he has done more, and I cannot forgive." [51]

In printing these letters Hogg sought to tone down Shelley's opinions by printing " religionist " for " Deist," " philosopher " for " Atheist," " intolerance " for " Christianity," etc., and for half a century succeeded in his amiable deceit.[52] But Shelley's father had good information on which his growing alarm was based. Even Tom Medwin [53] saw enough to convince him that Bysshe had now gone most of the way from the mild agnosticism of *The Necessity of Atheism* to the actual militant atheism of *Queen Mab*.[54] He ascribed the change to the consequences of Shelley's expulsion. Hogg's later belief was that Shelley would have settled down harmlessly enough had not the expulsion and ensuing antagonism stimulated him to more extensive controversy.[55] Shelley himself was aware of the change. " I *once* was an enthusiastic Deist," he wrote Janetta Phillips shortly after his return to Field Place, " but never a Christian." [56]

The cancelling of Hogg's invitation to Field Place by no means ended Shelley's desire to see Hogg and his sister Elizabeth united without benefit of clergy. His letters were full of this plan, nor did he abandon it entirely until after his own elopement. Much of what Shelley had to say consisted in arguments against Hogg's despair. He himself was afraid that Elizabeth was now lost to the cause of true enlightenment:

I will not deceive myself; she is lost, lost to everything; Intolerance has tainted her — she talks cant and twaddle. . . . A young female, who only once, only for a short time, asserted her claim to an un-

136

fettered use of reason, bred up with bigots, having before her eyes
examples of the consequences of scepticism. . . .[57]

The only excuse for still hoping was implied in a more general
observation in the same letter when he countered Hogg's assertion that mankind " ever has been a slave to the vilest of errors "
by asserting that there was still no proof that it always would be.

On the eve of seeing Elizabeth again, Shelley found it necessary to protest against some objections Hogg had made to his
scheme. Hogg appeared to favour vulgar matrimony on his expected income of six hundred pounds. The money, Shelley argued, was too much and quite a secondary matter; as for matrimony, that might do for the vulgar mass, who were already
corrupt beyond all hope, but it was beneath men of virtue and
honour. " For God's sake, if you want more argument, read the
Marriage Service before you *think* of allowing an amiable, beloved female to submit to such degradation." [58]

As hopes for Elizabeth faded, Bysshe was cheered by the prospect of new converts. Most important of these was his younger
sister's friend Harriet Westbrook, the beautiful blonde girl whom
he had met during the Christmas holidays, and who had befriended him during the lonely days in London. At the beginning he felt quite grateful to Harriet for her kindness and had
some doubts as to whether it would be a real kindness on his part
to enlighten her in return. He now learned that she was suffering persecution at school for her friendship with him:

They will not speak to her; her schoolfellows will not even reply to
her questions; she is called an *abandoned* wretch, and universally
hated, which she remunerates with the calmest contempt.[59]

Hogg may have betrayed some ironical amusement at the situation that was now developing, or something else may have
caused Bysshe to stand for a second half-listening to the worldly
suspicion that had made him doubt the proffered friendship of
Gibbons Merle. A day or two later he informed Hogg:

My poor little friend has been ill, her sister sent for me the other
night. I found her on a couch pale; her father is civil to me, very
strangely; the sister is too civil by half. She began talking about

l'Amour. I philosophized, and the youngest said she had such a headache, that she could not bear conversation. Her sister then went away, and I stayed till half-past twelve.[60]

Both Harriet and Eliza, he concluded, would make excellent crushers of intolerance, though Eliza might require " some taming."

When Harriet was " compelled " to return to school, Shelley accompanied her to Clapham. Thereafter for a week or two he spent most of his time at Miss Westbrook's [61] and reached the conclusion that Eliza was a much more amiable being than he had first supposed. When he left London he had " arranged a correspondence " with the two sisters.[62] One letter directed to Shelley during this correspondence fell into his father's hands (even though addressed in care of Captain Pilfold) and has been preserved. In it Eliza cautioned Shelley against saying anything at Field Place to indicate his intimacy with the Westbrooks.[63] Mr. Timothy Shelley must have realized that another danger was threatening, but he seems to have given no sign. Eliza's fears for Shelley's secrecy were probably unnecessary. Not even Medwin, who was in frequent conversation with Shelley in London, was told about the Westbrook sisters.

Bysshe actually entered Field Place via Cuckfield, Captain Pilfold's home. That sympathetic uncle first had Shelley in his own home and then persuaded Mr. Timothy Shelley into an agreement. On May 15 Bysshe wrote to Hogg from Field Place and announced an agreement by which he was to receive two hundred pounds a year and the right to live where he chose. Rather airily he also informed Edward Graham that he had received two hundred pounds a year, " free agency etc.," adding: " he looks rather blue today but the Capt. keeps him in tol. order." [64] To neither did he mention that he had agreed to enter some profession.[65] He probably failed to realize that the profound uneasiness and distrust that the last few months had generated in his father, together with his own impulsive instability, rendered any agreement only a temporary one.

One sentence in Shelley's letter to Graham quoted above seems to be connected with a little-known juvenile poem written evi-

dently within the week of May 15, 1811, immediately after Shelley's return to Field Place. To Graham Shelley had mentioned
receipt of an anonymous letter by Mr. Timothy Shelley accusing
him and his wife of drunkenness and Mrs. Shelley of immorality
with Graham. "We all laughed heartily," he concluded, "and
thought it a good opportunity of making up." Soon afterwards
Shelley was sending Graham a rhymed letter on the episode.
He described "old Killjoy" as blue with jealousy and resentment, and acquitted Graham of "cornuting old Killjoy's brow,"
largely because there was no temptation.[66] This unfilial piece of
doggerel is best regarded as an ill-judged expression of Shelley's
occasionally wild sense of humour rather than as a serious libel
upon his parents. The instability of the youth who wrote it is
well illustrated by the fact that within six months he was directly
and passionately accusing his mother of the very crime he had
first laughed at as an absurdity.[67]

Elizabeth was ill with a fever when Bysshe reached home, and
his father did all he could to prevent their association. When
Bysshe did see her he was gravely disappointed. She was now
gay and worldly — quite dead to the cause, but still capable of
resuscitation. He offered Hogg comfort by suggesting that it
was really an abstraction that he loved — an abstraction that had
been for a brief time a beautiful reality. Now (June 16), after
several times trying some mysterious experiment recommended
by Hogg, he found Elizabeth still unmoved: "You and your mad
friend!" she jeered. "Those, whom I have seen, and who have
seen me, may have some *little excuse* for their folly." [68] Beyond
this she would not talk with him.

When Elizabeth did talk, a few days later, it was to talk
pointedly of matrimony and to answer Shelley's objections to it
with the scornful exclamation: "'This, then, is the honourable
advice of a brother!'" [69] Hogg, too, still cherished the word
"matrimony," in spite of the "ineffable, sickening disgust" with
which Shelley regarded "this most despotic, most unrequired
fetter which prejudice has forged." [70] It was the one point on
which Shelley felt he could never agree with Hogg's principles.
Bysshe now desired Hogg to come secretly to Field Place, sleep
on a mattress in his rooms, and walk with him only at midnight.

Looking from the windows, he might see Elizabeth on the lawn.[71] But Hogg did not come, and after a brief unsuccessful courtship by John Grove in August [72] and a rumoured engagement to Edward Graham that enraged Shelley against his mother,[73] she passed out of the lives of the two friends, a fallen spirit who even as a poet was now seen by her brother to be distinctly inferior to Miss Brown and Miss Phillips.[74]

Life at Field Place was not at all satisfactory to the returned prodigal. His father ("this killjoy, as I name him") was still offended and suspicious and his formerly much-admired Elizabeth was now entirely unsympathetic and even avoided him. Mary and Hellen were in school at Clapham, and the two youngest children, John and Margaret, were too young to be enlightened. Hellen, who had stood by Harriet Westbrook when her schoolmates deserted her, "would be a divine little scion of infidelity, if I could get hold of her." [75] There was of course his mother, whom he regarded as rather liberal-minded, since she believed that religious forms and creeds were of much less importance than good character.[76] She, at least, was no slave to intolerance, and she sympathized with Bysshe's friendship for Hogg,[77] but she felt that the weather was the safest subject of conversation with her son.

Much of Bysshe's time was taken up in writing. To Hogg he wrote several times a week. The Westbrook sisters must have heard from him nearly as often, judging by the position they occupy in his letters to Hogg. Harriet was at first horrified by his opinions, and required considerable argument.[78] The Reverend Mr. Faber required an occasional epistolary ministration. Janetta Phillips, at Oxford, received two letters from Shelley, but was too much shocked at his views to encourage further correspondence. He continued, as in London, to write a few poems, which still gave no promise of future greatness. And of course he read. Field Place was far inferior to Oxford and London as a provider of the kind of books he most wanted. In Captain Pilfold's library he found (or kept) George Ensor's *National Education,* which he read with approval. He became quite enthusiastic over the beauties of Miss Sydney Owenson's novel *The Missionary,* which had just been published by Stockdale, and he ordered Scott's latest poem, *The Vision of Don Roderick.*

Some of his time he spent with his genial uncle, Captain Pilfold, at Cuckfield, a short ride from Horsham. The Captain was such a bluff, hearty fellow that Shelley could ignore the fact that he had fought with distinction under Nelson. He had won Shelley's gratitude by inducing Mr. Timothy Shelley to come to an agreement with his son. In return Shelley enlightened him and was immensely pleased when at dinner one day the Captain completely disabled a local " red-hot saint " with a broadside from *The Necessity of Atheism.*[79]

It was during one of the first of these stays with Captain Pilfold that Shelley became acquainted with Miss Elizabeth Hitchener, mistress of a near-by school at Hurstpierpoint of which the Captain was a patron. She was of somewhat humble parentage, but her point of view was liberal. Though not at first convinced by Shelley's glowing arguments against Christianity, she was at least willing to consider them. A correspondence immediately sprang up. Shelley sent her copies of Locke, Southey's *The Curse of Kehama,* and Ensor's *National Education.*

Miss Hitchener had the misfortune to meet Thomas Jefferson Hogg about a year later, just as she was being ushered out of Shelley's life, and so fell heir to one of his merciless and probably prejudiced descriptions. " The heroine was tall and thin, bony and masculine, of a dark complexion; and the symbol of male wisdom, a beard, was not entirely wanting. She was neither young nor old; not handsome — not absolutely ill-looking," and had " a prim, formal, didactic manner and speech." [80] This was after Miss Hitchener had already come to be regarded by Shelley himself as a " brown demon "; at first Shelley saw her quite differently. She enjoyed the esteem of the community [81] despite the fact that her father had been a smuggler, named Yorke, before he acquired a public-house and the name of Hitchener. At the age of twenty-nine she was an imaginative, impulsive, quick-spirited woman whose somewhat radical political and religious views probably found few sympathizers among her associates until Shelley appeared.[82]

Shelley's early letters to Miss Hitchener were devoted to her enlightenment with a quite impersonal ardour. He said he would as soon believe in a God as not, but that he was now fully convinced that none existed.[83] He wished to convince her likewise, first, because truth would be served thereby; second, because the dissemination of such a view would be the readiest way of eradicating Christianity, the great foe of real virtue. Since Elizabeth's real aim was to serve virtue, he argued, she was herself no longer a Christian, and should cease to attribute her virtue to "a spurious, irrational (as proved), disjointed system of desultory ethics" and "insulting, intolerant theology." We may believe in God as the essence of the universe, a synonym for "*the existing power of existence*," [84] he conceded, but not as a personified Being.

Elizabeth [85] felt her orthodoxy shaken by this first onslaught, but not destroyed. Her belief in God, she said, was based on a *feeling*, not on reason; but the God she believed in certainly sanctioned the full use of human faculties, and she was quite willing to devote these faculties to the question of His existence. She professed herself unmoved by the usual Christian fears and hopes of a future life, but unwilling as yet to wound others by declaring herself no Christian; moreover she found in the sacred writings much that strengthened her impulses to virtue. To this Shelley answered that virtues might occasionally be incident to Christianity, but they were not the essence of it — Christianity was essentially opposed to virtue. Atheism, he concluded, was nothing to be afraid of; they both believed in Truth, and Truth could be established in philosophy or politics only after religion was overcome.

Here the correspondence came to a pause — or at least there are no extant letters from Shelley to Elizabeth Hitchener between June 25 and July 15, 1811. On both sides it was marked from the beginning by expressions of fervent esteem for each other's character; the argument came to be based upon character almost as much as upon abstract reasoning. Miss Hitchener, from the first, assumed the position of a trusting and admiring disciple who does not follow all the way simply because she is unable to do so at once.

142

WHILE this correspondence was beguiling the tedium of Field Place with the education of still another crusher of intolerance, the newspapers carried a story of events in London that stirred the young poet to scorn and indignation. The Prince Regent, whose name was already odious to liberals and radicals, gave a most extravagant fête at Carleton House on June 19. Conservative papers revelled in the magnificent details of scarlet uniforms and gold lace. They wrote admiringly of the artificial stream of pure water running between mossy banks down the length of the two-hundred-foot table. The opposition condemned the heartless expense while people were starving. Shelley regarded it as the prelude to Revolution. " It is said that this entertainment will cost £120,000; nor will it be the last bauble which the nation must buy to amuse this overgrown bantling of regency," he wrote to Miss Hitchener,[86] and proceeded to compare it with the corrupt luxury of decaying Rome. At about the same time he wrote to Edward Graham with elaborate irony, to notify him that there would soon be an ode for him to set to music — " my loyal endeavour to magnify, if magnification be possible, our Noble Royal Family." He signed himself Philobasileus and adorned the outside of the sheet with a translation from the *Marseillaise*.

It is perhaps a sign of a certain strain of secrecy in Shelley, noticed by both Hogg and Peacock, that he could express himself so indignantly about the Carleton House fête to Miss Hitchener and yet not mention that he was writing or had just written a poem on the subject. Charles Grove later remembered that Shelley " wrote a poem on the subject of about fifty lines, which he published immediately, wherein he apostrophized the prince as sitting on the bank of his tiny river; and he amused himself with throwing copies into the carriages of persons going to Carleton House after the fête." [87] Of this poem all trace has been lost except four worthless lines that were handed on from memory to W. M. Rossetti by Shelley's grandson, the Reverend William Esdaile.

Shelley had been at Field Place less than a week before he began planning to leave it. This was partly due to an arrangement agreed upon with Hogg when the two separated in Lon-

don. " In less than a month," says Hogg,[88] " our pleasant student
life was to recommence at York, and to be continued there . . .
for a year. At the expiration of the year it was to be calmly enjoyed in London for an indefinite period, during the remainder
of our lives."

Moreover, at Field Place Shelley felt continually bored and
frustrated. In the old days, before he went to Oxford, there had
been some companionship with his father; they had formerly
read a good bit together.[89] Now his father was a contemptible
worldling, " a no-*ist,*" professing " no-*ism,* but superbism and
irrationalism." [90] He had pretty completely alienated Elizabeth
from the right side and had tyrannically sought to keep Bysshe
entirely separated from her. Field Place was no longer the
happy little kingdom it had once been. About June 27 he wrote
to Hogg:

I am a perfect hermit: not a being to speak with! I sometimes
exchange a word with my mother on the subject of the weather,
upon which she is irresistibly eloquent; otherwise all is deep
silence! I wander about this place, walking all over the grounds, with
no particular object in view. I cannot write, except now and then
to you — sometimes to Miss Westbrooks. . . . My hand begins to
hurry, and I am tired and ennuied.[91] The only thing that has interested me, if I except your letters, has been one novel. It is Miss
Owenson's Missionary, an Indian tale; will you read it? It is really
a divine thing. . . .[92]

Bysshe had recently received two invitations. Before leaving
London [93] he had been asked by Thomas Grove and his wife to
visit them at their home, Cwm Elan, in Radnorshire, about
which his interest had some time earlier been aroused by Harriet Grove. Later " old Westbrook " had invited Bysshe to accompany him and the two daughters to their house in Aberystwith, Wales. Shelley's first move [94] was to instruct Hogg to take
lodgings for him at York; he intended to leave Field Place in two
weeks, spend a week with the Westbrooks in London, and then
join Hogg. Four days later [95] he was telling Miss Hitchener that
he was going to spend a week in London and the rest of the summer in Wales. Perhaps the " Wales " really stood in his own

mind for York, which must not be mentioned where it might possibly get back to his father. From London he intended to proceed on foot " for the purpose of better remarking the manners, and dispositions of the peasantry." [96] But to Hogg he wrote two days later that he might not go beyond York on his way to Wales.[97]

Shelley also told Hogg that he was going to " pedestrianize," but if he did he left no notes on the " peasantry." In London, whether he stayed with " old Westbrook," Graham, or the Groves, he was so heavily occupied for several days with some mysterious " pressing and urgent business " [98] that the result was a short nervous illness that prevented his calling on Elizabeth Hitchener, who was in town at the time.[99] He reached Cwm Elan on July 14 or 15.

Thomas Grove's ten-thousand-acre estate was five miles southeast of Rhayader, the nearest post office, in Radnorshire, South Wales. Thirteen years before Shelley arrived, another poet, William Lisle Bowles, had spent part of a summer there as the guest of Mr. William Grove, and had celebrated its wild beauty in one of the best of his blank-verse poems, written on the spot.[100] With feeling the Wiltshire parson described the deep, narrow glen through which the Elan descends to join the Wye, the wild confusion of slate and limestone crags, the " wreathed waterfall," the thick woods of oak and ash, the birch " in lonely glens lightwavering " — all this on the one hand, and on the other, green pastures and light blue smoke ascending from a quiet cottage. To him they carried a meaning of natural and spiritual peace.

Shelley noticed these natural beauties readily enough. " Here are rocks, cataracts, woods and Groves," [101] was his first somewhat unawed impression. He wrote to Hogg [102] that the scenery was divine — and he was bored. But to Elizabeth Hitchener he showed not only a flash of real feeling for his surroundings, but also a clear perception of the reason why his recent tendencies had been away from such appreciation:

Nature is here marked with the most impressive character of loveliness and grandeur, *once* I was tremulously alive to tones and scenes . . . the habit of analysing feelings I fear does not agree with this. . . .[103]

145

Whether or not Bowles's poem graced the library table, Shelley's "lone walks" must have brought him close to the older poet's mood at one point:

> And lo, the foot-way plank, that leads across
> The narrow torrent, foaming through the chasm
> Below; the rugged stones are wash'd and worn
> Into a thousand shapes, and hollows scoop'd
> By long attrition of the ceaseless surge,
> Smooth, deep, and polished as the marble urn,
> In their hard forms. Here let us sit, and watch
> The struggling current burst its headlong way,
> Hearing the noise it makes, and musing much
> On the strange changes of this nether world.
> How many ages must have swept to dust
> The still succeeding multitudes, that "fret
> Their little hour" upon this restless scene,
> Or ere the sweeping waters could have cut
> The solid rock so deep.[104]

With the scientific musings that such a scene must have aroused in Shelley there must almost certainly have been feelings more painfully personal. Harriet Grove had been here before him; in the happiest spring of his life, during those long moonlight walks in which they had felt the quiet beauty of the Sussex countryside, she had filled him with the desire to see these wilder scenes [105] — so proper, Shelley still thought, for Gothic-novel settings. That was little more than a year ago, and meanwhile Harriet Grove had been completely alienated from him; she could no longer correspond with him, and by October expected to be married to the "clod of earth" to whom she had become engaged. In arguing with Hogg against yielding to despair because Elizabeth seemed lost to him, Shelley was probably arguing also with himself. What Hogg felt for Elizabeth, he had argued, was a passion, not reason, and reason should conquer passion.[106]

It certainly never occurred to Shelley as possible that *he* would be married to another before Harriet Grove's marriage — though Hogg was evidently beginning to read the signs. Shelley set him straight:

CWM ELAN

Reprinted by permission from R. Eustace Tickell: The Vale of Nantgwillt, London, 1894

Your jokes on Harriet Westbrook amuse me: it is a common error
for people to fancy others in their own situation, but if I know anything about love, I am *not* in love. I have heard from the Westbrooks,
both of whom I highly esteem.[107]

Cwm Elan did no more than Field Place to assuage Shelley's
restlessness and boredom. "All very dull, stale, flat, and un-
profitable," he complained to Hogg; "indeed, this place is a
very great bore." [108] "I am now with people who, strange to say,
never *think*," he told Miss Hitchener; [109] "I have however much
more of my own society than of theirs." Almost every letter to
Hogg reiterated his complaint: "I am all solitude, as I cannot
call the society here an alternative of it." "I do not see a soul;
all is gloomy and desolate. I amuse myself, however, with reading Darwin, climbing rocks, and exploring this scenery. Amusement! " [110] Occasionally he rode to Rhayader with Mrs. Grove
or, on Sunday, went to church, where the service was partly in
Welsh and a christening was performed "out of an old broken
slop-basin." [111] Erasmus Darwin's combination of science with
poetry impressed him quite sufficiently to leave its marks on
Queen Mab (1813) and on his later poetry.[112] He also re-read
The Missionary and read the newspapers. Occasionally there
were letters from his mother, Elizabeth, and probably Captain
Pilfold and Edward Graham; more frequently he heard from
Hogg, Harriet Westbrook, and Elizabeth Hitchener. With Miss
Hitchener the discussion had swerved, apparently at her desire,[113] from religion to politics, and Shelley became eloquent
on the subject of Equality. With Hogg there was the question
of Elizabeth. Hogg had actually visited Sussex, slipped into
Warnham Church incognito, and obtained a glimpse of Elizabeth.*[114]* He was now more in love than ever. Shelley continued
to forward to Hogg all the letters that Elizabeth wrote to Shelley,
but he no longer had any hopes himself, and he sought earnestly
both to abolish Hogg's despondency and to persuade him that
he was not genuinely in love.[115] To J. J. Stockdale, who had been
pressing him for the debt still due on *St. Irvyne*, Shelley imparted the news of further literary labours: "I am at present
engaged in completing a series of moral and metaphysical essays

— perhaps their copyright would be accepted in lieu of part of my debt? " [116]

Shelley's principal desire ever since he had returned to Field Place had been to effect a reunion with Hogg. His visit to Wales had been part of a scheme to realize this desire. He would accept Mr. Westbrook's invitation for a week, then he would join Hogg in York, or, if Hogg would only make a clandestine visit to Field Place, he would accompany him to York direct.[117] But he reckoned without Mr. Timothy Shelley's firm resolve to keep his son away from Hogg's influence. Timothy Shelley had informed Bysshe that he might go to York, but would receive no money from him if he did. Whereupon Bysshe had been forced to go to Cwm Elan, his announced destination, and plan from there to rejoin Hogg under the name of Mr. Peyton.[118] Caution was necessary, for the Honourable Member, whose "headpiece" Bysshe had thought "unequal" to it,[119] had recently developed a disconcerting knowledge of his plans. Shelley had recently paid two debts, and until his finances were recruited a little, he *had* to stay at Cwm Elan.[120] Nor is it at all unlikely that the Honourable Member's headpiece was also capable of this conclusion. At any rate, Bysshe stayed, very unwillingly.

So FAR as may be inferred from Shelley's letters to Hogg, Harriet Westbrook occupied a place in his thoughts distinctly subordinate to his desire to rejoin Hogg and even to his waning hopes for rescuing his sister Elizabeth for Hogg from the "machinations of worldly interests." He mentioned Harriet a number of times [121] and still intended to visit the Westbrooks at Aberystwith, but he seemed genuinely amused at Hogg's jokes on the subject. No doubt his anti-matrimonial arguments contributed to his sense of security. All of Hogg's arguments in favour of matrimony had failed to convince him. If Hogg's jokes caused him to think again, he must have reflected that the Westbrook sisters were also perfectly acquainted with his anti-matrimonial views. Nevertheless, he should have seen plainly that matters were becoming quite serious with Harriet:

The frequency of her letters became greater during my stay in Wales, I answered them; they became interesting. They contained complaints of the irrational conduct of her relations, and the misery of living where she could *love* no one. Suicide was with her a favorite theme, her total uselessness was urged as its defence.[122]

Suddenly, only three or four days after writing: " If I know anything about love, I am *not* in love," Shelley astonished Hogg with the information that he was leaving for London immediately to rescue Harriet Westbrook.[123]

What had occasioned this sudden action, and precisely what did it mean? Ever since her friendship with Shelley had become known in the school, Harriet had been persecuted on that account and Shelley had known of it and had praised her courage. Once one of her teachers had caught her reading one of Bysshe's letters; it had been seized and read, and Mr. Timothy Shelley had been summoned to help save the school from corruption.[124] One schoolmate [125] thought that Harriet had been expelled. She had not been expelled, but her position had been made so thoroughly uncomfortable that she was resolved not to return to school after her holiday at Aberystwith.

It is possible that " old Westbrook " had not been supplied with all the facts in the case; at any rate he insisted upon her returning. She appealed to Shelley for advice, and Hogg received the startling letter already mentioned:

My dear Friend,

You will perhaps see me before you can answer this; perhaps not; Heaven knows! I shall certainly come to York, but *Harriet Westbrook* will decide whether now or in three weeks. Her father has persecuted her in a most horrible way, by endeavouring to compel her to go to school. She asked my advice: resistance was the answer, at the same time that I essayed to mollify old W[estbrook] in vain! And in consequence of my advice *she* has thrown herself upon *my* protection!

I set off for London on Monday. How flattering a distinction! — I am thinking of ten million things at once.

What have I said? I declare, quite *ludicrous*. I advised her to resist. She wrote to say that resistance was useless, but that she would fly with me, and threw herself on my protection. We shall have £200 a year: when we find it run short, we must live, I suppose, upon love! Gratitude and admiration all demand that I should love her *for ever*. We shall see you at York. I will hear your arguments for matrimonialism, by which I am now almost convinced. I can get lodgings at York, I suppose. Direct to me at Graham's, 18 Sackville Street, Piccadilly.[126]

Harriet's distress and need of his help have always seemed a sufficient explanation for Shelley's action in rushing to London and even for his changed attitude toward matrimony, after having previously combated Hogg's arguments so long and stoutly. Harriet herself has never been given credit for affecting his opinions except through her helplessness. It is quite possible, however, that the arguments by which Shelley was now suddenly " almost convinced " came not from Hogg, but indirectly from Harriet, by way of that surest of all means of influencing Shelley — a book. This book was Amelia Opie's *Adelina·Mowbray, or the Mother and Daughter* (1804). Hogg had mentioned it, and Shelley had answered: " I have not read ' Adeline,' but shall, as soon as I can get it." A few days later [127] he informed Hogg in a postscript:

Miss Westbrook, Harriet, has advised me to read Mrs. Opie's "Mother and Daughter." She has sent it hither, and has desired my opinion with earnestness. What is this tale? But I shall read it to-night.

In his bored and almost bookless solitude Shelley would have examined any new book. Under the special circumstances there can be no doubt at all that he examined this one in which the ingenuous Harriet was so earnestly interested. If he read only a few pages, it would have been impossible not to finish it, for he would certainly have recognized himself as the hero and possibly Harriet as the heroine.

Glenmurray, the hero of *Adelina Mowbray*, was a very idealistic, high-minded young author·of good family and moderate means who had become odious to the orthodox on account of his publications. His books had formed the social and moral opinions of Adelina, before she knew the author. She, too, was a very high-minded person, who fully shared his views on the evils

150

of matrimony, but not on religion. When they met at Bath and fell in love, she was quite willing to unite her fortunes with his in a pure and constant free-love union. To protect her against the persecution of society, he was willing to flout his principles by a marriage, but she would not allow him to do so, as long as they both believed in the justice of the principles. Persecuted by a stepfather who was in love with her, and harshly treated by her mother, she was soon forced to flee abroad with Glenmurray. Up to this point the book described a situation that was remarkably like that of Shelley and Harriet. The remaining two-thirds of the book emphasized the disastrous consequences of unmarried love until both Glenmurray and Adelina recorded their convictions that it is condemned by its results.

It would be a matter of great interest to know what comment Shelley made to Harriet on this story. All we know is that in less than two weeks Harriet, persecuted at home, threw herself like Adelina on the protection of the man who had led her in persecution's way; and that Shelley for the first time expressed doubt of his anti-matrimonialism. Afterwards, though clinging to his general views, he twice justified his own marriage because of the disproportionate sacrifice entailed upon the unmarried wife.[128] This was exactly the conclusion Glenmurray reached in *Adelina Mowbray*.

Whether the sending of *Adelina Mowbray* was the suggestion of a mature woman who had observed that Shelley's conduct was unusually influenced by books and whose actions for some time previous suggest matrimonial designs,[129] or whether it was the independent idea of a schoolgirl desperately in love, who can say? At any rate it seems difficult to accept as pure coincidence. Charles Clairmont, who knew but did not reveal the details leading up to Shelley's elopement with Harriet, described them as " so very peculiar as could never have happened to any but one of so very strange a turn of mind as himself." [130]

Shelley hastened immediately to London, moneyless as he was, except for ten pounds just received from Hogg. He did not stay at Graham's lodgings in Sackville Street, where he had told Hogg to address him, but went direct to the Groves', in Lincoln's Inn Fields. It was best to refrain from telling Graham what had brought him. To do so would bring interference from Field Place if Graham proved loyal to his benefactor, or unpleasant consequences for Graham if he proved loyal to Shelley. John Grove and Tom Medwin were also kept in ignorance, and Elizabeth Hitchener, who lived too near Cuckfield and Field Place to be a safe confidante, was told briefly only that " particular business " [131] had occasioned his return. Only Charles Grove, to whom Shelley had written from Cwm Elan of his " summons to link his fate with another," [132] was taken into his confidence.

Shelley found Harriet very much depressed:

I was shocked at observing the alteration of her looks. Little did I divine its cause; she had become violently attached to *me*, and feared that I should not return her attachment . . . prejudice made the confession painful. It was impossible to avoid being much affected, I promised to unite my fate with hers. I staid in London several days, during which she recovered her spirits.[133]

In the midst of the events themselves, there was the necessity of giving Hogg some account of them. From his two letters to Hogg [134] we learn that Shelley considered Hogg's friendship his paramount interest; that he was giving Harriet's situation his whole time and thought; and that he still remained in London, " embarrassed and melancholy." Hogg had disapproved Shelley's intention, and Shelley assured him twice that his arguments on the question of matrimony (which were the same as Mrs. Opie's in *Adelina Mowbray*) were now Shelley's. It would appear that Harriet, like Adelina Mowbray, had scruples about allowing him to sacrifice his principles, and required argument. But Shelley was now " a perfect convert to matrimony."

From the testimony of Charles Grove and of Shelley's letters to Hogg at the time, one would conclude that Shelley had practically decided on matrimony from the time he left Cwm Elan — but this is only one side of the confused state of his emotions. In one of his letters to Hogg he seemed to contradict himself by adding: " Not that I suppose it to be likely that *I* shall directly be called upon to evince my attachment to either theory " [135] — that is, of marriage or free love. To Elizabeth Hitchener, after the marriage, he conveyed the impression that he had

accepted matrimony as a last resort, some days after he had
reached London.[136] He was certainly not in love, in the full
sense of the word, though his letters and conduct rather suggest
that he was nearer being in love than he realized. Sympathy
and chivalry, at war with an intellectual conviction, must have
had several victories and defeats before the final decision was
made. But when Shelley made his trip to Field Place after a
few days in London, he had decided. This visit was for the
purpose of securing funds for the elopement that he afterwards
spoke of as if it was not then decided upon.[137] He did see
and talk with Elizabeth Hitchener — but not about Harriet.[138]
Hogg's ten pounds were probably exhausted, and a mail-coach
trip to Edinburgh for two would cost about thirty guineas in
fares and tips, with expenses after arrival still to be provided.[139]
His financial stringency at Cwm Elan had taught him something
— a very little — about the disgraceful importance of cash, and
Charles Grove, his only confidant, must have mentioned the
point as worth consideration. He applied to his kinsman,
Thomas Charles Medwin, keeping him in ignorance of his purpose, and received a loan of twenty-five pounds.[140] He may have
borrowed smaller sums from his Grove cousins, Tom Medwin,
Captain Pilfold, or Edward Graham, though no record of it
now exists. He expected his quarterly allowance of fifty pounds
in a short time, probably on September 1, and he expected,
vainly as it turned out, to borrow again from his uncle Thomas
Medwin. These sums, if realized, would have been ample for
his immediate needs.

These activities had not gone unnoticed by the poet's suspicious father. Returning from Field Place, Shelley had airily
informed Hogg[141] that Mr. Timothy Shelley was in London
" wondering, possibly, at my London business. He will be more
surprised soon, possibly! " Shelley himself would have been
surprised had he known that his father was investigating rumours that had reached him about Shelley and Harriet. He
instructed Whitton to call on Mr. Grove (apparently John) and
find out exactly what was happening. Whitton thought the matter very serious. However, Mr. Grove was out of town, so the
inquiry had to be delayed. As soon as he could get written

authority from Mr. Shelley, Whitton promised to go direct to
Mr. Westbrook himself. Whitton took the matter so seriously
that he also wrote to Sir Bysshe Shelley about it.[142] Both Whitton letters are dated August 26. Shelley and Harriet were at
that time well on the way to York.

RETURNING to London about August 13,[143] Shelley found Harriet still in a state of painful indecision.[144] There were many
meetings with Harriet, to some of which Charles Grove accompanied his friend. Finally the decision was reached; they would
elope to Edinburgh.[145] From a coffee-house in Mount Street,
near Harriet's home, Shelley wrote a note appointing an hour at
which he would have a coach waiting for her there. On the next
day, August 25, Shelley and Charles appeared early at the
coffee-house and ordered breakfast. They were far ahead of the
appointed time, and as they waited Shelley threw oyster shells
across the street and remarked nervously: "Grove, this is a
Shelley business!" Soon Harriet appeared, they entered the
coach, and were off for the inn from which the northern mails
departed.[146] The Edinburgh mail did not leave until seven or
eight in the evening, and for a whole day they all waited within
the Bull and Mouth Tavern, sheltered behind its grotesque
plaster sign of a gigantic open mouth holding a bull. Nevertheless, Shelley was seen and recognized by a Mr. Dunn, an acquaintance of the family, but what might have been disaster
was turned by Shelley to profit. The next letter Shelley wrote
to his father was turned over to Mr. Whitton with the following
endorsement: "Sunday morning, ye 25th Aug., he borrowed
£10 from Mr. Dunn, saying he was just come from Wales, and
was going home directly he had paid his fare."[147] At seven
or eight Bysshe and Harriet entered the coach, and Charles
went home.

Ahead, for the fugitives, lay two hundred miles of tiresome
travel, a night and a day on the Great North Road, with little
to break the monotony except stops in noisy inn-yards for meals
or for a change of horses before they reached York, about midnight. During a pause at York Shelley wrote a note to Hogg,

asking him to send ten pounds to Edinburgh at once. Leaving this note at the inn to be delivered next morning, they were off again, through Northallerton, Durham, with its memories of feudal warriors, and Newcastle-upon-Tyne, with its ugly reminders of modern industry. Near Durham he posted a note to his father asking that his personal property be sent to Charles Grove — and saying nothing about Harriet. From this point on, there were three routes they might have taken,[148] but if they followed the same route taken by Hogg a few days later they passed through Alnwick, Berwick, and Dunbar, with many fine sights of the sea. The road was dusty and the meals served at the inns — an important point with Hogg, if not with Shelley and Harriet — were execrable.

The entrance to Edinburgh was through mean, narrow streets. The travellers had passed two nights in a mail coach, had suffered more than fifty hours of jolting, and were almost without money. Nevertheless, when Hogg found them a few days later — having been on the point of going somewhere on vacation when Shelley's note reached him, and deciding at once for Edinburgh — they were bright and happy. On the long journey Shelley had struck up a conversation with a young Scotch advocate [149] who had explained how they might marry according to Scottish law. Two men certified falsely that they were of legal age and had been six weeks in Edinburgh, a certificate was issued on August 28, and they were married either on that day or the next.[150]

Meanwhile Mr. Timothy Shelley had received his son's letter, posted en route. He immediately hurried up to London. Mr. Whitton's papers seem to show that he sought means of disinheriting his son, only to find that " there was not any power of revocation and new appointment." They had a long talk with Mr. Westbrook and Eliza. Next day there was a further conference, Eliza being absent and John Grove and Mr. Westbrook's solicitor present. Whether any common course of action was agreed upon is uncertain, but for himself Mr. Timothy Shelley resolved to stop his son's allowance and pay no attention to his letters. Mr. Westbrook seems also to have resolved to make no financial provision for his daughter, at least for the present.[151]

Chapter VII

EDINBURGH, YORK, AND KESWICK

DIFFICULTIES WITH THE FAMILY; HOGG'S TREACHERY;
FRIENDSHIPS WITH ELIZABETH HITCHENER
AND AT KESWICK

IF the purlieus of Edinburgh had seemed squalid and mean to
Hogg as he entered it a few days after the runaways, there was
no reason why the city itself should not have thrilled all three
of its new residents with its physical beauty and its literary and
historical associations. It was one of the handsomest cities in
Europe; for a century at least it had been a literary centre second
only to London. It had been the home of David Hume and
Thomas Campbell, and was now the home of Francis Jeffrey
and the great *Edinburgh Review*. Walter Scott lived near by.
The house in which the Shelleys were married, that of the
Reverend Joseph Robertson at 225 The Canongate, seems to
have been also the house in which David Hume wrote his
History of England,[1] but his young admirer who had written
The Necessity of Atheism, partly under his spell, appears not
to have known of it. In fact, Shelley was not much interested
in the scenic and traditional attractions of the Athens of the
North. Hogg showed some slight professional interest in the
law courts, and Harriet and Hogg both enjoyed the natural
beauty more than Shelley. Harriet alone displayed an enthusiasm for historic scenes.

When Hogg arrived, the young couple were already established in a comfortable ground-floor suite of rooms at 60 George

156

Street. Their landlord, a hostler named William Cumming, had listened sympathetically to Bysshe's story of present financial stringency and future expectations and had agreed to wait for his money. It is possible that he continued to wait for some of it, for the intended short stay in Edinburgh was prolonged to five weeks, chiefly because the young couple themselves were waiting for funds. Hogg's advent was of little help financially, for he had only the money that had been intended for his own vacation, and his father [2] declined to send him any more when he learned through Mr. Timothy Shelley that the two young men were once more together.

Shelley told later [3] that the landlord stipulated in return for his forbearance that the bridegroom should pay for a supper at which the landlord and his friends were to celebrate the wedding. The guests continued celebrating long after the young couple had retired to their room. Finally they attempted to invade the bridal chamber to " wash the bride with whiskey," but were repelled by the groom at the point of a pistol. If this adventure really occurred it left no aftermath of ill feeling on either side, for Hogg (who never heard of it apparently) found everything harmonious when he arrived.

Even Hogg found the living arrangements comfortable and pleasant enough. His own top-floor bedroom contained a bed that he thought might well have been softer. The doors slammed somewhat noisily, but that extremely important item to him — food — " was abundant and excellent." He had a particularly pleasant word for the shortbread, and noted Shelley's almost gluttonous enjoyment of the honey. The maid-of-all-work, named Christie, provided the party with considerable entertainment by her distracted dartings to and fro in response to frequent calls for the tea-" kittle," and her naïve answers to questions. Discovering that her voice grated harshly on Shelley's supersensitive ears, Hogg and Harriet practised quizzing her at length for his special benefit, until in real or pretended agony he would beg Harriet to send her out.

There was naturally a great deal of the long, ardent talk that had formerly been part of the joy of Oxford and of Poland Street, discussions in which Harriet's part, though unequal, must have been interested and zestful, for one recognizes the tone of such talk in her letters to Elizabeth Hitchener a few months later. Shelley frequently brought in whole armfuls of books secured from some library to which his Scotch travelling companion had probably introduced him. They included a number of French books: modern French philosophy, novels, and some of the works of Buffon.

With the introduction of books, Harriet came into an unexpected prominence. In words which her critics have slighted, Hogg makes it plain that Harriet was unusually well educated for her age:

I have seldom, if ever, met with a girl who had read so much as she had, or who had so strong an inclination for reading. . . . Her reading was not of a frivolous description; she did not like light, still less trifling, ephemeral productions. Morality was her favourite theme; she found most pleasure in works of a high ethical tone.[4]

While Bysshe occupied part of his mornings in translating a treatise of Buffon, Harriet translated her favourite novel of the moment, Madame Cottin's *Claire d'Albe*. Hogg saw the result — two volumes of exact, correct, and finely legible translation.

Harriet had a most pleasant voice and an extraordinarily distinct utterance. Reading aloud was her great joy. She read literally thousands of pages aloud, almost mercilessly. Hogg would have preferred conversation when Shelley was away, but "Whenever we were alone together, she took up a book and began to read, or more commonly, read aloud from the work . . . which she was reading to herself." [5] Yet he adds that

If it was agreeable to listen to her, it was not less agreeable to look at her: she was always pretty, always bright, always blooming; smart, usually plain in her neatness; without a spot, without a wrinkle, not a hair out of its place.[6]

Agreeable as it was to Hogg and doubtless to Shelley, the former was sometimes tempted to nod, but dared not. The bridegroom, more secure, occasionally nodded openly, and was fiercely stigmatized as an inattentive wretch.

The dry weather still held, and there was much to enjoy out-

158

side of the lodgings. Harriet insisted on an early excursion to
Holyrood and showed herself well read in whatever concerned
Mary Queen of Scots. After this expedition Bysshe returned
home to write letters, and Harriet and Hogg climbed to the top
of Arthur's Seat. The day was clear and sunny and the view was
excellent. Hogg observed that Harriet was modestly scrupulous
to protect her ankles against any rude disclosures by the stiff
wind that greeted their descent.

The daily routine was simple, and as much as possible like
that of the Oxford and Poland Street days: study and correspondence in the morning, walking in the afternoon, tea at dusk.
Occasionally they went forth into Prince's Street in the evening
to gaze at the famous comet, from which the eyes of the poet,
at least, wandered to the other starry systems with a speculative,
imaginative delight. More often their evenings were spent indoors, the hours gliding smoothly and pleasantly toward bed-
time as Harriet read aloud to them.

Sundays were then, as now, the longest days in Edinburgh.
Shelley felt terribly depressed by the relentless rigour of the
Sunday services that he attended with Hogg. In no very reverent spirit he and Hogg accompanied the maid Christie to the
Catechist and heard the dread question propounded: "Wha's
the de'il?" Shelley "burst into a shrieking laugh and rushed
wildly out of doors."[7] A grave citizen had previously reproved
him for laughing on the streets on the Sabbath, but on this
occasion he went unscathed.

There were always little corners of Shelley's life from which
Hogg and all the poet's successive closest friends were excluded, either from natural reticence or from a certain peculiar
secretiveness and love of mystery. Hogg saw Shelley go to the
post office before breakfast every morning and return with
letters; he knew that part of Shelley's mornings were taken up
with a rather heavy correspondence,[8] but he knew nothing,
apparently — nor do we — of what it was all about. The young
Edinburgh advocate who had given Shelley such unethical
advice about how to circumvent Scotch marriage laws saw him
several times later, but never with Hogg. Shelley also met
Charles Kirkpatrick Sharpe, who had eyed him somewhat

askance at Oxford and now proposed to give him a glimpse of Edinburgh society.[9]

In most ways the young couple must have found life pleasant in Edinburgh, even though Shelley expressed scorn for the "filth and commerce of Edinburgh" [10] and felt himself "chained" there through lack of funds. The difficulties of living on love were taking on a much more solid reality than when he had lightly mentioned them before hurrying from Cwm Elan to Harriet. Field Place continued ominously silent.

The only letters of Shelley's written during his five weeks' residence in Edinburgh that are now known are three letters to his father.[11] In the first of these, as in his letter written en route, he made no mention of Harriet, nor did Hogg mention her in his early letters from Edinburgh. After waiting for two weeks and learning in the meantime that his father knew all about the elopement and was deeply offended, Shelley wrote again to repeat his request for money and to deprecate his father's anger. He was willing to admit that he had "perhaps acted with impoliteness" in eloping without informing his father. His soothing admonitions, however, were slightly flavoured with a very impolite sarcasm:

To distrust your own mind . . . which the duties of legislation demands to be unruffled, which the happiness of your family requires calm, which your own peace needs to be unaffected by the base passion of anger, is certainly as wrong as it is inconsistent with the Christian forbearance and forgiveness with which you are so eminently adorned. The world, too, which considers marriage as so venial a failing, would think the punishment of a father's anger infinitely disproportioned to the offence committed.

Hearing nothing in reply to this, Shelley waited almost another fortnight and then wrote once more, taking the precaution of having Hogg address the letter, lest his father send it on to Whitton unopened.[12] The reason for his father's silence was now quite clear to him, he said. But marriage was not a crime, and his secrecy, though possibly annoying, had been necessary. He then proceeded to lecture his father at length on the Christian duty of forgiveness:

I appeal to your duty to the God.whose worship you profess, I appeal
to the terrors of that day which you believe to seal the doom of mortals, then clothed with immortality — Father, are you a Christian?
Judge not, then, lest you be judged. Remember the forgiveness of
injuries which Christians profess and if my crime were even deadlier
than parricide, forgiveness is your duty. What! will you not forgive?
How then can your boasted professions of Christianity appear to the
world, since if you forgive not you can be no Christian — do not
rather these hypocritical assumptions of the Christian character
lower you in real virtue beneath the *libertine* atheist . . . ? [13]

The letter concludes with a respectful request for the overdue
quarterly allowance of fifty pounds. All three letters show an
effort to avoid the appearance of disrespect while still cherishing
its substance. What should have been the main purpose — to
secure a desperately needed fifty pounds — Shelley jeopardized
by a reckless desire to display technical skill in argument, to
laugh in his sleeve at Christianity, and to convict his father of
hypocrisy. His letters were far better calculated to win the approbation of Hogg than of Mr. Timothy Shelley. In a Gothic
novel or an abstract epistolary warfare they would have served,
but not in a personal crisis. In fact, they suggest that the author
hardly saw his own predicament as an actual situation.

Mr. Timothy Shelley, however, was no romantic. He had
already warned Hogg's father that Shelley was travelling north
with a "young female" and might join Hogg at York, and he
had duly apprised Mr. Hogg of the reunion at Edinburgh.[14]
The shock of Bysshe's flight, the painful interviews with the
Westbrooks, and the unsatisfactory nature of his son's letters
threw him into a state of anxiety and emotional distraction in
which he talked loosely to friends and neighbours about his
family misfortunes. Gossip must have spread rather widely, for
it soon came to Whitton's ears, and he immediately wrote to
urge the wisdom of keeping private griefs as private as possible.[15] Knowing that Mr. Westbrook would furnish the fugitives with no money and that Hogg's funds were sufficient only
for himself, Mr. Timothy Shelley made no answer to his son's
letters.

HAD it not been for Captain Pilfold the culprits might have been starved into absolute surrender, or, more probably, into acts of reckless desperation. The genial Captain wrote frequent cheerful and lively letters and supported the garrison with cash. " To be confoundedly angry," he observed, " is all very well; but to stop the supplies is a great deal too bad! " [16] Perhaps the funds sent by Captain Pilfold were augmented by money secured by Hogg from sources unknown to his father; at any rate the party felt rich enough to leave Edinburgh by post-chaise instead of coach. They were off to York, to carry out the plan agreed upon before Harriet had entered into their schemes — a year at York together while Hogg finished his legal training there, and then London " for ever." The return to York was a leisurely three days' jaunt through mud and mist. It was a rather dreary journey, with occasional fine views, even through the rain. Within the chaise Harriet sought with indifferent success to spread cheerfulness by reading one of Holcroft's novels aloud.

The somewhat cheerless mood in which they reached York was not improved by learning that Hogg's former comfortable quarters had been let in his absence. Through crooked little streets in the mist and the dim twilight they sought other lodgings. Finally they engaged and entered into immediate possession of lodgings at No. 20 Coney Street. Hogg resumed his work in the conveyancer's office and was thereafter unavailable to his friends from nine to five, though he spent most of his evenings with them.

Both the lodgings and the landladies, the Misses Dancer, impressed Hogg as mean and dingy.[17] York itself seems to have affected Shelley somewhat similarly. He was totally unimpressed by the Roman bridge, the Norman castle, and the beauties of York minster. To him they were merely so many thousands of hours of human labour, misused to perpetuate human abuses.

Shelley immediately wrote a brief note to his father (postmarked October 5) to notify him of the new address and to repeat his desire that the books, papers, and clothes he had requested nearly six weeks before should be sent to him. This

162

EDINBURGH FROM ST. ANTHONY'S CHAPEL, 1831

Engraved by W. J. Cooke from a painting by Lieutenant Colonel Batty

YORK MINSTER

Engraved by E. Finden from a drawing by F. Nash

time his father complied, without comment. A week later Shelley wrote to acknowledge their receipt and to repeat, more
briefly, the arguments he had already urged against his father's
treatment of him. Shelley was beginning to realize that the
estrangement was now really radical: "*Obedience* is in my
opinion a word which should have no existence . . . you regard it as necessary." [18] After an unflattering reference to his
father's errors as due to a mind "not of the highest order," he
concluded somewhat hopelessly: "I would be your aff. dut. Son,
Percy B. Shelley." [19] The next day he appealed to his grandfather. But Sir Bysshe was in accord with Mr. Timothy Shelley and ignored the letter. With nerves already strained by
his father's policy of aloofness, Shelley now heard of the letters in which Mr. Timothy Shelley had warned Hogg's father
against him. From his point of view a cold, heartless silence
on the part of his father was now aggravated by treacherous,
stealthy persecution. Throwing all caution and tact to the
winds, he wrote his father a furious letter accusing him of libel,
treachery, persecution, and cowardice, ending:

I shall take the first opportunity of seeing you; if *you* will not hear
my name, *I* will pronounce it. Think not I am an insect whom injuries destroy . . . had I money enough I would meet you in London
and hollow in your ears Bysshe, Bysshe, Bysshe . . . aye, Bysshe till
you're deaf.[20]

Almost on the heels of this letter he took coach to see his father
face to face.[21]

MEANWHILE Shelley had reopened his correspondence with
Elizabeth Hitchener. After a silence of about six weeks he wrote
to her (probably October 8) to announce his marriage and to
justify it against the anticipated criticism that it violated his
principles. His justification was that no one should have to
forfeit reputation or political rights except for moral transgres-
sions. It was better to avoid these penalties by marrying rather
than to undertake a hopeless individual effort to correct the
popular prejudice. He wished to resume correspondence and he

hoped that Elizabeth could pay him and Harriet a visit or even live with them, now that Harriet's presence would remove any notion of impropriety in their friendship.

Elizabeth's answer to this letter was quite cordial. She did not consider that Shelley had intentionally deceived her about the marriage; she quite approved of it as an act of justice due to Harriet; and she expected the happiest results from the union. Far from being offended at Shelley's conduct, she would consider herself the great loser if their correspondence were broken off, for Shelley had really opened her mind, and she regarded him as the brother of her soul. Though she could not visit the young couple at that time, she hoped to do so later.[22]

The cordiality of this letter, contrasting with his father's hostile attitude, precipitated one of the most remarkable letters Shelley ever wrote. To this physically unattractive country school-teacher ten years his senior, whom he had known less than five months and with whom his previous relations had been almost impersonal, Shelley now expressed the most ardent devotion. She was the sister of his soul and was to share equally with his mother and sisters and Hogg (the brother of his soul) in any property he was to inherit. She was dearer to him than any of his blood kindred, being bound by a stronger tie than the mere accident of family relationship. This relationship he boldly called love, but he made it quite plain that to his mind it was a sexless love. The state of mind was so intensely Shelleyan, so characteristic of one side of the man at various times for the rest of his life, that it should be pondered by everyone who would try to understand Shelley's extraordinary personality. Nor should it be forgotten that it was written on the same day, apparently, as the furious letter to his father quoted above:

I write to-day [Shelley begins], because *not* to answer such a letter as yours instantly, eagerly — I will add, gratefully — were impossible, but I shall be at Cuckfield on Friday night. My dearest friend (for I will call you so), *you* who understand my motives to action which, I flatter myself, unisonize with your own, *you,* who can contemn the world's prejudices, whose views are mine, I will dare to say I *love:* nor do I risk the possibility of that degrading and contemptible interpretation of this sacred word, nor do I risk the supposition that the lump of organized matter which enshrines *thy* soul excites the love which that soul alone *dare* claim. . . . Henceforth will I be yours — yours with truth sincerity and unreserve. Not a thought shall arise which shall not seek its responsion in your bosom, not a motive of action shall be unenwafted by your cooler reason . . . and, [by] so doing, do I not choose a criterion more infallible than my own consciousness of right and wrong, (tho' this may not be required) for what conflict of a frank mind is more terrible than the balance between two opposing importances of morality . . . this is surely the only wretchedness to which a mind who only acknowledges virtue its master can feel. — I leave York to-night for Cuckfield where I shall arrive on Friday. That mistaken man my father, has refused us money, and commanded that our names should never be mentioned. . . . Sophisticated by falsehood as society is I had thought that this blind resentment had long been banished to the regions of dullness comedies and farces, or was used merely to augment the difficulties, and consequently the attachment of the hero and heroine of a modern novel. I have written frequently to this thoughtless man, and am now determined to visit him, in order to try the force of truth, tho I must confess I consider it nearly as hyperbolical as "music rending the knotted oak." Some Philosophers have ascribed indefiniteness to the powers of intellect; but I question whether it ever would make an inkstand capable of free-agency. Is this too severe. But you know *I* like the god of the Jews set myself up as no respecter of persons, and relationship is considered by me as bearing that relation to reason, which a band of straw does to fire. I love you more than any relation, I profess you are the sister of my soul, its dearest sister, and I think the component parts of that soul must undergo complete dissolution before its sympathies can perish. . . .

After some interesting speculations on immortality, necessity, and the proper use of money, Shelley concluded:

. . . Henceforth I shall have no secrets for [?from] you; and indeed I have much then to tell you; wonderful changes! Direct to me at the Capt.'s until you hear again, but I only stay two days in Sussex, but I shall see you.

Sister of my soul, adieu.

With, I hope, *eternal* love,

Your

PERCY SHELLEY.[23]

LEAVING Harriet in Hogg's care, Shelley set out for Sussex very possibly on the same coach that carried the so radically different letters he had just written to his father and to the sister of his soul. After three days and nights on the outside of a coach he reached Cuckfield on Friday morning, October 18. He immediately wrote to Miss Hitchener and asked her to dinner at Captain Pilfold's for the 21st. On Sunday the 20th he saw his father, who referred him to Whitton, to whom Shelley wrote at once to ask for an appointment. The next day Mr. Shelley wrote Captain Pilfold a rather stiff little note in the third person singular to inform him that Bysshe's conduct prevented his being received at Field Place and that all dealings between Shelley and his father had been placed in the hands of Mr. Whitton, "that no other person may interfere." [24] Shelley called on Sir Bysshe and learned again that Sir Bysshe stood with the squire of Field Place. To be received again by his family, his grandfather told him, he would have to learn to be dutiful and obedient. Even Whitton preferred not to talk with him and asked him to communicate his business in writing rather than in an interview.

Once more Shelley flew into a violent passion, this time over another matter, with his mother as the object. He had recently heard a rumour that his mother was promoting a match between his sister, the once perfect Elizabeth, and Edward Graham. He managed to see one or both of them at Field Place and treated them to a terrifying outburst of some sort, for on October 25 Mr. Timothy Shelley wrote to Whitton that they were exceedingly frightened, " and now, if they hear a Dog Bark, they run upstairs "; adding that he himself had thought of a special bodyguard.[25]

Before leaving, Shelley wrote his mother a letter that was almost furious in tone:

I suspect your motives for so *violently*, so *persecutingly* desiring to unite my sister Elizabeth to the music master Graham. I suspect that it was intended to shield *yourself* from that suspicion which at length has fallen on you. If it is unjust, prove it.[26]

"That suspicion" evidently refers to the anonymous charges against Mrs. Shelley and Edward Graham over which everyone

166

had made merry five months earlier. Shelley's father considered it "too absurd and ridiculous for a thought," though Shelley had already told his mother that it was his sole reason for making the journey from York.[27] At the same time (October 22) he dashed off a note to Elizabeth adjuring her to "speak truth" in case his mother showed the accusing letter to her husband.[28] To Elizabeth Hitchener and Charles Grove he spoke of his mother's "base" conduct in strong terms.[29]

Because his long-cherished plan of uniting Elizabeth to Hogg seemed checkmated by his mother, even though he himself had long since lost hope, Shelley now sneered at his old friend Graham as a "music-master" and denounced his only remaining ally at Field Place. Fortunately the letters were read only by Whitton, to whom they were sent unopened by Mr. Shelley. Whitton described them vaguely to Mr. Shelley and wrote to Shelley to ask permission to destroy them, saying that they had come to him unopened.[30] These letters which his family never saw were unnecessary to their conviction that he was mad — not definitely and totally, so as to require confinement, but actually dangerous when excited, and highly unpredictable. Within the next two weeks Mr. Timothy Shelley's letters to Whitton three times referred to Shelley's "perturbed," "disordered," and "untoward" mind, which would "not stop at any abuse of his parents" and which might be worked up "to such a Pitch as to do mischief to himself or some others." [31]

The visit to Sussex had left matters worse than they had been before. Shelley had talked with a kinsman, Thomas Medwin, about the legality of his Scotch marriage and had made arrangements for a marriage settlement of seven hundred pounds a year on Harriet whenever the money became available. He had received some comfort from Captain Pilfold, who accompanied him to London even after receiving Mr. Shelley's note, and he had had an evening's conversation with Elizabeth Hitchener at the Captain's house. He had got nothing from either his father or Captain Pilfold and he had come to regard his mother almost as an enemy. After a tiresome and dispirited journey he was back in York by October 26. One of his first actions on arriving was to write a letter to his father complaining of the continued withholding of his allowance and boldly accusing him of several libels.[32]

In York he found a note from Whitton, redirected from his London hotel, informing him that in future all communication with Timothy Shelley must be through Whitton, and asking leave to destroy the two letters to Elizabeth and his mother. Whitton's language can hardly be called insulting,[33] but Shelley was enraged to words stronger than any he had yet used. He returned the letter to Whitton "for his cool reperusal" and admonished him "when he deals with gentlemen (which opportunity perhaps may not often occur) to refrain from opening private letters, or impudence may draw down chastisement upon contemptibility." [34] Whitton's comment on this, to Sir Bysshe, was: "I have had from P. B. Shelley the most scurrilous letter that a mad viper could dictate." [35]

Whitton's letter had also informed Shelley that the Duke of Norfolk was interested in his difficulties and would be glad to talk with him. His Grace had been interested in Bysshe since the Eton days and had at one time cherished a design of seating him in Parliament when he came of age, as the member for Horsham. He had probably heard of the family difficulties at the time of the elopement. Meeting Timothy Shelley at a public dinner on October 22, two days after Shelley's visit to Field Place, he expressed some civil interest in the matter. Mr. Shelley had referred him to Whitton and he had interviewed Whitton on the 24th and had hoped to see Bysshe himself next day.[36] When Bysshe learned of this from Whitton's letter, having already been urged by Charles Grove to seek the Duke's help, he seized upon it as the one remaining chance of reaching an understanding with his father. On October 28 he addressed a dignified and very sensible-sounding letter to the Duke. He explained that the letters he now addressed to his father (letters " calculated to make his considerations of my proceedings less severe "!) were turned over to Whitton, and he requested the Duke to endeavour to persuade his father toward a more tolerant course of action. Lest the Duke should have been prejudiced against Mr. Medwin by Mr. Shelley's possible accusations, Bysshe assured him that Mr. Medwin had not knowingly aided in the elopement.[37] On November 7 the Duke of Norfolk wrote to both Bysshe and his father, telling the former he would interfere, though with little hope of success, and asking the latter to discuss the matter with him at Horsham on the 10th. The meeting took place at Horsham, and nearly two weeks later, November 23, the Duke wrote to invite Bysshe, Harriet, and Eliza to Greystoke.[38]

SHELLEY had intended to bring Eliza Westbrook from London to York, but he found Eliza at York ahead of him. Hogg's mother had learned with alarm that her son was alone in York with the "young female" against whom Mr. Timothy Shelley had already warned her husband. She had written to Harriet at once, representing the impropriety of the situation, and Harriet, whose sense of propriety was, in Hogg's opinion, almost prudishly careful, had replied "much in the stile of a Gentlewoman," civilly declining Mrs. Hogg's offer to write to her friends.[39] If we assume that Harriet immediately summoned Eliza, she would have arrived at the time she did arrive, a day before Shelley.

In Harriet's eyes Eliza was almost superhumanly perfect, a foster-mother who was always beautiful and always right. To Hogg she was probably a considerable annoyance and certainly (in retrospect) a subject for malicious ridicule. In his opinion her advent at once reduced Shelley to servitude in his own home; thereafter his only chance of a happy marriage was to say firmly: "Either Eliza goes, or I go." [40]

From the days of the blessed advent [Hogg writes], our destinies were entirely changed. The house lay, as it were, under an interdict; all our accustomed occupations were suspended; study was forbidden; reading was injurious — to read aloud might terminate fatally; to go abroad was death, to stay at home the grave! Bysshe became nothing; I, of course, very much less than nothing — a negative quantity of a very high figure. . . . Before the angelic visit, we had never heard of Harriet's nerves, we had never once suspected that such organs existed; now we heard of little else. "Dearest Harriet, you must not do that; think of your nerves . . . Harriet, dear, you must not eat this; you are not going to drink that, surely; what-

ever will become of your poor nerves? Gracious Heaven! What
would Miss Warne say? " [41]

There was another reason for Hogg's dislike of Eliza Westbrook that he chose not to state. Even had she received no
warning from Hogg's mother, Harriet would probably have
written (and possibly did write) to urge Eliza to come to her
as a protection against Hogg. The story Hogg attempted to
conceal by publishing Shelley's letters in garbled form has
long been guessed at, but it has remained obscure and even
somewhat doubtful until the recent discovery of the correct
text of Shelley's letters to him. [42]

Shelley had left Harriet in Hogg's care expecting that he
would at least make her evenings less lonely. This Hogg did,
according to his own account, by listening every evening to
readings from " staid and instructive books," by conversing on
the regular topic of what Bysshe might be doing at the moment,
and by hearing the extravagant praises of Eliza, who was to
accompany Bysshe on his return. [43] But Harriet told a far different story. [44]

Unwillingly, in response to Shelley's insistence that she elaborate her vague hints of Hogg's unworthiness, Harriet told
how he had taken advantage of Shelley's absence to attempt
to seduce her. He had already fallen deeply in love with her
in Edinburgh; he had declared his love in York, before Shelley
left; Harriet had repulsed him and held her tongue, hoping to
hear no more of it. As soon as Shelley was out of the way, Hogg
renewed his suit, beseeching Harriet with arguments some
of which must have seemed dangerously similar to doctrines
she had heard Shelley approve. When Shelley heard this he
frankly marvelled that she had been able to withstand the
persuasive sophistry of a man whom he himself found it so
difficult to stand against. Yet Harriet not only withstood his
pleas; she convinced him of the utter unworthiness of his conduct. Hogg then proposed to confess to Shelley in a letter, but
this Harriet forbade, fearing its effect on Shelley's state of mind.

As soon as he heard this story, Shelley immediately sought
out Hogg and took him for a long walk in the fields. Pale and

remorseful, Hogg confessed the whole story. Whatever resentment Shelley may have felt at the insult and distress to Harriet
was dwarfed by the profound shock of disillusion as to Hogg.
He who had been " but little below perfection " was now revealed in all his baseness as " a mistaken man — vilely, dreadfully mistaken." Scorning as he did the conventional views of
marriage and monogamy, Shelley did not find it so hard to
pardon Hogg as might be expected; to Elizabeth Hitchener,
his sole confidante at the time, he wrote:

I told him that I pardoned him freely, fully, completely pardoned,
that not the least anger against him possessed me. His vices and
not himself were the objects of my horror and my hatred. I told
him I yet ardently panted for his *real* welfare; but that ill-success
in crime and misery appeared to me an earnest of its opposite in
benevolence. I engaged him to promise to write to me. You can
conjecture that my letters to him will be neither infrequent nor
short.[45]

As soon as they could arrange to do so, Shelley, Harriet, and
Eliza Westbrook left York, keeping Hogg ignorant of the time
of their intended departure. An " investigation " which Shelley
had agreed upon with Hogg [46] was quite suddenly abandoned.
Accompanied by Eliza, the Shelleys left York probably on November 1 or 2.[47] One evening Hogg turned up at their lodgings
(which had been changed after Shelley's return) and found
merely a note of farewell. Harriet and Eliza wished to go to
the Lakes; Shelley, with no preferences of his own, listlessly
agreed. To deceive Hogg, in case he should follow them, they
pretended to be going to Richmond. It is indicative of Eliza
Westbrook's strong hand in the proceedings that when communications with Hogg were re-established Shelley admitted
this ruse but denied knowing of it at the time. After some days
of tiresome travelling they arrived at Keswick, probably on
November 5 or 6.[48] Here for possibly a week they took lodgings
with Mr. Daniel Crosthwaite, a portrait painter, at Town Head.
On November 12 Shelley dated a letter to Elizabeth Hitchener
from Chestnut Cottage.

For a month after the flight from York the mails were laden with agonized, partly incoherent letters between the two young men, whose ruptured friendship was the greatest agony that either of them had ever been called upon to endure.[49] In his first letter Shelley wrote with a reasonable control of his own feelings. He assured Hogg that he deceived himself either by false reasoning or by real passions which obscured true reasoning — and in either event he pronounced the result " disgusting and horrid." Still eager to be a friend to Hogg, he could not help expressing a fear that his professed conversion was not genuine. Except for a promise to write again next day, it would almost appear that this letter was intended to be final. Hogg's reply was evidently an impassioned one. He was suffering exquisite and undeserved misery; he protested how much he had " loved " and " adored " — apparently both Shelley and Harriet. Calmly at first Shelley answered that in the late crisis Hogg's love had really been only for himself, that this was the cause of all their present misery, and that he was as wretched as Hogg, and undeservedly so. Growing suddenly impassioned, he argued earnestly with Hogg to desert his weakness, master himself, and become again the " superior being," the " best, the noblest of men," whom he had formerly known and loved. Acknowledging that he was " half-mad " and was writing wildly, he declined in one breath to see Hogg again until further convinced of his recovery; then encouraged him to hope for an eventual reunion; then invited him to " come . . . dearest, best-beloved of friends . . . share my fortunes, enter into my schemes "; then seemed to hint that their reunion might come only after death. " Is all past, like a dream of the sick man which leaves but bitterness. . . . Oh how I have loved you. I was even ashamed to tell you how! and now to leave you *for ever.* . . . no not for ever. Night comes. . . . Death comes. . . . cold calm death almost I would it were to-morrow then is another life. . . . are you not to be the first there. . . . Assuredly dearest dearest friend reason with me . . . I am a child in weakness." [50]

Hogg's letters were no less emotional. Having failed to convince Shelley that he had mastered his passion, he seems to have thought he could persuade him by a philosophic "investigation" that it was not evil. He urged that he could live with the Shelleys and keep his love for Harriet within bounds, and at the same time he protested that his love was undying and wrote Harriet letters filled with such fervid compliments that she was indignant and Shelley was more than ever persuaded that it would never do to rejoin Hogg at York or permit him to come to Keswick. Time might effect a cure, but until he was convinced that it was right and safe he would not risk Hogg's dangerous presence, much as he still longed for the renewal of their association. How Harriet had withstood him in the first place was frankly a marvel to Shelley. He was partly convinced now of Hogg's sincerity, but he was equally convinced of his self-deception. Hogg's vague hint of a duel was passed by Shelley almost without comment, except to Elizabeth Hitchener. More than once Hogg threatened suicide if he could not regain his friend's confidence. In one of his own moments of greatest distress Shelley spoke of dashing himself from the cliffs, but he now met Hogg's threat with the assurance that he would certainly *say* he was convinced, but that the actual state of his beliefs could be altered only by a change in Hogg himself.

It may seem strange, as Hogg doubtless argued, that Shelley could take such a stand in apparent opposition to his own previous beliefs. But Shelley based his conduct not upon his theories of marriage, which he frankly reasserted, but upon his duty to Harriet. Exclusive cohabitation, he reminded Hogg, was a monopoly on which he set little value and of which he had frequently expressed disapproval. He said quite frankly that merely sharing Harriet's love with a friend was not a disquieting thought, he might even bring himself to resign to Hogg his own sexual claims. He thought himself almost free of "prejudice" on this point. The trouble was with the "prejudice" of others. It was a matter of which society had made a great fetish. Hogg himself was not entirely free of its influence, and Harriet considered it of vital consequence. Though he did not say so, it is quite possible that Shelley still remembered Mrs. Opie's novel which had probably influenced him in marrying Harriet instead of living with her in "free" love. At any rate, Hogg

173

would never be able to live with the Shelleys and suppress a passion which Harriet's " prejudice " made it impossible for her to tolerate. Without doubting Hogg's virtues altogether, Shelley did not believe that he could refrain from " deceiving " himself again if the old friendly intimacy were renewed.[51]

In his next letter Shelley made his position even more definite. If only the possession of Harriet's person were involved, he protested, how gladly would he return to York with Harriet. He believed himself incapable of jealousy in such matters; in fact, he was inclined to think the " Godwinian plan " of love the best. Could Harriet feel as he did about the innocence of free love, he would consider himself a base slave to prejudice if he opposed Hogg's wishes. But the case was quite different. Harriet's opinions of right and wrong were the only ones that could determine the morality of the present situation. Harriet clung so firmly to her " prejudice " that her whole happiness hinged upon Shelley's support. Since Harriet's happiness was his responsibility, he continued, even against his own theories, to support her desires. So senseless seemed the world's opinion on these matters, and yet so binding upon him because Harriet shared it, that he even hinted of suicide as an escape from it.[52] These arguments were in the main repetitions of what had already been urged or implied. But Hogg, as Shelley partly perceived, was scarcely in a state of mind to listen to reason.

While Shelley was thus conducting the most distracting correspondence of his whole life he was also settling himself and his family in a new environment. Chestnut Hill Cottage was really four contiguous cottages on a hill-top a mile out of Keswick. The group still stands and is duly listed in the current *Baedeker*. In the best of the four — the only one with a bow-window — the Shelleys and Eliza lived as long as they remained in the region. The rent was moderate — two and a half guineas weekly at first, with linen, later reduced to one guinea, without linen.[53] There was a pleasant old-fashioned garden below the cottages which was not let with their part of the house, but which Bysshe and Harriet were allowed, in Harriet's naïve phrase, to " run about in " when they were tired of sitting indoors.[54] Here they could obtain an excellent view of two lakes, Derwentwater and Bassenthwaite. All around were the cloud-capped mountains, not so wild as those to which Shelley had given only perfunctory admiration in Wales, but perhaps as beautiful.

For nearly a month after reaching Keswick Shelley was too absorbed in the aftermath of Hogg's treachery to allow for more than passing mention, in letters to Elizabeth Hitchener, of the surrounding scenery as a " sweet spot " or as " awfully beautiful." Thereafter he showed himself increasingly aware of the beauty and majesty of external nature. On November 23 he described the natural environment to Elizabeth Hitchener with real ardour:

I have taken a long *solitary* ramble to-day. These gigantic mountains piled on each other, these water-falls, these million-shaped clouds tinted by the varying colours of innumerable rainbows hanging between yourself and a lake as smooth and dark as a plain of polished jet — oh, these are sights attunable to the contemplation. I have been much struck by the grandeur of its imagery. Nature here sports in the awful waywardness of her solitude, the s[ummits] of the loftiest of these immense piles of rock seem but to elevate Skiddaw and Helvellyn. Imagination is resistlessly compelled to look back upon the myriad ages whose silent change placed them here; to look back when perhaps this retirement of peace and mountain-simplicity was the Pandemonium of druidical imposture, the scene of Roman Pollution, the resting-place of the savage denizen of these solitudes with the wolf. — [55]

Again, on December 11:

Oh how you will delight in this scenery! These mountains are now capped with snow, the lake, as I see it hence, is glassy and calm. Snow-vapours, tinted by the loveliest colours of refraction, pass far below the summits of these giant rocks. The scene, even in a winter sunset, is unexpressibly lovely. The clouds assume shapes which seem peculiar to these regions. What will it be in summer? [56]

In contrast with the stimulating natural environment, Shelley found the people disappointing — a result, probably, of his growing perception of economic ills. At Edinburgh he had been disgusted with the spirit of commerce; at York he had been im-

175

pressed with the tremendous waste of human comfort represented by the labour that had gone into religious monuments. He now found that humanity had been debased by commerce even in rural Keswick:

In fact, my friend, at this Keswick, though the face of the country is lovely, the *people* are detestable. The manufacturers with their contamination have crept into the peaceful vale, and deformed the loveliness of Nature with human taint. The debauched servants of the great families who resort contribute to the total extinction of morality. Keswick seems more like a suburb of London than a village of Cumberland. Children are frequently found in the River, which the unfortunate women employed at the manufactory destroy. Wales is very different, and there you shall visit us.[57]

Life went on very pleasantly in the little cottage overlooking the two lakes. Whatever Hogg's gloomy prognostications from the influence of Eliza Westbrook, no evidence of their truth was yet apparent. Harriet's continued worship of her as " more than Mother," to whom she owed everything,[58] was still only a potential danger. Shelley regarded her complacently enough as a prospective convert, a rather superior woman, prejudiced, but amiable, and definitely progressing in enlightenment.[59] The usual reading aloud and the usual walking abroad continued. The walks might be taken alone or in a group, and sometimes included a visit to the local museum of natural history or a stroll past the house to which the great Southey was expected soon to return. Shelley undertook to induct Harriet into his own pleasure in boating and incurred or barely escaped an accident on one such occasion.[60]

Once it seemed as if they might have to seek new lodgings. Their landlord, Mr. Gideon Dare, appeared one day in late November to ask them to move elsewhere. " The country," he informed Shelley, " talks very strangely of your proceedings. Odd things have been seen at night near your dwelling." Mr. Dare was with some difficulty satisfied by Shelley's explanation that the " odd things " were really some experiments with hydrogen gas with which he had been entertaining Harriet and Eliza.[61]

176

KESWICK, FROM SOUTHEY'S HOUSE

Artist unknown

DURING most of their stay at Keswick the Shelleys were in an even worse state of finances than when they left York. Negotiations with the family stood at a stalemate. On November 26 Shelley wrote to Thomas Medwin (a lawyer) to inquire if there was no possible way of raising money on his expectations; four days later he wrote in desperation to say that he was now desirous of raising money even at the ruinous rate of seventy per cent:

We are now so poor as to be actually in danger of every day being deprived of the necessaries of life. . . . I would thank you to remit me a small sum for immediate expenses. . . . Mr. Westbrook has sent a small sum, with an intimation that we are to expect no more; this suffices for the immediate discharge of a few debts; and it is nearly with our very last guinea that we visit the Duke of N[orfolk], at Greystoke, to-morrow.[62]

This visit, contrary to Shelley's expectations, was to lead to a financial arrangement. After the Duke of Norfolk, in the midst of his efforts to mediate between Shelley and his father, learned that Bysshe had moved from York to Keswick, he came to reside for a fortnight in his castle of Greystoke, near Penrith, and fourteen miles from Keswick. From Greystoke, on November 26, he wrote to invite Shelley, Harriet, and Eliza to visit him. On December 1, in the midst of a storm of snow and sleet, the little party reached Greystoke, where they remained for eight or nine days. When they arrived, and again on December 12, the Duke wrote to Mr. Timothy Shelley.[63]

The Duke of Norfolk stood in a position of friendship to both parties and had been at some pains to acquaint himself with Mr. Timothy Shelley's point of view. What he said to Bysshe and wrote to his father is unknown, except that he urged Bysshe to write a letter expressing genuine regret at the sorrow he had occasioned his father. This Shelley did, on December 13. His letter was dignified, earnest, and entirely lacking in those expressions that his father had previously read only as sneers and defiance. " Accept my apologies," he wrote, " for the uneasiness which I have occasioned; believe that my wish to repair any

177

uneasiness is firm and sincere." Though he still insisted on his freedom of expression, it was with a tact that had previously been absent:

I hope you will not consider what I am about to say an insulting want of respect or contempt; but I think it my duty to say that however great advantages might result from such concessions, I can make no promise of concealing my opinions in political or religious matters. I should consider myself culpable to excite any expectation in your mind which I should be unable to fulfill.[64]

To this letter his father replied somewhat stiffly, but with a glimmer of encouragement: he was glad the Duke of Norfolk had convinced Bysshe that he had acted erroneously toward his parents; he could never admit into his family the principles that had caused Shelley's expulsion from Oxford; but he trusted everything would " in due time and proper Probation be brought to an excellent work." [65] This seemed encouraging to Shelley. He wrote on December 23 to express his pleasure, and to inform his father that Mr. Westbrook was now allowing Harriet two hundred pounds a year. His own principles, he said, had not changed; he expressed them " with coolness and moderation " upon occasion, but he hoped his father would not object to his way of thinking.[66] By January 26 Shelley's allowance of two hundred pounds had been restored. Perhaps Timothy Shelley was somewhat shamed by Mr. Westbrook's conduct, which may explain his ungracious accompanying remark that he did it to prevent Bysshe's cheating strangers.[67]

At about this time Shelley heard from Captain Pilfold that Mr. Timothy Shelley and Sir Bysshe were planning to provide him with an immediate income of £2,000, on condition that he entail the estate upon his eldest son. There is no evidence that such a plan, if formed, was ever submitted to Shelley, but in repeating the rumour to Elizabeth Hitchener, Shelley rejected with scorn the idea that he could be bribed blindly to entail £120,000 upon a person who might use it for pernicious purposes.[68]

Shelley was now sure of an income, but he was also sure that he had hitherto been estimating his father's attitude much too lightly. For the first time he realized clearly that Field Place was definitely closed to him as long as he held the opinions that he knew he would never abandon. This would cut him off from Hellen, Harriet's friend, the only one left in the family whose sympathy he felt was not already alienated from him. Like Elizabeth and Hogg, she would also be lost to the cause of virtue. He made one pathetic effort to save her both for himself and for the cause. Disguising the superscription for the benefit of the Horsham postman, he enclosed to Allen Etheridge, his father's huntsman, a letter which the latter was to deliver secretly to Hellen. In this letter he adjured Hellen to continue to love him, to think always for herself:

I need not tell you how I love you. I know all that is said of me, but do not you believe it. You will perhaps think *I'm* the Devil, but, no, I am only your brother, who is obliged to be put to these shifts to get a letter from you. How do you get on with your poetry, and what books do you read. . . . *Thinking,* and thinking without letting anything but *reason* influence your mind, is the great thing.[69]

Hellen's letters of reminiscence, written long after Shelley's death and published in Hogg's biography, show that she did remember him with affection. But this letter never reached her. Allen Etheridge, like a faithless henchman in a Gothic novel, carried it straight to Mr. Timothy Shelley, who endorsed it and turned it over to Whitton to be preserved with the other documents in the case.

The visit to Greystoke was for Harriet and Eliza an agreeable interlude in a rather secluded existence. They seem to have made a favourable impression upon the Duke and his other guests. These guests included Lady Musgrave, Mr. and Mrs. Howard, James Brougham (brother of the Whig statesman and *Edinburgh Review* editor), and Mr. William Calvert (brother of Wordsworth's patron, Raisley Calvert). Shelley held forth on his social and political views, as he usually did, but his joy in the company was not unmixed. They were aristocrats. In the rôle of thorough democrat to which he stood committed with Elizabeth Hitchener, Shelley felt that these associations were disgusting:

Fatigued with aristocratical insipidity, left alone scarce one moment by those senseless monopolizers of time that form the court of a Duke, who would be very well as a man, how delightful to commune with the soul which is undisguised — [70]

— that is, with Miss Hitchener. Yet this impression, genuine enough in Elizabeth's spiritual presence, must be discounted by the fact that after having solicited the good offices of the Duke he wrote to Miss Hitchener: " In truth I do not covet any ducal intercourse or interference." [71]

ON THE return to Keswick, probably December 9, Shelley found a number of letters from Hogg awaiting him. They appear to have convinced him that all his earnest efforts to bring Hogg to reason were hopeless, at least for the present. The next day he wrote Hogg a letter which was evidently intended to be final. He proclaimed flatly that a reunion with Hogg was "*impossible.*" It would be tantamount to the destruction of Harriet's peace. He painted a plain picture of Harriet's depression at the mere sight of one of Hogg's letters and of her doubts of his own love whenever he said anything to palliate Hogg's behaviour. Hogg's society was a fascination hard to forgo; his friendship a blessing " worthier of attainment than fame or sensuality or the attachment of all other beings." But Harriet's happiness was his prime responsibility and he would not allow even his friendship with Hogg to interfere with it, nor was any association with Hogg possible without such a result. He no longer thought Hogg perfect, but he thought him capable of great things, and he knew of nothing except Harriet's happiness that could make him resign Hogg's friendship. He hoped (but doubted) that Hogg would be as willing to resign his passion, for Shelley's sake, as Shelley was willing to resign Hogg's friendship for Harriet's.[72] The hectic, almost incoherent tone of most of the earlier letters is here missing. Calmly and plainly Shelley renounced the greatest friendship of his life.

The renunciation, as it turned out, was not final, but there can be no question that Shelley thought it so at the time. His

hope, expressed in other letters to Hogg, that a period of separation might cure Hogg's madness, was a very doubtful one at best.
Conventional minds will perhaps wonder that it cost so much
distress to arrive at a firm determination to do what was so obviously " the right thing." For Shelley, however, in such a matter " the right thing " might be supposed difficult to determine,
and Hogg was in some respects at this time fully as dear to him
as Harriet. The wonder, if any, should rather be that Shelley
reached and adhered to his conclusion.

This is apparently the last letter from Shelley to Hogg until
the next December. All along Shelley had kept Elizabeth Hitchener informed of his correspondence with Hogg. Two passages
in letters to her written shortly after this letter show that Shelley
considered it a valedictory to his dearest friend: " He is incapable of being other but the every-day villain who parades St.
James's Street, tho' even as a villain will he be eminent and imposing." " He has too deeply plunged into Hypocrisy for *my* arguments to effect any change. I leave him to his fate. . . . How
I have loved him *you* can *feel*, but he is no longer the being
whom perhaps 'twas the warmth of my imagination that pictured." [73]

It was shortly after the return from Greystoke, about the time
that Hogg's renovation was finally abandoned, that Shelley gave
up the idea of taking a house near Miss Hitchener in Sussex and
began to think of going to the aid of the oppressed Irish. The
first reference to this scheme is in a letter of December 11 to
Miss Hitchener.[74] For three weeks thereafter little or nothing
more was said of it; then, in January, his letters suddenly became
alive with the topic.

WHILE the Irish scheme was slowly taking form, the Shelleys
were making useful friendships in the neighbourhood with the
Calverts and Southeys. At Greystoke Shelley had particularly
noticed the interest taken in him by Mr. Calvert and had been
surprised to find that gentleman well acquainted with his personal history. This is perhaps not quite so strange as Shelley

thought. Mr. Calvert was a good friend of the Duke, and lived not far from the Shelleys, at Windybrow, near Keswick; it is rather evident that the Duke had already engaged him to keep an eye on the young couple. After the return from Greystoke he and his family were most friendly to the Shelleys, as long as they remained at Keswick.

The Calverts were well known and well liked in the region, and Mr. William Calvert had two other qualities that made him congenial to the young poet — he was a political liberal and he was an amateur scientist, the owner of an electrical machine, a water-clock, and an instrument for measuring altitudes by tri-angulation. Between the Calverts, Wordsworths, and Southeys subsisted a close and friendly intimacy that continued with their children. "Zombi," one of the most distinguished of all Southey's highly gifted cats, was a present from the Calverts.

Perhaps the last personal reminiscence of Shelley was uttered by Mr. Calvert's daughter, Mary (Mrs. Joshua Stanger, who died in 1890). When she was a venerable old lady, Mrs. Stanger used to recall Shelley's visits to her father's house as one of her earliest memories — she was eight years old at the time:

"Yes, to be sure, dear sir, I did see Shelley plain, and I remember his eyes and his hair, and how troubled he was because, when he came to unfold the packet, the workbox he had brought for Mr. Calvert's little girl, as he used to call me, was not to be found. But I think I remember best the sort of look that came upon my father's and upon Southey's face when he talked, and how I and my brothers were hurried out of the room, lest we should hear the conversation." [75]

Robert Southey, whom Shelley had quoted at Oxford and had enthusiastically recommended to Miss Hitchener, was from the first one of the greatest attractions that Keswick held for Shelley. He had hardly been settled there a week before he informed Miss Hitchener that he had been " contemplating the outside " of Southey's house.[76] In the midst of scenery that was " awfully beautiful," he wrote two days later, " the object most interesting to my feelings is Southey's habitation." By November 23 he had still not seen Southey, being erroneously informed that he was absent on a journey, but he promised himself and Miss Hitchener that " on his return I will not be slow to pay homage to a *really* great man." One reason for being very humble to Mr. Dare when that gentleman wished to oust his lodgers was that Shelley wished to stay and see Southey. The meeting was so long delayed that the inevitable disillusion began before the two men saw each other. On December 15 he wrote to Miss Hitchener:

Southey has changed. I shall see him soon, and I shall reproach him [for] his tergiversation. — He to whom Bigotry, Tyranny, Law was [sic] hateful, has become the votary of these idols in a form the most disgusting. — The Church of England, its Hell and all, has become the subject of his panegyric, the war in Spain, that prodigal waste of human blood to aggrandize the fame of statesmen, is his delight, The constitution of England . . . are inflated with the prostituted exertions of his Pen. I feel a sickening distrust when I see all that I had considered good, great, and imitable, fall around me into the gulph of error. . . . Wordsworth (a *quondam* associate of Southey), yet retains the integrity of his independence; but his poverty is such that he is frequently obliged to beg for a shirt to his back.[77]

Within a few days after this (between December 15 and 26) Shelley became acquainted with Southey. " We first met Southey at his [Calvert's] house," Shelley informed Miss Hitchener. " He has been very kind to us. The rent of our cottage was two guineas and a half a week, with linen provided. He has made the proprietor lower it to one guinea, and has lent us linen himself." [78] Shelley's opinions at first were considerably more favourable than his letter of December 15, quoted above, would suggest. In spite of different opinions about the Irish, Catholic Emancipation, and Parliamentary reform, he discovered that Southey was " great and worthy," " an advocate of liberty and equality " (but in the future), a professing Christian who was in reality a deist (a discovery not to be made from Southey's letters and publications of the period), " a man of virtue," a stubborn, inferior reasoner, but a great poet.[79] He was somewhat impressed by Southey's belief that a revolution was inevitable; they talked together about the poet James Montgomery and sympathized equally in his trials; Shelley even discovered that South-

183

ey's notion of Deity was quite similar to his own. "He says I ought not to call myself an atheist, since in reality I believe that the universe is God. I tell him I believe that God is another signification for the Universe. I then explain. . . . Southey admits and believes this." In politics and ethics they differed amicably over the place of expedience, Southey holding that it ought to be the ground for politics, but not morals, Shelley arguing that politics should be considered merely an extension of morals, an idea which he emphatically reasserted eight years later in the third chapter of his *Philosophical View of Reform.* On such occasions Southey generally concluded by assuring Shelley — who could see no logic whatever in the assertion — that " when you are as old as I am you will think with me." [80] So ardent an idealist and so acute a reasoner as Shelley could not fail to perceive the strain of opportunism in Southey's views.

It speaks well for Southey's kindly and genial interest in his young friend that Shelley at first judged Southey as leniently as possible and phrased his judgment with the sensitive sympathy he usually reserved for only those with whom he felt himself entirely *en rapport:*

I am not sure that Southey is *quite* uninfluenced by venality. He is disinterested, so far as respects his family; but I question if he is so, as far as respects the world. His writings solely support a numerous family. His sweet children are such amiable creatures that I almost forgive what I suspect. His wife is very stupid: Mrs. Coleridge is worse. Mrs. Lovel[l], who was once an actress, is the best of them.[81]

Shelley must have been often in Southey's home. A house so full of books was sure to attract him. Hogg quotes some later remarks of Shelley representing Southey as discouraging too great familiarity with his books,[82] but we have Southey's own testimony to having interested Shelley in reading Berkeley. This book, it is true, was the property of Charles Lloyd, and Shelley was still too much the disciple of Locke and the sensational philosophy to be impressed by Berkeley as much as by a very unBerkeleyan pencilled note of Lloyd's: " Mind cannot create, it can only perceive." [83] From Harriet, however, we learn that

LAKE WINDERMERE, FROM THE FERRY HOUSE

Engraved by W. Taylor from a painting by T. Allom

GRETA HALL,
SOUTHEY'S HOME AT KESWICK

Artist unknown

Southey did lend his own books to the Shelleys.[84] Even that "stupid" woman Mrs. Southey could make teacakes of such a quality that Harriet was instructed thereafter to have teacakes every evening, "for ever." [85]

Southey took an unusual interest in the young radical, who affected him like his own ghost, who was "just what I was in 1794." He was pleased at Shelley's pleasure in meeting a man who, in his own too confident phrase, "perfectly" understood him and did him "full justice." Writing thus to his friend Grosvenor C. Bedford,[86] Southey furnished him with a short sketch of his friend's youthful misfortunes and gave him to understand (somewhat prematurely, as we have seen) that the young man was already turning from atheism to Berkeley under his guidance.[87] To his friend John Rickman, two days later, Southey wrote even more fully and enthusiastically. Through Rickman he hoped indirectly to influence Mr. Timothy Shelley in his son's behalf. He even became in this letter the first prophet of Shelley's greatness. "Unless I am greatly deceived," Southey pronounced, "there is every reason to believe he will become an honour to his name and his country." [88]

Relations between the Southeys and Shelleys continued on a pleasant personal footing as long as the Shelleys remained at Keswick. The Southeys all opposed Shelley's growing inclination to leave Keswick for Ireland. Shelley, however, was becoming more and more convinced that Southey was merely a time-serving deserter from the only cause that mattered. To Elizabeth Hitchener he expressed himself with some feeling:

I do not think so highly of Southey as I did. It is to be confessed that to see him in his family, to behold him in his domestic circle, he appears in a most amiable light – I do not mean that he is or can be the great character which once I linked him to. His mind is terribly narrow, compared to it. *Once* he *was* this character, – everything you can conceive of practised virtue. – Now he is corrupted by the world, contaminated by Custom: it rends my heart when I think of what he might have been! [89]

A fortnight later this sorrow had acquired a definite cast of stern indignation:

185

He has *lost* my good opinion. No private virtues can compensate for public language like this [quoting from the *Edinburgh Annual Register* several sentences of Southey's sneering at Sir Francis Burdett and praising George III]. . . . I can only exclaim with Bolingbroke, "Poor human nature!". . . Southey's conversation has lost its charm; unless it be the charm of horror at so hateful a prostitution of talents.[90]

To the several sharp personal disillusionments he had experienced in the last year — Harriet Grove, Elizabeth Shelley, Hogg — was thus added his first disillusion in a public character whom he had once regarded as a champion of virtue. Within a few months, in Ireland, he was to be similarly disappointed with John Philpot Curran and with people in the mass. Experience was beginning slowly to modify his views of human nature.

Shelley never met Wordsworth, whom he considered still staunchly true to humanity. Coleridge was not in the district while Shelley was there; he later expressed regret that Shelley's association had been with Southey instead of with him:

I *might* have been of use to him, and Southey could not; for I should have sympathized with his poetics, metaphysical reveries, and the very word metaphysics is an abomination to Southey, and Shelley would have felt that I understood him.[91]

Another Laker better qualified than Southey to trade subtleties and intensities with Shelley was De Quincey. They did not meet, and perhaps never heard of each other at the time. De Quincey also regretted later that he had not met Shelley. Within a few years he was one of the first important contemporary writers to see true genius in Shelley's poetry. John Wilson's review of *The Revolt of Islam* was very largely influenced by De Quincey's admiration for the poem and was the beginning of a series of criticisms in *Blackwood's Magazine* that were in many respects quite favourable.

ONE man of letters, William Godwin, had already exerted more influence on the mind of Shelley than Southey fondly hoped to exert. His *Political Justice* had been a bugle-call to English radical thought in the middle 1790's, but in the country's subsequent absorption in war Godwin had been almost forgotten. While William Godwin and his wife kept up their obscure publishing business in Skinner Street, specializing in harmless books for children (such as the *Tales from Shakespeare,* by Charles and Mary Lamb), what was left of the old revolutionary radicalism revolved mainly around such men as Sir Francis Burdett and the fight against the encroachments of government. Some of Godwin's earlier disciples had already turned conservative; only his correspondence and the occasional accession of a young disciple reminded him of his former eminence. Until about a year before, Shelley had supposed him dead; he had then received misleading information and had apparently relapsed into his former belief until better informed at Keswick.[92]

In the same letter in which Shelley stated his suspicion that Southey was no longer " quite uninfluenced by venality," he informed Miss Hitchener that he admired Godwin as much as ever and that he intended to write to him that day or the next, and to call on him later in London if Godwin failed to answer.[93] His first letter to Godwin is dated January 3, 1812. Thus began a long series of letters, forty-three of which are extant, continuing for the rest of Shelley's life. It is doubtful if Shelley's opinions (except of Godwin himself) would have been much affected had he never discovered that Godwin was still living; but the moment in which he decided to make Godwin's personal acquaintance completely altered the subsequent course of his life.

In introducing himself Shelley used an instinctively tactful Godwinian approach — he represented himself as taking a liberty unsanctioned by custom, but supported by reason. The name of Godwin, he continued, had always roused him to admiration and reverence; it had seemed a luminary too dazzling for the surrounding darkness. He had thought of Godwin as among the honourable dead. Having learned " with inconceivable emotions " that Godwin was still alive, he wished ardently to share the benefits of his intellect on a more intimate footing. After a paragraph in which he sought to characterize himself, he concluded with an earnest, persuasive request that Godwin should answer; if he did not, Shelley would still seek him out when he came to London and endeavour to show himself worthy of Godwin's friendship.

The paragraph of self-characterization is interesting as showing Shelley's opinion of himself at the age of nineteen. It is modest without being self-consciously so. If his persecutions seem slightly overstressed, it is because Godwin is supposed to have suffered longer and greater ones:

I have but just entered on the scene of human operations; yet my feelings and my reasonings correspond with what yours were. My course has been short, but eventful. I have seen much of human prejudice, suffered much from human persecution, yet I see no reason hence inferable which should alter my wishes for their renovation. The ill-treatment I have met with has more than ever impressed the truth of my principles on my judgment. I am young, I am ardent in the cause of philanthropy and truth; do not suppose that this is vanity; I am not conscious that it influences this portraiture. I imagine myself dispassionately describing the state of my mind. I am young; you have gone before me, I doubt not are a veteran to me in the years of persecution. Is it strange that, defying prejudice as I have done, I should outstep the limits of custom's prescription, and endeavour to make my desire useful by a friendship with William Godwin? [94]

Godwin was immediately interested. His journal shows that he answered Shelley's letter on January 6 [95] and from Shelley's reply it is evident that he asked for more particular information, something that would give his new correspondent a more definite personality in his eyes. Shelley immediately complied with an inaccurate sketch of his life in which the reading of *Political Justice* is made the key to all his subsequent career.[96]

Godwin's reply to this letter may be inferred from Shelley's answer to it. On two points Godwin must have rather surprised his young admirer. He expressed some doubts as to the wisdom of embarking on a campaign of radical action and publication too early in life. He also showed himself doubtful about Shelley's attitude toward his father. This, from the man who had taught him his scornful view of the claims of parenthood, must have been a mild shock even to Shelley's adoration. Nevertheless Godwin was genuinely interested. He promised his help

188

and friendship. The calm, passionless estimate of Shelley that was slowly forming in Godwin's mind is implicit in this letter; he waited until he had received four letters and then delivered his Olympian verdict with characteristic insensitive coldness:

I have read all your letters (the first perhaps excepted) with peculiar interest, and I wish it to be understood by you unequivocally that, as far as I can yet penetrate into your character, I conceive it to exhibit an extraordinary assemblage of lovely qualities not without considerable defects. The defects do, and always have arisen chiefly from this source, that you are still very young, and that in certain essential respects you do not sufficiently perceive that you are so.[97]

Coming from a supposedly purer fountain, this rather shrewd analysis did not irk Shelley as Southey's similar remarks had done.

It is generally assumed that Godwin's interest was stimulated by the information conveyed in Shelley's second letter that he was heir to an income of six thousand pounds. This may well be true. Godwin was already involved in the financial difficulties into which he was to sink deeper and deeper until after Shelley's death. His principles as well as Shelley's sanctioned his right to his disciple's money. It should be stated in Godwin's favour, however, that at the same time he was adopting another protégé who was without money and for whom he was making arrangements by which he could attend a university.[98]

Shelley immediately proceeded to amplify his previous effort at self-analysis and to explain himself on the points that had aroused Godwin's uneasiness.[99] He was *not* angry with his father; on the contrary he had always desired a reconciliation if it could be obtained without injury to the independence of his opinions. His father may have *acted* for his welfare, but he had certainly not *felt* for it. " I never loved my father — it was not from hardness of heart, for I have loved and do love warmly." Godwin's implied fear that Shelley was inculcating his beliefs too soon and too promiscuously elicited the remark that he " was not ignorant that vanity and folly delight in forwardness and assumption "; that between affectation and self-distrust there was a genuine modesty which he hoped he did not overstep in ad-

189

vancing his opinions. " I will not again crudely obtrude the question of atheism on the world." He believed that he could at the same time improve his own powers and " diffuse true and virtuous principles " without being too forward or presumptuous. Above all, he was deeply grateful that the man whose teachings had inspired him when those of all other tutors and advisers filled him with disgust should now be his friend and counsellor. " That William Godwin should have a ' deep and earnest interest in *my* welfare ' cannot but produce the most intoxicating sensations."

There can be no doubting the genuineness of this intoxication; it overflowed into his next letter to Elizabeth Hitchener. He quoted a part of one of Godwin's letters and promised to send her the others:

Godwin has answered my letters, and he is now my *friend;* he shall be yours — share with me this acquisition, more valuable than the gifts of Princes. His letters are like his writings, the mirror of a firm and elevated mind. They are the result of the experience of ages, which he condenses for my instruction. It is with awe and veneration that I read the letters of this veteran in persecution and independence. He remains unchanged. I have no soul chilling alteration to record of his character. . . .[100]

In his next letter to Godwin, written just before his departure from Keswick, Shelley presumed modestly to disagree as to the value of early authorship. He further explained (since Godwin still seemed uneasy about his filial relationship) that he wished his father well, but despaired of conciliation " when I see how rooted is his prejudice against me." He explained his marriage as he had done to Hogg, but not exactly as he had explained it to Elizabeth Hitchener. Finally — and inevitably — he hoped that Godwin and his family would visit him next summer in Wales.

SHELLEY's stay at Keswick was far from being a simple round of afternoon walks, occasional social calls, and letter-writing. The studies which he had transferred from Oxford to London and

later to Edinburgh continued, mainly in the mornings and evenings. He was quite conscious of expanding intellectual powers.
As he studied he sought to express these growing powers in prose
and verse. Harriet feared that he was working too hard for his
health and also that he might be writing himself into prison.[101]
From December 11, 1811 until the beginning of February he
was engaged on no less than five literary projects, all but one of
which were completed, or nearly completed, by the latter date.

The first of these projects he mentioned first to Miss Hitchener
on December 11 and again on December 26 and January 2,
only to say that he was laying it aside as not suited to the present
temper of his mind.[102] It was a poem to picture first " the manners, simplicity and delights of a perfect state of society, tho'
still earthly," to be followed by a picture of heaven — and Elizabeth Hitchener's aid would be necessary to make it all that it
should be. The idea may never have reached the stage of pen
and paper before it was laid aside, but anyone familiar with the
way in which many of Shelley's finest poems lie dormant in his
youthful letters will see in it the first formless state of the latter
part of *Queen Mab* and of the spiritual paradise described first
in *The Revolt of Islam* and most fully and triumphantly in *Prometheus Unbound.*

Another project first mentioned along with the abandoned
poem was a collection of his early verse.[103] It was " about to be
sent to the printer," with an explanatory preface, two weeks
after the project was mentioned. By January 2 it was presumably ready for the press and Shelley was looking for a printer.
Since " the poor cannot understand and w[oul]d not buy my
poems " Shelley proposed to print them " expensively " and use
the anticipated proceeds to help finance his more popular radical productions. Shelley's own judgment was that they were inferior and would " be only valuable to philosophical and reflecting minds who love to trace the early state of human feelings
and opinions, — who can make allowances for some bad versification." This volume he never published, but some of its contents later became known.[104]

The volume of essays was probably a continuation of the series
of " moral and metaphysical essays " Shelley had offered to

191

Stockdale on August 1.[105] He first mentioned them to Miss Hitchener on December 26, as intended for publication in the summer. By January 2 he had written about a hundred and fifty pages of them. Since they were metaphysical and not likely to prove popular, he designed to print them in Dublin " expensively," like the poems. What happened to them after they reached Ireland is unknown. Shelley's powers of expression in prose were at this time so far in advance of his poetical ability, and the moral and metaphysical speculations in his letters were frequently so keen and mature, that the loss of these essays is far more deplorable than the failure to recover his poems would have been. It is quite likely that they are echoed from time to time in the letters to Miss Hitchener. All of Shelley's published essays except the " Defence of Poetry " appeared posthumously and are dated conjecturally. Some of these conjecturally dated 1815 may actually have been written in 1812; it is probable at any rate that they were influenced by what was then written and lost.

Still another work that has been lost was the novel *Hubert Cauvin*,[106] designed to " exhibit the cause of morals and opinions in France during the latter years of its monarchy." It was to deal with some of the leading passions, but would pointedly exclude sex. About two hundred pages had been written when Shelley first mentioned it to Miss Hitchener, on January 2. Shelley expected to finish it early in February and print it in a cheap edition in Dublin. *The Revolt of Islam,* written and published six years later, had for its principal object the encouragement of those who had been led to despair by the failure of the French Revolution by presenting an ideal revolution properly based and conducted.

Except for a few scraps in his letters and several poems reprinted by Professor Dowden, the only one of Shelley's literary undertakings at Keswick that has been published is his *Address to the Irish people*.[107] It is the only one that he mentioned to Godwin, his new spiritual guide, who disapproved of juvenile literary efforts. When he mentioned it first to Miss Hitchener on January 20 it was already sufficiently advanced for him to describe and quote from it. His design was to print it on rough, cheap paper so that it could be posted up on vacant walls, as Tom Paine's writings had been. The work must have been practically completed at Keswick, since Shelley was able to send Miss Hitchener a proof-sheet eight days after reaching Dublin. Its further history belongs to the next chapter.

Toward the middle of January, Shelley's quiet routine of study, writing, and discussion received a rather violent interruption. At this time he was suffering from nervous attacks severe enough to cause him to resort to laudanum for relief.[108] Only a day before he recovered from his nervous attacks he was the victim of a physical assault, either real or imaginary. At about seven o'clock on the evening of Sunday, January 19, Shelley stepped outside the door of their cottage to investigate an unusual noise. He was immediately knocked senseless by an unseen assailant. Fortunately he fell inside the cottage and the assailant was afraid to proceed with his supposed design of robbery. Mr. Dare, who lived in another of the four cottages, was attracted by the commotion, snatched up a gun or pistol, and rushed upon the scene, whereupon the assailant or assailants fled into the night.[109] There had recently been a number of robberies in Keswick, so that there is nothing inherently improbable in the story, but the general impression among the neighbours was that Shelley had suffered an illusion rather than an attack.[110]

UNDER the sunshine of Elizabeth's approval,[111] " ideas, millions of ideas," [112] crowded into Shelley's consciousness. His expression of a few of them to her furnishes the best available evidence of the state and growth of Shelley's mind during the period of their correspondence. After the correspondence acquired its emotional tone there is less direct mention of books. Southey's *Bridal of Fernandez*, Lord Kames on love (both of which Shelley may not have read), Godwin's *Enquirer*, *St. Leon*, *Political Justice*, and *Caleb Williams*, which he characterized and had read, Paley's *Moral Philosophy* and the *Edinburgh Annual Register*, both of which he quoted,[113] practically complete the list. From the reopening of the correspondence after Shelley's marriage there is a definite, increasing vein of hostility to soldiers and commerce, leading straight toward the denunciatory passages in *Queen Mab* in 1813. The whole story is well summed up in one passage:

I have been led into reasonings which make me *hate* more and more the existing establishment, of every kind. I gasp when I think of plate and balls and titles and Kings. I have beheld scenes of misery. — The manufacturers are reduced to starvation. My friends the military are gone to Nottingham. . . . Curses light on them for their motives, if they destroy one of its famine-wasted inhabitants.[114]

The earlier argument of democracy versus aristocracy somewhat lapsed, more by consent than through any change in Shelley's opinions. Shelley continued his attack on Christianity as immoral, incredible, and oppressive.[115] " You seem to doubt Christianity," he wrote to the still-hesitant Elizabeth on January 2. " I do not: I cannot conceive . . . even the possibility of its genuineness." His views of marriage were but slightly altered by his own experience. He still thought it " an evil — an evil of immense and extensive magnitude," " monopolizing, exclusive, jealous " — but an evil so ingrained in human nature by custom that the remedy would be difficult.[116]

The changes that a few months had brought about in Shelley's relationships with Hogg, Miss Hitchener, and Harriet prompted several interesting comments on friendship and love, chiefly in relation to each other.[117] Ordinary love, like marriage, Shelley characterized as selfish; it was inferior to friendship in that the essence of the latter was unselfish sympathy. Shelley still believed with Locke that " the senses are the only inlets of knowledge," [118] but this view must have been unconsciously weakening under the influence of a strong yearning to believe in immortality. This yearning probably owes something to his unwillingness to regard his friendship with Miss Hitchener as mortal.[119]

Perhaps enough has been said already to show not only Shelley's surprising mental maturity in 1811 (in spite of the obscuring emotional ardour) but also the amazing extent to which the mature Shelley was dormant in the youth of eighteen and nine-

teen. On the latter point, however, considerably more might be
added. Thus, in a letter to Hogg on June 16, 1811, he seems to
forecast his " Sensitive Plant " (1821) in a sentence possibly
inspired by Erasmus Darwin's *Loves of the Plants* or a passage in
George Ensor in which it is suggested that plants may have feelings of their own. " Perhaps," Shelley writes, " the flowers think
like this [that there is a future life]; perhaps they moralize upon
their state, have their attachments, their pursuits of virtue;
adore, despond, hope, despise. Alas! then do we, like them,
perish; or do they, likewise, live forever? "[120] Again, the letter
of June 20, 1811 to Miss Hitchener [121] contains the skeleton idea
of *Alastor* (1816), which in turn owes some of its scenery and
much of its basic idea to Miss Owenson's novel *The Missionary,*
twice read and greatly admired by Shelley at about the time the
letter was written. The central idea of *Prometheus Unbound*
(1819) may be deduced from the following sentences of a letter
written to Miss Hitchener on October 18, 1811:

I have long been convinced of the eventual omnipotence of mind
over matter; adequacy of motive is sufficient to anything, and *my*
golden age is when the present potence will become omnipotence.
. . . Will it not be the task of human reason, human powers? [122]

Shelley's views of good and evil in human nature, as he expressed them in *Prometheus Unbound,* are accurately stated
in another letter to Miss Hitchener:

You must not *quite* despair of human nature. Our conceptions
are scarcely vivid enough to picture the degree of crime, of degradation, which sullies human society — but what words are equal to
express their inadequacy to picture its hidden virtue? [123]

The germ of the prose note on Necessity in *Queen Mab*
(1813) may be found in a comment to Miss Hitchener on
October 15 or 16, 1811:

Certainly everything is connected, both in the moral and physical
world there is a train of events, and tho' not likely it is impossible
to deny that the turn which my mind has taken, originated from
the conquest of England by William of Normandy.[124]

Again, in a letter to Hogg, dated by the editors of the Julian
edition November 8, 1811, occurs the sentence: " Night comes;

Death comes! Cold, calm Death. Almost I would it were to-morrow." [125] Years afterwards echoes of this passage occur both in the opening lines of *Queen Mab* and in the poem " To Night." Finally the phrase: " soul of my soul," [126] which Shelley employed in a letter to Godwin on January 10, 1812, is a variation of the similar phrases applied to Elizabeth Hitchener in various letters and occurs again in 1821 translated into Greek — *Epipsychidion* — as the title of a poem which reflects a repetition of the Elizabeth Hitchener experience and employs at least one figure of speech — the life-giving sun — as it was employed in the earlier episode.

Shelley's insistence to Southey that politics are really an extension of morality anticipates the same argument in the third chapter of his *Philosophical View of Reform* (1819) and is implicit throughout his " Defence of Poetry " 1821). Individually it would be easy to overstress the importance of any one of these passages, but collectively they indicate clearly enough that much of Shelley's most mature works grew slowly from seeds evident in his correspondence when he was a mere youth.

It seems odd that at the very time Shelley was demonstrating a remarkable intellectual acuteness in his letters, combined with a real power of clear expression, he was enclosing to Elizabeth Hitchener perfectly mediocre poems that contained not a single hint of the power of those later poems whose ideas were already vaguely germinating in his mind. Perhaps the reason for this seeming enigma is to be found partly in the fact that he had not yet abandoned prose as his first-chosen medium and partly in the fact that he found nowhere in his reading the ideas that he wished to express except in a prosaic medium. Also, his immediate bent was for more direct influence upon human reform than poetry could exert. Thus it is no surprise to find him undertaking a mission to Ireland.

THE project of going to Ireland was first mentioned to Miss Hitchener on December 11, 1811, after the earlier plan of taking a house in Sussex had been abandoned.[127] At that time it was necessarily a vague idea, to be put into effect in the summer, following an expected visit from Miss Hitchener. As yet there were no funds for it. But by January 20 the plan was definitely settled. Shelley was " eager and earnest " to be gone; he considered the state of Ireland as " constituting a part of a great crisis in opinions." If only Elizabeth would join, what might not be accomplished by " two hearts panting for the happiness and liberty of mankind " — like Laon and Cythna of later date? Southey's company was no longer an inducement to linger, and the scheme was now financially feasible, since Captain Pilfold promised £50, and the Duke of Norfolk might lend £100. The anticipated sale of the recent poems and essays would swell the total, and the restoration of Shelley's £200 allowance, announced a few days later, was expected soon.[128] The *Address to the Irish People* was already well started.[129]

Thereafter the Irish project formed part of every letter until they sailed.[130] The date of departure from Keswick was soon set for February 3. Shelley assured Godwin that his Address could not " excite rebellion " or " ' widen the breach between the Kingdoms ' " [131] — a phrase probably quoted from one of Godwin's letters to him. Elizabeth Hitchener, who had declined a pressing invitation to be one of the party, displayed considerable anxiety lest Shelley should be attacked, imprisoned, assassinated, prosecuted, or persecuted by spies. These rather flattering apprehensions 'were certainly not abolished by two remarks of Shelley's. "What think you of my undertaking? Shall I not get into prison? " he inquired on December 11. On January 29 he urged her to " share with us the noblest success, or the most glorious martyrdom." [132] It was perhaps even more pleasant to reassure Elizabeth than to communicate adventurous alarm. She was told that the government had desired the deaths of other radicals, naming Paine, Godwin, and Burdett, but in vain; political assassination was out of fashion. Shelley proposed to be very careful, study Blackstone, and use the law for his own protection. Not everybody who went to Dublin got killed or arrested, he observed comfortingly; Harriet and Eliza were not afraid.[133]

Hogg, to conceal his lack of actual knowledge, later represented the Irish adventure as a sudden unaccountable whim. He seems to have forgotten Shelley's interest while at Oxford in the case of Peter Finnerty. He perhaps did not know Shelley's acquaintance with the works of George Ensor, an Irishman whose books on reform show an interest in Ireland's woes even when the general subject is English.[134] Nor was he privileged to read the letters to Elizabeth Hitchener and Godwin, in which Shelley's increasing sense of social and economic wrongs is paralleled by a strong Messianic urge:

We have but a certain time allotted us in which to do its [life's] business: how much does it become us to improve and multiply this time; and to regard every hour neglected, misspent, or unimproved, as so much lost to the cause of virtue, liberty, and happiness.[135]

After three weeks of mounting enthusiasm Shelley, Harriet, and Eliza sailed from Whitehaven, " a miserable manufacturing sea-port Town," [136] on the night of February 3, 1812. The last week in Keswick had been spent with the Calverts — a week of vile, stormy weather which was rendered less depressing by the cordial hospitality of Mrs. Calvert. Shelley found slight encouragement for his undertaking. Their friends were all violently opposed except Mrs. Calvert, who heartily wished them success. Southey was sorry to see them go. But Shelley, keyed for action against wrongs that Southey's conduct encouraged, " passed Southey's house without *one* sting." In the letter he wrote to Elizabeth while waiting for the tide at Whitehaven, he recorded his doubt even of Southey's private character, " stained and false as is his public one." [137]

In the short space of five months Shelley had eloped with a girl he did not really love, married her against his own anti-matrimonial principles, acted with such mad frenzy at Field Place that all of his family were terrified of him, and separated from a friend he virtually adored to protect in the exercise of a " prejudice " a wife he was only beginning to love. At the same time he was developing to fever-pitch the extraordinary friend-

SOUTHEY IN 1814

Engraved by Henry Meyer from a drawing by Jackson, for the frontispiece of the New Monthly
Magazine, *No. 1*

ship he had formed with Elizabeth Hitchener. Such a series of occurrences would have seemed incredible in the novels of Shelley's boyhood, but in life they are fully verified facts. To make them appear fully rational is perhaps beyond the power of the biographer. Whatever understanding is achieved must be reached mainly through a study of Shelley's extraordinary letters at the time. They give evidence of an emotional intensity quite capable of transforming or even abolishing hard stubborn " facts " and also exhibit an occasional clear view of those facts and even of the writer's own personality that would not discredit the cool, shrewd judgment of a far older and completely dispassionate writer. They show a really astonishing grasp of ideas, including the clearly recognizable germinal ideas of some of the greatest works of his maturity. The fact that Shelley was only nineteen at the time may help explain the physical and emotional phenomena, but only renders the mental phenomenon more surprising. For whatever light it may throw upon the situation, one should examine more closely the most fully documented and perhaps the most important element in the situation, Shelley's friendship with Elizabeth Hitchener.

During the whole of the residence at Keswick, and in fact until the following autumn, Elizabeth Hitchener occupied the same high pedestal on which Shelley suddenly placed her shortly after his arrival at York. To others, even Godwin, he wrote with some restraint. Nothing of this sort could apply to Elizabeth, whom he called the " sister of *my soul*," " the friend of my heart," " my second self," even (in words anticipating his later doctrine of intellectual beauty) " the stronger shadow of that soul whose dictates I have been accustomed to obey." [138] From her he proposed to conceal nothing, he would " pour out " his " whole soul " to her.[139] " To *you* I tell everything that passes in my soul, even the secret thoughts sacred alone to sympathy." [140] He continually assured her of the high value of her friendship to his personal happiness and of her intellect and character to the great cause of truth and justice. The defection of Hogg, which he described as " indeed dreadful," so " terrible, dismaying " that his reason " almost withered "; [141] the sickening discovery that Southey, once a great voice for freedom, had sold himself to the oppressors, seemed to him as trivial as " gnat-bites " against his confidence in Elizabeth and hers in him. Her existence was a proof that humanity was not all bad and that virtue still existed: " Be *you* but false, and I have no more to accomplish, my work is done, my usefulness is ended." [142] It was an exceptional letter in which he neglected to assure her of the sustaining power of her letters, her sympathy, or her friendship, or in which he did not plan to take up a residence near her, invite her to visit in his home (either temporarily or " for ever ") [143] or offer to place his funds equally at her disposal.[144] He was not exclusive, however, or " monopolistic," as in his opinion a lover in the ordinary sense would have been. One letter asking Miss Hitchener to come to live with his household the next summer in an old Welsh castle expressed hope that the party might be increased by the following persons: Captain and Mrs. Pilfold and their children, the " dear little Americans " Elizabeth was tutoring, Elizabeth's spiritual mother, Mrs. Adams, and William Godwin.[145]

Shelley's financial prospects have been suggested [146] as the reason for Miss Hitchener's interest in him, but the evidence of the letters themselves is against this supposition. Shelley was always seeking to overcome her hesitation in accepting his offers of money, entertainment, and equality. Not only did Shelley share his closest thoughts with her — his opinions of himself, his hopes of having children, his cautious recourse to laudanum as a relief from nervous pain, and his intention of abandoning the drug — but he showed a similar interest in her concerns — the inconveniences of holding advanced notions in a narrow, conservative community, her comparatively ignorant and socially inferior parents, her " spiritual mother," Mrs. Adams, her humilating experience with a young pupil named Anne who was well on the road to enlightenment when she suddenly turned against her instructor.

Harriet loyally accepted Miss Hitchener at Shelley's estimate and welcomed her with cordial, admiring, little-sisterly letters. To her there seemed no difficulty in regarding Elizabeth as a coadjutor on a different plane rather than as a competitor for her husband's affections. The distinction was so clear in Shel-

ley's mind as reflected in the letters (and also, in Miss Hitchener's, so far as the written evidence goes) that it is not at all
incredible that it should be instinctively apparent to Harriet.
Even Eliza Westbrook allowed herself to be referred to in
Harriet's letters as Elizabeth's admirer.

Elizabeth's superiority to Harriet in Shelley's eyes was due
to her absence, which made her easier to idealize, and to her
intellectual and moral qualities. Shelley regarded her as " one
of those beings who carry happiness, reform, liberty, wherever
they go." [147] " Your pen . . . ought to trace characters for a
nation's perusal." " That tongue of energy, and that eye of fire,
would awe them [the Irish Tories] into native insignificance."
" I perceive in you the embryon of a mighty intellect which may
one day enlighten thousands." [148] She whom he regarded as in
many respects a superior was to be a necessary partner in his
poems and essays. The inferiority on these points of the sixteen-
year-old Harriet to the thirty-year-old Elizabeth was true and
was tacitly acknowledged by all the parties — though Shelley's
letters to Elizabeth show a growing respect for Harriet on this
plane, as well as a growing love on the plane that " my dear
Harriet " best understood.

Nor is Shelley's estimate of Elizabeth as absurd as it appears
in the sorry light of what happened a year later when Shelley
had advanced much further in experience and intellect and
when Elizabeth's physical presence extinguished her spiritual
halo. Her letters are badly written and, like Shelley's, are
marred by excessive sentimental expression. This is merely to
say that the sentimental novels of the day, often written in the
form of letters, exercised a natural effect on the epistolary style
of both writers. Beneath her epistolary deficiencies Elizabeth
Hitchener was undoubtedly a woman of more than commonplace intellectual strength. The woman she is sometimes described as being does not study and discuss Locke as intel-
ligently as she did, nor does she suggest or inquire about
Xenophanes or recommend Parkinson's three-volume *Organic
Remains of a Former World*.[149] In the year of Shelley's death
she published a poem, *The Weald of Sussex,* which, though
mediocre in expression, shows sense and reading and is cer-

201

tainly superior to the poems Shelley wished her to help him write. Merely to stimulate and understand the philosophic and metaphysical discussion with which Shelley's letters to her are loaded demands more intelligence than some of their subsequent readers have possessed. Exaggerated as Shelley's opinions of Miss Hitchener were, they had a real basis — and her importance to him in 1811 and 1812 must be measured by his judgment of her at the time.

If Shelley was happy at Keswick [150] in spite of his disappointment in Hogg and Southey and his growing sense of social injustice and human depravity, the cause lies partly in the natural environment, a consciousness of his own increasing powers, his augmented love and respect for Harriet, and the neighbourly kindness of the Calverts and Southeys. Mainly, however, it is to be found in the complete joy he took in his correspondence with Elizabeth Hitchener. Here the life of ideas and generous emotions that to him was the real essence of existence could still flourish unchecked, completely independent of an outer world to which his earlier experience had fitted him so imperfectly. Here he could find utter happiness in being — for himself and the sister of his soul — his own ideal of himself.

Never again in his relations with other individuals was Shelley to let himself go so utterly as in the letters to Elizabeth Hitchener. As the pressure of later events forced him more and more into a realization that complete companionship is possible only within one's own thoughts, the same ardour found expression in more generalized form in such poems as *Prometheus Unbound* and *Epipsychidion*. Yet even in the abandon of attempting to share his very soul with another, Shelley was capable of that clear, matter-of-fact objectivity which from time to time throughout his whole life permitted him to regard himself calmly and sensibly from an almost alien viewpoint. "Certainly," he stopped to observe in the midst of a fervent letter to Elizabeth, "any one who got hold of this letter would think I was a Bedlamite . . . well, you do not; and my reputation for *madness* is too well-established to gain any firmness or addition from this letter.[151]

Chapter VIII

THE UNSETTLED REFORMER:

IN IRELAND

DUBLIN; ADDRESSES AND NEWSPAPER NOTICES; PROJECTS AND FRIENDS; DISILLUSION AND RETURN TO ENGLAND

WITH Harriet and her sister, Shelley sailed from " miserable," " filthy " Whitehaven, with its " horrible inn," on midnight of February 3, 1812. By next morning, presumably, they were in the Isle of Man,[1] where they must have lingered for five or six days. Thereafter their vessel encountered a storm which drove it to the north of Ireland. After twenty-eight hours of tossing and rolling that proved most fatiguing for Harriet and Eliza, they reached Dublin on the night of February 12.[2] The next day they were settled in lodgings at Mr. Dunn's, a woolen-draper's, 7 Sackville Street, and Bysshe was writing to inform Miss Hitchener of their safe arrival.

A few years before 1812 Dublin was a city of nearly 200,000 inhabitants, living, on the average, ten or twelve people to the house.[3] It had some of the broadest streets and finest public buildings in the Kingdom, particularly the former House of Parliament; it also had one of the most numerous and ragged beggar populations in Europe. Sackville Street, where the Shelleys first lodged, began at the river Liffey, which bisected the town, and ran north. It was the broadest street in Dublin and one of the finest, but it exhibited the extraordinarily mixed features that were rather characteristic of the city as a whole.

At its entrance by Carlisle Bridge, only three houses from Shelley's lodgings, passers-by were constantly annoyed by the solicitations or blasphemous quarrels of ragged and dirty coal-carriers. The name plates of its residents included "Peers, Pastrycooks, and Perfumers; Bishops, Butchers, and Brokers in old furniture, together with Hotels of the most superb description, and a tolerable sprinkling of gin and whiskey shops." [4]

A short distance across the bridge Shelley could see the walls and grounds of Trinity College, a sight which Hogg next year thought was worthy enough, but hardly exciting to one who had seen Oxford. Across Grafton Street to the west of Trinity College stood the fine building that had housed the Parliament until Ireland ceased to have one; it was now the National Bank — to be called a Temple of Mammon in Shelley's address at the Fishamble Street Theatre. Perhaps a half-mile to the east of this building rose the dirty red-brick walls of Dublin Castle, from which Ireland was governed by the Lord Lieutenant and the "Castle Junto" of place-men. At the western edge of the city were the extensive quarters of the military.

The "state of Ireland" which Shelley so confidently hoped to ameliorate may be summarized in the Johnsonian phrase: "complicated misery." [5] A country of something less than five million inhabitants was hopelessly divided in race, creed, and economic interests. The Anglican Irish, scarcely more than a million, constituted the Protestant Ascendancy, owned nine-tenths of the land, and completely dominated all branches of the government. The Presbyterian Irish — about half a million people in the north — were economically more prosperous than the Catholic Irish, but were under similar civil disabilities. This should have been an incentive to unite with the Irish Catholics, except that it was counterbalanced by a strong religious antagonism. More than three million Irish Catholics lived miserably under a system of absentee-landlordism and rack-rent middlemen, their local and national affairs, their scant educational opportunities, and their social and economic life completely dominated by the Protestant Ascendancy.

Though the Irish had a Parliament of their own until 1800, it was composed entirely of Protestants and was utterly servile

THE CASTLE, DUBLIN, IN 1817

Artist unknown

to the English interests as expressed by the Lord Lieutenant, except when these interests failed to coincide with the vested privileges of the Protestant Ascendancy. The considerable alleviation of conditions achieved in the late eighteenth century mainly by the Irish Volunteers and by the Catholic Relief Act of 1793 was largely wiped out in the aftermath of the Rebellion of 1798. This rebellion, born of Ireland's despair and the hopes held out by the French Revolution, was suppressed by a non-Catholic militia, with an ill-disciplined ferocity that completely sickened such professional soldiers as Lord Cornwallis. Its aftermath of torture and deportations included such pleasant devices as suspending prisoners by one arm so that the downward pull could be relieved only by resting one bare foot on a sharp stake. Unwilling witnesses were made more compliant by fitting them with caps lined with hot pitch that could be removed only by removing hair and skin at the same time. The Habeas Corpus Act was suspended, martial law was declared, and the system of extreme Protestant Ascendancy was revived.

Such was the condition of Ireland before the passage of the Act of Union with England in 1800. The Union had been achieved with great difficulty by Pitt at the cost of wholesale promises and the further corruption of an already corrupt electorate. A strong influence in favour of the Union was the promise to lighten Catholic disabilities. Catholics who wished an opportunity to share in the government were easily convinced that their object would be more readily secured from the Parliament in London than from an Irish Protestant Parliament that rightly considered full Catholic participation its own death warrant.

In 1812, Irish Catholics were still waiting for this promise to be redeemed. Pitt had made one or two efforts, perhaps not sufficiently determined, and had been frustrated by the opposition of George III. In 1805, 1808, 1809, and 1810, petitions for Catholic relief presented by Irish members were decisively rejected by Parliament. Since Catholics were organizing into committees all over Ireland, the authorities of Dublin Castle revived the Convention Act of 1793, which admitted the right of petition but declared unlawful all bodies appointed by delegation or having any representative character. Another persecution was begun, but the Catholic petitions continued. In 1812 the question of Catholic relief was twice brought before Parliament and twice rejected. When Shelley reached Ireland early in 1812, he found Catholics still endeavouring to obtain relief by petitioning Parliament.

The time seemed especially opportune, for in March certain limitations imposed on the powers of the Regent would expire and the English Whigs, mostly friends of Catholic emancipation, expected with his help to dominate the government. Also a new Parliamentary election was held toward the end of the year. Both hopes proved bitterly delusive; the Regent " ratted " and the Tories swept the election; but it seemed at the time a moment of opportunity. On the 28th of February an aggregate meeting of the friends of Catholic Emancipation was to be held in the historic old Fishamble Street Theatre, to be addressed by one of the principal veterans of their cause, Daniel O'Connell.

LIKE his father and the Duke of Norfolk, Shelley had supported Catholic emancipation before he entered Oxford. His interest in the case of Peter Finnerty probably turned his eyes first upon Ireland as a special centre of religious and civil oppression. An account of Finnerty's unjustifiable imprisonment, in a cell sixteen feet by nine, with fourteen other persons, appeared in Leigh Hunt's *Examiner* for February 24, 1811, where Shelley was very likely to have read it in following the *Examiner's* account of Finnerty's more recent prosecution in England. Godwin's friend the Irish patriot John Philpot Curran had boldly but ineffectually defended Finnerty; it was this circumstance, probably, that led Shelley to the reading of Curran's speeches, from which he could learn more about conditions in Ireland.[6] When he acknowledged Godwin's letter of introduction to Curran with the remark that he was acquainted with Curran's speeches he might have gone further and stated that the *Address to the Irish People* that he was taking to Dublin was considerably influenced by that fact.[7] While at Keswick, where he sometimes argued the Irish question with Southey, he prob-

ably read some of the incidental comments on Ireland that
appeared during the year in the *Examiner,* the *Edinburgh Annual Register* and the *Edinburgh Review.* A fair amount of
information was necessary to avoid glaring errors even in so
general a document as his *Address,* but there is no indication
that Shelley made anything like a thorough study of the situation before he embarked on his venture. Despite his really
remarkable powers of intellectual assimilation he was probably
no better informed than all the other English friends of the
Irish who, according to their intended beneficiaries, never understood the situation sufficiently to make their aid effective.

One qualification, however, Shelley had in abundance —
enthusiasm. He had no sooner got settled in lodgings than he
set about the publication of his *Address to the Irish People.*
While this was going through the press, and afterwards, his
optimistic hopes overflowed in letters to Elizabeth Hitchener.
At the same time he conducted with Godwin a more reasoned,
dispassionate correspondence, better suited to the philosophic
calm of *Political Justice.* Harriet shared his enthusiasm completely. Even Eliza Westbrook caught the fever. Between completing a red cloak and acting as custodian of the family finances
("in some hole or corner of her dress") she found time for
culling extracts from Tom Paine to be used in a later attack
on religious intolerance.[8] At the same time Shelley was thinking
of another volume to be composed of moral and ethical extracts
from the New Testament.[9] The letters from Miss Hitchener
that had been awaiting Shelley's arrival, he assured her, added
energy to his hopes and "tenfold activity" to his exertions.[10]
True, he now saw that her coming to Ireland was impracticable,
but summer would come soon, when Elizabeth should join them
in Wales and add her strength and energy to the crusade. The
newly established Mexican republic inspired him to four stanzas
of energetic verse better than any of his previous poems; he
enclosed them to Elizabeth, along with some lines to Ireland,
as "lineaments in the picture of my mind." "My 'Address,'"
he informed her, "will soon come out. It will be instantly followed by another, with downright proposals for instituting associations for bettering the condition of human-kind. I — even

I, weak, young, poor, as I am — will attempt to organize them, the society of peace and love. Oh! that I [may] be a successful apostle of this only true religion, the religion of Philanthropy." "At all events," he added as a rather astonishing climax, "I *will* have a Debating Society, and see what will grow out of that."[11] His emotion ran so high that one whole paragraph of oratorical prose in this letter will scan almost regularly as blank verse. Some of the lines were, in fact, printed as verse, with only slight changes, in *Queen Mab* and in the poem "To Ireland."[12] To Godwin, however, after detailing his plans, he simply stated: "A crisis like this ought not to be permitted to pass unoccupied or unimproved."[13]

THERE was, in fact, a vast difference between Elizabeth Hitchener's whole-hearted, almost ecstatic support of Shelley's mission and Godwin's dry scepticism. Since *Political Justice* in twenty years had done little to change England (as Shelley rather tactlessly reminded Godwin), the philosopher saw small hope of his young friend's changing Ireland in less than two months. He distrusted Shelley's youthful tendency to rush into print. The pervading principle of *Political Justice,* he reminded Shelley, was that little progress and much mischief were to be expected from reform "associations"; Shelley's course, in spite of his desire to avoid violence, might easily "light again the flames of rebellion and war."[14] Shelley's answer that the associations he contemplated were of a special sort, and really in accord with *Political Justice,*[15] provoked Godwin to an almost impassioned declaration that this was not really so:

Shelley, you are preparing a scene of blood! If your associations take effect to any extensive degree, tremendous consequences will follow, and hundreds, by their calamities and premature fate, will expiate your error. . . . Do not be restrained by a false shame from retracting your steps. . . .

I wish to my heart you would come immediately to London.[16]

Godwin, who knew something of Ireland from Curran, was dreading an outcome that might very well have happened, but that actually fell almost ludicrously short of fulfilment. Shelley's first step was to procure publication of his *Address to the Irish People*. The printing was concluded about ten days after he reached Dublin; and Shelley enclosed the completed pamphlet to Godwin on the 24th, the day it came from the printers.[17] It was advertised in the Dublin *Evening Post* on the 25th and 29th of February and the 3rd of March. Probably Shelley also sent copies with personal notes to various friends of the Irish cause, but of this no record remains except an apparently unanswered note dated February 25, introducing himelf and his pamphlet to the Irish patriot Hamilton Rowan. A copy sent to Mr. Timothy Shelley was similarly unnoticed, except for a dry comment in a letter from Mr. William Whitton to Sir Bysshe, to the effect that young Mr. Shelley was now engaged in enlightening the Irish. Mr. Timothy Shelley, who was ill at the time, quite possibly never read it.[18]

Shelley's principal means of publication was through his rather unprepossessing Irish servant, Daniel Hill (or Healey).[19] Within two days he had distributed four hundred of his fifteen hundred copies, sixty of them to public-houses. Every day his servant distributed them to "multitudes" of people, sometimes with the embarrassing misinformation that the author was only fifteen years old. Both Shelley and Harriet took a hand. Standing in the balcony of their Sackville Street lodgings, they would watch until someone came along who "looked likely" and throw him a pamphlet; or they would walk the streets and give them to passers-by. It was deadly serious business to Percy, but Harriet's complete sympathy with the cause did not preclude some amusement at the means adopted for forwarding it: "For myself, I am ready to die of laughter when it is done, and Percy looks so grave, yesterday he put one into a woman's hood of a cloak. She knew nothing of it, and we passed her. I could hardly get on, my muscles were so irritated." [20] By March 18 most of the copies had been distributed.[21]

On March 2 appeared another address to the Irish, Shelley's eighteen-page octavo pamphlet entitled *Proposals for an Association of those Philanthropists, who Convinced of the Inadequacy of the Moral and Political State of Ireland to Produce*

Benefits which are Nevertheless Attainable are Willing to Unite to Accomplish its Regeneration. Though intended for a better class of readers, the *Proposals* merely repeat the substance of the *Address,* with a more detailed account of the proposed association and with less of the repetition that marks the more popular document.

Both pamphlets fully justify Shelley's claims in his letters to Miss Hitchener and Godwin that the government could find nothing in them on which to base a prosecution. While making it clear that he considered Ireland deeply wronged by the Act of Union and the withholding of Catholic emancipation, Shelley repeatedly asserted that violence on the part of the Irish would only ruin their cause. Mobs and secret societies, he insisted, led directly to the methods of the oppressor and tended to justify them. The only remedy was virtue, to be attained through sobriety, moderation, and wisdom. To the force of virtue, and to that only, all government must succumb as soon as virtue prevailed among the governed, for the absence of virtue was government's only excuse for existence. He assured his readers that Catholic emancipation was sure of achievement within the near future, and that the abolition of the Union, which was even more to be desired, would certainly be achieved eventually. Even if the Regent, on whom the Irish now pinned their hopes, should fail them (and Shelley seemed to anticipate — correctly — that he would), there was a trend in the times that would inevitably fight for Ireland.

He warned his readers that when they achieved their aims they would probably be disappointed. Poverty, vice, and oppression would not thereby be abolished any more than they were in England already. Ireland should be regarded as the starting-point of a movement that should *truly* emancipate the human spirit, not only in Ireland, but elsewhere — a movement that could be grounded only in wisdom and virtue and that would take longer than one generation to reach its goal.

Shelley's counsel of perfection must have fallen a little discouragingly upon the ears of men already exasperated to the point of vigorous action. It was scarcely practical advice in the circumstances, but for a young man of twenty, engaged in a hopelessly Utopian project, it was astonishingly true and wise. Eight years later, when Demogorgon in *Prometheus Unbound* delivered his final wisdom to the liberated human spirit, his message was almost exactly like that of the youthful Shelley in the following passage from his *Address to the Irish People:*

I wish you, O Irishmen, to be as careful and thoughtful of your interests as are your real friends. Do not drink, do not play, do not spend any idle time, do not take every thing that other people say for granted — there are numbers who will tell you lies to make their own fortunes, you cannot more certainly do good to your own cause, than by defeating the intentions of these men. Think, read, and talk; let your own condition and that of your wives and children, fill your minds; disclaim all manner of alliance with violence, meet together if you will, but do not meet in a mob. If you think and read and talk with a real wish of benefiting the cause of truth and liberty, it will soon be seen how true a service you are rendering, and how sincere you are in your professions; but mobs and violence must be discarded. The certain degree of civil and religious liberty which the usage of the English Constitution allows, is such as the worst of men are entitled to, although you have it not; but that liberty which we may one day hope for, wisdom and virtue can alone give you a right to enjoy. This wisdom and this virtue I recommend on every account that you should *instantly begin* to practise. Lose not a day, not an hour, not a moment. — Temperance, sobriety, charity, and independence will give you virtue; and reading, talking, thinking and searching, will give you wisdom; when you have those things you may defy the tyrant. It is not going often to chapel, crossing yourselves, or confessing, that will make you virtuous; many a rascal has attended regularly at Mass, and many a good man has never gone at all. It is not paying Priests, or believing in what they say that makes a good man, but it is doing good actions, or benefiting other people; this is the true way to be good, and the prayers, and confessions, and masses of him who does not these things, are good for nothing at all. Do your work regularly and quickly, when you have done, think, read, and talk; do not spend your money in idleness and drinking, which so far from doing good to your cause, will do it harm. If you have any thing to spare from your wife and children, let it do some good to other people, and put them in a way of getting wisdom and

virtue, as the pleasure that will come from these good acts will be
much better than the headache that comes from a drinking bout.
And never quarrel between each other, be all of one mind as nearly
as you can; do those things, and I will promise you liberty and
happiness. But if, on the contrary of these things, you neglect to
improve yourselves, continue to use the word heretic, and demand
from others the toleration which you are unwilling to give; your
friends and the friends of liberty will have reason to lament the
death-blow of their hopes. I expect better things from you; it is
for yourselves that I fear and hope. Many Englishmen are prejudiced against you, they sit by their own fire-sides, and certain rumours artfully spread are ever on the wing against you. But these
people who think ill of you and of your nation are often the very
men who, if they had better information, would feel for you most
keenly; wherefore are these reports spread, how do they begin?
they originate from the warmth of the Irish character, which the
friends of the Irish nation have hitherto encouraged rather than
repressed; this leads them in those moments when their wrongs
appear so clearly, to commit acts which justly excite displeasure.
They begin therefore, from yourselves, although falsehood and
tyranny artfully magnify and multiply the cause of offence. — Give
no offence.[22]

    As a means of hastening the desired conclusion, Shelley pro-
posed associations of philanthropists who by constant activity
and discussion should ascertain and forward the ends of true
virtue. Such associations, if they forswore secrecy and violence, could accomplish much, for was not discussion the main
avenue to truth? Shelley frankly admitted that such an association would be opposed by the priesthood, the aristocracy,
and the government. Though it would not be contrary to the
English Constitution, that fact would not necessarily ensure it
against danger from the government. No one, therefore, should
join it who was not willing to undergo persecution, if necessary,
for the sake of humanity.

    Incidental to his argument for the usefulness of such an as-
sociation as he proposed, Shelley boldly faced the two greatest
discouragements that liberals and radicals had to meet — the
comparative failure of the French Revolution, and the inferences commonly drawn from the new Malthusian theory of

population. The first subject, as shown by his letters and his description of his lost uncompleted novel, *Hubert Cauvin*, had for some months been one of his important interests. He asserted that the French Revolution had conduced to war, vice, and misery because the doctrines of philanthropy and freedom were but shallowly understood. Voltaire was a flatterer of kings, Rousseau was an encourager of dangerous passions, while Helvetius and Condorcet had drawn their conclusions unsystematically, and even these conclusions were not well understood by a people who were driven to revolution before they were morally and spiritually fitted for it. The Revolution had adopted some of the very vices of tyranny, particularly violence. A philosopher like Godwin, and associations for the non-violent opposition of tyranny, such as that now proposed, might well have turned the French Revolution into a complete success. Eight years later, in his *Philosophical View of Reform*, Shelley's criticism of the French Revolution was essentially the same.

The Malthusian theory of the pressure of population, which was everywhere being used by the privileged classes to justify a complacent attitude of *laissez faire*, seemed to Shelley no argument against an attempt to achieve a greater measure of happiness: "War, vice, and misery are undeniably bad, they embrace all that we can conceive of temporal and eternal evil. Are we to be told that these are remedyless, because the earth would, in case of their remedy, be overstocked?"[23]

To illustrate the contemptibility of such reasoning, Shelley fell back upon analogy:

To how contemptible a degradation of grossest credulity will not prejudice lower the human mind! — We see in Winter that the foliage of the trees is gone, that they present to the view nothing but leafless branches — we see that the loveliness of the flower decays, though the root continues in the earth. What opinion should we form of that man who, when he walked in the freshness of the spring, beheld the fields enamelled with flowers, and the foliage bursting from the buds, should find fault with this beautiful order, and murmur his contemptible discontents because winter must come, and the landscape be robbed of its beauty for a while again? Yet this man is Mr. Malthus. Do we not see that the laws of nature perpetually act by disorganization and reproduction, each alternately becoming cause and effect? The analogies that we can draw from physical to moral topics are of all others the most striking.[24]

Here again we have an illustration of the close connection between the supposedly immature reformer and the mature poet. The same analogy and its use formed the basis seven years later for one of Shelley's most perfect assaults upon pessimism, his " Ode to the West Wind."

Considered together, the two pamphlets show a great deal of penetrating political philosophy combined with a naïve ignorance of political tactics. Shelley was right in predicting the inevitability of Catholic emancipation and the abolition of the Union; he was right (at least for a hundred years to come) in sensing the temper of the age as progressively liberal. His exposition of the manner in which the law of libel was abused to muzzle the freedom of the press showed a very clear knowledge of the devices still used by reactionary governments. His picture of the economic ills resulting from the Act of Union through its added encouragement to absenteeism is theoretically sound, though actually it is probably still doubtful as to whether the Union benefited or injured Ireland economically.[25] In insisting upon the ultimate obedience of government to opinion, and the inevitable dependence of all true emancipation on a denial of violence and special privilege and a cultivation of wisdom through patience, tolerance, temperance, and free discussion, he was announcing a political creed from which he varied little to the end of his life, a creed that today is considered rather more liberal than radical. Shelley's radicalism was always more social and moral than political.

And yet Godwin was probably justified in fearing that Shelley's associations, if formed, would lead to bloodshed. Shelley was assuming a membership of Godwins and Shelleys, rather than Irishmen. Irishmen had already advocated assassination as the only remedy and were to advocate it again in later years. Moreover, Irishmen were faced with an immediate emergency; they had little patience with Shelley's assertion that this was trifling in comparison with the intellectual emancipation of their descendants. To Catholics and Protestants alike he insisted on the cruelty and intolerance of their creeds in the past and practically admitted that he was a deist. He preached temperance to a people to whom drink was almost the only refuge from reality, and the cultivation of knowledge to a people who were tragically without the means of cultivating it. The great majority of them were unable even to read his exhortation. " Three-fourths of the Catholics," says one historian of the times, " probably could not read and write." [26]

No notice was taken of the *Address* and the *Proposals* by the government, from which Shelley anticipated at least resentment and an effort to tamper with his mail.[27] Little more notice was taken by the Irish patriots. Even the Sussex papers to which Shelley seems to have furnished a copy of the *Address* declined to comment.[28] His Irish friends pronounced his sentiments noble, but lacking in expediency. " They . . . hold *expediency* to be necessary in politics," Shelley informed Elizabeth Hitchener, " inasmuch as it is employed in its utmost latitude by the enemies of innovation. I hope to convince them of the contrary of this." [29] But the Irish, like Southey a few months before, clung to expediency.

ON FEBRUARY 28, two days before the second of his pamphlets was published, Shelley made a personal appearance before the friends of Catholic emancipation. This meeting was held in the historic Fishamble Street Theatre, which had welcomed Handel to Ireland seventy-one years earlier. Lord Fingal, leader of the Catholic cause, presided. The principal address was by O'Connell, one of the most distinguished patriotic orators of the day. Many Protestant friends of the Irish cause were present. According to the account that appeared in the London *Morning Chronicle*, the theatre was brilliantly illuminated and " the boxes were filled with ladies, full dressed." [30] These " full dressed " ladies probably included Harriet Shelley and Eliza Westbrook. When a resolution was proposed thanking the Protestants for their encouragement, Shelley arose and spoke for more than an hour. His speech was reported during the next few days in six accounts of the meeting.[31] According to the published reports, after introducing himself as a sympathetic Englishman ready to devote himself to the Irish cause, Shelley condemned the English treatment of Ireland, expressed regret at the rumoured lukewarmness of the Prince Regent, endorsed Catholic emancipation, but pronounced the repeal of the Union still more important, and deprecated political and religious intolerance. The newspapers were kind enough to mention only the applause that greeted the more popular sections of his speech.

Shelley himself was by no means elated by his speech. To Elizabeth Hitchener he wrote:

I do not like Lord Fingal, or *any* of the Catholic aristocracy. Their intolerance can be equalled by nothing but the hardy wickedness and intolerance of the Prince. My speech was misinterpreted. I spoke for more than an hour. The hisses with which they greeted me when I spoke of *religion*, though in terms of respect, were mixed with applause when I avowed my mission. The newspapers have only noted that which did not excite disapprobation.[32]

Behind this comment, as in the case of the pamphlets, lies Shelley's contempt of political expediency. The meeting was controlled by Irish Catholic nobility and gentry whose view of reform was quite different from Shelley's. They were intolerant Catholics to whom criticism of historical Catholicism was repugnant. They wished least of all to alienate possible English support for Catholic emancipation by agitation to dissolve the Union. Their new champion, therefore, did not rouse them to unqualified enthusiasm. They applauded the sentiments that pleased them, and avoided entangling themselves with the speaker's program. Not even the authorities of Dublin Castle took him seriously. They were indeed concerned with the activity of the Catholic Association, whose meeting at the same theatre some months earlier they had sent messengers to disperse under the odious Convention Act. Two emissaries had been sent out to report on the proceedings of this meeting, but their two reports paid no attention to Shelley's speech.[33] One auditor, Chief Baron Woulfe, an Irish judge, remembered Shelley's speech many years later, chiefly for the odd style of its delivery. " The speaker would utter a sentence; then pause, as if he were taking time to frame another, which was slowly enunciated, the whole speech having the effect of unconnected aphorisms." [34]

The earlier reports of Shelley's speech had been brief and somewhat guarded. A week later, however, on March 7, the *Weekly Messenger* printed a highly laudatory article entitled " Pierce Byshe Shelly, Esq." Shelley sent copies to Godwin, to his father, and to Elizabeth Hitchener, the last of whom he instructed to insert it in the Sussex papers. As the first introduction of Shelley to the readers of any periodical, preceding by three years Leigh Hunt's brief notice of Shelley in the *Examiner,* this article should be quoted entire:

The highly interesting appearance of this young gentleman at the late Aggregate Meeting of the Catholics of Ireland, has naturally excited a spirit of enquiry, as to his objects and views, in coming forward at *such* a meeting; and the publications which he has circulated with such uncommon industry, through the Metropolis, has set curiosity on the wing to ascertain who he is, from whence he comes, and what his pretensions are to the confidence he solicits, and the character he assumes. To those who have read the productions we have alluded to, we need bring forward no evidence of the cultivation of his mind — the benignity of his principles — or the peculiar fascination with which he seems able to recommend them.

Of this gentleman's family we can say but little, but we can set down what we have heard from respectable authority. That his father is a member of the Imperial Parliament, and that this young gentleman, whom we have seen, is the *immediate* heir of one of the *first* fortunes in England. Of his principles and his manners we can say more, because we can collect from conversation, as well as from reading, that he seems devoted to the propagation of those divine and Christian feelings which purify the human heart, give shelter to the poor, and consolation to the unfortunate. That he is the *bold* and *intrepid* advocate of those principles which are cal-

217

culated to give energy to truth, and to depose from their guilty eminence the bad and vicious passions of a corrupt community; — that a universality of charity is *his* object, and a perfectibility of human society *his* end, which cannot be attained by the *conflicting* dogmas of religious sects, *each* priding itself on the extinction of the *other,* and *all* existing by the mutual misfortunes which flow from polemical warfare. The principles of this young gentleman embrace *all* sects and all persuasions. His doctrines, *political* and *religious,* may be accommodated to *all;* every friend to true Christianity will be his religious friend, and every enemy to the liberties of Ireland will be his *political* enemy. The weapons he wields are those of reason, and the most *social benevolence.* He deprecates violence in the accomplishment of his views, and relies upon the mild and merciful spirit of toleration for the completion of all his designs, and the consummation of all his wishes. To the religious bigot such a *missionary of truth* is a formidable opponent, by the political monopolist he will be considered the child of Chimera, the creature of fancy, an imaginary legislator who presumes to make laws without reflecting upon his *materials,* and despises those considerations which have baffled the hopes of the most philanthropic and the efforts of the most wise. It is true, human nature may be too depraved for such a hand as Mr. Shelly's to form to anything that is good, or liberal, or beneficent. Let him but take down *one* of the rotten pillars by which society is *now* propped, and substitute the purity of his own principles, and Mr. Shelly shall have done a great and lasting service to human nature. To this gentleman Ireland is much indebted, for selecting *her* as the theatre of his first attempts in this holy work of human regeneration; the Catholics of Ireland should listen to him with respect, because they will find that an enlightened Englishman has interposed between the treason of their own countrymen and the almost conquered spirit of their country; that Mr. Shelly has come to Ireland to demonstrate in his person that there are hearts in his own country not rendered callous by six hundred years of injustice; and that the genius of freedom, which has communicated comfort and content to the cottage of the Englishman, has found its way to the humble roof of the Irish peasant, and promises by its presence to dissipate the sorrows of past ages, to obliterate the remembrance of persecution, and close the long and wearisome scene of centuries of human depression. We extract from Mr. Shelley's last production, which he calls "PROPOSALS FOR AN ASSOCIATION, &C." [35]

218

After quoting extensively from Shelley's *Proposals,* the article concludes:

We have but one word more to add. Mr. Shelly, commiserating the sufferings of our distinguished countryman Mr. Finerty, whose exertions in the cause of political freedom he much admired, wrote a very beautiful poem, the profits of which we understand, from *undoubted* authority, Mr. Shelly remitted to Mr. Finerty; we have heard they amounted to nearly an hundred pounds. This fact speaks a volume in favour of our new friend.[36]

Such a renegade Englishman as this could not be allowed by the Anglo-Irish to escape unscathed. The Dublin *Journal,* a government organ, published two indignant letters, one signed " An Englishman," dated March 7; the other signed " A Dissenter," dated March 21.[37] The former sarcastically congratulated the Irish on acquiring " so *patriotic* and *enlightened* an advocate."

If it revolted against my principles, Mr. Editor, to hear such language from one of my own countrymen, you will readily conceive that my disgust was infinitely heightened to observe with what transport the invectives of this renegade Englishman against his native country were *hailed* by the assembly he addressed. Joy beamed in every countenance and rapture glistened in every eye at the aggravated detail.[38]

" A Dissenter," like " An Englishman," deplored the manner in which Catholic public meetings were used as springboards to notoriety by young " literary nondescripts and political adventurers," and proceeds thence to a scornful comment on Shelley's two pamphlets. For a dissenter, the casual effectiveness with which he brings to view the aspects of the pamphlet best calculated to damage the author in the eyes of the Catholic gentry is rather remarkable:

He proposes to " exterminate the eyeless monster Bigotry," and " make the teeth of the palsied beldame Superstition chatter." This, which is doubtless designed as an allegorical allusion to the Romish Church, must, if actually accomplished, be its death . . . he proposes to make us all " kneel at the altar of the common God " and to

" hang upon that altar the garland of devotion," figures which Deism
borrows from the old Heathen mythology. . . . That the abolition of
the aristocracy of the country is a feature in his picture of Utopian
amelioration, though, for reasons obvious, but lightly touched, and
as yet kept in the shade, is evident from the manner and connexion
in which he disapproves " of other distinctions than those of virtue
and talent." [39]

Neither of these attacks mentions Shelley by name.

By the time this press comment appeared, Shelley had already gained a clearer notion of the difficulties of his undertaking. Writing to Godwin on March 8, he confessed:

I had no conception of the depth of human misery until now.
The poor of Dublin are assuredly the meanest and most miserable
of all. In their narrow streets thousands seem huddled together, —
one mass of animated filth. With what eagerness do such scenes as
these inspire me! How self confident, too, do I feel in my assumption to teach the lessons of virtue to those who grind their fellow
beings into worse than annihilation. These were the persons to
whom, in my fancy, I had addressed myself: how quickly were
my views on this subject changed; yet how deeply has this very
change rooted the conviction on which I came hither.[40]

To Elizabeth Hitchener two days later he related with even
greater passion and indignation some of his more practical
experiences among the poor:

I cannot recount all the horrible instances of unrestricted and un-
licensed tyranny that have met my ears, — scarcely those which
have personally occurred to me. An Irishman has been torn from
his wife and family in Lisbon, because he was an expatriat[e], and
compelled to serve as a common soldier in the Portuguese Army,
by that monster of anti-patriotic inhumanity *Beresford,* the idol of
the belligerents. You will soon see a copy of his letter, and soon
hear of my or Sir F. Burdett's exertions in his favour. He *shall* be
free. This nation shall awaken. It is attended with circumstances
singularly characteristic of cowardice and tyranny. My blood boils
to madness to think of it. A poor boy, whom I found starving with
his mother in a hiding-place of unutterable filth and misery, whom
I rescued, and was about to teach to read, — has been snatched, on

a charge of false and villainous effrontery, to a magistrate of Hell, who gave him the alternative of the *tender* or of military servitude. He preferred neither, yet was compelled to be a soldier. This has come to my knowledge this morning. I am resolved to prosecute this business to the very jaws of Government, snatching (if possible) the poison from its fangs. A widow-woman with three infants were taken up by two constables. I remonstrated, I pleaded: I was everything that my powers could make me. The landlady was overcome. The constable relented: and, when I asked him if he had a heart, he said — "To be sure he had, as well as another man, but — that he was called out to business of this nature sometimes twenty times in a night." The woman's crime was stealing a penny loaf. She is, however, drunken, and nothing that I or anyone can do can save her from ultimate ruin and starvation. I am sick of this city, and long to be with you and peace. The rich *grind* the poor into abjectness, and then complain that they are abject. They goad them to famine, and hang them if they steal a loaf.[41]

Such experiences as these stimulated Shelley's determination, but in another sense they were profoundly depressing. As he realized the comparative futility of his efforts, he sickened more and more of Dublin's hopeless misery. In the letter quoted above he confessed that the Association moved slowly, that he found himself more hated as a freethinker than loved as a friend of freedom. Though he had "set some men's minds afloat," he doubted if his Association could be set up in Dublin, or even in Wales. He still thought that in Sussex, with Elizabeth's strong help (she was projecting a radical book-club), it would be feasible.

SHELLEY's disillusion was probably aided by his disappointment in John Philpot Curran. One of his first actions in Dublin had been to call at Curran's house, on the south side of St. Stephen's Green, with a letter of introduction from Godwin. This was on February 14, two days after the Shelleys reached Dublin. Curran was not at home. Shelley called again before the 24th. Again Curran was not at home, nor had he called on Shelley, though presumably Shelley had left Godwin's letter and his

221

address. By the 27th he had still not seen Curran and was beginning, rather naturally, to cultivate a dislike for him. On March 8, his stay in Ireland already half finished, Shelley wrote to Godwin: " I have not seen Mr. Curran. I have called repeatedly, left my address and my pamphlet. I *will* see him before I leave Dublin." At length Curran called, and Shelley dined twice at Curran's house before leaving Ireland. He was disappointed, as he had prepared himself to be. The brave and eloquent defender of the rebels of 1793 was by now Master of the Rolls — actually a member of the government, though still a liberal. Others than Shelley thought that the fire had largely gone out of him. Shelley recognized his great powers, but thought his conversation hardly elevating and his " incessant comicality " tiresome. In short, as he courteously informed Godwin, he could now admire Curran only as Godwin's friend.[42] A few months later Harriet expressed to Miss Nugent a much more forthright opinion than could be offered to Godwin: " I cannot bear Curran; what use is he to your country! " [43]

From another association, however, Shelley gained some encouragement that was not entirely disinterested. The probable author of the laudatory article on " Pierce Byshe Shelly " was John Lawless, a republican patriot, later the editor of the *Weekly Messenger.* Shelley made his acquaintance early in March and referred to him as " a valuable man " in a letter of March 10 to Elizabeth Hitchener. In the same letter Harriet also commented: " Has Percy mentioned to you a very amiable man of the name of Lawless? He is very much attached to the cause, yet dare not act. . . . We have this Morn'g been introduced to his wife." [44] Within four days a scheme was broached by which Shelley expected " soon " to " have the command of a Newspaper with Mr. Lawless." [45] He was also engaged in helping Lawless write a history of Ireland that was to expose the iniquity of English government. Though the book was eventually published by subscription,[46] Shelley's chapters were not finished when he left Ireland. He carried them to England on his return; they were read with delight and indignation by Elizabeth Hitchener, and were subsequently lost. Shelley's last extant letter from Ireland is to Thomas Medwin, Senior, en-

deavouring to raise a loan of £250 for completing the publication. At that time (March 20, 1812) two hundred and fifty
pages were already in print. It is not known whether or not
Shelley secured this sum, but it has been suspected that Lawless
did not suffer financially by his friendship with the young lib-
erator. Hogg hinted that Shelley's puff in the *Weekly Messenger* was "perhaps for a valuable consideration." [47] Frederick William Conway, who was editor of the *Weekly Messenger*
in 1812, stated thirty years later that he had known Shelley
slightly in 1812 and that " he was made the pecuniary dupe of
a person not less sincere in his politics, but in money matters
less honest." [48] Later, after Lawless had been imprisoned for
debt, Harriet flatly charged that he had swindled Shelley.[49]
Whether or not " Honest Jack " Lawless deserved his sobriquet
in financial matters, he was honest enough in his views of Shelley's mission. " Mr. L.," Shelley testified, " though he regards
my ultimate hopes as visionary, is willing to acquiesce in my
means." [50]

A more fortunate friendship had begun shortly after Shelley
circulated his *Address*. An elderly seamstress, whose heart beat
warm for Ireland, was offered one of the pamphlets by a vendor,
probably Shelley's servant, Daniel Hill or Healey, of whom she
inquired some particulars about the author. As soon as she
could she called at his address. Shelley was not at home, but
he returned the visit, and thus began a lasting friendship with
Miss Catherine Nugent. Harriet furnished Elizabeth Hitchener
with the following pleasing account of her:

I believe I have mentioned a new acquaintance of ours, a Mrs.
Nugent, who is sitting in the room now and talking to Percy about
Virtue. You see how little I stand upon ceremony. I have seen
her but twice before, and I find her a very agreeable, sensible
woman. She has felt most severely the miseries of her country, in
which she has been a very active member. She visited all the
Prisons in the time of the Rebellion, to exhort the people to have
courage and hope. She says it was a most dreadful task; but it was
her duty, and she would not shrink from the performance of it.
This excellent woman, with all her notions of Philanthropy and
Justice, is obliged to work for her subsistence — to work in a shop

which is a furrier's; there she is every day confined to her needle. Is it not a thousand pities that such a woman should be so dependent upon others? She has visited us this evening for about three hours, and is now returned home. The evening is the only time she can get out in the week; but Sunday is her own, and then we are to see her. She told Percy that her country was her only love, when he asked her if she was married. She called herself *Mrs.*, I suppose on account of her age, as she looks rather old for a *Miss*. She has never been out of her country, and has no wish to leave it.[51]

Miss Nugent lived at 101 Grafton Street, and it may have been on her account that the Shelleys changed their lodgings between March 8 and 10, from 7 Sackville Street to 17 Grafton Street. She dined with the Shelleys and spent the evening with the ladies when Shelley's affairs carried him away from home, perhaps more often than is indicated by Harriet's two surviving notes of invitation.[52] Harriet carried on an intermittent correspondence with her until January of 1815.[53] Miss Nugent obviously admired Shelley and regarded the young couple as " very much attached " to each other. Harriet she remembered as " an amiable and unaffected person — very young and very pleasing." [54]

Miss Nugent was a witness, though not a victim, of a rather important change in the Shelleys' mode of living. Both Shelley and Harriet had become Pythagoreans, and " Shelley spoke as a man believing in the metempsychosis." But though they did not eat animal food themselves, they tolerated it in others, so that Miss Nugent could be invited to dine on " a murdered chicken." A letter of Harriet's to Elizabeth Hitchener [55] shows that the new regimen had begun about March 1 and that after two weeks' trial they were both delighted with it.

Shelley's company, rather neglected for the first week or two in Ireland,[56] became more sought after when his *Address* was seen to promise to " spare no pains where expenditure may purchase you real benefit." This expression had immediately alarmed Godwin, who elicited the explanation, not furnished to the Irish, that the expenditure referred to pains rather than money. The article on " Pierce Byshe Shelly " had presented him as heir to one of the first fortunes in England and financial benefactor to Peter Finnerty. Thus on March 10 Shelley noted sadly: "I have daily had numbers of people calling on me: *none* will do. The spirit of Bigotry is high." [57] He found few republicans and few nascent deists.[58] The Catholic aristocracy, whom he disliked utterly,[59] evidently wished to have no dealings with him. Roger O'Connor, Hamilton Rowan, and John Philpot Curran, all veterans of the earlier fight for freedom and still associated with the cause, pointedly neglected to encourage his efforts, though Curran called upon him when it was too late and Rowan preserved his letter and pamphlet. Even John Lawless thought his scheme visionary. Everybody talked detestable cant about expediency. A warm, friendly letter from Mrs. Calvert, who had encouraged the Shelleys when they left Keswick, now doubted the possibility of their success.[60] Shelley recollected that his best friend among his relations, Captain Pilfold, had opposed the venture from the first.[61] Even the indomitable Miss Hitchener now urged him to leave Ireland.[62] He and Harriet had seen misery and poverty before, but never so much of it as now surrounded them. The overwhelming, ever present need for amelioration of every description intensified his growing sense of inability to make his own aid effective.

While these convictions were being slowly evolved from his own experience, Shelley continued to defend his conduct to Godwin, whose every letter sought to convince him of his errors. Nothing could exceed the deference with which Shelley treated Godwin's destructive criticism and humbly admitted faults in himself that Godwin had not explicitly charged him with. He acknowledged that he was young, over-confident, inexperienced, and egotistic; he acknowledged and praised Godwin's superior wisdom and earnestly hoped that he would continue his guidance. But he could not see that his course was either wrong or dangerous. He said nothing to Godwin about his personal efforts among the poor, his two publication schemes with Lawless, or the two propagandistic broadsides, *Declaration of Rights* and *The Devil's Walk*, that he had not yet circulated.[63] With a characteristic stubbornness so quiet and courteous that it almost appeared to be acquiescence he continued

225

on his course until convinced by events. He was then quite willing that Godwin should credit himself with the conversion. By March 18 he admitted to Godwin, not that his scheme for an " Association " was wrong, but that it was " ill-timed."

I have withdrawn from circulation the publications wherein I erred, and am preparing to quit Dublin. . . . But I submit; I shall address myself no more to the illiterate. I will look to events in which it be impossible that I can share, and make myself the cause of an effect which will take place ages after I have mouldered in the dust; I need not observe that this resolve requires stoicism. . . . I have seen and heard enough to make me doubt the omnipotence of truth in a society so constituted as that wherein we live.[64]

That very day Shelley addressed to Miss Hitchener a box containing the remaining copies of *An Address to the Irish People* and a number of copies of his broadside, *A Declaration of Rights,* which he had printed, but not circulated, in Ireland. *The Proposals for an Association* was not included; perhaps all the copies of it were in circulation, since Harriet says in the accompanying letter: " Percy has sent you all his Pamphlets," etc.[65] It is more likely, however, that he later brought them to England himself.

There is no evidence that the departure from Ireland was hurried, least of all by police interference. A plan to spend the summer in Wales had been formed before they came to Ireland and had been kept alive in the letters to Miss Hitchener. Both Shelley and Harriet in their letters of March 18 had stated that they intended leaving Ireland about April 7, unless, as Harriet added, a suspension of the Act of Habeas Corpus should force them to leave earlier. Habeas Corpus was not suspended, and the Shelleys left Dublin on Saturday, April 4.

The only official interference they experienced during their stay of seven weeks was from English, not Irish, officialdom. They had sent both letters and pamphlets under newspaper covers to Godwin, Mr. Westbrook, Elizabeth Hitchener, and possibly even to Mr. Timothy Shelley. Discovery by the postal authorities led to the recipient's being required to pay a high rate. Thus Godwin's copy of Shelley's *Address* cost the straight-

ened philosopher £1 1s. 8d.[66] The box directed to Elizabeth
Hitchener was opened for examination at Holyhead and its
contents were considered suspicious enough for an official report, to be mentioned more at length in the next chapter. A
copy of Harriet's letter was in due time sent from the Home
Secretary's office in London to the office of the Secretary for
Ireland, in Dublin. On April 8, four days after the Shelleys
left Dublin, Mr. Wellesley Pole returned it without comment.[67]

The journey from Dublin to Holyhead was a tedious voyage,
tacking against adverse winds, that consumed thirty-six hours
instead of the expected twelve. Having eaten nothing during
this time, they landed at two o'clock on a wet, stormy morning
and stumbled forward over a rough stone causeway to an inn
a mile away. Here, as Harriet informed Miss Nugent, they
" immediately began *upon meat*"; otherwise she feared Shelley and Elizabeth, " weakened by the vegetable system," might
have both descended to early graves.[68]

In his first letter to Elizabeth Hitchener after returning to
England Shelley thus dismissed the Irish sojourn: " We left
Dublin because I had done all that I could do; if its effects were
beneficial, they were not greatly so. I am dissatisfied with my
success, but not with the attempt." [69] The effect on Shelley,
however, was far greater than that on Ireland. He had opened
an active campaign of human amelioration toward which he
considered his whole life should be dedicated. He had learned,
or partly learned, that patriots may be almost as ignorant, intolerant, selfish, and grasping as tyrants; that between a clear
abstraction of justice in a benevolent, philosophic mind and its
effective application to conditions in a wretched community,
even the professed friends of justice interposed almost insuperable obstacles. His devotion to reform and his confidence in
its ultimate achievement remained unshaken, but the same surprising philosophic maturity that marked his *Address to the
Irish People* had taught him that genuine and lasting enlightenment was far more a matter of the distant future than he had
previously supposed. At close hand he had seen at its worst
all the effects of tyranny against which *Queen Mab* was soon
to be written.

Chapter IX

THE UNSETTLED REFORMER:
IN WALES AND DEVONSHIRE

DIFFICULTIES IN WALES; PLANS AND ACTIVITIES;
AT LYNMOUTH; NEW FRIENDS; DEVELOPING
INTELLECTUAL AND POETIC POWERS;
DISASTROUS PROPAGANDIZING

EVEN as they landed at Holyhead the Shelleys were under suspicion there as dangerous radicals. They did not know it and perhaps never heard of it afterwards. Already the box sent from Dublin to Elizabeth Hitchener on March 16 had been opened by the surveyor of customs at Holyhead to see if its contents were dutiable. He had found its contents — *An Address to the Irish People, A Declaration of Rights,* and Harriet's letter to Miss Hitchener [1] — all very alarming. He had called in the local postmaster, whose authority was involved on account of the letter. Each had reported the suspicious letter and the "inflammatory" Irish papers to higher authority. The inspector of customs went over the head of his local board and reported his "important" find directly to Lord Sidmouth, Secretary of State for the Home Department, in a letter dated March 30. On the next day the postmaster addressed a letter to the secretary of the General Post Office, London, describing the contents of the box and quoting the part of Harriet's letter which he considered most "dangerous to Government." The Home Department seems to have taken no action, beyond referring the matter to the Secretary for Ireland, in Dublin, who, as we have seen, returned the papers without comment. Very probably Miss Hitchener's box was forwarded to her shortly afterwards with no account of its adventures.[2]

Sir Francis Freeling, Secretary to the General Post Office, sent his communication to the Postmaster General, Lord Chichester, who answered from his seat of Stanmer Park, in Sussex, on April 5. He knew something of Shelley and Miss Hitchener already, he informed the Secretary. Shelley was "a most extraordinary man," had married "a Servant or some person of very low birth," and had addressed the Catholic Convention;[3] Miss Hitchener, though of low origin, he understood, was well spoken of. He undertook to have a watch placed upon her actions.[4]

Unconscious, therefore, of the petty-official excitement they had created, and restored after the hardships of the voyage by vicious but fortifying animal food, the party of three set out on Tuesday, April 7. For a whole week they went from inn to inn in North Wales, always hoping to find a place to settle and always disappointed.[5] Shelley had hoped to settle in Merionethshire, the home of young Fleetwood in Godwin's novel,[6] just as he had earlier settled in Poland Street because of the association of the name. Failing to find even temporary accommodation there, they came to rest on April 14 at Nantgwillt, Rhayader, Radnorshire, in South Wales.

Shelley was now on familiar ground, Rhayader being only five miles from Cwm Elan, where he had spent most of the previous summer. His cousin Thomas Grove helped him with the initial arrangements for leasing a house with two hundred acres, only a mile and a half from Cwm Elan. Living on the place while the negotiations for completing the lease were in progress, Shelley and Harriet fell deeply in love with it. It seemed ideal for the scheme they had been nourishing since the previous autumn at Keswick. Elizabeth (or Portia, as she was to be called, to avoid confusion with Harriet's sister, Eliza) was to live with them; her apartment was already picked out. Her father might accompany her and cultivate some of the arable land that went with the place. Some of the land could be sub-let, in order to reduce the rent. Godwin and his family might be induced to join them for the summer. The largest room was to be equipped, on credit, as a library, an extravagance which seemed justifiable to Shelley when he considered that this establishment was for the benefit of the human race.[7] Later Miss Nugent was also invited to visit Nantgwillt.[8]

The Irish campaign, in fact, had been thought of from the first as only one phase of a general campaign against oppression. Ireland had been chosen because it seemed to offer the best combination of time and place for such a beginning. During the sojourn in Dublin scarcely a letter to Elizabeth Hitchener or to Godwin had been without its pressing invitation to visit the Shelleys in Wales for the summer. Elizabeth was expected to resign her school and stay " for ever." Shelley and Harriet both argued vigorously against her objections to giving up her own means of livelihood and becoming a dependant. In Wales, Shelley argued, their combined forces could accomplish much. Meanwhile Shelley had gone on with his campaign in Ireland, and Elizabeth, apparently in a more cautious way, in Sussex. She even suggested that the whole movement might be transferred to Sussex, where she was then supposed to be distributing the contents of the box that had been detained at Holyhead. The departure from Ireland, therefore, was more a shift of base than a surrender.

IMMEDIATELY the house was found, Elizabeth and Godwin both received glowing descriptions of it and a renewal of the former pressing invitations. The house was large and comfortable and possessed an authentic ghost; the neighbourhood was quiet and well stocked with witches, fairies, and hobgoblins; the scenery was grand and inspiring. But there were two important difficulties to be overcome.

The first of these was to secure their possession of the house. The rent was £98 a year, but the furniture and stock must be bought outright for £500. On April 24 Shelley wrote to his father to ask for an advance of the purchase money, or at least the use of his name for security. The next day he wrote to ask

Mr. Thomas Medwin to go on his bond for six or seven hundred pounds in order to make the completion of the transaction possible. On May 5 Mr. Timothy Shelley declined, through Whitton, either to advance the money or to give security.[9] Mr. Medwin's answer is unknown, but may be inferred from the failure of the negotiations. Finally, during the first week in June, Mr. Hooper, the possessor of the house, became angry at Shelley's inability to complete the bargain, and the Shelleys left his house between June 3 and June 6 to stay with the Groves at Cwm Elan until they could find a new home.

The second difficulty arose over Elizabeth Hitchener. No sooner had her stubborn objections to giving up her financial independence been beaten down by the combined earnestness of Shelley and Harriet than local gossips in Sussex began to whisper. These whispers came back to Elizabeth through Shelley's aunt, Mrs. Pilfold. It was said that Elizabeth was to live with the Shelleys as Shelley's mistress; that she had refused to become Shelley's mistress before his marriage but had now consented under the impression that the relationship would be disguised by Harriet's presence. Shelley pronounced the talk absurd, and suspected that it had all originated in the fertile brain of Mrs. Pilfold, seeking to retain the services of a competent teacher for her children by manufacturing rumours and detailing them to Elizabeth as coming from general gossip.

I unfaithful to my Harriet! *You* a female Hogg! Common sense should laugh such an idea to scorn, if indignation would wait till it could be looked upon! — But, my friend, I do not believe there are any reports abroad in the country concerning us; Mrs. P[ilfold] of Cuckfield is the origin of them all. . . . She has made these reports, and then reported them to detain you. I see how it is. She has imposed on her husband. *His* nature is as open and unsuspecting as hers is artful and intriguing.[10]

To Elizabeth, however, such rumours were not thus lightly to be brushed aside. Captain Pilfold seemed to accept them and advised against her joining the Shelleys. Her father, who had objected to the plan from the first, now grew quite stubborn in opposing it. "Both he and the Captain," Shelley fumed,

" seem at least to share some of their qualities with the mule." [11] Elizabeth was so deeply distressed by the situation that she asked Shelley to reconsider the whole scheme. She actually became ill with worry.

Shelley professed to be indifferent to any effects the scandalous talk might have upon him personally, but the effect upon Elizabeth made him indignant. He undertook to settle with the Captain and Mr. Thomas Hitchener out of hand. To the former he wrote a letter " calculated to make his soul start back to see it," and received the answer that he disbelieved " the ' Mistress ' business " but that Shelley " certainly was very much attached " to Elizabeth, a charge which Shelley enthusiastically admitted, while denying anything like love in the Captain's understanding of the word.[12] To Mr. Hitchener he wrote a polite note, explaining his and Harriet's desire to have Elizabeth live with them and requesting him somewhat austerely not to " endeavour by parental command to change the decision of [a] free-born soul." [13] The reply was evidently unsatisfactory, for Shelley then accused him even more sternly of having agitated his daughter into actual physical illness by asserting a right he did not possess. " Neither the laws of Nature, nor of England," he announced, " have made children private property." [14]

Personal inconvenience, even Elizabeth's, might be borne with some philosophy, but a threat to Shelley's most cherished plans always provoked his fixed determination to succeed, and sometimes elicited hectic outbursts of passion. The passion in this case, so far as indicated by surviving evidence, vented itself on his aunt, " fertile in instant expedients, prepared to tell a thousand falsehoods," a mistress of " ever-ready calumny." [15] Neither she nor the " swinish multitude " who made calumny effective should be allowed to destroy a long-established plan for human betterment. " Are we," demanded Shelley, " or are we not to sacrifice the immediate energizing of those reforms which the thoughtless and the everyday beings cannot conceive of as practicable or useful? — to sacrifice these plans, ideas communicated, ameliorated, and passed thro' the fire of *unbiassed* discussions — those plans which your soul can-

not help bursting now to realize." [16] Such arguments, loyally
backed by Harriet and even Eliza, finally won Miss Hitchener's
somewhat nervous consent to go through with the original
plans.

By June 2 it was all settled that Elizabeth was to join them
in a fortnight. In case Nantgwillt had to be given up, she offered her own house for the party, but Shelley thought this too
near his relatives and the gossip-mongers for their plans to
operate unhampered.[17] Nantgwillt did have to be abandoned,
as we have seen, before Elizabeth could reach it, and the union
had to be postponed until a satisfactory home could be found.

The strain of the unsuccessful effort to secure Nantgwillt
and the somewhat more successful one to counteract the efforts
of the Sussex gossips perhaps contributed to the illness suffered
by both Harriet and Percy before the affair was settled. Harriet
was ill with an intermittent bilious fever from shortly before
April 24 to about May 7. Though Shelley realized that the
nature of the illness was slight, he became alarmed at Harriet's
weakness and lassitude. The nearest doctor was summoned
from forty miles away, and Harriet recovered. Within a week
after Harriet's partial recovery Shelley himself became ill with
what he described as an " inflammatory fever " that was serious
enough to prevent his writing to either Elizabeth or Godwin for
a fortnight.[18]

On June 2, as soon as he felt able to write, he addressed a
short letter to his grandfather, Sir Bysshe, in an attempt to ascertain the baronet's financial intentions when Shelley should
come of age about fourteen months later. The inquiry probably
had a bearing on the efforts to raise money for securing the
house and farm at Nantgwillt, or it may have been related to a
partly formed design of going to Italy for Shelley's health, until
he should have attained his majority.[19] Nothing came of either
the inquiry or the Italian project.

Naturally, the campaign for enlightenment languished during
these distresses. Elizabeth was instructed to distribute among
the Sussex farmers the *Declaration of Rights,* which Shelley
did not know had been detained by the authorities at Holyhead.[20] She was also inculcating her radical political and re-

ligious views among her students. Shelley wrote some verses
" On Robert Emmet's Tomb " and " To Ireland," both glorifying
unselfish patriotism.[21] In a letter to Elizabeth Hitchener quoted
in the previous chapter, Shelley had expressed his determination
to secure the freedom of an Irishman who had been impressed
into the Portuguese army.[22] This man, Redfern by name, had
written a pitiful letter to a Mr. Reynolds, apparently a friend of
Miss Nugent. Copies of this letter were printed and brought to
England for distribution. He now planned to distribute them at
once. Whether they were seen by anyone except Elizabeth
Hitchener remains uncertain.[23] It is quite probable that either
Shelley or Miss Hitchener attempted to insert the letter in the
Sussex newspapers. A clipping labelled in Mr. Timothy Shelley's hand: " Lewes paper, 1st June, 1812 " which was found
among the Whitton papers acknowledged receipt of " the address of P. B. S., Esq.," but declined to comment on " the accompanying letter " lest public comment would " direct, with
greater severity, the lash of tyranny and oppression against the
object of his commiseration, who appears to be completely
within their power." [24]

SHELLEY continued to read and to plan further reading. Godwin, suspecting a deficiency of historical ballast, recommended
a course of reading in the literature of the " chivalric age."
This resulted in Shelley's listing a few such books he had previously read, with an implied promise to read more.[25] He had
just finished reading Baron d'Holbach's *Le Système de la nature*,
which appeared to him " a work of uncommon powers." [26] Thus,
shortly before *Queen Mab* was to be written, we find Shelley
tending a little more to use poetry as a vehicle for his radical
feelings, and strengthening those feelings by an appreciative
reading of one of the books that was to influence *Queen Mab*.
Poetry as a means of conveying the deepest truth to a nation —
George Ensor's idea, which Shelley had commended to Miss
Hitchener a year before — was soon to be attempted in *Queen
Mab*. At the same time the poetry of intense personal emotion,
in which he was later to achieve pre-eminence, was also showing

definite development. In rather smooth tetrameter verses Shelley composed a poem of 154 lines entitled " The Retrospect: Cwm Elan, 1812."

This poem is rather important as Shelley's own comment on the significance of his first year of married life. Against a background of the natural beauty of the environment, he described his feelings when he visited the place in 1811 and as he felt a year later. During the first visit, Shelley said, he was desperately unhappy, but not entirely from unrequited love or unsympathetic relatives; rather it was a feeling that his whole world was out of sympathy with him. In the course of one year this had all been changed to happiness, for which he paid glowing tribute to Harriet:

> O thou! whose virtues latest known,
> First in this heart yet claim'st a throne;
> Whose downy sceptre still shall share
> The gentle sway with virtue there;
> Thou fair in form, and pure in mind,
> Whose ardent friendship rivets fast
> The flowery band our fates that bind,
> Which incorruptible shall last
> When duty's hard and cold control
> Had thawed around the burning soul,
> The gloomiest retrospects, that bind
> With crowns of thorn the bleeding mind;
> The prospects of most doubtful hue
> That rise on Fancy's shuddering view
> Are gilt by the reviving ray
> Which thou hast flung upon my day.[27]

ON MAY 26, shortly before the Shelleys left Nantgwillt for Cwm Elan, an event occurred that was somewhat exciting to the defenders of the freedom of the press. Daniel Isaac Eaton, a London bookseller, had been brought to trial on March 6, under the law of blasphemous libel, for publication of the Third Part of Thomas Paine's *The Age of Reason*. Liberals had published letters in his defence,[28] but he had been sentenced on May 15 to exposure in the pillory and eighteen months' imprisonment.

It was on May 26 that he was first placed in the pillory. The diarist Crabbe Robinson attended the scene and noted in his entry for the day that the usually rough mob was quite sympathetic with him and bought accounts of his trial on the spot. A more detailed and sympathetic relation appeared in the *Examiner* for May 31. This account probably reached Shelley just about the time he had to give up Nantgwillt. Shortly thereafter he expressed indignation at Eaton's treatment and asked Godwin if he would criticize an address he proposed to write and publish on the subject.[29] He was at work on it within the week,[30] but it was not completed and printed until July.

The Shelleys and Eliza Westbrook were to stay at Cwm Elan only until the arrival of their next quarter's allowance would enable them to find lodgings elsewhere. Though Harriet soon found Cwm Elan delightful, she was at first hardly enthusiastic over Shelley's cousin and his wife — " a very proud man," and a " very pleasant woman, tho' too formal to be agreeable." [31] Mrs. Thomas Grove, on her part, was greatly pleased with Harriet and was sorry to see her leave.[32] The little servant-girl who carried the post-bag at Cwm Elan had equally pleasant memories of Shelley, based probably on a fused recollection of both his visits. In 1878, sixty-six years after the events, she told a friend of Professor Dowden how "a very strange gentleman . . . and so nice-looking" had bought a little brass kettle for her at the sale at Nantgwillt House, how he had sailed a tiny wooden boat on the mountain streams, had used a five-pound note for a sail, and had once shipped an unwilling cat on his vessel as the crew.[33]

The Shelleys intended to take a house at Ilfracombe, in North Devonshire, sixty miles from Rhayader, and Elizabeth Hitchener was to join them there.[34] Within another week, however, Elizabeth's continuous accounts of her persecutions determined Shelley and Harriet to rush to her aid. The plan was therefore altered; they would go to Chepstow, where the Wye flows into the Severn. There they would take a cottage recommended by Godwin; they would install Eliza Westbrook there to wait for their return, and they would be with Elizabeth in Sussex within a week. How to get out of Sussex with Elizabeth, after having confounded the enemy, was something of a problem, since there was only enough money left to get to Hurstpierpoint; but one or the other would certainly be able to borrow the needed sum.[35]

This plan also had to be abandoned, since they found on their arrival at Chepstow that the cottage they were to occupy was not only too small, but unfinished. Shelley's letter to the owner, Mr. Eton, who boarded with Mrs. Godwin, was seen by Godwin and raised some doubts in his mind as to whether or not his unseen friend might be, after all, another votary of luxury.

Not being able to stop at Chepstow, the little party continued toward their original destination of Ilfracombe, abandoning perforce their intended expedition to raise the siege of Hurstpierpoint. When we next hear of them, through a letter of Harriet to Catherine Nugent, they have been settled for five or six days in Lynmouth, then as now regarded as one of the most beautiful villages in England.

We . . . came to this place in our way to Ilfracombe and the beauty of it has made us residents here for the summer months, when we think of going to London for the winter. It combines all the beauties of our late residence with the addition of a fine bold sea. We have taken the only cottage there was, which is most beautifully situated, commanding a fine view of the sea, with mountains at the side and behind us. Vegetation is more luxuriant here than in any part of England. We have roses and myrtles creeping up the sides of the house, which is thatched at the top. It is such a little place that it seems more like a fairy scene than anything in reality. All the houses are built in the cottage style, and I suppose there are not more than 30 in all. We send to Barnstaple for everything, and our letters come but twice a week. It is 18 miles from [here], therefore we ought to be able to [paper torn — ? manage] very well on a horse to get there. We have an immense precipice to descend into this valley, about 2 miles in length, which no carriage can come down.[36]

To this very attractive picture Shelley added several details in two letters to Godwin about a week later. Harriet, he said, thought its beauty even surpassed Nantgwillt. The climate was

so mild that roses bloomed there in winter. The picturesque
Valley of Stones, near by, was so impressive that Shelley never
tired of rhapsodizing about it later, and left scrawled on many
a fly-leaf and in letters and notebooks the crude little sketches
of crags and rocky spires to which the memory incited him.[37]
The house was small and very plainly furnished, but there was
at least a sufficient number of bedrooms and beds.[38]

It was perhaps just as well that their living-quarters were
modest and inexpensive. Godwin could no longer wonder if
they had rejected Chepstow cottage because of extravagant
views of living unbecoming to disciples of a democratic philosopher. Moreover, the Irish expedition and the expenses at
Nantgwillt had made serious inroads on their funds, and economy was for a while necessary. It was possible for Shelley to
borrow money on his expectations, but only at such an exorbitant rate that he declined to do so, as he had done once before,
when reduced to almost his last shilling in Keswick. He considered that he held his money and prospects in trust for the cause
to which he had devoted his future. " The involvement of my
patrimony would interfere with schemes on which it is my
fondest delight to speculate. I may truly therefore be classed
generically with those minors who pant for twenty one, though
I trust that the specific difference is very, very wide." [39]

Conditions now looked much brighter for the prosecution
of Shelley's schemes. Godwin and Elizabeth Hitchener were
both invited to join them. Godwin's invitation, this time, was
not urgently pressed, since Harriet felt some doubt as to whether
the simple accommodations were suitable for an elderly semi-
invalid. But if Godwin could not come they hoped at least
for a visit from Fanny Imlay, the daughter of Mary Wollstonecraft and Gilbert Imlay, whom Godwin had brought up as his
own daughter after the death of Mary Wollstonecraft. Elizabeth Hitchener was coming through London to Lynmouth and
could accompany her.[40]

Elizabeth reached London on July 14 on her way to Lynmouth, where she duly arrived shortly afterwards, fresh from
Skinner Street, having eaten supper and spent the night with
the Godwins. Her impression of Godwin was not altogether

LYNMOUTH

From an aquatint in the British Museum after the original by William Daniell, R.A., published c. 1818

complimentary. He saw very little of his own family, and then only at stated hours, she reported, and thought himself " such a very great man." Harriet was for the moment quite put out with Godwin, not merely from Elizabeth's account, but from his refusing to allow Fanny Imlay to visit the Shelleys " just because he had not seen our faces." [41] Godwin had said that he could never feel that he really knew people until he had seen them.

Godwin's belief that correspondence alone may be a delusive basis for friendship was soon to be miserably justified in the case of Harriet and Elizabeth, now called " Bessy " by the Shelleys. Of this, however, Harriet's first impressions give only the slightest hint:

Our friend, Miss Hitchener, is come to us. She is very busy writing for the good of mankind. She is very dark in complexion, with a great quantity of long black hair. She talks a great deal. If you like great talkers she will suit you. She is taller than me or my sister, and as thin as it is possible to be. . . . I know you would love her did you know her. Her age is 30. She looks like as if she was only 24 and her spirits are excellent. She laughs and talks and writes all day.

A week later, describing the indignation and depressed spirits which " Bessy " felt at the facts chronicled in Shelley's " Pieces of Irish History," Harriet remarked: " She possesses too much feeling for her own happiness." [42]

" Bessy's " presence was at first the great inspiration to Shelley that he had so constantly assured her it would be. There was walking, talking, arguing, and reading aloud such as the Shelleys had not experienced since the Edinburgh days with Hogg. Numerous plans for action were discussed. Since the Dublin printer, Stockdale, refused to complete printing the poems left in his hands unless he should receive part payment in advance, Shelley asked his friend John Lawless to get the manuscript back. He began to send out copies of his defence of Daniel Isaac Eaton, and opened relations with an English publisher, Thomas Hookham, of Old Bond Street, London, of whom he ordered a number of books. [43] He went ahead with the plan for publishing the Irish history (which Harriet referred to as " Pieces of Irish History ") by subscription.[44] He wrote two poems, " The Voyage," a three-hundred-line fragment, and " A Retrospect of Times of Old." Much more important, he was definitely launched on the writing of *Queen Mab*. A letter of August 18 to Thomas Hookham, publisher, shows that he had by no means given up the fight for Ireland, and was also active in other directions.

Since this letter introduces two new characters into the circle of Shelley's acquaintance, it may well be quoted entire:

> *Lynmouth Barnstaple*
> *August* 18, 1810 [*sic*]

Dear Sir

Your parcel arrived last night for which I am much obliged. Before I advert to any other topic I will explain the contents of mine in which this is enclosed. In the first place I send you 50 copies of the " Letter " [to Lord Ellenborough]. I send you a copy of a work which I have procured from America, and which I am exceedingly anxious should be published. It developes, as you will perceive by the most superficial reading, the actual state of republicanized Ireland, and appears to me above all things calculated to remove the prejudices which have too long been cherished of that oppressed country, to strike the oppressors with dismay.[45] I enclose also two pamphlets which I printed and distributed whilst in Ireland some months ago (no bookseller daring to publish them). They were on that account attended with only partial success, and I request your opinion as to the probable result of publishing them with the annexed " suggestions " in one pamphlet, with an explanatory preface, in *London*. They would find their way to Dublin. You confer on me an obligation, and involve a high compliment by your advice. I shall if possible prepare a vol. of essays, moral and *religious* by November; but, all my MSS. now being in Dublin, and from peculiar circumstances not immediately obtainable, I do not know whether I can. I enclose also by way of specimen all that I have written of a little poem [*Queen Mab*] begun since my arrival in England. I conceive I have matter enough for 6 more cantos. You will perceive that I have not attempted to temper my constitutional enthusiasm in that Poem. Indeed, a Poem is safe: the iron-souled Attorney general would scarcely dare to attack

" genus irritabile vatum."

The Past, the Present, and the Future are the grand and comprehensive topics of this Poem. I have not yet half exhausted the second of them.

I shall take the liberty of retaining the two poems which you have sent me — Mr. Peacock's — and only regret that my powers are so circumscribed as to prevent me from becoming extensively useful to *your friend.* The poems abound with a genius, an information, the power and extent of which I admire, in proportion as I lament the object of their application. Mr. Peacock conceives that commerce is prosperity; that the glory of the British Flag, is the happiness of the British people; that George III. so far from having been a warrior and a Tyrant, has been a Patriot. To me it appears otherwise; and I have rigidly accustomed myself, not to be seduced by the loveliest eloquence or the sweetest strains to regard with intellectual toleration [that] which ought not to be tolerated by those who love Liberty, Truth, and Virtue. I mean not to say that Mr. Peacock does not love them; but I mean to say that he regards those means [as] instrumental to their progress, which I regard [as] instrumental to their destruction. See *Genius of the Thames,* p. 24, 26, 28, 76, 98. At the same time I am free to say that the Poem appears to be far beyond mediocrity in genius and versification, and the conclusion of " Palmyra " the finest piece of poetry I ever read. I have not had time to read the Philosophy of Melancholy, and of course am only half acquainted with that genius and those powers whose application I should consider myself rash and impertinent in critisizing, did I not conceive that frankness and justice demand it.

I should esteem it as a favor if you would present the enclosed letter to the Chevalier Lawrence. I have read his Empire of the Nairs, nay, have it. Perfectly and decidedly do I subscribe to the truth of the principles which it is designed to establish.

I hope you will excuse, nay, and doubt not but you will, the frankness I have used. Characters of any liberality are so wondrous rare that the sooner they know each other, and the fuller and more complete that knowledge is, the better.

Dear Sir,

Permit me to remain

Yours very truly

PERCY B. SHELLEY

I am about translating an old " French " work, professedly by a *M. Mirabaud* — not the famous one "La Systême de la Nature." Do you know any thing of it? [46]

241

This letter contains Shelley's first mention of Thomas Love Peacock, who was to play such an important part in his subsequent life. According to Peacock's grand-daughter, Edith Nicolls, the two had met while the Shelleys were at Nantgwillt, during April and May,[47] but Shelley here seems to be writing about a man he has not met, and the first meeting is much more likely to have occurred in London in early November. Until Shelley took up his residence at Bracknell, however, in July of the next year, the future friends were only casually acquainted and saw each other not more than three or four times.[48]

The Chevalier Lawrence, to whom Shelley enclosed a letter, was another of Hookham's authors. He had published in 1811, eleven years after it had appeared in German, a Utopian romance entitled *The Empire of the Nairs; or, The Rights of Woman.* Shelley had read it during the spring. He now addressed a cordial letter to the author, introducing himself and proclaiming his enthusiastic adherence to its doctrines. It had convinced him, he said, that he had hitherto been ignorant of the greatest argument against matrimony, " viz., prostitution both *legal* and *illegal.*" [49] *Queen Mab* and *Laon and Cythna* were demonstrably influenced by the reading of *The Empire of the Nairs.*[50]

SHELLEY now felt himself more definitely settled for a while than he had been for some months previously. He was temporarily without illness or worry and was happy in the love of Harriet. The long-desired presence of Elizabeth Hitchener was a strong and as yet unclouded source of stimulation. The epistolary discussions with Elizabeth Hitchener that had given place to matters of more immediate moment since the trip to Ireland were turned into oral discourse by " Bessy's " presence; such discussions now appeared in his correspondence with Godwin. Having read Baron d'Holbach's *Le Système de la nature* with admiration for the materialistic philosophy, but with some suspicion that it was tainted with selfishness and sensuality, he argued that there was no more necessary connection between materialism and disinterestedness than be-

tween a round cricket ball and a square box. He could see
nothing except word-juggling in Berkeley's immaterialism. He
even challenged Godwin's infallibility by doubting, courteously
but firmly, the high value placed upon classical studies in one
of Godwin's *Enquirer* essays. Shelley's arguments were similar
to those advanced by George Ensor. One telling argument,
however, that Ensor would hardly have pressed placed Godwin in a rather ridiculous position for further argument;
namely, " I do not perceive how one of the truths of *Political
Justice* rest[s] on the excellence of ancient literature." [51]

The books previously listed as ordered from Hookham on
July 29 were not the first Shelley had ordered from him, nor were
they by any means the last. His letters to Hookham thereafter are full of lists of books to be sent and statements that
packages have arrived or failed to arrive. During the month
of December Shelley's extant letters show orders for nearly
seventy different works, some consisting of several volumes.
Hookham and Clio Rickman, another London bookseller, were
his providers.[52] Hogg, who was best acquainted with Shelley's
early habits with books, has left the following account:

A large share of his scanty income, amounting in the whole to
a considerable sum during some fifteen years that he was constantly
a purchaser, was always expended upon books; so that, wherever he
happened to be, he was commonly in possession of a tolerable library, comprising several choice works. I used to think him extremely lucky in buying books, for he frequently picked up a rare
and valuable author at a very moderate price; or, to do him justice,
I should perhaps rather say, that he was active, observant, and intelligent in such purchases, as he was in all other matters.
When he changed his residence, and he often changed it — too
often, indeed — he hastily chose some new domicile, where he resolved to remain " for ever "; thither his books were at once dispatched, but with so wild a precipitance, and such headlong hurry,
that ancients and moderns alike missed their way. And when he,
on the spur of the moment, quitted his eternal abode, as he was
wont, the books were left behind to follow him to his lately elected
and perpetual home: but they sometimes remained unheeded.
He had a good library expecting his return in a cottage at Kil-

larney; and at I know not how many other places in the British Isles, and in other states of Europe. I have many times thought, what an excellent collection of valuable books the poor poet would have owned, if all his different libraries, scattered about in distant localities, had been brought together under one roof and in one large room.

To lend Bysshe a book was to bid it a long farewell, to take leave of it for ever; and, indeed, the pain of parting was often spared, for he bore away silently, reading it as he went, any work that caught his attention.[53]

Here we may well pause for a glance at the nature and quality of what Shelley was writing at this time. The " Pieces of Irish History," as Harriet called them, have been lost, and can be judged only by their powerful effect on the over-sensitive " Bessy." The two poems previously mentioned, " The Voyage " and " A Retrospect of Times of Old " are among the still un-published manuscripts in the Esdaile family, but they have been described by Professor Dowden.[54] The former, he says, deals with the characters, hopes, and aspirations of a returning company of voyagers and breaks off with the seizure of a re-turning sailor by the press-gang. The latter has " much in com-mon with those earlier pages of *Queen Mab,* which picture the fall of empires, and celebrates the oblivion that has overtaken the old rulers of men and lords of the earth. . . . It possesses a visionary largeness which corresponds with the mood into which the sea and the mountain solitudes had lifted Shelley's spirit." The former was Shelley's first effort in the mixture of blank verse and irregular unrhymed verse in which *Queen Mab* is written, while the latter is quite similar to *Queen Mab* in content.

Two other poems among the Esdaile manuscripts testify to the strength of Shelley's love for Harriet.[55] One is four lines of a birthday sonnet, presented to Harriet presumably on Au-gust 1, asserting that Harriet's love will always be as ardent and her thoughts always as pure as at present. The other is a seventy-two-line tribute in blank verse that very definitely suggests Wordsworth's tribute to his sister in " Tintern Abbey." From the point of view of Shelley's development as a poet these

verses afford some hints of the power of expressing passionate
personal devotion that was to become one of his distinctions.
They also show how deep and genuine Shelley's love for Harriet had become:

> . . . O thou most dear,
> 'Tis an assurance that this Earth is Heaven,
> And Heaven the flower of that untainted seed
> Which springeth here beneath such love as ours.
> Harriet! let death all mortal ties dissolve,
> But ours shall not be mortal! The cold hand
> Of Time may chill the love of earthly minds
> Half frozen now; the frigid intercourse
> Of common souls, lives but a summer's day;
> It dies, where it arose, upon the earth.
> But ours! oh, 'tis the stretch of fancy's hope
> To portray its continuance as now,
> Warm, tranquil, spirit-healing. . . .

Here, certainly, was no prophecy of what was to happen within
a few short years.

THE protest against the punishment of Daniel Isaac Eaton was
now finished, in the form of a twenty-three-page open letter
to Lord Ellenborough, who presided at Eaton's trial. Presumably he is addressed because he constantly interrupted and
hampered Eaton's speech in his own defence and practically
instructed the jury to bring in a verdict of guilty.[56] Shelley
wasted little time, however, in condemning the judge:

It is true, my Lord, laws exist which suffice to screen you from the
animadversion of any constituted power, in consequence of the
unmerited sentence which you have passed upon Mr. Eaton; but
there are no laws which screen you from the reproof of a nation's
disgust, none which ward off the just judgement of posterity, if that
posterity will deign to recollect you.

He then proceeds to the two larger points involved, the injustice
of punishing any man for his beliefs, and the reasonableness
of the views for which Eaton was punished.

On the first of these points Shelley used arguments already mostly familiar to readers of his letters:

That which is false will ultimately be controverted by its own falsehood. That which is true needs but publicity to be acknowledged. It is ever a proof that the falsehood of a proposition is felt by those who use power and coercion, not reasoning and persuasion, to procure its admission. . . . Do you think to convert Mr. Eaton to your religion by embittering his existence? You might force him by torture to profess your tenets, but he could not believe them, except you should make them credible, which perhaps exceeds your power. . . . Belief and disbelief are utterly distinct from and unconnected with volition. . . . Volition is essential to merit or demerit. . . . No man is accountable for his belief, because no man is capable of directing it. Mr. Eaton is therefore totally blameless . . . the supposition that any revelation from an unknown power, avails to palliate a persecution so senseless, unprovoked, and indefensible, is at once to destroy the barrier which reason places between vice and virtue, and leave to unprincipled fanaticism a plea, whereby it may excuse every act of frenzy, which its own wild passions, and the inspirations of the Deity, have engendered.

Shelley's attack upon Christianity was no less an important object with him because the logic of the particular situation required him to make it ancillary to the defence of Eaton's rights as a citizen. He avowed boldly that Eaton's opinions seemed to him "more true and good than those of his accuser." The very existence of numerous books and articles demonstrating the truth of Christianity, he argued, was a proof that its truth was subject to question. If Christianity were really true, such questioning could only confirm it, but if Christianity after all should be false, such men as Eaton would deserve thanks for destroying error. Shelley's own belief that Christianity was a purely historical development, perverted by its professors, is quite clear from his description of it:

Christianity is now the established religion; he who attempts to disprove it must behold murderers and traitors take precedence of him in public opinion, tho', if his genius be equal to his courage, and assisted by a peculiar coalition of circumstances, future ages may exalt him to a divinity, and persecute others in his name, as he was persecuted in the name of his predecessor in the homage of the world.

The same means that have supported every other popular belief have supported Christianity. War, imprisonment, murder, and false-hood; deeds of unexampled and incomparable atrocity have made it what it is. We derive from our ancestors a belief thus fostered and supported. — We quarrel, persecute, and hate for its maintenance. — Does not analogy favour the opinion, that as like other systems it has arisen and augmented, so like them it will decay and perish; that as violence and falsehood, not reasoning and persuasion, have procured its admission among mankind; so, when enthusiasm has subsided, and time, that infallible controverter of false opinions, has involved its pretended evidences in the darkness of antiquity, it will become obsolete, and that men will then laugh as heartily at grace, faith, redemption, and original sin, as they now do at the metamorphoses of Jupiter, the miracles of Romish Saints, the efficacy of witchcraft, and the appearance of departed spirits?

Had the christian religion commenced and continued by the mere force of reasoning and persuasion, by its self-evident excellence and fitness, the preceding analogy would be inadmissible.[57]

The author was still under twenty years of age, but the argument and the style are anything but juvenile. The ideas are clearly conceived and are more firmly and sharply expressed than those of the Irish pamphlets. No reader not knowing the author would suppose him to be a youth whose practical judg-ment was as yet so far in arrears of his more abstract power of thought that he was seriously planning a seminary of world enlightenment based mainly on the assistance of a girl just escaped from boarding-school and a radical-minded, intense spinster who had given up a school in the country in order to become a partner. Occasionally the letter affords a glimpse of the latent moral fervour that was to contribute to the nobility of such later prose as the "Defence of Poetry." Like many products of eighteenth-century rationalism, it is a very effective appeal to reason, in a matter in which reason has always been subservient to emotion.

Had the *Letter to Lord Ellenborough* been published, it might very well have brought a government prosecution upon the author. Shelley was quite aware of this and took considerable precautions. The "Letter" was printed under his personal supervision, without the name of either author or printer, at the shop of a Mr. Syle, printer and bookseller of Barnstaple. A thousand copies were ordered. On July 29 Shelley sent twenty-five advance copies to Hookham,[58] and on August 4 he had sent copies to Catherine Nugent, Lord Stanhope, and Sir Francis Burdett.[59] On August 18, as we have seen, he sent Hookham fifty additional copies. Miss Nugent was warned that the pamphlet must not be published, and Hookham was given permission to show them only to "any friends who *are not informers.*" On the day following Shelley's second shipment to Hookham the arrest of Shelley's servant, shortly to be described, so frightened Mr. Syle that he destroyed all of his remaining copies and sought vainly to recover the copies previously released.[60] So complete was the destruction that only one copy of the pamphlet has since been discovered.[61]

EVER since Shelley had left Ireland, as he later told Medwin, he had been conscious of police surveillance.[62] If this was at first only fancy, it soon came to have a basis in fact. The villagers of Lynmouth observed strange deeds — deeds that in perilous times, shortly after the assassination of the Prime Minister, required patriotic attention. The slender, enthusiastic, shrill-voiced young man who had moved into the only vacant house in the village and who employed an Irish manservant and a foreign-looking "female servant" (probably Miss Hitchener) had been seen to mail many packages and as many as sixteen letters a day. Many of his packages and letters were directed to that well-known radical and enemy of the assassinated Perceval, Sir Francis Burdett. He was known to have with him large chests so heavy that three men could scarcely lift them. These were thought, correctly, to contain papers, since they were probably the boxes of publications Shelley had brought from Ireland. He had been seen to row out from shore a little distance and throw overboard a number of dark-green bottles, also to launch from the rocks curiously fitted little boxes, wrapped in bladder, rosined, waxed, and equipped with masts, sails, and lead ballast. When recovered and opened, the boxes proved to contain copies of *A Declaration of Rights*, and the bottles when broken gave up copies of a ballad entitled *The Devil's Walk*.[63] How should suspicious and matter-of-fact countrymen guess that the young stranger was peculiarly given to launching small boats, generally of paper, and would be for the rest of his life, that such actions gave him a mysterious symbolical pleasure, and that he was writing sonnets at home to express the pleasure and hope he derived from such symbolical launchings? [64]

These suspicions had existed at Lynmouth since the Shelleys arrived, but one would judge that their object was unaware of them. If his landlady, Mrs. Hooper, heard of them, her conduct shortly afterwards suggests that she was unimpressed. She must have known that her niece, whom she had adopted as a daughter, was helping Shelley cut the printer's name off the title pages of some of his radical literature.[65]

Having symbolically enlisted Ocean and Air in the cause of freedom, Shelley unluckily sought to add Earth, the third member of his "beloved brotherhood," through the agency of his blundering Irish servant, hitherto a rather useless dependant. Daniel was given a supply of the *Declaration of Rights* and *The Devil's Walk* and sent into Barnstaple with instructions to distribute them and post them on the sides of buildings. Thus the persistent reformer was finally putting into practice the technique announced in Keswick, before he went to Ireland, of printing popular propaganda on cheap paper and posting it up, as Thomas Paine had done. Dan, however, had been insufficiently warned of the danger or he had been too clumsy to avoid detection; he soon found himself in the local jail. He was charged, not with sedition, but with an offence that was too self-evident to be denied: circulating printed matter without the printer's name. He was fined twenty pounds on each of ten counts and was sent to jail for six months in default of his fine.

Under questioning, Dan clung loyally to the story with which he had probably been furnished. He had been accosted on his way to Barnstaple by a gentleman in black, totally unknown to him, who had given him five shillings to distribute some papers in the village. Having learned something of Shelley's recent actions in Lynmouth, the authorities were not much impressed with this story. When they heard Dan repeat his story to Shelley, who should have seemed annoyed with him, they were more impressed by Shelley's strange omission to upbraid him for scattering sedition. Within a day they also knew that Dan's papers were the same as those launched by Shelley at Lynmouth. They refused, therefore, to yield to Shelley's arguments for Dan's release, but they allowed him to purchase certain liberties for his servant within the prison, at the cost of fifteen shillings weekly.

No doubt the local authorities preferred to take no action against the son of a member of Parliament, unless they were assured of strong backing. Accordingly the town clerk was instructed to write a letter placing all the circumstances before Lord Sidmouth, Secretary of State for the Home Department. This letter and the ensuing official correspondence lay forgotten in the Record's Office Depot, Clifford's Inn, until 1870, when it was discovered by Mr. W. M. Rossetti.[66]

On August 22, two days after the town clerk wrote his first letter to Lord Sidmouth, the local postmaster sent a shorter account to Sir Francis Freeling, Secretary of the Post Office, with a copy of the *Declaration of Rights*. Sir Francis referred the letter to Lord Chichester, reminding him that the handbill was the same as that intercepted at Holyhead in the spring. Both gentlemen agreed to refer the matter to the Home Office. Henry Drake, the town clerk at Barnstaple, having investigated Shelley's career at Lynmouth, reported further details in a letter dated September 9. The accumulated data were referred to the departmental legal adviser, who, fortunately for Shelley, advised that no legal action should be taken against Shelley, but that his behaviour should be watched.

This action, which had been suggested by Lord Sidmouth on receipt of the first letter, was again recommended to the all too willing authorities of Barnstaple — but Shelley had meanwhile left the neighbourhood. In these proceedings there is no mention of the " Letter to Lord Ellenborough " said by Dowden to

have been mailed by Shelley to Lord Sidmouth shortly before
this incident. If Lord Sidmouth ever received and read it he
could not have failed to connect it with the more recent excitement from the same little town. What would have been the
recommendation of the legal advisers had this far more important document been added to the papers referred to them?

The arrest of Daniel Hill destroyed Shelley's plans for a
quiet, economical seminary of radicalism at Lynmouth as completely as his failure to secure Nantgwillt had uprooted his
earlier plan. Though he was responsible for Dan's imprisonment, he lacked the two hundred pounds necessary for his
release and could only mitigate his discomforts with a weekly
stipend. A new move was necessary, and there was no more
money than there had been when the Lynmouth cottage had
been taken, partly from motives of economy. The discomforts
of being a minor of limited funds and great expectations were
bad enough (though his minority may have had some weight
in averting a prosecution by agents of the Home Office), but
when the expectations included danger of arrest it was obviously necessary to make a fresh start elsewhere.

The little rose- and myrtle-bowered cottage saw sudden
activity and a quick need for funds. A five-pound note recently
received by mail in two equal sections, to prevent theft, could
not be changed in the neighbourhood. The friendly Mrs.
Hooper loaned them twenty-five shillings and consented to
wait for her rent. She even went forth and borrowed three
pounds for them from one of her neighbours, and Shelley himself seems to have borrowed from another.

Thus, when the town clerk of Barnstaple went to Lynmouth
a day or two before September 8, he found that Shelley and
his household had lately departed for Ilfracombe, evacuating
Lynmouth at about the same time the Russians evacuated Moscow. From Ilfracombe, when the sleuth arrived, they had already departed for Swansea. Here one of Shelley's old Eton
acquaintances was surprised by a sudden call from Shelley,
" in a state of great distress and difficulty." " We had an opportunity of rendering him a service," wrote Captain Gronow,
" but we could never ascertain what had brought him to Wales,

though we had reason to suppose it was some mysterious *affaire du cœur.*" [67] If the service was a moderate loan, Shelley's ability to make prompt restitution to his landlady is the more easily explained.

Leaving Lynmouth about August 29, the Shelleys missed by three weeks a visit from William Godwin. Godwin had decided to spend his annual vacation visiting and travelling in the region of Devonshire and South Wales and had written on the 13th of September to apprise the Shelleys of his coming. On the afternoon of the 18th he reached Lynmouth to find that the Shelleys had been gone for three weeks and had of course failed to receive his advance notice. Their landlady, "a good creature," who "quite loved the Shelleys," informed him that after a stay of nine weeks and three days they had left in a great hurry, with the financial assistance already described, and that they had already returned the borrowed money.[68] Though they still owed her thirty pounds for lodgings, she was obviously not at all uneasy.[69] If Mrs. Hooper knew of the recent suspicions and inquiries concerning Shelley, she gave Godwin no inkling.

Godwin was tired, half-ill, and considerably disappointed. Since he is commonly represented as being purely and uniformly selfish in his attitude toward his young disciple, it should be set down here that the letter he wrote to his wife showed no irritation, but a genuine concern for his protégés. He solaced himself with Mrs. Hooper's news that the Shelleys would be in London in two weeks and with a stroll through the Valley of Stones, whose picturesque beauty Shelley must have praised to him as he did later to Hogg.

Chapter X

THE UNSETTLED REFORMER:

IN WALES, LONDON, AND IRELAND

THE TREMADOC EMBANKMENT; NEW ASSOCIATIONS
IN LONDON; EXIT MISS HITCHENER; DOMESTIC
HAPPINESS AND INTELLECTUAL PROGRESS IN WALES;
FINANCIAL DIFFICULTIES;
MYSTERIOUS ASSAULT, AND FLIGHT TO IRELAND

THOUGH the Shelleys had thought it wise to leave Lynmouth
without delay, they were by no means so frightened as to
abandon their plans. They had not intended to stay in Devonshire through the winter, but had intended at one time to spend
the winter in London and at another, probably earlier, to go
to the Vale of Llangollen.

For five weeks after leaving Lynmouth the Shelleys with the
two Elizabeths were in Wales. The town clerk of Barnstaple
could trace them no farther than Swansea, at the southern extremity of South Wales, but it is clear from references in letters
written a little later that a large part of this period was spent
in the village of Tremadoc, in North Wales, about a hundred
miles from Swansea. How and when they got there is a matter
for conjecture. On leaving Lynmouth, however, Shelley had
written a sonnet hailing the

Mountain piles
That load in grandeur Cambria's emerald vales,

253

so that it is reasonable to assume that the party continued through Swansea toward Llangollen in North Wales, about forty-five miles west of Tremadoc. Possibly they turned aside before they reached Llangollen or else arrived to find that no suitable quarters were available; at any rate Harriet was disappointed in her hope of taking up residence there.[1]

Once in the neighbourhood of Tremadoc, Shelley could never have resisted being drawn to see it. The whole region was full of the praises of William Alexander Madocks, M.P., who had demonstrated in the village named for him that modern science, united with intelligence and philanthropy, could overcome the brute forces of nature. Even the guide-books sang the praises of the man who could create a model village where previously had been three feet of water at low tide, and rich fields of grain where three years before were only treacherous sterile sands.

Tremadoc was a village of from eighty to a hundred houses, built in the form of an oblong, and containing a handsome market-house, with assembly-rooms above, a bank, " a handsome new church, a comfortable inn, and a great number of good shops." [2] Having built this town and reclaimed some two thousand acres from the sea, Mr. Madocks proceeded to the still more difficult undertaking of completing a dike across the estuary of Traeth Mawr to shut out the sea completely. Parliament had given him in 1807 a grant of the sandy marshes he was to recover. The embankment was to be a mile long, a hundred feet wide at the base and thirty feet wide on top, and was to carry a safe road between the counties of Carnarvon and Merioneth.[3]

In 1812 the undertaking was complete, with the exception of a gap of about a hundred yards in the centre, through which the tide rushed with concentrated strength. At ebb tide " the waters within, retained by the embankment, poured through its two points an impetuous cataract, curling and boiling in innumerable eddies, and making a tumultuous melody. . . ." [4] As long as the embankment remained uncompleted the work already accomplished would be jeopardized by storms and high tides. Six months before the Shelleys' arrival, this had

TREMADOC EMBANKMENT IN 1810

Engraved by M. Dubourg from a drawing by H. W. Billington

actually happened. The *Gentleman's Magazine* for April 1812 carried the following news note dated February 15:

Mr. Madock's new embankment, at *Tre Madoc,* was greatly injured by a high wind and tide. In the second week after the accident, 400 men, with 200 horses, and 67 carts, were employed in repairing the breach.

The gap was still unclosed when the Shelleys came to Tremadoc, and in fact for some years afterwards.[5] The unaided resources of Mr. Madocks were insufficient to complete the undertaking and aid was being sought in the surrounding countryside. It was a perfect opening for a recently uprooted philanthropist who believed in a future made glorious by science and who could undertake the rescue of a small community as readily as that of a persecuted schoolgirl or an oppressed nation.

Mr. Madocks was not then in the neighbourhood, but Shelley immediately made the acquaintance of Mrs. Madocks and the local superintendent, Mr. John Williams. He offered to rent Mr. Madocks's house, Tremadoc, for one year, furnished. This brought about an investigation of Shelley by Mr. Madocks's cautious and sceptical London agent, S. Girdlestone. After an interview with Shelley's father-in-law, who declined to accept financial responsibility, Mr. Girdlestone concluded that Shelley would be an undesirable tenant and declined to rent to him except on terms which the young man could not meet.[6] Shelley subscribed a hundred pounds to the embankment fund,[7] and threw himself with enthusiasm into the task of inducing others to give. He seems to have suffered some illness during September, for after he had been a month in London he wrote to Mr. Williams: " I am much better than when you saw me last. If I can find time today I shall write to the Dr." [8] The doctor was probably William Roberts, a surgeon of Carnarvon, whose second attempt to collect his fee, after thirty-two years, brought to light the previously unknown fact that Shelley was arrested for debt while living in Tremadoc.[9]

The arrest occurred at Carnarvon, twenty miles from Tremadoc, near the end of September 1812. It was for a debt of sixty or seventy pounds, at the suit of some person who must remain unknown, since the Carnarvon County Records contain no trace of the incident. This is undoubtedly the affair referred to in the concluding sentence of Shelley's first letter to John Williams (November 7) after his return to London: "Mr. Bedwell will settle the £70 affair." Mr. Bedwell, in fact, had already begun settling the matter. On November 5 he wrote to Mr. John Evans, a Carnarvon solicitor:

My principal reason for troubling you with the present is in relation to an action against Mr. Percy B. Shelley who was arrested in your town — some month or two since for I believe Sixty pounds or thereabout — Mr. John Williams of Tre Madoc and Mr. [William] Roberts — Surgeon were I understand Bail — and I think Mr. Rumsey Williams was concerned for the Plaintiff — Mr. Shelley is just returned here from Sussex and altho' under Age which might be a Bar to these proceedings — he is not desirous to avail thereof — I have therefore to request you will see Mr. Williams and obtain particulars of Debt and Cash and first seeing same as proper get this business settled without further expense for which you will value upon me at the shortest date you please to include all Charges (the amount of which I cannot know) and adding your own thereto for the adjustment advise the Amount for my government in Cause.
I am Dear Sir
Your very obed. Serv.
JOHN BEDWELL.[10]

On September 28, within a few days of his arrest, Shelley's efforts in support of the embankment reached a climax. On that day a number of local gentry met in Beaumaris, at the home of Lord Bulkeley, Lord Lieutenant of Wales and Keeper of the Rolls. His Lordship himself was present and proposed the health of Mr. Madocks and of John Williams, "whose perseverance and fortitude had saved from ruin a great national work and whose integrity had borne him out among the incessant trials and fatigues of his duty." John Williams then rose and testified that it was through Shelley's providential intervention that he had been able to " employ so many men as, in the event of his meeting with public encouragement, would fortify the Embankment against any apprehended danger." He then introduced Shelley, who made a modest speech.

In the partly quoted, partly paraphrased account given three days later in the Bangor *North Wales Gazette,* Shelley said that " he was proud that Mr. Williams permitted him to place himself on an equality with him; inasmuch as one yet a novice in the great drama of life, whose integrity was untried, whose strength was unascertained, must consider himself honoured when admitted on an equal footing with one who has struggled for twelve years with incessant and unparalleled difficulties, in honesty, faithfulness and fortitude." Continuing, he praised the patriotism of Mr. Madocks, whom he " had never seen," and spoke briefly on the nobility of such a great work of benevolence as the embankment. " How can any one look on that work," he concluded, " and hesitate to join me, when I here publicly pledge myself to spend the last shilling of my fortune, and devote the last breath of my life to this great, this glorious cause." Sir Robert Williams then rose, thanked Shelley for his " honourable and liberal exertions," and proposed his health.

There is some evidence to indicate that Shelley's impulsive promise was more substantial than it has seemed in the light of later events. It must refer to something in addition to his subscription of one hundred pounds, from the fact that John Williams had evidently realized upon that sum or its promise. Williams was in constant communication with Mr. Madocks in London and Boston, and Mr. Madocks must have heard of the hundred pounds some time previously. Shelley's proposals involved realizing enough money on his expectations of inheritance to be of such material assistance in completing the embankment that Mr. Madocks might then easily take the risk of letting him a furnished house on his mere promise to pay.[11] The following letter from Madocks to Williams is evidently an answer — or the evasion of an immediate answer — to " handsome proposals " made through Williams immediately before this meeting — proposals involving an interview between Mad-

257

ocks and Shelley or Williams in Boston. It is addressed to John
Williams at No. 23 Conduit Street, London (as if Williams had
almost immediately left Wales for London) and is marked " To
be forwarded to him ":

My Dear John,

I have sent a few lines under cover to Mrs. Bridger for you and
I repeat the substance of them in this. *Do not* think of coming here
[Boston] or Mr. Shelley until you hear again from me.

The interest Mr. Shelley takes in the Embankment and his proposals on the subject are very handsome. When I have considered
the matter more fully *in London* I shall be better able to express my
feelings on the subject and on his handsome conduct. It requires,
however, much consideration before I lay myself under so great
obligation to a gentleman to whom I am a stranger, and there are
very many points still further to be considered. Write to me by
return of post. In great haste

                                                   W. A. MADOCKS

You will receive a letter from me in Conduit Street on Monday
[Wednesday crossed out] morning.[12]

Whatever Shelley's proposals were, one of the points to be
further considered must have been the practicability of raising
money during his minority. Mr. Madocks's London attorney,
J. Girdlestone, was cautious on this point and sceptical of Shelley on other matters. Very possibly Mr. Madocks had received
other letters from Tremadoc that caused him to hesitate. Elizabeth Hitchener had been talking rather largely and enthusiastically about Shelley's previous radical activities, and conservative local patriots by no means approved. A Mr. Robert Leeson of Morfa Lodge was particularly incensed after reading
one of Shelley's pamphlets supplied by Miss Hitchener. "An
envious, unfeeling sort of man," as Mrs. Williams described him,
he was already nursing a hatred that was later to produce
considerable ill feeling.*[13]*

SHELLEY and his party left Wales for London almost immediately after the meeting at Beaumaris, in accordance with
earlier plans made at Lynmouth to be in London by October 3.

They arrived there in time to have dinner with Godwin on October 4.[14] They had reached London two or three days earlier and Shelley had gone on to Sussex. His immediate purpose in Sussex may have been to raise money to discharge the debt for which he had been arrested; at any rate, Mr. John Bedwell took the debt in hand for him on November 5, immediately after his return to London. Undoubtedly he also tried to raise funds for the embankment, which still lacked at least £18,000 or £19,000 of the £20,000 deemed necessary for its completion.[15] Shelley's Sussex friends were not impressed by the emergency in Wales, or by the opportunity of saving so distant a countryside from the sea. From their answers Shelley described them as " cold, selfish, and calculating animals, who seem to have no other aim or business, on earth, but to eat, drink, and sleep." [16] The campaign for funds was continued from London, but with no recorded success. The Duke of Norfolk was given his opportunity to contribute, which he evaded with practised politeness and ease.

During the six weeks (October 4–November 13) that the Shelleys spent in London they had ample opportunity to enjoy the personal presence of their long-venerated guide, William Godwin. Godwin was at that time a short, thickset man of fifty-seven, with a fair complexion and a large, bald forehead. In his plain, dark, old-fashioned clothes and with his reserved, didactic manner he looked like the dissenting minister he once had been. His indistinct articulation and a sort of sharp, dry catch in his voice were capable of enhancing the effect when his conversation, as sometimes happened, turned unpleasant.[17] But Godwin was genial to his young disciple, and his family were equally so. For six weeks Shelley and Godwin talked together three or four times weekly, sometimes at family dinners in Godwin's Skinner Street household, sometimes at dinners at the Shelleys' hotel, sometimes in walks together and sometimes in calls upon each other.[18]

An occasional party to these meetings was Fanny Imlay (or Godwin, as she was called), the daughter of Mary Wollstonecraft and Gilbert Imlay, who had come into Godwin's family with his marriage to Mary Wollstonecraft. She was at this time between eighteen and nineteen years of age, a plain-featured, modest, sweet-spirited girl whom the Shelleys liked instantly. Even the second Mrs. Godwin, whom Charles Lamb and others detested, they admired at this time for her friendliness to them and her competence as sole and determined manager of the Juvenile Library she conducted. The Godwins' only son, William, was then a boy of nine, with whose romps Shelley showed his sympathy by helping him explode fireworks. Mary, Godwin's daughter by his first wife, Mary Wollstonecraft, who at fifteen was considered still a child, was absent on a visit to Scotland, and arrived home only three days before the Shelleys left London. Since the Shelleys dined at the Godwins' house the day after her return, it is very likely that the first fateful meeting of Shelley and Mary occurred on October 11, 1812, without impressing itself on the memory of either.[19]

The Shelleys were delighted with the whole Godwin family, of whom Harriet gave a full and enthusiastic account to her Irish friend, Catherine Nugent. " G.," she concluded, " is very much taken with Percy. He seems to delight so much in his society. He has given up everything for the sake of our society. It gives me so much pleasure to sit and look at him. Have you ever seen a bust of Socrates, for his head is very much like that? " [20]

The subjects discussed by the philosopher with his disciple while Harriet looked on and thought of Socrates are occasionally noted by Godwin in his highly abbreviated, staccato journal entries — " Matter," " spirit," " atheism," " utility," " truth," " the clergy," "Church government," and the " characteristics of German thought and literature " are all noted.[21] Godwin mentions reading part of *Queen Mab,* from which it is to be inferred that Shelley's first important poem was also a topic of their conversation. Other topics apparently not listed, but almost certainly discussed, were Shelley's finances and style of living, his relations to his family, Elizabeth Hitchener, and the great embankment project at Tremadoc. If Godwin urged uncongenial advice on these subjects — and on the first two his advice was sure to be so — it might further explain a sudden change in Harriet's opinion of him, as expressed in her next account

WILLIAM GODWIN

Engraved by Roberts from a painting by Thomas Kearsley

of Godwin to Miss Nugent, after the Shelleys had returned to Tremadoc.

One of Godwin's friends was a Mr. John Frank Newton, author of an essay, *The Return to Nature* (1810), in which he championed vegetable diet. Early in November,[22] after one of the Godwin-Shelley family dinners, Shelley indulged his youthful love of fireworks by slipping away with young William Godwin, who was going to explode fireworks with Mr. Newton's son. After the fireworks Shelley accompanied young Newton home and introduced himself to the family. The Newtons were cultivated people of somewhat Bohemian tastes, who believed in nudism for children, as well as in vegetarianism. They took to Shelley at once. Mr. Newton thought that he had never before met " so young a man who had acquired so much real knowledge of numerous authors." [23] The Shelleys left London on the 13th, so that the development of this new friendship had to be left for their next visit.

Although it is not a matter of written record, the Shelleys undoubtedly developed their friendship with Thomas Hookham, Jr., the young publisher of slightly radical tendencies with whom Shelley had in some way become acquainted before going to Lynmouth. It was at Hookham's rooms in New Bond Street, in all probability, that Shelley conversed two or three times with Thomas Love Peacock, shortly before returning to Wales.

The same crowded week that marked the foundation of the two new friendships also marked the re-establishment, on an altered basis, of an old one. Since parting from Shelley at York in 1811, Hogg had completed his training as a conveyancer, returned to London, and entered as a student in the Middle Temple, in accordance with his original plans. He was also gaining practical experience in the office of a special pleader. Though he was developing into quite a young Tory, who now thought Sir Francis Burdett a foolish fellow and much too noisy, he had by no means forgotten his radical friend. He had inquired about Shelley of John Grove, but had met a significantly frosty profession of ignorance. When Hogg had about given up the search, Shelley, seeking for his old friend among the law offices, traced him to his lodgings through the special pleader for whom he worked.

Thus, when Hogg was settling himself quietly to his tea and his book one evening in early November he was (to abridge his own fortissimo account) roused by a violent knocking at the street door and the sound of rapid feet upon the stairs. As he looked up, the door flew open and Bysshe rushed into the room. "Bysshe looked, as he always looked, wild, intellectual, unearthly. . . . He had ten thousand things to tell me, and as he told me a thousand at least of them at a time without order, and with his natural vehemence and volubility, I got only a very indistinct notion of his history during the preceding year." [24]

The next day Hogg dined with Shelley, Harriet, and Eliza, Elizabeth Hitchener apparently being absent. He found Harriet as cordial and as radiantly healthful as ever, and Eliza as distantly polite and as alarmed over Harriet's "nerves" as she had been in York. Harriet, who had become a thorough Irishwoman, sought to elicit his indignation over the fate of Robert Emmet and received a crusty Tory rejoinder. Shelley said nothing about Ireland (though there were a number of Irish books scattered about), but was extremely enthusiastic about Welsh scenery; Eliza sang the praises of Mr. and Mrs. Madocks. Not a word was said about the Godwins; Hogg supposed even many years later that Shelley did not see Godwin until he was next in London. The Shelleys were even then packing their belongings to set out for Wales the next morning, though they told him they expected to return in a short while to take up permanent residence in London.

Evidently the Shelleys remained in London a few days longer, for Hogg called at least once more, just in time to witness Elizabeth Hitchener's last day in a household where her presence had come to be regarded as odious. He had called to go walking with Shelley, but was "summarily condemned to walk with the two spinsters," both of whom he despised. Back and forth through St. James's Park and the neighbouring parks Hogg walked with them arm in arm, for what seemed to him a very long time, his "two jewels," as he sardonically called them, quarrelling incessantly with each other. "The lovely Eliza attacked the foe with haughty contempt; the bearded precep- tress defended herself and offended her enemy with meek con- tumacy." Though Elizabeth's departure had already been set- tled, there was a time during the ensuing dinner when it appeared to Hogg as if she might reassume her old spell. In answer to a question from Hogg she began again with fluency and animation on her favourite subject of the rights of women. "Presently Bysshe quitted his chair, and came and stood before her, listening with attention, and looking enthusiastic, as if his former interest had in some measure revived. The sisters eyed him with manifest displeasure, as a person holding treasonable communications with a public enemy." [25]

It was Hogg's belief that Eliza Westbrook thought Miss Hitchener personally disgusting and resented her presence and influence over Shelley, that she soon converted Harriet to her point of view, and that between them they rendered her odious to Shelley.

"The lady I have so often mentioned to you, of the name of Hitchener, has to our very great happiness left us," Harriet soon informed Miss Nugent.

We were entirely deceived in her character as to her republicanism, and in short everything else which she pretended to be. We were not long in finding out our great disappointment in her. As to any noble disinterested views, it is utterly impossible for a selfish char- acter to feel them.[26]

These reasons are too entirely Shelleyan for anyone else to be their author; it is Harriet, as usual, adopting and expressing Shelley's ideas. The next point may well have originated with either Harriet or Eliza:

She built all her hopes on being able to separate me from my dearly loved Percy, and had the artifulness [sic] to say that Percy was really in love with her, and [it] was only his being married that could keep her within bounds now.

After explaining how Miss Hitchener had been invited to live with them, she concludes: "It was a long time ere we could possibly get her away, till at last Percy said he would give her £100 per annum. And now, thank God, she has left us never more to return."

Shelley's comment to Hogg, about a month after Miss Hitchener's departure, shows on the one hand a superior sense of obligation and on the other hand a more intense disgust than Harriet's:

The Brown Demon, as we call our late tormentor and schoolmistress, must receive her stipend. I pay it with a heavy heart and an unwilling hand; but it must be so. She was deprived by our misjudging haste of a situation, where she was going on smoothly: and now she says that her reputation is gone, her health ruined, her peace of mind destroyed by my barbarity; a complete victim to all the woes mental and bodily, that heroine ever suffered! This is not all fact; but certainly she is embarrassed and poor, and we being in some degree the cause, we ought to obviate it. She is an artful, superficial, ugly, hermaphroditical beast of a woman, and my astonishment at my fatuity, inconsistency, and bad taste was never so great, as after living four months with her as an inmate. What would Hell be, were such a woman in Heaven? [27]

Godwin, who must have known something of what was happening, risked no comment. On Sunday, November 8, the day of Hogg's second visit to the Shelleys, he recorded the whole matter in his diary with his usual succinctness: " Call on E. Westbrook (E. H. *congé*)." [28]

Elizabeth Hitchener returned to Sussex in an embittered state of mind. She had given up her school to follow an enthusiastic vision that had ended in utter disillusion and, if not local disgrace, at least local discredit and ridicule. When she attempted to set up another school she was unable to secure a single pupil.[29] She proceeded to tell Captain Pilfold and his wife exactly the sort of person she considered their nephew to be. She wrote to John Williams at Tremadoc to warn him against Shelley and to express wild threats as to what she intended to do. Williams wrote to Captain Pilfold refuting some of her charges that involved conduct toward himself and received the Captain's assurance of his continued faith in his favourite: " Mr.

Shelley is my nephew, and I need not tell you *how* difficult
I found it, to reconcile Miss Hitchener's story with their known
moral and virtuous good characters." [30] Williams enclosed to
the Shelleys one of her wild letters and received an answer in
which Shelley treated her with scorn and characterized her as
" a woman of desperate views and dreadful passions but of
cool and undeviating revenge." [31]

This certainly sounds like the novels that had formed Shelley's earlier reading. With considerably less desperation and
passion than he ascribed to her, Elizabeth could have embarrassed him, and possibly had him arrested, for a debt of a
hundred pounds, borrowed from her in June. No such feelings
were in evidence a short time afterwards when another friend
from whom Shelley had parted called upon her. Gibbons Merle,
who in earlier days had carried messages from Shelley to Miss
Hitchener, called upon her some time after her separation from
the Shelleys. He found her at her father's house, " sitting alone
and in melancholy mood, with one of Shelley's works before
her. Her fine black eye lighted up, her well-formed Roman
countenance was full of animation when I spoke of Shelley. But
she did not allude to her elopement, nor did I touch upon a
theme which might have been painful." [32] Unless a few lines
in her poem " The Weald of Sussex " (1832) reflect a kindly
memory of Shelley, this is our last glimpse of Miss Hitchener
in relation to her early friend. Shelley's memory of her in later
years was scarcely so sentimental.[33] In Italy, in the last two
years of his life, he used to quote with peals of laughter the first
line of a poem in which she asserted her favourite contention,
equal rights for women: " All, all are men — *women* and all! " [34]

THE departure of the Shelleys and Eliza Westbrook from London occurred on November 13, within less than a week after
the separation from Elizabeth Hitchener and the reunion with
Hogg. It was a departure fully as sudden as the earlier and
more famous departure from York. In two letters written six
days earlier Shelley had stated that he was leaving for Wales
in a few days.[35] Hogg had known it for about a week. Yet

the Shelleys invited the Godwins and Fanny Imlay to dinner with them at their hotel on November 13 and left without warning or explanation before their guests arrived. This abrupt disappearance could hardly have been a second flight from Hogg, whose company had been sought and was to be sought again in Tremadoc and Ireland, nor can it be easily credited to financial pressure, because Shelley was representing himself to his mother at the time as in financial matters " to a certain degree independent." Neither could it have been a crisis in affairs at Tremadoc, for he had recently heard from Williams that the embankment was doing well.

Fanny Imlay wrote to Shelley expressing some sense of injury at this treatment. The Shelleys moved about, she complained, like characters in a modern novel. Shelley's reply admits the injury, but merely heightens the mystery as to its reason:

I know that I have in some degree forfeited a direct claim to your confidence and credit, and that of your inestimable circle. . . . It must, indeed, I confess it, have appeared insensible and unfeeling, it must have appeared an ill return for all the kind greetings we had received at your house, to leave it in haste and coldness, to pass over the enlightened and zealous benevolence of Godwin, ever inventive for good, and never deterred or discouraged in schemes for rectifying our perplexed affairs — to bid not one adieu to one of you. But had you been placed in a situation where you might justly have balanced all our embarrassments, qualms and fluctuations; had seen the opposite motives combating in our minds for mastery, had felt some tithe of the pain with which at the length we submitted to a galling yet unappealable necessity, you would have sympathized rather than condemned, have pitied rather than criminated, us unheard.[36]

It has always seemed natural to discount Hogg's insistence upon Shelley's irrational appearances and disappearances as part of his attempt to screen himself in the matter of Shelley's sudden departure from York. Here, however, is an instance made to Hogg's order that Hogg did not make or even know about. But if a rational explanation exists, it might be sought in the relations of Shelley and Godwin. Perhaps Godwin knew and opposed Shelley's plan for returning to Wales and living in a house that was certainly beyond his means, even if the rent would not have to be paid until later. He could scarcely have known of it without opposing it. He may also have pressed Shelley too hard on the matter of reconciliation with his family. The greatly altered nature of Harriet's next account of the Godwins suggests that the Shelleys may have left London in order to avoid unpleasantness with their philosophic guide:

. . . Godwin he, too, is changed, and [filled] with prejudices, and besides, too, he expects such universal homage from all persons younger than himself, that it is very disagreeable to be in company with him on that account, and he wanted Mr. Shelley to join the Wig [sic] party and do just as they pleased, which made me very angry, as we know what men the Wigs [sic] are, now. He is grown old and unimpassioned, therefore is not in the least calculated for such enthusiasts as we are. He had suffered a great deal for his principles, but that ought to make him more staunch in them, at least it would me.[37]

After the two hundred and sixty miles of travel in a post-chaise, the latter part of it through beautiful mountain scenery around Capel Curig and Snowdon, the Shelleys were back in Tremadoc by about the middle of November. In a poem of eight Spenserian stanzas written at about the time of his departure Shelley welcomed the freedom of the Welsh mountains as symbolical of the freedom of the human spirit by which Reason would eventually triumph over poverty and oppression.

Mr. Madocks's handsome new residence, Tanyrallt, a short distance outside the village, had been secured at a rental beyond their present means, with the privilege of deferring payment until Shelley reached his majority. The completion of the embankment was still highly doubtful. Shelley constantly travelled about the region with Mr. Williams, canvassing for subscriptions and urging that men and materials be sent for repairs. Through Shelley's influence a loaded vessel is said to have been sunk in the breach and total destruction of the embankment was averted.[38] Mrs. Williams has recorded that he was in the office from morning till night helping her husband write letters about embankment affairs. Two such letters survive, almost sternly requesting the dilatory Mr. John Evans to pay his subscription.[39] The funds fell so low that Mr. Madocks was frequently unable to pay his labourers, who were forced to support their large families through moonlight cultivation of small spots of poor ground.[40] There was considerable misery that winter and some of Shelley's time was employed in endeavouring to relieve the distress of the labourers. Mr. Madocks (who must have had it from others, since he himself was not present) often spoke enthusiastically to Medwin in later years of the poet's " numerous acts of benevolence, his relieving the distresses of the poor, visiting them in their humble abodes, and supplying them with food and raiment and fuel during the winter." [41] Mrs. Williams also testified later to Shelley's kind-heartedness, and told of his relieving the distress of a poor widow with a five-pound note.[42]

Shelley was probably much happier in these little offices of personal charity than he was in his dealings with persons of higher social rank or in his effort to save the embankment. Urging reluctant subscribers to make their promises good is an unpleasant task at best, and Shelley lacked the unscrupulous geniality of the most successful solicitor. The constant pressure of details foreign to his experience and taste was undoubtedly a trial. " I have been teased to death for the last fortnight," he wrote to Hogg.[43] " Had you known the variety of the discomfitures I have undergone, you would attribute my silence to anything but unkindness or neglect. I allude to the embankment affairs."

Impatience with " embankment affairs " led easily to disillusion and suspicion about the embankment itself and its projectors. Harriet was surely echoing Shelley when she recanted all her former good opinions of Mr. Madocks. She had heard the local stories of his lively company brought down from London for theatrical entertainments, " insulting the spirit of nature's sublime scenery." He had substituted for a fine natural prospect, merely " to please his stupid vanity," " nothing but a sandy marsh uncultivated and ugly to the view." " The harm that man has done through his extravagance is incalculable. Here he built the town of Tremadoc, and then almost ruined

its shopkeepers by never paying their just debts. We have
been the means of saving the bank from utter destruction, for
which I am extremely glad, as that person who purchases it
will reap very great benefit from it." [44]

The Shelleys were far from being universally popular with
their neighbours and the squires and professional men of the
surrounding neighbourhood. Not to mention the natural coldness with which provincial communities are apt to view self-
appointed exhorters and collectors from the outside, Shelley
provided a number of his neighbours with causes for more
active antipathy by his frankly expressed views on politics and
religion. Shelley must have felt some occasional sense of strain
even between himself and John Williams, for Williams was
a devout and active churchman. Wales had little use for atheism and republicanism, even if the latter was, as Shelley assured
Hogg, far removed from pot-house democracy.[45] Peacock was
condemned by a lady as " worse than a murderer " because he
was an infidel. This particular incident Shelley could view with
a touch of humour, but the general state of mind that it indicated aroused him to indignation:

There is more philosophy in one square inch of your counter than
in the whole of Cambria; it is the last stronghold of the most
vulgar and commonplace prejudices of aristocracy. Lawyers of unexampled villainy rule and grind the poor whilst they cheat the rich;
the peasants are mere serfs and are fed and lodged worse than
pigs, the gentry have all the ferocity and despotism of the ancient
barons without their dignity and chivalric disdain of shame or
danger.[46]

Even during the Shelleys' first stay at Tremadoc the animosity
of Robert Leeson was open and avowed. It now involved Shelley in suspicions of his good friend John Williams, since
Leeson indicated Williams as the source of his information
about Shelley's radical activities in Ireland.[47] As he was leaving
Tremadoc, Shelley wrote to Williams to reproach him, but without intending, as he later made plain, to charge him with
treachery. The matter produced a temporary coolness between
them without breaking off their friendship.[48]

SHELLEY had written from London [49] to assure his mother that his marriage had made him " one of the happiest of men," lacking only harmony with the rest of his family to make him absolutely the happiest. At Tremadoc, when alone with Harriet, he continued to be " happiest of the happy." [50] Harriet was a rather indifferent housekeeper, according to Hogg, but she loved reading, had a warm heart and a pleasant, easy disposition, and had made remarkable progress in adopting and echoing Shelley's opinions on practically all matters that he considered important. More than one poem written at Tremadoc deals with Shelley's love for Harriet and his happiness at finding in her a spirit ardent as his own for truth and justice. In the matter of the Irish she was if anything more Irish than Shelley himself. She was now studying Latin under Shelley's tutelage and hoping soon to be able to write a Latin letter to that confirmed classicist, Jefferson Hogg. When Fanny Imlay rather implied that Harriet was a " fine lady," Shelley protested warmly that she was not:

The ease and simplicity of her habits, the unassuming plainness of her address, the uncalculated connexion of her thought and speech, has ever formed in my eyes her greatest charms; and none of these are compatible with fashionable life, or the attempted assumptions of its vulgar and noisy eclat.[51]

As usual, Hogg and Miss Nugent were both invited to visit them at their secluded, verandaed " Italian villa," with its bare steep rocks behind and its view of the embankment, the sea, and the mountains.

Both Shelley and Harriet desired children, and they knew now that Harriet was to have a baby in the spring. Shelley continued to rejoice in his vegetarianism, to which he gave principal credit for an improved state of health; Harriet occasionally ate meat and intended to continue this mild heresy until spring.

In this seclusion Shelley continued to follow his own private pattern of life, which not even expulsion from Oxford, estrangement from family and friends, financial difficulties, or marriage had ever seriously altered. The vexations of Tremadoc might retard but could not halt the continued progress of *Queen Mab*.

They might reduce the number of letters to Hogg and Godwin,[52] but correspondence, as always with Shelley, continued.

To be sure, the correspondence with Hogg was no longer on the unrestrained, confidential basis that had existed before the painful episode that had separated them at York. Shelley never gave complete confidence where he did not sense complete sympathy, and both he and Hogg now realized, even if they had not done so at York, that their views of religion and society had grown far apart. Hogg frankly wondered if this had not produced a less cordial feeling on Shelley's part toward his old friend, to which Shelley replied that since principles were involuntary matters he could not condemn Hogg for any belief that he sincerely held. He did not accuse Hogg of insincerity, and he did not think that he himself could be accused of bigotry or factionalism:

I certainly am a very resolved republican (if the word applies), and a determined sceptic; but although I think their reasonings very defective, I am clearly aware that the noblest feelings might conduct some few reflecting minds to Aristocracy and Episcopacy. Hume certainly was an aristocrat, and Locke was a zealous Christian.[53]

The relationship with Thomas Hookham, Jr., was gradually expanding into something more than a mere business connection. Book orders and arrangements for publication were occasionally interspersed with more personal comments on such subjects as Peacock, Harriet's progress in Latin, and financial affairs. Since Hookham's leanings were radical, Shelley and Harriet sometimes interjected a remark or comment as from one radical to another. Thus it was, now that Hogg was no longer in complete sympathy, that Shelley and Harriet turned to Hookham for co-operation in giving aid and comfort to victims of tyranny in the larger world beyond Tanyrallt and Tremadoc.

Since Shelley had indignantly condemned the sending of troops to Nottingham in November 1811, the Luddite riots had spread over the north until frame-breaking was a common and almost

271

regular occurrence, not always unaccompanied by violence. Troops and local authorities seemed powerless to protect the machines believed by most labouring men to be the direct cause of their distress. In March 1812 Parliament had passed the terrible Frame-Breaking Bill, making the destruction of any manufacturing machinery a capital offence. Lord Byron, a pale, hypersensitive newcomer to the House of Lords, had devoted his maiden speech to a vain warning against its blundering savagery. He painted a picture of a frame-breaker dragged into court, a man " meagre with famine, sullen with despair, careless of a life which your Lordships are perhaps about to value at something less than the price of a stocking-frame," a man surrounded by starving children whom his best efforts could not provide with a livelihood. Two things, he caustically asserted, would still be wanting to convict such a man, " twelve butchers for a jury, and a Jeffreys for a judge! " [54]

The bill had passed, however; eight convicted Luddities had been hanged at Chester in May, and eight more at Manchester in June. More recently, before a large and very silent throng at York, seventeen more had been executed under heavy military guard, on January 9 and 16. The Shelleys were greatly concerned about the children whom, in Byron's scathing phrase, these victims had been " nefariously guilty of lawfully begetting." On January 31 Harriet wrote to Thomas Hookham:

I see by the Papers that those poor men who were executed at York have left a great many children. Do you think a subscription would be attended to for their relief? If you think it would, pray put down our names and advertise it in the Papers. Put down my Sister's name, Mr. Shelley's and mine for two guineas each; if this meets with your approbation we will enclose the sum.[55]

Before Hookham could put this commission into effect he received a letter about another subscription that Shelley considered a more important matter. Leigh Hunt, with his brother John, had for the fourth time been indicted by the government, this time on a charge that could hardly fail to bring a conviction. In the pages of their *Examiner* they had opposed to the Tory flattery of the Prince Regent a scornful picture of " a corpulent

gentleman of fifty " who was " a violator of his word, a libertine
over head and ears in debt and disgrace, a despiser of domestic
ties, the companion of gamblers and demireps, a man who has
just closed half a century without one single claim on the gratitude of his country or the respect of posterity." [56] Shelley had
followed the trial in December and had commented with interesting perspicacity on Brougham's inability to secure an
acquittal. The only real defence, Shelley remarked, was an
avowal of the indicted statement, which would have rendered
Brougham himself liable for treason and libel.[57] Sentence was
pronounced on February 4, 1812: the brothers were to pay a fine
of £500 each, suffer imprisonment in separate prisons for two
years, and give securities totalling £750 each for good behaviour during five years.

It seemed to Shelley that such a sentence set the seal of
abjectness and slavery upon England for ever. Boiling with
indignation at its " horrible injustice and tyranny," he wrote
to Hookham to urge an immediate subscription to pay the fine
of £1,000:

Hunt is a brave, a good, and an enlightened man. Surely the public
for whom Hunt has done so much will repay in part the great debt
of obligation which they owe the champion of their liberties and
virtues; or are they dead, cold, stonehearted, and insensible, brutal-
ized by centuries of unremitting bondage?

Though " rather poor at present " he enclosed £20 and wished
ardently that he might " wallow for one night in the Bank of
England." [58]

Shelley also wrote to Hunt. " It was this imprisonment,"
Hunt wrote in his autobiography, " that brought me acquainted
with my friend of friends, Shelley. I had seen little of him before; but he wrote to me, making me a princely offer, which at
the time I stood in no need of." [59] The " princely offer " could
hardly have been an offer to pay the fine, as Hunt remarks in
the next paragraph that " Some other persons, not at all known
to us," offered to raise money to pay the fine. The offer was
declined, as were also two others from government sources,
one to remit the imprisonment, and another to remit the fine,

in return for an undertaking not to publish further comment on the Regent. The fine was actually paid by the Hunts themselves, who were financially handicapped for many years afterwards by its crippling effects. Leigh Hunt explained in an editorial in the *Examiner* for February 21 that they must insist on assuming the responsibility for their own actions. Later he disclaimed merit for this genuinely magnanimous action in language that is rather surprising: "for I was destitute, at that time, of even a proper instinct with regard to money." [60]

It was perhaps as well for Shelley that Leigh Hunt did not accept his princely offer. He had never been able, since he and Harriet had been assured of a combined allowance of £400, to live easily within that amount. They had attempted, with or without success, to borrow additional money on which to go to Ireland, had returned to England financially straitened, had been able to command only £13 when leaving Cwm Elan, had borrowed £100 from Elizabeth Hitchener in June, had been living in a small cottage at Lynmouth to recoup their finances, and had been straitened again on their hurried departure and forced to borrow a small sum and postpone payment on a lodging bill. A little later Shelley had been arrested for debt. After returning to Tremadoc from London they spent money on personal charities and on a rather large bookseller's account. Whether or not they actually paid their subscription to the embankment or any part of the £100 recently promised Miss Hitchener, they were in financial difficulties again, even though their rental for the cottage of Tanyrallt was not expected of them till the next year. On December 4, 1812 Shelley spoke of himself as "not having a sixpence of ready money"; [61] when he wished to start the subscription for Hunt he described himself as "rather poor at present." He was still in debt £30 to Dr. Roberts of Carnarvon for professional services and for a loan. Presumably he was generally known to be in debt to tradesmen, else his enemy Leeson could not have told everywhere that he was leaving suddenly in order to avoid paying his debts. When he did leave Tanyrallt suddenly, he had no

funds on hand and had to appeal to Hookham.[62] Shortly thereafter he had to borrow £100 from Williams's brother Owen. He
owed the Madocks estate £350, and he expected to be unable
to clear his credit in Tremadoc unless he could raise a loan
of £400.[63]

Though Shelley seemed at this time quite incapable of living
within his income, he was acutely aware of its insufficiency to
meet his need for relieving the distresses of others. He longed
ardently not only to " wallow in the Bank of England for one
night," but for his coming of age, after which money could more
easily be obtained. To Hogg it seemed that the £400 would
have been quite ample for the Shelleys' unostentatious style
of living, had a great part of it not been wasted on costly flittings
to and fro and on the needs of others. Neither Harriet nor her
sister, in Hogg's opinion, was at all better qualified than Shelley
himself to see that their income was carefully managed.[64]

In his difficulties Shelley was advised by Hogg to seek again
the mediation of the Duke of Norfolk with Mr. Timothy Shelley. It is quite likely that Godwin also gave him similar advice,
in connection with his desire that Shelley become a regular
Whig. Early in December, therefore, Shelley proposed to write
" a long and wheedling letter " to His Grace. " I have no hopes,
however," he added,

of bending my father, but by the mere force of gross interest, and
therefore suppose it equally impossible, that he should come to terms
before I am of age, as that he should hold out at the expiration of
my minority.[65]

A letter was written to the Duke of Norfolk, whose failure to
answer it left Shelley unworried:

Do you know, I cannot prevail upon myself to care much about it.
Harriet is very happy as we are; and I am very happy. I question if
intimacy with my relations would add at all to our tranquillity. . . .
I can say to my conscience, " I have done my best "; but I shall not
be very unhappy if I fail.[66]

Nevertheless, Shelley did write to his father a friendly letter,
now lost. The answer left matters not greatly improved. Mr.

Shelley expressed appreciation of his son's inquiries and good wishes and regret that there had been difficulties between them. He hoped that the Welsh mountains might produce " Reflections that you well know would be so congenial to my own sentiments, as well as those of yr. Mother." [67] Thus Shelley, who believed that opinions were utterly incapable of voluntary change, was expected to change his opinions if he wished to change his relations with his family.

STUDY, writing, and publication plans went on steadily. Shelley asked Godwin to recommend a plan of reading and study, and on December 10 Godwin sent him a long letter [68] containing some excellent suggestions, some of which are reflected in the titles of the books Shelley ordered within the next three weeks. The books on the substantial list previously ordered were mostly received and read at Tanyrallt. [69]

At this point, therefore, it might be well to pause and consider somewhat more in detail the books by which Shelley was surrounded as he wrote his first important poem. Classified according to subject, these titles show that Shelley was acting very seriously on Godwin's belief that he needed to ground himself more thoroughly in the growth and nature of the institutions on which modern society is based. " History," Godwin had said, " is a detail of all that man has done in solitude or society," adding that Greek and Roman history are especially valuable. " I am determined to apply myself to a study that is hateful and disgusting to my very soul," Shelley assured his principal agent, " but which is above all studies, necessary for him who would be listened to as a mender of antiquated abuses. I mean that record of crimes and miseries — History." [70] Accordingly, nearly a third of the books he ordered were histories. This list covers the range of Greek and Roman history with particular thoroughness, but Byzantine, Renaissance Italian, Jewish, Scottish, English, American, Indian, Brazilian, and Peruvian history are not omitted.

Almost as many more titles fall within the general range of philosophy, religion, and metaphysics. Such reading as they

represent had been Shelley's particular pleasure and interest
ever since it had supplanted his early love of sensational novels.
Had Shelley not turned from metaphysics to poetry, thought
Mary Shelley, he might have presented the world with a really
important theory of the mind.[71] Such writers as Epicurus, Diderot, Condorcet, Paine, Hume, and Godwin he was in most
cases already acquainted with. These, together with a few
others not in the lists, such as Helvetius, Holbach, Volney, and
Lucretius, constitute the backbone of that logical, materialistic
system of thought which brought everything to the bar of infallible Reason and there judged it by the evidence of infallible
sense. It had dominated Shelley's view of human life and institutions and was at this moment reaching one of its most effective poetic expressions in *Queen Mab*.

Other volumes in the list bear evidence, as *Queen Mab* does
also, that the side of his nature that could not content itself
for ever within the bounds of eighteenth-century rationalism
was already vaguely beginning to assert itself. Berkeley, whom
he had rejected almost with scorn when read at Southey's suggestion a year earlier, he now ordered for himself. Mary Shelley was to conclude later that he was a disciple of Berkeley.[72]
Spinoza and Kant, both so much more congenial to his later
beliefs that the Encyclopædists, he did not comment upon particularly at this time, but he insisted that he wanted all of
Kant's works (though he could hardly have read at this time
any that had not been translated from the German) and he
later worked on a translation of Spinoza. After a few months
Hogg observed in the poet's London lodgings a Latin edition
of Kant which Shelley had spent considerable pains to secure
and which he seemed totally to neglect. Shelley had known
Plato slightly already, but was to know him as an important
influence only later.

Science was still an active interest. Medicine and physiology
are represented in his order lists by Spallanzani, Celsus (assuming that Shelley meant the author of *De Medicina*), Hippocrates, and "Trotter on 'Nervous Temperament' and on
'Drunkenness'"; astronomy by Ptolemy. The physical sciences
were represented by Erasmus Darwin's poems and notes (rein-

forced, possibly, by the microscope he had asked his mother to forward from Field Place); the elementary science of language by Horne Tooke and Lord Monboddo. The list of poetical and dramatic works is only slightly smaller than the philosophical and historical. The classical languages are well represented, but are outweighed in number by the English poets. In particular it is to be noted that, except for Milton, all the English poets who most notably affected the formation of Shelley's poetic style are on the list — Spenser, Shakespeare, Southey, Wordsworth, and Coleridge. One wonders if Godwin's blunt but penetrating observation after reading a part of *Queen Mab* in manuscript could have caused Shelley to begin deliberately to lay the foundation for a better style. "*You* have what appears to me a false taste in poetry," Godwin had written in the letter previously quoted. "You love a perpetual sparkle and glittering, such as are to be found in Darwin, and Southey, and Scott, and Cambell."

The completion of *Queen Mab* was now in sight. "I expect to have *Queen Mab* and the other Poems finished by March," Shelley informed Hookham, adding that *Queen Mab* would be equipped with long, philosophical notes, which seemed to him to be a safer way of expressing radical beliefs and to have the added merit of freeing the poem of an excess of didactic matter.[73] Hogg had advised Shelley, among other things, to write the poem in rhyme. A part of Hogg's advice Shelley professed to have taken, but he rejected rhymed verse in favour of "blank heroic verse" and "blank lyrical measure," pointing to Milton's *Samson Agonistes*, the Greek choruses, and Southey's *Thalaba* as precedents. It may be that Hogg advised a more moderate expression of views, for Shelley returned to the subject to state: "As I have not abated an iota of the infidelity or cosmopolicy of it, sufficient will remain, exclusively of innumerable faults, invisible to partial eyes, to make it very unpopular." [74] By February 19 the poem was finished and transcribed and Shelley was at work on the notes. It was not to reach Hookham, however, until about a month later.[75]

The "other Poems" mentioned several times by Shelley [76]

were the shorter poems written from time to time since his return from Ireland. The manuscripts are still in the possession of the Esdaile family, which allowed Professor Dowden to quote all that has yet been printed from them, with the exception of three poems later printed by Shelley himself.[77] Shelley informed Hookham that they would amount to about 2,800 lines,[78] and contemplated publishing them as "a volume of Minor Poems." He was not at all sure that they would "stand the criticism even of friendship"; some of them were "abrupt and obscure"; some of the later ones, however, he felt conveyed "a meaning in every word"[79] and had the merit of "breathing hatred to government and religion but . . . not too openly for publication." Such of these poems as have been printed show a very decided growth in power of expression over the poems that had been left in Ireland for publication. The principal influences on the style were Southey, Campbell, Wordsworth, and Scott.

The efforts to recover the volume of poems left in Ireland still continued. Lawless having failed to secure it, Miss Nugent was urged more than once to recover it by hook or crook.[80] Yet when she had persuaded the Dublin printer to release the poems, Shelley failed to publish them, as well as most of the shorter poems written since leaving Ireland. He had already outgrown them.

The "Biblical Extracts" begun in Ireland was now also ready for publication. It would sell best, Shelley thought, made up into an attractive little volume of the size and type of Godwin's *Essay on Sepulchres* and offered in a limited edition as a Christmas or an Easter gift-book. Apparently it had a preface by way of antidote to "Biblical poison."[81] Hookham was to arrange for publication by Daniel Isaac Eaton, if possible, but was to see to it in any event that 250 copies were printed. Since the Shelleys expected to find some of these copies in a box to be received early in February, it is quite possible that the volume was printed, but no trace of either volume or manuscript has since been discovered. Even more shadowy is the nature and fate of another work that may have been Shelley's, entitled

" God Save the King," which seems to have been sent to Tany-rallt after the Shelleys' departure, and which was apparently too seditious to be sent through the customs.[82]

In spite of occasional nervous irritations over embankment affairs, and an accumulation of debts that seemed to be lightly regarded, Shelley and Harriet were quite happy at Tanyrallt in the winter of 1812–13. Shelley was in good health and was making good progress with his reading and writing; Harriet was coming along in her Latin studies and was providing herself with some new songs — Irish melodies, simple ballads, and old sentimental songs like " Robin Adair " and " Kate of Kearney " — to add to the pleasure of long winter evenings in their isolated cottage.[83] As matters stood thus, with increasing domestic happiness balanced by growing irritations with the local environment, Shelley was suddenly driven from Wales by a mysterious occurrence that has never been satisfactorily explained.

ON FEBRUARY 26 their faithful servant Daniel Hill found his way back to them, having just been released from the Barnstaple jail. That night, between ten and eleven o'clock, half an hour after the Shelleys had retired to bed, but while the servants were still up, Shelley thought he heard a noise in one of the parlours. The night was a wild and stormy one, with the wind making a noise like thunder and the rain falling in torrents. It is an interesting fact that Shelley was expecting trouble and had loaded a pair of pistols that very night in anticipation. Armed with his pistols, he went downstairs and heard steps retreating through the billiard-room. Following the sound through an adjoining small room, he saw a man in the act of leaving through one of the windows. The man fired at Shelley and missed; Shelley then attempted to fire, but his pistol flashed in the pan. In the ensuing hand-to-hand struggle Shelley was knocked down, but after some struggling on the floor he managed to fire his second pistol. The marauder, apparently wounded in the shoulder, sprung up shrieking: " By God, I will be revenged! I will murder your wife. I will ravish your sister.

By God. I will be revenged! " — and disappeared through the window.

After this the whole household assembled in the parlour and remained there for two hours, but eventually retired to bed, leaving Shelley and Daniel Hill on guard. Three hours later, at about four o'clock, Shelley sent Dan to ascertain the time. While he was out of the room a man thrust his hand through the window and fired at Shelley, presumably with a pistol. The bullet went through the window curtain and through Shelley's flannel gown. Shelley's pistol again flashed in the pan, but he had armed himself with an old sword since the first affray, and he attacked the marauder with this. Dan Hill returned to the room just in time to cause the flight of the assailant, who had almost wrested the sword from Shelley's grasp. Harriet, rushing down the steps at the sound of the pistol-shot, reached the room after the marauder had vanished.[84]

Such are the details of a most harrowing experience, as related by Harriet two weeks later. Answering an agitated summons the next morning, John Williams found Shelley in a most distressing nervous condition and elicited an account of the affair somewhat at variance with Harriet's.[85] According to this account, Shelley had seen a face against the window and had fired at it, shattering the glass. He had then rushed out upon the lawn, where he saw the devil leaning against a tree. As he told his story to Williams, Shelley seized pen and ink and sketched this vision upon a wooden screen and then attempted to burn the screen in order to destroy the apparition.[86] The screen was saved with some difficulty, but was subsequently lost, not, however, before a copy of Shelley's sketch was made.[87] This copy testifies most eloquently that what Shelley thought he saw was not a man, but a veritable devil.

So careful and well-disposed a biographer as Professor Dowden concluded from this evidence that Shelley's mind was undoubtedly unhinged " to a certain degree " whether or not there was an actual struggle.[88] Thus the matter stood until " revelations " made about 1862 and first published in 1905 convinced subsequent biographers that Shelley's wild story was entitled to almost literal belief.

On the high plateau back of Tanyrallt, accessible by rude steps cut in the cliff, lay a small farm known as Pant Ifan. According to local tradition Shelley sometimes climbed the steps and wandered about on the plateau, which was used largely for grazing sheep. Several times he encountered sheep that seemed hopelessly ill and shot them in order to end their misery. This was resented by the farmers on the plateau. The owner of Pant Ifan some time later was Robert Williams, son of the postmaster at Tremadoc. He was known locally as Robin Pant Ifan. In 1862 and earlier he used to descend to Tanyrallt and tell how with several wild companions intent on frightening Shelley from the community he had fired a pistol through the window at Tanyrallt and when Shelley's pistol flashed in the pan had climbed through the window and grappled with him. Two young daughters of Mr. Greaves, then the owner of Tanyrallt, heard him tell his story and repeated it many years later to Miss Margaret L. Crofts, who gave it to the world in 1905.[89] This story has ever since been uncritically accepted as true,[90] despite its conflict with the physical evidence found on the scene next morning and despite the obvious fact that a man who could descend a high straight cliff in 1862 could not have been old enough fifty years earlier to grapple with a young man of twenty. Neither of Mr. Greaves's daughters believed his story.[91] My own scepticism has led me to an investigation of his age, which reveals that in 1813 Shelley's fully accredited assailant was three years old.[92]

This leaves the Tanyrallt " assault " exactly where Hogg, Peacock, and Professor Dowden left it — a story in two versions, quite inconsistent with each other, both flatly contradicted by a prompt informal examination of the scene which could discover only one set of tracks — Shelley's own — and the marks of only one bullet, which must also have been Shelley's, since it was fired from within the room, toward the window. A further discrediting circumstance overlooked by Shelley's sceptical friends and all subsequent biographers was the state of visibility at the times Shelley " saw " the marauder. The moon was nearly through its fourth quarter, with only a slight decrescent rim of its surface showing. On a stormy night, among

SHELLEY'S TANYRALLT ASSAILANT

From Shelley's sketch as copied by Miss Fanny Holland, and publish-
ed in the Century Magazine, *October 1905*

trees and in a mountainous country, such a slight, low-hung moon could have furnished no illumination at all, even had it been visible.[93] Whoever has tried to keep a straight path on a cloudy, moonless night will find it hard to believe Shelley saw anything, much less a figure he could sketch. The figure that Shelley sketched — a devil rather than a man — is the final proof that what he saw was seen in his imagination and not with the physical eye.

Were it not for a series of such experiences running through Shelley's whole life, such an incident might not be worth a lengthy and careful investigation, but in relation to the others, and to Shelley's mental constitution, it is important to learn as far as possible in each instance what actually happened. In this case it is evident from the freshly primed pistol that Shelley either expected an attack or wished his family to believe so. If he deliberately staged the whole show, as Leeson charged, the after-effects on his mind and health could not have been so serious as they were. Therefore his imagination must have dwelt upon some real or imaginary threat until it anticipated and produced the thing threatened. Three slight circumstances link this occurrence with the assault at Keswick on the night of January 19, 1812. In both cases there is no evidence that anyone but Shelley saw his assailants; his friends in both cases thought the attack imaginary, and the former attack had been preceded — hence possibly suggested — by local alarms. The latter attack also had such a prelude. The Chester newspapers, published on the borders of Wales, took a rather special interest in Welsh news. They were the papers most apt to be read in North Wales by English readers who could not read the Welsh papers. On September 18, 1812 the Chester *Chronicle* carried particulars of three murders in Wales and charged that "the assassinations that have taken place in this country within the last eight months have been unequalled in point of number and aggravation for a century before." In this article, headed "Two More Murders in Wales," or in the events about which it is written, lies sufficient imaginative stimulation for a young man who believed himself persecuted and knew that he had incurred local hatred. The language and conduct of

Shelley's assailant smack strongly of the Gothic novel and suggest that he was evoked by some local stimulus acting upon the scores of such novels in Shelley's mind. This suggestion is strengthened by the sequel. In 1815, in London, Shelley was so strongly convinced that the same assailant was following him with murderous intent that he would not go out alone at night.[94] This obsession closely resembles the plight of Caleb Williams in Godwin's novel, which Shelley had read before, and of which he ordered a copy on December 24, 1814, immediately before the obsession was noted.

Harriet Shelley believed Shelley's story at the time, and her sister Elizabeth is said to have told it as a true story to Shelley's children many years later.[95] But Harriet came to doubt the reality at least of the continued persecution,[96] and both Hogg and Peacock disbelieved it utterly from the start. After visiting the scene only five or six months later and discussing the matter with the neighbours, Peacock was satisfied that Shelley had suffered a delusion.[97] Hogg stated that the matter had been carefully investigated by people acquainted with the locality and the conditions, and that neither he nor anyone he had ever met believed that an attack had occurred. After considering that Dan Hill might possibly have been at the bottom of the commotion in the house, he concluded that

Shelley was in a nervous, unsettled state, which was far more likely to be the parent of imaginary aggressions, than the fruit and offspring of a real attack, on the mind of a man of remarkable and unquestionable courage.[98]

It is of little actual importance that the assault upon Shelley almost certainly never happened. The essential reality was mental rather than physical. It was possibly a mental state that loaded the pistols in advance; it was certainly a mental state that made Shelley tell two stories of the events that differ so widely in essential details as partly to negate each other. The devil Shelley saw was certainly not real, but he was so real to Shelley that he sketched a picture of him and then sought to destroy him by destroying the picture. Throughout his whole life there were times when the reality of events existing only in his own mind far transcended the reality of ordinary physical occurrences. In 1818 an autobiographical character in his " Julian and Maddalo " speaks of himself (lines 445–6) as one who could see the absent with the glance of fantasy.

The after-effects were also much too real for anyone to suppose that Shelley deliberately fabricated the story, as an escape from creditors or for any other motive. In Mr. Williams's opinion he was actually out of his right mind immediately after the experience. The Shelleys at once quit Tanyrallt and took refuge in the house of Mr. Nanney, the solicitor-general for the county, a friend of theirs who lived seven miles distant from Tanyrallt. Shelley suffered an illness of several days, brought on, as he said, " by watching, fatigue, and alarm," [99] Either just before or immediately after this illness he wrote most urgently to Hookham: " I have just escaped an atrocious assassination. Oh send the £20 if you have it — you will perhaps hear of me no more." His state of mind was still so agitated that he concluded his letter with the awkward, unusual phrase: " friend, Percy Shelley." [100] To this Harriet added an explanatory note, saying that Shelley was dreadfully nervous from having been up all night. It thus appears that the Shelleys expected and guarded against a repetition of the attack. Years afterwards, in fact, Shelley ascribed certain physical pains to the pressure of the Tanyrallt assailant's knee upon his body.[101] He believed then and later than his assailant was Mr. Leeson.[102]

The Shelleys did not wait to receive the supplicated remittance from Thomas Hookham, but set out for Ireland as soon as they could put their affairs in order. Shelley sought to borrow twenty-five pounds through John Williams in order to pay some small debts, but as he repeated the request from Ireland, it is to be assumed he did not wait for an answer.[103] By March 6 they were at Bangor Ferry, on their way to Ireland. En route they had been greatly cheered by receiving a remittance from Hookham, enough, Shelley assured him, to relieve them from all pecuniary difficulties.[104] After a tedious, stormy passage, on March 9 Shelley, Harriet, and Eliza arrived in Dublin and put up at the home of " Jack " Lawless, or near by, whence Shelley wrote to Williams for a loan, describing their financial condition as so desperate that "I do not think that we can manage to live until the arrival of Mr. Caldecott's expected loan." [105]

The little party lingered in or near Lawless's home at 35 Cuffe Street, Stephen's Green, for about a fortnight. Thence Shelley forwarded the manuscript of *Queen Mab* to Hookham, who was asked ("if you do not dread the arm of the law, or any exasperation of public opinion against yourself") to print 250 copies, on fine paper, "to catch the aristocrats: they will not read it, but their sons and daughters may." The "long, philosophical and Anti Christian" notes and the other poems would be sent later.[106] They also wrote two or three letters to Hogg, urging him to join them in Dublin and promising to return to London with him.[107] Very likely they saw Miss Catherine Nugent again. Had they been less hurried they might have made the acquaintance of Miss Sydney Owenson, recently become Lady Sydney Morgan, of whom they had learned through Miss Nugent after they had left Ireland the previous year. She had been away from Dublin during their former visit, but in 1813 was presumably again in the city, in the centre of the little group of Irish sympathizers. Shelley and Harriet had both read and admired some of her work, and Harriet had expressed a desire to meet her.[108] There is no record of such a meeting taking place, however.

HAVING already planned to visit his friends in Wales during March, Hogg found it convenient to accept their altered invitation. After a journey of tremendous discomforts he arrived in Dublin very tired and very hungry, having been about two days in the same wet clothes, without sleep, and, worst of all for Hogg, almost without food. The Shelleys, he found, had gone on to Killarney. Hogg wrote to them and sat down to wait. The additional 240 miles to Killarney appealed neither to his pride nor to his much-wounded love of comfort. For a week or ten days he lingered, seeing Dublin and its society under the genial tutelage of "Honest Jack" Lawless. Many of the people he met knew Shelley and spoke cordially of him.

THE LAKES OF KILLARNEY

Engraved by George Cooke

Still he heard nothing from Killarney. His money and his time being almost exhausted, he started back to London, leaving Dublin on March 30, only a day before Shelley and Harriet arrived to meet him, after two days and nights of hard travelling from Killarney.[109]

Why they had gone to Killarney (or even to Ireland) was something Hogg could never explain, particularly as they complained afterwards of the expense and the discomfort. It seems likely, however, in view of their considerable interest in scenery, that they may have gone partly to see the beautiful lakes. Shelley commented upon this beauty five years later, when he wrote to Peacock that only the arbutus islands of Lake Killarney could compare with the beauty of Lake Como,[110] but this single remark is almost the only remaining record of Shelley's visit. Hogg learned from him, however, that they had taken a cottage on an island and had moved into it with Eliza Westbrook, Daniel Hill, and a large number of books, most of which had been brought from Tanyrallt or Dublin.[111] The lake was too much beset with sudden gusts and whirlwinds for Shelley to have engaged much in the boating that he loved, even had there been time. Certainly he could have had little time to write the notes to *Queen Mab* there, as has been suggested, for he had been absent from Dublin only nine days, half of which were spent in hard travel.

When Shelley and Harriet hastened to Dublin to join Hogg they left Eliza in the cottage in command of Daniel Hill and the accumulation of books. In Dublin they decided to follow Hogg to London, as soon as they had rested from the recent long journey and could find money for the trip. Money having been found, Shelley and Harriet reached London on or shortly before April 5 and put up temporarily at the home of Mr Westbrook, in Chapel Street. Eliza was left to hold the fort — perhaps to hold off the landlord — on the banks of Lake Killarney. According to Hogg, Shelley was openly delighted to be rid of her company. " He made no secret of his satisfaction, but often gave vent to his feelings with his accustomed frankness and energy. The good Harriet smiled in silence. . . ."[112] This is the first sign of Shelley's distaste for a woman he later came to hate as a principal cause of his misfortunes. Very soon, however, Eliza arrived in London with Daniel Hill. Thereafter, as long as the Shelleys remained in London, she lived partly in her father's house and partly with them.

Chapter XI

SHELLEY COMES OF AGE:

FINANCIAL AND MATRIMONIAL

TROUBLES

QUEEN MAB; FINANCIAL DIFFICULTIES; THE NEWTON
AND BOINVILLE CIRCLES; SHELLEY AT TWENTY–ONE;
ANOTHER JOURNEY; DOMESTIC CRISIS;
VISIT TO FIELD PLACE

WHEN Shelley reached London, during the first week of April 1813, he must have been fairly accustomed to unsettled conditions of living. Wales, Edinburgh, York, the Lake country, Ireland, Wales again, Devonshire, London again, Wales, and Ireland once more — all had known his restless presence within a year and a half. London again, Bracknell, Edinburgh again, Windsor, and once more London — so the tale was to continue at a somewhat slower tempo, to the end of his days. It was a situation certainly not without importance in the crucial turning-point of his life, for which the stage was even now being slowly prepared.

The Shelleys remained a short while with Harriet's father at 23 Chapel Street and then moved to Cooke's Hotel near by, on Albemarle Street. The first extant letter of Shelley's from Cooke's Hotel was written about May 17,[1] after he had probably been there for some time. For over a month Harriet at least was so busy with " the hurry and bustle of a city " [2] that she wrote no letters at all before May 21. Shelley also seems to have been too busy for a while to write, for on May 3 John Lawless became disturbed at not having heard from him since the departure from Ireland and wrote to Hogg to inquire about him.[3] The " hurry and bustle " may have been partly due to a number of those apparently spontaneous, mysterious engagements to or from which Shelley was always flitting, according to Hogg.[4] It was perhaps also due in part to financial and family negotiations and to seeing *Queen Mab* through the press.

By May 21, when Harriet wrote to Miss Nugent, *Queen Mab* was in the press and Shelley seemed on the verge of reconciliation with his family. The Duke of Norfolk was again willing to help; John Grove, who had recently seen Mr. Timothy Shelley, dined with Bysshe and Harriet and urged Bysshe to write to his father; and Bysshe's mother and sisters were anxious to see him at Field Place. Bysshe had written his father: " If however, I could convince you of the change that has taken place in some of the most unfavourable traits of my Character and of my willingness to make any Concessions that may be judg'd for the Interest of my Family, I flatter myself that there would be little further need of his Grace's Interference." [5] Harriet expected to be at Field Place in a week or two.

Mr. Timothy Shelley thought that the most unfavourable trait of his son's character was atheism; he wrote at once to propose that Shelley inform the authorities at Oxford that he had returned to Christianity. To Shelley's reply that his beliefs were unchanged he answered that until they were changed he would be obliged to refuse communication with him except through the Duke of Norfolk.[6] It was evident to both Shelley and Harriet that a genuine reconciliation was now impossible.[7] Shelley wrote to the Duke of Norfolk to thank him for his friendly interest. " I was prepared," he wrote,

to make my father every reasonable concession, but I am not so degraded and miserable a slave as publicly to disavow an opinion which I believe to be true. Every man of common sense must plainly

see that a sudden renunciation of sentiments seriously taken up is
as unfortunate a test of intellectual uprightness as can possibly be
devised.[8]

Mr. Timothy Shelley had been made stubborn and unreasonable by long disappointment, but it is hard to see how even he
could deny the truth of Shelley's complaint. His wife and
daughters, although in general they supported the father against
the son, evidently did not support his last position. They corresponded with Shelley and Harriet, furnished information as
to Mr. Timothy Shelley's movements, and began planning a
secret visit of Shelley to Field Place, in his father's absence.

Queen Mab left the press probably in May or June 1813, adding
another danger to the financial troubles with which Shelley
was beset. " Indeed, a poem is safe: the iron-souled Attorney
general would scarcely dare to attack," Shelley had assured
Hookham when sending him a " specimen " of the poem almost
a year before.[9] Shelley made it safer by limiting the edition to
250 copies and taking good care that none of these got into
the wrong hands. No copies were sold; only about seventy
copies were disposed of during the poet's life.[10] Whenever the
poet presented anyone with a copy it was his practice to remove
the title page, the dedication, and the imprint at the end of the
volume.[11] The title page bore Shelley's name as both author
and printer, with the address of Shelley's father-in-law: " 23,
Chapel Street, Grosvenor Square." If this was actually Shelley's
address at the time, the poem must have been published early
in May.

The dedicatory poem, "To Harriet " * * * * * [12] shows that in
1813 Shelley not only loved his wife, but actually idealized her:

> Whose is the love that gleaming through the world,
> Wards off the poisonous arrow of its scorn?
>   Whose is the warm and partial praise,
>   Virtue's most sweet reward?

Beneath whose looks did my reviving soul
Riper in truth and virtuous daring grow?
   Whose eyes have I gazed fondly on,
   And loved mankind the more?

Harriet! on thine: — thou wert my purer mind;
Thou wert the inspiration of my song;
   Thine are these early wilding flowers,
   Though garlanded by me.

Then press into thy breast this pledge of love;
And know, though time may change and years may roll,
   Each floweret gathered in my heart
   It consecrates to thine.

The plan of the poem is quite simple. The heroine, Ianthe, lies asleep while her disembodied soul is carried aloft by Queen Mab. From an immense distance she views the past, present, and future of the world, and is instructed by the fairy queen in the significance of what she sees. The voice of Queen Mab is that of Shelley at twenty and twenty-one, with overtones from most of the radical literature he had been reading since he left Eton, and especially during the preceding year. Volney's *Ruins of Empire,* a French Revolutionary work combining history, travel, and radical philosophy, probably furnished the idea of a supernatural revealer and interpreter. Lucretius may have suggested the general notion of a philosophic poem with a somewhat scientific bias that should treat religion as corrupt and selfish superstition. Tom Paine's denunciation of the cruelty of the ancient Jews seems to have inspired Shelley's similar observations. Voltaire, Godwin, Baron d'Holbach, and J. F. Newton are acknowledged sources for various ideas. Most of the philosophical thought is so much the common property of eighteenth-century radical philosophy, and even sometimes of the ancient Epicureans, that it is futile to attempt to assign it to any one particular source. Shelley had read extensively and acutely and had assimilated his reading.

The ideas which the poem was written to express were mainly ideas that Shelley had held for several years already and that he was to continue to hold, with surprisingly little modification, for the rest of his life. They may be briefly summarized thus: The spirit of Nature and of life is Necessity, a passionless, impartial force knowing no limits or decay. It extends throughout the whole universe and governs every minute action of every atom of the natural world, and every whim of thought. Nothing acts but as it must act and was predestined to act, without the variation of a hair, from the first instant of time. Mankind is naturally virtuous and happy, but man has degenerated through the growth of certain evils. Eventually these evils must perish of their own corruption, restoring humanity to virtue and happiness. At present, however, "man's all-subduing will" tolerates his own evils, which depend upon selfishness, superstition, lust, and an animal diet that carries with it the seed of moral and physical evil.[13] God (as in Volney and Voltaire) is a depraved creation of the human mind, a celestial tyrant on an earthly model. Human ignorance and selfishness, as best shown in priestcraft, kingcraft, and commerce, are the causes of tyranny and warfare. Marriage is an expression of selfishness and a violation of individual liberty. It becomes an intolerable tyranny as soon as either party grows tired of it. These are the lessons of the past and present and the basis for hope for the future.

The figure of Ahasuerus, the Wandering Jew, fiercely symbolizes the victim of Christianity, which to Shelley was the worst of all tyrannies. In *Queen Mab* the age-long sufferings of Ahasuerus are hardly mentioned, but nearly two hundred lines of impassioned diatribe are put into his mouth in which he asserts the cruelty and injustice of God, ridicules the doctrine of atonement, presents Christ as a vengeful, hypocritical demagogue, and stands forth against celestial tyranny,

> Mocking my powerless tyrant's horrible curse
> With stubborn and unalterable will —

a clear prototype of the Shelleyan Prometheus.[14]

The lyrical passages, in the unrhymed irregular verse of Southey's *Thalaba* and *The Curse of Kehama,* are certainly as good as their models; the regular blank verse, while far inferior in musical and imaginative quality to Shelley's later blank verse, is quite adequate to its purpose, which is more rhetorical than poetic. The poem is spirited, clear, and well planned. It was taken up by the radicals in 1821, and in the next twenty years went through at least fourteen pirated editions. The followers of Robert Owen, generally regarded as the father of English socialism, took the book as a kind of Bible and frequently quoted texts and passages from it in their ephemeral periodicals.[15] None of Shelley's later poems, intellectually and imaginatively superior as they are, has had half the effect of *Queen Mab* on the actual behaviour of men, or on its author's subsequent fortunes. During the two years following its first appearance Shelley carefully revised the poem, possibly for a later edition; a part of this revision he reprinted in his *Alastor* volume in 1815, as " The Dæmon of the World." Two men were found guilty of blasphemous libel by English courts for publishing *Queen Mab*.[16]

To characterize such a poem merely as " juvenile," as nineteenth-century editors and biographers have generally done, is a prime evidence of inability to " see Shelley plain." Intellectually Shelley ceased being merely juvenile about the time he entered Oxford. *Queen Mab* is in fact the early culmination of Shelley's steady purpose to wage war on every form of oppression. He had already learned in Ireland that in particular situations practical concessions must be made, that actual improvement comes very slowly. This was a principle that he always kept in mind when addressing himself to reform at any particular time and place. It did not inhibit him when, as in *Queen Mab*, he considered the subject of reform poetically, which to him was synonymous with ideally. He was always far more radical under ideal than under practical conditions. Later, under the influence of experience and a changing concept of reality, he removed his mission one step further from active, practical radicalism by taking as his purpose the dissemination of " beautiful idealisms of moral excellence," as he stated in the preface to *Prometheus Unbound*. The underlying principles of his belief, however, never varied greatly from those set forth in *Queen Mab*.

The circumstances under which it circulated naturally prevented *Queen Mab* from attracting attention at the time. Shelley was in the somewhat ridiculous position of having achieved a complete expression of his mission only to feel obliged to conceal it. It must have been his impatience at this circumstance that prompted him to follow it with two pamphlets that could be published, dealing with two of its most important subjects, the evils of eating animal food, and the tyrannies of religion. The first of these was *A Vindication of Natural Diet,* dated 1813 on the title page and priced at one shilling and sixpence. It repeats the *Queen Mab* note on vegetable diet, with slight alterations and additions. There was no reason why Shelley should have printed it anonymously except that it was presented as "one in a series of notes to Queen Mab, a Philosophical Poem." [17]

The second, *A Refutation of Deism, in a Dialogue,* also anonymous, is dated 1814, and probably belongs to the early spring of that year. Here Shelley had the problem of repeating and elaborating the most dangerous ideas in *Queen Mab* without being prosecuted. He accomplished it by presenting his ideas as an argument between Theosophus, a deist, and Eusebes, a Christian. Superficially it might have been written by any well-read, fair-minded clergyman capable of such a clear and flexible prose style as Shelley had now attained. Shelley states his object in the Preface — to show that "Deism is untenable," that "there is no alternative between Atheism and Christianity," and that "the existence of a God can be argued only from Divine Revelation." In the end Theosophus, the deist, is apparently overcome; he abandons his defence of deism and admits that in preference to atheism he would "endeavour to adopt" — not Christianity — but "so much of the Christian scheme as is consistent with my persuasion of the goodness, unity, and majesty of God."

While he was being led to this equivocal conversion, Theosophus made a devastating attack on Christianity. Eusebes, arguing against the deist's grounds for believing in God, made short work of his argument from design, thus destroying one common basis of Christian faith while asserting the sufficiency of another, revelation. In 101 pages of argument Shelley manages to develop more fully and subtly than in *Queen Mab* all his arguments against Christianity without once seeming to champion them. No reader of *Queen Mab* could be deceived for a moment by such ironical praise of Christianity as " The morality of the Christian religion is as original and sublime as its miracles and mysteries are unlike all other portents." On the other hand, no reader not already acquainted with Shelley's views would be inclined to question its face value. The irony throughout is certainly subtle enough to serve one of Shelley's purposes, safety; but it is altogether too subtle to have served effectively the other, an exposure of Christianity. Neither pamphlet, in fact, seems to have had much circulation. No contemporary comment has ever been recorded, and only eight copies of the former and five of the latter have since been discovered.[18]

It was probably during the negotiations with his father that the Shelleys moved from Cooke's Hotel in Albemarle Street [19] to lodgings in Half-Moon Street, which they occupied until some time in June.[20] Even though there was no longer hope of a genuine reconciliation, there was still the possibility that Mr. Timothy Shelley might be induced to rescue his son from the financial difficulties into which he had been sinking. Hogg speaks of " many valuable hours " consumed in the hotel " in the dull diplomacy of his father's agents." [21] Evidently they came to naught. If the Duke of Norfolk made any further representations to Mr. Timothy Shelley [22] they were without apparent financial results. Early in June, probably, the Shelleys left their lodgings in Half-Moon Street and moved to Pimlico.

For the last year Shelley's expectation of reaching a financial settlement upon attaining his majority had encouraged his tendency to spend beyond his means. This hope being now disappointed, he turned in real desperation to Mr. Thomas Charles Medwin, who had previously aided him with money and legal advice.[23] Harriet's confinement was being hourly expected, and he hoped that Mr. Medwin might see him through

the attendant financial difficulties. Again Shelley sought information that would facilitate an appeal to the dealers in
post-obits against whom Mr. Medwin had previously warned
him: " I know that I am heir to large property. How are the
papers to be seen? Have you the least doubt but that I am
the safe heir to a large landed property? Have you any certain
knowledge on the subject? " [24] This correspondence practically
coincides with an undertaking to assume William Godwin's
financial worries along with his own. Godwin had to raise
three thousand pounds. " More than twelve months ago," wrote
Godwin on August 27, 1814, Shelley " undertook by his assistance to rescue me from my pecuniary difficulties." [25]

Mr. Medwin's attempt to arrange an interview was somewhat hampered by Shelley's inability to leave Harriet until after
the birth of her child. On June 28 [26] Shelley asked him for an
early interview, informing him at the same time that Harriet
had been safely delivered of a daughter and was rapidly recovering. Mr. Medwin came to dinner with the Shelleys on
July 7 (causing Shelley to break an engagement with Hogg),[27]
but the amount and precise nature of his aid is uncertain. Possibly he was the source of a belief expressed soon afterwards
by Harriet that the Shelley family could and would deprive Shelley of his right to inherit — a belief which was kindly dissipated
by Mr. Timothy Shelley himself, in an interview — probably
his last — which Shelley somehow managed to obtain with him
about the end of August.[28]

There was a pressing danger that Shelley would be arrested
for debt. Bailiffs actually did lock a door upon the shrinking
figure of Mr. Thomas Jefferson Hogg, proclaiming that he was
Mr. Percy Bysshe Shelley, and under arrest for debt.[29] Harriet
was assured by Shelley's sister that Mr. Timothy Shelley was
doing everything in his power to prevent Shelley's arrest. Yet
his desperate financial condition continued unabated and soon
led to raising money on post-obits.

A minor worry not unconnected with their financial difficulties was the faithful Daniel Hill, who had returned to England with Eliza Westbrook. There was nothing for him to do,
and very little that he could do, except eat. While still at

Cooke's Hotel Dan overate to the extent of bringing on an illness and had to be removed to a hospital. Here, according to the unsympathetic Hogg, he was cured largely by the substitution of hospital for hotel fare. Both Harriet and Bysshe were so pleased with his constant loyalty that they were unwilling to get rid of him, even though he was an expense and something of a nuisance. He was supposed by his employers to be homesick for Ireland, but when they sent him home in July or August, Dan turned quite insolent. He bore to Dublin, to the ear of John Lawless, a tale of wrongs at the hands of the Shelleys that caused "Honest Jack" (already regarded by the Shelleys as dishonest) to write Shelley a letter of protest.[30]

DESPITE financial difficulties, the Shelleys did not find their life in London unpleasant. Harriet was jolly and easy-going, Shelley too genuinely careless of mere creature comforts to be disturbed by circumstances that sorely grieved their most constant visitor. Even in retrospect Mr. Thomas Jefferson Hogg counted it a triumph of friendship to have endured their hospitality for the sake of their company. Ordering a dinner was a sacred rite to Hogg, but to Shelley it was an embarrassment and an impertinence, and to Harriet a matter of indifference. "Ask Harriet," Shelley would cry out in desperate self-defence. "Whatever you please," Harriet would say by way of ordering. Harriet had known nothing of housewifery when she married and had learned nothing since. The result was that Hogg was condemned to dinners for which he felt a profound disrespect:

Some considerable time after the appointed hour, a roasted shoulder of mutton, of the coarsest, toughest grain, graced, or disgraced, the ill-supplied table; the watery gravy that issued from the perverse joint, when it was cut, a duty commonly assigned to me, seemed the most apt of all things to embody the conception of penury and utter destitution. There were potatoes in every respect worthy of the mutton; and the cheese, which was either forgotten or uneatable, closed the ungenial repast. Sometimes there was a huge boiled leg of mutton, boiled till the bone was ready to drop out of the meat, which shrank and started from it on all sides, without any sauce, but with turnips raw, and manifestly unworthy to be boiled any longer. Sometimes there were impregnable beefsteaks — soles for shooting-shoes. I have dropped a word, a hint, about a pudding; a pudding, Bysshe said dogmatically, is a prejudice. I have wished that the converse of the proposition were true, and that a prejudice was a pudding, and then, according to the judgment of my more enlightened young friends, I should never have been without one.[31]

Had not Shelley and Harriet been practising vegetarianism with renewed fervour (even though they did not require conformity in their guests), it might have been better for Hogg's comfort. In theory Shelley quite agreed with Mr. Newton about alcoholic drinks; he never tasted whisky, and drank beer and weak wine only occasionally, and never of his own initiative.[32] Shelley did not really object to physical comforts, as Hogg shrewdly noticed; he accepted them with a gracious ease when they came his way in the natural course of events; but he objected on principle to luxury and ostentation, and he thought of food quite simply as necessary if one were to continue long to learn and propagate the truth, but not in itself important. Thus he ate when he felt hungry and when it was convenient. He would dash into a shop, buy a loaf of bread, and break off and eat pieces from it as he walked along. In his pockets he generally carried raisins with which occasionally to supplement the dry bread. The spot where he sat reading or writing was often ringed about with crumbs. As he munched his bread, whether in a coffee-house, at home, or on the street, he sometimes practised what seemed to Hogg totally unconscious marksmanship with bread pellets. Deeply immersed in his own thoughts, he would roll a bread pellet between his fingers and flip it with his thumb unerringly toward its mark — a portrait, an image, or the nose of a pedestrian or fellow diner. He never missed, and he was never suspected by any of his human victims because he was never himself actually conscious of being the offender.

Shelley often prepared a dish for himself called panada, which a French lady had shown him how to make by soaking bread in hot water, squeezing out the water, and sprinkling the bread with pounded sugar and grated nutmeg. Having previously eaten a large bowl of this delicacy, he was often quite indifferent to regular meals. He objected, on theory, to muffins and crumpets with tea, because they were apt to be buttered, but when the buttered muffins were served him without comment he would eat them without noticing the defilement to which they had been subjected. Between Harriet's incompetence and their combined indifference they came to rely largely upon penny buns as an accessory to tea.[33] Habits such as these might well be supposed to be injurious to health — as indeed Peacock did suppose a year or two later — but their early effects at least were not noticeably harmful. Harriet, according to Hogg, was as energetic as ever; Shelley bounded up and down steps and delivered his fine bravura knocks at his friends' doorways with undiminished vigour. He was reported by Harriet to be in perfect health.[34]

Much of Shelley's activity in London had to do with mysterious goings and comings about which Hogg knew nothing and concerning which he chose to be tolerantly amused. From Hogg's ignorance we may assume that they were mainly concerned with Shelley's radical and philanthropic interests, to which he knew his friend had ceased to be sympathetic.

For the rest, there were his friends, old and new, and his books. Thomas Hookham lived near Cooke's Hotel and the Half-Moon Street lodgings; Chester Street, where the Newtons lived, was within easy walking distance. At Hookham's house, probably at his shop while *Queen Mab* was going through the press, there must have been occasional talks with Thomas Love Peacock.[35] Hogg was frequently on hand for discussions and long walks through the London streets. Edward Graham and John Grove were seen occasionally, though John Grove soon left London to enter the University of Edinburgh. A Mr. Ryan, whom the Shelleys had known in Dublin, saw them several times between early May and late June of 1813.[36] Toward the end of June, John Williams of Tremadoc was in London and in contact with the Shelleys.[37]

For over two months there was little association with the Godwins, an odd circumstance that is partly explained by Harriet's resentment of Mrs. Godwin's " dreadfully disagreeable " disposition,[38] which may have led her, among other things, to speak her mind about the last dinner invitation she had received from the Shelleys.[39] Shelley told Godwin quite frankly of Harriet's feelings, and Godwin, to whom complaints of his spouse's temper were certainly no surprise, appears to have persuaded Mrs. Godwin to attempt to remove this feeling. At least on June 9, the day after Godwin called, his journal records that " M. J." (Mary Jane Godwin) called on Shelley, and after that date intercourse between the two families was more frequent, but the interchange of dinners that had formerly gone on so briskly was not renewed. Shelley's half-uncle, John Shelley of Penshurst, called upon him several times in London and urged him to visit Penshurst, but Shelley declined. He rather liked his uncle, who thought Mr. Timothy Shelley unreasonable toward his son; but he had been to Penshurst before and he did not like his aunt or the society she entertained.[40]

There were, of course, plenty of casual contacts of which little or no record survives. Hogg speaks of Harriet's Quaker doctor, the distinguished and preternaturally silent " Dr. John S.," and of a slight acquaintance Shelley formed with the Earl of Oxford.[41] Many persons who were in Hogg's opinion mere cranks or adventurers imposed upon Shelley at this time. They saw in him a young man of good prospects, whose debts would be paid and who would be given a reasonable allowance in a few months when he reached his majority. To some of them he probably listened with more sympathy than Hogg knew of, but by others he was keenly annoyed. One such visitor who seems to have annoyed only Hogg was a nameless young poet who delighted Harriet by talking most desperately on one of her own favourite subjects — an intention to commit suicide. " There was no end of obtrusion," Hogg complained:

the word intrusion is not strong enough. One person wanted to teach Harriet Italian; another, probably, would have given, or sold to Eliza, instructions in Hebrew, or Arabic; but the greater number, without any excuse or pretense, forced themselves upon him. He was a rock to which limpets stuck fast, and periwinkles attached themselves.[42]

Among all of his London friends the Newton family seemed to Shelley the most delightful. Even the usually disdainful Hogg pronounced this family to be truly elegant and testified that Shelley derived great delight and great advantage from their company. Some time before the middle of May [43] Shelley took Hogg with him to dine at their home. Hogg was startled to see five healthy, happy, completely nude children rush to the door to greet Shelley. They fled incontinently to the nursery when they saw him accompanied by a stranger. Hogg was on this occasion so impressed with the Newtonian theory and practice of nudism, about which he had not been warned, that he actually failed to comment upon the food; but this oversight he later remedied by a general account of vegetarianism as practised by the Shelleys and Newtons. Hence we know that on this, as on later occasions, he drank distilled water, tea or coffee, and ate bread-cakes with little or no butter, fruits, vegetables, and possibly honey. Mr. Newton himself, in the book from which Shelley drew some of the information incorporated in the long note on vegetarianism in *Queen Mab*, has given a general account of the meals in his household, meals often eaten by the Shelleys:

Our breakfast is composed of dried fruits, whether raisins, figs, or plums, with toasted bread or biscuits, and weak tea, always made of distilled water with a moderate portion of milk in it. The children, who do not seem to like the flavour of tea, use milk with water instead of it. When butter is added to the toast, it is in a very small quantity. The dinner consists of potatoes, with some other vegetables, according as they happen to be in season; macaroni, a tart, or a pudding, with as few eggs in it as possible: to this is sometimes added a dessert. Onions, especially those from Portugal, may be stewed with a little walnut pickle and some other vegetable ingredients for which no cook will be at a loss, so as to constitute an excellent sauce for all other vegetables. As to drinking, we are scarcely inclined, on this cooling regimen, to drink at all; but when it so happens, we take distilled water, having a still expressly for this purpose in our back kitchen. [44]

" Certainly their vegetable dinners were delightful, elegant and excellent repasts," Hogg testified. [45] He became himself a vegetarian for a while and recalled with some enthusiasm, long after he had relapsed into a carnivorous state, the "soups in great variety," all "the finest and best" vegetables "dressed with care and skill," plain, stewed, or artfully disguised, and the fruits, puddings, seed-cakes, and numerous confections of his vegetarian days.

Shelley reached the height of his vegetarianism in this environment. He argued that eating animal flesh was the basis not only of human disease, but of human vices as well. Man had only to confine himself to a harmless Newtonian diet in order to free himself from disease and from the various social and political evils to which he is at present addicted through his predatory, carnivorous habits. In practice, Shelley was a strict vegetarian only among the orthodox, but when alone or with non-vegetarians he sometimes lapsed. He could be as unconscious of his food as of any other physical circumstance, and it may be quite true, as Hogg reports, that in the Lake region a few months later he was seen settling down to a solitary meal of cold boiled beef.[46]

The well-appointed home of the Newtons was almost a second home to Shelley while he was in London. Mr. Newton was a man of knowledge and refinement. He was Godwin's contemporary rather than Shelley's, being forty-six years of age in 1813, but he was an agreeable companion for the poet, anxious like Shelley to improve humanity, preaching his hobbies with almost Shelleyan devotion and resourcefulness. He elaborated a theory that the ancient signs of the zodiac in the temple at Dendera constituted a vegetarian allegory and he could think of almost anything as related to this mystical significance. Thus he imagined that a public-house having four horseshoes for a sign had faithfully preserved therein the meaning of the four quarters of the zodiac — even though the astonished innkeeper denied any such knowledge and seemed to think the mystic four more closely connected with the number of shoes expected by the horse.[47] Newton was so impressed with the potential value to humanity of the notes he supposed Horne Tooke must have written in his copy of Newton's *Return to Nature* that he commissioned a friend to bid as much as two hundred guineas for it at the sale of Horne Tooke's library. (It was bought for him for eighteen pence, with the leaves still uncut.[48])

Mrs. Newton, the daughter of a wealthy West Indian planter who had retired to England, was an attractive, sympathetic woman, the mother of five very healthy and well-trained young children. She was quite competent to express critical opinions of English literature and was an accomplished musician. While Mrs. Newton was making music with some fellow artist, Shelley, whose musical tastes were simpler than those of the performers, often retired to a corner of the room and told ghost-stories to the children.[49] The Newtons had a considerable acquaintance among people of culture and influence, which might have been of greater service to Shelley had he co-operated a little more fully with their well-intentioned efforts. The Chevalier Lawrence, with whom Shelley had previously opened a correspondence, was a visitor at their house and also at Shelley's.[50] Although Hogg does not mention names, it is clear from his account that most of the efforts to introduce Shelley to various people originated within the friendly, ad-miring group of which the Newtons seem to have been the centre. It was Mrs. Newton who successfully introduced Shelley to the gaieties of Vauxhall Gardens, with its multitude of twinkling lights, its fireworks, and its lively music. A mere mundane critic, seeing him there with Mrs. Newton, remarked Hogg, " might have declared that there was a most desperate flirtation between them; a more spiritualized observer . . . would discern in their union a strong and close sympathy, and would describe and designate it as such."[51] Shelley also at-tended dances at this time, at least occasionally.

It was thought that the sympathy and sprightly common sense of the Countess of Oxford might be a great advantage to the eccentric young poet; the Countess herself was interested and spoke of him with kindness and regard, but before a meet-ing could be brought about the Earl and his Countess departed for Italy.[52] An artist employed to paint a portrait of Dr. Samuel Parr, the classical scholar and liberal Whig and churchman, praised Shelley very highly to Hogg and expressed a desire to arrange a meeting between Shelley and Parr, but the meeting

never came off, though other friends of Shelley's, probably the
Newtons, cherished the same desire.[53] It was also planned to
make Shelley acquainted with Fanny Burney, but he either neglected or evaded the opportunity.[54] Hogg several times endeavoured to bring about meetings between Shelley and various
people of his acquaintance and was never so angry with his
friend as when people would come to town, or dinners would
be arranged, only to discover at the last moment that the poet
was nowhere to be found.[55]

Through the Newtons the Shelleys became acquainted with
Mrs. Boinville and her circle. Mrs. Boinville was an older sister
of Mrs. Newton. Her husband, a distinguished but penniless
French émigré and a friend of Lafayette, had returned to
France under the Consulate and had rendered valuable service
to Napoleon. He died during the retreat from Moscow, on
February 7, 1813, not long after the death of Mr. Collins, his
wife's father. The double sorrow had turned Mrs. Boinville's
hair perfectly white by the time the Shelleys made her acquaintance in April or May 1813. Shelley sometimes called her Mai-
muna, from the character in Southey's *Thalaba,* whose

> face was as a damsel's face,
> And yet her hair was white.

When the Shelleys left their lodgings on Half-Moon Street,
probably about the middle of June, it was in order to live only
a few doors away from Mrs. Boinville, who with her eighteen-
year-old daughter, Cornelia, occupied a house in a quiet street
in Pimlico.[56] Hogg speaks of Shelley as being warmly attached
to Mrs. Boinville, which rather understates the case, according
to Shelley's own testimony:

I could not help considering Mrs. B[oinville], when I knew her, as
the most admirable specimen of a human being I had ever seen.
Nothing earthly ever appeared to be more perfect than her character
and manners. . . . Cornelia, although so young when I saw her,
gave indications of her mother's excellences, and, certainly less fas-
cinating, is I doubt not, equally amiable and more sincere. It was
hardly possible for a person of the extreme subtlety and delicacy of

Mrs. Boinville's understanding and affections to be quite sincere and constant.[57]

From this it is easy to guess that if any of Shelley's letters to Mrs. Boinville could be found [58] they would in some respects resemble the letters to Elizabeth Hitchener. When the Boinville family moved to Bracknell, Berkshire, thirty miles from London, the Shelleys followed them about the middle of July, and took a house in Bracknell known as High Elms House. Harriet described the move to Catherine Nugent as one " merely for convenience," which may refer equally well to avoiding association with the Middlesex bailiffs and preserving association with the Boinvilles.

The circle of people who forgathered in June and July of 1813 at Mrs. Boinville's house in Pimlico and later at Bracknell overlapped somewhat with the Newton circle but contained probably more French émigrés and more political and social radicals. Hogg, in spite of his conservative prejudices, approved of Shelley's friendship with the Newtons, but heartily disliked most of the company in which he found him at Mrs. Boinville's. Mrs. Boinville herself he thought " an amiable and accomplished old lady, and tolerably agreeable, but too much of the French school to be quite so "; but " the greater part of her associates " he thought were simply " odious." [59]

This " rabble rout " Hogg endured for a while for Shelley's sake, but he thoroughly disapproved of the " higgledy-piggledy ways " and half-baked sentiments with which in his opinion they were debasing his friend. Once he practically kidnapped Shelley from their very door. " Come along," he exclaimed, " let us take a walk together, let us leave the sentimentalists to ripen for the gallows by themselves! " After a long walk through the fields, ending in a coffee-room at Kensington, Shelley remarked with a sigh: " How I wish I could be as fastidious and exclusive as you are, but I cannot — " [60] In the domestic misfortunes that were even then being prepared for Shelley, Hogg did not hold his Bracknell associates altogether innocent.[61]

With the ladies of both these circles of friends Shelley

was extraordinarily popular. His romantic personal beauty, his harmless eccentricity, gentle manners, and earnest enthusiasms made him, in Hogg's opinion, irresistibly attractive to them. They called him by affectionate names and thought elegant society his proper vocation [62] — hence the desire to introduce him to the Countess of Oxford. One elderly "blue," who took mustard in her coffee because she had once seen Frederick the Great do so, was a great admirer and friend of the young poet and expressed keen disappointment when he failed to attend her lecture on the evils of wearing stays.[63] Mrs. Newton and Mrs. Boinville were both obviously very fond of him. To the young and intellectual and to the sentimental Shelley's company was particularly attractive. Since his eloquence and enthusiasm commonly waxed brightest when other people should normally be ready for bed, it frequently happened that he sat up all night enthralling two or three young ladies with his talk of wisdom and virtue.[64] One of his greatest admirers was a beautiful young perfectionist to whom Hogg rendered himself temporarily displeasing by suggesting that when perfectibility arrived she might take an apartment with Hogg in a huge hollow emerald. In various conversations with Hogg she spoke of Shelley with warmth, admiration and enthusiasm. "I would gladly, oh, so gladly, give half of all I possess if he were an habitual . . . even an occasional visitor. Cannot you bring him to me?" She quoted a conversation between herself and another lady in which they praised Shelley as "so modest, so reserved, so pure, so virtuous" and agreed that he would make terrible havoc among the ladies if he were at all rakish.[65]

It is quite possible that Hogg's anecdotes of Shelley as a ladies' man are somewhat exaggerated by his constant desire to make a good story, but even as Hogg tells them it is evident that Shelley was interested in ladies only as they were interested — or seemed interested — in the ideas that were all-important to him.[66] The Shelley Hogg knew in the spring and summer of 1813 was only superficially different from the Shelley he had met three years earlier at Oxford.

The whole soul of my ardent and imaginative young friend was inflamed at this period of his life, by a glowing desire to witness and to promote the improvement and progress of civil society. He had translated an essay, or treatise, of some French philosopher, on the Perfectibility of the Human Species; and he read his translation aloud to me.[67]

Having devoted himself as a youth to the overthrow of tyrannies, he had developed while at Oxford a perfectly satisfactory method of fitting himself for his part. This consisted mainly in much reading and much discussion. In this most important item his expulsion from Oxford was never allowed to make any difference.

There was now a much greater diversity between the political and social views of the two friends than had formerly existed, but Shelley was not intolerant of honest disagreement. The old walks with Hogg were resumed, even though they were less frequent and the discussions more reserved than in earlier days of more complete sympathy and confidence. Hogg would call for Shelley at his lodgings or at the Newtons' or Boinvilles', or Shelley would call at Hogg's lodgings, and they would take long walks across the fields or through the streets, generally winding up at some coffee-house for tea. Sometimes, in lieu of the walk, Shelley and Hogg would sit up all night, discussing books and playing chess. Doubtless there were other walks and many other discussions, of which Hogg never knew, with Peacock, Hookham, the Chevalier Lawrence, Mr. or Mrs. Newton, and Mrs. Boinville.

Hogg has little to say concerning the discussions that took place during his walks with Shelley, but he has left a rather vivid impression of the walks themselves. Through many unknown London streets, said Hogg, " I always let him lead the way and followed his guidance: his course and choice of direction were erratic and uncommon, and he would dart across the road and quickly enter some unpromising, ill-omened street or passage, and hurry me along it: I have often wondered by what impulse he was thus borne along. His flight was to escape

from, not to pursue; to get away from some object for which
he had conceived a sudden dislike." [68] It is just possible that
on some of these occasions he was seeking to escape from the
" conversation." Hogg annoyed Shelley by laughing at Godwin's *Political Justice.* " You laugh at everything! " Shelley complained on another occasion. " I am convinced that there can
be no entire regeneration of mankind until laughter is put
down! " When Hogg was in such a mood Shelley told him that
his mind was " not fitted for the reception of truth." [69]

THE reading of books went forward as steadily as ever. During the spring, while living in the Half-Moon Street lodgings,
Shelley would sit long hours in a little projecting window looking so bright and happy, that Mrs. Newton compared him to
some young lady's lark, hanging outside for air and song.[70] No
matter how many books he may have left behind at various
lodgings, Shelley never required more than a few days to as-
semble a respectable library at his next stop. In the little sitting-
room on Half-Moon Street books were arranged in rows on the
floor, they occupied the recesses on either side of the fireplace,
were piled in disorder on tables and chairs, and were heaped up
under the tables. The only ones that Hogg mentioned by title
were the neglected Latin translation of the works of Immanuel
Kant, and Sir Walter Scott's *Rokeby,* hot from the press, with
which Harriet demonstrated all her old powers of reading
aloud.[71] Perhaps she also continued reading aloud from the
books with which she had first entertained Hogg in the room
at Cooke's Hotel — Drummond's *Academical Questions,* Smith's
Theory of Moral Sentiments, Bishop Berkeley's works, and
Southey's *Chronicle of the Cid.*[72] Shortly afterwards, at Bracknell, Shelley read with intense admiration C. M. Wieland's
Agathon.

On occasion Shelley also read aloud, usually some sublime
passage from the *Iliad* or the *Odyssey,* both of which he had
read through more than once. He read " with extreme rapidity,

animation, and energy, raising his shrill voice, until it equalled
the crowing of a cock; nor would he cease before he reached the
end of the book, and then closing it, he laid it gently upon the
ground, and lifting up his eyes to the ceiling, he exclaimed with
heartfelt pleasure, 'Hah!' remaining for some minutes in an
attitude of veneration, wholly absorbed in pleasure and admiration." [73] He often read Homer as he lay in front of the
fire, striking the flame from the coals with shovel or fire-iron,
gradually acquiring an eyestrain and a very ruddy colour in
the cheek next the fire. Similarly he pored over various moral
and metaphysical writers, giving somewhat closer attention to
the materialists than to the idealists.

In order that he might extend his reading even more widely,
Shelley now took up the study of Italian with Hogg. Their
instigators and tutors were " certain amiable and elegant friends
and associates whose favourite studies were the Italian language
and literature, some of whom even had formerly resided in
Italy," [74] including, apparently, Mrs. Boinville and her daughter.
Though Hogg applied himself industriously, he was soon far
outdistanced by Shelley, whose quickness and insight made
him a better linguist. Through Tasso's *Jerusalem Delivered*
they proceeded at an even and equal pace, emerging in the
end "more than half Crusaders and not altogether indisposed
to enlist under the sacred banners of Godfrey." But when they
came to the *Orlando Furioso* Shelley discovered that romance
and paladins "were his own proper, peculiar element." He
was borne away on an enthusiastic flood of magic and marvels;
parts of it he read again and again, sometimes aloud. He dis-
coursed upon it "with wild rapture" during his walks with
Hogg. Petrarch was read under the tutelage of a lady who considered herself a prey to pensive melancholy. She found and ex-
pounded beauties of sentiment and expression in Petrarch's long
devotion to Laura which made him for her the greatest of all
poetic lovers, an attitude in which Bysshe, but not the flippant
Hogg, fully concurred. [75]

With his mental horizon thus steadily expanding, and with
a number of pleasant associates, the year 1813 and the early
months of 1814 were for Shelley and Harriet an " auspicious,

beneficial, and happy period." [76] In the things that mattered most — reading and discussion — Shelley was doing precisely as he had done at Oxford.

IN 1813 and 1814 Shelley printed his first significant volume, realized the hopelessness of reconciliation with his father, and made a decision that changed and complicated his future more than any other event in his life. It is important, therefore, to see as fully and clearly as we can just what sort of person he was at this time. Hogg, even though not always reliable, must be our principal authority. [77]

A youthful army officer who met Shelley in the early summer of 1814 described him as slender, rather delicate-looking, with a slight gentlemanly stoop, an unusually small head, dark, rather unkempt hair, expressive eyes, a beautifully fair complexion and very fine features, with a somewhat careless attitude toward clothes, a frank, simple, earnest way of talking, and a natural good breeding in all of his actions. [78] Hogg never remembered seeing Shelley in a greatcoat or cloak, even in coldest weather. His waistcoat was generally only partly buttoned, his shirt-collar commonly unbuttoned, and his neck-cloth either cast aside or lost. He wore a hat in the streets as a reluctant concession to custom, but when walking in the fields he generally went bareheaded. The wild appearance of his hair was due partly to his habit of plunging his head in cold water several times daily and afterwards frequently running his fingers through his hair to separate it and facilitate drying. [79]

The idea that Shelley's health was at this time particularly delicate is definitely rejected by Hogg. Like Harriet, he was constantly indulging in talk about suicide; he even told Hogg a purely fanciful story about having attempted suicide when rejected by an imaginary young lady shortly before entering Oxford. He suffered occasionally from certain painful infirmities and at times coughed violently and felt pains in his side and chest. He sometimes thought he was consumptive and declared that he broke blood-vessels and spat blood, but Hogg watched closely and could never get any confirmation of this assertion. It was his opinion that Shelley's constitution and general health were good and that the occasional indispositions were due to habitual imprudence of dress and diet rather than to constitutional weaknesses.[80] Peacock seemed to think that Shelley suffered from little more than bad diet.[81] The money-lenders from whom Shelley borrowed consistently from 1813 until he left England evidently agreed with Hogg and Peacock. These unsentimental dealers in post-obits did not hesitate to risk large sums on the probability that Shelley would survive his father or grandfather or both, and only one of them thought it worth while to protect the risk by insuring Shelley's life.

Nothing about Shelley impressed Hogg more strongly than his extremely sympathetic and fanciful imagination. " He lived and moved and had his being under the absolute, despotical empire of a vivid, fervid fancy." [82] This led him sometimes to identify himself completely with the subject of his thought or fancy. A few passing remarks about a fabulous shorthand writer who eventually abbreviated his system to absolute zero led Shelley to the unconscious study of blank sheets of paper for invisible symbols. A consequent remark about the extreme fatigue probably endured by Tiro, the supposed inventor of shorthand, caused Shelley a few minutes later to exhibit the same fatigue that his fancy imputed to Tiro.[83]

The same tendency could produce positive delusions of much longer duration. After having read somewhere an account of a rare disease called elephantiasis, characterized by an enormous swelling of the legs, Shelley observed that an old woman sitting opposite him in a crowded stagecoach possessed legs of an extraordinary thickness. He immediately imagined her to be a victim of this disease and feared that he had contracted it from her. Soon he discovered unmistakable symptoms in himself, nor could the ridicule or expostulations of his friends disabuse him of his conviction. One day while sitting in an armchair talking to Mr. and Mrs. Newton, he fell writhing upon the floor and informed his startled hosts that he had elephantiasis.[84] He was persuaded to consult an eminent physician, who also failed to destroy the illusion. Convinced that he was doomed to an early and horrible death, he went about in great dejection examining his friends, even young ladies at a dance, for signs of the cracked and roughened skin that was supposed to be a symptom of the disease. He persisted in the delusion for several weeks and then gave way to some more cheerful exercise of the imagination.[85]

Shelley was often the creature of sudden impulse when there was no question of delusion. His friends were not surprised if he sometimes vanished for a while, abruptly and without apparent cause. "No human being," says Hogg, with his usual love of sweeping statements, "no poet, was ever less punctual; he had no perception, no notion of time."[86] He "could follow no other laws than the golden law of doing instantly whatever the inclination of the moment prompted."[87]

He took strange caprices, unfounded frights and dislikes, vain apprehensions and panic terrors, and therefore he absented himself from formal and sacred engagements. He was unconscious and oblivious of times, places, persons, and seasons, and . . . quickly and completely forgot all that he had repeatedly and solemnly promised; or he ran away after some object of imaginary urgency and importance, which suddenly came into his head.[88]

It is hard not to regard this statement as exaggerated, yet Peacock did not offer to amend it, and his own less strongly worded account, as well as other incidental evidence, supports the general truth of Hogg's assertion. Hogg seems not to have considered the possibility that such a person as he described might break solemn promises through never having been fully aware of making them.

Shelley was not entirely without a sense of humour, a rather odd one that was sometimes related to his imaginative assimilation of other characters. An acquaintance named Graham (who may or may not have been Edward Fergus Graham) had become involved in a ridiculous flirtation with a fair admirer who turned out eventually to be quite mad. One day Shelley called on him and was received in a state of extreme panic, being mistaken at first for the vengeful husband. The details of Graham's fright and of the inamorata's mad letters seemed so ludicrous to Shelley that he often related the story, acting parts

313

of it, "shrieking with paroxysms of the wildest laughter." [89]
Shelley liked to relate another droll story of a madwoman, and
he occasionally listened to such stories with pleasure. His
natural mood was quite grave and serious, "yet occasionally
he could be merry notwithstanding the strong aversion for
laughter and ridicule which he habitually and vehemently expressed." [90] When he did laugh, his mirth was sometimes wild
and uncontrollable. Hogg was considerably embarrassed by
Shelley's bursting into sudden laughter during a conversation
at Bracknell with an elderly French émigré whom he considered
absurd. At another time, when Shelley accompanied Hogg into
the dining-hall of Lincoln's Inn, he was suddenly smitten with
the weighty triviality of the great Sir Thomas Plumer's remarks
and rushed from the room with wild shrieks of laughter. Such
"unexpected, vehement, irrepressible bursts of laughter were
often distressing," at least to Hogg, who was left to do the explaining. [91] Hogg's constant emphasis on the wildness of Shelley's laughter conveys an almost maniacal suggestion that seems
excessive. Peacock saw more deeply and truly into the nature
of Shelley's sense of humour when he remarked that Shelley
(four years later) would laugh at nothing which offended good
feeling or perverted moral judgment, and for that reason what
seemed to him truly ludicrous presented itself with greater
force, and he "laughed heartily." [92]

Did Hogg himself see Shelley simply as a queerly dressed,
impatient, impulsive, wildly enthusiastic, unreliable food-fad-
dist and ladies' darling whose very laughter was tinged with
a maniacal suggestion? The answer is plainly "No." Allowing
for his characteristic exaggeration [93] and occasional misunderstanding, his account rings true. Not all the details are verifiable
from other sources, but the picture is not contrary to the inferences to be drawn from Shelley's own letters, it is refuted
by no independently known data, and is supported in general
by Peacock and in its most fantastic detail, the elephantiasis
delusion, by both Peacock and Madame Gatayes. The trouble
lies not with the incidents but with Hogg's farcical sense of
humour and his insensitiveness. Hogg himself is so emphatic
about the attractiveness of Shelley's conversation and person-

ality that his fundamental admiration is obvious enough, and Hogg was never the kind of person to waste his admiration on fools. By his insensitive *fortissimo* methods he spoiled the picture, not for himself, but for over-sensitive defenders of the poet who would themselves sometimes spoil the picture in an opposite direction.

Hogg commonly records his observations for the intrinsic interest of each detail. Once the reader seeks to connect them with one another in terms of character he finds precisely what he would have expected to find had he read all the other materials except Hogg. He finds that in 1813 and 1814 Shelley was a mild-mannered, impulsive young man with a natural fondness for the society of women and children, and a strong love of literature dealing with magic, violence, and rescue, whether of a holy city, in Tasso, or a damsel to be sacrificed to a sea-monster, in Ariosto. All this, with his fondness for fireworks and the tales of magic he loved to tell the Newton children, was purely and simply an extension of his early years into his young manhood. The worship of Love in which he revelled in reading Petrarch and Wieland had been foreshadowed by his own early letters to Hogg. The habits of study and perambulating discussion were the Oxford life continued. The metaphysical, anti-religious, and revolutionary ideas of his youth were still present, though Hogg says less about them than one would expect. Even this seems less remarkable when we recall the points on which Hogg and his friend were now least in sympathy and also that when Hogg wrote of them all Shelley's surviving friends were more or less apologizing for or unconsciously disguising his radicalism into something acceptable to Victorian liberalism. Whatever the young ladies may have thought about it, the all-night sessions of serious talk with them that evidently puzzled Hogg were too much like the early missionary efforts with his own sisters, the Westbrook sisters, and Elizabeth Hitchener not to be essentially the same thing.

Through practically all the phenomena of conduct that Hogg's account presents run three very definite threads that were already well established by Shelley's previous conduct: an extreme sympathetic capacity to become the person with whom his imagination was for the moment engaged, a tendency to act upon momentary impulse, and a simple, intense preoccupation with his own sense of mission which made it quite natural for him genuinely to ignore details of food, clothing, and conventional social obligations. Here, if anywhere, was a young man whose imaginative childhood persisted side by side with a highly sensitive and sophisticated intellectual penetration; and in whom an absorbing purpose of subconscious fixity coexisted with a naïve impulsiveness that rendered him — superficially — a person unpredictably erratic. Here also was the same young man not inconsistent with the rough and ready judgments of most of the people who observed and commented upon Shelley between the time he entered Syon House Academy and the time he left Oxford.[94]

We need not here discuss the well-worn question of the relation between genius and insanity, the attractive paradox that clarity of purpose and insight may itself become so terribly intense as to constitute insanity. One is simply compelled to perceive that, at least between the ages of twenty and twenty-three, Shelley was on the verge of insanity as it is ordinarily recognized. He had a delusion of persecution which Hogg barely recognizes in a few chance phrases[95] but which is clear from his earlier letters to Elizabeth Hitchener and Godwin, and from his attitude toward his father and toward Robert Leeson of Tremadoc; Peacock clearly recognized it as important in the early summer of 1816.[96] His wild impulsiveness and the extreme sensibility by which he could assimilate to himself the experience of others had a definitely recognizable pathological tinge and somewhat obscured from observation a singleness of purpose that amounted at times — as indicated in the Elizabeth Hitchener letters — almost to obsession.

A sudden alteration of health or an unusual mental shock might at any time result in conduct inconsistent with his basic character as a friendly, well-mannered young man of intellectual acuteness and great personal charm. He could write to Hogg (June 23, 1811): "I can find an excuse for madness, because I myself am often mad"; in letters to Elizabeth Hitchener he could refer semi-humorously to his reputation for madness; he could behave at Field Place in October 1811 in a manner that convinced his father and apparently his mother and sisters of temporary madness; he could furiously accuse his mother on the basis of an anonymous letter that he had shortly before pronounced ridiculous; and he was later to endow practically all of his autobiographical characters — Laon, Lionel, and the Madman of " Julian and Maddalo " — with various degrees of occasional madness. The conclusion seems inescapable. Tom Medwin saw and stated it quite clearly: " Insanity hung as by a hair suspended over the head of Shelley." [97] And yet it would be a most stupid error indeed to substitute this possible Shelley of some particular moment for the much more apparent and stable character that was respected and loved by most people who knew him.

NEITHER Hogg nor Peacock has much to say of Harriet during the residence in London. In Cooke's Hotel and in Half-Moon Street she had been full of good health and good humour and as devoted as ever to reading aloud. The birth of Ianthe in June seems a reasonable explanation for the fact that we do not hear of her presence in the various companies in which Hogg so frequently described Shelley. The Newtons sometimes saw her in her own home,[98] and presumably in theirs, and it is to be supposed she exchanged neighbourhood visits with the Boinvilles after she and Shelley moved to Pimlico to be near them. Eliza Westbrook, of course, was in constant attendance on her.

The Shelleys named their little daughter Eliza Ianthe, Ianthe for the heroine of *Queen Mab*, and Eliza for Harriet's sister, probably, rather than Shelley's. She was a beautiful, healthy child, but there was a slight defect in one of her eyes that Hogg thought may have been a source of some chagrin to the mother, who never acceded to his hints that he would like to see Ianthe. In fact, Hogg never did see Ianthe, then or later, a fact which did not prevent his stating a belief that Shelley was not particularly interested in his child.[99] Peacock, who often saw Shelley with Ianthe after she was a few months old, definitely corrects Hogg on this point. Shelley was extremely fond of his daughter and spent a great deal of time walking up and down the room with the child in his arms, singing a queer song of his own composition. The music consisted of three notes in a minor key; the words sounded like monotonous repetitions, " Yáhmani, Yáhmani, Yáhmani, Yáhmani." [100] Hogg himself quotes a letter of Shelley's in which affection for Ianthe is quite evident,[101] and in September Shelley wrote a sonnet in which he expressed his love for Ianthe and her mother.[102] Harriet made a rapid recovery after the birth of her child and was soon as lively and rosy as ever, " at times perhaps," says Hogg, with what may be intended as a significant pun, " rather too rosy." [103]

As soon after Ianthe's birth as seemed practicable, probably about the middle of July 1813,[104] the Shelleys moved to Bracknell, where they planned to stay until the spring. While they were at High Elms, as their new home was called, the Shelleys saw little of Hogg. He never visited Bracknell while the Shelleys were there, and though he saw Bysshe during various trips to the city, he was himself absent on his northern vacation from the beginning of August until the end of October. It was probably during this time that they set up a carriage, a vehicle which Hogg never beheld, but which nevertheless caused him, as we have seen, to be arrested for debt in mistake for Shelley. Peacock, who had previously been absent in Wales, returned during Hogg's absence and visited at High Elms. The Newtons, with their children, also made the Shelleys a visit, probably in late September or early October. After their return Mrs. Newton wrote to Hogg, who had not heard from the Shelleys since his departure in early August, that his friends were all well and happy, but had recently embarked upon a journey to the north:

Since their arrival in the north, where, I imagine, necessity will fix them for some time, we have had no tidings of them. The lady, whose welfare must be so important in your estimation was, as usual, very blooming and very happy, during the whole of our residence at Bracknell: Ianthe grown surprisingly, and Miss Westbrook ever smiling and serene. They have made an addition to their party, in the person of a cold scholar [Peacock] who, I think, has neither taste nor feeling. This Shelley will perceive, sooner or later; for his

318

warm nature craves sympathy, and I am convinced he will not meet
with it in his new acquaintance.[105]

Hogg was completely surprised at Shelley's undertaking a
journey which he regarded as sudden, utterly causeless, and
wildly extravagant.[106] In this case, however, the motive was
more substantial than the sudden impulse of a particular moment, or the " thick-coming fancies " which, in Peacock's phrase,
" almost invariably preceded his change of place." [107] Harriet
had foreseen the probable necessity of such a move from their
first arrival at Bracknell, and there can be little doubt that Mrs.
Newton understood the nature of the " necessity " she mentioned in her letter to Hogg. Shelley was in constant fear of
the bailiffs and had already escaped arrest only by accident
when Hogg had been arrested for Shelley's debt. The removal
to Bracknell had been occasioned, in Harriet's view, by " convenience," and the journey to the lakes by " necessity." [108] Shelley owed bills at Tremadoc that came due on his coming of
age, and other creditors were doubtless awaiting that date with
some eagerness. But August 4 came and went without any
financial settlement with Mr. Timothy Shelley. It only made
it a little easier for Shelley, no longer a minor, to arrange post-
obits at a perfectly ruinous rate. The fear of arrest continued,
even after his return from the north.[109] The best Shelley could
do was to arrange an interview with his father for November.[110] Meanwhile it was wise to vanish from his creditors. The
Shelleys' departure from Bracknell was indeed secret, and involved further secrecy as to their destination,[111] but it was not
sudden.

A LONG journey with a wife, an infant, and two guests required
some preparation. Shelley bought a coach, which was probably
deemed necessary for the infant Ianthe, who could hardly be
expected to risk the chances of having to ride " outside " in
a public conveyance. Harriet's detractors later instanced this
coach as a proof of her extravagance and love of show. Having
bought the coach on credit, Shelley next sold to a money-lender

named Starling a £2,000 post-obit bond for £500.[112] On Monday, October 5, the Shelleys, Eliza Westbrook, and Peacock started for the Lakes. The new carriage could not carry six passengers and all of their luggage, so a package and a box were left behind for Thomas Hookham to forward by coach. Monday night found the travellers at Warwick; in about a week they had completed their journey of more than three hundred miles and had reached their appointed inn on Lake Windermere, at Ambleside. This was no other than Lowood Inn, an inn of the same name and location as that from which Casimir Fleetwood, in Godwin's novel that Shelley admired, introduced himself by letter to his philosophic friend somewhat as Shelley introduced himself to Godwin. Once more Shelley was trying to settle in a spot made attractive by one of Godwin's novels. He intended to take a furnished house and remain till spring, but no suitable house could be found, and the people of the region did not recommend themselves as neighbours.

The Shelleys did not see Southey, who was away from Keswick at the time, and was at the moment on the point of becoming poet laureate, thus openly affiliating himself with the forces of reaction and becoming an object of scorn to the liberals and radicals. They did carry out their intention of seeing their old friends the Calverts. The visit lingered long in the memory of the Calverts' little daughter (later Mrs. Stanger), to whom the Shelleys announced they had brought a present of a work-box. But on unpacking the luggage it was found that the work-box was not there.[113]

Lingering only a few days among the Lakes, the party set out for Edinburgh, which they reached probably not more than a week before October 20. Here, as at Bracknell and then at Ambleside, they intended at first to remain for the winter. Shelley expected to find in Edinburgh a more tolerant society and a higher regard for literature than in London. Harriet, at least, was very happy with the thriving little Ianthe, " so fair, with such blue eyes," and with the retrospect of the two " happiest and longest years of my life " to which she was inspired by being once more in the city and even the neighbourhood in which she had been married.[114] Shelley was zealously pushing forward his self-education, reading Tacitus, Cicero, Homer, and Hume, and making a start to fulfil his determination to master the physical sciences. Despite his opinion that Peacock was too lacking in generous enthusiasm, he found pleasure in Peacock's scholarly conversation and his easy-going, unbigoted, if slightly cynical enlightenment.[115] John Grove was in Edinburgh completing his medical education; his conversation was not inspiring, but he was a useful family ally, and it is probable that he saw something of the little party at No. 36 Frederic Street.

Probably it was through John Grove that Shelley met another medical student, a young Brazilian named Joachimo B. Pereira, hitherto known only from Peacock's account as Baptista.[116] He was also a victim of parental tyranny, a frank, warm-hearted, gentlemanly young man, forced to study medicine against his inclination. He shared earnestly in Shelley's enthusiasms, adopted the vegetable diet, and began a translation of *Queen Mab* into Portuguese. This translation was to be introduced by a sonnet beginning: " Sublime Shelley, cantor di verdade," and ending, " Surja *Queen Mab* a restaurar o mundo." The translation was probably never completed, on account of the attractive young Brazilian's early death, and the sonnet survives only in the two lines that Peacock recalled.[117] It was the first of at least fifteen poems written to or about Shelley during his lifetime and within the year of his death.[118]

Nevertheless, Shelley was very soon discontented with the idea of remaining in Edinburgh all winter. He wrote to Hogg on November 26 that he expected soon to return to London alone.[119] The £500 raised on a post-obit early in October lasted apparently less than two months, and on November 28 Shelley was writing to an unidentified person earnestly requesting him not to decline accepting a draft of £30, " as the consequence would be, *our being driven out of our lodgings.*"[120] Before the return journey could be undertaken, the carriage in which they had arrived required a complete overhauling, at a cost of nearly £14. The cautious coach-maker, John Dumbreck, insisted upon his money before he would release the carriage. Eventually he released it on the guarantee of " Mr. William Dumbreck, of the Hotel St. Andrews Square " — the hotel at which the Shelleys probably ate their meals, since it seems to have been the nearest to their Frederic Street lodgings.[121]

SHORTLY before the 10th of December Shelley was back in London,[122] not alone, but with the rest of his party. During the next two or three weeks he saw Godwin and the Newtons frequently. Two brief undated notes, his only extant correspondence between November 28 and the following March, were written from Godwin's house at 41 Skinner Street. During the remainder of December Hogg was again in frequent association with the Shelleys, both at their lodgings and at the home of the Newtons. Near the end of the year the Shelleys took a furnished house at Windsor, a neighbourhood familiar to Shelley from his Eton days, and only eight or ten miles from the home of the Boinvilles at Bracknell. Here they lived for about two months, Shelley spending much of his time in town or with the Boinvilles,[123] Harriet and Eliza probably spending considerable time in London at the Westbrook house.

Shelley's time immediately after his return to London seems to have been largely taken up with financial matters. He had attained the age of twenty-one on August 4, but he was no nearer financial security than before the flight to Edinburgh. The financial pressure was embarrassing. Harriet wrote to Tremadoc to authorize the sale of the furniture left in Tanyrallt cottage for the benefit of Mr. S. Girdlestone, Mr. Madocks's London agent.[124]

It is very likely that some of the five hundred pounds raised in October went to Godwin's needs, thus beginning what was to prove the greatest single drain on Shelley's finances for most of the remaining years of his life. On November 12, nearly a month before Shelley's return from Edinburgh, Godwin's journal contains the significant entry: "Shelley, deed, etc." The same journal mentions Shelley's presence in Godwin's house on December 10, 11, and 12, immediately after his return. Two undated notes, supposed by the editors of Shelley's letters to have been written at this time, were endorsed from 41 Skinner

Street and show that Shelley was trying to raise more money. Before leaving London it had been his intention to raise only enough money on post-obits to pay his own debts.[125] But Godwin was an exception. We have already seen that Shelley assumed Godwin's burdens before September 1813. Now, at a time when his own financial position was desperate, he seems even to have given them pre-eminence.[126]

Hogg had seen neither of the Shelleys between the time he left town in early August and the time they returned from Edinburgh in early December. When the intimacy was renewed late in December, Hogg observed that Harriet had changed considerably since the birth of Ianthe.[127] On July 31, less than six months earlier, Shelley had written a poem for Harriet's birthday entitled " Evening: To Harriet " picturing " our close-woven happiness " as something in which it would be unthinkable to pick flaws. A tender sonnet to Ianthe, written in September 1813, asserted that she was

> Dearest, when most thy tender traits express
> The image of thy Mother's loveliness.

Harriet, on her part, had written to Catherine Nugent as late as October 20 that her two years of marriage with Shelley had been the happiest and longest years of her life.

In December and January Hogg found Harriet as healthy, cheerful, and vigorous as ever, but she had given up all effort to share Shelley's intellectual interests. Her old habit of reading aloud and her former devotion to study were now completely abandoned. Shelley seemed to accept her mental complacency as a settled fact and no longer urged her to cultivate her mind. Instead of reading to Hogg when he called and Shelley was away, she now proposed a walk, during which her conversation dwelt largely on the bonnets and caps displayed in millinery-shop windows. When Hogg called he often found either Shelley or Harriet at home alone. Harriet had gone out with Eliza or was at her father's, or Shelley was prosecuting his financial schemes in London or had gone to Bracknell to visit with the Boinville circle.[128] Whether from hard necessity or indifference to his home, Shelley now kept rooms both at Mrs. Boinville's at Bracknell and at the lodgings of his publisher in London, Thomas Hookham.[129] Harriet still talked of suicide as happily as ever. A surgeon who was called in for some slight operation on Ianthe was rather shocked by this talk and by her un-emotional observance of his procedure and went away with the conviction that she was a person incapable of genuine sympathy.[130]

The removal to Windsor did not, of course, lessen Shelley's financial difficulties, other than to make him less conspicuous to London bailiffs. On March 4, after two months more of uncertainty, Shelley sold to Andrew John Nash and George Augustus Nash a post-obit of £8,000 for £2,593, 10s., but the transaction was not completed by signing the indenture until July 12. Half of the proceeds of this bond went to Godwin, whose share, when all expenses were paid, came to £1,120.[131] Meanwhile Shelley made one more attempt to persuade his father and grandfather to relieve him. He had employed a Mr. Amory, a solicitor, who had called upon Mr. Timothy Shelley at Field Place and received assurances that he was genuinely concerned over his son's financial difficulties. Mr. Shelley talked to Sir Bysshe on the matter, but refrained for the present from suggesting what then seemed to him a good solution: namely, to pay the debts, give Shelley an allowance, and bond him to stay within the terms of the settlement. The debts were evidently considerable, for Sir Bysshe talked of selling Castle Goring, and Mr. Timothy Shelley had some doubts as to Shelley's ability to pay them with post-obits.[132]

Expressing an apparently genuine gratitude for his father's concern, Shelley wrote on March 13 to inform him that he could no longer delay selling post-obit bonds for a considerable amount, unless he received relief. He did not mention the bond for £2,000 he had already sold to Starling before leaving for Lowood Inn, Ambleside, nor the larger bond for £8,000 which he had arranged to sell on March 4; perhaps Mr. Amory had informed his father of the first, and the successful issue of his appeal could still cancel the other. He did point out that the sale of post-obits at ruinous rates (usually three or four to one) would completely frustrate his grandfather's desire to keep the estate intact, assuming that Shelley would outlive his father and grandfather. He knew that his father could do little in the matter without the concurrence of Sir Bysshe, but he hoped that Sir Bysshe would realize the danger to the estate of forcing him to adopt such a disastrous last expedient.[133]

This letter, Mr. Shelley remarked in turning it over to Whitton, "would not at all suit his grandfather's notions." "And on my own part," he added, "I would rather he would first acknowledge his God, then I might be led to believe his assertions.[134] If Shelley ever wrote to his father after this, the letter has not been preserved. His financial hopelessness in April is shown by a letter from his lawyer saying that Shelley had tried in vain to raise money on his expectations and that during his grandfather's life his family was unable to help him.[135] By July 12, when he completed the sale begun on March 4, Shelley had evidently given up hope of relief from his father and grandfather. This sale was primarily, if not entirely, for Godwin's benefit.[136] Meanwhile Mr. John Williams had been pressing Shelley in April and May for a settlement of old Tremadoc accounts, the non-payment of which he represented as causing him considerable personal distress. Shelley offered another post-obit, but the matter remained unsettled.[137]

WHILE living at Windsor, Shelley spent much of his time with the Boinvilles, who were still at Bracknell, ten miles away. Hogg made a brief visit there, unfortunately during Shelley's absence, slept in Shelley's disordered, book-strewn bedroom, and reported on the society that Shelley kept. Mrs. Newton was then visiting her sister, Mrs. Boinville. The two sisters and Cornelia Turner [138] were "never weary of the sweet courtesies of making tea"; hours were late, meals were, to Hogg's chagrin, rather irregular, sketchy affairs, but there was plenty of good bread and butter and sprightly conversation. Wieland's long, weary romance of *Agathon,* in a French translation, was at that time the favourite reading of the group. Against Hogg's scepticism, the ladies championed it as a demonstration of the superior value of purely Platonic love, an estimate which Shelley heartily endorsed. There was a young Frenchman [139] present who characterized Shelley to Hogg as " a man of splendid talents and overwhelming eloquence, but . . . very eccentric." He told how Shelley had improved on Wordsworth's " Highland Boy " by navigating a small stream at the bottom of the garden in the family wash-tubs, one after another, until the bottoms dropped out of each in turn.[140]

Peacock, who was occasionally with the Boinville circle in the company of Shelley and Harriet, was regarded with disapproval by the more fervent theorists because he sometimes laughed at them. Harriet often laughed with him.[141] To one who has noted how faithfully Harriet's earlier letters reflected Shelley's prejudices and enthusiasms this may seem a slight indication of a developing lack of sympathy. More serious differences were appearing about Ianthe. Harriet declined to suckle the child herself and engaged a wet-nurse whom Shelley did not like. In a recent medical book he had read repeated statements of the dire effects of wet-nursing.[142] Peacock told (but did not print) Shelley's horrified reaction to Harriet's " unnatural " conduct:

The nurse's soul would enter the child. All day he tried to persuade Harriet to do her duty, walking up and down the room, crooning old songs to the child in his arms. At last, in his despair, and thinking that the passion in him would make a miracle, he pulled his shirt away and tried himself to suckle the child.[143]

Shelley had begun to dislike Eliza Westbrook some time before; he now hated her with all his heart and soul:

It is a sight which awakens an inexpressible sensation of disgust and horror, to see her caress my poor little Ianthe, in whom I may hereafter find the consolation of sympathy. I sometimes feel faint with the fatigue of checking the overflowings of my unbounded abhorrence for this miserable wretch. But she is no more than a blind and loathsome worm, that cannot see to sting.[144]

In this mood Shelley no longer expected to find sympathy at home except " hereafter " in Ianthe. He was indeed in a very depressed state of mind; he had been staying with the

Boinvilles for a month, endeavouring to escape, as he phrased it, " from the dismaying solitude of myself," and dreading the inevitable return to his own fireside. He was still interested in reading; he even resumed his Italian with Cornelia as his helper — Cornelia, whom he now regarded as no longer cold and reserved, but as inheriting " all the divinity of her mother." Except for pleasant moments that he owed to the ministering kindness of Mrs. Boinville and her daughter he now regarded life almost as a disgusting burden.¹⁴⁵ He confessed to Cornelia that the reason for his lingering late in conversation with her was that he " dreaded the visions which pursued him when alone at night." ¹⁴⁶

On March 22, less than a week after his dejected letter to Hogg, Shelley remarried Harriet. According to his sworn statement before Surrogate Samuel J. Meyrick, his purpose was " to obviate all doubts which have arisen or may arise touching the validity of the said [Scotch] marriage." ¹⁴⁷ Even though Shelley may have considered this marriage as a purely legal precaution, it is still evidence that Shelley and Harriet were not seriously at odds when it occurred. A far more natural procedure in that case would have been to secure the annulment of a marriage whose irregularity he could demonstrate, instead of confirming it at the cost of another irregularity. Whatever alienation existed between Shelley and Harriet, therefore, belongs principally to the month of April.

In March or April the Shelleys seem to have left Windsor and taken a house at Bracknell. Soon thereafter Shelley reoccupied his room at the Boinvilles'.¹⁴⁸ Mrs. Boinville wrote to Hogg on April 18: " Shelley is again a widower; his beauteous half went to town on Thursday with Miss Westbrook, who is gone to live, I believe, at Southampton." ¹⁴⁹ From this it would appear that Shelley's intense hatred for his sister-in-law was recognized and was being met by her withdrawal. A poem written at Bracknell in April ¹⁵⁰ reveals the same mood in which Shelley had written to Hogg a month earlier. In this poem he pictured his reluctant, sad return from the Boinvilles' to his own home. Clouds and gathering winds made the black midnight a fit symbol of his hopeless mood as " duty and dereliction," aided apparently by pressure from Mrs. Boinville, drove him back to his "sad and silent home." Under the influence of Mrs. Boinville's "ungentle mood" Cornelia did not dare urge him to linger, but in the hopeless "solitude" of his home he would always remember "the music of two voices and the light of one sweet smile."

The voices were those of Mrs. Boinville and Cornelia; the sweet smile was obviously that of Cornelia alone, whom he calls his "lover" in an earlier line. It is evident from the fact that Shelley left the Boinvilles' unwillingly, under pressure, either that his affection for Cornelia was felt to be showing un-Platonic symptoms or that Mrs. Boinville realized that his continued stay was producing misery in his own home.

CORNELIA TURNER was certainly no Elizabeth Hitchener. She was young, accomplished, physically attractive, and spoke the language of sentimental sympathy and Platonic love. Did these charms, in Shelley's extremely depressed state of mind, destroy his loyalty to Harriet, whose imperfections were now becoming apparent; or was his evident attraction to her simply another and more difficult attempt at an innocent Platonic love such as that for Elizabeth Hitchener, which Harriet had tolerated for a while, and such as his second wife was also to encounter? The evidence supports either conclusion and establishes neither.

In the letter of March 16 to Hogg, Shelley had enclosed the following lines:

> Thy dewy looks sink in my breast;
>   Thy gentle words stir poison there;
> Thou hast disturbed the only rest
>   That was the portion of despair!
> Subdued to Duty's hard control,
>   I could have borne my wayward lot:
> The chains that bind this ruined soul
>   Had cankered then — but crushed it not.

These lines he had explained as "the vision of a delirious and distempered dream, which passes away at the cold clear light

328

of morning. Its surpassing excellence and exquisite perfections have no more reality than the colour of an autumn sunset." In the same letter he had characterized Cornelia as a divine crea- ture, " the reverse of everything bad." In April he had written a poem in which he had plainly referred to Cornelia as his " lover." To Mark Twain and to many others this could not possibly mean anything except that Shelley was frankly in love with Cornelia.[151] In most circumstances it could hardly be otherwise, but in the peculiar circumstances of the present case it is still inconclusive.

To a literalist Shelley's use of the word " love " must always constitute a pitfall; in a circle which believed that the only real love was sentimental or Platonic love, the word " lover " would hardly mean to Shelley what it meant to Mark Twain. It is easier to see a Platonic rather than a carnal lover in one who confesses, as Shelley did to Cornelia, that he seeks her company as a protection against terrifying visions when alone at night. Yet Shelley's own words prove that this " love " was in conflict with " duty," which should not be true of Platonic love. Mrs. Boinville, with the happiness of two families at stake, obviously saw more in duty than Shelley did, and required him to go home — showing plainly that she regarded the situation as dangerous. Harriet said later that Shelley fell in love with Cornelia and paid her such marked attention that her husband carried her off to Devonshire; Jane Clairmont, who knew the Boinvilles, supported this with a statement that the Boinvilles indignantly broke off his acquaintance at the time, but not Harriet's.[152] Whatever the real state of Shelley's mind toward Cornelia Turner, it seems plain that Cornelia's mother was alarmed and that Harriet felt she had a just grievance against Shelley.

Shelley seems to have reasoned with himself very much as Mrs. Boinville must have reasoned with him. In a poem evi- dently addressed to himself he speaks of having

> . . . sought in starry eyes
> Beams that were never meant for thine,
> Another's wealth. . . .

He describes a state of spiritual loneliness made more intense by realizing the faithlessness of the smiles of either Harriet or Cornelia. His own soul, changed to a fiend, tempts him to a pursuit he knows would be disastrous. He concludes:

> Be as thou art. Thy settled fate
> Dark as it is, all change would aggravate.[153]

Much more definite than this is another poem, entitled " To Harriet " and written in May, soon after Shelley's expulsion by Mrs. Boinville. This poem begins:

> Thy look of love has power to calm
>   The stormiest passion of my soul;
> Thy gentle words are drops of balm
>   In life's too bitter bowl;
> No grief is mine, but that alone
> These choicest blessings I have known.

The last two lines of this stanza are obviously not a full catalogue of Shelley's griefs, but the stanza and those that follow furnish conclusive proof of Shelley's love for Harriet in May 1814, after his expressions of supposed love for Cornelia Turner. The remaining stanzas go much further, in fact. Shelley admits that he has incurred Harriet's scorn or resentment, but he pleads that " a slight endurance " on her part will give him lasting happiness and cure a deep misery of soul. He begs her to reject any " erring guide " counselling remorselessness, and to yield to her own fine nature and pity him if she cannot love.[154]

THE affair with Cornelia Turner, whatever its real nature, was over. How Harriet received Shelley's appeal to her generosity is not known, except that she copied the poem in her own hand for preservation. It has been falsely accepted as a fact that she " assumed an attitude of hard alienation towards her husband " and soon separated from him of her own free will, though expecting probably to return after he had been duly chastened.[155]

In fact, Harriet remained at home after Shelley left the

home of Mrs. Boinville.[156] Shelley appears to have remained at
home also, with the usual frequent visits to London [157] made
necessary by his financial dealings. On June 18 Shelley went
to London to conclude the sale of his post-obit bond of eight
thousand pounds to Andrew John Nash and George Augustus
Nash. Harriet was then still at home. Unexpected delays postponed the conclusion of Shelley's transaction day by day until
July 6. Godwin, who was to receive half the proceeds of the
sale, thought it necessary for Shelley to be on the spot, and
Shelley remained. In order to escape arrest for debt, Shelley avoided his known haunts, lodged in Fleet Street, and
took his meals with the Godwins. During the first week of this
period (June 18–25) Shelley daily expressed his impatience
with the delay. In September Shelley and Harriet had formed a
plan of returning to Nantgwillt, in Wales,[158] and Shelley was
now anxious to be relieved of his London engagement in order
to put this plan into effect. When Godwin held him to his
London engagement, he begged to be allowed to return to
Bracknell to visit his family for one night only.[159] Harriet was
awaiting his return to Bracknell as late as June 25 and evidently
went to Bath only because Shelley was held in London against
his will.

Had the money from the post-obit been secured at the time
it was expected there is every reason for supposing that Shelley
and Harriet would have retired with Ianthe to Nantgwillt, there
to attempt to recapture some of their former happiness. In the
seclusion of Nantgwillt the future lives of Harriet and Shelley
might have avoided the cataclysm that was even then impending. Harriet was young enough, and sufficiently devoted and
frightened, to return to her former habits of reading and study
and become once more the disciple that Shelley craved. Limitations of mind and character, however, probably made it impossible for her to go much further along that road than she
had already gone — and motherhood introduced interests that
clashed with discipleship. Possibly Harriet lacked the imagination to perceive that the recent flurry over Cornelia Turner
was perhaps an effect rather than a cause, that Shelley was
physically and spiritually ill, from reasons that were not en-

tirely domestic, and that Cornelia Turner was only the straw at which he grasped, rather blindly and deliriously.

Harried by duns and bailiffs, almost hopeless of financial succour from his family, flitting from residence to residence, lacking the former undivided sympathy and encouragement of his wife, Shelley had gone to Mrs. Boinville's home in March in a state bordering upon nervous and physical collapse. " Seriously," Mrs. Boinville had then written to Hogg, " I think his mind and body want rest. His journeys after what he has never found, have racked his purse and his tranquillity." [160] Sleep, he told Cornelia Turner, only brought hideous dreams. At the same time he described himself to Hogg as " a feeble, wavering, feverish being " of exhausted energies. " I have sunk into a premature old age of exhaustion which renders me dead to everything, but the unenviable capacity of indulging the vanity of hope, and a terrible susceptibility to objects of disgust and hatred." [161] In these moods Shelley was capable of such wild and irrational behaviour as had previously convinced his father that he was not always entirely sane. The hatred of Eliza Westbrook accompanying the present mood may have had a rational basis, but it was definitely pathological in its expression and evidently seemed so to both Hogg and Peacock. The letter to Hogg, the two poems written at Bracknell in March and April, and the poem to Harriet in May, all suggest a state of complete mental and physical exhaustion of which his domestic unhappiness was only a contributory cause and may have been primarily an effect.

This was a state of mind to which Shelley was subject throughout his life. With her abundant, cheerful health and her rather ordinary extroverted mind it may be doubted if Harriet was fully equipped to recognize and cope with such a situation, even with the best will to do so. Cornelia Turner was only an incident, but what of the mood? Some of its causes still remained, in spite of the superficial restoration of domestic happiness. Cornelia Turner had vanished, but what if the next straw should prove more substantial, and even exhibit a reciprocal power of grasping? At the very moment that Shelley was preparing to retire with Harriet and Ianthe to Wales he

332

was on the verge of just such a situation. It was this that Harriet had to fear, more than the absurd shortcomings attributed to her by later biographers.[162]

During a temporary lull in his attendance upon the money-lenders, very probably about the first week in June,[163] Shelley made a visit to Field Place — the last time he was ever allowed to cross the threshold. In Mr. Timothy Shelley's absence with the three youngest children, his wife seized the occasion to invite Bysshe home for a short, secret visit. Upon his arrival Shelley was cordially welcomed by his mother, his two older sisters, Elizabeth and Mary, and the old butler, Laker. Everybody entered into the conspiracy of silence. For walking out a disguise was perhaps necessary and was in any case a pleasant thrill. Captain Kennedy, a young officer quartered at Horsham who spent some of his evenings at Field Place, contributed a military uniform which Shelley did not disdain to wear. The cap was much too large for his unusually small head and came down over his eyes. As "Captain Jones" his shambling walk and stooped shoulders did no very great credit to military smartness, but Shelley thoroughly enjoyed his disguise. Captain Kennedy, a youth of sixteen, was most favourably impressed with Shelley's earnest, sincere manner, his generosity, his praise of Sir James Mackintosh and Godwin, his reading aloud from a translation of Goethe, and his "exquisitely metaphysical" but "by no means clear" or fixed views of spiritual matters.[164] If plans were made looking to Shelley's reunion with his family, they were almost immediately frustrated by Shelley's conduct after his return to London.

Chapter XII

ELOPEMENT AND FOREIGN TRAVEL

IN LOVE WITH MARY GODWIN; ATTEMPTED SUICIDE; FLIGHT WITH MARY; RETURN TO ENGLAND; EFFECTS OF THE JOURNEY

ON June 8 Thomas Jefferson Hogg had been listening to the trial of Lord Cochrane with a certain complacence, since he himself had drawn up the information against the defendant. After an hour or two he strolled forth for a walk and in Cheapside fell in with Shelley. They walked along together through Newgate Street to Skinner Street, where Shelley asked Hogg to come in and wait for a few minutes while he settled some brief business with Godwin.

In they went, through Godwin's shop, to the family living-room upstairs, a room shaped like a quadrant, with windows in the arc, a fireplace in one radius, a door in the other. The walls were covered with bookshelves filled with old books, for Godwin, as Charles Lamb is said to have remarked, had read more books not worth reading than any other man in England. Over the fireplace hung Opie's portrait of Mary Wollstonecraft. Godwin was out; Shelley paced the creaking floor with impatient footsteps, fuming at his absence. Then the door was softly opened a little, a thrilling voice called: " Shelley! " Hogg caught a glimpse of the speaker as Shelley darted through the door to speak with her; she was a young girl, fair-haired and fair-skinned to the point of paleness, with a piercing look. She was dressed, rather oddly for London, in tartan. Shelley returned in a moment with the announcement that there was no use waiting for Godwin. " Who was that? " Hogg asked

as they resumed their walk. Shelley replied: " The daughter of
Godwin and Mary." It was about this time that Mary Godwin wrote in the book she was using for her Latin exercises:
" Shall I write a poem on receiving a cordial shake of the hand
from an esteemed and excellent person ah I cannot write
poetry."

In the year and a half that had elapsed since their first meeting Mary Godwin had ceased to be a child.[1] Ten months of
open air and sea-bathing, reading and day-dreaming in Scotland
had restored and fortified her health and improved her mind.
When she was fifteen her father had described her as " very
pretty," " singularly bold, somewhat imperious, and active of
mind," adding: " her desire of knowledge is great, and her perseverance in everything she undertakes almost invincible." [2]
Young Robert Baxter, in Scotland, was supposed by his family
to have been very much in love with Mary before her departure
for London.[3] The Baxter family remembered her at sixteen
as agreeable, vivacious, and sparkling, with fair hair and a
clear, bright white complexion.[4] She admired the character
and principles of her mother, perhaps the more by contrast
with the acerbities of the present Mrs. Godwin, who sometimes nagged her for reading too much. At such times it
was her custom to slip away to St. Pancras Churchyard and
read her book under the willow tree that shaded her mother's
grave.

Such a person at fifteen would hardly have been ignored by
Shelley at the time of their first meeting if the acquaintance
had not been immediately interrupted. At sixteen and a half,
seeing Shelley almost daily, it was all the more certain that
she should attract his interest — and no less certain that he
should attract hers. When Hogg first saw her, Shelley had
been in and out of the Godwin household rather constantly for
five or six weeks. Beginning on June 18 and continuing until
July 7, Shelley took practically all his meals with the Godwins.

If any dangerous attachment developed before June 26 it
was not evident to the Godwins nor to Shelley, for as late as
June 25 Shelley was planning to acquire Nantgwillt, in Wales,
as a retreat from the world for himself and his family. That

Godwin observed nothing means little, but it means much that Mrs. Godwin did not, for she was already aware of possible danger. Before this she had noted Shelley's attentions to Fanny Imlay and had suspected that Fanny was in love with Shelley, though not that Shelley was in love with her. On May 23 she had sent Fanny on a visit to Wales to remove her from the danger of falling in love with Shelley. She had also noted a strong brother-and-sister friendship between Shelley and her own daughter, Jane Clairmont, when the latter came home to Skinner Street for the Christmas vacation.[5] When Godwin first spoke to Shelley about his attentions to Mary and received the answer (according to Mrs. Godwin) that it was only his manner with all women, there was no reason why even Mrs. Godwin should not believe him. Hogg would certainly have believed it; very probably Shelley believed it himself.

In words that have only recently come to light Shelley himself has described what next followed:

I speedily conceived an ardent passion to possess this inestimable treasure. In my own mind this feeling assumed a variety of shapes. I disguised from myself the true nature of my affection. I endeavoured also to conceal it from Mary, but without success. I was vacillating and infirm of purpose: I shuddered to transgress a real duty, and could not in this instance perceive the boundaries by which virtue was separated from madness, *where* self-devotion becomes the very prodigality of idiotism. Her understanding was made clear by a spirit that sees into the the truth of things, and affections preserved pure and sacred from the corrupting contaminations of vulgar superstitions. No expressions can convey the remotest conception of the *manner* in which she dispelled my delusions. The sublime and rapturous moment when she confessed herself mine, who had so long been hers in secret, cannot be painted to mortal imaginations. . . .[6]

It was Mary, then, who precipitated a declaration that might or might not have happened otherwise. This was on Sunday, June 26, 1814 — William Godwin, in a letter soon to be quoted, fixes the date precisely.

Within the next four days Shelley wrote the following poem:

TO MARY WOLLSTONECRAFT GODWIN:
JUNE, 1814

I

Mine eyes were dim with tears unshed;
  Yes, I was firm — thus wert not thou; —
My baffled looks did fear yet dread
  To meet your looks — I could not know
That anxiously they sought to shine
And longed to soothe and pity me.

II

To sit and curb the soul's mute rage
  Which preys upon itself alone;
To curse the life which is the cage
  Of fettered grief that dares not groan,
Hiding from many a careless eye
The scorned load of agony.

III

Whilst you alone, then not regarded,
  The faithful you alone should be,
To spend years thus, and be rewarded,
  As you, sweet love, requited me
When none were nigh — Oh I did wake
From torture for that moment's sake.

IV

Upon my heart your accents sweet
  Of peace and pity fell like dew
On flowers half dead; — thy lips did meet
  Mine tremblingly; thy dark eyes threw
Their soft persuasion on my brain,
Turning to bliss its wayward pain,
Charming away its dream of —— .

V

We are not happy, sweet! our state
  Is strange and full of doubt and fear;
More need of words that ills abate; —
  Reserve or censure come not near

337

Our sacred friendship, lest there be
No solace left for you and me.

VI
Gentle and good and mild thou art,
  Nor can I live if thou appear
Aught but thyself, or turn thine heart
  Away from me, or stoop to wear
The mask of scorn, although it be
To hide the love thou feel'st for me.[7]

According to Godwin's and Shelley's view on marriage, Godwin should have found no logical objection to the union of Shelley and Mary. Shelley waited only until his loan for Godwin's benefit had been completed. What then happened has been described by Godwin himself:

On Sunday, June 26, he [Shelley] accompanied Mary and her sister, Jane Clairmont, to the tomb of Mary's mother, one mile distant from London; and there, it seems, the impious idea first occurred to him of seducing her, playing the traitor to me, and deserting his wife. On Wednesday, the 6th of July, the transaction of the loan was completed; and on the evening of that very day he had the madness to disclose his plans to me, and to ask my consent. I expostulated with him with all the energy of which I was master, and with so much effect that for the moment he promised me to give up his licentious love and return to virtue. I applied all my diligence to waken up a sense of honour and natural affection in the mind of Mary, and I seemed to have succeeded. They both deceived me.[8]

Godwin immediately required Shelley to discontinue all visits to Skinner Street. Soon thereafter, probably in the second week of July, Shelley sent Mary a copy of *Queen Mab* with the encouraging inscription: " You see, Mary, I have not forgotten you." Under the dedication to Harriet, Shelley wrote: " Count Slobendorf was about to marry a woman who, attracted solely by his fortune, proved her selfishness by deserting him in prison " — which looks like a cryptic indictment of Harriet. To these inscriptions Mary added the following:

July 1814. This book is sacred to me, and as no other creature shall ever look into it, I may write in it what I please — yet what shall I

MARY WOLLSTONECRAFT GODWIN

Painting by John Opie. Reprinted by permission of the National Portrait Gallery

write? — that I love the author beyond all the powers of expression, and that I am parted from him, dearest and only love — by that love we have promised to each other, although I may not be yours, I can never be another's. But I am thine, exclusively thine.

> " By the kiss of love, the glance none saw beside,
>   The smile none else might understand,
> The whispered thought of hearts allied,
>   The pressure of the thrilling hand."

I have pledged myself to thee, and sacred is the gift. I remember your words: " You are now, Mary, going to mix with many, and for a moment I shall depart, but in the solitude of your chamber I shall be with you." Yes, you are ever with me, sacred vision.

> " But ah! I feel in this was given
>   A blessing never meant for me,
> Thou art too like a dream from heaven
>   For earthly love to merit thee." [9]

DURING the week before the fateful declaration of June 26 Harriet, as we have seen in the previous chapter, was at Bracknell, and Shelley was begging Godwin's consent to visit her. Soon afterwards Harriet went with Ianthe to Bath. Within two or three days after June 26, perhaps on that very day, Shelley's letters to her suddenly ceased. Harriet became alarmed and wrote to Thomas Hookham:

My Dear Sir

You will greatly oblige me by giving the enclosed to Mr. Shelley. I would not trouble you but it is now four days since I have heard from him which to me is an age. Will you write by return of post and tell me what has become of him as I always fancy something dreadful has happened if I do not hear from him. If you tell me that he is well I shall not come to London; but if I do not hear from you or him I shall certainly come as I cannot endure this dreadful state of suspense. You are his friend and can feel for me.

                                        I remain yours truly
                                                H S [10]
6 Queens Square
     Bath

Allowing two days for the distance between London and Bath, one supposes that Shelley answered Harriet's letter immediately. On July 14 Harriet arrived from Bath at his request. He told her that he was desperately in love with Mary, that both he and Mary had thought of committing suicide, and that her generosity ·could save them. The version of the crisis which he then gave Harriet was later repeated by her, with her own colouring, in a letter to Catherine Nugent:

Mary was determined to seduce him. She is to blame. She heated his imagination by talking of her mother, and going to her grave with him every day, till at last she told him she was dying in love for him, accompanied with the most violent gestures and vehement expostulations. He thought of me and my sufferings, and begged her to get the better of a passion as degrading to him as herself. She then told him that she would die — he had rejected her, and what appeared to her as the sublimest virtue was to him a crime. Why could we not all live together, I as his sister, she as his wife? [11]

To Harriet, Shelley's proposal appeared monstrous, but she behaved with considerable self-control and presence of mind. Alarmed more by Shelley's present desperate mood than by any fear that she had lost his love permanently, she allowed him to believe that if his present feelings were not a passing fever she would not continue to oppose them. The wild surge of hope and relief with which Shelley viewed Harriet's apparent attitude is seen in the following letter, written within a few hours of the interview:

My Dearest Friend,
Exhausted as I am with our interview, and secure of seeing you tomorrow at 12, I cannot yet refrain from writing to you.
I am made calmer and happier by your assurances. It is true that my confidence in the integrity and disinterestedness of your conduct has ever remained firm; but I dreaded lest the shock might inflict on you some incurable unhappiness; lest you should doubt the continuance of my affection for you, lest you should see, what I so deeply felt, nothing but misery and despair.

My spirit turned to you for consolation, and it found it; all that vulgar minds regard as so important was considered by you with consistent and becoming contempt. Feeling still persuaded that my affection for you was undim[in]ished, you offered to my view, and anticipated for yourself that pure and lasting happiness which is the portion only of the great and good.

For this, dearest Harriet, from my inmost Soul, I thank you. This is perhaps the greatest among the many blessings which I have received, and still am destined to receive at your hands. I loathed the very light of day, and looked upon my own being with deep and unutterable abhorrence. I lived — Mary too consented to survive — I lived in the hope of consolation and happiness from you, and I have not been deceived.

I repeat (and believe me, for I am sincere) that my attachment to you is unimpaired. I conceive that it has acquired even a deeper and more lasting character, that it is now less exposed than ever to the fluctuations of phantasy or caprice. Our connection was not one of passion and impulse. Friendship was its basis, and on this basis it has enlarged and strengthened. It is no reproach to me that you have never filled my heart with an all-sufficing passion; perhaps you are even yourself a stranger to these impulses, which one day may be awakened by some nobler and worthier than me; and may you find a lover as passionate and faithful, as I shall ever be a friend affectionate and sincere!

Shall I not be more than a friend? Oh, far more — Brother, Father of your child, so dear as it is to us both, for its own sake and because we love each other.

Mrs. Boinville deeply knows the human heart: she predicted that these struggles would one day arrive; she saw that friendship and not passion was the bond of our attachment. But I derided her shortsighted prophecies — I! who was so soon to become the object of their completion.

Can your feelings for me differ in their nature from those which I cherish towards you? Are you my lover whilst I am only your friend, the brother of your heart? If they do not, the purest and most perfect happiness is ours. I wish that you could see Mary; to the most indifferent eyes she would be interesting only for her sufferings, and the tyranny which is exercised upon her. I murmur not if you feel incapable of compassion and love for the object and sharer of my passion.

341

If you want to draw on the Bankers before I see you, Hookham will give you the checks.

Adieu. Bring my sweet babe. I must ever love her for your sake.

Ever most affectionately yours

P. B. SHELLEY [12]

On the next day, Friday, July 15, Harriet and Shelley called on Godwin together, and Godwin called on Harriet in Shelley's absence; on Saturday Godwin called on the two together and went out in a coach with Shelley alone.[13] According to Mrs. Godwin, Harriet also called on the Godwins alone:

She was very much agitated, and wept, poor dear young lady, a great deal. . . . She implored us to forbid him our house and prevent his seeing Mary. . . . We sympathized with her, and she went away contented, feeling, as she said, quite sure that, not seeing Mary, he would forget her. We then spoke to Mary on the subject, and she behaved as well as possible — approved our renouncing his acquaintance, and wrote a few lines to Harriet to pray her not to be unhappy, as she would not see Mr. S— again.

Jane Clairmont, who copied this letter, added on her own authority that she accompanied Mary to Chapel Street and heard Mary assure Harriet that she would discourage Shelley's love for her.[14]

If Harriet was correctly quoted by Mrs. Godwin, it seems very clear that she loved Shelley and still believed in his love for her. She was becoming frightened, but she still regarded the affair with Mary as a sudden infatuation from which Shelley would suddenly recover, like the affair with Cornelia Turner, which she mentioned during the same interview. Her subsequent letters to Catherine Nugent suggest that she cherished the same hope for some time after the actual elopement. As late as November 15 Mrs. Godwin reported her as still confident of Shelley's return to her. But the reassurance she received from Mary was not sufficient; she distrusted Mary. Her instinct and observation told her that this was far more serious than the affair with Cornelia Turner. She was expecting to become a mother again in December, and the shock was too great for her. Something of the agony of the next two weeks, both for herself and for Shelley, may be gathered from Harriet's brief account to Catherine Nugent:

You may suppose how I felt at the disclosure. I was laid up for a fortnight after. I could do nothing for myself. He begged me to live. The doctors gave me over. They said 'twas impossible. I saw his despair, the agony of my beloved sister; and owing to the great strength of my constitution I lived; and here I am, my dear friend, waiting to bring another infant into this woful world.[15]

MARY WOLLSTONECRAFT GODWIN at sixteen and a half was probably fully as bold and determined as her father thought her at fifteen. If she had earlier resolved to make Shelley love her, she now appears to have formed an honest intention of discouraging his love. She concurred in her father's decision to forbid Shelley the house. For a short while [16] thereafter, tranquillity seemed to be restored. During this time, on July 22, Godwin had a talk with Jane Clairmont and wrote again to Harriet.[17] He continued to visit Shelley and to discuss philosophy, logic, and history with him, still confident, seemingly, of the power of calm philosophy over passion.

Then one day a wild and dishevelled Shelley entered the Skinner Street shop in Godwin's absence and rushed upstairs. Gone now was all the Spartan self-control he had urged upon Hogg when the latter was similarly possessed. He had tried that, and it was no good. How could he ever have written so ignorantly, less than three years ago: "Love is not a whirlwind, that it is unvanquishable"? He pushed Mrs. Godwin violently aside and walked straight up to Mary. "They wish to separate us, my beloved, but Death shall unite us." He offered her a bottle of laudanum. "By this you can escape from tyranny."

"This," he said, taking a small pistol from his pocket, "shall reunite me to you." Mary turned pale as a ghost; Jane Clairmont, who was in the room, shrieked again and again. Mrs. Godwin rushed out for aid and returned with Mr. Marshall, a friend who was waiting downstairs to have dinner with the family. Between them they persuaded Shelley to go home. Mary wept and was so distressed that she hardly knew what she said. As well as she could remember it after Shelley left, she had said to him: " I won't take this laudanum; but if you will only be reasonable and calm, I will promise to be ever faithful to you." [18]

There was another brief period of quiet.[19] Mary seemed to be still adhering to her resolution. Fanny Imlay was away from home on a visit. Jane Clairmont, of a bolder nature than Fanny, was to some extent Mary's confidante and sympathizer.[20] Shelley also needed a sympathizer. Hogg may have left town a week early for his northern vacation, or Shelley may have felt (as Hogg's subsequent conduct showed) that he would have been an uncomfortable confidant. At any rate it appears from Shelley's letter of October 5 that Hogg was ignored until he was confronted with a *fait accompli*. Instead, Shelley sent Peacock an urgent summons to come up from the country. Peacock arrived and was deeply shocked and surprised at the condition in which he found Shelley:

Nothing that I ever read in tale or history could present a more striking image of a sudden, violent, irresistible, uncontrollable passion, than that under which I found him labouring when, at his request, I went up from the country to call on him in London. Between his old feelings towards Harriet, *from whom he was not then separated,* and his new passion for Mary, he showed in his looks, in his gestures, in his speech, the state of a mind " suffering, like a little kingdom, the nature of an insurrection." His eyes were bloodshot, his hair and dress disordered. He caught up a bottle of laudanum, and said: " I never part from this." [21]

What Peacock saw was precisely what Shelley himself had once described as the worst possible state for such a person as himself: " For what conflict of a frank mind," he had once philosophized to Elizabeth Hitchener, " is more terrible than the balance between two opposing importances of morality . . . this is surely the only wretchedness which a mind who only acknowledges virtue its master can feel." [22]

One midnight the Godwins' door-bell rang violently; it was the master of the house in which Shelley lodged, come to say that Shelley had taken a violent dose of laudanum and was at

death's door. When Mr. and Mrs. Godwin hastened to him
they found him already in the hands of a doctor, who was
forcing him to walk up and down the room. For the next day,
while Mrs. Godwin nursed him, he could say nothing beyond
" Yes " and " No " — which was, in fact, about all he would ever
have desired to say to Mrs. Godwin. The Godwins procured a
man and a woman who watched over him until Mrs. Boinville
came upon their notification. Harriet must have been still too
ill to attend Shelley; she is not mentioned in Mrs. Godwin's
account, and Shelley is spoken of as being in lodgings at Hatton
Gardens, whereas Harriet was at her father's house in Chapel
Street. Mrs. Boinville stayed with Shelley a week until he had
recovered.[23]

Shelley's recovery was hastened, Mrs. Godwin suspected, by
secret notes from Mary. His spirits rose and he promised not
to attempt suicide again. Mrs. Godwin was right; Shelley had
bribed the shop porter at Skinner Street to convey notes between him and Mary. There was no further hesitation, at least
on his part, as to what was to be done. Mary still needed persuasion, but that can hardly have been difficult when Shelley
was so determined and when her own emotions argued so
strongly on his side. Mary and Jane used to take a walk every
day in the neighbourhood of the Charterhouse. Here Shelley
would join them, and Jane would walk up and down at a distance, while Shelley and Mary sat and talked in one of the
arbours.[24] It was here that Shelley overcame Mary's reluctance
to elope by assuring her that Harriet no longer loved him and
was in fact an adulteress. He declared, as Jane Clairmont later
testified,

that Harriet did not really care for him; that she was in love with a
Major Ryan; and that the child she would have was certainly not
his. This Mary told me herself, adding that this justified his having
another attachment.[25]

It would seem that Jane had some doubts on the point, for she
added that neither her mother nor the Boinvilles had ever heard
of Mr. Ryan. But there was a Mr. Ryan,[26] and it is hardly to

be doubted that Mary accepted Shelley's story of Harriet's infidelity with him. In no normal sense of the word does it seem possible for Shelley himself to have believed her unfaithful at this time. It had not been a fortnight since he himself had testified eloquently to Harriet's nobility and fidelity. In all subsequent references to Harriet's two children he plainly assumed paternity. Charles Clairmont, who drew his information from Shelley, later expressly exonerated Harriet from this charge while condemning her on other grounds.[27] Either Shelley knew at the time that his argument was false, or else its truth was so utterly necessary to him that he believed it himself because he so intensely longed to do so.[28]

SHELLEY had already informed Harriet that she could draw money through Hookham.[29] In the hands of a lawyer named Tahourdin, Shelley had placed deeds and settlement papers providing for a separation from Harriet and for a separate maintenance for her, as soon as the amount of maintenance and the separation itself were agreed upon. There was money in the hands of his bankers.[30]

By the night of July 27 Shelley and Mary could delay no longer. Shelley ordered a chaise to be ready at four o'clock in the morning, and "watched until the lightning and the stars became pale." At four o'clock Shelley was waiting. Mary joined him, then left him again for a short time — possibly to leave the note that Godwin found on his dressing-table an hour later. "How dreadful did this time appear; it seemed that we trifled with life and hope; a few minutes passed, she was in my arms — we were safe; we were on our road to Dover." [31]

Jane Clairmont was with them; she would be useful as an interpreter, since neither Shelley nor Mary possessed her fluency in French. Doubtless she, too, needed liberation from "tyranny." But during the dash to Dover — and in Shelley's later account of it — she was ignored as thoroughly as Byron's George III, after he had crept into heaven. As the sun rose higher, the heat became excessive; it was one of the hottest days for many years. Mary was ill and faint with the heat and the

DOVER

Engraved by E. Finden from a drawing by C. Stanfield

CALAIS

Engraved by E. Finden from a drawing by S. Prout

strain and leaned her head listlessly against the side of the chaise. Shelley sat in the middle, whispering consolation to her, while Jane, very much alone, sat on the other side, watched the landscape whirl past, and felt as if the end of the world had come. It was necessary for Mary to rest at every stage, and it was extremely necessary to keep ahead of the pursuit. They knew Godwin's early-rising habits; they probably guessed pretty accurately what had been happening in Skinner Street — Godwin's finding Mary's letter at five o'clock, the prompt inquiries among neighbouring livery stables, Mrs. Godwin's departure to overtake them. They did not know that Mrs. Godwin had had to wait for the evening mail coach, which would still get her to Dover in time for the next Calais packet.[32]

Shelley hurried the flight by every possible means, imagining pursuers at his heels. At Dartford they took four horses instead of two. Reaching Dover at four o'clock, they found that the packet would not sail until next day. Had they waited for it Mrs. Godwin would have caught them in England. Taking time only for Mary to refresh herself with a sea-bath and for Shelley to interview the customs officers and engage a small boat, they set sail ahead of the packet, at six in the evening.

For the first time they felt safe. The cliffs slowly receded, the sails flapped in a flagging breeze, and the moon came up over a slow, heavy Channel swell. Soon, however, the breeze freshened into a gale, Mary became so ill that she could scarcely move, and Shelley himself was almost too exhausted to support the weight of her head against him. As the winds grew more violent and contrary, what had been promised as a passage of two hours lengthened into a whole night. A thunder-squall caused their small boat to ship water in a manner that alarmed even the sailors. For a few moments, at least in his own opinion, Shelley faced death with his beloved:

Mary did not know our danger; she was resting between my knees that were unable to support her; she did not speak or look, but I felt that she was there. I had time in that moment to reflect, and even to reason upon death; it was rather a thing of discomfort than horror to me. We should never be separated, but in death we might not know and feel our union as now.[33]

The wind changed once more and drove them on toward Calais. They landed in the early dawn, on Friday, July 29. " Mary, look! " Shelley exclaimed, " the sun rises over France." Completely worn out, they engaged a room at Dessein's Hotel and rested until evening.

Before the evening was over, Mrs. Godwin reached Calais on the packet Shelley had refused to wait for. Godwin, who knew how Shelley hated her, had made her promise not to see him, lest he do her some personal violence.[34] In the evening a Captain Davison came to Shelley with the information that a fat lady had arrived who claimed that he had run away with her daughter. Jane spent the night with her mother and promised to return to London with her, but next day she thought better — or worse — of her promise and decided to remain with the culprits. Mrs. Godwin had expended all her feelings and persuasions on the previous argument; she now left without a word, and Shelley passed her on the street as she made her way back to the dock.

What was the meaning of the strange and agonizing series of events culminating in the breathless final dash to Dover and Calais? Shelley's friends were puzzled, and apparently all but Peacock were offended. When Shelley in his distraction had summoned Peacock to· London, Peacock had remarked with evident surprise: " It always appeared to me that you were very fond of Harriet." Shelley had answered: " But you did not know how I hated her sister." This was true, but it was an inadequate explanation even in Shelley's eyes. After having discussed the matter with both Shelley and Harriet, Peacock asserted vigorously that there was no estrangement and "no shadow of a thought of separation " until Shelley fell in love with Mary, but that he was then utterly lost and might well have said: " *Ut vidi! ut perii!* " [35]

The real nature of Shelley's conduct goes so deeply into certain phases of his character that it must be examined somewhat in detail. Harriet's view was that Shelley was bewitched by the fact " that her name was Mary, and not only Mary, but Mary Wollstonecraft." [36] She might have added Godwin also, to include both the illustrious parents whom Shelley himself

348

makes a part of Mary's attractions in his dedicatory poem to
Laon and Cythna.

It is abundantly clear, then, from the testimony of Godwin,
Shelley himself, Harriet, and Peacock, that Shelley's love for
Mary Godwin was a sudden, powerful, and almost paralysing
emotional explosion. Harriet's explanation, and Shelley's false
statement about Major Ryan, also suggest that it was accompanied by delusions and by that curious idealizing confusion
of facts between the world existing in Shelley's mind and the
world of reality. His elopement with Harriet had curiously
paralleled a book he had just been reading and had been accompanied by the same circumstances of " tyranny " and threatened suicide as the present situation. He had already twice
paralleled the actions of Godwin's hero Fleetwood, in following
him into Merionethshire and later to Lowood Inn on Lake Windermere, and he was soon to follow him to another spot made
memorable by the novel. Only recently he had re-enacted
Wordsworth's " Highland Boy " with the Boinville wash-tubs at
Bracknell. And at Bracknell he had also read Wieland's *Agathon,* the emotional excitement of whose philanthropic and
philosophical-sentimental hero much resembled his own. Agathon also had veered between two loves, a spiritual and a
sensual, abandoned one for the other, and ultimately found
happiness by living with them *both* on a Platonic basis, having
meanwhile discovered that the first one was really his sister.
Was the proposal of a similar *ménage à trois* which Shelley
made to Harriet suggested by this book? [37] At any rate Harriet's
statement that Shelley had fallen in love with an idea rather
than a reality was not mere spite, but showed a considerable
insight into Shelley's peculiar nature. Mary Wollstonecraft was
at that time, and for some years after, rather more of a goddess
for Shelley than William Godwin was a god. During the next
six or seven weeks Shelley read two of Mary Wollstonecraft's
books and sent to Harriet to ask for another. The very name
was magic.

Explosion though it was, however, and attended by irrational
mental phenomena as it seems to have been, Shelley's sudden
infatuation with Mary could hardly have occurred but for cer-

tain fairly normal facts that made some such occurrence easily possible. The union with Harriet, as Shelley perceived too late, was in the beginning "not a union of passion" — certain comparisons made by Hogg in 1811 between his own nature and Shelley's seem to support Shelley's testimony on this point. Later the case seemed to be altered, but it may only have seemed so, in Shelley's ignorance of real passion.

A much more substantial reason for Mary's victory and Harriet's defeat is to be found in another remark Shelley made to Peacock in the stress of his indecision: "Every one who knows me must know that the partner of my life should be one who can feel poetry and understand philosophy. Harriet is a noble animal, but she can do neither." [38] Staunch friend of Harriet as he continued to be, Peacock could not contradict this opinion when he later came to Harriet's defence against Lady Shelley and her *Shelley Memorials*. He could testify impressively to her beauty, good taste, and frank, spontaneous manner. He could say with truth that she was well educated, read well, and wrote well, that she was fond of her husband and accommodated herself in every way to his tastes. "If they mixed in society, she adorned it; if they lived in retirement she was satisfied; if they travelled, she enjoyed the change of scene." Still honesty compelled him to add that no one who knew both Harriet and Mary could deny that Mary was intellectually better suited to the poet's needs, nor would he deny that a man who lived so totally in a world of ideas as Shelley had a peculiar need of such sympathy. [39]

With a naturally apt mind, Harriet had been able in her letters to reflect Shelley's political and social views with remarkable fidelity, as if they were her own. When she got beyond this she showed that her mind was quite naïve and certainly not interested in philosophy and poetry for their own sake, but only — as far as she could go — for Percy's. She belonged naturally far more to a world of brisk physical cheerfulness and unquestioned conventions than to the speculative, literary, and unconventional atmosphere to which Mary had been long accustomed at Godwin's shop and home in Skinner Street. Shelley could never propose to "form" Mary's mind, as he proposed to Harriet even after the elopement; [40] instead, he considered rather absurdly that Mary's mind was far superior to his own. [41]

Long ago Shelley had set himself with almost deadly tenacity to the mission of making mankind listen to a better notion of right and wrong. It is probable that his depression of the previous spring was caused partly by a subconscious apprehension of Harriet as no longer a partner in this purpose, a feeling that he honestly denied when it was first forced upon his conscious attention. The feeling found conscious expression only after a catastrophe in which it had already been a cause. Thus at the crisis of Shelley's life the partly hidden, unchanging purpose in his character merged with the unstable, sudden, and superficially erratic side of his nature to produce his elopement with Mary Wollstonecraft Godwin.

SCARCELY had Mrs. Godwin taken her dejected way to the Dover packet before Shelley's party were again on the road, fugitives no longer. That same evening they left Calais for Boulogne, where they spent the night. Next morning they again climbed into a queer-looking, two-wheeled, un-English-looking vehicle called a cabriolet. The stiff-peruked postilion resumed his interminable cracking of the whip. Travelling all day on July 31, and day and night on August 1, they reached Paris about two o'clock in the afternoon of August 2 and engaged lodgings at the Hôtel de Vienne. The excessive heat continued, and Mary continued to suffer from it.

They remained in Paris for six days, from August 2 until the evening of August 8. Shelley's first action was to look over with Mary the contents of a box containing some of her youthful compositions, together with letters she had received from her father and friends, including Shelley. Characteristically, he was interested in the " productions of her mind." They visited the Tuileries, the Louvre, and Notre Dame, but found nothing remarkable except a " terribly impressive " painting of the Deluge. For the first day or two Mary was still ill. The spectre of financial difficulties had already reappeared, but they were too happy in each other to be dejected by it. " The morning [August 7] passes in delightful converse. We almost forget that we are prisoners in Paris; Mary especially seems insensible to all future evil. She feels as if our love would alone suffice to resist the invasions of calamity." On August 4 Mary reminded Shelley that it was his birthday, upon which Shelley remarked gallantly in his journal: " I had thought it had been the 27th June." [42]

The financial situation was in fact quite embarrassing. They had reached Paris almost penniless. On his birthday Shelley sold his watch and chain for eight napoleons, five francs. Tavernier, a French man of business through whom he hoped to raise funds, proved dilatory or unwilling; in Shelley's words he was " an idiot." Shelley felt sure that he could interest Miss Helen Maria Williams, an English authoress and heroine of the Revolution who had been known to both of Mary's parents. He located her home with some difficulty, only to find that she was out of town. An obscure French author named M. R. de Sair, with whom they once or twice dined and breakfasted, took them to a banker, who refused to advance them anything. Fortunately Tavernier gave them " a remittance of £60 " on August 7, and they were enabled to pay their bills in Paris and proceed on their journey.

A letter from Hookham reached Shelley the day after their arrival, and a second, delivered by Tavernier, on August 6. The first letter was characterized by Shelley as " cold and stupid " and contained the news that " Mrs. Boinville's family were reduced to the utmost misery by the distant chance of their being called upon in the course of a year to pay £40 for me. He did not send the money " — meaning probably money that should have been sent to the Shelleys rather than the Boinvilles, for it was on the next day that Shelley sold his watch and chain. The second letter Shelley described merely as " dull and insolent." Apparently Hookham resented the elopement on Harriet's behalf.

WITH money in hand they now prepared to resume their journey. They were headed for Switzerland — more precisely for Uri, a district made sacred to Shelley by Godwin's novel *Fleet-*

PARIS IN 1819, PONT LOUIS XVI

Engraved by E. Finden from a drawing by Captain Batty

wood.[43] Jane and Shelley went to market and bought an ass, which turned out to be too weak to carry a burden and accompanied them to Charenton merely as a companion. Next morning at Charenton they sold the ass and bought a mule, losing heavily on the transaction. Hence to Guignes, nine leagues distant. Shelley led the mule and Mary rode it, with the exception of eight miles during which Jane rode and Mary walked.

Beginning with their flight from London, Shelley and Mary kept a journal,[44] from which we may compile the following timetable of their journey until they turned back toward England:

Monday, August 8: Paris to Charenton.
Tuesday, August 9: Charenton to Guignes.
Wednesday, August 10: Guignes to Provins.
Thursday, August 11: Provins to Nogent to St. Aubin to Trois
    Maisons.
Friday, August 12: Trois Maisons to Echemine to Pavillon to Troyes.
Saturday, August 13: Remain at Troyes.
Sunday, August 14: Troyes to Vandeuvres to Bar-sur-Aube.
Monday, August 15: Bar-sur-Aube to Chaumont to Langres.[45]
Tuesday, August 16: Langres to Gray.
Wednesday, August 17: Gray to Besançon to Mort.
Thursday, August 18: Mort to Noe to Maison Neuve to Pontarlier.
Friday, August 19: Switzerland — St. Sulpice to Neufchâtel.
Saturday, August 20: Remain at Neufchâtel.
Sunday, August 21: Neufchâtel to Soleure.
Monday, August 22: Soleure to Zoffingen and beyond.
Tuesday, August 23: Reach Lucerne about 10.00; by boat to Brunen.
Wednesday, August 24: Remain at Brunen.
Friday, August 26: Decision to return to England.

The journey had been planned as a pedestrian one, the ass to carry the light luggage and one of the ladies occasionally. With the incompetent ass replaced by a mule, this plan worked for three days. Mary and Jane, clad in black silk gowns, rode by turns, Shelley leading the mule and carrying a light basket of fruit and bread. Their heavy luggage was to follow. Mary, who was still ill from time to time, did most of the riding. At Trois Maisons, however, Shelley strained his leg so badly that it was impossible to walk, so Mary surrendered the mule and

Shelley rode for the rest of the day. Six days later Jane also was "very unable to walk." At Troyes they engaged a voiture and sold the mule, having lost, from ass to voiture, fifteen napoleons on their ownership of livestock. Thereafter all rode, even though the driver engaged at Troyes proved surly and obstinate and finally left them when they came to mountainous country. The mule of the next driver went lame shortly after they crossed the Swiss frontier. At Neufchâtel, just as the money they had secured in Paris was running low, Shelley visited a banker and returned with a large canvas bag full of silver, the equivalent of about thirty-eight pounds.

Most of the country over which they passed between Paris and the Swiss frontier had been laid desolate by war within less than six months. It was here that Napoleon had fought his last desperate, brilliant campaign in the winter and spring of 1814 to keep the invaders from Paris. Their Parisian landlady had warned them that the region was lawless and blasted, that the ladies would surely be "*enlevées*" by disbanded soldiers. They saw no outlaws, but they saw a record of military ferocity and desolation that left its impression not only upon their journal but upon their later writings.

At Guignes they slept at the same inn and in the same beds that Napoleon and his staff had occupied only shortly before. Nogent had been completely desolated by the Cossacks; its bridge was broken and its houses were in ashes. Most of the little villages had been burned, the cows had been killed or driven away, the fields were no longer cultivated. Echemine, Pavillon, and practically every village they saw before reaching Troyes had been completely ruined. It was the same in the outskirts of Troyes and beyond toward the Swiss frontier. On the road to Troyes they met an old man who said his children had been murdered by the Cossacks. For the first time Shelley beheld the actual physical effects of warfare, for which he had long entertained an abstract horror. It impressed itself on his mind more than the somewhat matter-of-fact contemporary chronicle reveals. Three years later he wrote in the preface to *Laon and Cythna* (1817): "I have seen the theatre of the more visible ravages of tyranny and war; cities and villages reduced

to scattered groups of black and roofless houses and the naked
inhabitants sitting famished upon their desolated thresholds."
In the poem he presents his most vivid and realistic picture of
a countryside desolated by warfare. Mary also retained a lasting
impression, and in a novel written after Shelley's death she drew
a picture of war-ruined villages that is practically a paraphrase
of the accounts set down in her journal in 1814.[46]

Perhaps the travellers judged the inhabitants without sufficiently considering that the war might have been partly responsible for some of their present characteristics. The beds
almost everywhere after they left Guignes were "infinitely detestable." At one place they slept in the afternoon sunshine on
the clean moss in a near-by forest, at another they sat the night
through by a kitchen fire, at still another, Trois Maisons, Jane
asserted that she was kept horribly awake by the rats putting
their cold paws on her face. The inhabitants seemed never to
have washed, and were so very unamiable and inhospitable that
the travellers "could hardly pity them." The village cabaret at
Echemine surpassed in filth any Irish cabin that Mary had ever
read of and any Scotch cabin she had seen; they could hardly
swallow their food. Jane's journal scarcely mentions a town
without remarking incidentally that it was dirty, but of the
little village of Mort, where they passed the night of August 17,
she remarks: "Perhaps never dirt was equal to the dirt we saw."
At Pontarlier, their last day in France, Mary recorded emphatically: "We sleep, for the first time in France, in a clean bed."

What with Mary's illness (on the 8th she recorded "one horrible spasm"), the lameness in turn of Shelley, Jane, and the
mule, the continued dirt and discomfort, and the uncertainty
of additional funds, one might naturally conclude that this unusual honeymoon tour was a very dismal one. But such was
not the case. The high spirits of the wayfarers that had been
proof against the pessimism of their Paris landlady remained
high. Hookham's letters that had seemed dull and insulting in
Paris might well have caused a sense of foreboding for what
awaited their return to England, but neither journal contains
a single note of apprehension. Jane was a natural enthusiast
who, beginning with Charenton, thought various places "won-

derful "; Shelley and Mary were too much in love to regard physical discomforts. All three were lovers of romantic scenes, whether of mountains and streams and pine forests or of quaint old towns like Provins and Besançon. "The approach to Provins is most beautiful," wrote Shelley (August 10); "a ruined citadel, with extensive walls and towers, stood above the town; the cathedral was beyond; it formed one scene. We slept at a little old woman's whose beds were infinitely detestable." Jane indulged in a rapturous description of the environs of Besançon.

Resting in a shady grove near Vandeuvres, Mary recorded that "The moss was so soft, the murmur of the wind in the leaves was sweeter than Aeolian music we forgot that we were in France or in the world for a time." [47] To all three travellers the first view of the Alps as Mary described it was plainly a much more significant matter than all of the difficulties of the journey:

Two leagues from Neufchâtel we see the Alps; hill after hill is seen extending its craggy outline before the other, and far behind all, towering above every feature of the scene, the snowy Alps; they are 100 miles distant; they look like those accumulated clouds of dazzling white that arrange themselves on the horizon in summer. Their immensity staggers the imagination, and so far surpasses all conception that it requires an effort of the understanding to believe that they are indeed mountains.[48]

Shelley might have reflected with truth as he saw Mary write such passages as these, that here was something beyond Harriet's possibilities. Neither of the two journals, however, indicates any knowledge that Harriet still existed as a possible shadow on their enjoyment. At Troyes, while they waited a day, Shelley had written to Harriet,[49] "to shew you that I do not forget you." The letter ignores the possibility that Harriet might be unhappy, or even unsympathetic with the present expedition. He assured Harriet that he was her best friend and adviser and urged her to join him in Switzerland, bringing with her the deeds then in his lawyer's hands that had been prepared to legalize the separation and provide a settlement for her.

At Brunen they had hoped to stop for the winter. Brunen is situated on the narrow strait which joins the main body of the Lake of Lucerne with a bay of the lake known as the Lake of Uri. Across the strait was the Canton of Uri, where Fleetwood's philosopher friend Russigny had resided in Godwin's novel, *Fleetwood*. A short distance down the lake was the chapel of William Tell, which Russigny had shown to Fleetwood while descanting nobly on the freedom of the Swiss. Once this fact is recalled, it is easy to guess why Shelley knew in Paris, several days before the other details of the excursion were arranged, that he was going to Uri. He had already stopped in Poland Street for the sake of freedom and in two other places for the sake of Fleetwood.

But Mary could not endure the filth of their apartment, and it proved impossible to procure a house. They rented a two-room apartment for six months, moved in, and received with somewhat scant politeness a visit from the old abbé and the local doctor. It was on the 25th that they took possession. Shelley immediately set to work on a new romance, *The Assassins*, which Mary wrote down at his dictation. This fragmentary novel, never finished, seems to have been imagined somewhat after the general plan of Johnson's *Rasselas*. The Assassins (whose real nature was then unknown) were depicted as an isolated sect practising a purer form of religion than the rest of the world could understand or accept.[50] Next day Shelley worked on his romance until three o'clock, after which they suddenly decided to return to England as soon as the laundress appeared with the clean linen. Only the circumstance of the linen's being too damp to pack postponed their departure until the next day.

Of the money received at Neufchâtel, only twenty-eight pounds remained.[51] No more was procurable except by Shelley's presence in London. It was not only necessary to return, but to return by the cheapest route possible. Accordingly they decided to make the return entirely by water by descending the Rhine. The excellent financial reasons for immediate departure appear in Mary's later account,[52] but not in the contemporary journal. To Jane, at the time, it seemed that they were leaving because either Mary or Shelley disliked the stove in their new quarters. On the morning of their departure (August 27) she wrote in her journal: "Most laughable to think of our going to England the second day after we entered a new house for six months — All because the stove dont suit"; and at the end of the day: "How wild the people in London will think us — all because the stove did not burn brightly and there were too many Cottages."

Descending the Reuss from Lake Lucerne to the Rhine and following the Rhine to Rotterdam, they completed a journey of 800 miles in thirteen days, at an expense of £28. Their timetable may be pieced together from the three accounts as follows:

Saturday, August 27. Brunen to Lucerne.

Sunday, August 28. Lucerne to Dettingen.

Monday, August 29. Dettingen to Loffenburg to Mumph. Hence to Rheinfelden and one league beyond by voiture and on foot. Hence to Basel by boat.

Tuesday, August 30. Basel to Thauphane.

Wednesday, August 31. Thauphane to a village beyond Strasbourg. Sleep on boat.

Thursday, September 1. Hence beyond Mannheim. Sleep on boat.

Friday, September 2. Past Mannheim toward Mayence (3 hours ashore). Sleep on board.

Saturday, September 3. To Mayence.

Sunday, September 4. Mayence to Bingen to Braubach to Kens.

Monday, September 5. Kens to Coblenz to Bonn. Bonn to Cologne by land, post. Thereafter by land.

Tuesday, September 6. Cologne to Clêves, by diligence and cabriolet.

Wednesday, September 7. Clêves by Nimeguen to Triel by post.

Thursday, September 8. Triel to Rotterdam by post. Embark for England.

Friday and Saturday, September 9 and 10. Wind-bound at Marsluys.

Sunday and Monday, September 11 and 12. En route to Gravesend.

Tuesday, September 13. Reach Gravesend.

Their mode of conveyance by water and by land varied considerably. They floated in moderately comfortable little pas-

senger-boats known as water-diligences, in a freight-boat, and
once in a conveyance which Mary called a canoe because
it was the most primitive type of boat she could imagine —
a long, narrow, flat-bottomed boat of unpainted deal, so crazily
knocked together that it leaked at every seam.[53] Their first land-
conveyance was a cabriolet that broke down and left them to
continue on foot. From Bonn to Cologne they travelled by slow
post-coaches that seldom exceeded a mile and a half an hour;
thereafter they journeyed to Clêves by diligence and cabriolet,
which they found if anything slower. Finally, in Holland they
travelled by post-chaise about as rapidly as in England.

The journey started somewhat inauspiciously with Jane suffering an attack of "horrors" at Lucerne that was sufficient to
delay their departure for Dettingen. From her own journal it
is easy to infer that this was caused by a hypersensitive reading
of *King Lear*. The next day a fellow traveller was so boorishly
insolent that Shelley knocked him down.[54] Thereafter the journey was without particular incidents. The three travellers
simply talked and read, endured discomforts, admired the
scenery, and loathed their fellow travellers. Mary was still
in somewhat precarious health, and all were occasionally exhausted or famished.

Their fellow passengers were mostly Germans compelled, like
themselves, to travel by the very cheapest method. On the
second day (August 28) Mary's journal speaks with loathing
of "the horrible and slimy faces of our companions in voyage."
"Our only wish," she added, "was to absolutely annihilate such
uncleanly animals," whom she designates a few lines later as
"loathsome 'Creepers.'" "Never did I see such a set as were
in the boat with us," wrote Jane on the same day. "Their mirth
was [word crossed out] and loud and unmeaning; their eyes
were shiny . . . leering blasphemy and horror on the be-
holder." On September 4 (having met a few more tolerable
passengers meanwhile) Jane wrote: "Nothing could surpass
the [word crossed out] Manners that prevailed in the Cabin
below — Drinking, smoking, singing, and cracking jokes of a
disagreeable nature — We sat upon the deck the whole day
with one or two tolerable men who smoked it is true but were

brought to own it was wrong." The next day she wrote: " Never
was a more disgraceful set than the common order of people of
Germany. Your soul shrinks back to its inmost recesses when
by accident you set your eye over countenances grimed with
mental and bodily depravity." In her published account Mary
repeated these opinions, somewhat condensed and mollified.
They were republicans, but they were also English travellers of
the early nineteenth century. These people were " canaille "
(Jane's word). When one of them who spoke a little English
sought to talk with them, they frightened him off by talking
dangerously of cutting off the heads of kings.

Both contemporary journals show that the travellers enjoyed
the journey. The swift green waters of the Reuss, the foaming
rapids of the Reuss and the upper Rhine, thrilled them with admiration and a mild sense of danger. Shelley counted this experience a part of his education when in the Preface to *Laon and
Cythna* he came modestly to examine his fitness to speak out as a
poet: " I have sailed down mighty rivers, and seen the sun rise
and set, and the stars come forth, whilst I have sailed night and
day down a rapid stream among mountains." Jane's journal,
much less laconic than that of Shelley and Mary, grows enthusiastic on almost every page, but Mary's journal is somewhat more
restrained than formerly. Occasional passages, however, like
the following, written on August 30, her birthday, show that
her feeling for the beautiful and the romantic was still undulled:

The Rhine is violently rapid to-day, and although interrupted by
no rocks, is swollen with high waves; it is full of little islands, green
and beautiful. Before we arrived at Thauphane the river became
suddenly narrow, and the boat dashed with inconceivable rapidity
round the base of a rocky hill covered with pines.

A ruined tower, with its desolate windows, stood on the summit
of another hill that jutted into the river beyond. The sunset was
illumining the mountains and the clouds, and casting the reflection
of its hues on the agitated river. The brilliance and colourings in the
circling whirlpools of the stream was an appearance entirely new,
and most beautiful.[55]

In Holland they travelled at good speed over well-kept roads
squeezed so tightly between canals at times that carriages could

COBLENZ

Engraved by S. Fisher from a drawing by C. Stanfield

COLOGNE

Engraved by M. J. Starling from a drawing by W. L. Leitch

not pass one another. They reached Rotterdam on the evening
of September 8, with only twenty écus left in the exchequer.
A captain was found who would take them to England for
three guineas each, to be paid on arrival. On the next day they
sailed and reached Marsluys in the evening, where they were
held in port for two days by contrary winds. Both Shelley and
Mary were seasick on the first day's voyage out. By the next
day they were sufficiently recovered to argue with a passenger
about the slave trade, and on their arrival at Gravesend (September 13) they were able to persuade the captain, though
" with great difficulty," to trust them for their passage-money.

They had reached home without a penny and apparently
without a care. The whole of their extraordinary excursion of
six weeks had been care-free, almost high-spirited. Nowhere
in either of their two journals is there any note of dejection or
any feeling that they had plunged themselves into a complicated and difficult situation, except that Mary once permitted
herself a moment of sadness at the thought of Godwin deserted
and almost alone.[56]

NOT even during this exciting period did Shelley forget his
character as an apostle and devotee of freedom. At Paris his first
interest was to make himself further acquainted with the possibilities of Mary's mind. Here was a new companion-in-arms
rather than a mere disciple, as his sister Elizabeth and Harriet
had been. On the way to Switzerland and back again, whenever there was a good opportunity, Shelley and Mary read together. On August 17 it was Mary Wollstonecraft's romance
Mary, a Fiction; on the 31st it was her *Letters from Norway.*
On August 23 and 25 it was the Abbé Barruel's *Mémoires pour
servir d'histoire du Jacobinism* — in which Shelley had long ago
discovered a stimulation certainly unintended by the reactionary author. On the 24th it was Tacitus; on the 27th and September 4 it was Shakespeare. On Saturday, September 10, the
journal states, " Mary begins ' Hate ' and gives Shelley the
greater pleasure," and on September 11, " Mary writes more of
her ' Hate.' "

Jane was another recruit. Her journal shows considerable thoughtful reading of Shakespeare, Rousseau, and Mary Wollstonecraft. On the very day that Mary started " Hate," Jane's journal carried the information that she, too, was becoming an author: "Write a story. . . . Write all day. . . ." It was to deal with " the workings and improvement of a mind which by common people was deemed the mind of an idiot." Shelley had declared that he was not in the least in love with Jane, " but she is a nice little girl, and her mother is such a vulgar, commonplace woman, without an idea of philosophy, I do not think she is a proper person to form the mind of a young girl." [57] One supposes therefore that it was because Shelley had assumed her philosophic guardianship that on August 21 " Shelley and Jane talk concerning Jane's character." Two months later Shelley was setting her lessons in French, Italian, Latin, and history.[58]

With the stimulation of Mary and Jane as companions in the fight for liberty, Shelley had continued the fight himself in beginning *The Assassins*, which he resumed during the two days' wait at Marsluys.[59] Very dimly the more abiding aspects of his future poetry may be seen taking shape in the incidents and impressions of his unusual marriage-tour-without-marriage. Except for his earliest writings, which are almost purely sensational, Shelley's poetry and prose up to this time had been an argumentative and hortatory plea for justice. He had seen and loved mountains and lakes before, but they had not excited him to the discovery that beauty may be regarded as an end in itself, or that through a just apprehension of beauty the universal sympathy for which he longed might be attained. Two years later, in the midst of the Alps again, he was to find and give expression to that conception of Intellectual Beauty which entailed a somewhat revised idea of his poetic mission. For this the journey of 1814 had already laid a definite basis in the eager response to natural beauty shown by the journal of Shelley and Mary, and in several passages in *The Assassins*. " All that was wonderful and lovely was collected in this deep seclusion," he writes of the happy valley of the Assassins. " The fluctuating elements seemed to have been rendered everlastingly permanent in forms of wonder and delight." Following these sentences comes the description of the valley, obviously drawn from one before Shelley's eyes at the time. " No spectator," he concludes, " could have refused to believe that some spirit of great intelligence and power had hallowed these wild and beautiful solitudes to a deep and solemn mystery." It was this " Power " that Shelley alluded to in the Preface to his next important poem, *Alastor* (written in 1815), as " that Power which strikes the luminaries of the world with sudden darkness and extinction, by awakening them to too exquisite a perception of its influences." From this to the " Hymn to Intellectual Beauty " and " Mont Blanc " was but a short step. The tour had definitely awakened Shelley (to use his own words in referring to it) to " the inconstant summer of delight and beauty which invests this visible world." [60]

Chapter XIII

DISASTER AND RELIEF

PARIAHS IN LONDON; DIFFICULTIES OVER HARRIET,
GODWIN, AND JANE; LOVE IN EXILE; HOGG AND
PEACOCK; MARY ATTEMPTS FREE LOVE; BIRTH
OF A SON AND DEATH OF A GRANDFATHER;
MARY'S MOTHERHOOD AND ILL HEALTH;
EXIT JANE

SHELLEY's little party reached London at about three o'clock on the afternoon of Tuesday, September 13. Their first care was to obtain money. A call on Shelley's bankers, Martin and Call, revealed that there was none on deposit. Shelley's moderate drafts from the Continent, aided probably by cheques drawn by Harriet, had exhausted his small balance. They then proceeded to the Hookhams'. Only Edward Hookham was at home, and he was none too cordial. From the Hookhams' they drove to Pall Mall to the home of the Voiseys.[1] Here they received their first taste of bitterness; Mrs. Voisey was very indignant with them over their recent conduct. Henry Voisey was kind, however, and ran ahead of them to Chapel Street to notify Harriet of their coming. Jane and Mary remained in the coach two hours, feeling rather neglected and abused, while Shelley talked with Harriet. Probably it was from her that Shelley obtained enough money to discharge his coachman.[2] By this time it was dark. They went to the Stratford Hotel in Oxford Street, dined, and went early to bed.

Next morning, after the party had talked over their situation and read the newspapers, Shelley made another call on Har-

riet. Evidently Harriet was not prepared to accept the new
situation, for Mary noted after the interview that she was " a
very odd creature" and Jane mentioned, without further detail, " her very strange behaviour." Shelley wrote a number of
letters, and called on Hookham, returning with some clothes [3]
and a copy of Wordsworth's *Excursion,* which they read aloud
that night with little joy. " Much disappointed," Mary recorded
of it; " he is a slave." After dinner they moved into new lodgings
at No. 56 Margaret Street, Cavendish Square. They were now
settled, or as settled as they were ever to be during the distressing months that awaited them.

The story of that period is a rather monotonous chronicle of
fruitless attempts to raise money, dodge bailiffs, and reach an
understanding with Harriet, made tolerable for Shelley only
by finding in his new love a recompense for the loss of friendships and freedom of action. The two journals kept by Jane
Clairmont and by Shelley and Mary jointly [4] preserve a detailed
record of daily events. For the ten days following their removal to Margaret Street Jane's journal (with the quoted or
condensed passages I have inserted in parentheses from Mary's
parallel account) presents the following picture of their daily
life: [5]

Thursday Sept. 15

Rise and breakfast at nine — Send again to Maria Smith's [6] — Letter
from her. Shelley goes to Harriet. Meet Hookham there — Recon-
cilement. Bring him home — He writes to Voisey. Read Emile —
Write my Common Place Book — Dine at six [several words crossed
out] — till eleven — Shelley reads us the Ancient Mariner. Get our
Boxes from Hookham's. Read in the Excursion — the story of Margaret very beautiful. [line crossed out] (". . . Mary reads the
Excursion all day, and reads the ' History of Margaret' [7] to P. B. S.
. . . He reads part of Caleb Williams to us.")

Friday Sept. 16th

Rise at nine — Breakfast — Read Rasselas — and De l'origine de l'ine-
galite des Hommes — Curious and weak letter from Harriet with
Shelley. [one word illegible] I write to Papa and Charles — Letter
from Turner. Hookham Dines — Just before dinner about six, Mama

and Fanny pass the Window — Shelley runs out to them. They won't speak — Hookham quits us early — Voisey at tea — He explains Dr. Gall's system — Departs about 1/2 past ten — Mary retires — Shelley is writing to Papa and I am reading the notes to Queen Mab when we hear stones at the Window — Look out and there is Charles — Joyful meeting — He stays till three in the Morning — Tells us about their Plan of putting me in a Convent — (" Read the ' Excursion ' and ' Madoc.' . . . Mrs. Godwin and Fanny pay a visit to the window but refuse to speak to Shelley when he goes out to them." Charles talks also of the conduct of William Godwin, Jr., and of money affairs in Skinner Street.)

Saturday Sept. 17th

Rise at eleven — Breakfast — Mr. Cooper's attorney calls — Shelley goes to Insurance Office with him — Write and read all morning. Dine at 1/2 past six — Write to Charles. Shelley reads aloud the Curse of Kehama. They go to Bed at ten. Sit up till one writing [word crossed out]. Read the Lara of Lord Byron. (Mary reads " Madoc " all morning.)

Sunday Sept. 18

Rise late. Read Emile. Write. Very lazy. Mr. Peacock calls he and Shelley Walk he dines and goes soon after — Curious Accounts of Harriet. To Bed early. (" Mary receives her first lesson in Greek. She reads the ' Curse of Kehama ' while Shelley walks out with Peacock." . . . In the evening " we talk, study a little Greek and go to bed.")

Monday Sept. 19th

Rise late — Shelley goes to Ballachey's Read the Curse of Kehama and Emile. Hookham calls at dinner time. he goes early — Read the Sorcerer and Political Justice. Admire the Sorcerer very much. (" Shelley goes to Ballachy's [8] receives notice that the sale is Wednesday. Mary reads Greek and ' Rasselas ' . . . Mary reads ' The Sorcerer.' Shelley writes his romance. Write to Amory." [9])

Tuesday Sept. 20th

Rise late. Shelley goes to Ballachey's Read Emile — Write also. Dine at Seven — Shelley reads aloud Thalaba till Bed time. (" Shelley writes to Hookham and Tavernier [10] . . . Mary reads ' Political Justice ' all the morning. Study Greek. . . .")

Wednesday Sept. 21*st*

Rise late — Shelley goes with Hookham to the Sale — Is obliged to
buy the Reversion etc. — Write and learn Greek characters. Hookham dines. Goes early. Write Greek again. (Mary reads Greek. In
the evening Shelley reads one canto of " Thalaba " and goes to bed
tired and sleepy.)

Thursday Sept. 22*nd.*

After Breakfast walk out with M and S — Search for Drawings. Return at 4. Read Greek. Letter from Harriet. Mean and worldly —
Sit up till one reading the Monk. (". . . Mary reads ' Political Justice '; Shelley writes Greek." Shelley hears Harriet has gone out of
town and receives a letter from her " in a far different style." " Shelley draws, and Mary reads ' The Monk ' all evening.")

Friday Sept. 23*rd.*

Finish the Monk. Walk after breakfast with M and S. Go to Hookham's and Priestly's in Holborn — Buy a Greek Anacreon, and the
Life of Johanna Southcott [*sic*]. When we get home find a letter
from Papa. Very prejudiced [these two words are crossed out but
they are legible; two others which follow are illegible]. Read Greek
— Hookham dines — Shelley reads Thalaba aloud in the Evening.
Write a little Greek and learn four tenses of the Verb to strike —
(". . . at a bookseller's buy a guineas worth of books. . . .")

Saturday Sept. 24*th.*

Shelley and Mary to Ballachey's. Learn εἰμι. Read Lewis Tales
of Wonder and Delight. Shelley reads aloud Thalaba in the Evening finishes it. Write Greek — Read Smellie.

Sunday Sept. 25*th*

Write Greek. Read Smellie Philosophy Natural History. Mr. Pea-
cock dines. Shelley and he go to Mr. Warre's in Norfolk Street.
(Mary reads " two odes of Anacreon before breakfast," draws, reads
" Political Justice," walks out with Shelley.)

During this period of ten days Shelley wrote two letters to
Harriet, on September 15 and 16,[11] that are not noted in either

journal. In both letters Shelley strove for a better understanding based upon Harriet's acceptance of Shelley's love for Mary as something not to be tampered with or reviled. "My attachment to Mary," he uncompromisingly asserted, "neither could nor ought to have been overcome." He still professed a strong friendship for Harriet and deprecated her tendency to confide her troubles to others whose influence he distrusted. "I deem myself," he protested, "far worthier and better than any of your nominal friends." Hence it was "not well" that Harriet should wound him with reproach and blame when he was still perpetually concerned about furthering her best interests. Shelley hoped at first that Harriet might still consent to accept his view of the situation and come to live with him and Mary on these terms. He consulted Basil Montagu, Godwin's legal friend, on the subject.[12] Harriet was still recalcitrant. Shelley warned her that their friendship must fall to a lower level unless she could respect the confidence he reposed in her. Indiscretions such as her recent one of divulging his address to an attorney might lead to his arrest by the bailiffs. He desired to make a settlement upon Harriet without delay, and he wished her to determine at once the future nature of their friendship:

Consider how far you would desire your future life to be placed within the influence of my superintending mind: whether you still confide sufficiently in my tried and unalterable integrity to submit to the laws which any friendship would create between us; whether we are to meet in entire and unreserved faith or allow our intimacy to subside.

These letters did not change Harriet's point of view. She did nothing to further the execution of Shelley's deed of settlement because it would have set the seal of finality on what she still hoped was only a temporary aberration.

ON SEPTEMBER 26 Shelley, Mary and Jane moved to new lodgings at Mrs. Page's, 2 or 5 Church Street, Pancras. In his letter of September 16 to Harriet, Shelley had said that a move would soon be necessary, because he feared his present address was becoming known to creditors. Since his return from the Continent Shelley was no less anxious to avoid bailiffs than just before his elopement, when he feared arrest for debt. If the fourteen hundred pounds or more presumably retained by Shelley from the post-obit sale in July had been applied to creditors, the effect was negligible.

For nearly a month life in the Pancras lodgings followed the same dreary constricted pattern as before. Nearly every day Shelley went about his unsuccessful efforts to raise money. Sometimes with Hookham, sometimes with Peacock, Mary, or Jane, he called on brokers or lawyers or at the Westminster Insurance Office. It is not always clear from the daily accounts whether the men mentioned were lawyers or money-agents, but the former seem to have been mainly Amory, Tahourdin, and Tavernier, and the latter Pike, Finnis, Ellis, Homerton, and, most frequently, Ballachey. On October 5 Shelley had hopes of obtaining four hundred pounds at the rate (exorbitant even for post-obits) of six to one; but six days later even this hope was disappointed, all because a certain Mr. Lawrence, of the Westminster Insurance Office, was (in Mary's opinion) too conscientious. Mary's record of the failures became almost fatalistic. October 18: " Shelley goes with Peacock to the lawyers but as usual does not succeed." October 19: " Shelley goes to the City and meets with total failure." October 22: " Shelley is out all the morning at the lawyers, but nothing is done." On October 22 one of his creditors, Starling, found him at home and forced him to sign a bill at one month, with no real prospect of being able to meet it. His regular allowance was mortgaged to Hookham, from whom he was able to obtain enough money to live on and small sums to meet one or two sudden emergencies. Under these circumstances Shelley had to explain to Harriet that it was impossible to send her any more money at present, much as he felt the humiliation of her dependence on " that selfish fellow," as he now called her father.[13]

There had been a reconciliation with Hookham, who had condemned the elopement. For a while Hookham came frequently to their lodgings for dinner, breakfast, or for an evening call. Occasionally Shelley or Jane called at Hookham's. But the reconciliation was by no means proof against relapse. On October 20, after Hookham had come to breakfast, Mary confided bitterly to her journal that " that man comes strictly under the appellation of a ' prig.' " Much worse opinions were to come.

Hogg was in Yorkshire on his regular autumn vacation and is not even mentioned in the two journals prior to October 4. Almost certainly Hogg had by this time heard of the elopement from Harriet, Peacock, or the Newtons. In spite of his patronizing air he had always been fond of Harriet.[14] Perhaps he felt as Southey did when Shelley called upon him in London at about this time. " A man ought to be able to live with any woman," Southey had said. " You see that I can, and so ought you." Pointing to the portrait of Mary Wollstonecraft, whom he greatly admired, Southey expressed bitter regret that her daughter should have been so misled.[15] On October 4 Shelley wrote Hogg a letter which from internal evidence appears to be his first letter to Hogg since the elopement.

Shelley began his letter with an account of his courtship of Mary and the subsequent elopement. Apparently he had not heard from Hogg since these events, and he was anxious to be reunited with his friend and to have Hogg perceive and share his new-found happiness. Never before, Shelley proclaimed, had he known the real meaning of the word contentment. He announced himself a completely changed man — an assertion which the usually sceptical Hogg probably found not hard to believe when he remembered the Shelley he had recently observed. He felt a new unity in his character replacing a former collection of jarring and discordant impulses. He was in fact a new man, a man far more true to himself, far more capable of genuine friendship, and far more useful to humanity. And all this change, he asserted, was due to Mary. Without the stimulation and support of her presence he felt himself quite worthless. A letter from Hogg would make his happiness complete.[16]

Shelley's eloquence left Hogg unmoved. Nearly two weeks later (October 17) Shelley received an answer which Jane described as very cold, and Mary wrote in her journal: " Few friendly spirits in the world." The Newtons, if they were still in London, ignored Shelley completely.[17]

Peacock, whose friendship Shelley regarded as a cold, selfish one,[18] and Hookham, who was also somewhat under suspicion, were the only two of his former friends who associated with Shelley during the first month after his return. Mrs. Boinville, either because of the financial risk to which Shelley had exposed her or because she disapproved of his recent conduct, wrote a letter which Mary described (October 11) as "cold and sarcastic" and Jane as "very sneering."[19] On October 20 Jane remarked in her journal: "We still hear nothing of any friend of Mr. Shelley's." This winter, in Peacock's opinion, was the most solitary period of Shelley's whole life.[20] Even his mother no longer wished to see him.[21]

Peacock's company, however, was constant. There were very few days when he did not call. Often he came for breakfast or dinner and accompanied Shelley when he went forth on his financial rounds. Occasionally Jane or Shelley walked to the apartment in Southampton Buildings where Peacock lived with his mother. Sometimes the whole party walked together in the fields, where Shelley once or twice indulged his juvenile love of fireworks. Their favourite walk was over Primrose Hill to a pond called the Lake of Naugis, where they would launch paper boats [22] and fire-boats. It was in the midst of his new interest in fire-boats that Shelley turned again, on October 4 and 5, to making chemical experiments. On some days Peacock called at the Pancras lodgings more than once. After he had called the second time on October 6 both Jane and Mary recorded: "Peacock stays wearying us all the morning." Later Mary seemed to resent his presence so much that she deliberately omitted mention of him in her journal. Occasionally Shelley and Mary went by themselves to Mary Wollstonecraft's tomb in St. Pancras Churchyard, to recollect the early days of their love or to read Godwin's *Essay on Sepulchres.*

PEACOCK was hand-in-glove with the Shelleys in a wild scheme about which one could wish that the two journals furnished more details. On September 30 Mary, Jane, and Shelley walked to Hampstead Heath. Here, in the happy hunting-ground of

eighteenth-century highwaymen, they discussed " the possibility of converting and liberating two heiresses," who are not
identified in Mary's journal, but whom Jane mentions as " poor
Eliza and Helen " — presumably Shelley's sisters. After all that
had happened since the spring of 1811, Shelley still seemed to
think it possible to proceed with his early design of making his
two sisters " divine little scions of infidelity." Some sort of project was formed and was submitted to Peacock for his criticism
when he dropped in a little later to talk and dine. The plan was
to kidnap the two girls from their boarding-school and flee
with them to the west of Ireland, where with Peacock and
" Marion " they would found a little seminary of radical opinion
such as Shelley and Miss Hitchener had once planned for
Nantgwillt in Wales. " Marion " was Marianne de St. Croix,
whom Peacock loved, but was too poor to marry. That the
supposedly cold, sceptical Peacock entered briskly into such a
scheme is more intelligible when it is seen that it included providing for his marriage to Marianne.

On the next day Peacock, Shelley, Jane, and Mary walked
to Hackney. Here, while Shelley and Peacock kept out of the
way, Mary and Jane called at Mrs. Hugford's school and saw
" Eliza, Helen, and Anne." That evening was given over entirely to discussion of " our running away scheme." The next
day (October 2), according to Jane, they discussed their plan
all day and far into the night. Such a scheme called for money,
which Shelley still hoped to raise, and for the young ladies'
consent, about which anyone but a Shelley should have felt
distinctly sceptical. For lack of one or both of these essentials
it either failed, or else it was suddenly abandoned in a manner
which Hogg at least would have called characteristic. After
the four days in which these plans occupied most of their time,
we hear nothing further about them except for an entry in
Jane's journal for October 6, saying that Shelley had written
a letter to Mrs. Hugford, a part of which he read aloud.
Whether it was written as a part of the scheme or merely for
amusement seems uncertain from Jane's description of it as
" terrible nonsense."

If this fantastic incident indicates that Shelley's mind still

THOMAS LOVE PEACOCK IN 1803

*Reprinted from Peacock's Works, Vol. VI, London, 1893, by permission of
the publishers, J. M. Dent & Sons*

operated at times peculiarly within the world of his early novel-
reading [23] and even had power to draw other minds under the
same spell, an occurrence which closely followed it will suggest
even more strongly the atmosphere of Gothic horror. On the
night of October 7 Mary went rather early to bed. Shelley and
Jane sat up over the fire, talking late into the night, an occasional
practice of theirs which one suspects Mary did not entirely approve. For some time the talk was of oppression and reform, an
association of philosophical people, the cruel punishments suffered by soldiers, Shelley's two favourite sisters, Hogg, Harriet, and Elizabeth Hitchener. At one o'clock Shelley observed
that it was the witching hour of night; was it not horrible, he
asked, to feel the silence of night tingling in one's ears? The
conversation turned upon " unaccountable and mysterious feelings about supernatural things." Shelley repeated his former
question; Jane thought his expression indescribably melancholy
and awe-inspiring. By two o'clock they were both so stricken
with awe that they scarcely dared breathe. " Did you ever read
the tragedy of ' Orra '? " Shelley asked when, after long hesitation, Jane was on the point of going to her room. " Yes," Jane
answered (and might have added that she had recently been
reading Monk Lewis). Then: " How horrible you look —take
your eyes off." And: " Good-night." [24]

Shelley was too disturbed to sleep; he was preparing to read
for the rest of the night when Jane rushed down the stairs in a
state of complete terror — her cheeks and even her lips deathly
white, eyes wide and staring, hair stiff and erect, skin drawn
into innumerable wrinkles. Shelley calmed her with some difficulty, and learned that a pillow, which she had just been staring at in the middle of her bed, had been moved instantly to
a chair, through no discoverable human agency. For the rest
of the night they sat by the fire, fearing that their candle would
not last till daylight, and engaging at intervals in awful conversation " relative to the nature of these mysteries." As daylight
was returning, Jane was again overwhelmed by Shelley's terrible
expression, which she later described to him as " a mixture of
deep sadness and conscious power over her." Shelley was unable to calm her; she fell into convulsions, shrieked, and writhed

on the floor. (This is Shelley's phraseology; Jane says simply: " I was ill.") The next day Jane was ill and melancholy most of the day. If Shelley had a psychological explanation for Jane's horrors (which, after all, he shared), he did not express it in his account, and Jane's remark: " I did not feel in the way he thinks I did," must go unexplained.

Peacock laughed at this story, but his derision did not prevent Jane from falling into horrid thoughts of ghosts that kept her awake all night. Even Shelley betrayed a touch of humorous scepticism when similar mysteries occurred a week later. On that night, October 14, Jane walked in her sleep and groaned horribly for two hours. Other acts of levitation occurred in her room. " The chimney-board," Shelley observed, " is found to have walked leisurely into the middle of the room, accompanied by the pillow, who, being very sleepy, tried to get into bed again, but sat down on his back." Mary's comment on October 18 leaves little doubt as to what she thought of these midnight sessions of terrifying conversation. " I go to bed soon; but Shelley and Jane sit up [" till two," in Jane's account], and, for a wonder, do not frighten themselves."

Even Mary, whose imagination was under better nervous control, was not proof against the fears that were to some extent justified by their precarious situation. On October 12 she received a letter which she apparently feared to open. After deliberating for some time she burned it. The next day, having meanwhile kept her counsel, she announced what she had done. Immediately there was "much dispute and discussion concerning its probable contents." " Alarm," continues Mary's account. " Determine to quit London." Possibly Jane was not told of this new threat, for all she records is: " Long talk about removing." They sent to Hookham for five pounds in order to meet the emergency. Then they changed their minds and all three went to Drury Lane to occupy box seats for Kean's performance of Hamlet — which they found so disappointing that they left in disgust at the end of the second act. When they returned to their lodgings they were again smitten with alarm. Calling a coach, they drove to the Stratford Hotel and spent the night there.

MAINLY unreal as all these excursions and alarums may have
been, Harriet at least was a difficulty not likely to vanish with
clear morning sunlight. Between September 14 and October 26
Shelley wrote ten letters to Harriet, but apparently did not see
her.[25] The first and second of these letters, as we have seen,
sought vainly to commit Harriet to an acceptance of the new
modus vivendi. Shelley had the advantage of the strong influence he had always exerted over Harriet's mind and of an
absolutely inflexible confidence in the rectitude of his own
actions and intentions. His position throughout was firm and
consistent. Harriet, although stubbornly resolved not to give up
the fight, was from the first unfortunate and inconsistent in her
manner of waging it. She hoped to win Shelley back,[26] yet she
could not abstain from wounding him by making violent attacks
on the woman with whom, according to her theory, he was in-
fatuated. She reproached him for doing her a great injury,
while at the same time Shelley reproached her for acting basely
and ignobly by refusing to accept the inevitable. She who had
always taken her opinions from him now took the advice of
people he despised; she even consulted a lawyer. Although
Harriet explained that she did not intend bringing legal action,
Shelley continued to resent this as an imputation on the generosity of his intentions toward her. Her letters were characterized by Jane and Mary in occasional phrases in their journals
as " mean and worldly " (September 22), " very civil " (October 5), or " cheerful " and " good-humoured " (October 11).

By September 27 Harriet was in need of money from Shelley,
who was unable to send it either then or for some time later.
As Shelley's affairs grew more desperate, the situation reversed
itself and he was compelled to call on Harriet for aid in order
to avoid arrest for the bill of Charters, the coach-maker. Harriet promised on October 23 to raise the money,[27] and on October 25 Shelley wrote her a most urgent letter to request haste.
He said that his " antient illness " had returned upon him,
that Harriet alone now stood between him and prison, and that
although all their valuables had been sold to buy food, Mary
and Jane had " very near perished with hunger." [28] Whether
or not Harriet quieted Charters at the time, his bill was a source

of later annoyance and remained unpaid until after Shelley's death.[29]

On October 10 Harriet wrote that Eliza was not with her and that she was alarmed over her approaching confinement. Shelley and Peacock called on her doctor, who was out. They then sent a porter, who returned with an oral message from Harriet and a letter from Dr. Sims, stating that Harriet's condition, while not very favourable, was not particularly dangerous. Next day Harriet wrote a cheerful letter, in which she made several suggestions for improving Shelley's health, concerning which he had complained in his letter of the preceding day.

Harriet took the story of her misfortunes to Shelley's solicitor, Amory, who sympathized with her and declined for a while to continue as Shelley's representative. Shelley interpreted this as an act of deliberate malice on Harriet's part. Shelley and Mary also believed that Harriet was spreading the story that Godwin had encouraged their love-affair, and Harriet appears to have admitted and defended doing so.[30] If Harriet really believed this, in the face of what she had seen, she had reached the point of those who seek solutions for their difficulties by believing only what they wish to believe. Five or six weeks later Harriet called on the Godwins and told them of a rumour being circulated that Godwin had sold Mary and Jane to Shelley for £800 and £700 respectively, a story which she said she assured everyone was a wicked calumny.[31] Also in her letter to Catherine Nugent [32] she charged Godwin only with being the father of Shelley's pernicious theories. This seems fairly good evidence that Harriet's more extreme charges against Godwin were the expression only of a particularly reckless state of mind. Shelley's household, lacking this evidence, believed otherwise. On October 30 Jane wrote in her journal: " We talk over Harriet's plan of ruining Papa."

Shelley was now convinced that the highest type of friendship was no longer possible between him and Harriet, because there was no further possibility of the complete confidence on which such friendship must rest. As early as September 26 he sharply denounced Harriet's character: " I was an idiot to ex-

pect greatness or generosity from you, that when an occasion
of the sublimest virtue occurred, you would fail to play a part
of mean and despicable selfishness. The pure and liberal principles of which you used to boast that you were a disciple, served
only for display. In your heart it seems you were always en-
slaved to the vilest superstitions, or ready to accept their support for your own narrow and worldly views. You are plainly
lost to me for ever. I foresee no probability of change." [33] These
words were written when Shelley was indignant at the "basest
and blackest treachery" that he thought Harriet was embarking
on by engaging a lawyer. Later letters were less excommuni-
catory in tone, but came to the same thing in the end: "Do not
mistake me. I am and will be your friend in every sense of the
word but that most delicate and exalted one. I solemnly protest
to you that not the slightest unkindness or enmity toward you
has ever entered my heart." [34] Since the confidence that Shelley
demanded as a prerequisite for the highest friendship involved
Harriet's desertion of the "selfish and worldly wretches" who
were her advisers, and her complete acceptance of Shelley's
point of view, Harriet could not hope to be "ranked among the
wise and good" [35] without abandoning her own case completely.
Naturally the difficulty remained unsettled.

While matters were taking this course with Harriet, Godwin
and his wife still continued, as Jane had written on September 23, "very prejudiced." On October 15 a letter from Godwin
to Jane urged her to leave the Shelleys,[36] but Shelley advised
her against it and she declined. Five days later Peacock called
upon Godwin, whose stubborn refusal to have anything to do
with his daughter and her lover was distressing to both of them.
Godwin refused even to talk about Shelley with anyone but an
attorney. Except for a long talk between Jane and Mr. Marshall
on the 12th, the Shelleys were for some time practically ignorant
of what was happening in Skinner Street. Then, on October 22,
Fanny Imlay, who was forbidden by the Godwins to see or
talk with the truants, heard some news that was of vital importance to them.

Thomas Hookham, according to her information, was planning to betray Shelley to his creditors. Fanny wrote a warning

note and waited in a field near by while a small boy delivered it. When Shelley and Jane ran out to talk with her she screamed and ran away. They followed her to Skinner Street, and Jane sent in a note to her brother, Charles Clairmont, which brought him out for an interview. Charles claimed to know nothing of any treachery on Hookham's part, but next morning Jane managed to obtain a talk with Fanny which fully confirmed her warning. Mary thought that Hookham had been set on by Harriet. Shelley and Peacock set off to seek Hookham, who either could not or would not be found. Shelley wrote to Harriet appealing for aid, and Harriet answered, as we have seen,[37] promising to raise money for the carriage-maker, Thomas Charters — with whom, it would seem, Hookham had been " plotting."

Shelley, Mary, and Jane seem to have been perfectly convinced of Hookham's treachery. If they were right, Hookham changed his mind again by October 27, when he agreed to offer bail for Shelley in case of his arrest. Thus Shelley was still in danger. A letter to Harriet at this time stated that it was now necessary for him to go into hiding until November 6.[38]

AT NINE O'CLOCK [39] on the night of Sunday, October 23, Shelley left his lodgings to take up a furtive existence until the bailiffs could be faced. He went into hiding none too soon, for the very next day suspicious callers arrived whom Mary and Jane took to be bailiffs. Thereafter until November 9 there were only two nights (those of October 29 and November 5) that Shelley spent at home. These were Saturday nights when at midnight debtors were immune from arrest for twenty-four hours. During this period he had to meet Mary by stealth, taking whatever precautions he could against her being followed. Mary's journal for the sixteen days shows only two days in which it is not clear that they met, most commonly for two hours at a time. On some days they met more than once, and on most days they wrote to each other — desperate, impassioned little notes, generally, that show why the absolute nadir of Shelley's physical fortunes was not, after all, the most depressed period of his life. Peacock's lodg-

ings had already been agreed upon as a point of contact. On
the first day Mary sought for him vainly at Peacock's, then up
and down Fleet Street, until she finally found him in a coffee-
house, and returned home in a cab "tired to death." Thereafter they met at Peacock's, in Holborn, at St. Paul's, at Gray's
Inn Gardens, and at unnamed hotels and coffee-houses, shifting
the meeting-places constantly in order to foil the bailiffs. Meanwhile these minions called at least once (October 26), in their
unimaginative way, at the Pancras lodgings, departing empty-
handed and angry.

Shelley also saw Peacock and Jane occasionally, and corresponded with Jane. At Peacock's (on November 7) he met
Hogg, but the meeting did nothing to encourage him. Hogg
was very witty but very cold, and asked Shelley about his "two
wives." Hogg's coldness to Shelley was matched by Mary's loss
of her best friend, Isabel Baxter, in whose home she had been
visiting shortly before her elopement. Isabel's fiancé, Mr. David
Booth, wrote Mary a letter, received on November 3, terminating the friendship. "So all my hopes are over there," Mary
wrote in her journal. "Ah! Isabel; I did not think you would
act thus." Shelley, flitting from inn to inn, received the following comment on Isabel:

I know her unexampled frankness and sweetness of character. . . .
I am indeed disappointed. I did think Isabel perfectly unprejudiced.
She adores the shade of my mother. But then a married man — it is
impossible to knock into some people's heads that Harriet is selfish
and unfeeling and that my father might be happy if he chose.[40]

SOME of the Godwins' friends were shunning Skinner Street
since the elopement; the Godwins were in an almost hopeless plight financially,[41] and were repulsing with cold reproach
Mary's efforts at reconciliation. They even threatened and
punished Fanny Imlay for seeing Mary. Knowing that Mrs.
Godwin disliked her, Mary detested her in turn and held her
responsible for Godwin's intransigence. Concerning Godwin,
she could only record in her journal the somewhat mournful
comment: "Oh! philosophy." Under these circumstances, with
Shelley a fugitive, Mary learned that in February or March

she was to have a baby. Jane, whose flightiness of character had already become a mild source of worry to Shelley, was occasionally captious to both Shelley and Mary, was thinking of returning to the Godwins, and actually did return for a day or two.

Shelley learned all the discouraging news in his furtive interviews and certainly felt it as an added burden upon his spirits. He considered himself still responsible for Godwin's debts as well as his own. On November 5, before he had attained security from his own creditors, he eased matters somewhat for the Skinner Street household by "settling" one of Godwin's creditors, Lambert. His own desperation was somewhat assuaged by the confidence, shared by him and Mary since before October 25, that their danger would be over on November 6, a confidence proved sound by the event.

Shelley's quarterly income was now only half what it had been before Mr. Westbrook's allowance stopped, and it was mortgaged to Hookham, from whom he obtained at least some of it for living-expenses. With Mary and Jane he was living on four pounds a week, which he considered very good management [42] but which was nevertheless slightly in excess of his annual two-hundred-pound allowance. While he was in hiding a brief period came when they were faced with the imminence of actual hunger. On the 24th of October Shelley's microscope was pawned or sold to a Skinner Street pawnbroker named Davison, for five pounds, and his pistols seemed destined to go the same way. Jane's journal for October 31 contains the significantly simple entry: "Mrs. Page [their landlady] wants some money." On November 1 Shelley was dining with Mary and Jane at the Cross Keys Inn, in St. John Street. Shelley and Mary had previously spent the night of October 20 at this inn. On their second visit the landlord became impertinent (as Jane saw it) and refused to send up the meal without a payment. Jane went to Hookham for money, but failed to get it. She then went to Peacock's, but failed to find him. Before evening Shelley secured some cakes from Peacock, and Hookham sent money to pay the bill. On November 4 Jane's journal states: "This is the Morning on which S will receive money — If he does not I know not what we shall do."

The letters that were exchanged between Shelley and Mary during the sixteen days of Shelley's exile from his home are tense with the strong emotion that is oddly missing in the brief and usually toneless daily records kept by Mary and Jane. In the early days of Shelley's hiding, before Hookham's " conversion," that " sly little rascal " of the journals was an object of almost apostolic wrath in Shelley's letters. " I care not for the Hookhams," he wrote on October 24. " I'll tear their hearts out by the roots with irony and sarcasm if I find that they have dared to lift a thought against me." The next day he wrote: " I will make this remorseless villain loathe his own flesh in good time. He shall be cut down in his season. His pride shall be trampled into atoms; I will wither up his soul by peacemeal " [*sic*] — which sounds rather as if Monk Lewis had undertaken to rewrite one of the more bloodthirsty of the Psalms. Thereafter the violence ended and Shelley and Hookham seemed to be co-operating. On October 30, when Hookham warned Shelley that he might be arrested if he returned to the London Coffee House, Mary wrote in her journal, somewhat scriptually also: " This man has repented him of his wicked deeds."

Both Shelley and Mary gave occasional utterance to a feeling of despondency. " Oh, my love," Mary wrote on October 25, " you have no friends; why then should you be torn from the only one who has affection for you? " On the 24th Shelley wrote:

My imagination is confounded by the uniform prospect of the perfidy and wickedness and hardheartedness of mankind. Mary most amply redeems their blackest crimes. But I confess to you that I have been shocked and staggered by Godwin's cold injustice. The places where I have seen that mans fine countenance bring bitterness home to my heart to think of his cutting cruelty.

Mary felt Godwin's alienation very keenly and was also deeply hurt at the defection of Isabel Baxter. She now felt at times almost an outcast — a newer feeling for her than for Shelley — but her love for Shelley seemed to be intensified by her complete dependence on him. " Goodnight, my love — " she concluded a letter on October 28,

to-morrow I will seal this blessing on your lips — dear, good creature, press me to you, and hug your own Mary to your heart. perhaps she will one day have a father till then be everything to me
love — . . . . Oh we must meet soon, for this is a dreary life I am
weary of it — a poor widowed deserted thing no one cares for her —
but ah — love is not that enough — indeed I have a very sincere affection for my own Shelley.

But Good night I am woefully tired and so sleepy. I shall dream
of you, ten to one, when you, naughty one, have quite forgotten me.

Take me — one kiss — well, that is enough. to-morrow! [43]

Shelley's letters to Mary, in spite of occasional depression,
were hopeful. They abound in such expressions as " this will
not last," " we shall soon be restored to each other," " but this
will soon pass," " I am full of business and hopes," " a few days,
perhaps a few hours will terminate our difficulties." [44] His
greatest privation was his separation from Mary, his greatest inspiration the hope of being reunited with her in security. " This
separation is a calamity not to be endured patiently; I cannot
support your absence," he wrote on October 24.[45] On the 25th:

I shall see you to-night, My beloved Mary fear not. Have confidence
in the fortunate issue of our distresses. I am desolate and wretched
in your absence; I feel disturbed and wild even to conceive that we
should be separated. But this is most necessary, nor must we omit
caution even in our unfrequent meetings. Recollect that I am lost if
the people can have watched you to me. I wander restlessly about;
I cannot read or even write. But this will soon pass. I should not
infect my own Mary with my dejection; she has sufficient cause for
disturbance to need consolation from me.[46]

" How hard and stubborn," he wrote on the 27th,

must be the spirit that does not confess you to be the subtlest and
most exquisitely fashioned intelligence; that among women there
is no equal mind to yours! And I possess this treasure! How beyond
all estimate is my felicity! Yes; I am encouraged — I care not what
happens; I am most happy.[47]

On October 28 he wrote:

Your thoughts alone can waken mine to energy; [my mind] without
yours is dead and cold as the dark midnight river when the moon

is down. It seems as if you alone could shield me from impurity and
vice. If I were absent from you long I should shudder with horror
at myself. My understanding becomes undisciplined without you.
I believe I must become in Mary's hands what Harriet was in mine.[48]

The last note written to Mary during his period of hiding (November 8) concludes:

My dearest, best love only one more day, and we meet. Your affection is my only and sufficient consolation. I find that I have no personal interest in any human being but you, and you I love with my whole nature.[49]

In their present adversities Shelley and Mary looked forward
to a retreat from the world as soon as the necessary funds could
be secured. With characteristic tenacity Shelley still clung to
his old dream of Nantgwillt, in Wales, where he had once been
happy with Harriet and had planned to retire with her only
about a month before he eloped with Mary. He had written to
the owner, Mr. Hooper, on or shortly before October 28. On
November 3 Mary was impatient for the answer:

No answer from Hooper — I wish he would write. Oh how I long
to be at our dear home, where nothing can trouble us, neither friends
or enemies! Don't be angry at this you know my love that they are
all a bad set; but Nantgwillt — do you not wish to be settled there in
a house you know love with your own Mary — nothing to disturb
you, studying, walking and other such like amusements — oh its
much better, believe, not to be able to see the light of the sun for
mountains than for houses.[50]

Shelley expected an answer from Hooper on the 5th.[51] Evidently there were insuperable difficulties, but Shelley's desire
for a Welsh retreat persisted. Eight months later he was considering the possibility of leasing or buying a home in Merionethshire.[52]

For about two months after Shelley returned to the Pancras
lodgings his daily existence, as shown by Mary's journal,[53] was
quite similar to that shown by the extracts from the two journals

quoted earlier in this chapter. When Shelley went out walking in the evening, Claire Clairmont — she had recently dropped the Jane [54] — accompanied him more often than Mary, possibly because the latter was not always well. He would not walk alone at night, as Claire informed her mother, because he feared assassination. He believed that Mr. Leeson, his fancied assailant at Tanyrallt, was following him with a dagger.[55] Visits to money-lenders and lawyers — particularly the latter — continued, but they were less frequent and less urgent than formerly. Though an immediate crisis had been surmounted, there were still enough unpaid bills to make an occasional change of lodgings not inadvisable. On November 9 they moved to Nelson Square. On November 11 Hookham thought it worth while to try to collect twenty-four pounds, in answer to which Mary's journal records noncommittally: "Shelley goes to him." At about the same time Shelley appears to have furnished Harriet with some money.[56] On the 26th of December they were looking for another house, in Hampstead, and on January 7 they were again searching for a house. Whether or not they found one during January is rendered uncertain by the loss of several pages from Mary's journal.[57]

Claire was becoming more and more a problem. Shelley had been aware of this possibility for some time. On October 14 "Jane's insensibility and incapacity for the slightest degree of friendship," as Shelley wrote in the journal, led him to some serious moralizing on the danger of "giving away to trivial sympathies." This was occasioned, as we learn from Claire's journal of the same date, by a "quarrel with Shelley" in which she said "a thousand unkind things, meaning none." She quarrelled similarly with Mary on the 19th, and on November 4 she professed herself greatly disappointed in Shelley, whom she ordinarily regarded as almost perfect.

For two days after Shelley's return Claire was gloomy and sullen. Shelley had no sooner talked her into a good humour than she was again upset by news from Skinner Street. Charles Clairmont and Fanny Imlay were now in more constant contact with Shelley's household than formerly, and Fanny Imlay called or wrote occasionally, though she was still subject to heavy

threats in case she talked to Mary. Having been falsely informed that Mrs. Godwin was about to die, Claire returned to
Skinner Street. In two days she was back again. Mrs. Godwin
was in no danger, Shelley disapproved of her action, and she
could stand Skinner Street no longer. " I wish this girl had a
resolute mind," Shelley complained to his journal on November 14, the day before her return. On the 24th Claire became
quite ill with an inflammation of the liver and had to be bled.
The next day she was again in ill humour, and again Shelley
sat up with her that night and " talked her into reason " (Shelley's phrase). On December 19 Shelley wrote in the journal:
" Clara imagines that I treat her unkindly. Mary consoles her
with her all-powerful benevolence. I rise (having already gone
to bed), and speak with Clara; she was very unhappy; I leave
her tranquil." Claire was by nature destined to remain a problem, especially to Mary, a problem that waxed and waned from
time to time and that occasionally taxed Mary's patience to the
breaking-point.[58]

Godwin's proceeds from Shelley's post-obit sale shortly before
the elopement with Mary had been insufficient to meet all of
his obligations at the time, and his financial situation had meanwhile grown steadily worse. Shelley had expected from the
first to meet an obligation of Godwin's for two hundred pounds
falling due on December 1. Early in November Godwin received a letter from Longdill, Shelley's solicitor, saying that
Shelley had requested him to pay this bill. Godwin was still so
resentful of Shelley's treatment of him and of the consequent
rumour crediting him with having sold Mary and Claire to Shelley that he wished to refuse Shelley's aid. He agreed to accept
the money only under the combined persuasions of Mr. Marshall, Mrs. Boinville, and Cornelia Turner. Still refusing to
thank Shelley, he consented grudgingly to Mrs. Godwin's doing
so, through Longdill.[59] One of Godwin's other creditors, a
wealthy money-lender named Lambert, particularly aroused
Claire's indignation. On November 7 she wrote in her journal:

Lambert is worth 300,000 £ and he oppresses and insults Godwin for
the paltry sum of a hundred and fifty — pretending at the same time

to admire his energy and talent — and it is for these people that Godwin has sacrificed his happiness and well-being — that he refuses to see his daughter and Shelley — the two people he loves best in the world.

Shelley, as he thought, had " settled " Lambert on November 5, but on the 14th he was still dealing with him, and on the 22nd he offered him a post-obit in payment of Godwin's debt. Another of Godwin's creditors, Hogan, was apparently quieted for the moment.

On December 7 Skinner Street affairs reached another crisis — there was no money to pay the rent, which was likely to be demanded at any time. One hundred pounds was needed, ninety of which Shelley secured next day from Hookham. At the same time Shelley must have been relieved to hear from Charles Clairmont that another of Godwin's friends was bestirring himself. Francis Place was said to be endeavouring to raise money on Shelley's post-obit to meet a debt of twelve hundred pounds owed by Godwin to Hume.[60] For a short time after this Godwin's difficulties seemed to be quiescent. They were beyond solution, however, and, like Claire Clairmont, were a constantly recurring difficulty to the end of Shelley's life.

From such occasional entries in the journal as " Go to 'Change . . . to Lambert's, receive £30 " (November 14), " Shelley . . . goes to Tahourdin's and other lawyer's holes " (November 28), " out all day with those detested lawyers " (November 30), " out among the bad all morning " (December 2), one sees that both on his own account and on Godwin's Shelley was still busy with the London money-lenders. Outside of London he vainly sought by correspondence during November and December to raise money from " a farmer," Sir John Shelley,[61] and an unnamed person in Wales. An application for an increase in his annual allowance of two hundred pounds from his father was denied on December 10.[62] On December 21, after visiting Pike's and the Insurance Offices, Shelley entered into another post-obit agreement under which he was to receive £3,000 for £10,000. He did not do this without first endeavouring to raise the necessary sum — £1,200 for Godwin's debts and £300 for his own — through his own family. William Whitton discussed legal ways and means with Mr. Timothy Shelley, who was anxious to prevent the sale of another post-obit, but Sir Bysshe's consent was necessary, and he was too old and feeble to be consulted.[63] The comparatively favourable rate Shelley received when he sold his post-obit may have been due partly to this news about Sir Bysshe's health. It also indicates that Shelley and Mary were correct in suspecting that the loan-sharks had endeavoured to take advantage of his necessity during the time he was in hiding.[64]

Since the return from the Continent Shelley's health had continued good. From the beginning of their journal on July 28 until the end of the year he is mentioned only four times as being unwell, and in each case the context shows that the illness interfered not at all with his regular activities and was not mentioned on the days preceding or following.[65] Shelley's statement to Harriet: " These vexations have induced my antient illness," [66] reflects, obviously, a state of alarm rather than a state of fact. Both Mary and Claire, while generally in good health during September and October, suffered more occasional fits of ill health than Shelley.[67]

FROM November 9, when Shelley returned to his lodgings, until after the new year began, Peacock seems practically to have disappeared. He was not once mentioned in the journal as calling, and only five times during the same period is a member of Shelley's household mentioned as calling at Peacock's.[68] During this time Peacock was involving himself in a matrimonial tangle that might have served just as well in one of his novels as the love-affair of Scythrop in *Nightmare Abbey*, which is intended to represent Shelley's difficulties. Peacock was supposed to be in love with Marianne de St. Croix, whom Mary Shelley rather disliked, but whom the Shelleys were willing to aid him in marrying. This did not prevent Peacock from arguing cynically about Love.[69] The Shelleys knew nothing of what was happening until Peacock's mother sent for Shelley and told a distressing story of how Peacock had taken up with a rich heiress and was then (January 3) living with her. Mrs. Peacock, Marianne de St. Croix, and Shelley all felt miserable, and Shelley immediately wrote to Peacock. Within a week Peacock also felt miserable, when, after spending money on the scale of " Charlotte's " supposed wealth, he discovered that she had nothing. On January 12, in Shelley's temporary absence, Mary received a letter from Peacock in prison, saying that his debt was forty pounds. She sent two pounds, and Shelley on his return instituted some fruitless inquiries about " Charlotte." " There is a terrible mystery in the affair," Mary remarked,[70] without suggesting a solution.

In November Hogg returned to the fold, gradually, with caution on both sides. Since he had treated Shelley's earlier advances coldly, almost sarcastically, Shelley received his first visit, on November 14, with some misgivings. If Hogg liked Mary, Shelley decided, they might still be friends, in spite of radical differences in their sympathies.[71] Hogg did like Mary, and Mary was sufficiently pleased with his conversation " on many interesting subjects " to forget for the moment that she was ill. Thereafter Hogg was a frequent caller, whom Mary found increasingly interesting.[72] He generally stayed until midnight and talked or argued on such subjects as virtue, love of wisdom, free will, necessity, the law, the sexes, and sport. He described so graphically a remarkable vision of a deceased former lover who appeared to him in a dream that Claire was precipitated into another exhibition of her " horrors."

Among Hogg's amusing anecdotes, unfortunately merely mentioned in the journal, were stories of Dr. Lambe and Mrs. Newton and " a funny account of Shelley's father, particularly of his vision and the matrimonial morning." [73] But though Mary found him interesting from the first, she was very cautious in deciding that she really liked this friend of Harriet's who was invariably on the wrong side of an argument. In her opinion he bungled his arguments on virtue, was " quite wrong, but quite puzzled " on some other points, and was in general " sadly perverted " in his notions. By December 4, however, she admitted liking him better than before, though she feared he was

" *un enfant perdu.*" Through December her liking steadily increased. Thereafter, if any doubt remained, it must have been dispelled by the receipt, on New Year's Day, of a gallant little note and a present. For the next few months, as long as Shelley and Mary remained in London, Hogg was an intimate of their household. He came to be referred to occasionally as Jefferson or as Alexy, from his novel *Prince Alexy Haimatoff*, which they had all read and Shelley had reviewed on November 16 before Hogg began calling.[74]

SHELLEY's earlier efforts to come to an agreement with Harriet had ended in her forbidding him to call on her and in a threat from Shelley to cease writing to her unless she changed her manner.[75] For a few weeks, apparently, they neither saw nor heard of each other. Harriet was expecting the birth of her child about the end of December, but it was born a month prematurely, on November 30. It was a boy, very healthy for an eight-months child, and very like its father.[76] Harriet named him Charles. Shelley first heard of it on December 6, in successive letters from Hookham and Harriet — the latter signing herself, as Mary noted with two exclamation points: " *a deserted wife!!*" When Shelley immediately began writing announcement circulars, Mary could not help thinking of the child she was expecting. She commented bitterly that Charles's birth should be announced with ringing of bells, " for it is the son of his *wife.*" [77]

Harriet, too, had her bitterness, having possibly hoped that Charles's birth might detach Shelley from Mary. " Oh, my dear friend," she wrote to Catherine Nugent, " what a dreadful trial it is to bring children into the world so utterly helpless as he is, with no kind father's care to heal the wounded frame. . . . I have seen his father; he came to me as soon as he knew of the event; but as to his tenderness to me, none remains. He said he was glad it was a boy, because he would make money cheaper. You see how that noble soul is debased. Money now, not philosophy, is the grand spring of his actions." [78] This interview was painful to Shelley as well, as reflected in Mary's brief account of it on December 7: " Shelley calls on the lawyers and on Harriet, who treats him with insulting selfishness."

After this Harriet gave up all hope of Shelley. On December 20 she wrote him a letter threatening him with her lawyer.[79] A month later she wrote again to Catherine Nugent: "I am sorry to tell you that my poor little boy has been very ill. He is better now. . . . I am truly miserable, my dear friend. I really see no termination of my sorrows. As to Mr. Shelley I know nothing of him. He neither sends nor comes to see me. I am still at my father's, which is very wretched. When I shall quit this house I know not. Everything goes against me. I am weary of my life. I am so restrained here that life is scarcely worth having. . . . I live for others. At nineteen I could descend a willing victim to the tomb. How I wish those dear children had never been born. They stay my fleeting spirit when it would be in another state. How many there are who shudder at death. I have been so near it that I feel no terrors. Mr. Shelley has much to answer for. He has been the cause of great misery to me and mine. I shall never live with him again. 'Tis impossible. I have been so deceived, so cruelly treated, that I can never forget it. . . . Is it wrong, do you think, to put an end to one's sorrow? I often think of it — all is so gloomy and desolate." [80]

Here we have a fairly accurate warning of what was to happen two years later. The old careless talk of suicide that Hogg had found ridiculous had now acquired a basis. Shelley was lost; she lacked the moral and intellectual strength to begin a new life; her home was intolerable, and was likely to become more so as she lived more and more upon her sense of injury. It may have been a petty yielding to this sense, or it may have been real necessity that caused her on January 2 and 3 to send her creditors to Shelley. Mary wrote in the journal for January 2, 1815: "Harriet sends her creditors here; nasty woman. Now we must change our lodgings." The next day Shelley wrote simply: " Creditors from Harriet." It was not until January 7 that they looked for new lodgings, and it was not until about February 8 that they actually moved.

AT ALMOST the precise moment that Harriet was giving up Shelley for lost, a strange and almost incredible situation was developing between Shelley, Mary, and Hogg. The gallant little note accompanying Hogg's New Year's present to Mary was swiftly followed by a declaration of his love. One can scarcely doubt that Hogg's declaration was made with Shelley's knowledge and encouragement. Mary was by this time genuinely fond of Hogg, but her own letters to him show that this fondness was fully as much on Shelley's account as her own. Unlike Harriet, she found no difficulty in subscribing to the theories of both Shelley and Hogg against the exclusive rights of matrimony. She was at the time expecting to become a mother in April or May, so that for months to come the matter would have no physical importance.

Theoretically, Mary yielded at once — openly, affectionately, and in full confidence that she was thereby adding to Shelley's happiness. Addressing Hogg as " Dearest Hogg," she acknowledged his declaration of love, and stated her belief that he was so generous and disinterested that one could not help loving him. Their acquaintance had been so brief that she had not previously thought of loving him, though she already regarded him with a deep affection which she felt sure would in time turn into a passion, such as Hogg richly deserved.

They would then be as completely happy as the angels who sang for ever. Perhaps Mary thought this comparison might seem a little flat to one rather incredulous of angels, so she added another — as happy as the lovers in the world of perfection that Jane Clairmont was so fond of praising.[81]

This honest expression was followed by two notes dated conjecturally January 4 and 6, in the first of which Mary asked Hogg to call and console her while Shelley and Claire were absent on a number of errands, and in the second of which she asked him to accompany her to an exhibit. The next day, January 7, Mary granted Hogg's request for a lock of her hair, and gave him even more explicit statement of her feelings toward him. Her affection for him, though not yet exactly what he desired, she felt to be growing daily.

She asked only for time to be able to make him completely

391

happy. She reminded him that in any event there were physical causes which made it necessary to wait — causes to which Shelley as well as Hogg must be subject. If, as Hogg protested, it was in her power to make him happy, she would certainly try to do so, but it was a matter of time. Meanwhile they could hope, and need not be too prudent. As Mary later teased Hogg with being a " Prince Prudent," it would seem that the idea of prudence in the interim was Hogg's rather than Mary's. Mary's signature, " most affectionately yours," seems a true index to the state of her emotions.[82]

Whatever letters may have been written to Hogg during the next sixteen days have been lost. In her letter of January 23 Mary unconsciously made it quite clear why she was willing to look forward to a passion which she had honestly stated she could not feel at present. Addressing Hogg now as " my own Alexy," Mary expressed her anticipated pleasure in the fulfilment of their love after the birth of her baby. Hogg would teach her Italian and they would read many books together. Their greatest happiness would be in Shelley, and everything they did would make him happy. This prospect is followed by a really passionate assertion of her utter devotion, not to Hogg, but to Shelley.[83]

It was obviously Shelley's pleasure in beholding her union with Hogg that in Mary's eyes constituted the chief attraction, for both herself and Hogg, in their anticipated union! One thinks of Shelley's desire for Hogg's union with his sister Elizabeth, of the Hogg-Harriet affair, of Shelley's later affection for Jane Williams followed by her union with Hogg. One thinks also of Shelley's free-love theories and of the tendency to fixed ideas that he sometimes showed and wonders if this is an extraordinary coincidence, or a fixed idea with both Shelley and Hogg, or if it is not in fact slightly insane.

If, after this, Hogg is to be regarded as attempting a seduction, he must surely be conceded to be an original genius in his method. Shelley's last poem to Harriet had stated his grief that her love was for him alone.

Mary's journal gives no hint of any unusual emotional situation between herself and Hogg, but it does show that during

January and February he was regarded as practically a member of the family. He introduced chess as an amusement, constituted himself Mary's Latin-teacher, went walking, and read — sometimes aloud, like Harriet. When Shelley and Mary were both ill on February 14 Hogg remained for the night.

A gap of six days in the journal (February 17–23) indicates that Mary was having difficulties over her unborn child. On February 22, apparently, the baby was born, more than two months before its time. The doctor (who arrived five minutes too late) had small hopes that the child would live. Shelley was too agitated and exhausted to be of much help; on the contrary he was ill for several days and on February 26 had a spasm. Both Mary and the child improved, however, and by March 2 were ready to move to new lodgings. During this time Hogg was with them every evening until eleven, and when the child was born he spent the night in the house. Even Mrs. Godwin softened her animosity to the extent of sending some linen by Charles Clairmont. Then, on March 6, Mary woke up in the night to find that her child was dead. Hogg was immediately summoned and again spent the night.

Mary was in wretched health and spirits. Shelley, having consulted Dr. Pemberton on February 28, was told that abcesses were forming on his lungs and that he was dying rapidly of consumption.[84] Claire was a domestic problem; Godwin's difficulties still hung over the whole family like a heavy pall. Hogg, whose vacation began on March 10, decided to forgo his usual vacation trip to his beloved Yorkshire and remain with his friends. Thereafter, until April 17, he lived in the same lodgings with the Shelleys.[85]

DURING the very week that Hogg declared his love for Mary, Shelley received news that radically changed his prospects for the rest of his life. On January 7 Shelley wrote in the journal: " See the death of Sir Bysshe in the papers. Hookham calls, and is very gracious." Sir Bysshe died on January 5. As he was over eighty-three years old and had been for some time too feeble to be consulted on matters of business, his death could hardly have been a surprise for one whose constant dealings with money-lenders involved frequent questions about the baronet's health. Mr. Whitton, who was Sir Bysshe's attorney, notified Shelley through Amory and begged Amory to prevent Shelley's going to Field Place at present, since his presence there would be " most painful to Mrs. S." [86]

Shelley went to Sussex in spite of this indirect request. He was accompanied by Claire, perhaps because Mary was still feeling weak and ill. Leaving Claire at Slinfold, a village near Horsham, Shelley appeared at his father's door on January 12 and was refused admission by order of his father, now Sir Timothy. While the will was being read, Shelley sat before the door reading *Comus* in Mary's pocket edition of Milton. Dr. Blocksome emerged and informed Shelley that his father was very angry with him. Mr. John Shelley-Sidney, Shelley's half-uncle, who had always been rather friendly to Shelley, emerged next and observed that it was a most remarkable will. For an explanation of its meaning Shelley was referred to Whitton. Whitton informed him that night that he was now the next heir to the income on a hundred thousand pounds provided he would entail the estate. He gave Shelley a general notion of the will and its codicils and promised a more detailed explanation after the funeral.[87] The funeral took place next day, but Shelley did not attend. His feelings about his grandfather had not changed from those he had formerly expressed to Elizabeth Hitchener: "He is a bad man. I never had respect for him: I always regarded him as a curse on society. I shall not grieve at his death. I will not wear mourning: I will not attend his funeral." [88] It was a promise more easily kept than Shelley had supposed.

Mr. John Shelley-Sidney, of Penshurst, would seem to the average layman to have been quite correct in characterizing Sir Bysshe's will as a remarkable one. On January 20 Shelley received from Whitton a copy of the will and its various codicils, together with an assurance of Sir Timothy's willingness to concur with him in executing its provisions.[89] The estate consisted of a residuary personal estate of £143,675, 12*s.*, 5*d.*, and of

certain entailed real properties that had been added under
different settlements. The settlement of 1782 comprised the
Michell estates which had belonged to Sir Bysshe's first wife,
while that of 1791 comprised the estates inherited from Edward
Shelley of Field Place. Sir Bysshe's will provided that both
these estates be held for life by Timothy Shelley and after him
by Percy Bysshe Shelley, and thereafter by sons of Percy Bysshe
in order of seniority. If Percy Bysshe died without male issue,
the succession was to pass to Timothy Shelley's second son,
John, by whom it must be entailed upon his eldest son. These
estates were to be increased by the trustees (William Whitton
and a Mr. Du Cane) through the investment of one half the
residuary personal property in real estate to be subject to the
same regulations. No one could inherit either of these estates
without agreeing to resettle it according to the terms of Sir
Bysshe's will. There was one portion of his estate, however, his
inheritance under the will of his brother, John Shelley of Field
Place, worth £800 a year, to which Percy was heir in tail male
after his father, for the resettling of which Sir Bysshe's will made
no provision.[90] The total value of the estate, personal and real,
was estimated at about £200,000.[91]

By providing for the augmenting of the entailed estates, Sir
Bysshe had hoped to make it to the interest of his grandson to
accept them and prolong the entail. Unless he did so agree, he
could, if he survived, execute certain legal forms after his father's
death and become absolute owner in fee simple; and with this
prospect he could encumber the estates before his father's
death, thus defeating his grandfather's ambition of transmitting
a large undivided estate.[92]

The settled estates of which Shelley could not be deprived
after his father's death were valued by his solicitor, Longdill,
in 1817 at £80,000.[93] Shelley had always objected to entailing
estates, on the ground that it placed great economic power in
the hands of one who might be entirely unworthy of it. Moreover, it suited his own desires better to be in possession of an
adequate income without encumbrances. It was possible under
Sir Bysshe's will to achieve this by selling to his father the re-

version of the John Shelley estate, valued at £18,000. Through an oversight this part of the estate had not been tied up with the other settlements in the fifth codicil, which had been added to Sir Bysshe's will shortly after Shelley's elopement with Harriet. Sir Timothy had the best of reasons for desiring to buy it. It could thus be added to the entail and freed from possible encumbrance by Shelley, and the price would enable Shelley to pay his debts and live on a scale that would protect Sir Timothy against uneasiness caused by Shelley's financial distresses. It would be a partial protection against post-obits based on the rest of Shelley's inalienable expectations. It would also insure the inheritance of a larger proportion of the estate by Shelley's younger brother, John, in whose hands Sir Timothy thought it would be safer.

Sir Bysshe's will required Shelley to decide within a year whether or not to prolong the entail. Shelley's decision against it was made instantly, but after learning that his father hoped he would so decide he did not instantly announce it. This, and various legal complications, somewhat delayed the execution of his agreement with his father.

On March 8, 1815, however, Shelley executed a deed poll by which he declined to participate in the conditional benefits of his grandfather's will and renounced for himself and his heirs for ever all benefits conditioned upon his resettling his eventual inheritance in accord with his grandfather's wishes. Godwin heard of this act in prospect and asked for a copy of the codicil; he feared that Shelley was acting rashly.[94] Longdill also advised Shelley against this procedure. He was purchasing freedom in the use of his eventual inheritance of about £80,000 by depriving himself and his son of a much larger expectation. The half of Sir Bysshe's residuary personal estate thus renounced amounted to over £70,000. Shelley's annual income, if he had complied with Sir Bysshe's will, would have been from £12,000 to £14,000, after the death of Sir Timothy.[95]

Being thus freed from entailing the remainder of his expectations, on May 13 Shelley entered into an indenture with his father by which he sold him the reversion of the estates devised by the will of John Shelley for the sum of £7,400 and an annuity of £1,000 to be paid quarterly during their joint lives, secured against the rental of certain of Sir Timothy's estates. Estimating the John Shelley property to be worth £11,000, the legal advisers agreed that a £1,000 annuity approximated its present value to Shelley. In the outcome the total sum paid by Sir Timothy until the annuity ceased with Shelley's death amounted to approximately £15,000.[96] Shelley's first quarterly payment was received on June 24, 1815.

As soon as his arrangements with his father were completed Shelley made provision for Harriet by sending her £200 for the payment of her debts and arranging that £200 annually should be withheld from his annuity and paid to Harriet or to her order. With the £200 Harriet still received from her father, this gave her an income of £400 annually, and Shelley an income of £800. Shelley saw Harriet three times in April 1815, about producing their child in some Chancery proceedings that were necessary in connection with Shelley's recent agreement with his father. On the first of these occasions, April 10, Mary's journal reports Harriet " in a surprisingly good humour "; but on the last, April 22, Shelley was " much teased with Harriet." Three or four days later Harriet's attorney informed him that unless he made " a handsome settlement " upon her she would prosecute him for atheism.[97] Thereafter, until Shelley produced Charles again in court, in March 1816, he appears to have had no contact with Harriet.[98]

The agreement reached with Sir Timothy was operative from the time it was reached, but its legal basis seemed very uncertain to Whitton and Longdill. Until certain questions were settled Sir Timothy could not actually sign the agreement without risking his own inheritance under a clause debarring from the enjoyment of benefits any heir who sought to defeat the purposes of the will. A friendly Chancery suit by Shelley to clear this point was decided in Shelley's favour on April 20. Before May 13 Sir Timothy had paid nearly £1,800 on Shelley's account. The financial memorandum signed by Shelley and his father on May 13 is as follows:

1815	B. forward	£1781.13.6
May. Messrs Wimburn & Co., to obtain the relinquishment of a contract for £10,000 Post Obit security agreed to be granted		160. 2.
Messrs North and Co.		32. 7.
Mr. Viner		48.
Mr. Laing		44. 4. 6.
Mr. Starling in discharge of a Post Obit Security to the Amo't of £2000.		833. 7. 6.
		2899.14. 6.
13th Paid Mr. Percy Bysshe Shelley		4500. 5. 6.
		£7400. 0. 0.

13 May 1815

Witness	T. SHELLEY [signed]
WILLIAM WHITTON [signed]	PERCY BYSSHE SHELLEY [signed] [99]

Although this memorandum shows Sir Timothy's expenditure of the exact amount specified in his agreement with Shelley, it would appear that he must have spent other sums in addition, and also that Shelley's debts were still not all paid. The agreement provided that all encumbrances on the estate must be removed.[100] The post-obit sold in July 1814 for Godwin's benefit was still outstanding. It had brought £2,600, and Nash, the owner, now refused to sell it back for £4,500. A suit in Chancery brought in Shelley's name but at his father's expense [101] was finally decided in Nash's favour on May 28, 1818, after which the post-obit was presumably bought back at Nash's price. But even Shelley's price, if paid, would have exhausted his cash, and there were still the £200 sent to Harriet, the bill of Charters, the coach-builder, some of Shelley's Welsh debts, and probably others. On April 17 Shelley's solicitors had written to W. Williams (brother of John) saying that Shelley was making an arrangement with his family which would enable him to pay all debts.[102] But the letters of D. E. Varney quoted in the Appendix to this work show that though some of Shelley's Welsh debts were paid at this time, others were not, because Shelley had failed to list them all, and the money was exhausted. Other debts contracted before May 1815 were, like that to Charters, also unpaid at the time of Shelley's death. Added to all this was Shelley's obligation to Godwin, which he had entered as a debt of £1,200. Shelley sent Godwin £1,000 of this at once, expecting to pay the rest in November, when Sir Timothy was to make him another payment for resigning the reversion of other parts of the estates than the portion covered by the £7,400. But £200 of this "debt" of £1,200 to Godwin Shelley reserved for his own expenses, according to his understanding of his agreement with Godwin. His father-in-law understood it differently, and considerable bitterness resulted.[103]

Although the Chancery proceedings in April 1815 had terminated favourably to the arrangement with Sir Timothy, new difficulties occurred to the lawyers over another passage in the will. This occasioned another friendly Chancery suit, ostensibly over the right of Sir Timothy to cut timber on one of the properties involved. Not until March 22, 1816 did Chancery give an opinion, which Shelley characterized as "doubtful and hesitating."[104] During these protracted proceedings Shelley's financial position stood thus: If his arrangement with his father held good (which was eventually the case), he would continue to receive £800 annually and Harriet £200. If it proved invalid, he had no income, but held the reversion of landed property of from £6,000 to £8,000 a year and could raise money on his definite expectations.[105] Meanwhile any attempts to raise money outside of his annuity must be kept a secret from his father, lest it jeopardize the whole arrangement.

ALTHOUGH the death of Sir Bysshe Shelley did not immediately provide Shelley with funds, it did improve his credit. On the very day Shelley learned of Sir Bysshe's death the journal notes: "Hookham calls, and is very gracious,"[106] and on February 23: "£30 from Longdill." Nevertheless, Shelley's little family were still restless lodgers. On February 8 they moved from Nelson Square to Hans Place, and on March 2 to still other lodgings, unnamed.[107] On March 28 they looked at another house, which they may or may not have taken.[108] The bailiffs were still unimpressed by Shelley's expectations and were still hunting for him, at least occasionally. By the last week in April no place in London seemed safe. Apparently leaving Claire in London, Shelley and Mary took lodgings at the Windmill Inn, Salt Hill, whence Mary wrote coquettish letters seeking to persuade the prudent Hogg to join them. From this rural retreat Shelley still made the necessary but perilous calls upon his London solicitor, Longdill. How long they remained here is uncertain. Shelley had written to Hogg that they were to stay "one day and one — " the last word being now lost. Mary's last extant letter from Salt Hill is dated April 26. Eleven days of Mary's journal covering the period April 24 to May 5 have been torn out, but on May 5 the Shelleys were again living in London. On May 13 the two indentures signed with Sir Timothy Shelley give Shelley's address as Marchmont Street, Brunswick Square.

While the Shelleys were at Salt Hill, Mary wrote to Hogg on April 25 and 26 three letters that constitute the last documents in their love-affair. The three troubled months that had elapsed since her letters of early January had given added proofs of Hogg's kindness and had placed him in possession of the pet names (the Maie and the Dormouse) which Shelley sometimes used with Mary. But either the personal contacts of several weeks' living in the same lodgings or the shock of her own grief and despondency during that time would seem from these letters to have altered Mary's feelings and possibly Hogg's. The later letters deal with other circumstances besides Hogg's love, which is mentioned but once. Mary is chiefly concerned to induce Hogg to visit them, which he ("Prince Prudent") seems too cautious to risk. There is no further mention of passionate love in the future. The emotion is limited to affectionate, coquettish admonitions and entreaties.[109]

Did Hogg ever attain his original desire, which Mary and Shelley were once both willing to grant him? The answer is uncertain, but a brief anticipation of the next few years indicates a negative conclusion. From the latter part of May until August the Shelleys were away from London, apparently not in Hogg's company. During this period there is no extant letter to Hogg from either Shelley or Mary. Mary's one extant letter to Shelley does not mention Hogg, nor does Shelley's one letter to Hogg mention Mary. From early September 1815 to early May 1816, while the Shelleys were living at Bishopsgate, Hogg was a frequent visitor. But William Shelley was born during this period on January 24 — and it is quite clear from numerous references by Shelley and Mary that they entertained no doubt that Shelley was the father. During February, March, and April, with a new baby to engross her attention, it hardly seems probable that Mary should have admitted Hogg's desires, if they still persisted. On the contrary, it must have been during this time, or even before, that Mary developed an active dislike of Hogg, for as soon as the Shelleys were settled at Marlow, after their summer in Switzerland, Mary wrote to Leigh Hunt that she disliked Hogg and thought him " more disagreeable than ever," adding: " I would not have him come every week to disturb our peace by his ill humour and noise for all the world." [110] When Hogg did visit Marlow it was to stay with Peacock, not the Shelleys. From September 1815 to 1818 all of Shelley's five extant letters to Hogg are rather reserved and impersonal in tone, and only one of them mentions Mary.

If these facts, from their nature, suggest only a general improbability, they seem to be rather positively reinforced by a hitherto puzzling entry in the journal of Dr. John William Polidori immediately after meeting Shelley in Switzerland in June 1816. " He married," Polidori wrote of Shelley, " and a friend of his liking his wife, he tried all he could to induce her to love him in turn." [111] The inference is that Shelley's inducements failed. Polidori's information came either directly from Shelley or from Byron through Claire Clairmont. Shelley's own letters show that it could not apply to the Hogg-Harriet situation of 1811; hence it can only be taken as indicating the failure of Shelley's passing desire for a free-love union of Hogg and Mary.

Under these circumstances one need not draw extreme conclusions from a very interesting passage in a letter from Shelley to Hogg dated January 1818, even though it does seem to show that Mary's would-be affair with Hogg had Shelley's approval. Shelley wrote that he would be glad to see Hogg again and yield him his share of " our common treasure." He reported Mary as saying teasingly that she would not go to London, but he promised that they need not fear again being deprived of " this participated pleasure." [112]

This letter seems scarcely in line with Mary's known distaste for Hogg after 1815 or with other circumstances which have already been considered. Probably either the " common treasure " and the " participated pleasure " mean nothing more than a renewal of the old friendly intimacy (and even that would seem a vain hope), or else Shelley had originally been in the grip of an obsession, like his earlier unsuccessful design of uniting Hogg and Elizabeth Shelley — an obsession strong enough to return even after intervening circumstances had rendered its fulfilment impossible.

Mary recovered slowly, working and reading as much as she could, and netting a purse which she presented to Hogg on March 14. She constantly dreamed about her dead child. On March 13 she wrote in the journal: " Shelley and Clara go to town. Stay at home; net, and think of my little dead baby. This is foolish I suppose yet, whenever I am left alone to my own thoughts, and do not read to divert them, they always come back to the same point — that I was a mother and am so no longer." Soon she was able to take pleasure in the exhibition of Lucien Bonaparte's pictures (March 17), the birds at Bullock's Museum (March 18), the wild animals at Exeter Change (March 22), and " all the fine things " at the British Museum, such as ores, fossils, and statues (April 7). By April 18 Mary was able to commit, under similar circumstances, the same sin with Hogg that Harriet had so devastatingly committed. On that day " Jefferson and the Maie go for bonnets after dinner with Clara." Throughout this period Peacock called occasionally, for breakfast, dinner, or a walk culminating in the sailing of paper boats.

DURING all this time, until Shelley procured money from his father in May,[113] Godwin's affairs continued as perplexing as ever. On March 19 Charles Clairmont described the Godwins' condition so gloomily that Mary wrote in her journal: " I am

afraid nothing can be done to save them." On April 21: "Fanny
comes, and gives us an account of Hogan's threatened arrest of
my Father. Shelley walks home part of the way with her." Godwin was ill. He still refused to see Mary, though even Mrs.
Godwin urged that he see her. In his necessity he condescended
to an exchange of letters with Shelley on financial matters only,
but his one letter was in "a style of freezing coldness." [114]

Claire Clairmont was becoming a more constant source of
irritation than formerly. Mary's "powerful benevolence" that
had previously soothed Claire in one of her moods had worn
thinner under stress of Mary's own sufferings. Perhaps Mary
was jealous of the attention Shelley paid to Claire.[115] "Very
unwell," Mary wrote in her journal for March 11. ". . . Talk
about Clara's going away; nothing settled; I fear it is hopeless.
She will not go to Skinner Street; then our house is the only
remaining place, I see plainly. What is to be done?" The next
day's entry contains the decidedly edged remark: "Very quiet
in the morning, and happy, for Clara does not get up till 4."
Two days later there was another conference between Shelley
and Mary over Claire which left Mary feeling that the prospect
was "more dismal than ever; not the least hope" — a conclusion
she pronounced "indeed hard to bear."

One reason why Claire could not return to Skinner Street was
that Mrs. Bishop, Fanny Imlay's aunt, objected. Mrs. Bishop
was planning to take Fanny into the girls' school that she conducted in Dublin with her sister, and she felt that Fanny's association with Claire would cause unfavourable gossip. Mrs.
Godwin sent Mrs. Bishop's letter to Shelley, to show him that
he had deprived Claire of a home. Shelley replied that he
would never regret having saved a victim of prejudice and
promised to provide for Claire in his will. The Shelleys appear
to have advertised for a position for Claire, probably as governess or companion.[116] A Mrs. Knapp, one of Mrs. Godwin's
acquaintances, considered taking Claire into her house. On
May 6 Godwin was to see Mrs. Knapp about the matter; on
the 8th Shelley and Mary called on her and learned that she
could not take Claire. In the end Claire went to stay with a

Mrs. Bicknell, a widow, at Lynmouth.[117] Thence she wrote to Fanny Imlay, giving a cheerful picture of her environment and state of mind.[118]

Mary was greatly relieved at Claire's departure. When Shelley took a walk with Claire the day before she left, Mary recorded acidly: "Shelley and the lady walk out." When Shelley accompanied Charles Clairmont out, on the day of Claire's departure (May 13), Mary became so anxious at his failure to return promptly that she went out to meet him. Gratefully Mary wrote in her journal: "I begin a new Journal with our regeneration."

"REGENERATION" was not too strong a word to apply to the situation of the Shelleys on May 13, 1815, when Mary began her new journal. A source of domestic friction had just been removed from their home. On the very same day Shelley had concluded financial arrangements with his father by which most of his debts were paid and he was guaranteed an income of £800 a year after a deduction for Harriet. Not until this moment was he really safe from arrest and imprisonment. For nine months he had precariously defended himself either by temporary financial arrangements or by flight from the bailiffs. At the same time an almost equal load had been lifted from Mary's mind — and to a large degree also from Shelley's — by securing £1,000 for Godwin, without which he too was in daily peril of a debtors' prison. Coincidentally the distress and danger resulting from inability to provide for Harriet was abolished. Finally, Shelley had in hand at least £200 in cash, reserved from the £1,200 claim he had put in for Godwin.[119]

For more than nine months the Shelleys had been to only one or two operas or plays. Their amusement away from home had been limited to walks, paper-boat sailing, one or two lectures (for instance, "Garnerin's Lecture on electricity, the gasses, and the phantasmagoria" on December 28), two or three visits to the British Museum, the Zoological gardens, and the exhibit of a particularly admired statue of Theocla on Jan-

CLAIRE CLAIRMONT

Copy by Emory W. Price of the oil painting by Amelia Curran. By permission of the British Museum

uary 5 and 6. These, however, were trifling privations for Shelley. Far greater was the mental stress of the vain effort to settle matters with Harriet, the continual dodging of bailiffs and trying to arrange financial expedients with grasping money-lenders, Mary's danger when her child was born, the domestic friction between Mary and Claire (and possibly even with Mary about Claire), the falling-off of old friends, and particularly the animosity and distress of Godwin. He had rather expected and would always expect misunderstanding and persecution, but to be misunderstood and scorned by one whom he still reverenced as the author of *Political Justice* was peculiarly hard to bear. One day when Godwin and Charles Clairmont met Shelley by accident on the street, Godwin remarked to Charles on the great pity that one so beautiful as Shelley should be so wicked.[120]

The effect of such continuous mental stress upon Shelley's literary production was devastating. He had vowed to devote his life to the abolition of tyranny, and in nine months he had written for a part of one day (September 19) on *The Assassins* and part of one evening (November 16) on a review of Hogg's novel *Memoirs of Prince Alexy Haimatoff*.[121] The immense difference in poetic quality between *Alastor*, written in the autumn of 1816, and the earlier *Queen Mab* indicates that Shelley must have written considerable practice verse between writing these two poems, but almost the only record of it is an unfinished poem in the back of one of Claire Clairmont's journals.[122] One day Shelley suddenly asked Peacock: " Do you think Wordsworth could have written such poetry, if he had ever had dealings with money lenders? "[123] In August, when both his health and his spirits had greatly improved, Shelley wrote to Hogg: " My health has been considerably improved under Lawrence's care, and I am so much more free from the continual irritation under which I lived as to devote myself with more effect and consistency to study." [124]

The " continual irritation " was more mental than physical; it almost certainly aggravated Shelley's physical illnesses. The actual daily record of Shelley's illnesses for the nine months after his return to England strongly supports the opinions of Hogg and Peacock that he exaggerated his ill health. From September 1814 to January 1815, as we have seen, Shelley was ill only four days, not in succession — less than Claire or Mary — which did not prevent his describing his health to Harriet as desperate. Thereafter, until May 13, Shelley is mentioned as being ill in only six of the daily journal entries — February 14, 24, 25, 26 and March 19 and 25. He may also have been ill on some of the days for which entries are now missing, and he was presumably not well on the two days (February 28 and March 14) on which he called upon Dr. Pemberton. On none of these days, except possibly February 25, was he too ill for reading and study. Two of his attacks (February 26 and March 25) were spasms, presumably like those witnessed by the Newtons in 1813 and the Hunts in late 1816 or early 1817. The only period of successive illness was for several days in February during a time of great nervous strain following the birth of Mary's baby. Physically, at least, Shelley would seem not to have been so ill as Mary Shelley's note to *Alastor* has led biographers to believe. Very probably, as Mary wrote later, "His nerves, which nature had formed sensitive to an unexampled degree, were rendered still more susceptible by the state of his health "; [125] but the more important influence was the reverse, that of nerves upon health. The imaginary " consumption " vanished in a sudden improvement of general health shortly after the various nervous strains were removed on May 13.

Neither health nor nerves were allowed seriously to interfere with the important business of reading and study. For Claire and Mary, as well as for Shelley, this was both a duty and a recreation. Shelley regarded them as of the elect, who were to be fitted by reading and study for a war against tyranny and injustice. This was why he objected to Claire's return to her mother, " a vulgar, commonplace woman, without an idea of philosophy . . . not . . . a proper person to form the mind of a young girl." [126] Having failed in his attempts to " form the mind " of Harriet, he was now presented with another opportunity.

He continued setting Claire lessons in French, Latin, Italian, Greek, and history, and discouraged her study of music.[127] On September 18 Mary began Greek under Shelley's tutelage (as Harriet had formerly begun Latin), and kept at it steadily, no doubt encouraged by the little scraps of Greek that Shelley made it a point to insert in most of the otherwise hurried, impassioned notes that he wrote her while living in concealment. One of these notes concludes: "If you are inclined to work over any Latin, read Cicero's 'Paradoxa,' one particularly concerning Regulus. Adieu, my own beloved, my Mary. Good night." [128]

Mary and Claire were both willing, intelligent pupils whose journals show a great amount of reading and study, but there are slight indications that Shelley thought they were not always sufficiently industrious. One of Mary's letters promises: "I will be a good girl and never vex you any more. I will learn Greek and — but when shall we meet when I may tell you all this . . . ? " [129] After receiving two letters from Shelley, Claire experienced a fit of remorse for having spent "three very idle inactive days." Remembering "what Shelley said in Margaret Street," she registered "new vows," not to be broken, by which Shelley should be agreeably surprised.[130]

Except possibly for the sixteen days when he was a semi-fugitive, hardly a day went by in which Shelley and Mary did not read. Daily records like that of February 6, 1815 may be taken as almost a pattern: "Read Gibbon all morning. Shelley reads Livy. Shelley writes and sends letters. After dinner read Gibbon (finish vol. 2) Hogg comes at nine. Work. He goes at half-past 11. Talk a little, and then go to bed." At the end of 1814 Mary made a list of the books each had read since the journal was started. The list comprises sixty volumes read by Shelley and sixty-two by Mary, and omits three volumes that according to the daily record should have been credited to each. All but three or four of these were read after the second week in September,[131] averaging for Shelley about twenty volumes a month. In the first four months of 1815 Shelley's pace slowed perceptibly, but he nevertheless read considerably.[132] Twelve hundred pages in seventeen days Shelley characterized (February 13) as "desultory," even though a large part of it consisted of Latin and Greek in the original. Almost all the rest of the books read had a direct application to Shelley's interest in poetry and revolutionary reform.

THE " new journal " which had been begun to celebrate the Shelleys' " regeneration " unfortunately is lost from May 13, 1815 to July 21, 1816. In the scarcity of other materials, very little is known of the events of Shelley's life until he settled at Bishopsgate, probably on August 3, 1815.[133] In June Shelley and Mary were touring the southern coast of Devonshire, intending soon to lease a house and settle down. From Torquay Shelley wrote to his Tanyrallt friend, John Williams, to ask about houses for rent or purchase in Merionethshire.[134] After a visit to Clifton, Shelley returned to London to continue looking for a house, and Mary remained for a while at Clifton. By July 27 she was impatient at the delay and separation:

> We ought not to be absent any longer; indeed, we ought not. I am not happy at it. When I retire to my room, no sweet love; after dinner, no Shelley; though I have heaps of things *very particular* to say; in fine, either you must come back, or I must come to you directly.

House-hunting, she urged, was much too long and uncertain a task to be undertaken separately. She also feared that perhaps Claire was with Shelley:

> Pray, is Clara with you? for I have inquired several times, and no letters; but, seriously, it would not in the least surprise me, if you have written to her from London and let her know that you are without me, that she should have taken some such freak.

She was determined to be with Shelley on August 4, his birthday, either in Clifton or in London; and she was grieved that they were not to be together on the anniversary of their elopement:

> Tomorrow is the 28th of July. Dearest, ought we not to have been together on that day? Indeed we ought, my love, as I shall shed

some tears to think we are not. Do not be angry, dear love; your Pecksie is a good girl, and is quite well again, except a headache, when she waits so anxiously for her love's letters.[135]

This is the last we hear of either Shelley or Mary until they were settled at Bishopsgate, early in August 1815.

Between March and September, including the months when Shelley's actions and movements are least known, a mysterious monthly magazine called the *Theological Inquirer, or Polemical Magazine,* flourished briefly in London. It appeared and disappeared without attracting the least public notice. At a time when Shelley was still entirely unknown to the British press this magazine commented upon or reprinted works of Shelley in each of the first five numbers, twice in every number except June. No other subject seemed to interest the *Theological Inquirer* nearly so much, yet not once did it mention Shelley by name. Remembering Shelley's notion of founding a periodical in Ireland and his part later in founding the *Liberal* in Italy, it is difficult to resist the suspicion that he had a considerably more important connection with this periodical than surviving evidence substantiates.

The magazine was a rather able vehicle of philosophic radicalism, conducted by Erasmus Perkins, A.B., of Clarendon Square, Somerstown, a mysterious person whose name seems to have been omitted from all the London directories and all the English lists of college and university graduates. In the prospectus for *Collectanea Sceptica,* a book he designed publishing at this time, he described himself as "author of Essays on Religious Persecution, A Dissertation on the Moral Sense, and lecturer on Biblical Criticism, Metaphysics, Ethics, etc." Eight letters "On Religious Persecution" signed Erasmus Perkins appeared in Cobbett's *Political Register* in 1814 and 1815, the last on April 8, 1815; and a note in the July issue of the *Theological Inquirer* mentions two articles received from the *Political Register* — otherwise Erasmus Perkins seems to be only a name, and perhaps a dubious one.

The first number (March) of the *Theological Inquirer* republished anonymously, without comment, the first part of Shelley's *Refutation of Deism*, which was concluded in the April number. Errors in Shelley's previous printing of the essay were so completely corrected that it is hard not to suppose the editor had been furnished with a copy corrected by Shelley himself.[136] In the March issue also appeared the first instalment of a long exposition of *Queen Mab*, signed F., which was continued in April and May and concluded in July. The mysterious F. professed not to know the poet and claimed to have been introduced to the poem on the Continent in 1814 by the dramatist Kotzebue, after which he bought *six* copies in Berlin. This rather unconvincing account may or may not be related to the fact that Shelley and Mary both read in 1815 "Kotzebue's account of His Banishment to Siberia." In his exposition F. managed to quote, with generous praise, about a third of the entire poem, omitting the more dangerous passages. He described *Queen Mab* as a paradise for poetry-lovers, and the author as a genius and a philosopher of the first rank. The same F., who contributed a number of poems to the magazine, also contributed to the July number an "Ode to the Author of 'Queen Mab,'" the first poem ever published about Shelley. All this anonymous Shelleyana appearing in the *Theological Inquirer* attracted no attention from other periodicals, but stimulated several letters from readers of the *Inquirer*. One, under the obvious pseudonym Eunomus Wilson, contributed and commented upon a *Queen Mab* passage not mentioned by F. Another, Mary Anne, wrote several letters taking issue with the *Refutation of Deism*, pointing out truly in the beginning that its real purpose was to discredit Christianity, and ending in the July number with a letter completely recanting her attack. Both F. and Mary Anne were favourably remarked upon in notes by the editor.

Considering that less than seventy copies of *Queen Mab* were in circulation at this time and that all these had been given away by Shelley himself, one feels certain that Shelley knew and connived with "Erasmus Perkins," "F.," and probably "Mary Anne" and "Eunomus Wilson." If Shelley financed this periodical that was so peculiarly interested in his writings it must have been out of the twelve hundred pounds withheld from Godwin in July 1814, which seems otherwise to have

vanished. Who were " Erasmus Perkins " and " F."? Until more
definite information appears the whole episode remains tan-
talizingly obscure.[137] At least during his apparent inactivity in
the spring of 1815 Shelley had the pleasure of feeling that his
missionary purposes were being carried forward by a well-
written periodical, that *Queen Mab* had been published in part,
and that he had been hailed in a published poem as a bold and
inspired prophet of freedom, at present unknown, but destined
for future greatness:

> O! how thy rich, poetic page
> My growing wonder did engage:
> Methought with Fairy Mab I soared, to trace
> The vast immense of universal space.
> While with the pure unspotted soul
> That from Ianthe's bosom stole,
> I shed the sacred drops of Feeling's birth,
> To view the moral desart of the earth:
> And oft I cursed " th' almighty fiend,"
> Who from his empyrean lean'd
> And poured the venom'd vial of strife
> To damp the hope of human life.
> These truths the voice of nations shall proclaim
> In coming times, and know, and bless thy name: —
> Hail then, immortal bard! hail to thy future fame! [138]

Chapter XIV

PEACE AT BISHOPSGATE

HAPPINESS AND HEALTH; *ALASTOR;* DEVELOPMENT
AS POET AND THINKER; DIFFICULTIES WITH
GODWIN, HARRIET, AND THE COURT OF
CHANCERY; CLAIRE'S LIAISON WITH
BYRON; DEJECTION AND DEPARTURE
FOR SWITZERLAND

THE LOW-ROOFED furnished cottage that Shelley took at Bishopsgate was situated down a short road or lane close to the Rhodo-
dendron Walk, Windsor Park, and was so secluded that "even
the tax-collector didn't know it."[1] In front of the cottage
stretched Bishopsgate Heath; to the west was Chapel Wood and
Virginia Water. Standing on the edge of the more ancient part
of the forest, it was shaded by gnarled and decayed oaks of
great antiquity struggling for supremacy with an energetic
growth of younger trees. A garden, enclosed with a light railing, provided Shelley and Mary with flowers.[2]

Here they could employ their pet names of Pecksie, the
Elfin Knight, and the Maie in more privacy and security than
they had previously enjoyed in the harried months following
their return from the Continent. One moment of light-hearted
playfulness stands undated after the last entry in the journal
broken off on May 13. Mary hastily scribbled on a blank page
a simple domestic recipe concerning aniseed and spermaceti.
Opposite it Shelley wrote a heavily humorous Gothic burlesque
of it: "9 drops of human blood, 7 grains of gun-powder, 1-2 oz.
of putrified brain, 13 mashed grave worms — the Pecksie's doom
salve. The Maie and her Elfin Knight." Mary had recovered

from the ill health and low spirits attending the birth and death
of her first child and was looking forward to the birth of another
child in January or February.

At the end of two weeks in her new home at Lynmouth Claire
had written to Fanny Imlay a letter full of enthusiasm for her
new life and surroundings. " After so much discontent, such
violent scenes, such a turmoil of passion and hatred, you will
hardly believe how enraptured I am with this dear quiet spot
. . . I am never disappointed, for I know the extent of my
pleasures; and let it rain or let it be fair weather, it does not
disturb my serene mood. This is happiness, this is that serene
and uninterrupted rest I had long wished for. It is in solitude
that the powers concentre round the soul, and teach it the calm,
determined path of virtue and wisdom." [3] Surely this indicates
both that the domestic scenes in Shelley's flitting *ménage à
trois* had been more violent than Mary's journal reveals, and
also that the changeable, impulsive Claire could become for
a while the echo of the philosophy Shelley preached to her. No
one knew how soon and how disastrously this calm philosophy
was to be shattered, but it is likely that neither Shelley nor Mary
expected it to last long.

Political events and the manifold ills of this world no longer
excited Shelley to a feverish determination to rectify matters
single-handed and at once. Napoleon's escape from Elba in
March, his quick mastery of France, the battle of Waterloo,
his banishment to St. Helena, and the reactionary plans of
the Allies moved Shelley much less deeply than one would
expect. The only echo of these events in the journal is a bare
mention, on March 23, of Napoleon's entry into Paris. Shelley
had concluded that the time for action was not yet, and could
only be prepared for, rather than precipitated, by writing. [4] It
was not always easy to feel so. In late August he wrote to Hogg,
apropos of " enormities " committed by the Allied troops in
France: " In considering the political events of the day, I endeavour to divest my mind of temporary sensations, to consider
them as already historical. This is difficult. Spite of ourselves
the human beings who surround us infect us with their opinions;
so much as to forbid us to be dispassionate observers of the

questions arising out of the events of the age." [5] Napoleon's downfall interested him to the extent of evoking a sonnet, " Feelings of a Republican on the Fall of Bonaparte," regretting the event only as the victory of a worse tyranny even than Napoleon's.

Hogg was in the north on his annual vacation, but Peacock was near by, at Marlow, and was a frequent caller. Charles Clairmont, who had given up his idea of going to Australia at Shelley's expense, was again on hand with another scheme for which he needed financial assistance. Though Charles was a financial leech, his letters indicate that he was by no means stupid company. In Peacock, who was professedly given up to idleness during the summer, Charles found a delightful companion, in spite of disparaging remarks from Shelley. Together — joined sometimes no doubt by Shelley and Mary — they took daily walks to such neighbouring historic spots as Virginia Water, Cooper's Hill, Windsor Castle, Old Windsor, and Runnymede. Charles was waiting until Shelley could find money to pay his expenses to Ireland to investigate a business opportunity at Enniscorthy.[6] Claire, who was already restless at Lynmouth, was to accompany him. That the money was eventually found is shown by Shelley's order to his bankers, dated October 9, 1815, to send ten pounds to " Miss Clairmont, Post Office, Enniscorthy, Wexford, Ireland." [7]

BUT while the money for Charles was still to be sought the whole party — Shelley, Mary, Charles, and Peacock — embarked about the end of August upon a ten-day boat excursion up the Thames.[8] Since his first acquaintance with boating on the Thames at Eton, Shelley had descended the Rhine in a boat, for a considerable part of its length. He now wished to ascend from Old Windsor to the source of the Thames. Between flat green banks, past many little villages and the large town of Reading, they followed the river's leisurely windings to Oxford, where they remained from seven in the evening till four the next day. Here, while Oxford was on vacation, Shelley showed his companions the Bodleian Library, the Clarendon Press, various college quadrangles, and "the very rooms where the two noted infidels, Shelley and Hogg . . . pored . . . over the . . . boundaries of human knowledge."[9] Here Shelley felt ill, consulted a doctor, and even thought of abandoning the trip. Peacock, who had an idea that the trouble was caused by Shelley's diet of bread and butter, tea, and occasionally lemonade made with a powder, offered a rival prescription: "Three mutton chops, well peppered."[10] Shelley took Peacock's prescription and lived by it for the rest of the journey. Success was obvious and immediate. He "rowed vigorously, was cheerful, merry, overflowing with animal spirits, and had certainly one week of thorough enjoyment of life."[11]

In a day or two they had reached Lechlade, about fourteen miles from the source of the Thames. They had already decided to pass from the Thames to the Severn by a canal that joined the Thames at Lechlade. Shelley's enthusiasm was now so high that he proposed a complicated journey by connecting canals and rivers. They must cross North Wales and several inland counties to Durham and the Lakes, thence to the Tweed and the Forth, and eventually, after two thousand miles of rowing, reach the Falls of Clyde. The very first canal, however, proved insuperable, since the party could not afford a fee of twenty pounds that was demanded. They resumed their original intention of pushing to the source of the Thames, but were halted three miles above Lechlade by shallow water and by water-weeds too thick and high to be overcome. So, turning back to Lechlade, they started next morning on the homeward voyage. In four days they were back at Windsor. All of his fellow travellers commented on the remarkable improvement in Shelley's health and spirits. "He has now the ruddy healthy complexion of autumn upon his countenance," Charles Clairmont wrote after their return, "and is twice as fat as he used to be."[12]

An unmistakable mark of Shelley's growing power is seen in the poem written on one of the two days spent in the inn at Lechlade. The opening descriptive stanzas of "A Summer-

Evening Churchyard, Lechlade, Gloucestershire," show a latent
metrical subtlety not yet fully mastered. With certain slight
touches of influence from eighteenth-century churchyard verse,
they are nevertheless entirely free from any significant influences of the sort, even though Shelley, like every other poet,
knew Gray's "Elegy" and had often walked in the churchyard
at Stoke Poges. The elegiac note of the concluding stanzas is
the characteristically Shelleyan one that occurs with increased
power many times in his later poetry.

> The dead are sleeping in their sepulchres:
> And, mouldering as they sleep, a thrilling sound,
> Half sense, half thought, among the darkness stirs,
> Breathed from their wormy beds all living things around,
> And mingling with the still night and mute sky
> Its awful hush is felt inaudibly.

> Thus solemnized and softened, death is mild
> And terrorless as this serenest night:
> Here could I hope, like some enquiring child
> Sporting on graves, that death did hide from human sight
> Sweet secrets, or beside its breathless sleep
> That loveliest dreams perpetual watch did keep.

A week after his return to Bishopsgate, Shelley wrote to Hogg
in a very cheerful tone: "The exercise and dissipation attached
to such an expedition have produced so favourable an effect
on my health that my habitual dejection and irritability have
almost deserted me, and I can devote six hours in the day to
study without difficulty. I have been engaged lately in the
commencement of several literary plans which, if my present
temper of mind endures, I shall probably complete in the winter." [13]

Charles Clairmont returned from Ireland with a somewhat
surprising project for which he requested Shelley's financial
support. He proposed that Shelley lend him money to become
owner or part owner of the distillery business he had gone to
Enniscorthy to investigate. Despite the fact that Shelley had
taken his occasional glass of negus as an undergraduate at

Oxford, it is a little surprising to find that he apparently had no strong objections to the nature of Charles's project. Charles showed numerous letters, estimates, and documents indicating a return of twenty or twenty-five per cent on the investment. Shelley promised the necessary funds at the usual rate of interest, as soon as he could conclude his arrangements with his father. He even went further and offered to procure the funds immediately " on the same terms as he is now settling with his father, which is about £100 for £65." [14]

But Charles felt obliged eventually to make good Shelley's sacrifice, in addition to repaying the amount secured. Since he knew that no business could stand such a strain, he followed Godwin's example and appealed to Francis Place, ostensibly for advice. Knowing that Place despised Shelley and might refuse to countenance the project on that account, Charles embarked upon a really eloquent, if somewhat inaccurate, defence of Shelley's conduct toward Harriet. Place, however, was unimpressed. He replied briefly and dryly that even if the project looked as promising to him as to Charles, he would not invest in it on his own account, much less withdraw his money from present investments to lend to another. " Neither can I consent," he added, " to take the chance of being involved in any transaction between you and Shelley." [15] Whether from his own scruples at accepting Shelley's sacrifice or from Shelley's inability or unwillingness to secure the money, Charles was lost to the distilling business.

Ironically enough, it may have been Harriet, whose character he had handled so unmercifully in his letter to Place, who blasted Charles's business opportunity. Since April, apparently, there had been no contact between Shelley and Harriet. About November, however, Harriet demanded an additional allowance for the support of the two children. This Shelley refused. He offered to take Ianthe into his own home and urged a deed of separation. Harriet, on the advice of friends, would consent to neither, whereupon Shelley threatened to withdraw Harriet's present allowance of two hundred pounds. Harriet's father and her attorney, Mr. Desse, then called upon Mr. William Whitton to see if Sir Timothy would provide for one of the children on condition that Mr. Westbrook provide for the other. If not, they proposed to bring proceedings against Shelley in the Ecclesiastical Court for alimony and in the Court of Chancery for separate maintenance for the children, alleging Shelley's religious opinions as grounds for refusing to yield him custody of the children. The probability that the highly dangerous *Queen Mab* would be offered in evidence of his religious opinions may have influenced Shelley to drop his threat; but Sir Timothy was unmoved by the threat to his own peace of mind involved in such proceedings. He accepted Whitton's advice [16] and declined to take any further action, and the Westbrooks appear to have accepted the *status quo*.

SHELLEY was now relatively free from the bailiffs, money-lenders, and physical and nervous weakness that had inhibited his writing for almost a year. As soon as he found a house at Bishopsgate, he settled himself with his usual determination to writing and study. Of his ten extant letters between August and January, only two have any connection with money-lenders, while the two to Hogg reflect his new energy, and four to book-dealers [17] concern such orders for books as he had been unable to resume since his elopement with Mary. One of the literary projects he referred to in writing to Hogg after the Thames boating expedition was undoubtedly the volume of verse published as *Alastor, or the Spirit of Solitude; and Other Poems.* The autumn months were warm and dry; the cool oak shades of Windsor Great Forest and the grassy borders of the Thames offered ideal seclusion for the study and thought that was going into *Alastor*. The new poem was one that could hardly have been credited to the author of such a vigorous, objective call to arms as *Queen Mab*. Physical sufferings, ill health, and the loss of friends had, as Mrs. Shelley wrote, " brought home to him the sad realities of life . . . inclining him rather to brood over the thoughts and emotions of his own soul than to glance abroad." [18] He still indulged his earlier hopes of human regeneration, but he had realized more keenly the difficulty of their fulfilment.

The theme of *Alastor,* according to Shelley's Preface, is that concentration upon high and lofty ideals may bring with it an avenging fury,[19] which makes the actual world seem dark and dead to those who have pursued perfection too far. Even an idealist cannot subsist without human sympathy. Such a ruin, however, is glorious, Shelley hastens to add, compared with the slow and poisonous decay of those selfish beings who are " deluded by no generous error, instigated by no sacred thirst of doubtful knowledge." Unfortunately, Shelley's criticism of himself — for the over-idealistic poet as described in both the Preface and the poem is undoubtedly Shelley [20] — goes too much against the grain to be perfectly clear and consistent. The young poet's progress to an untimely death is presented with such sympathy that no one who had not read the Preface would suppose that the author intended the poem as a criticism of him. In fact, it is hard to see how Shelley regarded his young poet's death as untimely, since (lines 305, 365) it seems to have been deliberately sought. Shelley had only recently read the works of Kirke White, whose untimely death, like that of Chatterton, may have made him feel that a pathetic death was the proper end for an unappreciated young poet.

Like Shelley, the young poet of *Alastor* was nurtured " By solemn vision and bright silver dream," sought " The fountains of divine philosophy," and left an " alienated home " as a mere youth to pursue knowledge to its utmost bounds. Like Shelley, too, he was a vegetarian. His wanderings in his search were more those of Shelley's reading than of Shelley's actual footsteps, but the beauty of the scenery derives from Shelley's own impressions of the Alps, the Rhine, the Thames, and Windsor Forest. Like Volney, a favourite author with Shelley, the young poet visited the ruins of ancient empire, and like Shelley's friend Newton he was enthralled by " the Zodiac's brazen mystery " in ancient temples. His ruin started when in a dream he beheld a vision of a veiled maid whose " voice was like the voice of his own soul." In his sleep he sought to clasp this vision and succeeded. More and more wasted by his own intensity, he pursued it beyond the bounds of sleep, until after many wanderings that are not always easy to follow he expired in a green recess by a lonely mountain stream. Shelley himself continued to seek a human prototype of ideal beauty until in the last year of his life he repeated as the result of his own experience a conclusion quite similar to the one he wished his readers to draw from *Alastor.* "The error," he wrote to John Gisborne, "consists in seeking in a mortal image the likeness of what is perhaps eternal." [21]

Mrs. Shelley suggested [22] that Shelley's recent expectation of death partly accounts for the tone of the poem. But Shelley had been freed from this fear and was enjoying excellent health when he wrote *Alastor.* His preoccupation with death, both in *Alastor* and in many later poems, is so noticeable as to have suggested a belief that his whole art was really dominated by it.[23] Such a strain seems more likely to have been based upon something more convincing than an expectation that had already passed. Its sources can be sought more securely in a blend of Gothic romance, metaphysical speculation, and "graveyard" poetry, originating in Shelley's youth. He had at least planned,[24] as he claimed in *Alastor,* to make his bed

> In charnels and on coffins, where black death
> Keeps record . . . .

The blank verse of *Alastor* is quite different from and greatly superior to that of *Queen Mab.* One seeks to account for the difference by consulting the written record of Shelley's reading and learns that between the dates of the two poems Shelley read much Shakespeare, Spenser, Milton, and Wordsworth, and one finds a few definite echoes, especially of the two later poets, in *Alastor.*[25] Echoes, however, do not make good blank verse. Even study and constant practice from good models do not necessarily produce more than a correct mosaic style that has no distinctive character of its own — nor is there any proof of constant practice in Shelley's case.[26] Yet in little more than two years he progressed from an undistinguished matter-of-fact blank verse to an imaginative, subtly modulated style that is practically on a par with his high models without being in the slightest sense subservient to them. The hero of the poem might be a little pathetic and the detail a trifle confusing, but the solid intellectual background, the descriptive power, and the

mature technique told anyone who cared to listen that here was
a poet who could do other things equally well. At twenty-three
Shelley was entitled to rank with the really important poets of
his age.

Shelley had put too much of himself into *Queen Mab*, however, to abandon it utterly. While he worked on *Alastor* he
was also working on a recension of *Queen Mab* that could be
published with it. Other passages than the highly dangerous
ones that constituted the real heart of the poem had been praised
in the *Theological Inquirer*. The copy of the original edition
from which he worked has been preserved and indicates a great
deal of studied revision.[27] The result, renamed " The Dæmon of
the World. A Fragment," was hardly a happy one; the most impassioned passages were omitted, and the effort to improve a
metre he had already cast aside could hardly be regarded as
more than good practice. The emasculation of such a spirited
outburst must have subjected Shelley to some of the same
qualms he imagined Wordsworth now felt. Nor did it profit
anything. Just enough of the indignant reformer remained in
the turn of a few phrases to cause two reviewers to suspect that
here was a young poet not to be criticized without a healthy
orthodox suspicion. Such ideas may have been fostered by Shelley's avowal of republicanism in the sonnet on Napoleon, and
the sonnet rebuking Wordsworth for deserting his high principles, both published in the *Alastor* volume.

By January 16, 1816 *Alastor* had been printed in sheets by
S. Hamilton, a printer of Weybridge, and Shelley was in search
of a publisher. On that date he sent the sheets to John Murray,
Byron's publisher, who apparently declined to publish them. On
the advice of Carpenter and Son, Old Bond Street, who had
agreed to be co-publishers, the poem was offered to Baldwin,
Craddock, and Joy, Paternoster Row, whose name precedes that
of Carpenter and Son on the title page. Shelley expected publication about the middle of February.[28] From Field Place Sir
Timothy Shelley wrote to Whitton on February 27: " P. B. has
published a poem with some fragments, somewhat in his usual
style, not altogether free from former sentiments, and wants to
find out one person on earth the Prototype of himself." [29]

To Southey, with a copy of *Alastor,* went a graceful little note expressing gratitude for Southey's friendship while Shelley was at Keswick. Shelley made no mention of Harriet or Mary, and offered as excuse for his failure to write from Ireland "the disappointment of some youthful hopes, and subsequent misfortunes of a heavier nature" that were really subsequent to his return from Ireland. "The true weight of this apology," he concluded, "you cannot know. Let it be sufficient that, regarding you with admiration as a poet, and with respect as a man, I send you, as an intimation of those sentiments, my first serious attempt to interest the best feelings of the human heart, believing that you have so much general charity as to forget, like me, how widely in moral and political opinions we disagree, and to attribute that difference to better motives than the multitude are disposed to allege as the cause of dissent from their institutions." [30]

The reviews of *Alastor* were far from encouraging.[31] All three of the reviewers who deigned to notice the volume in 1816 agreed in vigorous condemnation of its obscurity. The *Monthly Review* scornfully professed inability to obtain a clue to Shelley's "sublime obscurity" — "till an address to Mr. Wordsworth explained in what school the author had formed his taste." Shelley was advised in his next publication to benefit his readers ("if he has any") by "an *ordo,* a glossary, and copious notes . . . explanatory of his meaning." The *British Critic,* acknowledging considerable experience with "profound and prosing stupidity," professed itself "not a little delighted with the nonsense [of *Alastor*] which mounts, which rises, which spurns the earth and all its dull realities." After a merrily sarcastic illustration of some of the offending passages, the review concludes: "A man's hair singing dirges, and a boat pausing and shuddering, are among the least of his inventions; nature for him reverses all her laws, the streams ascend." The *Eclectic Review* was a little more just and dignified. It quoted a passage to show Shelley's "very considerable talent for descriptive poetry," and gave Shelley's own explanation of the poem's meaning, but found the explanation inadequate. "All is wild and specious, untangible and incoherent as a dream. We should be utterly at a loss to convey any distinct idea of the plan or purpose of the poem." It comments suspiciously " that every indication of the Author's belief in a future state of existence, and in the moral government of God, is carefully avoided " except one profane reference to a God " ' profuse of poisons.' " So well justified were these suspicions by Shelley's later career that the *Eclectic* never reviewed another work of Shelley's during his lifetime.

If Shelley had hoped that his new moderation would procure a fair critical reception for *Alastor,* he was deceived. One out of three critics still caught a faint whiff of brimstone. It is not necessary to suppose that the critic knew something of Shelley's private history or even that the volume would have been favourably received had it been pious and conservative. In spite of new subjects and trends in poetic technique introduced by Cowper, Burns, Blake, and Wordsworth, there was not in England in 1815 a single review that did not respect the views expressed in Dr. Johnson's *Rasselas* on the dangers of imagination far more than Wordsworth's still-derided Preface to *Lyrical Ballads. Alastor* was in fact, and without prejudice, contrary to the prevailing idea of poetic excellence.

ONE of the literary designs Shelley mentioned to Hogg was undoubtedly a series of moral and metaphysical essays, perhaps a continuation of the design he first formed at Keswick.[32] These essays are important landmarks in the growth of his beliefs and capacities. In one of these fragments, " On Love," occurs Shelley's first definition of love as complete human sympathy merging into universal sympathy — a significant idea underlying much of his later poetry:

It is that powerful attraction towards all that we conceive, or fear, or hope beyond ourselves, when we find within our own thoughts the chasm of an insufficient void, and seek to awaken in all things that are, a community with what we experience within ourselves. If we reason, we would be understood; if we imagine, we would that the airy children of our brain were born anew within another's; if we feel, we would that another's nerves should vibrate to our own, that the beams of their eyes should kindle at once and mix and melt into our own, that lips of motionless ice should not reply to lips quivering and burning with the heart's best blood. This is Love. This is the bond and the sanction which connects not only man with man, but with every thing which exists. We are born into the world, and there is something within us which, from the instant that we live, more and more thirsts after its likeness.[33]

Within two or three years Shelley came to perceive that this was an ideal practically unattainable for most mortals. For himself, not until shortly before his death did he confess that " the error . . . consists in seeking in a mortal image the likeness of what is perhaps eternal." Yet the paragraph preceding this idealistic definition of Love contains an unconsciously realistic suggestion of its difficulty: " I know not the internal constitution of other men, nor even thine, whom I now address. I see that in some external attributes they resemble me, but when, misled by that appearance, I have thought to appeal to something in common, and unburthen my inmost soul to them, I have found my language misunderstood, like one in a distant and savage land."

The prose fragment, " On Life," if indeed it was written in 1815, shows that by this time Shelley had abandoned Locke for Berkeley, whom he had rejected in 1812.[34] " I confess that I am one of those who am unable to refuse my assent to the conclusions of those philosophers who assert that nothing exists but as it is perceived." [35] In one passage on dreams,[36] a subject on which Shelley had been making notes as early as 1811, he comments on the strong emotional effect sometimes produced by seeing in dreams sights that when previously seen in waking hours produced no such effect. Starting to give an instance from his own experience, he was so " overcome by thrilling horror " that he was forced to break off writing.[37]

If at the age of twenty-three Shelley possessed to an almost excessive degree the nervous and physical sensitiveness usually found in great poets, he had also attained the intellectual depth and subtlety and the just estimate of imagination and human sympathies that are also necessary. Man, he asserted, was not merely a moral and intellectual being, " but also, and pre-eminently, an imaginative being." [38] He believed that words often obscure rather than elucidate the real significance of life, because they are instruments of logic that are ill-adapted to in-

tuitive perceptions and are encrusted with all the trite associations of long and hackneyed use.[39] Hence the delusion of seeking through words alone to arrive at the cause of life, for
" cause " itself is only a word, expressing only " a certain state
of the human mind with regard to the manner in which two
thoughts are apprehended to be related to each other," whereas
the " cause " of life or mind may be entirely dissimilar to the
mind.[40] The human mind, in fact, like the infinite variety of
life itself, is much too intricate for exploration through the
medium of words. " But thought can with difficulty visit the
intricate and winding chambers which it inhabits. It is like a
river whose rapid and perpetual stream flows outwards; like
one in dread who speeds through the recesses of some haunted
pile, and dares not look behind. The caverns of the mind are
obscure, and shadowy; or pervaded with a lustre, beautifully
bright indeed, but shining not beyond their portals." [41]

Here we have, if not the source of Shelley's significant use
of images in his poetry, at least their intellectual justification.
Words in their logical meaning being by nature often inadequate to the uses of great poetry, images and symbols may sometimes be employed to speak more directly to the imagination
and intuition. The passage itself is built of images all of which
occur in *Alastor*. Clouds, caves, and serpents, probably, had
already acquired some symbolic significance to Shelley; but
after 1815 we find an increasing use of clouds, serpents, eagles,
boats, streams, veils, caverns, in an attempt to make poetry express more justly the extreme subtlety of the matter with which
it must deal in order to widen the scope of human understanding.

At the same time Shelley was laying a philosophical foundation for the optimistic view of human nature that is so characteristic of his poetry. In the fragmentary " Speculations on
Morals " he admits that there are human impulses to inflict
pain, seize power, and exhibit revenge, pride, and selfishness
— impulses that cannot be abolished by the anticipation of reward or punishment in a future existence. But the behaviour
of children, he argues, demonstrates that there is also a powerful, fundamental benevolence in human nature. A very young

child is sensitive to its own pain but insensitive to its mother's pain. This is because it has not yet learned to associate pain with its signs and indications; but as soon as this lesson is learned, it is distressed by the signs of pain in those most dear to it. We are selfish in direct ratio to our limitations of experience and knowledge. "Thus an infant, a savage, and a solitary beast, is selfish, because its mind is incapable [of] receiving an accurate intimation of the nature of pain as existing in beings resembling itself. The inhabitant of a highly civilized community will more acutely sympathize with the sufferings and enjoyments of others, than the inhabitant of a society of a less degree of civilization. He who shall have cultivated his intellectual powers by familiarity with the finest specimens of poetry and philosophy will usually [sympathize more] than one engaged in the less refined functions of manual labour. . . . The only distinction between the selfish man, and the virtuous man, is that the imagination of the former is confined within a narrow limit, whilst that of the latter embraces a comprehensive circumference." [42] In this passage Shelley anticipates his profound defence of poetry as the language of the one power — Imagination — by which men's natures are ennobled. Chivalry, he continues, was founded on a theory of self-sacrifice, love possesses its extraordinary power only because of its element of disinterestedness. The love of fame, sometimes justly condemned as selfish, is not always so; it is frequently no more than a high desire that the feelings of others should sympathize with our own, and thus operates to draw us out of, rather than into, ourselves.

MARY's second child was born on January 24, a healthy, amiable infant with smooth rosy cheeks and auburn hair.[43] On January 25 Shelley concluded one of his patient, impersonal business letters to Mary's estranged father: "Fanny and Mrs. Godwin will probably be glad to hear that Mary has safely recovered from a very favourable confinement, and that her child is well." [44] Godwin's continued refusal to see either Shelley or Mary did not prevent their naming the child William.

As long as the parents remained in England William throve and was a source of joy to them.

The winter of 1815–16 passed agreeably and quietly. Hogg had returned from his northern vacation and was a frequent visitor. He might be on the wrong side of a moral or meta-physical argument, but he told amusing stories, and he knew and loved learning. Despite certain Toryish trends since leaving Oxford, he still hated tyranny and priestcraft.[45] Peacock, like Hogg a lover of the classics, was constantly dropping in from Marlow. The winter, as Hogg said, was a mere Atticism.[46] Of course there were arguments and high discussions, during which Peacock stored up a few points for the character of Scythrop, in which he was to make mild fun of Shelley the next year.[47] These arguments were always amiable, however; even when Peacock argued against his " delusions," Shelley maintained his position with a sweet, inflexible courtesy.

When the weather permitted, Shelley spent considerable time on the water or among the oaks of Windsor Great Park. There were many country rambles. Bracknell, where some of Shelley's friends of 1813 still resided, was not far away. On the heath just above Bracknell was a pool of clear water, with firm, clean banks, that was the best place Shelley ever found for launching paper boats. Shelley could seldom pass a pool of water without launching a flotilla. If no other paper was handy, he made his boats from whatever letters happened to be in his pockets at the time. Peacock, who had known the sport before Shelley, en-couraged him. Hogg, on the other hand, cordially abominated the practice, particularly if it interrupted a brisk walk on a cold winter day. Other visitors than Hogg or Peacock were dis-couraged. There was one exception, a Quaker doctor named Pope, who came over occasionally from Staines to discuss theol-ogy with Shelley. Despite Shelley's reluctance on account of differences in point of view, Dr. Pope urged the poet to express himself, for, as he said, " I see thee art very deep." [48]

Peacock tells an amusing incident of Shelley's efforts to avoid a boresome caller: " Amongst the persons who called on him at Bishopsgate, was one whom he tried hard to get rid of, but who forced himself on him in every possible manner. He saw

427

him at a distance one day, as he was walking down Egham Hill, and instantly jumped through a hedge, ran across a field, and laid himself down in a dry ditch. Some men and women who were haymaking in the field, ran up to see what was the matter, when he said to them, 'Go away, go away; don't you see it's a bailiff?' On which they left him, and he escaped discovery." [49]

The legal difficulties in completing his financial agreement with his father seemed no nearer solution than ever. This need not have disturbed Shelley on his own account. Sir Timothy had cleared off the post-obits and paid most of Shelley's bills, and was regularly paying the annuity of £1,000. If it should be finally decided that the agreement between Shelley and his father was void, Shelley would then be the next heir to the estates he was trying to resign, and could immediately raise on his expectations all the money he was likely to require. The difficulty was not Shelley's needs, but Godwin's. These Shelley could not meet out of his annuity, nor could he raise money on post-obits until the courts had passed on his agreement with his father. He had given Godwin £1,000 at the time of his first settlement with Sir Timothy in April. There was to have been a final settlement with Sir Timothy in November, after which Godwin would receive another sum, probably £1,200.[50] This was prevented by the legal complications that had arisen.

When Mr. Hogan, the most urgent of Godwin's creditors, had brought suit in October 1815, or earlier, Shelley tried unsuccessfully to satisfy him by offering security for Godwin.[51] Thereafter the matter seems to have lapsed until January, when Godwin again became desperate. He could not see why Shelley's present position made it impossible to raise the money he needed. Shelley replied in a series of patient explanations showing a remarkable lucidity and comprehension of legal and financial complications.[52] No one who has examined the complex legal documents could maintain after reading Shelley's letters that he was incapable of understanding practical affairs; when he failed in practical matters it was only through sheer insufficiency of interest. Godwin, despite his business fiascoes, had a keen analytical mind and considerable first-hand knowledge of legal and financial technicalities, but in this affair Shelley showed a grasp of reality almost ridiculously superior to Godwin's.

Godwin needed between £200 and £300 to satisfy Hogan, his most pressing creditor, and about £1,000 more to satisfy other obligations not so immediately urgent. Francis Place had already forsworn helping Godwin further, having decided that he was perfectly selfish, unreliable, and unscrupulous in money matters.[53] Godwin's persistent misunderstanding of both Shelley's letters and the reports of his two go-betweens, Charles Clairmont and Mr. Turner,[54] may have been due as much to an unscrupulous desire of wearing Shelley down as to lack of comprehension. But Shelley still refused to jeopardize his whole prospects by entering into further post-obits. He did allow Godwin to enter into negotiations with money-lenders on his credit. Godwin obtained at Warnham a copy of the registry of Shelley's birth in order to facilitate these negotiations, a fact which came to Sir Timothy's notice and further increased Shelley's risk.[55] Shelley offered various expedients: he would sign a bond of security either alone or with Godwin; he would sell an annuity; he would even enter into negotiations with a Dr. Bethune who wished to buy all or part of Shelley's interest in one of the properties involved in Shelley's suspended dealings with Sir Timothy. But Sir Timothy must be kept in ignorance of everything, and Godwin's prospective lenders were too cautious and suspicious to proceed without securing papers from Whitton and Longdill, thus informing Sir Timothy of the proceedings. Late in February Shelley signed a deed of some sort that was to satisfy Hogan. He also tried desperately to raise a loan of £500 from Dr. Bethune[56] on his expectations, probably to satisfy Josiah Wedgwood, who was pressing Godwin for £500 due him.[57]

Godwin's creditors other than Hogan, however, were doomed to wait still longer. In the friendly suit to decide timber rights on the property in which Dr. Bethune was interested the Court of Chancery ruled that the timber must be cut and sold and the money paid into court to abide future equities in the matter, and that neither Shelley nor his father could touch the estates in question. This put an end to Shelley's hopes of obtaining money

429

from Dr. Bethune and also wrecked his previous agreement with Sir Timothy. Sir Timothy thereupon agreed to continue Shelley's present allowance and to advance him, in six weeks or two months, on post-obit, money sufficient to meet engagements contracted during the legal negotiations. Out of this he could spare £300 for Godwin, and he hoped to obtain £300 more for him through a negotiation that Hayward, Godwin's attorney, had in hand. This, too, was a post-obit transaction, which Shelley evidently considered sufficiently safe, now that the court had given judgment and he had concluded arrangements with his father.[58]

The long explanations with Godwin would have taxed the patience of anyone not subject, as Shelley was, to occasional fits of irritation and temper. Yet Shelley was uniformly courteous and considerate in everything that respected carrying out his obligation. He informed Godwin that his attitude toward his financial obligation would be in no sense affected by Godwin's treatment of him and Mary.[59] The good opinion of no one in the world was so valuable to Shelley as Godwin's. He had been cut to the quick by Godwin's repudiation of him. This he was forced to bear, but to bear Godwin's haughty tone of moral superiority and his talk of forgiveness was beyond even Shelleyan patience. "Perhaps," he warned Godwin early in the correspondence, "it is well that you should be informed that I consider your last letter to be written in a certain style of haughtiness and encroachment which neither awes nor imposes on me."[60] At one time it looked as if a personal interview might be necessary to explain the financial and legal complications. Shelley made it plain that if necessary he would consent even to this, though it would inflict the deepest dejection and pain thus to meet a man "who having been once my friend, would receive me with cold and haughty words."[61] Eventually he did make three apparently unsuccessful attempts to see Godwin.[62] It was excruciatingly bitter and depressing to realize that where his character should be best known it should be so thoroughly depreciated and scorned.[63] These feelings sometimes made him physically ill. He unsealed one letter to Godwin to add that he had been seized with symptoms of an irritable fever that would render him for a few days incapable of active exertion.[64]

Shelley's bitter disappointment was not due entirely to the mere fact that Godwin repudiated him. He had idealized Godwin, and now, like Francis Place, he was compelled to face the sorry conviction that Godwin had repudiated himself. This perception Shelley's natural delicacy inclined him to suppress, but continued provocation finally forced him to express it. " I lamented also over my ruined hopes, hopes of all that your genius once taught me to expect from your virtue, when I found that for yourself, your family, and your creditors, you would submit to that communication with me which you once rejected and abhorred, and which no pity for my poverty or sufferings, assumed willingly for you, could avail to extort. Do not talk *forgiveness* again to me," he continued with rising indignation, " for my blood boils in my veins, and my gall rises against all that bears the human form, when I think of what I, their benefactor and ardent lover, have endured of enmity and contempt from all mankind." [65]

In other letters Shelley apologized for these outbursts and begged Godwin to burn them. His stubborn idealism would permit him in calmer moments to recognize only those faults in Godwin that it was impossible to ignore. Had he not named his son for Godwin and was he not still, against his own inclinations, consistently following Godwin's early advice to make himself thoroughly acquainted with the early history of nations and institutions before rushing forth to reform them? " I respect you," he confessed with obvious truth, " I think well of you, better perhaps than of any other person whom England contains; you were the philosopher who first awakened, and who still as a philosopher to a very great degree regulate my understanding. It is unfortunate for me that the part of your character which is least excellent should have been met by my convictions of what was right to do. But I have been too indignant, I have been unjust to you. — Forgive me. — Burn those letters which contain the records of my violence, and believe that however what you erroneously call fame and honour separate us,

431

I shall always feel toward you as the most affectionate of friends." [66]

Godwin was not the only cause of Shelley's growing feeling of dejection. When it had seemed necessary to produce his son Charles in the last Chancery action, Harriet had refused to surrender the boy until forced to do so by an order of court.[67] In April the scornful reviews of *Alastor* were beginning to appear. Shelley had seen the anonymous *Queen Mab* warmly and continuously praised in the *Theological Inquirer;* he now saw a superior poem, in which he had gone out of his way to avoid offending popular prejudices, treated with a careless contempt utterly ruinous to the hopes of fame that were probably built on it. Before this, chiefly because of Godwin, Shelley had resolved either to desert England or to retire into some solitary region of the country, " hiding myself and Mary from that contempt which we so unjustly endure." [68] Italy was his ultimate destination, he thought, but he expected to spend a few years first in Cumberland or Scotland. He felt himself to be generally hated.[69] This feeling must have been considerably augmented by the reception of *Alastor*. On May 3, as soon as the settlement with his father made it possible to leave, Shelley was on his way to the Continent. " The motives which determined me to leave England and which I stated to you in a former letter," he wrote Godwin before sailing, " have continued since that period to press on me with accumulated force. Continually detained in a situation where I esteem a prejudice does not permit me to live on equal terms with my fellow-beings I resolved to commit myself to a decided step. I therefore take Mary to Geneva, where I shall devise some plan of settlement and only leave her to return to London and exclusively devote myself to business." [70]

PEACOCK, who may or may not have known the cogent reasons Shelley gave Godwin, assigns another reason for Shelley's departure. According to him, Shelley was restless, and was firmly convinced that his father and his uncle had designs against his liberty.[71] It seemed to Peacock almost a habit with Shelley, when he desired to change his residence, to be warned by some mysterious visitor that the change was instantly necessary in order to avoid dire peril. This time, as Peacock sceptically recorded, Shelley's warning came as follows:

One day as Peacock was setting out for a walk from the Shelley cottage at Bishopsgate he found that the poet had gone off with his hat, leaving his own inadequate small hat instead. Peacock settled himself to wait, and presently Shelley returned. " You know Williams of Tremadoc? . . . It was he who was here to-day. He came to tell me of a plot laid by my father and uncle, to entrap me and lock me up. He was in great haste, and could not stop a minute, and I walked with him to Egham." " What hat did you wear? " asked Peacock. " This, to be sure," said Shelley, indicating Peacock's hat that he had carried out with him. At Peacock's request he put it on again, and it came down over his face. " You could not have walked to Egham in that hat," Peacock announced. Shelley answered that perhaps he had carried the hat rather than worn it, and remonstrated with Peacock on his scepticism. " It is very hard on a man who has devoted his life to the pursuit of truth, who has made great sacrifices and incurred great sufferings for it, to be treated as a visionary."

But Shelley was determined to substantiate his story. He undertook to conduct Peacock to Williams at the Turk's Head Coffee House, in London. Next morning they set out on foot, but they had gone only a short distance when Shelley said he thought Williams had probably left a day early, and suggested that they walk through the forest instead of continuing to London. He would take other means of convincing Peacock. The matter was dropped for several days, after which Shelley reported to Peacock that he had received a letter and an enclosure from Williams. Peacock asked to see the letter. " I cannot show you the letter," Shelley replied, " I will show you the enclosure. It is a diamond necklace. I think you know me well enough to be sure I would not throw away my own money on such a thing, and that if I have it, it must have been sent me by somebody else. It has been sent me by Williams . . . to prove his identity and his sincerity." Peacock observed that

showing a diamond necklace would prove nothing except that
Shelley had such a necklace to show. " Then," said Shelley, " I
will not show it to you. If you will not believe me, I must submit
to your incredulity." [72]

WHEN Shelley and Mary sailed from Dover, Claire Clairmont
was with them, though Shelley did not mention her in his farewell letter to Godwin dated May 3. It was almost certainly on
Claire's account that the party was going to Geneva, which Shelley had not mentioned in connection with his plans, instead of
to Italy.

Claire's movements after she went to Ireland with Charles are
for some time uncertain. Presumably she returned with him,
but not to her old position in Lynmouth, where she had formulated her laudable resolutions a few months earlier. She is mentioned at times as being with the Shelleys, at times with the Godwins; and some of her letters give her address as 21 Noley
Place, Mary le Bonne, and 13 Arabella Row, Pimlico.[73] On
March 12, 18, and 21 Shelley wrote cheques in her favour for
£20, £10, and £11 respectively, which suggests that during
March she was living in London on Shelley's bounty.[74]

Lord Byron was at this time approaching the end of his glittering career as the liberal-minded, attractively cynical and
wicked author-about-town. A great lady had obtained entrance
to his apartments disguised as a page; a shy, precocious young
invalid named Elizabeth Barrett confessed later to herself that
she would have been delighted to follow him on his romantic
travels and serve as his page. The restless and impulsive Claire,
at loose ends in London, ambitiously " fell in love" with him
at a distance like many another. Claire, however, possessed
boldness and initiative; she believed thoroughly in the creed
of Godwin and Shelley and thus had no terrifying social and
moral inhibitions. Under the name of E. Trefusis she wrote
Byron that though an utter stranger she had loved him many
years, that her happiness was in his hands — that she placed
a reputation as yet unstained and an infinite capacity for af-

fection and devotion entirely at his mercy. Byron could not
be bothered. Assuming another name, " G. C. B.," Claire asked
for an appointment " on business of peculiar importance," which
Byron granted in a most forbidding manner and twice failed to
keep. Claire then under her own name wrote again, having previously either seen Byron or told her story in a letter. She now
wished his advice, as one of the subcommittee of the Drury
Lane Theatre, about her desire to become an actress. Byron
referred her to his friend Douglas Kinnaird. Omitting to see
Kinnaird, she then asked Byron's help in deciding between a
literary or a dramatic career, submitting a manuscript and talking also about the works and opinions of her one friend, Shelley.
Byron was still decidedly bored. He bade her write briefly
when she wrote and called her " a little fiend." This characterization caused Claire to ask Shelley (still ignorant, according to
her account, of her theatrical plans and hence presumably of
the connection with Byron) what he thought of her character,
to which Shelley gave a response which Claire reported in his
" exact words." " My sweet Child," she quoted Shelley as saying, " there are two Clares — one of them I should call irritable if it were not for the nervous disorder, the effects of
which you still retain: the nervous Clare is reserved and melancholy and more sarcastic than violent; the good Clare is
gentle yet cheerful; and to me the most engaging of human
creatures; one thing I will say for you that you are as easily
managed by the person you love as the reed is by the wind;
it is your weak side." [75]

Byron probably cared no more at this time [76] for Shelley's
opinion than for Claire. Lady Byron, however, had just left
him; he was irritable and harassed, and the persistent Claire,
though her cleverness and independence were obvious, was
doing her best to exhibit the submissive qualities that he most
admired. Claire had already proposed that they spend the night
together at some quiet place ten or twelve miles out of London.
He made counter suggestions and changed the date, but some
time before Byron left England (April 25) Claire was established as his mistress. On March 28 Byron wrote one of his finest

lyrics to her, if we are to accept the opinion of his biographers
and editors that Claire's beautiful voice was the inspiration of
the lines:

> There be none of Beauty's daughters
> With a magic like thee,
> And like music on the waters
> Is thy sweet voice to me.

It was probably immediately after Byron's departure that
Claire revealed her secret to Shelley and Mary in order to persuade them to go to Geneva instead of Italy.[77] Under their
former plan Hogg had supposed to the last minute that he was
to accompany them, nor was he undeceived until the party was
actually on its way to Switzerland. "Mauvaise honte or awk-
wardness" and "circumstances [which] have occurred since I
last saw you" and which were "more fit to be made the subject
of conversation than of a letter" were the only explanations
Shelley somewhat vaguely assigned Hogg for his unannounced
departure.[78] This situation may have been created by a sudden
change in Mary's attitude toward Hogg, but it is far more likely
to have been caused by Claire. As soon as they reached Paris,
Claire wrote to inform Byron that Shelley had yielded to her
"pressing solicitations" and that she would soon join him at
Geneva, under the name of Madame Clairville.[79]

Closely related psychologically with Shelley's attempt to convince Peacock that his journey was a flight from arrest is an
incident which Shelley related to Medwin five years later as
having occurred on the night before he sailed. On the night
before he sailed, as Shelley told Medwin, a genuine disciple,
young, beautiful, accomplished — a married woman of wealth
and social position — placed her life, her fortune, and her reputation entirely at his disposal. She had read *Queen Mab* and
was utterly devoted to its principles and its author, for whom
she renounced husband, home, and society. All she asked was
to be allowed to accompany him as his devoted lover and
disciple.

Unfortunately for the fulfilment of her devotion, Shelley was
still completely in love with Mary, to whom the extra disciple

that he had hitherto possessed in Claire seemed at times to be superfluous. Deeply touched, Shelley explained to the unknown lady as delicately as possible that he could not accept her devotion. Nevertheless she followed him to Switzerland and gazed at him from afar with a spy-glass. Later she followed him to Italy; she was once for one night in the same hotel in which he lodged; finally she talked with him again in Naples and died there while he was in the city.[80]

Muddled and confused as Medwin could be, there has never been any reason for suspecting his general good faith toward Shelley. Even had he been dishonest enough to attempt it, he could hardly have invented a story about Shelley so psychologically apt. For a hundred years scholars have been sceptically curious about this tale, without having been able to find a single circumstance to confirm it. The death in Naples of such a woman as Shelley described would almost inevitably have been traceable through obituaries, official death-records, and English consular reports — all of which are extant and contain no such traces. The woman who died in Naples in 1818 would appear never to have existed, and it will be seen later that Shelley invented or resurrected her in order to mislead Medwin's curiosity about what actually happened there. But the same woman in the spring of 1818 may have had a genuine existence in Shelley's mind. He had just lost a disciple when Claire's primary allegiance was transferred to Byron. Disciples, feminine by preference, were such a necessity that it is just possible he invented this one for his own consolation and even for a while believed in her.

437

Chapter XV

SWITZERLAND AND BYRON

JOURNEY TO GENEVA; LIFE AT HÔTEL D'ANGLETERRE
AND MONT ALÈGRE; EXCURSION
ROUND THE LAKE; FINANCES; ASSOCIATION
WITH BYRON; CHAMOUNI EXPEDITION;
LAST DAYS AT GENEVA

ON a " serene, starlight night," if Mary's fictionized version [1] of
the journey is literally true, Shelley, Mary, little William, and
Claire sailed from Dover to Calais. At Calais Mary wrote a
letter to her estranged girlhood friend Isabel Baxter, who apparently never answered it.[2] By May 8 they were in Paris. Here
they passed two days of dullness, bored by delays in obtaining
passport signatures and by the lack of any friends or acquaintances in the city. It had been less than a year since Waterloo.
Foreign troops were still quartered in France to support the
unwanted Bourbons, and Paris had ways of making English
tourists feel that they belonged to an unfriendly nation.[3] To
Shelley's party, however, this resentment was encouraging for
the cause of freedom.

From Paris to Troyes the journey repeated their travels of
1814. Passing through Dijon and Dôle, they reached the Jura
Mountains at Poligny. Over a steep, narrow road by moon-
light, with a dark ravine on one side and an overhanging precipice on the other, they came to Champagnolles at midnight,
in the midst of a driving rainstorm. They were now surrounded
by a natural grandeur that was not the less inspiring because
at that date and season it was tempered with considerable in-

convenience and danger. The rain had changed to snow; over the edge of the road they could see in the valleys below them impenetrable forests of huge pines almost buried in the deep drifts. At the village of Les Rousses a little bribery enabled them to proceed by a shorter and less dangerous route than their passport specified. Even so they completed the last stage of the journey only with the aid of four horses and ten men to support the carriage.

After this white wilderness of incessant snowstorms and penetrating cold the warm sunshine of Geneva and the hum of sun-loving insects was very pleasant. In the suburb of Sécheron, from their windows at Dejean's Hôtel d'Angleterre they looked over a sparkling blue lake to a sloping shore dotted with vineyards and country houses, with mountains rising in the background, ridge after ridge, until they reached their limit of imposing grandeur in Mont Blanc. " You know," Mary wrote to Peacock, " that we have just escaped from the gloom of winter and of London; and coming to this delightful spot during this divine weather, I feel as happy as a new-fledged bird. . . . The budding flowers, the fresh grass of spring, and the happy creatures about me that live and enjoy these pleasures, are quite enough to afford me exquisite delight, even though clouds should shut out Mont Blanc from my sight." [4]

Shelley shared these feelings, but with him they mingled with a newly realized love for England, now that it seemed possible that he might see England again only in brief visits. A man never fully realizes his love for England, he wrote to Peacock, until he has learned by foreign travel, as Wordsworth did, to put a just value upon his native land. England, he asserted, was of all countries the most free and refined. " Our poets and our philosophers, our mountains and our lakes, the rural lanes and fields which are so especially our own, are ties which, until I become utterly senseless, can never be broken asunder." [5]

BYRON, with his youthful physician, Dr. John William Polidori, had left England ten days before Shelley, but his route was the longer one through Belgium and the Rhine country. Travelling more slowly and pausing more often, he reached Geneva some ten days after the arrival of Shelley's party. The record of his journey, as preserved in the third canto of *Childe Harold's Pilgrimage,* had a thousand times more readers than the inconspicuous little volume in which Shelley and Mary told of their wanderings.[6] Rising defiantly from his domestic calamity with a vitality that compelled attention, he was ready to tell England in unmistakable terms that another great poet had appeared. But the "bleeding heart" that he bore with such tragic triumph over half a continent had somewhat annoying consequences in private life. At Geneva he found himself the cynosure of a whole battery of spy-glasses and telescopes.

Byron lounged into Dejean's Hôtel d'Angleterre on May 25, with the slight mortifying limp that could never be quite fully concealed — and Claire Clairmont had brought about a junction of literary influences [7] that was to have an important effect upon both men and upon English public opinion. Byron probably realized little more importance in the meeting at the time than the curious observers. He had read Shelley's *Queen Mab* with some admiration without even knowing the author's name;[8] he had heard Shelley's character praised by Claire; and he had read the *Alastor* volume very probably with some impatience, if one may generalize from his own taste and practice in poetry at the time. Claire's scornful characterization of her fellow travellers in Paris as "Otaheite philosophers" sounds suspiciously like an echo of some previously expressed opinion of Byron's.

As soon as Shelley's party reached Geneva they settled down into the quiet way of living always observed by Shelley whenever there was opportunity. Seeking only their own society, they spent the heat of the day in reading Latin and Italian. In the early afternoon they walked in the hotel garden "looking at the rabbits, relieving fallen cockchaffers, and watching the motions of a myriad of lizards" on the southern wall.[9] They hired a boat in which they sailed on the lake every evening from about six o'clock until ten. After Byron's arrival he and Polidori joined the nightly sailing parties. Mary, who could never enjoy a sea voyage, was almost hilariously delighted with their evening sails. As they glided home to their dock they never failed to take pleasure in the scent of flowers and new-mown grass, the chirp of the grasshoppers, and the song of the evening birds.

Soon Byron was to record his delight in the same phenomena:

> . . . and drawing near,
>   There breathes a living fragrance from the shore,
> Of flowers yet fresh with childhood; on the ear
>   Drops the light drip of the suspended oar,
>   Or chirps the grasshopper one goodnight carol more;
>
> He is an evening reveller who makes
>   His life an infancy and sings his fill.
> At intervals, some bird from out the brakes
>   Starts into voice a moment, then is still.[10]

So similar is Byron's observation to Mary's earlier description that one fancies either Mary or Shelley bringing up the subject one evening as their boat slipped silently to shore.

Until about June 1 both parties continued to live in Sécheron, at Dejean's Hôtel d'Angleterre. Shelley then moved his party to a little cottage called Mont Alègre, on the opposite side of the lake, exchanging a view of Mont Blanc for " dark, frowning Jura." Their boat was still a prime source of pleasure, though constant rains now kept them more often indoors. Frequent thunder-storms seemed often to them, as to Byron, impressively beautiful. "We watch them," Mary wrote, " as they approach from the opposite side of the lake, observing the lightning play among the clouds in various parts of the heavens, and dart in jagged figures upon the piny heights of Jura, dark with the shadow of the overhanging cloud, while perhaps the sun is shining cheerily upon us. One night we *enjoyed* a finer storm than I had ever before beheld. The lake was lit up — the pines on Jura made visible, and all the scene illuminated for an instant, when a pitchy blackness succeeded, and the thunder came in frightful bursts over our heads amid the darkness." [11]

In sunnier weather, on still afternoons, they listened to the monotonous simple ballads of the peasant women who worked as vine-dressers in the vineyard separating Mont Alègre from

the Villa Diodati. Sometimes at night they heard a more distinguished voice floating back from the darkness of the lake.
Byron, returning to his hotel with Dr. Polidori after his regular
evening visit to Mont Alègre, was chanting to the elements
Moore's "Tyrolese Song of Liberty." [12]

On June 10 Byron left his hotel and came to live at the Villa
Diodati, only seven or eight minutes' walk from Mont Alègre
through an intervening vineyard. Here he hoped (but vainly)
that he could be free from the telescopes. His unofficial observers had already been talking and writing. Back to England
were drifting stories that Byron, Claire, Shelley, and Mary were
living together in a state of general promiscuity.

Byron and Shelley were now much more often in each other's
company. Byron's odd young physician, Dr. John Polidori, was
also generally of the party, as were Claire and Mary. Every
morning Byron called at Shelley's cottage, after which the party
usually sailed on the lake. Every evening, when the weather
was fine, there was another sailing expedition. On one such
evening Byron burst into a strange wild howl of music that he
assured them was an Albanian song. At times they would vary
their boating with a stroll along the shores, Byron always bringing up the rear of the party, musing and trailing his sword-stick
as he walked.[13] Sometimes there were evening gatherings, generally at the Villa Diodati. The conversation often lasted until
early morning.

In such company the self-conscious Polidori was more than
apt to make himself ridiculous. Once at Mont Alègre he insisted on having the company hear a tragedy he had written.
Byron obligingly read it aloud and when the audience almost
laughed at a passage about "the goitered idiot of the Alps"
Byron remarked with perfect truth and gravity that he had read
worse things at Drury Lane. Polidori, said Byron, was "very
young and hot-headed . . . always in squabbles, and had no
kind of conduct." Naturally he was at times rather a trial to
others in the party. The growing friendship of Shelley and
Byron made him quite jealous. When Shelley outsailed him
in a sailing match, he wished to challenge him to a duel, but
was deterred by Byron's remark that though Shelley had scru-

LAKE LEMAN. VILLA DIODATI, MONT ALEGRE, AND
MONT BLANC IN BACKGROUND

Engraved by W. Hill from a drawing by W. H. Bartlett

VILLA DIODATI, BYRON'S RESIDENCE ON LAKE LEMAN

Engraved by E. Finden from a drawing by W. Purser

ples against duelling, he himself had none and would be glad to take Shelley's place.[14] Yet Polidori, as Byron remarked, was " not a bad fellow." On June 2, as we learn from his journal, he superintended the vaccination of little William Shelley, for which the father presented him with a gold chain and seal. Mary liked him well enough at times to call him her younger brother.[15]

Shelley and Byron were now joint owners of a sailing boat, which they planned to take on an excursion around the lake. About this time Polidori sprained his ankle as he scrambled too hastily to assist Mary up the rocky incline to Villa Diodati, and his disability was seized upon as an excuse for excluding him from the expedition. His irritation and jealousy passed all bounds and brought a sharp reproof from Byron. Polidori took this to be the prelude to dismissal and consequent ruin and retired to his room in mortification. He was preparing to commit suicide when Byron entered and soothed his feelings with such kindly generosity that the moody young man burst into tears.[16]

It was the usually silent Mary who produced the most tangible result of the nightly séances around Byron's fireside. Her novel *Frankenstein* has for its immediate background another of those curious incidents that illustrate Shelley's extreme susceptibility to suggestion. About a week before the boat trip the party was amusing itself during a spell of rainy weather by reading a collection of German ghost-stories translated into French under the title of *Fantasmagoriana, ou Recueil d'histoires d'apparitions, de spectres, etc.* On the night of June 16 there was much talk of these horrors around the fire at Diodati. Two nights later there was similar talk. Byron adduced Coleridge's recently published " Christabel," which he had seen in manuscript and partly memorized, as an admirable example of the poetic use of such materials. He quoted the lines describing the horrible secret of the witch's deformity. For a moment there was silence; then Shelley, who had been staring at Mary, uttered a sudden shriek, pressed his hands over his head, seized a candle, and fled from the room. It required Polidori's professional services with cold water and ether to restore him to anything like normality. As he looked at Mary he had been shocked into uncontrollable horror by seeing a vision of a woman he had once heard of who had eyes for nipples.[17]

On the conclusion of the first of these ghostly séances Byron proposed that each one present should write a ghost-story. " You and I," he gallantly promised Mary, "will publish ours to-gether." [18] Shelley began and abandoned a story based on his own life. Claire (who is ignored in Mary's account) had begun a story by the next evening, as had all but Polidori, according to his diary. Polidori, in Mary's account, started and abandoned a gruesome story of a woman with a fleshless skull for a head. By his own account he began a quite different story, threw it aside, and later finished and published it as *Ernestine Berchtold.* Byron began and abandoned a story called *The Vampire,* which Polidori later finished. It was published in 1819 and became quite popular under the supposition that it was Byron's.

Mary could not at first get an idea for her story. Every morning Shelley asked: " Have you thought of a story? "[19] Eventually the idea was suggested by a conversation between Byron and Shelley on the vital principle. Was it not possible, they speculated, to reanimate a corpse by electricity? Gradually she formulated her idea of a mechanical monster endowed with life by a student of magic and driven to criminal behaviour by the absence of human sympathy. Precisely when she began writing her story is uncertain, but she was being constantly encouraged by Shelley, and she probably began it before the journey to Chamouni.[20] The story was published the next year with a preface by Shelley, and achieved many more readers than any work of Shelley's during his lifetime.

THE excursion of Shelley and Byron round the lake began on the afternoon of June 23 and ended on July 1.[21] A long letter from Shelley to Peacock relates in detail the points visited and the impressions they aroused — Hermance, Nernier, Yvoire, Évian, Meillerie, St. Gingoux, the mouth of the Rhone, La Tour de Bouverie, Clarens, Chillon, Vevai, Ouchy, and Lausanne.[22] Between Meillerie and St. Gingoux a heavy windstorm sweeping straight up the lake raised such a sea that the boat appeared almost on the point of sinking. A stupid boatman mismanaged the sail so that the boat was nearly driven under water and then released it so suddenly that the rudder was broken and the boat became almost unmanageable. Byron, an excellent swimmer, took off his coat and waited for the boat to capsize; Shelley, unable to swim and knowing that Byron would attempt to save him, caught hold of a locker and declared his determination to sink with it rather than endanger another life by accepting Byron's aid.[23]

At Meillerie and Clarens both travellers were immensely impressed by the associations with Rousseau and his *Julie*. Byron wrote at once his famous stanzas beginning: " Clarens, sweet Clarens, birthplace of deep Love! "

> All things are here of Him, from the black pines
>   Which are his shade on high, and the loud roar
> Of torrents where he listeneth, to the vines
>   Which slope his green path downward to the shore,
>   Where the bowed waters meet him and adore,
> Kissing his feet with murmurs; and the wood,
>   The covert of old trees with trunks all hoar,
> But light leaves, young as joy, stands where it stood,
> Offering to him and his a populous solitude.[24]

As for Shelley, " I read ' Julie ' all day," he wrote; " an overflowing, as it now seems, surrounded by the scenes which it has so wonderfully peopled, of sublimest genius, and more than human sensibility. Meillerie, the Castle of Chillon, Clarens, the mountains of La Valais and Savoy, present themselves to the imagination as monuments of things that were once familiar, and of beings that were once dear to it. They were created indeed by one mind, but a mind so powerfully bright as to cast a shade of falsehood on the records that are called reality." [25] Some days later, when they were at Lausanne, standing among the old acacias through which Gibbon had taken his memorable stroll after regretfully ending the last page of his *Decline and Fall of the Roman Empire*, the harder-minded Byron had recovered sufficiently from the emotional intoxication of Rousseau to do justice to the " lord of irony " who studied long and deeply,

> And shaped his weapon with an edge severe
> Sapping a solemn creed with solemn sneer.[26]

Being rather a souvenir-hunter, he gathered some acacia leaves to send to his friend and publisher, John Murray. But Shelley was still so much under the influence of Rousseau's passion that he would pluck no memento of Gibbon for fear of outraging " the greater and more sacred name of Rousseau," compared with whom Gibbon was so " cold and unimpassioned." [27]

The castle of Chillon was to both poets a terribly significant monument, inspiring Shelley to a long prose passage and Byron to two famous poems written under its immediate stimulation. Here, however, Byron was the optimist and Shelley the pessimist. To Byron it typified, through Bonnivard, the " eternal spirit of the chainless mind." Shelley wrote: " I never saw a monument more terrible of that cold and inhuman tyranny which it had been the delight of man to exercise over man. It was indeed one of those many tremendous fulfilments which render the ' pernicies humani generis ' of the great Tacitus so solemn and irrefragable a prophecy." [28]

Elsewhere also Shelley was alive to the contrast between natural beauty and grandeur and the sorry effects of human perversity. The wretched appearance of the inhabitants of Évian he attributed to the fact that they lived under the tyranny of Savoy rather than the freedom of Switzerland — a " powerful illustration of the blighting mischiefs of despotism." At Clarens the ruins of the little chapel in the " *bosquet de Julie*," razed by the orders of the monks of St. Bernard, confirmed Shelley's former conviction that " if avarice could harden the hearts of men, a system of prescriptive religion has an influence far more inimical to natural sensibility." [29]

Before the journey was over, Shelley had composed a poem in which he sought to give a spiritual meaning to the unutterable beauty by which he felt himself surrounded.[30] In *Alastor* he had already found his old doctrine of a dispassionate Necessity too cold and rigid for his expansive sympathies. He had referred in the Preface to a " Power " whose exquisite influences it was dangerous to perceive too suddenly and fatal to ignore.

To this power in his "Hymn to Intellectual Beauty," he now gave a definite name and definite functions. It was "Intellectual Beauty," or beauty which can only be conceived as an idea, rather than experienced in its fullness. Even its shadow, Shelley asserts, is unseen, and visits the world infrequently, but is nevertheless the secret of all that is true and beautiful both in the natural world and in humanity. Poets, sages, and prophets have tried vainly to understand it and to give it a name. If it could only be understood and brought to keep firm state in the human heart, "Man were immortal and omnipotent." Shelley then relates how as a schoolboy he had first felt the existence of some such power and had dedicated himself to its service. He calls from their graves "the phantoms of a thousand hours" of hard study and intense pursuit of knowledge to testify to his zeal and constancy, and prays to be guided through life by the same spirit.

ON THE eve of starting his tour of the lake with Byron, Shelley found that he had by no means completely escaped the worries connected with Godwin and England. At the time Shelley left England, Godwin had been absent in Scotland arranging for the publication of his *Mandeville,* a novel for which he claimed extraordinary originality and with which he hoped to re-establish his finances.

The best he could do with his publisher was to obtain an advance of £200, for which he had to give a note payable on demand after January 1 if two volumes were not delivered by that date. This sum was immediately swallowed up by old obligations, and still William Taylor of Norwich was pressing him for an overdue debt and he had been obliged to give a Mr. Kingdon a note for £300 that might be presented for payment at any moment.[31] When he returned to London he found that Shelley, his only immediate hope, had gone to the Continent without having provided the long-promised financial succour.

Godwin was greatly disappointed; but he immediately set to work, as Shelley had advised, to obtain money from Mr. Bryant on Shelley's expectations. Bryant's client, Dr. Bethune, offered

447

£1,700 net for a thirty years' purchase of certain properties involved in the settlement of 1791, but could not proceed without a copy of the settlement, which Shelley's absence made it impossible for Godwin to secure.[32] From Évian, the first post-town on his tour, Shelley suggested means of securing a copy of the necessary settlement and authorized Godwin to go ahead, with due precautions as to the value of the property involved and the continued necessity of secrecy. " No person," he concluded, in apologizing for an apparent stiffness of tone, " can feel deeper interest for another or venerate their character and talents more sincerely, or regret more incessantly his own impotent loneliness, than I for you and yours." [33] Godwin went ahead, through his agent Mr. Hume, and apparently brought matters to the point where only an authorization from Shelley to Hume and Shelley's final signature to the deeds were needed to complete the transaction. Shelley undertook to do everything possible to facilitate matters,[34] but for some reason the transaction was never completed.

On either Godwin's or his own account Shelley was himself making efforts at this time to secure more money. He had already secured a sum of money on annuity, through R. Hayward, from a Mr. Billing. In May or early June he tried unsuccessfully to obtain a second advance from the same source.[35] At about the same time, through Longdill and Whitton, he requested that his annuity be increased from £2,000 to £2,500. " It is scarcely to be believed that a young man could be so inconsiderate," Whitton wrote to Sir Timothy, who declined the request. Sir Timothy went further. He would not complete the loan of £2,000 that had been agreed upon before Shelley's departure, nor enter into any new pecuniary account with him during his absence from England. He was offended at Shelley's sudden departure without notice and without having made any further provision for Harriet's children.[36] Shelley had known all along that he must soon return to England to complete his financial arrangement with his father. It was now clear to him that he would probably have to remain in England on his return.

A letter from Peacock confirmed Shelley's intention to return and settle in England. He had hoped to buy the house at Bishopsgate — if the owner would make it a post-obit transaction — but he now learned that it was planned either to demolish the house or radically to alter it. He wrote to Longdill to give up possession of the house on August 3, and commissioned Peacock to look after his possessions and secure another house in the same general neighbourhood. As yet he hardly expected to return before spring, after having made a tremendous boat trip. His plan was to descend to the mouth of the Danube, going thence to Constantinople, Athens, Rome, Tuscany, and southern France, "always following great rivers." But England, he now felt, was the " best of nations," and England should be his " perpetual resting place." Peacock was to take a house at long lease, for a " fixed, settled, eternal home." Shelley was already provided with a kitten for it, which by some means was increased to two when he reached England. Soon he was buying flower seed with which to colonize Alpine flowers in his English garden.

If Shelley never knew a real home since boyhood it was not through incapacity to appreciate its blessings. " You must shelter my roofless Penates," he adjured Peacock, in the letter just quoted, " dedicate some new temple to them, and perform the functions of a priest in my absence. They are innocent deities, and their worship neither sanguinary nor absurd. Leave Mammon and Jehovah to those who delight in wickedness and slavery — their altars are stained with blood or polluted with gold, the price of blood. But the shrines of the Penates are good wood fires, or window frames intertwined with creeping plants; their hymns are the purring of kittens; the hissing of kettles; the long talks over the past and dead, the laugh of children, the warm wind of summer filling the quiet house, and the pelting storm of winter struggling for entrance." [37] This surprising tribute to domesticity Shelley knew might seem amusing to Peacock, for he added: " In talking of the Penates, will you not liken me to Julius Caesar dedicating a temple to Liberty? " Shelley's attorney, Longdill, must have been of Peacock's opinion, for he sold the Penates, possibly for debts, without even consulting Shelley in advance.[38]

449

FOR three weeks more there was constant visiting back and forth between Mont Alègre and Villa Diodati. Day after day glided by in the old unhurried daily and nightly routine of sailing, walking, and discussing.

Shelley read less than usual while in Switzerland and as yet had written only one poem. Byron, on the other hand, had written " The Prisoner of Chillon " and most of the third canto of *Childe Harold* since his meeting with Shelley. Possibly Byron's genius, as Mrs. Shelley later suggested, inhibited Shelley's. Shelley was too genuinely modest, perhaps, to think of competition with a man whom most people were coming to regard as the greatest poetic genius of the age. On the other hand, he was far too deeply grounded in learning and good taste not to realize that on these grounds he was independent of Byron and possibly his superior. " Lord Byron," he wrote to Peacock, passing his judgment with calm equality, " is an exceedingly interesting person, and as such is it not to be regretted that he is a slave to the vilest and most vulgar prejudices, and as mad as the winds? " [39]

Frequent daily discussions between two such lively minds as Byron's and Shelley's must have been of great benefit to both. For Shelley, who thought too modestly of his own poetry to consider himself Byron's poetic peer, the advantage must have consisted mainly in an intellectual stimulation derived from Byron's strong vitality and sharp, incisive comments. In the midst of his enjoyment he could scarcely avoid the same quiet reassurance he must have attained once four years before in talking with Southey — a confidence that in mental powers he was already the equal of two of the great poets of the age.

Byron, who partly agreed with Shelley's political views and mainly disagreed with his social and religious ideas, respected his knowledge and was probably at times almost awed by his moral earnestness. Shelley saw in Byron a great potential force for truth and righteousness and sought tactfully to inspire him with a high moral purpose such as he himself had expressed in the " Hymn to Intellectual Beauty."

Shelley practically forced Byron to override his earlier prejudices and perceive the greatness of Wordsworth's poetry. In

450

Byron's phrase, Shelley constantly "dosed" him with Wordsworth.[40] The Wordsworthian tone of many of the best passages
in the third canto of *Childe Harold's Pilgrimage* show the effect
of Shelley's prescription. Byron was experiencing and expressing a new feeling, a confidence that he was not an isolated
being, but a portion of the nature by which he was surrounded:

> Are not the mountains, waves and skies a part
> Of me and of my soul, as I of them? [41]

This was coming rather close to Wordsworth's realization of
a spirit and a motion that

>   impels
> All thinking things, all objects of all thought
> And rolls through all things.

But Wordsworth's voice must have reached Byron strongly
coloured and reinforced by Shelley's constant talk on metaphysical subjects. On the last day of the excursion Shelley wrote
his "Hymn to Intellectual Beauty," in which he too found a
spiritual beauty which was the source of all that was worthy in
the human mind. The speculations by which he reached this
conclusion must have found frequent expression at the time
that both he and Byron were so similarly stimulated by the
natural beauty around them. Never before his association with
Shelley in Switzerland and never afterwards did Byron approach so near to a spiritualized view of Nature.

Mary was usually a silent listener during these conversations.
Yet they impressed themselves so deeply on her memory that
never after Shelley's death could she hear Byron talk without
unconsciously waiting for Shelley's eager answer. It was, she
recorded, "like thunder without rain," or like "any familiar
object . . . shorn of its best attributes," to hear Byron's voice
without Shelley's; it afflicted her with "unspeakable melancholy." [42]

AT HALF past eight on the morning of July 21, Shelley, Mary,
and Claire began their previously planned expedition to Cha-

mouni. William was left behind in the care of Elise, his Swiss nurse. Byron was expecting visitors from England and remained at Diodati. Four hours' travel through steamy hot lowlands brought the party to Bonneville, where the Alps began to close in on them. Beginning to ascend, they passed through Cluses and on to St. Martin (Sallanches), still following the valley of the Arve. Between Bonneville and Cluses they passed two waterfalls, one of them about three hundred feet high. Next morning, on muleback, they left the inn at St. Martin for Chamouni. Soon they passed another waterfall — two hundred and fifty feet of wavering, fluctuating spray that filled the valley with a wind-swept mist. As they climbed still higher, they could see gleaming glaciers and mighty pines above them, while far below was the rushing, foaming Arve, bordered by pines and fretted by boulders. They entered the vale of Chamouni, where the mountains spread apart sufficiently to permit cultivated fields, cottages, and little villages. The glacier of Boisson, dotted with conical and pyramidal towers and seamed with precipices, was now very close; the way became more dangerous. Behind them they heard a thunderous noise and turned to see an avalanche plunge down a ravine and turn from its course a stream they had crossed earlier in the day. Very much fatigued, they reached the inn at Chamouni at seven o'clock.

A paragraph of Shelley's letter to Peacock suggests that part of this fatigue may have been due to the excitement of almost intolerable beauty acting upon so highly sensitive a mind as Shelley's.

From Servox, three leagues remain to Chamounix. Mont Blanc was before us. The Alps with their innumerable glaciers on high, all around; closing in the complicated windings of the single vale: — forests inexpressibly beautiful — but majestic in their beauty — interwoven beech and pine and oak overshadowed our road or receded, whilst lawns of such verdure as I have never seen before, occupied these openings, and extending gradually becoming darker with their recesses. Mont Blanc was before us but was covered with cloud, and its base furrowed with dreadful gaps was seen alone. Pinnacles of snow, intolerably bright, part of the chain connected with Mont Blanc shone thro' the clouds at intervals on high. I never knew, I never imagined what mountains were before. The immensity of these aerial summits excited, when they suddenly burst upon the sight, a sentiment of extatic wonder, not unallied to madness — And remember this was all one scene. It all pressed home to our regard and to our imagination. Though it embraced a great number of miles the snowy pyramids which shot into the bright blue sky seemed to overhang our path — the ravine, clothed with gigantic pines and black with its depth below — so deep that the very roaring of the untameable Arve which rolled through it could not be heard above — was close to our very footsteps. All was as much our own as if we had been the creators of such impressions in the minds of others, as now occupied our own. Nature was the poet whose harmony held our spirits more breathless than that of the divinest.[43]

In the valley of Chamouni a little incident occurred that to a mind less dedicated than Shelley's might have typified the hardships of the emancipator. "In one village," wrote Mary in her journal, "they offered us for sale a poor squirrel, which they had caught three days before; we bought it; but no sooner had I got it in my hand, than he bit my finger, and forced me to let it go; we caught it however, again, and Shelley carried it some time; it appeared at length resigned to its fate, when we put it on a railing, where it paused an instant, wondering where it was, and then scampered up its native trees."[44]

After breakfast the next day, July 23, the party mounted mules for the difficult ascent to the source of the Arveyron. The last mile had to be negotiated on foot among treacherous boulders. Seated on a rock beside one of the streams of the Arveyron, they could see the river rolling impetuously from its cavern of ice. From the opposite glacier of Montanvert they could see masses of ice detach themselves and fall with such thunderous force that they were converted into powder. That evening Shelley went with the guide to visit another glacier, that of Boisson. The inexorable, devastating encroachments of these glaciers offered a grand and gloomy stimulation. The scientific side of his mind saw in them the gradual extinction of all life in the valleys in a smother of "avalanches, torrents, rocks and thunders." To his poetic mind they were a symbol of unutterable and incomprehensible power. Such thoughts, he wrote Peacock, were best reserved for later conversations. That evening, however, he transmitted some of these feelings into poetry.[45]

" MONT BLANC — Lines Written in the Vale of Chamouni," blends the river Arve and its parent mountain into one impressive symbol of Power. Through a scene of beauty and wild desolation,

> — Power in likeness of the Arve comes down
> From the ice gulphs that gird his secret throne.

In the journal and in Shelley's letter to Peacock the glaciers also were compared to rivers. Though Shelley does not expressly repeat the comparison in the poem, he paints a graphic picture of the " flood of ruin " rolling slowly down the heights and obliterating everything in its path. Shelley seems at first uncertain whether the general scene suggests " awful doubt " or a faith mild, solemn, and serene; [46] but in the end the various streams unite and out of the terrifying welter

> . . . one majestic River,
> The breath and blood of distant lands, for ever
> Rolls its loud waters to the ocean waves.

In like manner " the everlasting universe of things," sometimes bright and sometimes gloomy, flows through the human mind. For both the Arve and the glaciers the sources of power are the secret, remote, and inaccessible fastnesses of Mont Blanc, where " Power dwells apart in its tranquillity." The " everlasting universe of things " also flows from " hidden springs " which the poet does not undertake to lay bare, though he suggests that sleep may offer " gleams of a remoter world." This " secret strength " from which river and glacier derive power in Mont Blanc is the same which also governs thought and

> to the infinite dome
> Of heaven is as a law.

The poem is definitely marked with the influence of Wordsworth in both idea and phrase, but it has an essentially Shelleyan integrity. Its sentiment is hardly the pantheism (or Ne-

CHAMONIX: MER DE GLACE

Engraved by S. Fisher from a drawing by W. H. Barlett

cessity, as Hazlitt called it) of Wordsworth's " Tintern Abbey,"
but a somewhat uncertain amalgamation of Shelley's old doctrine of Necessity with his more recent concept of " Intellectual
Beauty." Its imagery, which is its essence, is the typically Shelleyan imagery of rivers, caves, and veils. Its hint that experience
is simply the universe flowing through the individual mind reflects the philosophy of Berkeley and shows that Shelley was
already well on the road to his later and more mature view
of the nature of reality. None of this is to be found in Wordsworth or in a poem by another of Shelley's favourite poets,
Coleridge's "Hymn before Sunrise in the Vale of Chamouni"
(1802). Shelley had doubtless read Coleridge's poem about a
sight he had never beheld, but he was far from regarding the
scene simply as an impressive proof that " Earth with her thousand voices praises God."

On the next day the party set out for the glacier of Montanvert. Rain fell in torrents, and the whole party were wet to
the skin. Half-way up they decided to return to the inn. Shelley, who went a little ahead, slipped or tripped, and fainted,
but was able to continue the journey a few minutes later. Next
morning they set out at nine and reached the top of Montanvert
at noon. The narrow valley through which they ascended is
thus described in Shelley's letter to Peacock:

It exhibits an appearance as if frost had suddenly bound up the
waves and whirlpools of a mighty torrent. We walked to some distance upon its surface — the waves are elevated about twelve or
fifteen feet from the surface of the mass, which is intersected with
long gaps of unfathomable depth, the ice of whose sides is more
beautifully azure than the sky. In these regions everything changes
and is in motion. This vast mass of ice has one general progress
which ceases neither day nor night. It breaks and bursts forever;
its undulations sink whilst others rise. From the precipices which
surround it the echo of rocks which fall from their aerial summits,
or of the ice and snow scarcely ceases for one moment. One would
think that Mont Blanc was a living being and that the frozen blood
forever circulated through his stony veins.[47]

They dined at a little inn on Montanvert. Here occurred an
incident, of which Mary's journal makes no mention, that was

destined for several years thereafter to be told around England to the detriment of Shelley's reputation. The generosity of a former tourist had provided an album in which a succession of visitors had inscribed their names, often with trite pious comments on the scene as a striking testimony to the glory of God. What Shelley felt as he read these inscriptions only Shelley could say; we only know that in his own way, inspired by the same sights, he had just finished an impassioned tribute to *his* notion of a supreme Power. Perhaps his predecessors seemed intolerably smug. Perhaps the excitement " not unallied to madness " with which he was filled prompted him to a last outburst of youthful exhibitionism. At any rate he inscribed his name, and after it the words:

$$\delta\eta\mu o\kappa\rho\alpha\tau\iota\kappa os \ \phi\iota\lambda\acute{\alpha}\nu\theta\rho\omega\pi o\tau\alpha\tau os \ \kappa\alpha\grave{\iota} \ \acute{\alpha}\theta\epsilon os$$

[democrat, great lover of mankind, and atheist].

That the inscription was at least partly exhibitionism is strongly suggested by the fact that Shelley had already written another almost identical inscription in the album of the Hôtel de Londres at Chamouni, and very probably a still earlier one at the inn at Sallanches where the party had spent the first night after leaving Geneva. One of these inscriptions, but certainly not the one at Montanvert, was noticed by Byron a month later when he visited the same region with Hobhouse, Scrope Davies, and Polidori. " Do you not think," said Byron to Hobhouse, " I shall do Shelley a service by scratching this out? " Whereupon, " with great care," he defaced the offending words, not dreaming that Shelley might have left similar records elsewhere. Within less than a fortnight after Shelley wrote his inscription in the hotel register at Chamouni, a group of English travellers were so unfavourably impressed by it that one of them could quote it accurately in a letter to the *Christian Observer* eight years later, and some time thereafter the page was cut out by another traveller and carried bodily to England. About a year after Shelley wrote the inscription at Montanvert, Robert Southey visited the same little inn, copied Shelley's inscription, and carried it back to England, where it was quoted in print to Shelley's disadvantage.[48]

THE weather was now unfavourable, and Mary was anxious to be with her child again. On Friday, July 26, the party started for Mont Alègre. Travelling in easy stages, they reached Villa Diodati at nine o'clock the next evening, July 27. "We converse with Lord Byron till 12," Mary records in the journal for that day, "and then go down to Chapuis [Mont Alègre] kiss our babe, and go to bed."

The month of August passed quietly in a routine not very different from that already established at Mont Alègre. Shelley and Byron were often together on the lake or at Diodati, unaccompanied by either Mary or Claire. Byron still dropped in upon the Shelleys occasionally for an hour's chat before dinner, but not so often as formerly. Mary seems not to have visited Diodati after August 13, and Claire only three times, all but once with Shelley. On August 13 Mary had written in the journal: "After dinner Shelley goes out in the boat with Lord Byron, and afterwards we all go up to Diodati" — followed by the one cryptic word: "War." If this meant a disagreement over Claire, it can hardly have been a serious one, for Claire returned to Diodati next day to copy Byron's poems and Byron thereafter called six times at Mont Alègre.[49]

Mary was writing her novel, reading almost every day, and keeping up her Latin studies. Shelley was reading also, mainly Lucretius and Pliny, but not so much as usual. Shelley's twenty-fourth birthday, August 4, was duly observed. Mary presented him with a telescope and made a fire-balloon for him to send up from the lake. The lake was too rough, so it was sent up from land, but it was not a success; it took fire too soon. Earlier in the day Mary and Shelley went out in the boat and Mary read to him aloud Book IV of Vergil. Almost every evening during the first part of the month they went up to Diodati, but there is no mention in the journal of Byron's calling at Mont Alègre except once, in response to a message. Almost the only extraordinary incidents were the arrest of Polidori at the instance of an apothecary who sold bad magnesia (the hot-headed "Poli" had "cassé ses lunettes et fait tomber son chapeau"), and an attack upon Shelley by an ill-tempered dog which apparently did no damage.[50]

There were occasional letters from England. A long letter from Fanny Imlay was a regular magazine of news. Coleridge, Fanny reported, was living at Highgate with an apothecary who had just caught him attempting to smuggle in laudanum; the Lambs had been spending a month in and near Bristol; Godwin was much depressed by Sheridan's death; Mr. Robert Owen, of Lanark, was a frequent visitor at Godwin's and talked optimistically of his schemes for reform (but Fanny couldn't see how the privileged classes were to be persuaded to relinquish their advantages). Many conditions and incidents (which Fanny detailed) showed that England was in an alarming political and economic condition. Godwin was sleepless and miserable over financial worries — " I think it is my duty to tell you the real state of the case, for I know you deceive yourself about things." As to her own situation, her aunt, Everina Wollstonecraft, was to be in London soon, and Fanny hoped then to settle the question of getting a position in her school at Dublin. Fanny represented herself as still in poor health and a terribly depressed state of mind; [51] but this was such a common state for the whole family that probably its serious meaning in Fanny's case did not become apparent to the Shelleys until some months later.

Charles Clairmont also wrote from Bagnères-de-Bigorre, in the Pyrenees. He had gone to Bordeaux to develop his French and learn Spanish, hoping this would open some commercial opportunity. Thence he had drifted to the Hautes-Pyrénées, whence he now wrote reams of delighted description. But the kernel of his letter was that he wished Shelley to finance him for six months while he studied Spanish and German. Shelley sent him ten pounds, which according to Charles's figures would support him for two months. [52]

Mary and Shelley went into Geneva only occasionally, mainly to make purchases. There was a book-dealer in Geneva, J. J. Paschoud, whose shop Shelley occasionally visited. This man may have been a fellow radical, for he commissioned Shelley to translate Godwin's *Political Justice* for him, but the commission was never executed. [53] The high narrow houses of Geneva seemed rather unattractive to the Shelleys, and their in-

458

habitants a shade too puritanical. Neither, for that matter, did Shelley or Mary think very highly of the Swiss peasants except when comparing them with people who lived under a political tyranny.[54]

BOTH Shelley and Mary are extremely reticent in their journals and letters about Claire. Despite its inauspicious beginning and Byron's account of its termination, her affair with Byron must have made her precariously happy for a while.[55] During this time it was a pleasure to her to write out the fair copies of the third canto of *Childe Harold's Pilgrimage*, "Monody on the Death of Sheridan," and "The Prisoner of Chillon." It is too much to suppose that the constant association of the two parties from the day of Byron's arrival was not partly due to Claire. But Claire's moody variability and even her independence and sprightly intelligence were not qualities that would long hold Byron's interest. Moreover, there were other forces at work. Madame de Staël, whose home at Coppet Byron frequently visited, was lecturing him severely on his way of living and persuading him to co-operate (though doubtfully) in her attempt to produce a reconciliation with Lady Byron. In England Byron's half-sister, Augusta Leigh, heard the wild rumours that had been sent home by prying tourists and wrote to remonstrate. Byron's reply, dated September 8, represents the affair as a trivial incident already terminated:

— as to all these "mistresses," Lord help me — I have had but one. Now don't scold; but what could I do? — a foolish girl, in spite of all I could say or do, would come after me, or rather went before — for I found her here — and I have had all the plague possible to persuade her to go back again; but at last she went. Now, dearest, I do most truly tell thee, that I could not help this, that I did all I could to prevent it, and have at last put an end to it. I was not in love, nor have any love left for any; but I could not exactly play the Stoic with a woman, who had scrambled eight hundred miles to unphilosophize me.[56]

Byron said nothing to Augusta about his knowledge that Claire was with child by him,[57] nor is there any mention of it

in the journal kept by Shelley and Mary. The day after their
return from Chamouni, however, Mary records: " Shelley reads
Lucretius, and talks with Claire." And five days later (August 2): " Shelley and Claire go up to Diodati; I do not, for
Lord Byron did not seem to wish it." [58] This, in all probability,
dates the beginning of Shelley's long and difficult service as
mediator between Claire and Byron. The three-cornered conversation looks very much like·a discussion of Byron's provisions
for his mistress and her child. He had already proposed to
Claire to place the child shortly after its birth in the care of his
half-sister, Augusta, but Claire objected. Possibly this was the
" war " so cryptically mentioned in Mary's journal for August 13. Byron finally agreed, according to Claire's statement,
to leave her in charge of the child, as its " aunt," until it was
seven years old.[59]

Claire's situation alone made it inadvisable to remain much
longer at Mont Alègre, for it would never do to allow Claire's
pregnancy to be associated with the local gossip already current.
At the same time Shelley received a letter from Longdill which
for financial reasons seemed to require his return to England.
" This," says Mary in the same entry previously quoted, " puts
us in very bad spirits."

Toward the end of their stay in Geneva Byron had three visitors.
Though Claire was at Diodati at least twice during " Monk "
Lewis's visit, there is no evidence that Mary and Claire ever
met Byron's guests — perhaps Byron was being particularly
careful what stories got back to England — but Shelley was
a good deal in their company. The first of these guests was that
still-flourishing veteran of the tale of terror Matthew Gregory
Lewis, better known as " Monk " Lewis, from his youthful novel
of *The Monk*, which had so thrilled Shelley's boyhood. Lewis
was at this time just entering the forties; he was a man somewhat aware of his literary importance, genuinely kind and hu-
mane, but still, in Byron's opinion, rather a bore. Lewis arrived
on August 14 and immediately began talking about German
literature and tales of terror. By reading aloud and translating

a part of Goethe's *Faust* he introduced Byron, and possibly
Shelley, to the greatest literary man of the age. Byron's *Manfred*, soon to be written, may have owed some Faustian traits
to this experience, as it may also owe something to Peacock's
theories of Ahrimanes, which were much in Shelley's mind and
probably his conversation at the time. Shelley was so impressed
with four tales of the supernatural that Lewis told around the
evening fire at Diodati that he summarized them all in his journal.[60] With his strong metaphysical interests Shelley believed
in ghosts, or at least Byron thought so.[61] He was somewhat disappointed that neither Byron nor Monk Lewis believed in the
supernatural, and was definitely scornful of their illogical argument that no one could believe in ghosts without also believing
in God.[62] Lewis must have talked also about the slaves on his
West Indian plantation, whose condition he had improved and
intended to secure. Two days after telling his ghost-stories
he drew up an ardently worded codicil to his will by which he
bound his heirs to respect the rights and privileges he had
established for his slaves. Byron, Shelley, and Polidori signed
the document as witnesses.[63]

Byron's other guests, John Cam Hobhouse and Scrope Davies,
arrived on the 26th, only three days before Shelley left Geneva.
Shelley spent the evening with them, dined with them next day
and spent the evening, and went out with them for a sail on
the lake. On the 28th Byron came down to say good-bye. Polidori, who had just been dismissed by Byron, came the same
day by himself; his last act was to tell Shelley some anecdote
that made Shelley's blood run cold with disgust. For the last
time Shelley's little party went out upon the lake in their beloved sailboat. The packing was finished and everything was
made ready for a departure early the next morning.[64]

THE journey to England took nine days and was without particular incident. Most of the first two days, from Geneva to Dijon,
was over a route already familiar. From Dijon to Versailles,
a little more than three days' travel, they followed a route new
to them, by way of Rouvray, Auxerre, Villeneuve, Le Guiard,

and Fontainebleau. From Versailles to Havre, by way of Aux-
onne, Rouen, and Gretor, was also through a region previously
unknown. The journal comments with scarcely more than routine interest on people, buildings, and countryside and hardly
contradicts Shelley's characterization of the journey as tedious.[65]

More than anything else the palaces at Fontainebleau and
Versailles interested Shelley and Mary as examples of the extravagance of tyranny. Versailles was magnificent, certainly,
but the orangery was "a stupid piece of expense" and there
was a pervading flavour of royal effeminacy — a Greek architect
could have done far better with less money and labour. The
splendid, costly tournaments of Louis XIV, as depicted in a
book of paintings at Versailles, seemed to show clearly why an
improverished people were goaded to fury and horrible excess.
The vacant rooms of the palace "imaged well the hollow show
of monarchy" — so well, indeed, that the image was remembered about a year later in *Laon and Cythna* when the victorious
people bring Laon to the tyrant's desolate palace whose

> sculptured walls vacantly to the stroke
> Of footfalls answered, and the twilight's gloom
> Lay like a charnel mist within the radiant dome.[66]

Shelley had seen more than an image, however; he had seen
an idea for a great poem that should deal with the French
Revolution. He somewhat diffidently recommended the subject
to Byron,[67] and when Byron did nothing with it he developed
it himself in *Laon and Cythna,* or *The Revolt of Islam,* as it was
renamed.

After a day's wait at Havre Shelley's party sailed for Portsmouth on September 7. The winds were unfavourable; Mary,
as usual, was seasick. When they reached Portsmouth over
twenty-six hours later Shelley too was "not well." From Portsmouth Shelley wrote a short letter to Byron and set off next
day to London.

Mary, Claire, Elise (the Swiss nurse), and little William
started for Bath, where they were to wait until their house at
Marlow was ready for occupancy. But this was probably not
the only reason for their going to Bath. It is evident from the

letters of Fanny Imlay and Godwin that the Skinner Street
household knew nothing of Claire's affair with Byron and its
impending result. They were to be kept in ignorance as long
as possible.

The sojourn in Switzerland had been of wonderful benefit
to Shelley. On his arrival Polidori, a physician, had described
him as consumptive, bashful, and shy. Many hours of mountain-
climbing and of boating in the wind and sunshine had produced a physical improvement. The association with Byron had
strengthened his confidence in himself, even though it may have
lessened his desire to write in seeming competition with a man
whom he thought a much greater poet. The shocks and increasing complexity of life had certainly diffused his earlier,
almost monomaniac singleness of purpose; but even as Fanny
Imlay was chiding him for not writing more he was firmly announcing in the "Hymn to Intellectual Beauty" that he had
kept and would keep his early vow to "free this world from
its dark slavery." Above all, he had acquired a much more
elevated sense of the grandeur and mystery of "this unfathomable world." "Before we return," Shelley had assured Peacock,
"we shall have seen, and felt, and heard, a multiplicity of things
which will haunt our talk and make us a little better worth
knowing than we were before our departure." [68] That these
things at least haunted their thoughts is shown by a later entry
in Mary's journal, written in the midst of the troubles they encountered soon after their return. "I am melancholy with reading the 3rd canto of *Childe Harold*. Do you not remember,
Shelley, when you first read it to me? One evening after returning from Diodati. It was in our little room at Chapuis. The
lake was before us, and the mighty Jura. That time is past, and
this will also pass, when I may weep to read these words, and
again moralize on the flight of time. Dear Lake! I shall ever
love thee . . . I think of our excursions on the lake. How we
saw him [Byron] when he came down to us, or welcomed our
arrival, with a good-humoured smile. How vividly does each
verse of his poem recall some scene of this kind to my memory!" [69]

Unfortunately the principal impressions of this visit that later

English travellers, including Southey, could get in Switzerland were the old rumours that made of the Byron-Shelley party a league of incest, and the damning entry that Shelley had made in the album at Mont Anvert.[70] Some of these travellers must have talked with a boatman who had often been on the lake with Byron and Shelley and could have given them a different impression. Shortly after Shelley's death this boatman thus expressed himself to Lady Blessington, who had known both Shelley and Byron:

Poor Mr. Shelley . . . ah, we were all sorry for him. He was a different sort of man [from Byron], so gentle, so affectionate, so generous; he looked as if he loved the sky over his head and the water on which his boat floated. He would not hurt a fly — nay, he would save everything that had life, so tender and merciful was his nature. He was too good for this world, and yet, lady, some of his countrymen whom I have rowed in this very boat have tried to make me think ill of him, but they never could succeed, for we plain people judge by what we *see,* and not by what we *hear.*[71]

Chapter XVI

BATH, LONDON, AND

THREE DISASTERS

MONEY MATTERS; SUICIDE OF FANNY; FRIENDSHIP
WITH LEIGH HUNT; HARRIET'S LAST DAYS AND
SUICIDE; MARRIAGE; DEFEAT IN CHANCERY

SHELLEY left Portsmouth for London on the afternoon of September 9. Byron had entrusted him with one of the fair copies of *Childe Harold*, Canto iii, to be conveyed to Murray, his publisher. Scrope Davies was bringing back a second copy for Murray, in case anything happened to the first, but it was Shelley who was to act as Byron's agent in settling the terms and making any necessary editorial decisions. Murray was "exceedingly polite" when Shelley left the poem with him on the 11th, but his cordiality must have waned somewhat when Shelley insisted that Byron's price was 2,000 guineas instead of the 1,200 guineas Murray had supposed.[1] At any rate, he omitted to send the proofs to Shelley for correction and answered Shelley's reminder by saying that Byron had instructed him to commit the proofs only to William Gifford.[2] By this time (November 20) Shelley suspected that Murray might bear him ill will on account of the extra £800 he had been obliged to pay for the manuscript. However that may be, it is certain Murray bore him ill will a year later, when he characterized Shelley to John Wilson Croker as "the vilest wretch now living" and promised to furnish him full information about "the vile author" of *Queen Mab*.[3]

465

Shelley had expected to have an interview with Longdill in London, but found that he was out of town, and was forced to await his return. After Switzerland, London seemed a "peopled desert"; his old lodgings at 26 Marchmont Street, where he was staying, seemed chill and lonely in the absence of Mary and Claire and the estrangement of Godwin. Fanny Imlay called on him there, reported the cheering news that Godwin was making excellent progress on his new novel, and was no doubt cheered in turn by Shelley's mistaken belief that Godwin's financial difficulties were now soon to be abolished.[4]

Quite possibly Shelley did not wait in London for Longdill's return, for by September 14 he was Peacock's guest at Marlow. From here he wrote to Mary conveying Peacock's invitation to join them in their search for a suitable house. Leaving the regular routine of reading and writing that she had immediately set up at Bath, and trusting "Itty Babe" to Claire and Elise (who were to make him some nightgowns in her absence), Mary joined Shelley and Peacock on September 19. The next five days were consumed mainly in conversation and in numerous walks throughout the neighbouring countryside. To Claire, left in Bath without ready money and with only a vague idea of the sewing she had undertaken, reports of these activities must have sounded a little excessive. "Don't over-walk Shelley," she wrote to Mary, "and pray make him get a great-coat."[5]

On the 24th Shelley went up to London to complete the financial settlement agreed upon with his father before he went to Switzerland. Sir Timothy, who was generally pretty well informed about his son's affairs, knew that Shelley still had a number of debts outstanding. He may even have known, through Longdill or Whitton, of Shelley's efforts to relieve Godwin, of which he would certainly have disapproved. Nothing could be more evident than his fear of future embarrassments to the estate and his complete lack of confidence in his son's ability to handle money. This fear was justified by the fact that in spite of the debts paid in 1815 and the income of £800, Shelley was now over £1,400 in debt. Sir Timothy made it an indispensable condition of completing his agreement that Shel-

466

ley should pay all of his past debts out of the money provided. With Longdill's assistance, he so managed that Shelley was " encompassed with such toils as were impossible to be evaded." Shelley had expected to have £500 or £600 left, out of which he would furnish the £300 that Godwin so desperately awaited. Instead, he had only £248 remaining. Most of this he now sent to Godwin with the bitter confession that he did not know how to provide the remainder.[6]

Though Shelley had very little actual money to disburse after his creditors were paid, he still had a considerable fortune in prospect. On the same day (September 24) that he completed his agreement with his father he also made his first will. To Harriet he left £6,000, to Ianthe and Charles £5,000 each, to Mary Jane Clairmont £6,000 to be invested in an annuity, and to Thomas Love Peacock £2,000 to be invested in an annuity. All these sums were placed in trust with Byron and Peacock, trustees. In addition, Claire was to receive £6,000 outright, Hogg and Byron £2,000 each, Peacock £500. The residue of his estate he bequeathed to Mary Wollstonecraft Godwin. It is natural that Shelley made no provision for Godwin, Fanny Imlay, or William Shelley. Godwin would have felt insulted by being mentioned, and a mention of Fanny or little William might call attention to their illegitimacy. It would be better to trust their fortunes to Mary, whose inheritance would comprise the bulk of Shelley's estate.[7] There is no record of Shelley's will at Somerset House, nor would Sir Timothy Shelley ever consent to its execution; but after Sir Timothy's death Shelley's will as amended in 1817 was carried out by his widow and his surviving trustee, Peacock.

WHILE in London, Shelley had another talk with Fanny Imlay, to whom he said nothing about the disappointment in store for Godwin. It is possible, as he led Fanny to believe, that everything was uncertain until he should hear again from Longdill; it is more probable (as Fanny later suspected) that Shelley knew at the time and would not or could not tell her. No one knew better than Shelley that Godwin's fate and that of his novel depended on securing the financial relief Shelley had promised. No one had a higher opinion than Shelley of Godwin's novels or of Godwin's importance to the cause to which Shelley was dedicated. To the end of his days Shelley considered Godwin the greatest living philosopher. If, as Fanny suspected, he did not deal openly with Godwin, it must have been from no unsympathetic motive.

" You know the peculiar temperature of Papa's mind," Fanny wrote to Mary on October 3. ". . . You know that it is of the utmost consequence, for *his own* and the *world's sake,* that he should finish his novel; and is it not your and Shelley's duty to consider these things, and to endeavour to prevent, as far as lies in your power, giving him unnecessary pain and anxiety? Shelley's letter came like a thunderclap. I watched Papa's countenance while he read it (not knowing the contents), and I perceived that Shelley had written in his most desponding manner."

Before the end of the year Godwin, and the world, were saved — at least temporarily, which was as much as could be hoped. Through Hayward, Shelley seems to have effected some kind of sale or loan that netted a hundred pounds more than Godwin's immediate need.[8]

Fanny had two other grievances against Shelley and Mary, which she stated with sisterly frankness. " I am angry with Shelley," she wrote (September 26), " for not giving me an account of his health. All that I saw of him gave me great uneasiness about him, and as I see him but seldom, I am more alarmed perhaps than you, who are constantly with him." Mary was certainly not alarmed, and made not a single comment in her journal on Shelley's health between September 8 and November 27; instead she recorded a steady, daily activity of reading and walking that makes Fanny's fears seem over-solicitous.

Fanny's other complaint touches upon a point in Shelley's character that has puzzled his biographers more, perhaps, than anything else. Mrs. Godwin had recently visited Bracknell, where Shelley had lived with Harriet, and had heard by accident some damaging stories told there by Harriet in a visit after Shelley had deserted her. These stories Fanny had repeated to Shelley as a warning against taking a house in that neighbourhood. When a letter from Mary showed her that they had been twisted into evidence of Mrs. Godwin's malignity, Fanny protested, and rose warmly to the defence of a woman who sometimes made her life miserable. " I either related my story very ill to Shelley," she wrote (October 3), " or he, paying little regard to what I might say, chose to invent a story out of his own imagination for your own amusement, which you too have coloured to your own mind, and made what was *purely accidental* and only occurred *once,* a story after the manner of ' Caleb Williams,' viz., of ' Mama pursuing you like a hound after foxes.' I do not choose to be made the author of a glaring *falsehood.* Mama and I are not great friends, but, always alive to her virtues, I am anxious to defend her from a charge so foreign to her character." She added that though Mrs. Godwin could never forgive Shelley for separating her from Claire, she would never do either Shelley or Mary " a deliberate or deadly injury " and was in fact anxious to speak as well as possible of both of them except in the bosom of the family. Thus Fanny Imlay, a devoted friend, seems to agree with Peacock and Hogg that Shelley's stories might sometimes be more imagination than fact, and offers still another suggestion that Shelley could translate his novel-reading into the plane of his actual living.

FROM September 25 to October 9 Shelley, Mary, and Claire led a placid, featureless existence at Bath, unconscious of impending tragedy. Shelley wrote Byron a friendly letter reassuring him about his affairs in England and encouraging him to fulfil his destiny as a great poet.[9] He took frequent walks, and read a variety of books — Lucian, Peter Pindar, the life of Holcroft, *History of the French Revolution,* Tasso, *Don Quixote* — some of them aloud, to Mary. Mary kept up her Latin, read even more than Shelley, took drawing-lessons, walked, and looked after her child. Claire interested herself in her music and the baby and awaited her own confinement in January. The first intimation of tragedy appears in Mary's journal entry for Wednesday, October 9: " In the evening a very alarming letter from Fanny. Shelley goes immediately to Bristol; we sit up for him till 2 in the morning, when he returns he brings no particular news." At the same time Fanny had written to Godwin: " I depart immediately to the spot from which I hope never to remove."

On the next day Shelley made a second visit to Bristol and secured information leading him to Swansea, where he went on the 11th. Godwin also set out for Bristol as soon as he received Fanny's letter, but at Bristol he turned back, having probably seen the account of Fanny's suicide in the *Cambrian* for October 12. Shelley learned at Swansea that Fanny had taken a room at the Mackworth Arms on the night of October 9, had dismissed the chambermaid, and had been found dead next morning. On the table was a bottle of laudanum and a note which read:

" I have long determined that the best thing I could do was to put an end to the existence of a being whose birth was unfortunate, and whose life has only been a series of pain to those persons who have hurt their health in endeavouring to promote her welfare. Perhaps to hear of my death will give you pain, but you will soon have the blessing of forgetting that such a creature ever existed as . . ." The signature, according to the account in the *Cambrian,* appeared to have been torn off and burned. Except for a few clothes she had with her only eight shillings sixpence and the watch that Shelley and Mary had brought her from Geneva. One article of clothing was marked " G." another " M. W." If the local authorities ever penetrated her decent, pathetic anonymity, the fact was never published. By reporting her simply as "found dead" the coroner's jury saved her from the disgraceful burial that English law still prescribed for suicides.[10]

On his return journey to London Godwin spent the night at Bath at a hotel only a quarter of a mile from Shelley's lodgings, but he did not call on Shelley's family. They learned later that Fanny had suddenly left Godwin's home, travelling through Bath to Bristol and Swansea without calling at Shelley's lodgings, and that she was ostensibly on her way to Ireland to see

her aunts, but did not have enough money with her to reach
Ireland.

No doubt in the miserable evenings that followed Shelley's
return to Bath all three of his household saw only too clearly
how the tragedy had been prepared. Fanny's unfortunate position in the Godwin household made her the scapegoat for the
two others who had escaped Mrs. Godwin's uncertain moods.
Her sensitive, sympathetic, rather brooding nature was especially susceptible to Godwin's miseries and her own feeling of
penniless dependence. Claire had taken notice of Fanny's despondency as early as May 28, 1815. " Now do not be melancholy," she had written from Lynmouth; " for heaven's sake
be cheerful; so young in life, and so melancholy." [11] She had
written bright, cheerful letters to Fanny from Switzerland; but
Fanny's melancholy had not been dissipated. In her letter of
May 29, 1816 to Mary and Shelley, Fanny had reported herself
in a somewhat better frame of mind as a result of talking with
an old friend of her mother's, but added: " I have determined
never to live to be a disgrace to such a Mother." [12] Her letter
of July 29 must have seemed in retrospect a clear warning: " If
you knew how I am harassed by a variety of trying circumstances I am sure you would feel for me "; " You ask about old
friends; we have none, and see none." She wrote of " the dreadful state of mind I generally labour under, and which I in vain
try to get rid of." [13] The mother whose memory Fanny adored
had been similarly subject to fits of depression and had once
attempted to drown herself.

Recently, however, Fanny's hopes of going to Ireland had
revived. Her two aunts, Mrs. Bishop and Miss Everina Wollstonecraft, were in London during the latter part of September,[14] on the visit that Fanny expected would settle her fate.
Perhaps it did. Fanny may have been informed that their recent
financial reverses made it impossible for them to receive her
for more than a visit or that they again believed that it would
ruin their school to employ a teacher both of whose " sisters "
had eloped with one man without marriage. Did Shelley's disappointment of Godwin's financial hopes, which fell at this mo-

ment, convince Fanny that she could never be more than a hopeless burden on others? She had only recently learned that she was not Godwin's child, but an illegitimate daughter born to her mother before she knew Godwin [15] — was this the additional straw that brought about her decision? Or had she learned that Claire was soon to give birth to an illegitimate child, thus ruining once more her hopes of a teaching position in Ireland? Only Fanny or some member of Shelley's household could answer these questions. The Godwins, at least, did not know of Claire's condition until 1817.[16] Miss Mary Hutton, an acquaintance of Fanny's aunts, felt sure that Aunt Everina had caused Fanny's suicide by declining to receive her in Dublin.[17] If Shelley's little circle knew, they kept silence. They could hardly help realizing that nearly all possible clues led, one way or another, to the elopement of Shelley and Mary. And being intensely certain that their action was not blameworthy, they could only feel a dumb misery.

Mary felt later that if Fanny had only waited until her marriage with Shelley she could have had a happy home at Marlow.[18] This indicates that Mary at least, who would have been a competent judge in such matters, took no stock in a theory stated later by Godwin that Fanny's death was due to a hopeless love for Shelley.[19] Shelley said nothing, except for two veiled references in a letter to Byron to an event preceding Harriet's death that was " a far severer anguish " and affected him " far more deeply." [20] In 1839 Mrs. Shelley published without comment the following lines, written by Shelley in 1817, which very probably refer to his last talk with Fanny, on September 24:

> Her voice did quiver as we parted,
>   Yet knew I not that heart was broken
> From which it came, and I departed
>   Heeding not the word then spoken.
>   Misery — O Misery,
>   This world is all too wide for thee.

Godwin, now that the last and most devoted of his daughters had gone, admitted that he was not surprised. It was a heavy blow, which he accepted with stoical, dignified resignation. All

that remained was to shield Fanny's name. " Go not to Swansea," he wrote to Mary,[21] " disturb not the silent dead; do nothing to destroy the obscurity she so much desired that now rests
upon the event. . . . We have so conducted ourselves that not
one person in our home has the smallest apprehension of the
truth." These wishes were rigorously observed. Neither Claire
nor Shelley in writing to Byron disclosed the fact that Fanny
was a suicide; even Charles Clairmont was kept ignorant, not
only of the nature, but even of the fact of Fanny's death. As
late as August 8, 1817 [22] he proposed to write to Fanny and inquired if the Shelleys often saw her. Even to his old friend
W. T. Baxter, Godwin could not bear to tell the whole truth:
" From the fatal day of Mary's elopement," he wrote, " Fanny's
mind had been unsettled, her duty kept her with us: but I am
afraid her affections were with them. Last Autumn she went
to a friend in Wales — and there was a plan settled about her
going from thence to spend a short time with her Aunts in
Dublin, but she was seized with a cold in Wales which speedily
turned to an inflammatory fever which carried her off." [23]

Claire wrote to Byron: " We have spent a most dismal time.
Fanny (the daughter of Mary Wollstonecraft and Imlay) has
died, and her death was attended by such melancholy consequences as (at least for me) can never be forgotten. Poor Shelley's health is broken up, and I never passed such wretched
hours. Everything is so miserable that I often wish myself quite
dead." [24]

Mary bought mourning, went steadily ahead with her *Frankenstein,* her Latin, her drawing, and her general reading —
and many years later converted Fanny's pathetic story to the
uses of fiction in *The Last Man.*[25] She began the study of chemistry with Shelley on October 28. Shelley wrote a little and continued his reading, finding particular pleasure in Montaigne's
Essays. Both Shelley and Mary went frequently for walks; Shelley even set out for Oxford, but was stopped by some mysterious
" men dressed in black " and decided to return to Bath. There
is no mention in the journal of Shelley's illness, and the fullness
and regularity of his daily occupations seem inconsistent with
the state of broken health that Claire ascribed to him.[26] On

473

October 26 he announced a resolution — and kept it through the 27th — to keep account of the weight of the food he consumed, but whether his interest was valetudinarian or strictly scientific does not appear.

FROM October 15 to December 5 life at 5 Abbey Churchyard, Bath,[27] pursued the regular tenor described above. A letter arrived from Byron on November 19. Shelley's answer provides an excellent example of the tact he could exercise in another's interest. It was evident to Shelley that Claire needed a moral support which Byron was too indifferent to offer, and he knew that Byron was far too proud and suspicious to tolerate a frank remonstrance:

Poor Clare's time approaches, and though she continues as well as women in that situation usually are, I think her spirits begin to fail. She has lost much of the animation and lightness which perhaps you do not ever remember in her. I shewed her your letter, which I should have withheld had I been aware of the wretched state into which it would have thrown her. I need not say that I do not doubt that you were as little aware of such an effect. But the smallest omission, or the most unpremeditated word often affects a person in a delicate state of health, or spirits. Any assurances which I could make to her of your correct intentions would be superfluous; she expresses the most unbounded confidence in you; and, as is natural, considers every imagined defect of kindness in me, as a breach of faith to you. I need not entreat you to believe that neither Mary nor myself will be deficient in every requisite attention and kindness. If you do not like to write to Clare, send me some kind message to her, which I will, to give suspicion his due, throw into the fire as a sacrifice.[28]

A long letter from Charles Clairmont [29] painted a glowing picture of life in the Pyrenees and sought to interest Shelley in emigrating to that region. He informed Shelley that an American friend of his, named Lovell, was greatly interested in *Queen Mab* and would shortly be in London, where he desired to meet the author. Incidentally, Charles owed Lovell £12, 18s., which Lovell had obligingly consented to receive from Shelley in London.

Another letter, to Godwin, shows that Shelley recognized extremes beyond which he would not go even in succouring genius. Godwin had urged Shelley to accept a proposal from a money-lender named Dawe. Shelley enclosed a rough calculation showing that he would be paying nearly twenty-five per cent and throwing away £2,800. "I lament exceedingly," he wrote, "that you supposed it possible, or even esteem it right. . . . I am persuaded that it is my duty not to submit to terms of so exorbitant a nature." The very principles which made him believe in the injustice of hereditary rights, he remarked, also taught him that it would be wrong to present such a "remorseless mean-spirited wretch" as Dawe with the power represented by £2,800. There were other and better means.[30]

Shelley was now about to take upon himself another pensioner, albeit one whose friendship was to be one of his principal pleasures during the rest of his life. He was already acquainted with Leigh Hunt, but the acquaintance had hardly been more than casual and had been interrupted by Hunt's imprisonment and by Shelley's vicissitudes of the last two years. In October Shelley had sent to Hunt's *Examiner* his "Hymn to Intellectual Beauty," signed with one of Mary's pet names, "Elfin Knight." This had been acknowledged by a note in the *Examiner* for October 6: "The Elfin Knight, the first opportunity." On December 1 Shelley received a letter from Hunt, and on the same date Hunt's *Examiner* contained a little article entitled "Young Poets." Briefly, before announcing more fully that John Keats and John Hamilton Reynolds were young poets of great promise, the reviewer (Leigh Hunt) encouraged "Percy Bysshe Shelley, author of *Alastor, or the Spirit of Solitude.*" As yet he had seen little of Shelley's work, "but if the rest answer to what we have seen, we shall have no hesitation in announcing him for a very striking and original thinker."

Despite the bold conclusion this was decidedly cautious praise. It filled less than half a dozen lines and was not to be compared with the full glowing tributes paid to the anonymous author of *Queen Mab* in the pages of that mysterious journal the *Theological Inquirer*. Here, however, Shelley's name was printed in bold capitals, the writer was a man whose good

475

opinion Shelley particularly esteemed, and his conditional encomium could not have been better phrased to please the young poet. Coming at a time of great discouragement, it lifted Shelley's spirits enormously. Before he saw the *Examiner,* apparently as a result of Hunt's letter of the same date, Shelley sent Hunt a present of a sum of money.

Two letters from Hunt to Shelley soon reached him at Marlow, where he had gone from Bath on December 5 to resume his search for a house. The eagerness with which he welcomed Leigh Hunt's friendship is expressed in a letter which should be quoted somewhat at length:

I have received both your letters yesterday and to-day, and I accuse myself that my precipitancy should have given you the vexation you express. Your letters, however, give me unmingled pleasure, and that of a very exalted kind. I have not in all my intercourse with mankind experienced sympathy and kindness with which I have been so affected or which my whole being has so sprung forward to meet and to return. My communications with you shall be such as to attempt to deserve this fortunate distinction. Meanwhile, let me lay aside preliminaries and their reserve; let me talk with you as with an old friend. . . . [One paragraph omitted.]

Next, will I own the " Hymn to Intellectual Beauty? " I do not care — as you like. And yet the poem was composed under the influence of feelings which agitated me even to tears, so that I think it deserves a better fate than being linked with so stigmatised and unpopular a name (so far as it is known) as mine. You will say that it is not thus, that I am morbidly sensitive to what I esteem the injustice of neglect — but I do not say that I am unjustly neglected, the oblivion which overtook my little attempt of " Alastor " I am ready to acknowledge was sufficiently merited in *itself;* but then it was not accorded in the correct proportion considering the success of the most contemptible drivellings. I am undeceived in the belief that I have powers deeply to interest, or substantially to improve, mankind. How far my conduct and my opinions have rendered the zeal and ardour with which I have engaged in the attempt ineffectual, I know not. Self love prompts me to assign much weight to a cause which perhaps has none. But thus much I do not seek to conceal from myself, that I am an outcast from human society; my name is execrated by all who understand its entire import — by those very beings whose happiness I ardently desire. I am an object of compassion to a few more benevolent than the rest, all else abhor and avoid me. With you, and perhaps some others (though in a less degree I fear) my gentleness and sincerity find favour, because they are themselves gentle and sincere: they believe in self devotion and generosity, because they are themselves generous and self devoted. Perhaps I should have shrunk from persisting in the task which I had undertaken in early life, of opposing myself in these evil times and among these evil tongues, to what I esteem misery and vice. If I must have lived in the solitude of the heart, fortunately my domestic circle incloses that within it which compensates for the loss. But these are subjects for conversation, and I find that in using the privilege which you have permitted me of friendship, I have indulged in that garrulity of self-love which only friendship can excuse or endure. . . . [Two paragraphs omitted.]

Last of all — you are in distress for a few hundred Pounds; — I saw Lord Byron at Geneva who expressed to me the high esteem which he felt for your character and worth. I cannot doubt that he would hesitate in contributing at least £100 towards extricating one whom he regards so highly from a state of embarrassment. I have heard from him lately, dated from Milan; and as he has entrusted me with one or two commissions, I do not doubt but my letter would reach him by the direction he gave me. If you feel any delicacy on the subject, may I write to him about it? My letter shall express that zeal for your interests which I truly feel, and which would not confine itself to those barren protestations if I had the smallest superfluity.

My friend accepts your *interest* and is contented to be a Hebrew for your sake. But a request is made in return which in courtesy cannot be refused. There is some little literary luxury, some enjoyment of taste or fancy you have refused yourself, because you have not felt, through the difficulty of your situation that you were entitled to indulge yourself in it. You are entreated, — and a refusal would give more pain than you are willing to inflict — to employ the enclosed in making yourself a present of this luxury, that may remind you of this not unfriendly contest, which has conferred a value on £5 which I believe it never had before.

Adieu,
Most affectionately yours,
P. B. SHELLEY

I will send you an " Alastor." [31]

477

Mary was writing Shelley news of little William and urging him to be prompt and sensible about choosing " our little mouse hole to retire to. . . . Give me a garden and *absentia Clara,* and I will thank my love for many favours." [32]

Shelley remained at Marlow only a week and then, commissioning Peacock to oversee the conditioning of the house and grounds he had leased, he proceeded to visit Leigh Hunt. Since shortly after his liberation from prison, Hunt had been living in a little cottage in the Vale of Health, Hampstead. Here, amid rural surroundings that have long since vanished, he maintained a cheerful, lively rendezvous for all of his friends and admirers who cared to walk or ride out from the city for an evening of literary or political comradeship. The accommodations were limited, and a bit haphazard; the guest might have to sleep on the sofa in Hunt's study, but the welcome was warm. Even in his essays Hunt is unusually companionable, but in his personal relations he was one of the most friendly and amiable men alive. A few months before Shelley's visit John Keats had already begun to drink deep of the somewhat imperfect poetic inspiration to be found in Hunt's cottage — long evenings of political liberalism, rather sentimental dilettantish enthusiasms for " nature " and " art," a demand for a radically new poetry that based itself too much on an uncomprehending scorn of Pope and Gray. At about the time Shelley visited Hunt, Keats was writing a sonnet in which he expressed himself as

> brimful of the friendliness
> That in a little cottage I have found,

and was packing somewhat loosely into the most ambitious poem he had yet attempted most of the Huntian enthusiasms and excesses that he was soon to outgrow. His " Sleep and Poetry " furnishes a partial catalogue of the art by which Keats was surrounded as he went to sleep on Hunt's study couch. Busts of the elder bards " smiled at each other "; fauns and satyrs snatched at the fruit of tree or vine; nymphs tripped the greensward or wiped " cherishingly Diana's timorous limbs "; Sappho, King Alfred, and Kosciusko gazed down from the walls

478

(possibly with a " wild surmise "); and Petrarch stepped forth to meet Laura. Four years later, in his poetic " Letter to Maria Gisborne," Shelley voiced a warm memory of the same room, with its irrepressibly cheerful host and its

> many a cast from Shout,
> With graceful flowers tastefully placed about;
> And coronals of bay from ribbons hung,
> And brighter wreaths in neat disorder flung.

Other frequent visitors at the time were Charles Lamb, William Hazlitt, John Hamilton Reynolds, Charles Cowden Clarke, B. R. Haydon, and James and Horatio Smith. Sooner or later, in the frequent visits to Hampstead that were to follow, Shelley became acquainted with nearly all of them. Shelley's first visit with Hunt lasted only two or three days; long enough, however, for him to feel distinctly pleased with his new friend and to make the acquaintance of Horace Smith and John Keats.

Horace Smith, already a successful banker and writer of light verse, had recently read some of Shelley's poems and was looking forward to meeting him. When Shelley entered the room, Smith observed him closely. He was " a fair, freckled, blue-eyed, light-haired, delicate-looking person, whose countenance was serious and thoughtful," with an earnest, odd-sounding voice and a stooped carriage. He was well-tailored, but careless of his appearance. Instantly Horace Smith concluded that here was a *gentleman.* A few moments later, observing Shelley's quiet detachment from a bantering, facetious series of sallies started by Hunt, Smith realized that here was a mind so deeply impressed with its own wrongs and those of the world that it was naturally more disposed to seriousness than to levity. When the whole party (which included Keats) sallied forth for a walk upon the heath, Smith attached himself to Shelley and listened with astonished sympathy while Shelley poured forth his ideals and aspirations in complete defiance of the conventional reticences. Like John Frank Newton before him, he was amazed at the extensive reading so young a person had at his command.[33]

479

NEVER did Shelley form friendships more in the nick of time. Already another calamity had befallen him, though he was not yet aware of it. He had been back in Bath only a day when, on December 15, he received a letter from Hookham conveying devastating news of Harriet.

Shelley had apparently heard nothing of Harriet's actions since June, when she had made an unsuccessful effort, through Peacock, to obtain an increased allowance.[34] There is no mention of Harriet in the journal of Shelley and Mary between its resumption on July 21, 1816 and Harriet's death. So far as Shelley's personal interest was concerned, she was by this time practically out of his life; he would have supposed that such an event as her death would be a matter of complete indifference to him.[35] That there were other obligations, however, which he had no thought of denying, is shown by his provision for Harriet and her children in his will of September 24. A few weeks after making this will, perhaps as a result of it, he had written to Thomas Hookham to ascertain Harriet's address. But Harriet had recently vanished from Hookham's ken also, and while he was still inquiring for her address, he received the news that she had destroyed herself. "This shocking communication," Hookham informed Shelley, "must stand single and alone in the letter which I now address you: I have no inclination to fill it with subjects comparatively trifling: you will judge of my feelings and excuse the brevity of this communication."[36]

About September 9, the day after Shelley's return to England, Harriet had left her father's house at 23 Chapel Street. There is no evidence other than Shelley's word that she was driven forth by the greed and jealousy of her sister Eliza; she had left her father's house twice before for brief visits or residences elsewhere.[37] She had rented the second floor of a house at 7 Elizabeth Street, Hans Place, in a neighbourhood that she knew had been frequented by Shelley during the year after he left her.[38] What name she gave is unknown, but she stated truly that she was married and that her husband was abroad. Both the landlady and her servant noticed that she appeared very gloomy and despondent, and the former testified at the inquest that she appeared to be pregnant. Her behaviour was quiet and en-

tirely respectable; she talked little, and spent much of her time
in bed. On Saturday, November 9, she asked for an early dinner, which was served to her at four o'clock and which she
scarcely touched. Before five o'clock she had left the house,
never to return. No one saw or heard more of her until December 10.

A week after her disappearance her family became uneasy
and employed William Alder, who had accompanied her to
the door when she engaged her Hans Place lodgings, to drag
the Serpentine and the neighbouring ponds in a search for her.
This indicates that Harriet's family knew of her residence at
Hans Place and were aware of the same lowness of spirits that
had been remarked by all who knew her in her last days. They
knew the curious attraction that suicide had held for Harriet
even in her happier days.[39] For this reason it is very probable
that they were not seriously alarmed by a farewell letter from
Harriet dated "Sat. eve," until they found that she had actually
disappeared. Harriet disappeared on a Saturday evening, November 9, presumably the same "Sat. eve" on which the following farewell letter was written:

My Dearest and much Beloved Sister, — When you read this letter,
I shall be no more an inhabitant of this miserable world. Do not
regret the loss of one who could never be anything but a source of
vexation and misery to you all belonging to me. Too wretched to
exert myself, lowered in the opinion of everyone, why should I drag
on a miserable existence? embittered by past recollections and not
one ray of hope to rest on for the future. The remembrance of all
your kindness which I have so unworthily repaid has often made my
heart ache. I know that you will forgive me — because it is not in
your nature to be unkind or severe to any. Dear amiable woman
that I had never left you, oh! that I had always taken your advice.
I might have lived long and happy, but weak and unsteady have
rushed on to my destruction. I have not written to Bysshe. Oh, no,
what would it avail, my wishes or my prayers would not be attended
to by him, and yet should he rec. this, perhaps he might grant my
request to let Ianthe remain with you always. Dear lovely child,
with you she will enjoy much happiness, with him none. My dear
Bysshe, let me conjure you by the remembrance of our days of happiness to grant my last wish. Do not take your innocent child from

Eliza who has been more than I have, who has watched over her with such unceasing care. Do not refuse my last request, I never could refuse you and if you had never left me I might have lived, but as it is I freely forgive you and may you enjoy that happiness which you have deprived me of. There is your beautiful boy, oh! be careful of him, and his love may prove one day a rich reward. As you form his infant mind so will you reap the fruits hereafter. Now comes the sad task of saying farewell. Oh! I must be quick. God bless and watch over you all. You dear Bysshe and you dear Eliza. May all happiness attend ye both is the last wish of her who loved ye more than all others. My children — I dare not trust myself there, they are too young to regret me and ye will be kind to them for their own sakes more than mine. My parents — do not regret me, I was unworthy of your love and care. Be happy all of ye, so shall my spirit find rest and forgiveness. God bless you is the last prayer of the unfortunate

HARRIET S.

To you my dear Sister I leave all my things; as they more properly belong to you than anyone and you will preserve them for Ianthe. God bless you both.[40]

   William Alder's search was unsuccessful, but a month later, on the morning of December 10, an out-pensioner of Chelsea Hospital who was walking along the Serpentine not far from Harriet's Hans Street lodgings noticed a body floating in the river. It was brought ashore and carried to the Fox public-house, near by. There it was recognized by the landlord's daughter, who knew Harriet,[41] and William Alder, who happened to live there. At the inquest it was also identified by the landlady and her servant. None of them, not even William Alder, identified it as the body of Harriet Shelley, however. Either Harriet was going under the name of Smith when she took lodgings, or the Westbrook family, notified by their friends at the Fox, prevailed upon them to identify it by that name in order to escape the disgrace of suicide. The body bore no marks of violence and a valuable ring was found on one of Harriet's fingers. This precluded a verdict indicating robbery and murder, but there still remained a possibility of death by accident. Though three witnesses had testified to Harriet's extreme depression, the verdict was not suicide, but simply: " Found dead in the Serpentine River." Some of the jurors, like the landlord's daughter and William Alder, may have known Harriet or her family. Had they brought in a verdict of suicide, Harriet must have been buried at the cross-roads.

The coroner's verdict was delivered on December 11, and *The Times* for the next day carried a brief notice of the death of " a respectable female far advanced in pregnancy." When and where Harriet was buried is unknown; the burial would have to be prompt and would be likely to be very quiet, so it probably occurred before Shelley reached London. In the parish register of Paddington, the late Mr. Roger Ingpen discovered that on December 13, 1816 Harriett Smith, of Mount Street, St. George's, Hanover Square, aged twenty-one, had been buried in that parish.[42] Very probably this refers to Harriet Shelley, who sometimes spelled her name Harriett,[43] who was twenty-one at the time of her death, and who would most probably have been buried on the 13th. The address is quite near that of Harriet's father and also of the Mount Coffee House, which he had conducted. From the same address, two days before, had been buried a Benjamin Smith, possibly an acquaintance of the Westbrooks, which may have some obscure bearing upon the name under which Harriet was buried.[44]

Thus, under a cloud of obscurities and imputations, ended the life of a beautiful girl whose pliable character yielded too readily, first to her sister's dominance, then to Shelley's, and again to her sister's. She entered Shelley's life with a threat of suicide if he did not return her love; she left it with the execution of her threat. The charges made by Shelley, Mary, the Clairmonts and Godwins that she subjected Shelley to some petty persecutions after he left her are at least partly true, though exaggerated. But even if they were entirely true they could hardly counterbalance the evidence of her last letter that she loved Shelley until she died.

It is very unlikely that Shelley ever saw Harriet's last letter. On December 15, when he received Hookham's letter announcing Harriet's death, he took a walk with Mary to discuss the situation and immediately set off for London. His main concern was the children; Harriet was already in her grave. The next day he wrote Mary the following letter:

I have spent a day, my beloved, of somewhat agonising sensations; such as the contemplation of vice and folly and hard heartedness exceeding all conception must produce. Leigh Hunt has been with me all day and his delicate and tender attentions to me, his kind speeches of you, have sustained me against the weight of the horror of this event.

The children I have not got. I have seen Longdill, who recommends proceeding with the utmost caution and resoluteness. He seems interested. I told him I was under contract of marriage to you; and he said that in such event all pretences to detain the children would cease. Hunt said very delicately that this would be soothing intelligence to you. — Yes, my only hope my darling love, this will be one among the innumerable benefits which you will have bestowed upon me, and which will still be inferior in value to the greatest of benefits — yourself — it is thro' you that I can entertain without despair the recollection of the horrors of unutterable villainy that led to this dark, dreadful death. — I am to hear to-morrow from Desse whether or no, I am to engage in a contest for the children. — At least it is consoling to know that if the contest should arise it would have its termination in your nominal union with me — that after having blessed me with a life, a world of real happiness, a mere form appertaining to you will not be barren of good.

It seems that this poor woman — the most innocent of her abhorred and unnatural family — was driven from her father's house, and descended the steps of prostitution until she lived with a groom of the name of Smith, who deserting her, she killed herself. — There can be no question that the beastly viper her sister, unable to gain profit from her connexion with me — has secured to herself the fortune of the old man — who is now dying — by the murder of this poor creature. Every thing tends to prove, however, that beyond the mere shock of so hideous a catastrophe having fallen on a human being once so nearly connected with me, there would, in any case have been little to regret. Hookham, Longdill — every one, does *me* full justice; — bears testimony to the upright spirit and liberality of my conduct to her: — there is but one voice in condemnation of the detestable Westbrooks. If they should dare to bring it before Chancery, a scene of such fearful horror would be unfolded as would cover them with scorn and shame.

How is Clare? I do not tell her, but I may tell you how deeply I am interested in her safety. I [need] not recommend her to your care. Give her any kind message from me, and calm her spirits as well as you can.

I do not ask you to calm your own — I am well in health tho' somewhat faint and agitated — but the affectionate attentions shown me by Hunt have been sustainers and restoratives more than I can tell. Do you, dearest and best, seek happiness — where it ought to reside in your own pure and perfect bosom: in the thoughts of how dear and how good you are to me — how wise and how extensively beneficial you are perhaps destined to become. Remember my poor babes, Ianthe and Charles. How dear and tender a mother they will find in you — Darling William, too! — My eyes overflow with tears. To-morrow write a long letter, and give me some answer to Hunt's message.

P. B. SHELLEY [45]

The sworn testimony of the coroner's inquest [46] disproves Shelley's statement that Harriet " descended the steps of prostitution until she lived with a groom of the name of Smith." The name Smith would seem to have been borrowed from a neighbour after Harriet's death. Shelley may have deduced his story from a garbled and second-hand account of the inquest, but Harriet was accompanied to the door of her last lodgings by one who had known her for five years as Harriet Shelley, and she lived there respectably alone until within a month of the time her body was found. There is not even any medical testimony to support the newspaper statement that Harriet was in " an advanced state of pregnancy," which seems to have been founded only on the landlady's impression that she seemed " in a family way " — an impression made plausible later perhaps by the appearance of a body that had been long under water.

So FAR had Harriet receded from Shelley's affections that she was merely " this poor creature " entitled to sympathy in the end, as in the beginning, because she was supposed to be the victim of oppression. " Every one does *me* full justice " sounds a little like the lady in *Hamlet* who protested too much. The threat against the Westbrooks, which he absolutely failed to make good in the subsequent proceedings, is pure melodrama — all that he ever charged in court against Eliza was that by promoting the marriage she became responsible for its consequences. All together it is scarcely the generous, high-souled letter that Shelley was accustomed to write. Perhaps it was impossible, under the circumstances, to do Harriet justice without condemning himself — and without his sense of rectitude he was nothing. How vital it was in this case may be seen from the passion with which he later rose to its defence against Southey: "I take God to witness, if such a Being is now regarding both you and me, and I pledge myself if we meet, as perhaps you expect, before Him after death, to repeat the same in His presence — that you accuse me wrongfully. I am innocent of ill, either done or intended; the consequences you allude to flowed in no respect from me. If you were my friend I could tell you a history that would make you open your eyes; but I shall certainly never make the public my familiar confidant." [47] Yet Shelley never told his friends anything to convince them of Harriet's guilt, nor did he show until several weeks afterwards that he was deeply disturbed by her tragic end. He was never more calm and self-possessed, Peacock observed, than in the early days of January.

Soon, however, Peacock observed that Harriet's fate caused Shelley "deep agony of mind," which he usually managed to conceal. One evening in 1817, as the two were walking and talking in Bisham Wood, Shelley fell into a gloomy reverie from which Peacock's sallies were powerless to rouse him. "There is one thing," Shelley remarked gloomily, "to which I have made up my mind. I will take a great glass of ale every night." "A very good resolution," said Peacock laughingly, "as the result of a melancholy musing." "Yes," said Shelley, "but you do not know why I take it. I shall do it to deaden my feelings, for I see that those who drink ale have none." The next day he reverted to this remark and explained its apparent oddity. "I will tell you what I would not tell anyone else. I was thinking of Harriet." [48]

Mary met the crisis with an immediate affection and loyalty

that inspire admiration. "Ah, my best love, to you do I owe every joy, every perfection that I may enjoy or boast of. Love me, sweet, for ever. I hardly know what I mean, I am so agitated." She sympathized in his indignation against the Westbrooks, and, most whole-heartedly, in his desire to obtain immediate possession of his children and those of a woman she had come to despise. "How very happy I shall be to possess those darling treasures that are yours. . . . Now I long more than ever that our house shall be quickly ready for the reception of those dear Children, whom I love so tenderly. Then there will be a sweet Brother and Sister for my William, who will lose his pre-eminence as eldest and be helped third at table, as Claire is continually reminding him. . . . Come back to reassure me, my Shelley, and bring with you your darling Ianthe and Charles." [49]

Shelley called twice on Eliza on December 17, but was unable to see her. He then sent his old friend Mrs. Boinville to see her, but without result. On the next day he wrote to her. From the fact that his letter does not mention Charles but seems to be wholly concerned with Ianthe one wonders if Eliza had not already informed him of Harriet's last wish that Shelley should have only Charles and of her own determination to carry it out. Shelley had already denounced Eliza to Mary as Harriet's murderess, and he repeated the charge a month later to Byron. Yet he now assured Eliza that he bore her no malice and that he gave no faith to the imputations cast on her conduct and that of her father. Such an astounding statement certainly lends support to the opinion of Shelley expressed by Godwin and Southey; but, at the risk of seeming to quibble, it must also be remarked that it may be only another example of two other well-marked characteristics — his belief at the moment, as Mary said, that everything he did was right, and his perfectly amazing capacity to believe what he wished.

Shelley told Eliza politely and firmly that he could never consent to leave Ianthe with her: "I cannot expect that your feelings toward the lady whose union with me you may excusably regard as the cause of your sister's ruin should permit you to mention her with the honour with which Ianthe must

487

be accustomed to regard the wife of her father's heart. To deal frankly with you, I cannot believe that you will refrain from inculcating prepossessions on her infant mind the most adverse to my views. I do not think the worse of you for this. . . . Nothing can shake my resolution."[50] He assured Eliza that it would be better to surrender the children at once, without useless delay. His friend Leigh Hunt would receive them for him and would be glad to attend her at any time she might appoint. If Eliza answered this letter there is no record of it. Shelley repeated his demands, but Eliza held fast to the children. They were in fact in the country, in the care of the Reverend Mr. John Kendall, of Warwick, who was later proposed by the Westbrooks as their permanent guardian.[51]

One of Shelley's first thoughts on hearing of Harriet's death was that the way was now open to legitimate his connection with Mary by marriage. He mentioned it in his first letter to Mary from London, and Mary in her reply stipulated only that it should take place in London. Sir Lumley Skeffington,[52] who was regarded as somewhat of an authority on matters of propriety, was consulted as to whether the marriage should take place at once. Peacock was also consulted. Both agreed that it should. Shelley returned to Bath and brought Mary up to London, where they spent some days with the Hunts. On December 28 Shelley and Godwin visited the office of the Vicar General and obtained a marriage licence. On the morning of the 29th, with Mr. and Mrs. Godwin as witnesses, a quiet marriage was performed at St. Mildred's Church, Bread Street. In writing to Claire that evening Shelley gave an account of the ceremony, " so magical in its effects," which Claire would find the " more provoking " because " unnecessary." " However," he added, " they will now be satisfied and quiet." Godwin, he wrote, was already treating him with almost distinguished courtesy, which he could not resist; but he could hardly endure Mrs. Godwin, or the unhappy associations of Skinner Street. No one at Skinner Street seemed as yet to have any suspicion of Claire's secret.[53]

From Godwin's journal and letters may be gleaned an interesting picture of how a philosopher who had attacked marriage regarded the marriage of a daughter who had offended him by acting on his principles. In the journal the marriage is disguised as a call: " Call at Mildred with P. B. S., M. W. G., and M. J." There is an abbreviated Latin reference to an earlier volume, presumably kept locked in his desk, in which a fuller entry is inserted.[54] To William Baxter he wrote: "Mrs. Shelley died in November last and on the 30th December Shelley led my daughter to the altar. I shall always look with poignant regret upon preceding events, but you can scarcely know what a relief that has brought to mine and Mrs. Godwin's mind. Mary has now (most unexpectedly) acquired a station and character in society. Shelley is not without faults, but he is not also without many good and even noble qualities, and if he had come into my family as a bachelor I should unquestionably have regarded his choice of my daughter as a subject of congratulation." [55] To his brother he was even more smugly uncommunicative: " I went to church with this tall girl some little time ago to be married. Her husband is the eldest son of Sir Timothy Shelley, of Field Place, in the county of Sussex, Baronet. So that, according to the vulgar ideas of the world, she is well married. . . . You will wonder, I daresay, how a girl without a penny of fortune should meet with so good a match. But such are the ups and downs of this world." [56]

Two days later they returned to Bath, but on January 6 Shelley set out again for London. Far from surrendering his children, the Westbrooks had now taken the offensive. Having first settled two thousand pounds in four-per-cent annuities on the children in order to bring them within the protection of the Court of Chancery, John Westbrook on January 10 (as " next friend " of the infants) filed a bill in Chancery [57] praying the court to appoint as guardians John and Eliza Westbrook or some other proper persons, and restrain their father from taking custody of them. This bill recited the history of Shelley's connection with Harriet and Mary and was supported by documentary and printed evidence in the shape of a copy of *Queen Mab*, the " Letter to Lord Ellenborough," and nine of Shelley's letters — eight to Harriet since the beginning of his love for Mary, and the letter Shelley had only recently written to Eliza. In one of the two supporting affidavits filed by Eliza this letter was very shrewdly turned against Shelley by quoting his reference to Mary as the lady whose union with Shelley Eliza " might excusably regard as the cause of her sister's ruin."

Shelley arrived in London with an idea of obtaining possession of his children by habeas corpus proceedings. But this would have no bearing on the decision of the Court of Chancery; moreover, it would require several weeks' time, during which the Court of Chancery would already have rendered a decision. He was forced, therefore, to meet his enemies on their own ground, which was a very dangerous ground for him. After talking with Longdill he stated the case thus to Mary:

. . . Their process is the most insidiously malignant that can be conceived. They have filed a bill to say that I published Queen Mab, that I avow myself to be an atheist and a republican, with some other imputations of an infamous nature. This, by Chancery Law I must *deny* or *admit* upon oath and then it seems that it rests in the *mere* discretion of the Chancellor to decide whether those are fit grounds for refusing me my children. They cannot have them at any rate; *my* father or *my* nearest relations are the persons whom the Chancellor will intrust with them if they must be denied me. It is therefore sheer revenge. If I admit myself or if Chancery decides that I ought not to have the children because I am an infidel; then the W[estbrook]s will make that decision a basis for a *criminal information* or common libel attack.[58]

Shelley was given five days in which to prepare an answer. Everything, he wrote Mary, except the happiness that was dependent on her alone, hung on the issue of this trial. If he could make his answer sufficiently convincing, the Chancellor might decide not to hear the case. It would be sufficient, in his opinion, if he could establish the truth of a statement Godwin had just made to him, that he had evidence of Harriet's unfaithfulness four months before the elopement.[59]

Shelley never seems to have supposed that Eliza's determination to keep the children may have been at least partly due to her fondness for Ianthe, whom she had tended since her birth.

490

In a letter to Byron written the day before he filed his answer to the bill of complaint he gives a very clear Shelleyan version of the situation:

My late wife is dead. The circumstances which attended this event are of a nature of such awful and appalling horror, that I dare hardly advert to them in thought. The sister of whom you have heard me speak may be truly said (though not in law, yet in fact) to have murdered her for the sake of her father's money. Thus did an event which I believed quite indifferent to me, following in the train of a far severer anguish, communicate a shock to me which I know not how I have survived. The sister has now instituted a Chancery process against me, the intended effect of which is to deprive me of my unfortunate children, now more than ever dear to me; of my inheritance, and to throw me into prison, and expose me in the pillory, on the ground of my being a REVOLUTIONIST, and an *Atheist*. It seems whilst she lived in my house she possessed herself of such papers as go to establish these allegations. The opinion of Counsel is, that she will certainly succeed to a considerable extent, but that I may probably escape entire ruin, in the worldly sense of it. So I am here, dragged before the tribunals of tyranny and superstition, to answer with my children, my property, my liberty, and my fame, for having exposed their frauds, and scorned the insolence of their power. Yet I will not fail; though I have been given to understand that I could purchase victory by recantation. Indeed, I have too much pride in the selection of their victim.[60]

The plain truth seems to be that the Westbrooks cared nothing about Shelley's opinions except to use them as a means of retaining Harriet's children. Otherwise they would certainly have brought a criminal action such as both Whitton and Shelley's advisers thought bound to succeed. The situation was a purely domestic one. The Westbrooks, rather than church and state, were the complainants; Shelley's treatment of Harriet, rather than his assault upon recognized institutions, was the cause of their action. Except letters to herself and Harriet, Eliza did not introduce as evidence any papers that Shelley had not printed. But Shelley was thoroughly convinced, in spite of the facts, that this was simply a case of tyrannous society seeking to crucify a philanthropist for his philanthropy.

Shelley filed his answer to the bill of complaint on January 18, 1817. He flatly denied that he had deserted Harriet — " this defendant and his late wife agreed, in consequence of certain differences between them, to live separate and apart from each other." [61] He asserted that he had left the children in Harriet's care only on her solicitation and on account of their tender age, that he had contributed regularly to their support, that he now wished to educate them to their proper station in life, and that as their father he was entitled so to do. One day before this answer was filed Mr. William Whitton, writing to inform Sir Timothy Shelley of the proceedings, expressed himself as perfectly certain that the Chancellor would not allow Shelley the custody of his children or even communication with them, and expressed a fear that the Chancery complaint, if opposed, would be followed by a criminal action.[62]

Both sides had engaged distinguished counsel. Sir Samuel Romilly, who represented the Westbrooks, was probably the most distinguished lawyer of the age. A few years earlier Sir James Mackintosh had said of him that his moral character stood higher than that of any other well-known living Englishman. It is probable that Shelley had already heard bitter words about him, for he was the first lawyer consulted by Lady Byron's family at the time of the Byron separation. Shelley had Charles Wetherell, Basil Montagu, and a Mr. Bell. A year later Wetherell was to be better known as the defender of the radicals Thistlewood and Watson. Godwin's friend Basil Montagu was a really wise and learned lawyer, but a better consultant than pleader; Bell, less polished and learned than Basil Montagu, was possibly his superior as a practical pleader.

The judge who now held Shelley's fate in his hands has been vividly sketched by Hazlitt as a good-natured, able judge, proverbially careful, impartial and conscientious in all matters not affecting his personal or political interests, but a man who never deviated an instant from a calm, placid support of the most out-and-out Toryism. "Lord Eldon has one of the best-natured faces in the world; it is pleasant to meet him in the street, plodding along with an umbrella under his arm, without one trace of pride, of spleen, or discontent in his whole demeanour, void of offence, with almost rustic simplicity and honesty of appearance — a man that makes friends at first sight, and could hardly make enemies if he would; and whose only fault is that he cannot say *Nay* to power, or subject himself to an unkind word or look from a King or a Minister. . . ." " The Lord Chancellor's impartiality and conscientious exactness are proverbial; and is [*sic*] we believe, as inflexible as it is delicate in all cases that occur in the stated routine of legal practice. . . . He delights to balance a straw, to see a feather turn the scale or make it even again; and divides or subdivides a scruple to the smallest fraction. He unravels the web of argument and pieces it together again; folds it up and lays it aside, that he may examine it more at leisure. He hugs indecision to his breast, and takes home a modest doubt or a nice point to solace himself with it in protracted, luxurious dalliance. Delay seems, in his mind, to be of the very essence of justice." [63]

Shelley's case was heard on Friday, January 24, 1817. Sir Samuel Romilly argued that *Queen Mab* proved clearly that Shelley's opinions on religion rendered him unfit to be the guardian of his children. Basil Montagu answered that *Queen Mab* was a youthful work that had never been published and that a man might write many things he did not intend his children to see. He therefore prayed Lord Eldon to dismiss the complaint, with costs. Further arguments by the defence are indicated by Wetherell's brief, which was prepared by Longdill. It asserted that not twenty copies of *Queen Mab* had ever got abroad, that only a few copies of the " Letter to Lord Ellenborough " had been printed, that the author himself could not find a copy of it, that Shelley's youthful diatribes against marriage could not be taken seriously in the light of the fact that he had married twice before he was twenty-five, that there was no precedent for depriving a parent of his children on the grounds of religious opinions alone, that the worldly interests of the children would suffer by their being taken from a father of prospective rank and fortune and given to a former coffee-house keeper and an illiterate, vulgar woman whose matrimonial scheming had produced the present situation.[64]

Lord Eldon listened with his usual air of careful impartiality and pronounced that he should have to consider the case further. After studying the petition and affidavits he would announce his decision at a future date. Any further hearings would be in the Lord Chancellor's private room. This was in effect an initial victory for the Westbrooks. The Lord Chancellor had not dismissed their complaint. Shelley was still deprived of his children, and a definite possibility was established that a criminal action might be based upon the Chancery evidence as soon as the case was concluded.

To pursue the Chancery case to its conclusion is to run ahead of other events in Shelley's life that paralleled its later stages. Lord Eldon took slightly over two months to consider. Meanwhile further arguments were advanced. The complainants shifted their emphasis from Shelley's attacks on religion to his attacks on matrimony. Shelley was hard at work on a written Declaration setting forth his defence. In this he had the assistance of Godwin and probably of Hunt. Godwin, though unsparing in some of his marginal comments on Shelley's manuscript, thought the result a better example of Shelley's mental powers than *Laon and Cythna*.[65] Shelley's document was finished by February 2, when Mary, who had come up to London to be with Shelley, records that she made a fair copy of it. " If I have attacked religion," Shelley wrote, ". . . I am punishable, but not by the loss of my children; if I have imagined a system of social life inconsistent with the constitution of England, I am punishable, but not by the loss of my children." Since the argument on religious grounds had been abandoned, Shelley went on to observe that the point on which the Chancellor had to decide the case seemed to be " not whether I shall teach my children religious infidelity, not whether I shall teach them political heterodoxy, but whether I shall educate them in immodest and loose sentiments of sexual connection." On this issue he stated boldly that he considered marriage, as it existed in England, " a mischievous and tyrannical institution " and would continue publicly to state his reasons for so thinking. If this, however, disqualified him as a guardian, then no man in England could ever protest against prevailing opinions without the fear of having the courts converted into instruments of private vengeance against him. In practice he sought to conform to the institution which in theory he condemned. Estranged from his former wife by "incurable dissensions," it had been a great grief to him that he could not at once marry the woman to whom he felt himself genuinely united, but he had done this as soon as possible.[66]

Having considered all these matters, Lord Eldon gave his judgment on March 27. He was still cautiously unwilling to commit himself to a sweeping decision. It was clear to him only that the children should not be placed in the exclusive care of their father, but it was not clear that they should be given to the Westbrooks. They should be brought up under a proper plan for their maintenance and education, and both sides were authorized to submit plans and nominate guardians. The Lord Chancellor's judgment, he was careful to state, was based not upon Shelley's opinions either religious or moral, nor upon his entering into an irregular union with Mary Godwin, but upon the fact that in his case immoral opinions had led to conduct that the court was bound to consider immoral. Furthermore he was convinced by the evidence adduced that Shelley would certainly inculcate similar opinions and conduct in his children if given sole custody of them. Shelley was restrained from intermeddling with the children until further order of the court, and one of the Masters in Chancery, Mr. William Alexander, was directed to submit a proper plan for the children's education and maintenance. Lord Eldon's judgment, he remarked, was not final.[67] He also observed, rather ominously, that any attempt to publish an account of the case would be treated as contempt of court.[68] Perhaps he had read Leigh Hunt's guarded comment or suspected from his conversations with Shelley that the young man might print his Declaration. True to his character as a cautious and careful lawyer who never lost sight of his political interests, he protected himself against the charge of religious intolerance by basing his decision on the safest possible legal grounds, while at the same time making sure, by preventing publicity, that the large body of religious bigots among his supporters would still suppose that his decision established the precedent of depriving blasphemers of their children. An appeal to Parliament was too hopeless to be considered; even the bar of public opinion, had Shelley been permitted to appeal to it, would have sustained the Chancellor, so reasonably and courteously was his opinion expressed.

Lord Eldon's decision had denied Shelley sole guardianship of his children, but had suggested that fit guardians of Shelley's choice might be approved. Even this miserable consolation was almost denied Shelley by the prejudiced Master in Chancery to whom the arrangements were referred. He reviewed the whole evidence in the case [69] and reached the conclusion that Shelley's character was such that even his nominee for the guardianship should be rejected. Shelley's nominee for the guardianship was his solicitor, Mr. P. W. Longdill. Longdill submitted (June 21) a detailed plan for the care and upbringing of the children that must have been very bitter reading to Shelley, who was forced to recommend it. In selecting Charles's first school, one conducted by an orthodox Church of England clergyman would be preferred. Ianthe, along with a considerable list of orthodox virtues, was to be taught to disregard fashionable clothes, which were " an apparent abandonment of all feelings of feminine Delicacy and Decency," and was to be shielded from the reading of most novels, of all books that might shake her faith in the Church of England, and even of Pope and Shakespeare except in expurgated editions. Both children were to be accustomed to morning and evening prayers, grace before meals, and regular Sunday attendance at church. For their maintenance they were to have the £80 income from the four-per-cent bank annuities deeded them by Mr. Westbrook, and Shelley was to supply whatever additional sums were needed. The Westbrooks submitted a counter-proposal on July 1, proposing as guardian the Reverend John Kendall, of Warwick, and also proposing that Shelley should add £120 to the annual £80 already possessed by the children. Yielding only to Longdill's outraged protest that if this plan were adopted Mr. Westbrook should at least pay the additional £120, Mr. William Alexander disallowed Longdill's proposal and recommended that of the Westbrooks on August 1, 1817.

Naturally both Longdill and the Shelleys were indignant at this biased effort to misapply the Lord Chancellor's decision and prefer an inferior proposal. Longdill appealed to Lord Eldon and secured a decision on November 10 directing Mr. Alexander to reconsider the matter on the basis of further proposals. This time Shelley proposed Dr. Thomas Hume, a reputable doctor of medicine who was a neighbour and friend of Longdill's and who submitted Longdill's former plan as the one he would propose. The Westbrooks proposed the Reverend Mr. Jacob Cheesbrough, a clergyman of Ulcomb, Kent, after rejecting with some rudeness a lady suggested to them by Sir Timothy Shelley. This time Shelley's proposal was approved by Mr. Alexander and confirmed by Lord Eldon. It was further decreed that Shelley might see his children once a month or twelve times a year in the presence of one or both guardians, that the Westbrooks might see them once a month unattended, and that Sir Timothy Shelley and his family might see them without restriction. By now, however (Lord Eldon's confirmation was dated July 25, 1818), the proceedings had been drawn out over eighteen months, and the Shelleys had already left England never to return. Shelley never saw Ianthe again. Charles he never saw either before or afterwards.[70]

497

Chapter XVII

LONDON AND MARLOW:

CLEARING SKIES

NEW FRIENDS IN LONDON; MARLOW; VISITORS AND
AMUSEMENTS; REFORM; CHARITIES; VISITS TO
LONDON; MIDSUMMER AT MARLOW

SHELLEY remained in London, very busy with lawyers and con-
sultants, until after the Lord Chancellor's first decision, on January 24. Mary continued awhile at Bath, pursuing her steady
routine of reading and writing, but becoming eventually so
uneasy at the accounts she received of the legal proceedings
that on January 26 she went up to London to join her husband.

It is typical of Mary's circumspection as a diarist that she
made no mention in the journal of the birth of Claire's child,
on January 12. Until February 18 Claire remained at Bath under her assumed title of Mrs. Clairmont. The child, a healthy,
beautiful girl, was temporarily named Alba (" Dawn ") until
the wishes of Byron ("Albè") could be consulted.

While in town, Shelley and Mary stayed with the Hunts,
dining and sleeping occasionally in Skinner Street, as convenience dictated. Shelley was busy writing out his second Chancery statement (copied by Mary on February 2) and interviewing counsel and advisers. About this time a long letter arrived
from Charles Clairmont. Charles was still in the French Pyrenees and had just discovered an ardent desire to marry his
landlady's daughter. He demonstrated that his happiness could
be securely founded on a gift of about eighty pounds.

Typical entries from Mary's journal for the period are:

Tuesday, Feb. 4 — Hear Hunt's music; dine with Hunt, Mrs. Hunt, and Miss K[ent] [1] at Godwin's; sleep at Hunt's.

Wednesday, Feb. 5 — Read "Tales of My Landlord;" walk on the Heath. Messrs. Keats and Reynolds sup at Hampstead.

Saturday, Feb. 8 — Shelley and Hunt go to London to attend the Chancery. Read the "Arcadia;" dine and spend the evening at H. Smith's. The suit is again put off.

Sunday, Feb. 9 — Walk with Shelley and Hunt to Brougham's in the morning; after dinner, read the "Arcadia." Several of Hunt's acquaintances come in the evening. Music. After supper, a discussion until 3 in the morning with Hazlitt concerning Monarchy and Republicanism.

Tuesday, Feb. 18 — Walk out with Mr. and Mrs. Hunt. Clare and William arrive. Conversation and music in the evening.

Sunday, Feb. 23 — We remain at Hunt's some time longer, and then Shelley, William, Clare and I depart for Marlow. Shelley returns Monday [March 3] . . . I go up to town the following day . . . I return Thursday, and the following week [March 9–16] we enter our house. . . .

There is no hint in the journal for January and February of any agitation or excitement over Harriet or the Chancery proceedings. But Shelley's letters tell a different story. To Byron, as we have seen, he wrote as one who had already undergone terrific strain and was even then facing the pillory, fine, and imprisonment. To Mary, before her arrival, he wrote of his danger, but added: " Now my darling Pecksie, don't fancy I'm disquieted so as to be unwell." [2] He informed Claire, after Mary's arrival, that he expected eventually to suffer imprisonment and fine as the result of a criminal prosecution. For the next few months, however, he considered himself safe — so that she should not agitate herself over the matter.[3] These letters sound a little too much like the mingled hints of danger and

assurances of safety in his earlier letters about the journey to
Ireland to be entirely convincing, nor is it easy to accept at full
value Leigh Hunt's statement that Shelley was for a while " torn
to pieces " [4] by anxiety and excitement over the recent events.
Undoubtedly, in spite of the negative testimony of the journal
and the positive statement of Peacock, Shelley was deeply
stirred, but he was also dramatizing himself in his letters. In
his real anxieties, which were deep enough, he had the consolation of having both Mary and Leigh Hunt at his side as
sympathetic helpers.

Leigh Hunt's precocious young son, Thornton, not only noticed and described Shelley's agitation over the Chancery trial,
but in almost the same breath described one of Shelley's physical seizures whose occurrences are generally to be noted at
such times. " The emotions that he underwent were but too
manifest in the unconcealed anxiety and the eager recital of
newly awakened hopes, with intervals of the deepest depression.
He suffered also from physical causes, which I then only in
part understood." After tracing the physical seizures to the " attack " at Tanyrallt he continues: " I can remember one day at
Hampstead: it was soon after breakfast, and Shelley sat reading,
when he suddenly threw up his book and hands, and fell back,
the chair sliding sharply from under him, and he poured forth
shrieks, loud and continuous, stamping his feet madly on the
ground. My father rushed to him, and, while the women looked
out for the usual remedies of cold water and hand-rubbing,
applied a strong pressure to his side, kneading it with his hands;
and the patient seemed gradually to be relieved by that process.
This happened about the time when he was most anxious for
the result of the trial which was to deprive him of his children." [5]

There was ample time between Chancery engagements to
become better acquainted with the circles that revolved around
Leigh Hunt and Godwin. In the month following Mary's arrival in town on January 26, her journal mentions a call on
Basil Montagu and a dinner with him at Godwin's, two calls
on Brougham, an evening with Keats, another with Keats and
Reynolds, and another with John and George Keats at Hunt's,
an evening call on Horace Smith, an evening with Charles and

WILLIAM HAZLITT

Engraved by Marr from a drawing by Bewick

Mary Lamb at Godwin's, and dinner with Basil Montagu and Mr. and Mrs. William Hazlitt at Godwin's.[6] Mary went several times to plays or operas, usually while Shelley was elsewhere. At Godwin's the talk was apt to be serious, punctuated occasionally by a pun from Lamb or by Godwin's abrupt, flat bark of a laugh or his rather snarling, cutting manner of insisting upon logic and accuracy.[7] At Leigh Hunt's there were often music — commonly Hunt's " sweet, small baritone "[8] in an Irish or Italian song — frequent puns and witticisms, an open forum for talk of all sorts. Whether strolling on the heath or holding forth informally after breakfast in his flowered dressing-gown, Hunt was a good raconteur and a sympathetic, discerning listener.

After the removal to Marlow, Shelley made frequent visits to town, where he usually stayed with the Hunts and associated with members of the Hunt circle. One member of the group who is known to have been a friend of Shelley's was Walter Coulson, then editor of the *Globe* newspaper, whose extensive miscellaneous information filled the others with awe-stricken wonder.[9] Another friend who·happens not to be mentioned in Shelley's letters at the time was Vincent Novello, the musician, later a friend of Mendelssohn's. Novello's home, with its admirable hostess, its music, and its attractive bevy of children, was the scene of more than one dinner where Hunt, Keats, Shelley, Charles Cowden Clarke, and the Lambs dined by mutual agreement on bread and cheese, celery, and Lamb's "Lutheran beer."[10] Mary Novello, later Mrs. Charles Cowden Clarke, at that time still in the nursery play-room, remembered standing on a chair in order to look out of the play-room window and catch a glimpse of the young poet of whom she had heard her parents talk.[11]

Shelley had known Southey, Godwin, Curran, and Byron before, and he had previously been a member of the Newton-Boinville circle; but never before in his rather lonely life had he been a member of a circle composed of people of genius, taste, or knowledge. His pleasure in their company was evident; the benefit to his own character and powers, though not demonstrable, must have been considerable.

501

In Leigh Hunt and Horace Smith, Shelley found two of his firmest and most valuable friends. To the end of his life Hunt thought Shelley the finest character he had ever met — so fine, in fact, that he sometimes half-doubted if Shelley were mortal in the same sense as other people.¹² The only possible fault he would admit in Shelley was "his occasionally condescending, though for the kindest purposes, to use a little double-dealing."¹³ Hunt began, in the early days of their friendship, by laughing at Shelley's naïve supposition that the editor wrote every word that appeared in the *Examiner;* soon, although older and more experienced, he was going to Shelley for advice in a spirit of humility that to Shelley seemed almost ridiculous.¹⁴ Shelley's opinion of Hunt was expressed for a small circle in his "Letter to Maria Gisborne" (1820) and for the world at large in his dedicatory letter published with *The Cenci.* To Maria Gisborne he characterized Hunt as "one of those happy souls which are the salt of the earth." To Hunt he wrote, in his dedicatory letter: "One more gentle, honourable, innocent and brave; one of more exalted toleration for all who do and think evil, and yet himself more free from evil; one who knows better how to receive, and how to confer a benefit, though he must ever confer far more than he can receive; one of simpler, and, in the highest sense of the word, of purer life and manners I never knew." Except for Hogg during a brief year of youth, Leigh Hunt was the best and fittest friend that Shelley ever knew.

Of Horace Smith, Shelley wrote to Maria Gisborne that his character combined enough "wit and sense, Virtue and human knowledge" to "Make this dull world a business of delight." "I know not what Horace Smith must take me for sometimes," Shelley once exclaimed to Hunt. "I am afraid he must think me a strange fellow: but is it not odd, that the only generous person I ever knew, who had money to be generous with, should be a stockbroker! And he writes poetry too; he writes poetry and pastoral dramas, and yet knows how to make money, and does make it, and is still generous!"¹⁵ Smith did not agree with Shelley on all points, and at times he did think Shelley an odd fellow, but odd mainly in the sense that his philanthropy was

" so utterly self-denying and unworldly " as to make him seem
a sort of *lusus naturæ* to " such a nation of Mammonites as the
English."

Horace Smith also felt, as he recalled one long intimate conversation with Shelley at Marlow, a mingled reverence and admiration for something unearthly in him.[16] Without a doubt,
Shelley would have made any sacrifice for either Hunt or Smith,
nor did he doubt their willingness to do the same for him. Shelley was Hunt's banker on all possible occasions after 1816, and
Horace Smith, to a less extent, acted in the same capacity for
Shelley.[17]

It will undoubtedly assist in the understanding of a very difficult character if we pause here to consider further what Shelley and his suddenly widened circle of acquaintances thought
of each other in 1817. Few people have ever had the greatness
to inspire such opinions as those expressed of Shelley by Leigh
Hunt and Horace Smith, even though cold criticism may subject
them to discount as posthumous idealizations. No such discount
could do more than reduce them to what would still remain a
remarkably impressive testimony. Not all of the Hunt and Godwin circles, however, so regarded Shelley. The Novellos, as
their daughter afterwards recalled, spoke of him with admiration, as did both the Clarkes in retrospect. But Godwin, for
all of his new courtesy, regarded his son-in-law as a person far
from perfect. He was quite aware, he said, that Shelley's temper
was " occasionally fiery, resentful, and indignant," and he had
but lately picked up some story apparently to Shelley's discredit.[18] After three years' further knowledge of Shelley he still
accused him of immorality and deceit and of being a lover of
falsehood for its own sake.[19] Lamb knew Shelley only slightly
and did not desire to know him better. Shelley thought well of
Lamb and was disappointed that " the calumny of an enemy "
had caused Lamb to avoid him.[20] Hazlitt, though he would
argue with Shelley against Hunt and Coulson on the subject
of a monarchy versus a republic, was very far from any real
sympathy with him. He regarded Shelley's enthusiasm as too
extreme to be of practical service to the radical cause. To him
Shelley had " a fire in his eye, a fever in his blood, a maggot in

his brain, a hectic flutter in his speech, which mark out the philosophic fanatic." [21] Hunt, who could not understand such feelings toward a brother-in-arms, thought Shelley might have offended the sensitive, resentful Hazlitt by " cutting him up " in conversation at Godwin's table.[22]

Henry Crabb Robinson, another guest of Godwin's, who seems to have met Shelley but once, was also rather unfavourably impressed, possibly because Shelley spoke with great bitterness of Southey as a renegade and made insinuations against Wordsworth. Much of his talk seemed to Robinson " vehement and arrogant and intolerant." [23]

Keats might well have been expected to take a great liking to Shelley, who was probably as eager to be of service to him in 1817 as in 1820. Tom Medwin quoted Shelley as saying that *Endymion* and *The Revolt of Islam* (earlier known as *Laon and Cythna*) were both written as the result of an agreement between the two young poets each to write a long poem within six months.[24] That Keats rather avoided Shelley seemed to Leigh Hunt to be due largely to his excessive consciousness of their different social stations and to the great difference in their poetic styles and interests.[25] His intellectual interests were far less extensive and subtle than Shelley's, some of which he probably regarded without sympathy. Both Shelley and Hunt seemed to him at times to be willing to see his abilities undervalued. It is a dangerous matter to advise an aspiring young poet not to publish, as Shelley advised Keats in 1817 — nor is it without significance that Keats reminded Shelley of this advice in 1820,[26] even though Shelley had helped him print his volume after advising against it.[27] Moreover, Keats was just becoming conscious that Hunt's influence upon his poetry was by no means wholly a good one, and he may have feared a similar effect from too much intimacy with Shelley. When Shelley invited him to Marlow he declined, explaining to Benjamin Bailey that he wished to keep his " own unfettered scope." [28] This looks as if Keats distrusted his own powers in close contact with Shelley very much as Shelley did in contact with Byron at Geneva. There was ample ground for such a feeling in a self-conscious, independent young poet who may have noticed that some of his lines already seemed to be tinged with echoes from *Queen Mab* and *Alastor.*[29]

By the 18th of March the house at Great Marlow [30] had been put in condition and the Shelleys were living in it.[31] Albion House, as it was called, was a fairly large, rambling, two-storey structure with a gabled roof and dormer windows, standing on West Street at some distance back from the Thames, on the edge of open country. One of its rooms, large enough for a ball-room, Shelley fitted up as a study, gracing it with life-size casts of Venus and Apollo. In the rear was a garden with a lawn, enclosed by high hedges. Here the view was partly obscured by a mound, behind which was a kitchen garden and a flower garden. Firs, cypresses, and apple trees made rather more shade than was desirable. Shelley had taken the house on a twenty-one-year lease before Harriet's suicide, hoping to settle there for many years, but it soon became evident that it was both too dark and too damp for comfort.[32]

To the Swiss cats, presumably transported from Bath, were added a dog which turned out to be too vicious to keep. Shelley wrote at once to London for Mawe's *Gardening Calendar.* A manservant and a cook were employed, in addition to Elise, the Swiss nurse. Fanny Imlay would have been relieved, had she been alive, to know that Mary took her advice and avoided some of the dangers of local gossip by engaging London servants, through Mrs. Hunt.[33] Later (April 29), with the aid of Vincent Novello's expert advice, a piano was selected in London and sent down for Claire's benefit.[34] Claire, incidentally, had resumed her maiden name and had no ostensible connection with her infant, who was given out to be the child of a friend, sent down from London for its health.

The Shelleys were hardly settled in their new home before they began inviting guests. Godwin was the first. In a letter beginning with a graceful apology for having vexed Godwin by failing to keep an engagement, Shelley adds: "We are immersed in all kinds of confusion here. Mary said you meant to come hither soon enough to see the leaves come out. Which leaves did you mean, for the wild-briar buds are already un-folded?"[35] Godwin arrived on April 2,[36] and for four days shared the pleasures of excursions by land or water to Maiden-head, Medmenham Abbey, and Bisham Wood.

On the evening of Godwin's departure the Hunts arrived with their four children and were added to an unidentified guest who had already been at Albion House a week.[37] Mrs. Hunt was ill; the weather was cold and disagreeable; but the society was good. "You shall never be serious when you wish to be merry," Mary promised Hunt before this visit, "and [shall] have as many nuts to crack as there are words in the Petitions to Parlia-ment for Reform." She had already assured him of complete indulgence in the matter of "sophas, hair brushes and hair brushers."[38] The Hunts remained for about a month, during a part of which, at least, Mrs. Hunt's sister, Elizabeth Kent, was also at Albion House — a considerable help with the children, since Mrs. Hunt was ill much of the time. Before the Hunts had left, Byron was given a pressing invitation, should he re-turn to England,[39] and Hogg was urged by Shelley to hasten his promised visit to Peacock.

"Ought we not to be happy?" Mary demanded on first com-ing to Great Marlow; "and so indeed we are, in spite of the Lord Chancellor and the Suspension Act."[40] Shelley's health, she added, had been very good. The presence of visitors did not hinder Mary's working steadily on the correction and copy-ing of *Frankenstein*, nor Shelley in his reading. Shelley was reading mainly Latin and Greek authors, the history of the French Revolution, and Spenser, from whom he often read aloud in the evening. Mary, in addition to her work on *Frank-enstein*, was keeping up her Latin studies and was reading ap-parently more books than Shelley. Only once before June (May 9) is Shelley mentioned as writing, but he had in fact been at work on *Laon and Cythna* since the latter part of April.

Occasionally Mary, like Shelley, gave some slight indication that the ordeal through which she had come had left its mark upon her. Remarkably self-controlled as she was, she was then only a girl of twenty. Instead of the calm classic beauty and repose which so excited the admiration of Mary Cowden Clarke

SHELLEY'S HOUSE AT GREAT MARLOW

Etching by A. Evershed, 1876, for the H. B. Forman edition of Shelley's Works. By permission of

Mr. M. B. Forman

a few years later, she seemed to the observant little Thornton
Hunt in 1817 to be a rather harassed, sharp-tongued, carelessly
dressed young woman who was not in the best of health. Since
Harriet's death she expressed herself to Shelley and the Hunts
with increased scorn of Peacock and with a reversion to her
original scorn of Hogg. In her journal she pointedly ignored
them both, as far as possible. What these two gentlemen could
have said about Mary was left unsaid, but one of Peacock's
reasons for declining to write an extended biography of Shelley was his dislike of Mary, after half a century. In old age he
confided to Robert Buchanan that he once refused to enter
Shelley's house at Marlow while Mary was at home.[41]

With constant rowing, sailing, and walking trips with various
friends, life at Great Marlow was much more social than it had
been at Bishopsgate. The new grand piano — still unpaid for
— was often called into service to duplicate the musical evenings
the Shelleys had enjoyed when visiting the Hunts. Hunt had
been enjoined by Mary to learn the *Ranz des Vaches* and the
Marseillaise in French and was assured that the piano would be
in tune for him. Claire's voice, according to her instructor, was
like a string of pearls.[42]

What all this meant to the poet is indicated by no less than
four unfinished poems,[43] all begun at Marlow under the influence of music. One begins:

> The silver key of the fountain of tears,
>   Where the spirit drinks till the brain is wild . . .

another:

> My spirit like a charmed bark doth swim
>   Upon the liquid waves of thy sweet singing.

The finest of these, " To Constantia Singing," which he all but
finished, shows how Claire's voice could cause Shelley to idealize
a girl with whose weaknesses he had been painfully familiar
for several years:

> In thine eyes a power like light doth lie . . .
> I have no life, Constantia, now, but in thee. . . .

"To Constantia Singing" and "To Constantia" contain a note of reproach that may well be Shelley's grief over Claire's desertion to Byron in 1816:

> Alas that the torn heart can bleed but not forget

and

> Such is my heart — roses are fair,
>   And that at best a withered blossom;
> But thy false care did idly wear
>   Its withered leaves in a faithless bosom!
> And fed with love, like air and dew,
>   Its growth —

But Shelley's sociability was limited to kindred spirits. For casual, time-killing mere acquaintances he felt a very distinct aversion. Before going to Marlow he notified the neighbours through his upholsterer that his family "would associate with no one in the village, would never go to church, and would [do] as they chose in defiance of public opinion." [44] "I am not wretch enough," he told Peacock, "to tolerate an acquaintance." [45] The poor knew him through his charities, and two or three local residents knew him through common interests. Among these were the brothers Tyler, who happened to be cultivated men, though linen-drapers' assistants, a Mr. Pilcher, and a Mr. Brooks, admirer of Robert Owen. [46] With Mr. Madocks, his local man of business, Shelley used to engage in long conversations on all manner of Shelleyan subjects.

Dr. Furnivall, whose son later founded the Shelley Society, lived not far away at Egham and continued to attend Shelley's family as in the Bishopsgate days. He recalled many a "dish of tea" with Shelley, accompanied by typical Shelleyan conversation. Once he arrived at Albion House just as Shelley, Peacock, and Hunt were concluding an animated conversation on suicide. It was a queer subject, if one remembers Harriet. Dr. Furnivall heard them all subscribe to Peacock's view that suicide was desirable, and though his professional business at the moment was concerned with the expected entrance of another life into the world, he did not scruple to offer the means of exit to anyone present who really desired them. All three survived this opportunity for extinction.[47]

Usually the villagers saw Shelley only at a distance, going or coming from his island retreat near Medmenham Abbey, dashing along through the streets or groves, regardless of all he met, sailing his paper boats on the river, or returning alone late at night from Bisham Wood. At such times there was not wanting an occasional touch of his earlier love for the fantastic; his head might be crowned with wild-flowers, or he might assert that he had been engaged in raising the devil, and repeat the incantation he had used.[48] Some of these occasions were probably enhanced by Shelley's love of repeating — "with wild energy," as Mary noted — "The Ancient Mariner" or Southey's "Old Woman of Berkeley."[49]

One local resident whose company Shelley had learned to dread while living at Bishopsgate happened to possess a name very much like that of a music master whom Peacock, at Shelley's request, engaged for Claire. When the musician called to complete the engagement, Shelley did not yet know his name and understood the servant to be announcing the arrival of his special abhorrence. Shelley sprang up from his chair in quick alarm. "I would just as soon see the devil!" he exclaimed, and straightway jumped through the window and vanished rapidly over the garden fence. Following a back path he arrived at Peacock's still much excited, and rushed in upon the surprised novelist with the exclamation: "Barricade the doors; give orders that you are not at home. Here is —— in the town."[50]

The humour of such incidents was not lost upon Shelley himself. When the purely ludicrous presented itself uncontaminated by a suggestion of social or moral wrong, he laughed heartily, as Peacock says he often laughed in recalling his flight from the bore. "He was playful," Mrs. Shelley observed, "and indulged in the wild spirit that mocked itself and others — not in bitterness, but in sport."[51] Once, within a few months of the same time as the former incident, Leigh Hunt and Shelley were riding to London together on the Hampstead stage when Shelley, moved by some impulsive dislike of an old lady who was a fellow passenger, yielded to one of his sudden impulses to

astonish. Being at that time rather fond of quoting the passage
in Shakespeare's *King Richard II* in which the King indulges
his misery, he startled the old lady into a state of alarm
by suddenly breaking forth most earnestly: " Hunt!

> For God's sake, let us sit upon the ground
> And tell sad stories of the death of kings.[52]

In his play with children Shelley could give free vent to his
boyish penchant for semi-frightful humour. His own son, whose
nickname had now graduated from Willmouse into Willy and
Will-man, was just cutting his teeth and learning to walk, and
was as yet too young for such entertainment. So also was Claire's
child, the delicately beautiful, blue-eyed, black-haired little
Alba. Hunt's four children were older, Thornton, the eldest,
being seven in 1817 and John five. These children, whether at
Hampstead or Albion House, treated Shelley as a member of
their own family. Thornton Hunt, looking backward over forty-
six years,[53] remembered obeying Shelley as he would his own
father, listening to Shelley's wildly imaginative tales very much
as the Newton children had done three years earlier, romping
with him almost as a fellow child, and taking long, talkative
tramps with him which sometimes ended in his being carried
home by his older companion. Once as they sailed paper boats
together on the pond on Hampstead Heath Shelley remarked
playfully that he should like to sail in one of these boats and be
shipwrecked; it would be of all possible deaths the one most
to be preferred. Sometimes, like an older playmate, Shelley
teased Thornton into exasperation. But what Thornton remembered most vividly, and what his father also recalled,[54] was
Shelley's pleasure in assuming a frightful, threatening aspect
which the Hunt children found deliciously dangerous. This was
known as "doing the horn," and consisted in screwing up his long
hair into a semblance of a horn, assuming a ferocious facial
expression, and advancing "with rampant paws and frightful gestures." The children were horribly impressed. They
did not suspect that the mature, metaphysical Shelley was find-

ing a psychological interest in the childish reaction to " grim impressions " in addition to the purely naïve pleasure he found in conveying them.⁵⁵

"What do you say to Mr. Shelley, Thornton? " asked Leigh Hunt, as he paused in writing a letter to Shelley, some months later.

" ' My love, and I shall be glad if he's happy.'

" ' What shall I say for you, John? '

" ' Why, why, *his* love; no, don't say *his* love: — say my love, and I shall be glad if he has got a great stone in his hand.' (Here he, and Thornton, and Mary burst into a loud fit of laughter.)

" ' What shall I say for you, Mary? '

" ' Say ' (hardly able to speak for laughter) ' that I shall be glad if he's love.' " ⁵⁶

Surely this smacks of camaraderie. It chimes truly with the recollection of Charles Cowden Clarke, who for sixty years remembered Shelley as " scampering and bounding over the gorse-bushes on Hampstead Heath late one night, — now close upon us, and now shouting from the height like a wild school-boy." ⁵⁷

At Marlow, Shelley had another small friend who remembered him vividly in later years. One day in early summer a little girl named Polly Rose, who lived in the neighbourhood, was somewhat startled to see a strange-looking, bright-eyed, bareheaded young gentleman emerge from the woods, with wreaths of wild clematis wound about him. He glanced at her observingly and hastened on, but in a short while returned with a young lady. They questioned her and then went to her mother with a request that they be allowed to take her into their home and educate her. Thus Shelley partly achieved for a few months his long-standing, persistent desire to adopt and educate a young girl. From that time Polly spent a part of almost every day at Albion House, took many of her meals there, and often slept there. The education appears to have consisted mainly in bed-time discussions between Polly and Mary of the questions previously discussed between Mary and Shelley. With Polly, as with the Hunt children, Shelley easily reverted to his own childhood. Often he would place Polly on a table and tilt it up until she slid to the bottom. Or he would place Polly and Claire (another child for the moment) on a table and run it rapidly from one end of the room to the other.[58]

Thornton Hunt remembered quite well during the crisis of the Chancery proceedings Shelley's agony of apprehension lest he be deprived of his children. After the blow had fallen Shelley believed that the Lord Chancellor might deprive him of little William also.[59] The knowledge that he was soon to be father of another child [60] probably heightened rather than lessened his sense of loss and injustice. He applied for permission for Harriet's children to visit Longdill for a fortnight, so that he might see them, and when the Westbrooks' attorney put him off and he was kept ignorant of the children's present location he appealed directly to the Chancellor, apparently without result.[61] Before this appeal, however, Shelley had written a poem, " To William Shelley," inviting his infant son to flee with him:

> . . . we must not stay
> Or the slaves of the law may rend thee away.
>
> They have taken thy brother and sister dear,
>   They have made them unfit for thee;
> They have withered the smile and dried the tear,
>   Which should have been sacred to me.
> To a blighting faith and a cause of crime
>   They have bound them slaves in youthly prime,
> And they will curse my name and thee,
> Because we fearless are and free.

At about the same time he wrote sixteen stanzas of strong, bitter invective, " To the Lord Chancellor," detailing the various curses under which he must lie, concluding:

> By all the hate which checks a father's love,
>   By all the scorn which kills a father's care,
> By those most impious hands that dared remove
>   Nature's high bounds — by thee — and by despair!
>
> Yes, the despair which bids a father groan,
>   And cry, " My children are no longer mine;

The blood within those veins may be mine own,
    But, Tyrant, their polluted souls are thine."

I curse thee, though I hate thee not; O slave!
    If thou couldst quench the earth-consuming hell
Of which thou art a dæmon, on thy grave
    This curse should prove a blessing. Fare thee well!

AT BISHOPSGATE in the previous year Shelley had reached the conclusion that the reformation of humanity was too long and difficult a matter to be pushed to an immediate conclusion by one ardent young reformer. "I am undeceived," he had confessed to Hunt in December 1816, "in the belief that I have powers deeply to interest or substantially to improve, mankind." Now, in 1817, "his life was spent more in thought than action — he had lost the eager spirit which believed it could achieve what it projected for the benefit of mankind." [62] Henceforth for the rest of his life Shelley was still an ardent crusader, but his efforts were directed almost entirely to preparing men's minds so that they would be ready when "that sure slow Angel" "watching the beck of Mutability" summoned them to a new order.[63]

This meant only that experience had taught him the wisdom of changing his tactics. His interests were unchanged. Writing from Switzerland he had demanded and received from Fanny Imlay long accounts of the state of popular unrest in England. Returning, he had eagerly followed the *Examiner's* gallant weekly assaults upon injustice and maladministration.

As the evils of unemployment, high taxes, high prices, and government repression had mounted steadily throughout the year 1816, as foreign markets had languished and incendiary fires, mendicancy, local riots and hunger marches of colliers and iron-workers increased, Hampden Clubs and clubs of Spencean Philanthropists had sprung up all over England and Scotland. The former, led by the moderate Major Cartright and the veteran champion of Parliamentary reform, Sir Francis Burdett, were quite reasonable champions of governmental reform; the latter, more visionary, championed community of land and the abolition of machinery. Both societies were soon sown with government spies and *agents provocateurs.* A secret committee of the House of Commons reported in 1817 that "nothing short of a revolution" was the real object of the Hampden Clubs. The mob spirit was very much alive all over England.

William Cobbett, suddenly reducing the price of Cobbett's *Political Register* in November 1816 from one shilling halfpenny to twopence, had become overnight one of the most powerful leaders of popular opinion. Thus he was instantly converted, by an alchemy best known to reactionary minds, into a "firebrand" and "incendiary." On December 2, 1816 a mass-meeting at Spa-fields had been exhorted to proceed at once to take what was wanted, and had proceeded to a considerable orgy of looting. This was the occasion for the famous trial of Watson and others for treason, a trial in which Shelley's Chancery counsel, Wetherell, ably secured an acquittal. While the House of Lords was being told by a secret committee that a traitorous conspiracy existed for overthrowing the government by general insurrection, the Corporation of London had petitioned the King to remove a number of specified grievances and urged Parliamentary reform. In this state of alarm the right of habeas corpus was suspended in 1817. Cobbett and other radicals who had been inaccessible to prosecution as long as they avoided libel, blasphemy, and incitement to violence, took flight to America; Leigh Hunt remained, kept up the fight, and became increasingly a target for Tory abuse. "I like the freedom of the press and quill," Byron jeered from Italy; "I like the Habeas Corpus (when we've got it)." [64]

Shelley watched all this with close interest, but without the feverish thirst for action with which he might have viewed it two or three years earlier. "The whole fabric of society presents a most threatening aspect," he wrote to Byron on November 20, 1816. "What is most ominous of an approaching change is the strength which the popular party have suddenly acquired, and the importance which the violence of demagogues has assumed. But the people appear calm, and steady even under situations of great excitement; and reform may come without revolution."

This is the language of a moderate reformer rather than of a political radical. Mary spoke in the same tone ten months later: "Have you seen Cobbett's 23rd number, to the Borough-mongers? Why, he appears to be making out a list for a pro-scription. I actually shudder to read it. A revolution in this country would not be *bloodless* if that man has any power in it." [65]

Before Shelley left London to take up his residence in Great Marlow, he had finished a thirteen-page pamphlet entitled *A Proposal for Putting Reform to the Vote throughout the Kingdom*. It was the first work of Shelley's to be published by Charles and James Ollier, two enterprising young liberal publishers whom Shelley had met in Hunt's circle. The pamphlet appeared within a day or two of either March 2 or March 20, as by "The Hermit of Marlow." [66] It passed entirely unnoticed except that Hunt commented on it briefly in the *Examiner* of March 2 and commended it in an editorial on the 29th. Southey listed it without comment among the titles at the head of his *Quarterly Review* article (January 1817) on the present disaffections, and the *Morning Chronicle* listed it on March 20. This must have been rather disappointing to Shelley, who had urged Ollier to advertise generously and had made personal arrangements for the disposal of forty or fifty copies, besides sending Ollier a mailing list of thirty-eight persons and institutions.[67] These were radicals or liberals with whom Shelley hoped his pamphlet might have practical results. Among the thirty-eight recipients designated by Shelley were two Hampden Clubs and such liberal leaders as Burdett, Brougham, Cobbett, the Lord Mayor of London, General Sir Ronald Crawford Ferguson, Lord Cochrane, Francis Place, and Major Cartright. The names of Curran, whom he had known in Ireland, William Taylor of Norwich, Mr. Madocks of Tremadoc memory, George Ensor and James Montgomery, of still earlier interest to Shelley, and Robert Owen of Lanark,[68] reflect a more personal interest.

Shelley's pamphlet proposed to call a meeting at the Crown and Anchor Tavern, in London, where a great meeting of delegates had already been held earlier in the year, to plan a house-to-house canvas of the United Kingdom on the one subject of whether or not the nation desired a Parliamentary reform that would make the Commons actually representative. Avoiding all questions likely to cause internal dissensions, this meeting should sit until it had completed practical details of the canvas and arranged to finance it by subscription. Shelley himself pledged a hundred pounds, one tenth of his income, toward the expenses. No man, Shelley maintained in the pamphlet, should be taxed without consent. Parliament should meet annually. Rather surprisingly he stated his opinion that the country was not yet ready for the universal male suffrage that public meetings and reform clubs were demanding, or for the abolition of kings and aristocracy. Such sudden action, he stated, would place the country in the hands of demagogues and mobs, " men who have been rendered brutal and torpid and ferocious by ages of slavery." Only by " many gradations of improvement " could the nation arrive at the best social and political system, a pure and stable republic.

In early March, when the Shelleys were staying with Peacock, Shelley and Peacock formed a design of putting their beliefs about reform into practice. Since no man could be legally taxed without his consent, and since Parliament, the taxing body, did not really represent the nation, they would refuse to pay taxes. Was not the country peppered with Hampden Clubs, and had not Hampden set the example of refusing to pay illegal taxes, in their own Buckinghamshire? Nothing happened, however, for no one except Mary and Leigh Hunt heard of their resolution, and neither of these was a tax-collector.[69]

AT ABOUT the time he was writing his temperate *Proposal*, Shelley had a personal experience which provoked him to more passionate expression. A poor woman whose son was on trial before one of the London courts was returning home one night with her son, walking through Hampstead. It was a bitterly cold night in mid-winter. Not far from Leigh Hunt's house the woman was overcome and sank to the ground in convulsions. Shelley came along as her son was trying to assist her and immediately applied for aid at the nearest houses. The occupants would not take the woman in or even allow her to be placed in an outhouse while Shelley went for the doctor. As Shelley was vainly arguing, a carriage drove up to a near-by house and an elderly gentleman and his family began to alight. Again the poet told his story, more hopefully, but the gentleman would hear nothing of it. Like the rest, he considered the woman an impostor — " Sir, your conduct is extraordinary! " " Sir! " cried Shelley, with sudden sternness, " I am sorry to say that *your* conduct is *not* extraordinary. . . . It is such men as you who madden the spirits and the patience of the poor and wretched; and if ever a convulsion comes in this country (which is very probable), recollect what I tell you: you will have your house, that you refuse to put the miserable woman into, burnt over your head." The two men then managed to convey the woman to Leigh Hunt's house, where Hunt, arriving about that time from the opera, found them holding her until the arrival of a doctor. Next day she was sufficiently recovered to be sent on to her home at Hendon.[70]

At Marlow Shelley continued his personal interest in the poor. Many of the inhabitants were lace-makers, whose trade suffered the usual fate of luxury trades at a time when many people were able to purchase only the barest necessities. These ill-paid, starving workers came to know Shelley well. He visited them in their cottages and attended their illnesses, for which he would prescribe and provide broth or pea soup. Once, being without money or writing-materials at the moment, he gave the shoes off his feet to a poor woman whom he found limping barefoot over the stones. Once " a portion of the warmest of Mrs. Shelley's wardrobe " was discovered to be missing; Shelley had impulsively given it to someone more needy. Shelley carried little money on his person, but he generally carried pencil and paper or a book. Many times Mr. Madocks, a neighbour who sometimes acted as Shelley's deputy and petty banker, received notes scribbled on notebook leaves or leaves torn from books, directing that the bearer be paid a specified sum, which might be as much as half a crown.

On Saturday evenings Shelley held audience with the poor at Albion House, a bag of coins at his elbow. When he was absent — and he was probably as unreliable in his engagements with the poor as with Godwin and Hogg — the coins and the authority were delegated to Mrs. Madocks. In the winter of 1817, as distress and cold weather increased together according to their immemorial association, Shelley bought some sheeting and twenty blankets, such as army officers were furnished with, for distribution among the needy. Some indication that his charity was not devoid of experienced prudence is furnished by the fact that each blanket was stamped with Shelley's name. During this winter Shelley contracted ophthalmia, as a result, Mary thought, of his visits to the poor.[71]

Practical as it was, Shelley's benevolence at Marlow had also a tinge of his doctrine of universal love and brotherhood which he expressed more clearly in his later poetry. *Alastor* had stressed the sympathy existing between the poet and wild creatures, and the Lady of the Garden in " The Sensitive Plant " (1820) carefully preserved the lives even of " all killing insects and gnawing worms." At Marlow Shelley dissuaded small boys from persecuting squirrels with stones and commissioned his gardener to buy living crayfish as they were hawked through the streets and return them to the Thames.[72]

Charles Cowden Clarke, when he visited Marlow some years after Shelley's departure, was told that the more well-to-do inhabitants of the village considered Shelley a madman. Tom Medwin, in 1835, found Shelley's name in Marlow still very much alive and highly cherished, particularly among the poor. Some ten years later William Howitt found that the poor still remembered him for his good deeds; the small gentry had never heard of him, and two or three shopkeepers recalled him only by " a bad joke on his boat, by his disbelief in the devil " (which rendered him " a very bad man "), " and by a forgotten bill." [73]

Daily life at Albion House was a matter of very simple routine. Leigh Hunt, an early visitor who spent all together nearly three months there, indignantly answered the current slanders on Shelley's private life by printing what he had seen:

This was the round of his daily life: — He was up early; breakfasted sparingly; wrote . . . all the morning; went out in his boat

GREAT MARLOW, 1814

Engraved by W. B. Cooke from a drawing by S. Owen

THE THAMES ABOVE LONDON: STONE AT STAINES, 1821

Engraved by W. B. Cooke from a painting by G. Arnold

or into the woods with some Greek author or the Bible in his hands;
came home to a dinner of vegetables (for he took neither meat nor
wine); visited, if necessary, "the sick and the fatherless," whom
others gave Bibles to and no help; wrote or studied again, or read
to his wife and friends the whole evening; took a crust of bread or
a glass of whey for his supper; and went early to bed. This is literally
the whole of the life he led.[74]

Mary's journal for this period, brief enough in its entries, concerns her own activities more than Shelley's, but does not clash
with Hunt's account. Another resident of the house, Polly Rose,
remembered that Shelley dined at five on bread and raisins and
read or wrote until ten, at which time Polly was sent to bed.

When Shelley was writing he sometimes spent most of the
day in his boat, or on a hill in Bisham Wood. A Marlow gentleman told Medwin that he sometimes spent whole nights in his
boat, taking up an occasional abode at a small inn down the
river.[75] Numerous and sometimes long were the walks he took
with Hunt, Hogg, or Peacock. "We took many walks in all
directions from Marlow," says Peacock, "and saw everything
worth seeing within a radius of sixteen miles. . . . We often
walked to London, frequently in company with Mr. Hogg. It
was our usual way of going there, when not pressed for time.
We went by a very pleasant route over fields, lanes, woods, and
heaths to Uxbridge, and by the main road from Uxbridge to
London. The total distance was thirty-two miles to Tyburn
turnpike. We usually stayed two nights and walked back on
the third day. I never saw Shelley tired with these walks.
Delicate and fragile as he appeared, he had great muscular
strength." [76]

In the numerous rowing and sailing excursions on the Thames,
Shelley often preferred steering to taking an oar, but when he
rowed he " could stick to his seat for any time against any force
of current or of wind, not only without complaining, but without being compelled to give in until the set task was accomplished, though it should involve some miles of hard pulling."
He did not shrink from towing his boat back to its moorings
after a row or sail of considerable length.

On landing from these excursions it was necessary to climb a steep bank before being able to enter Albion House from the rear. Once when young Thornton Hunt was present Shelley quite delighted him by his activity in assisting the ladies up the bank. "While others were content to accomplish the feat for one, he, I think, helped three up the bank, sliding in a half-sitting posture when he returned to fetch a new charge. I well remember his shooting past me in a cloud of chalk-dust, as I was slowly climbing up. He had a fit of panting after it, but he made light of the exertion." [77] When he went to Hampstead, as both Charles Cowden Clarke and Leigh Hunt observed, Shelley was full of exuberant vitality. Not until the end of June is there any indication in either the journal or in letters that Shelley's health was anything but vigorous. The late spring and early summer were sunny and serene, and time passed at Albion House, as Shelley wrote Byron, "in that tranquil uniformity which presents much to enjoy and leaves nothing to record." [78] "This was an agreeable year to all of us," Peacock recorded, including even the less serene months of autumn and winter. [79]

During his residence at Marlow, Shelley was frequently in London for short periods, whether on business or pleasure. At such times Leigh Hunt's cottage in the Vale of Health, Hampstead, was his second home, though he spent some evenings also at Godwin's. One such occasion arrived when Mary, after about a month of revising and transcribing, wrote finis to *Frankenstein* on May 14. A publisher must be sought. On May 22 Mary and Shelley left their guests at Albion House and went down to London for a few days, descending the river in their boat. The book was first submitted to Murray, who was sure, Mary thought, to be prejudiced against it by William Gifford. [80] At any rate he rejected it. Mary remained till the end of the month, Mrs. Godwin being mercifully absent in France. Shelley stayed only four days (May 22–6) during which he attended the opera (*Don Giovanni*) and an exhibition of sculpture and painting, dined with Hogg at Godwin's, and passed an evening with Hazlitt there.

On his visits to Hampstead, which sometimes lasted several

days, Shelley delighted in the rough broken ground. The fresh
northwest wind, as Hunt observed, gave him " an intoxication of
animal spirits." The city streets were apt to cause a sudden,
characteristic mood of depression. " Look at all these worn and
miserable faces that pass us," he burst out one day as he and
Hunt were walking in the Strand, " and tell me what is to be
thought of the world they appear in." [81]

" It was a moot point when he entered your room," Leigh
Hunt said, " whether he would begin with some half-pleasant,
half-pensive joke, or quote something Greek, or ask some question about public affairs. He once came upon me at Hampstead,
when I had not seen him for some time; and after grasping my
hands into both his, in his usual fervent manner, he sat down,
and looked at me very earnestly, with a deep, though not melancholy interest in his face. We were sitting with our knees to the
fire, to which we had been getting nearer and nearer, in the
comfort of finding ourselves together. The pleasure of seeing
him was my only feeling at the moment; and the air of domesticity about us was so complete, that I thought he was going to
speak of some family matter, either his or my own, when he
asked me, at the close of an intensity of pause, what was ' the
amount of the National Debt.' " [82]

In these visits to town Shelley became an assiduous frequenter
of the Italian opera. Seated in the old Italian Theatre, with its
comparatively quiet, decorous audiences, he would remark to
Peacock that it was " delightful to see human beings so civilized." Mademoiselle Mélanie, the principal danseuse there in
1817, enchanted him; he had never imagined before, he said,
such grace of motion. The music of Mozart, especially in *Nozze
di Figaro,* delighted him. He regarded the regular stage, however, as a corrupter of principles that were much dearer to him
than the entertainment of an hour. Miss O'Neill in Milman's
Fazio compelled his admiration to the extent that two years
later he hoped to secure her as Beatrice in *The Cenci,* but this
was the only play Peacock ever saw Shelley enjoy. In fact, Peacock, a confirmed theatre-goer himself, never enticed Shelley to
attend any other play except Sheridan's *School for Scandal.*
Here, in the fourth act, Shelley could hardly be persuaded to

remain in the theatre. " I see the purpose of this comedy," he protested. " It is to associate virtue with bottles and glasses, and villainy with books." He often talked of "the withering and perverting spirit of comedy." Peacock once sought to make him admire a finely written passage satirizing a withered old crone and a lazy maidservant in Beaumont and Fletcher's *Rule a Wife and Have a Wife*. Shelley's only comment was the indignant remark: " There is comedy in its perfection. Society grinds down poor wretches into the dust of abject poverty, till they are scarcely recognizable as human beings; and then, instead of being treated as what they really are, subjects of the deepest pity, they are brought forward as grotesque monstrosities to be laughed at." When the ludicrous did not involve even a temporary compromise with his terribly earnest logic of justice Shelley laughed all the more freely, but he could tolerate no trifling that might obscure the really important issues.[83]

By the end of June, Mary's brief, placid record of day-by-day events affords a slight premonition of impending trouble. Amplified by additions from contemporary letters, it shows clearly that several clouds were already threatening the serenity of Albion House:

Thursday, June 26. — Read Tacitus and Buffon.

Friday, June 27. — Read Tacitus and " Julie." [Godwin writes to Mary, inclosing an insulting letter he has received which apparently involves the Shelleys, mentioning a visit from Shelley on the 26th, a hopeful interview with Shelley and Longdill in an effort to relieve Godwin's financial distress. He has promised Shelley to visit Marlow again forty days hence, when he finishes *Mandeville*, and Shelley has informed him that by that time he and Mary expect to be in London — probably in order that Mary's baby may be born there.]

Saturday, June 28. — Read " Julie." Shelley returns at midnight. [From London, where he had gone with Mr. and Mrs. Hunt and Thornton, on the 25th.]

Sunday, June 29. — Read " Julie." Talk with Shelley. [Shelley writes to Leigh Hunt: " I have so constant a pain in my side, and such a depression of strength and spirits, as to make my holding the pen whilst I write to you almost an intolerable exertion. This, you know, with me is transitory." To this Mary added: " You may see by this letter that Shelley is very unwell. . . . He was well yesterday until the evening, but to-day he is worse than I have known him for some time."]

Monday, June 30. — (Mary) — Read " Julie." Shelley reads Homer. He is not well.

Tuesday, July 1. — Read " Julie." Shelley is very unwell; he reads Homer.

Wednesday, July 2. — Finish " Julie; " read Tacitus. Shelley reads Homer. He is better.

Thursday, July 3. — Read Tacitus; finish 3rd book; read Buffon. Shelley reads Homer.

Friday, July 4. — Read Tacitus. Shelley reads Homer. [Godwin writes to Shelley, referring to an unspecified sum of money he has borrowed from Shelley early in April and asking for a two weeks' loan of £100 or £150 to meet an immediate, urgent necessity.]

Saturday, July 5. [No entry July 5, 6, 7] — [On July 6 Shelley wrote Hogg that he and Peacock would be glad to see him at Marlow, though it was now too late for him to enjoy Hunt's company there. He discusses his classical reading and adds: " I am weak enough to employ myself in writing, though half conscious that my time might be better employed."]

Tuesday, July 8. — Read Tacitus; the " Persian Letters." Shelley reads Homer and writes; reads a canto of Spenser and part of the " Gentle Shepherdess " aloud.

Wednesday, July 9. — Read Tacitus and Buffon. Shelley reads Homer and Plutarch. [On July 9 Shelley wrote to Byron to urge him to make some early provision for Alba, whose continued presence at

Marlow was causing an embarrassing situation. " I have lately had a kind of relapse of my constitutional disease, and if the Chancellor should threaten to invade my domestic circle, I shall seek Italy; as a refuge at once from the stupid tyranny of these laws and my disorder."]

Thursday, July 10. — (Mary) — Read Tacitus. Shelley reads Spenser aloud. Read Buffon.

Friday, July 11. — Shelley reads Homer's Hymns. Finish 5th book of Tacitus. Shelley reads Spenser aloud.

Saturday, July 12. — Write from Pliny; read Tacitus. Shelley reads Homer's Hymns. Miss Kent and the [Hunt] children depart. William Cambden. Work.

Sunday, July 13. — Read Tacitus. Shelley reads " Prometheus Desmotes," and I write it. He reads Homer's Hymns. [Shelley writes Ollier a brief note asking him to send Coleridge's *Sibylline Leaves* " immediately."]

Monday, July 14. — Read Tacitus; transcribe; work. Books arrive from London.

Tuesday, July 15. — [No entry]

Tuesday, July 22. — Read Tacitus; " Clarke's Travels; " transcribe for Shelley. Shelley writes; reads several of the Plays of Aeschylus and Spenser aloud in the evening.

Wednesday, July 23. — [No entry]

Saturday, July 26. — Read Tacitus; read Miss Edgeworth's " Harrington and Ormond; " " Arthur Mervyn." Shelley reads the " Agamemnon" of Aeschylus, and walks to Hampden and Virginia Water. Hogg is in Marlow. [Hogg was visiting Peacock.]

Sunday, July 27. — [No entry]

Thursday, July 31. — Read Tacitus and " Clarke's Travels." Shelley goes to Egham; he reads Aeschylus and " Travels in the Kingdom

of Caubul." Read " Rasselas; " Make jellies, and work. Hogg returns to London, talking of ducks and women, a disagreeable letter
from Isabel.

Friday, Aug. 1. — [No entry]

If the whole of Mary's journal for the next six months could be
quoted with interpolations from the letters it would show to the
end the same regular round of reading and study which was now
second nature to both Shelley and Mary, with a gradual, un-
even acceleration of the disquieting forces, until in the end a
flight to Italy seemed the only answer to all problems at once.

Chapter XVIII

MARLOW AND LONDON:

CLOUDS GATHER

POETIC ACTIVITY; AUTUMN VISITORS; POOR HEALTH;

DEBTS AND DANGERS; PUBLICATION OF *LAON*

AND CYTHNA; LAST DAYS AT MARLOW;

LONDON PLEASURES, DEPARTURE

FOR ITALY

IT was a long time after the first faint warnings before Shelley realized that they must terminate in his departure from Marlow and England. While his present situation was gradually becoming more untenable he was obliviously and whole-heartedly committing himself to poetry. If under adverse circumstances he had clung to his reading with inflexible stubbornness, he had not forgotten that his studies were part of a still greater purpose to become a poet who could compel the world to listen to the truth as he saw it. As Thornton Hunt noticed, even in ordinary discussions it was a trait of Shelley's mind to brush aside all minor considerations and concentrate on the one single, sufficient factor.[1] Circumstances beyond control might wreck or completely modify his life externally, but his purpose continued the same, single and practically indestructible. The very intensity of this purpose, in fact, may be one reason for some of the difficulty in achieving it; so fine and subtle a mind as Shelley possessed must inevitably have solved many of the merely practical difficulties that beset him had he consistently thought them important enough at the time. He was always eminently practical in achieving publication.

While at Marlow, Shelley not only wrote a great deal, but, as before, stimulated both Mary and Claire to activity.[2] *Laon and Cythna,* considerably the longest poem Shelley ever wrote, " Prince Athanase," a fragmentary poem of over three hundred lines, a good part of *Rosalind and Helen,* and twenty-six shorter poems and fragments — a total of about six thousand lines — constitute Shelley's poetic production within a little less than a year. In addition he wrote the prefaces to *Frankenstein* and *History of a Six Weeks' Tour,* and his pamphlet on the death of the Princess Charlotte. He began his translation of the Homeric Hymns, dictated a translation from Spinoza,[3] marketed three volumes, and saw them through the press. These poems not only show " how full of passion and reflection were his solitary hours," [4] they *were* his solitary hours. Much more than the journal in which they are so briefly and seldom mentioned, they constitute the picture of Shelley in 1817. " He never wandered," said Mary, as she wrote of Shelley's life at Marlow, " without a book, and without implements of writing." [5]

Of the longer poems and fragments, *Laon and Cythna,* or *The Revolt of Islam,* as it was renamed, was apparently the first undertaken. Shelley states in the Preface that its composition occupied him for six months, and Mary's journal on September 29 records for September 23: " Shelley finishes his Poem, and goes up to town with Clare." This would date the beginning of the poem shortly after the middle of March. It is significant that on April 17 and 22 Shelley is recorded as reading " The History of the French Revolution " (Lacretelle's, apparently) and on April 23 Mary's journal states: " Shelley reads ' History of the French Revolution ' and Spenser aloud in the evening." This remark, with minor variations, runs through the journal like an irregular refrain until late in July. By that time the poem was three-fourths finished [6] and Shelley felt that his ear was sufficiently attuned to the harmonies of the Spenserian stanza to make further oral reading unnecessary.

Ever since he had visited Versailles it had been in Shelley's mind that someone should write a poem on the French Revolution that would show the real basis of revolutionary change and, by presenting the *beau idéal* of a revolution in contrast with the errors into which the French Revolution had fallen, show that the gloom and depression felt by so many liberals on account of its failure were really unjustified. He had first suggested the subject to Byron, but in vain — " our faithless Albè," as Mary now called him, was in too indolent a mood to pay serious attention even to Shelley's urgent letters about Claire and her child. As soon as the Chancery business would allow, Shelley himself took up the design he had urged upon Byron. Day after day he sought his " high prominence in Bisham Wood," [7] retreated to Medmenham Abbey, or moored his boat under an island or a chalky cliff. Alone in any of these spots with his " unbounded and sustained enthusiasm," Shelley went through the " ' agony and bloody sweat ' of intellectual travail." [8] These expressions of Shelley after Godwin had disappointed him by failing utterly to appreciate the poem at its proper worth may be a little intensified by the circumstances, but they are amply supported in the main by the poem itself and its Preface. " I felt the precariousness of my life," Shelley told Godwin, " and I engaged in this task resolved to leave some records of myself. Much of what the volume contains was written with the same feeling, as real, though not so prophetic, as the communications of a dying man." [9] In the Preface Shelley informed his readers that so far as the " education peculiarly fitted for a poet " was concerned, he had been fortunate. He was well acquainted with mountains, lakes, and streams; he had seen the effects of war in regions only recently devastated; he had seen large cities and large assemblies of excited men; had associated with men of genius, and had made himself acquainted with the best literature of ancient and modern times. The present poem was intended not only to test how great was the public desire for a better state of things, but also, for himself, whether or not he possessed the one most important requisite of a poet, the power of communicating his sensations and enthusiasms to others. He had written fearlessly, in the belief that contemporary criticism was a matter of only trifling moment, but his poem was narrative, and not didactic, hence the reader should not impute to the author opinions belonging more properly to his dramatic characters. Whatever certain characters said in their own persons, the author intended no attack upon the Supreme Being, but only upon the erroneous and degraded idea of Him.

The Revolt of Islam is too long and wandering to be capable of effective brief summary without radically changing its arrangement.[10] Shelley himself described the purpose and general content as follows:

For this purpose I have chosen a story of human passion in its most universal character, diversified with moving and romantic adventures, and appealing, in contempt of all artificial opinions or institutions, to the common sympathies of every human breast. I have made no attempt to recommend the motives which I would substitute for those at present governing mankind by methodical and systematic argument. I would only awaken the feelings, so that the reader should see the beauty of true virtue, and be incited to those inquiries which have led to my moral and political creed, and that of some of the sublimest intellects in the world. The Poem therefore (with the exception of the first Canto, which is purely introductory), is narrative not didactic. It is a succession of pictures illustrating the growth and progress of individual mind aspiring after excellence, and devoted to the love of mankind; its influence in refining and making pure the most daring and uncommon impulses of the imagination, the understanding, and the senses; its impatience at "all the oppressions which are done under the sun;" its tendency to awaken public hope, and to enlighten and improve mankind; the rapid effects of the application of that tendency; the awakening of an immense nation from their slavery and degradation to a true sense of moral dignity and freedom; the bloodless dethronement of their oppressors, and the unveiling of the religious frauds by which they had been deluded into submission; the tranquillity of successful patriotism, and the universal toleration and benevolence of true philanthropy; the treachery and barbarity of hired soldiers; vice not the object of punishment and hatred, but kindness and pity; the faithlessness of tyrants; the confederacy of the Rulers of the World, and the restoration of the expelled Dynasty by foreign arms; the massacre and extermination of the Patriots, and the victory of established power; the consequences of legitimate despotism, civil war, famine, plague, superstition, and an utter extinction of the domestic affections; the judicial murder of the advocates of Liberty; the temporary triumph of oppression, that secure earnest of its final and inevitable fall; the transient nature of ignorance and error, and the eternity of genius and virtue. Such is the series of delineations of which the Poem consists.[11]

Even to modern readers, more familiar than Shelley's contemporaries with the new style of poetry, *The Revolt of Islam* is far more difficult reading than Shelley could have anticipated. If he had any special fitness as a poet, Shelley informed Godwin, it was " to apprehend minute and remote distinctions of feeling, whether relative to external nature, or the living beings which surround us." [12] He had decided some time before that language itself might sometimes be inadequate to convey ideas and he had already begun to develop a symbolism which by appealing directly to the imagination and sympathies might heighten the effect of literal language. In *The Revolt of Islam* this use of symbols, while by no means necessary to the general meaning, undoubtedly puzzles the reader at times. This is particularly true when Shelley deliberately goes contrary to conventional notions and makes the serpent symbolize the good, in the eternal warfare between good and evil. The poem is rather overweighted with description, much of which is excellent poetry, but repetitious. Even Leigh Hunt complained mildly of the numerous similar descriptions of water scenes, and Byron said that its few readers could not understand it, " I for one." [13]

But the principal weakness of the poem is structural. The first canto, including a kind of survey of the French Revolution and a partly symbolical explanation of Shelley's philosophy of good and evil, is far too elaborate an introduction to a story. Having reached his story in the second canto, Shelley does not proceed directly, but allows his two protagonists to tell their stories individually, with a consequent effect of overlapping, stopping and starting again. Even with Shelley's clear outline in the Preface it is hard to follow and understand. One of the best summaries of the action of the story, and one of the justest

PEN SKETCH BY SHELLEY ON INSIDE COVER OF
MS. OF *LAON AND CYTHNA*

By permission of the Bodleian Library

criticisms it ever received, appeared in Leigh Hunt's *Examiner*. Hunt concludes:

The beauties of the poem consist in depth of sentiment, in grandeur of imagery, and a versification remarkably sweet, various, and noble, like the placid playing of a great organ. If the author's genius reminds us of any other poets, it is of two very opposite ones, Lucretius and Dante. The former he resembles in the Dædalian part of it, in the boldness of his speculations, and in his love of virtue, of external nature, and of love itself. It is his gloomier or more imaginative passages that sometimes remind us of Dante. The sort of supernatural architecture in which he delights has in particular the grandeur as well as obscurity of that great genius, to whom however he presents this remarkable and instructive contrast, that superstition and pain and injustice go hand in hand even in the pleasantest parts of Dante, like the three Furies, while philosophy, pleasure, and justice smile through the most painful passages of our author, like the three Graces.

Mr. Shelley's defects as a poet are obscurity, inartificial and yet not natural economy, violation of costume, and too great a sameness and gratuitousness of image and metaphor, and of image and metaphor too drawn from the elements, particularly the sea. The book is full of humanity; and yet it certainly does not go the best way to work of appealing to it, because it does not appeal to it through the medium of its common knowledges. It is for this reason that we must say something, which we would willingly leave unsaid, both from admiration of Mr. Shelley's genius and love of his benevolence; and this is, that the work cannot possibly become popular. It may set others thinking and writing, and we have no doubt will do so; and those who can understand and relish it, will relish it exceedingly; but the author must forget his metaphysics and sea-sides a little more in his future works, and give full effect to that nice knowledge of men and things which he otherwise really possesses to an extraordinary degree. We have no doubt he is destined to be one of the leading spirits of his age, and indeed has already fallen into his place as such; but however resolute as to his object, he will only be doing it justice to take the most effectual means in his power to forward it.[14]

The core of Shelley's optimism was that it was natural for men suddenly liberated from a long brutalizing tyranny to behave like brutes. Pessimism because they did so was unreasonable. Nations became liberal-minded only as the result of " resolute perseverance and indefatigable hope, and long-suffering and long-believing courage, and the systematic efforts of generations of men of intellect and virtue." [15] In the first canto, in the splendid conflict between the eagle of oppression and the serpent of righteousness, Shelley symbolized his belief that the contest between good and evil principles is everlasting — the serpent, though often defeated, is never slain, and always returns to the conflict. The disappointments of the French Revolution, therefore, were a mere incident. The ideal revolution described in the poem is crushed, but this is no reason for gloom — the serpent is merely recruiting his strength for another fight. In the operation of a vague principle of mutability [16] another opportunity would surely be presented, and if men only learned meanwhile to overcome revenge, envy, and prejudice and to depend solely on love, or universal sympathy, the final outcome could not be doubtful. Already Shelley, as he said in the Preface, felt aware of a " slow, gradual, silent change." Had not Malthus, he exulted, the very high priest of hopelessness, recently altered his *Essay on Population* so that it was now merely a commentary on the unanswerableness of *Political Justice*?

This long-range optimism contains more inspiration for the philosophic than for the practical radical, who will always be much more sympathetic with the vigorous, clear directness of *Queen Mab*. Nothing could be more sanely tempered than the view of revolutionary change set forth in the Preface and first canto of the *The Revolt of Islam*. And yet in its subsequent attacks upon kings, priests, outworn custom, and perverted religion the poem is quite as vigorous as *Queen Mab*. Shelley was still far too ardent and impetuous to submit his feelings consistently to the disciplined patience that his experience and his fine intellectual insight taught him were necessary. His revolution is brought about largely by the fact that both Laon and Cythna are freed by the tyrants to preach revolution. They go free through no compulsion except the power of persuasion — a piece of good fortune which escaped Bonnivard and which a practical revolu-

532

tionist no doubt would consider almost as miraculous as the liberation of Daniel or Saint Paul.

IT IS uncertain when Shelley began writing *Rosalind and Helen*. So complete was his absorption in *Laon and Cythna* that if *Rosalind and Helen* was begun first it was laid aside in order to concentrate on a poem which he held in much higher esteem. The love-story of Lionel and Helen is so similar to that of Laon and Cythna (both being autobiographical) that Shelley's comparative lack of interest in the poem might easily be explained by the fact that before finishing it he had already done the same thing more fully in another poem.[17] At any rate he threw the poem aside, either soon after he began *Laon and Cythna* or late in September, when his doctor placed a prohibition on further imaginative writing.[18] It was not complete at the latter date, when Mary referred to it as "my pretty eclogue," thus indicating a special interest in it which supports the evidence of the poem itself that it was written to justify the love of Shelley and Mary. In her journal for February 18, 1818 Mary wrote: "Copy Shelley's Eclogue." Shelley sent it to the printers before leaving London,[19] from which it seems fairly certain that in an earlier form the poem was finished in England. In its present form, however, it was finished in a few days during the summer of 1818, at the Baths of Lucca.[20]

In publishing the eight fragments of "Prince Athanase" in 1824 Mrs. Shelley dated the first and longest "December, 1817," the rest simply "Marlow, 1817." A fair guess at the time the poem was begun may be based on her journal entry for August 13: "Shelley writes; reads Plato's 'Convivium.'" Plato's *Convivium*, or *Banquet*, which Shelley later returned to with enthusiastic admiration, is perhaps the most important single key to Shelley's doctrine of Love. Here he found one of the noblest expressions of love as universal sympathy. Shelley's first name for his poem was "Pandemos and Urania," from the two types of love, the earthly and the spiritual, discussed in *The Banquet*. His young hero, very much like the poet in *Alastor*, seeking Ideal

Beauty throughout his travels, meets first an earthly lover by whom he is betrayed. Only on his death-bed does he meet the Uranian love he has been seeking. This is the story as Shelley planned it;[21] as written it consists mainly of two sketches of Prince Athanase and his friend Zonoras and a short, beautiful apostrophe to love:

> Thou art the wine whose drunkenness is all
> We can desire, [O Love!] and happy souls,
> Ere from thy vine the leaves of Autumn fall,
>
> Catch thee, and feed from their o'erflowing bowls
> Thousands who thirst for thine ambrosial dew; —
> Thou art the radiance which where ocean rolls
>
> Investeth it; and when the heavens are blue
> Thou fillest them; and when the earth is fair
> The shadow of thy moving wings imbue
>
> Its deserts and its mountains, till they wear
> Beauty [like some] light robe; — thou ever soarest
> Among the towers of men, and as soft air
>
> In Spring, which moves the unawakened forest,
> Clothing with leaves its branches bare and bleak,
> Thou floatest among men. . . .

Shelley seldom expressed to others the anguish and indignation aroused by his recent troubles, said Mary Shelley long afterwards; but his otherwise unexpressed passion and sense of injury found utterance in the poems written at Marlow.[22] A glance at these poems lends considerable support to Mrs. Shelley's statement.

Laon, Prince Athanase, and Lionel, Shelley's three heroes, are all very much alike and very much like Shelley, except that Prince Athanase is not primarily a radical but, like the poet of *Alastor*, a devotee of love and sympathy. Laon and Lionel both dedicate themselves to reform, Laon's dedication [23] being much like that of Shelley himself, as described in the " Hymn to Intellectual Beauty " and the " Dedication: To Mary." All three came to early and untimely death, and Shelley at the time of writing dwelt often on the idea of a similar death himself. Laon and Lionel both loved, in defiance of the marriage laws, women very much resembling idealizations of the Mary Shelley who is passionately described as the perfect mate in the " Dedication: To Mary." In *The Revolt of Islam* and " Prince Athanase " the hero is advised and befriended by an old man apparently intended to represent the Dr. Lind who had been Shelley's early friend at Eton.[24] There is also a " false friend " in *The Revolt of Islam,* who may or may not have autobiographical significance.[25] Lionel, like Shelley, had been bitterly disappointed in love before he met Helen.

Shelley's purpose in the poems of the Marlow period was, as he said himself, to fulfil his compelling sense of mission as well as he could while it was still possible. No one can read *The Revolt of Islam,* with its earnest enthusiasm for the improvement of humanity, and still doubt Shelley's statement. But it was also a necessity of Shelley's nature to feel justified. There was never a time in his life when his sense of rectitude was more necessary to him than in the year following Harriet's suicide and the beginning of the Chancery proceedings involving his children. Under the surface of his greater concern for the world may be clearly seen his keen feeling for his personal situation. Prince Athanase with his false and true loves offers a close parallel to Shelley's conception of his own history. *The Revolt of Islam* and *Rosalind and Helen* both show parents whose children have been torn from them by an exercise of tyranny, and both offer impressive examples of true love without marriage. *Rosalind and Helen,* in fact, is primarily the study of two unions, the fine love of Helen and Lionel without marriage, which closely parallels that of Shelley and Mary, and the legalized union of Rosalind and her husband, without love, which is apparently based upon Mary's impression from Isabel Baxter's father that Isabel's marriage to Mr. Booth was turning out badly. It is difficult to regard these parallels to Shelley's personal situation as accidental. Occasional passages in Shelley's letters show how closely his view of his own character tallies with those he assigns his three heroes. Three poems written during the same year — " Lines to the Lord Chancellor," " To William Shelley," and " Dedication: To Mary " — speak openly and intensely on the same themes.

THE relapse in Shelley's health in late June and early July mentioned in his letters to the Hunts and Byron was only temporarily alarming. July turned to August without any further alarm. Shelley's twenty-fifth birthday passed happily, though the brooch (probably to contain a miniature or a lock of hair) that Mary was to give him could not be presented on time because Marianne Hunt in London had neglected a shopping commission. In writing to chide her for this and to thank her for Shelley's birthday present from the Hunts (also still to come) Mary remarked: " We are all well here." Mary was expecting soon to be confined and wished to be provided with a nurse from London by August 20.[26]

The autumn brought several visitors to Marlow. One was Thomas Hookham, Jr.,[27] whose visit was probably to Peacock, since Mary Shelley did not see him.[28] On September 1 Mary's hopes were aroused by a short visit from Mr. William Baxter, the father of Mary's estranged girlhood friend Isabel Baxter. He remained only three days, but by the 25th he was again at Albion House, this time for a longer stay. He was delighted with Shelley and Mary, perhaps the more readily because he was himself a man of liberal sentiments. " He has taken a prodigious fancy to us," wrote Mary to Shelley during Shelley's absence in London, " and is continually talking of and praising ' Queen Mab,' which he vows is the best poem of modern days." [29] He had expected to find in Shelley " an ignorant, silly, half-witted enthusiast " with " morals that fitted him only for a brothel." Instead he had been astonished and delighted to find him " a being of rare genius and talent, of truly republican frugality and plainness of manners, and of a soundness of principle and delicacy of moral tact that might put to shame (if shame they had) many of his detractors; and, with all this so amiable that you have only to be half an hour in his company to convince you that there is not an atom of malevolence in his whole composi-

tion." [30] In his opinion his daughter's failure to answer Mary's
letters was due entirely to the opposition of her husband, Mr.
Booth, whose ill temper and jealousy bade fair to make Isabel
"another victim of that ceremony." He wrote to Isabel to warn
her that she herself would be the principal loser if she allowed
her friendship for Mary to cool.

The interruption in Mr. Baxter's visit was probably caused by
the birth of Mary's third child, Clara Everina, on September 2.
Unlike Harriet, Mary did not refuse to nurse her child, but it
must have amused the ironic Peacock, who remembered Shelley's agitation on the former occasion, to observe Shelley's complacence when Mary felt compelled to supplement her own milk
with that of a she-ass. The child throve, however, despite the
almost immediate resignation of the ass in favour of expected
offspring of her own.[31]

The Hunts arrived for a week's visit on September 19. It was
at this time, just as he was finishing *Laon and Cythna,* that Shelley's health became really alarming. Toward the end of a single
journal entry covering the dates September 1–19 Mary wrote:
"Shelley writes his Poem [*Laon and Cythna,* as yet unnamed];
his health declines." On September 24 Shelley wrote to Byron:
"My health is in a miserable state, so that some care will be required to prevent it speedily terminating in death. . . . They
recommend Italy as a certain remedy for my disease." [32] At the
same time Mary was writing to Shelley: "Ah! My love you cannot guess how wretched it was to see your languor and increasing illness. I now say to myself, perhaps he is better; but then I
watched you every moment, and every moment was full of pain
both to you and to me." [33]

During October and November Shelley's health mended only
from time to time; basically it remained the same.[34] Mary was
becoming more and more distressed. "When I see you, droop-
ing and languid, in pain, and unable to enjoy life," Mary wrote,
"then on your account I ardently wish for bright skies and Italian sun." [35] As the weather grew colder and the hours of sunlight shorter, the dampness and darkness of Albion House became more and more apparent; both felt that they could not
remain there much longer.

537

In writing to Godwin on December 7 Shelley gave a particular description of his ailment:

My health has been materially worse. My feelings at intervals are of a deadly and torpid kind, or awakened to a state of such unnatural and keen excitement that only to instance the organ of sight, I find the very blades of grass and the boughs of distant trees present themselves to me with microscopical distinctness. Towards evening I sink into a state of lethargy and inanimation, and often remain for hours on the sofa between sleep and waking a prey to the most painful irritability of thought. Such with little intermission is my condition. The hours devoted to study are selected with vigilant caution from among these periods of endurance. It is not for this that I think of travelling to Italy, even if I knew that Italy would relieve me. But I have experienced a decisive pulmonary attack, and, although at present it has past away without any very considerable vestige of its existence, yet this symptom sufficiently shows the true nature of my disease to be consumptive. It is to my advantage that this malady is in its nature slow, and, if one is sufficiently alive to its advances is susceptible of cure from a warm climate. In the event of its assuming any decided shape, it *would be my duty* to go to Italy without delay; and it is only when that measure becomes an indispensable duty that, contrary both to Mary's feelings and to mine as they regard you, I shall go to Italy.[36]

It would appear that Godwin or Peacock had again persuaded Shelley to try the medical efficacy of meat, for later in the same letter he remarks: " I ought to say I cannot persevere in the meat diet."

Long before this Shelley had consulted physicians who ordered him to discontinue writing and recommended a warmer climate.[37] Italy had already been practically decided upon, but Godwin was still kept ignorant of the decision, because he was almost certain to object. This threw an added burden upon Mary, who expected Godwin to come to Marlow for a visit. " He will talk as if we meant to stay here; and I must — must I? — tell fifty prevarications or direct lies. . . . I am sure that I shall never be able to support it. . . . Had you not better speak? You might relieve me from a heavy burden. Surely he cannot be blind to the many heavy reasons that urge us. Your health,

the indispensable one, if every other were away. I assure you
that if my Father said, 'Yes, you must go; do what you can for
me; I know that you will do all you can,' I should, far from writing so melancholy a letter, prepare everything with a light heart;
arrange our affairs here; and come up to town, to await patiently
the effect of your efforts. I know not whether it is early habit or
affection, but the idea of his silent quiet disapprobation makes
me weep as it did in the days of my childhood." [38]

Since Shelley's disorder had previously been generally coin-
cident with nervous excitement or exhaustion, one naturally suspects that some of the other "many heavy reasons" for departure may have had their bearing upon Shelley's health. He had
just finished a long and arduous poem of nearly five thousand
lines, into which, by his own testimony, he had thrown his heart
and soul, and the "'agony and bloody sweat' of intellectual
travail." He was also becoming more and more disturbed over
his inability to get Byron to realize the serious threat of Claire's
continuous presence at Albion House with her child. It was already being whispered that he conducted a harem at Albion
House and that Alba was his child. Mary complained of Claire's
restlessness and peevishness even while sympathizing with her
on account of the cause.

Between September 23, when he finished *Laon and Cythna,*
and October 24 Shelley was in London most of the time, consulting money-lenders, lawyers, and doctors, returning to Marlow only three times, for about twelve days all together. It was
during the first ten days of this period that affairs came to a decision. Mary, with a constitutional tendency to despair, was also
in a weak state of health from recent childbirth. Peacock irritated her by coming uninvited every day to dine, and to "drink
his bottle." Claire, who had accompanied Shelley to London,
returned to irritate her with ill humour, restlessness, and disturbing reports of the affairs Shelley was trying to settle in London. Godwin had recently taken umbrage at some real or imagined slight to his wife, whom he well knew both the Shelleys
disliked. Even Hunt, usually a most welcome visitor, annoyed
her by thoughtlessly neglecting to accompany her when he
knew she was too weak to walk alone.

The house was incredibly dark and clammy. Mary's letters to Shelley became more and more urgent. They *must* quit the house and go either to Italy or to the Kentish coast. She slightly preferred the latter, but would abide by Shelley's decision. Whether or not they went to Italy, Alba must go there, and soon. It would be unjust as well as impossible to keep her much longer, and ridiculous to rely upon any promises Byron might make in the matter — "We must decide to go ourselves, or send her, within a month." "You do not seem enough to feel the absolute necessity there is that she should join her Father with every possible speed." "But Alba. Indeed, my love, her departure must not be delayed. . . . After all, dear Shelley, indecision will be our bane." [39] Perhaps it would cost very little more to take Alba to Italy than to send her. Shelley agreed that Alba must join her father and on October 6 decided: "We must go to Italy, on every ground." [40]

ANOTHER reason for some worry was an increasing financial strain. The lease on Albion House had cost in the neighbourhood of twelve hundred pounds, and a good deal of money had been spent on furniture. [41] What Shelley's numerous petty local charities cost is unknown and was probably never known to Shelley himself — he was always careless about small sums and wrote out his money orders for Mr. Madocks, dispensed his coins on Saturday evenings, provided his soup, blankets, and sheets, with a very hazy notion of the aggregate cost. If Mary missed a pound note from her bureau her natural supposition was that Shelley had taken it to London with him without mentioning the fact.

Likewise he had no clear notion of the total amount of his debts to local tradesmen. Mary, with more exact ideas on such matters, became worried. "Do get the state of your accounts from your Banker," [42] she insisted. Shelley borrowed £250 from Horace Smith under the impression that it would be sufficient, but Mary wrote: "Your account of our expences is by very much too favourable. . . . Our debts at Marlow are greater than you are aware of, besides living in the mean time and articles of dress that I must buy." [43] For the first time, apparently, they now discovered that a large amount of Harriet's debts were still unpaid, and that Longdill had undertaken their payment — as indeed he was legally obliged to do. Longdill had a considerable bill of his own to submit, and there were the other expenses of the recent Chancery trial which Shelley now informed Mary " *must* be paid." [44]

Over and above all this were Shelley's regular pensioners. Claire was still dependent on him, and so was her brother Charles. [45] Leigh Hunt had ceased to assert his financial independence and was now accepting donations. So was Peacock, to whom Shelley made an allowance of a hundred pounds, though the regularity of payment is very doubtful. [46] Godwin, of course, was exigent as ever. His *Mandeville*, the proceeds of which were to relieve his distresses, was now published, [47] but the distresses still needed relief. Even the neighbours noticed how Hunt and Godwin had come to depend on Shelley. With obvious exaggeration one of them related that Hunt once carried away a load of furniture, that Godwin threatened to stab himself unless relieved, and that Shelley had to summon Peacock as a protection against their importunate voracity. [48]

Of the thirty-four extant cheques drawn by Shelley between June 28 and December 18, totalling £543 16s. 1d., sixty pounds went to Horace Smith, probably in repayment of a loan, £196 10s. 10d. to Godwin, £150 to Leigh Hunt, and £53 to " self or bearer." [49] Leigh Hunt has testified that on one occasion alone (undated) Shelley gave him £1,400, and Horace Smith asserted that to his knowledge Shelley gave Godwin and other literary men upwards of £5,000 in all. [50] Some of these undated gifts certainly occurred in 1817. In an unsuccessful effort to borrow money for Hunt, Shelley introduced himself to the banker poet Samuel Rogers in early July. [51] He did borrow money in small amounts from others besides Horace Smith. [52] It was no wonder, then, that Shelley turned once more to the post-obit brokers. This would probably have been necessary in any event. From September 23 to November 19 Shelley spent most of his time in London, [53] " much teased," as Mary noted in her journal for October 5.

Shelley was in fact considerably more teased by financial worries than Mary's journal makes clear. His debts in October amounted to more than £1,500.[54] Some of his creditors were becoming impatient. He had been in town only a short while when he was arrested for debt and held for two days, at the instance of no less a person than his uncle, the gallant Captain Pilfold, who had formerly been his champion. In the preceding March, Captain Pilfold had written or spoken to Shelley's father about some overdue obligation of Shelley's, and Sir Timothy, through Whitton, had declined to interfere. Just when Shelley was arrested and how released does not appear, but on October 16 Mary wrote: "You say nothing of the late arrest, and what may be the consequences." [55] Shelley hoped that Sir Timothy could now be prevailed upon to advance money in order to prevent the necessity of selling his reversion, but Sir Timothy was advised by Whitton that Shelley would soon sell his reversion in any case.[56]

At the same time Mary feared to urge Shelley to return to Marlow, lest he be arrested there. "Mr. Wright has called here to-day, my dearest Shelley," she wrote, "and wished to see you. I can hardly have any doubt that his business is of the same nature as that which made him call last week. You will judge, but it appears that an arrest on Monday will follow your arrival Sunday." [57] Nevertheless, Shelley did arrive on Sunday, accompanied by Godwin, and remained until Wednesday, without arrest.[58]

Thus Mary's fear that their affairs might be drifting toward an insuperable fiasco were not at all surprising. "Nothing is done . . ." she complained, "and indeed I do not expect anything to be done these many months." The necessity of a post-obit transaction meant further delay. "I wish to hear extremely the account of your money at the bankers." "You tell me that the Italian sun will be the best physician — be it so — but money, money." And still, whatever happened, "Godwin must not be left unprovided." [59] Just when Shelley solved his financial difficulties is uncertain. On December 17 he wrote Byron that he had been in weekly expectation of leaving England but had en-

countered constant, gradual delays in settling his affairs.[60] This
suggests that by that time he had the assurance of money, at
least. There is no evidence, however, that he secured the actual
cash until the end of January.[61]

It was also about the middle of December that the alarm over
Shelley's health subsided. Four days after describing his illness
to Godwin, Shelley wrote: " This dry and frosty weather fills me
with health and spirits; I wish I could believe that it would
last." [62] It may be significant that Shelley's worst state of health
again coincided almost exactly with a state of nervous worry
over other matters. After Italy had been decided upon and the
other worries abated, we hear no more of Shelley's poor health.

Very little of these worries was apparent to Shelley's visitors
or associates. Life at Albion House continued as usual, except
that Shelley was often absent in London. If the Hunts knew
that the Shelleys were in serious difficulties during October, they
left no mention of the fact, though they were visitors at Marlow
when Shelley went up to London on September 23 and for a little while afterwards. (They failed to remember the nursemaid
when they left, and Mary instructed Shelley in a postscript to an
otherwise anxious letter to " purchase a gown for Milly, with a
little note with it from Marianne, that it may appear to come
from her . . . it must be *stout*, such a kind of one as we gave to
the servant at Bath." [63])

In the midst of their worries Mary wrote to invite Hunt to
come down for another visit: " I have written to Hunt; but tell
him over and above that our piano is in tune, and that I wish he
would come down by Monday's coach to play me a few tunes.
He will jest, I think, but it would really give me the greatest
pleasure. I would make love to him *pour passer le temps,* that
he might not regret the company of his Marianne and Thornton.
I do not tell you to tell him the latter part of this message, but
you may if you please." [64]

Peacock, to Mary's disgust, often dined, took tea, or spent the
evening at Albion House. " This was an agreeable year to all of
us," he wrote long afterwards, without ever having been conscious either of Mary's dislike or of the secret difficulties of Shel-

ley and Mary. The only reason he ever stated for their departure from Marlow was Shelley's "spirit of restlessness." [65] Late in November Hogg was invited down; [66] he arrived on December 6. Twice Shelley brought week-end guests with him from London, Godwin on October 19 and Walter Coulson on the 24th. Godwin came down again for the week-end of December 20, to be followed the next week-end by Horace Smith. [67]

MEANWHILE, on November 8 Mary had joined Shelley in London, where they remained together till the 19th, calling on the Godwins, the Hunts, and Ollier and receiving calls from them and from Keats, Coulson, Mr. Baxter, and Mr. Booth. [68]

When Charles Ollier and Godwin called on the Shelleys on November 10 and 11, the conversation turned to a subject about which all liberals and radicals were suddenly concerned. Extravagant, profligate, and dull, the royal sons of the aged and insane George III had long forfeited the affections of the English people. Princess Charlotte, beautiful and gracious, was still young and naïve in matters of statecraft, but was known to be more favourable than her father and uncles to the reforms which many of the best minds in England felt must be achieved if a revolution was to be averted. When the Prince Regent, her father, deserted the liberal cause in 1812, it was reported all over England that Princess Charlotte of Wales had wept upon reading one of his speeches. Byron had published his "Lines to a Lady Weeping":

> Weep, daughter of a royal line
> A sire's disgrace, a realm's decay —

encountering thereby a storm of partisan vituperation that had no small part in producing his own downfall. The hopes of England were centred on the expectation that the Princess Charlotte would succeed her disgraceful father to the throne of England. On November 6 she died in childbirth. The whole nation was grief-stricken; to the advocates of reform the future now looked gloomier than ever. In Italy Byron interrupted the flow of his *Childe Harold's Pilgrimage* to insert six stanzas on a tragedy which, he asserted, made Freedom mourn and afflicted the nation with a " deep and immedicable wound."

What Shelley, Godwin, and Ollier said to each other on the subject can only be inferred from the pamphlet Shelley began writing as soon as the visitors had left. Next day he finished it and sent it to Ollier as the outcome of their conversation, with instructions to send it to press " without an hour's delay." [69] But although Shelley was in hot haste, there is no certainty that the pamphlet was ever printed before 1843. [70]

Shelley began his pamphlet by remarking that the death of a woman " young, innocent, and beautiful, snatched from the bosom of domestic peace," was a fit occasion for grief — and also a fit occasion for thought. How many thousands of people died likewise every year for whom none wept, for some of whom possibly the parish did not even furnish a coffin? He agreed that public grief was salutary when caused by public calamity. Yet at the present time a greater calamity than the death of Princess Charlotte was being almost neglected.

With this neat parallelism Shelley launched upon the real subject of his pamphlet. Almost at the time the Princess had died three ignorant labourers had been hanged and beheaded for taking part in the so-called Derby insurrection. Apart from the justice or injustice of the court, nothing could be more horrible than for man to shed the blood of man, thus stimulating revenge and hatred and loosing a long train of executions, assassinations, and proscriptions to remote time.

These executions, he continued, were the result of a desperate state of affairs. When the government had revived William III's methods of anticipating taxes by loans, they had piled up a huge public debt whose mere interest exceeded all the other expenses of government. Worse still, they had thereby created a new aristocracy, " petty piddling slaves who have gained a right to the title of public creditors, either by gambling in the funds, or by subserviency to government, or some other villainous trade." To support themselves and the country's two aristocracies labourers were now obliged to work sixteen hours a day for the same amount previously earned in eight. Discontent and disaffection became a positive danger to the government. Faced with the choice of despotism, revolution, or reform, the government had chosen the first and had sent forth spies to stimulate abortive revolts in order to instill terror by suppressing them.

Continuing, Shelley asserted the common knowledge that one of these spies, Oliver, had instigated the petty outbreak for which Brandreth, Turner, and Ludlam were executed. Two of them had so accused him in their dying statements. England's real grief should be that its rulers trampled upon human rights, imprisoned its critics at will, piled up a public debt which ensured a general calamity in the future, created a choice between anarchy and oppression, and conspired through spies and bloodshed to frighten the people into choosing the latter. Let England mourn, then, for a Princess who, like Liberty, was young, innocent, and lovely. But Liberty also was dead, and whereas the Princess had perished through natural causes, Liberty had been murdered. " Let us follow the corpse of British Liberty slowly and reverently to its tomb," he concluded with a dignified eloquence far removed from the partisan vehemence Crabb Robinson objected to in his conversation on the day Princess Charlotte died: " — and if some glorious Phantom should appear, and make its throne of broken swords and sceptres and royal crowns trampled in the dust, let us say that the Spirit of Liberty has arisen from its grave and left all that was gross and mortal there, and kneel down and worship it as our Queen."

The day after this pamphlet was dispatched, the Shelleys received an evening call from Mr. Baxter and his son-in-law, Mr. Booth. Though perhaps not so enjoyable as the dinner next day at Hunt's, with music afterwards,[71] this must have been one of the most interesting evenings during their visit. The Shelleys hoped that Isabel Baxter Booth would be allowed to accompany them to Italy. Mr. Baxter greatly liked and admired the Shelleys and had even become a temporary convert to vegetarianism; [72] but Mr. Booth had heard talk of Shelley and his opinions that made him deeply dubious. A self-educated, strong-minded little man of dynamic personality and odd appearance, Booth was radical in his political beliefs, but conservative and suspicious on social and moral questions. It must have required considerable persuasion on Baxter's part to bring him to the interview.

The argument was keen and well sustained on both sides. " I never met a man," Shelley testified, " by whom, in the short time we exchanged ideas, I felt myself excited to so much severe and sustained mental competition, or from whom I derived so much amusement and instruction." [73] But if Booth felt himself similarly extended it only increased his conviction that Shelley was a dangerous character. Not only was he not converted through Baxter's good offices, but within a short while he converted or overawed Baxter.

Baxter sought to discourage Shelley's friendship by ignoring his letters and invitations, but this Shelley would not have. Pressed for an explanation of his changed conduct, Baxter urged the difference in social station. Shelley could not believe this, after the intimacy that had already developed, and wrote Baxter a dignified protest. Mary's intimacy with the Baxter family, he said, was originally a matter of their seeking, not hers. But the friendship had meant much to her and she had grieved for three years over its interruption and had rejoiced when it seemed about to be renewed. They had thoroughly enjoyed the recent company of Mr. Baxter and were persuaded that there was not actually a sufficient difference in their views to cause a second rupture in their relations. Was not the change due to Mr. Booth's influence? Mr. Booth, to whom this letter was shown, answered angrily that he regarded Shelley's comments on himself (which were really rather flattering) as calumny, that he had never sought Shelley's friendship and so had a perfect right to decline it, that he had never accused Shelley of anything not avowed by Shelley, and that he objected to Shelley's principles and conduct.[74] So ended Mary's hope of renewing her dearest friendship.

WITHIN a fortnight after Shelley and Mary returned to Marlow trouble developed over the publication of *Laon and Cythna*. Shelley realized that the poem, repeating as it did the doctrines of *Queen Mab*, might bring dangerous consequences. But, as he wrote to Byron, " It *is* to be *published* — for I am not of your opinion as to religion &c., and for this simple reason, that I am careless of the consequences as they regard myself. I only feel persecution bitterly, because I bitterly lament the depravity and mistake of those who persecute. As to me," he continued almost as if he were mounting the scaffold at the moment, and enjoyed it, "I can but die; I can but be torn to pieces, or devoted to infamy most undeserved; and whether this is inflicted by the necessity of nature, and circumstances, or through a principle, pregnant, as I believe, with important benefit to mankind, is an alternative to which I cannot be indifferent." [75]

The poem was turned over to Buchanan McMillan, the Bow Street printer, with instructions to print 750 copies at Shelley's expense. By October 13 the first four sheets had been printed and submitted to a prospective publisher, along with a description of the poem.[76] Evidently the poem was declined. Probably on Leigh Hunt's advice Shelley then offered it to Charles and James Ollier, who had published the *Proposals for Putting Reform to the Vote*. Being young men of liberal principles who possessed a share of enterprise and courage, they accepted the poem and were almost ready to announce it for sale by the end of November.[77] Leigh Hunt gave it a preliminary puff by quoting eight stanzas in the *Examiner* for November 30. However, the printer was now causing delay over some corrections and perhaps also over the possibility of a prosecution for printing it. "That McMillan," the impatient poet complained, "is an obstinate dog and as troublesome as he is impudent." [78]

McMillan was no sooner settled than the Olliers became even more obstinate than he. Copies of the book entitled *Laon and Cythna* and postdated 1818 had already gone forth early in December when the Olliers suddenly became recalcitrant. "In the personal conduct of my Hero and Heroine," Shelley had written in the concluding paragraph of his original Preface, "there is one circumstance which was intended to startle the reader from the trance of ordinary life. It was my object to break through the crust of those outworn opinions on which established institutions depend. . . . The circumstance . . . was introduced, however, merely to accustom men to that charity and toleration which the exhibition of a practice widely differing from their own has a tendency to promote." He added in a footnote that

548

the sentiments connected with this circumstance were not the author's own. This circumstance was the fact that the two principal characters were brother and sister, who loved each other without benefit of clergy.

There seems to be no reason to doubt the complete honesty of Shelley's explanation. In commenting on the whispered charges against Byron, Shelley had spoken of them as " calumnies," which implies a disapproval of incest. But Shelley's desire to startle succeeded too well with the Olliers. They were convinced that publication of the book would convict them of condoning incest, as well as the other more ordinary attacks on social and religious conventions. They flatly refused to publish the book unless certain changes were made.

Shelley was now in an extremely trying situation. For months he had devoted most of his time and enthusiasm to the poem and was passionately committed to publishing it. The printing had been at his own expense; he could hardly afford to reprint the whole book. Even if he did, it would be damned in advance by the whisper that a fairly courageous publisher of known liberal tendencies had already washed his hands of it. Under circumstances that would have been infuriating even to a phlegmatic author he wrote Charles Ollier one of the most eloquent letters he ever penned. He pointed out that Ollier's fears were based on no circumstances that were not already to be foreseen when the book was accepted and that its withdrawal after having been actually published placed the author under a false and unjust imputation of deceit which would damage the work irretrievably. He appealed to Ollier's courage and liberal principles:

I beseech you to reconsider the matter, for your sake no less than for my own. Assume the high and secure ground of courage. The people who visit your shop, and the wretched bigot who gave his worthless custom to some other bookseller, are not the public. The public respect talent; and a large portion of them are already undeceived with regard to the prejudices which my book attacks. You would lose some customers, but you would gain others. Your trade would be diverted into a channel more consistent with your own principles. Not to say that a publisher is in no wise pledged to all the opinions of his publications, or to any; and that he may enter his protest with each copy sold, either against the truth or the discretion of the principles of the books he sells. But there is a much more important consideration in the case. You are, and have been to a certain extent, the publisher. I don't believe that, if the book was quietly and regularly published, the Government would touch anything of a character so refined, and so remote from the conceptions of the vulgar. They would hesitate before they invaded a member of the higher circles of the republic of letters. But, if they see us tremble, they will make no distinctions; they will feel their strength. You might bring the arm of the law down upon us by flinching now. Directly these scoundrels see that people are afraid of them, they seize upon them and hold them up to mankind as criminals already convicted by their own fears. You lay yourself prostrate, and they trample on you. How glad they would be to seize on any connection of Hunt's by this most powerful of all their arms — the terrors and self-condemnation of their victim. Read all the *ex officio* cases, and see what reward booksellers and printers have received for their submission.

He suggested a compromise by which Sherwood and Neely might become the principal publishers and the Olliers only secondary. This, while injurious to his interests, would not destroy them, as Ollier's sudden complete withdrawal would. In any event, he promised to continue to work for Ollier's best interests. He concluded:

I have just received a most kind and encouraging letter from Mr. Moore on the subject of my poem. I have the fairest chance of the public approaching my work with unbiassed and unperverted feeling: the fruit of reputation (and you know for *what purposes* I value it) is within my reach. It is for you, now you have been once named as publisher, and have me in your power, to blast all this, and to hold up my literary character in the eye of mankind as that of a proscribed and rejected outcast. And for no evil that I have ever done you, but in return for a preference which, although you falsely now esteem injurious to you, was solicited by Hunt, and conferred by me, as a source and a proof of nothing but kind intentions.

Dear Sir,

I remain your sincere well-wisher,

PERCY B. SHELLEY [79]

It soon appeared, however, that Ollier's demands could all be met by cancelling the title page and twenty-six pages of text and substituting new pages. "The contents of your letter this morning certainly alters the question," Shelley wrote Ollier two days later, probably referring to some such suggestion. He urged Ollier to see him at the first opportunity. Next day Ollier appeared at Albion House; he remained for two days and returned to London with the revised text ready to print.[80] The bulk of the revisions had to do with changing the relationship of Laon and Cythna from brother and sister to cousins. The title was changed from *Laon and Cythna* to *The Revolt of Islam*. In order to protect the change every effort was to be made to call in the few copies that had been prematurely issued under the original title.[81]

Peacock has left a vivid description of Shelley contesting every change point by point, protesting that his poem was ruined, refusing for a long time to alter a single line, yielding only on the united advice of his friends. "He contested the proposed alterations step by step, in the end, sometimes adopting, more frequently modifying, never originating, and always insisting that his poem was spoiled." [82] Peacock was undoubtedly a spectator and participator in the scene, as one of Shelley's local advisers. Though his memory concerning Shelley may sometimes be proved inaccurate, it is grotesque to suppose that his account of the present incident is completely fictitious. Shelley's conduct as Peacock describes it was too natural to Shelley (or any other poet!) to be entirely false.

Yet Peacock, like Hogg in other circumstances, has undoubtedly created a false impression that Shelley's behaviour in this crisis was totally impractical. There was in fact nothing that he could do but make the best of it. Not only did he do this as soon as the device of substituting cancel-leaves was suggested, but he even did it with a good grace. "The present edition of 'Laon and Cythna' is to be suppressed," he wrote to Thomas Moore; [83] " and it will be republished in about a fortnight under the title of 'The Revolt of Islam,' with some alterations which consist in little else than the substitution of the words *friend* or *lover* for that of *brother* and *sister*. The truth is, that the seclusion of my habits has confined me so much within the circle of my own thoughts, that I have formed to myself a very different measure of approbation or disapprobation for actions than that which is in use among mankind; and the result of that peculiarity, contrary to my intention, revolts and shocks many who might be inclined to sympathise with me in my general views. — As soon as I discovered that this effect was produced by the circumstance alluded to, I hastened to cancel it — not from any personal feeling of terror, or repentance, but from the sincere desire of doing all the good and conferring all the pleasure which might flow from so obscure a person as myself. I don't know why I trouble you with these words, but your kind approbation of the opening of the Poem has emboldened me to believe that this account of my motives might interest you." [84]

Once Shelley had seen the matter in this light, all his succeeding correspondence with Ollier bore upon the very practical details of hastening the publication, retrieving copies of the first edition, seeing that the poem was properly advertised and that review copies were sent out, and insisting that the *Alastor* volume be advertised along with it.[85]

WHATEVER agitation may have been caused by the difficulty with Ollier is not even hinted at in Mary's journal. She recorded simply on December 14: " Ollier comes down "; on December 15: " alterations for ' Cythna ' "; and on December 16: " Ollier goes up." Mary's reading went on steadily, and Shelley's was interrupted only on the day that the alterations were made. On the day of Ollier's arrival Shelley read Berkeley; on the day of his departure he began reading Lady Morgan's *France*. Throughout the month of December there were few days in which Shelley did not read Berkeley or Hume (two contrasting philosophers who well illustrate the difference between Shelley's youth and maturity), Gibbon, Lady Morgan's *France*, Shakespeare, or *Paradise Lost*. He was not too absorbed in his own difficulties to take an interest in the third trial of William Hone for treason, or to send two cheques to the fund raised for Hone's benefit following his acquittal.[86]

Christmas passed pleasantly and peacefully in reading and walking. On Christmas Eve Shelley indulged his bent for telling children tales of horror; his temporarily adopted ward Polly Rose listened with mingled terror and delight to the tale of Bürger's *Lenore*, told *con amore*.[87] Horace Smith arrived the day after Christmas on his last visit to the Shelleys at Marlow. He arranged to act as Shelley's London financial agent while Shelley was abroad, so that he might be saved brokerage and agency fees in receiving his income.[88] " Never, never shall I forget my last wandering with the poet," he wrote later:

as we stretched far away from the haunts of men, beneath the high over-arching boughs, which, forming around us a Gothic temple, with interminable cloisters, still opening as we advanced seemed to inspire him with the love and the worship of nature, and to suggest a fuller disclosure of his religious views than he had hitherto imparted to me. Becoming gradually excited as he gave way to his sentiments, his eyes kindled, he strode forward more rapidly, swinging his arms to and fro, and spoke with a vehemence and a rapidity which rendered it difficult to collect his opinions on particular points, though I have a clear recollection of their general tendency.[89]

Only a few more weeks now remained to be spent in Marlow. Shelley and Mary read steadily, as usual. Claire began the study of Italian. On January 3 Hogg arrived for a short visit. Shelley was ill again for two or three days, but his illness did not prevent the increase in the amount of Latin reading that generally occurred when Hogg was present.[90] Godwin came with his young son William, now a schoolboy; he arrived at a new financial misunderstanding with Shelley, and departed.[91] Shelley set about translating the Homeric Hymns, but was interrupted by a return of the ophthalmia he had contracted in visiting the poor. For a while thereafter he seems to have discontinued his reading, but Mary read to him occasionally and engaged him in chess.

On January 29 Shelley, Claire, and Peacock drove up to London in the family carriage. The primary object was to conclude Shelley's financial arrangements with Mr. William Willats, a dealer in post-obits, with whom Shelley signed the final papers on January 31. Shelley at once dispatched a sum of money to Godwin. By this time he had probably reached the conclusion that Francis Place had arrived at long before; namely, that no matter how large the sums turned over to Godwin, it was hopeless to look for an end to his demands. He sent Godwin only a part of the sum apparently agreed upon, stating frankly that he was resolved to keep in his own hands " the power conferred by the difference of the two sums." Godwin's reply was so prompt that it was dated on the same day on which Shelley concluded his loan. " I acknowledge the receipt of the sum mentioned in your letter. I acknowledge with equal explicitness my complete disappointment." After challenging Shelley to place the difference between the two sums in the hands of a banker, subject only to their joint signatures, he continued with bitter Godwinian dignity:

Since our last conversation at Marlow, I have reflected much on the subject. I am ashamed of the tone I have taken with you in all our late conversations. I have played the part of a supplicant, and deserted that of a philosopher. It was not thus I talked with you when I first knew you. I will talk so no more. I will talk principles; I will talk Political Justice; whether it make for me or against me, no matter. I am fully capable of this. I desire not to dictate. I know that every man's conduct ought to be regulated by his own judgement, such as it may happen to be. But I hold it to be my duty once to state to you the principles which belong to the case. Having done that, it is my duty to forbear. I would enlighten your understanding if I could; but I would not, if I could, carry things by importunity. I have nothing to say to you of a passionate nature; least of all do I wish to move your feelings; less than the least to wound you. All that I have to say is in the calmness of philosophy, and moves far above the atmosphere of vulgar sensations. If you have the courage to hear me, come; if you have not, be it so. What I have to say I *must* say, if I ever stand in your presence again; but I had rather it were without a witness.[92]

Whether or not Shelley accepted Godwin's challenge is unknown. We only know that with money in hand he returned to Marlow on February 5, having spent an agreeable evening at

HORACE SMITH

Engraved by Finden from a portrait by Maskerrier

the opera with Claire, Hogg, Peacock, and the Hunts,[93] and
having passed at least part of one evening in a sonnet-writing
contest with Hunt and Keats, the product of which was three
rather undistinguished sonnets on the Nile.[94]

SHELLEY remained in Marlow only long enough to help pack the
books. On February 7 he returned to London, leaving Mary
and Claire to complete the packing. Two days later Claire went
up with Alba and little William. Mary remained one day longer,
but was in London on the 10th, when they all went to the
opera to hear *Don Giovanni,* and *Acis and Galatea.* Next
day they were settled in lodgings at 119 Great Russell Street,
Bloomsbury Square.[95] By an odd coincidence — or was it another instance of Shelley's curious tendency to go to places with
Godwinian associations? — Shelley's landlord was named Godwin, but he was no relation of the Sage of Skinner Street.[96]

With their affairs practically settled, Shelley and Mary now
devoted themselves almost entirely to a round of social pleasures
quite rare in their experience. Reading seems for once to have
been neglected; the fact that Shelley is mentioned once (February 25) as "not well" seems to have made no difference. They
visited the Indian Library, Apollonicon, the "Panorama of
Rome," and the British Museum, where they saw the Elgin
Marbles and the "casts from Phidias." Twice they went to the
theatre, to see Milman's *Fazio* and Byron's *Bride of Abydos.*
Five times they went to the opera. Hogg and Peacock came to
dinner eight times together, once with the Hunts, and once or
twice separately. Four times they spent the day or evening with
the Hunts; once they dined with Horace Smith. All this in the
last seventeen days of February. Not once in the period does
either Mary's or Claire's journal mention Godwin.[97]

Shortly before the time set for their departure Shelley called
on Mr. Baxter and learned that Isabel Booth was in town. But
the determined Mr. Booth was still in the ascendant; Mary was
forced to record that Isabel "neither comes nor sends." Now
that they were embarking on foreign travels, it seemed wise to

christen the three children, at which time (March 9) Claire's child received the new name of Allegra. There were also one or two literary matters to be set straight.

On February 18 Mary copied Shelley's *Rosalind and Helen* (as it then existed) so that it could be left with the printers. During the autumn Peacock had written his best poem, " Rhododaphne," which Mary had copied for him in early December. Always generous in such matters, Shelley greatly admired the poem and had undertaken to review it. This review was probably written in London shortly before their departure; Mary finished copying it on February 23, and it was sent off to Hunt for the *Examiner,* where it never appeared.[98]

The last week in England is thus represented in Mary's journal:

Sunday, March 1 [covering March 1–9] . . . On Thursday, 5th, Papa calls, and Claire visits Mrs. Godwin. On Sunday, 8th, we dine at Hunt's, and meet Mr. Novello. Music.

Monday, March 9 — Christening the children. Horace Smith calls; he spends the evening here, with Godwin and Peacock. After they are all gone, Hunt comes, with Miss Kent; they go at 12.

Tuesday, March 10 — Packing. Hunt and Marianne spend the day with us. Mary Lamb calls. Papa in the evening. Our adieus.

Wednesday, March 11 — Travel to Dover.[99]

Mary forgot (or disdained) to state that Peacock had supper with the Shelleys on the evening of March 10, after he had attended the opera,[100] nor did she evidently think it worthy of notice that Shelley fell asleep during the visit of the Hunts, and so left England without a parting kiss from Marianne.[101]

The better part of a day was consumed in travelling from London to Dover by coach, through Chatham, Ospringe, and Canterbury. Dover by night, with its numerous lights twinkling from the low hill-tops, seemed almost a fairy city as they entered the outskirts. Next morning (March 12) the sea was quite rough, and it was only after some hesitation that they decided to embark without waiting for a smoother passage.[102]

From descriptions of Shelley during the previous year [103] it is possible to get a fairly adequate notion of his physical appearance as he left England for ever. He was a young man midway between twenty-five and twenty-six years of age, round-shouldered, narrow-chested, slender, and of somewhat better than average height when he abandoned his habitual stoop and stood erect. His hands and feet were rather large, but his general build was slight and hardly seemed sufficient to support the physical energy that he sometimes exerted. He walked with a lounging or weaving gait that contributed to a general suggestion of youthful immaturity. He dressed well, but carelessly, usually exposing to view a throat that appeared curiously small and undeveloped, and a thick, somewhat unruly thatch of wavy, golden-brown hair. His face was round and rather flat, with small features, receding chin, and nose slightly retroussé. Under the influence of dejection or ill health his fair, freckled face seemed rather pasty, but excitement or exercise easily brought the colour to his cheeks. Intensely blue eyes and a well-shaped mouth were his finest, most expressive features. In repose these features conveyed an impression of thoughtful, courteous attention, alert and gravely comprehending. Under stress of argument or excitement they reflected instantly Shelley's characteristic lively changes of mood. A vehement mood was emphasized by somewhat awkward gestures and by the conversion of a voice ordinarily low, clear, and distinct into a shrill, dissonant vehemence that sometimes made him seem to strangers more antagonizing than he intended to be.

His manners were gentle and sympathetic, with a simple native dignity born of his sincerity. Intimates like Hogg, Peacock, and Hunt soon learned that occasional unconventionalities were merely the unconscious expression either of abstraction or of sudden impulse. He had learned by bitter personal experience that intense conviction and utter sincerity of purpose, even when reinforced by extensive reading and study, are no guarantees against misunderstanding and partial frustration. The shock of this surprising discovery — the knowledge that even his particular idol, the author of *Political Justice,* could not do him personal justice — depressed and sobered him.

Without yielding anything of his fundamental beliefs and purposes, Shelley had come to realize that Godwin's first advice was sound, that he could accomplish little or nothing by premature direct action, that he must inform himself further about the origin and growth of the customs and prejudices he hoped to help overthrow. In moments of extreme depression he now doubted his ability to contribute significantly to this result even at long range. He had offered the public a volume of real distinction and had seen it contemned by reviewers who praised other poems that he knew were inferior. Nevertheless, in spite of occasional dejection, he continued to write poetry for publication, poetry that repeated most of the doctrines of *Queen Mab*. He even sought in two pamphlets to influence the public mind on matters of immediate reform. In these the studious moderation of his language and his proposals suggest that his conversation on similar subjects had grown less hectic and tumultuous than formerly. Enough of the former quality still remained to offend Crabb Robinson and Hazlitt, but to most people who have commented on Shelley in 1817, even to some like Mr. Baxter who were at first prejudiced by unfavourable reports, Shelley revealed a personality that was peculiarly winning and persuasive.

Superficially at least, he had attained a juster notion of the power and value of money. But Sir Timothy and his attorney were both convinced upon good evidence of his financial irresponsibility. Godwin and his friend Turner felt likewise, and so, undoubtedly, did Mr. Madocks and a number of small creditors whose accounts Shelley left unsettled. There were people in Marlow who knew him mainly by sight and local rumour who thought him a little crazy; and there were people in the same town, who knew him perhaps better, who thought him a kindly, sympathetic, and even practical-minded benefactor of the poor. Few if any of the people who had thought the youthful Shelley mad would say so now. He had achieved a kind of perspective on his own peculiar mental complexion and even wrote calmly of two of his autobiographical characters, Laon and Lionel, as having been mad for a time. Soon, in " Julian and Maddalo," he was to add a third, who also possessed the very Shelleyan quality of mistaking illusion for reality.

Philosophically he had come a long way since his early materialistic bias. As a convert to Berkeley's idealistic philoso-

558

phy, he was about ready to suggest that reality, so called, was actually illusion. His early ideas of love had become much more definite and important to him, largely on account of his reading in Plato. The old doctrine of Necessity had made way for the doctrine of Intellectual Beauty, which was already in process of being merged in his conception of the supreme importance of Love, or universal sympathy.

Recently he had associated intimately with Byron and Hunt and had come to know less intimately a number of other men of poetic and intellectual abilities. The esteem in which these men held his character and powers fortified his own confidence based upon continuous, thoughtful study.

As Shelley left England the sound of Leigh Hunt's favourable review of *The Revolt of Islam* was yet pleasant in his ears. The *Quarterly,* which could alone almost make or break an author, had not yet spoken, but its words would be none the softer for Leigh Hunt's praise. Shelley had in his luggage a copy of Hunt's *Foliage,* published late in 1817, containing two sonnets, one entitled " To Percy Bysshe Shelley, on the Degrading Notions of Deity," and the second simply " To the Same." That men should " defame the kindly and the wise " was no wonder, Hunt asserted in the first sonnet, because such men held an idea of Deity that converted beauty into ugliness and hatred. The truly wise, he continued in the second, should never be thwarted by such misunderstanding:

> The Spirit of Beauty, though by solemn quires
> Hourly blasphemed, stoops not from its calm end
> And forward breathing love, but ever on
> Rolls the round day, and calls the starry fires
> To their glad watch. Therefore, high-hearted friend,
> Be still with thine own task in unison.

The same theme of admiration and encouragement echoed from a more recent sonnet by Horace Smith, published in the *Examiner* for February 8 under the title " Sonnet: To the Author of *The Revolt of Islam* ":

> O thou bold Herald of announcements high,
> No prostituted Muse inspired thy story,

But human Love lent thee his wings to fly
　　Forward into a coming age of glory,
　　When Tyrannies and Superstitions hoary
Beneath the foot of Liberty shall lie,
　　And men shall turn from those oppressions gory
To worship Peace, and Love, and Charity.
The heart that could conceive so bright a day,
Is proof that it may come; — therefore shall they
　　Who live on tears and darkness, steep each tooth
In poisoned gall to make that heart their prey;
　　But thou shalt smile and pity, giving thy youth
　　To glorious hopes, and all-defying Truth.

SOURCES AND NOTES
Chapter I

GENERAL SOURCES

Note: Unless otherwise specified, all references in this work to Hogg's Life of Shelley, *Trelawny's* Recollections of Shelley and Byron, *and Peacock's* Memoirs of Shelley *are to the combined edition of all three books by Humbert Wolfe (London, 1933, 2 volumes) entitled* The Life of Percy Bysshe Shelley.

Thomas Allen: *History of the Counties of Surrey and Sussex.* 2 vols. London, 1829.

Thomas K. Cromwell: *Excursions in the County of Sussex,* etc. London, 1822.

H. B. Forman, ed.: *Shelley's Works.* 8 vols. London, 1876–80.

Thomas Jefferson Hogg: *The Life of Shelley,* ed. Humbert Wolfe. London, 1933.

Thomas W. Horsfield: *The History, Antiquities and Topography of the County of Sussex.* 2 vols. Lewes, 1835.

Roger Ingpen and Walter E. Peck, ed.: *Complete Works of Shelley,* Julian Edition. 10 vols. London, 1926–9.

Mark Antony Lower: *A Compendious History of Sussex, Topographical, Archæological, and Anecdotal.* 2 vols. London, 1870.

Mark Antony Lower: *The Worthies of Sussex.* Lewes, 1865.

W. MacIntosh: *Horsham, Its History and Antiquities.* London, 1868.

Thomas Medwin: *Revised Life of Shelley,* ed. H. B. Forman. London, 1913.

NOTES AND REFERENCES

[1] Lower (*Worthies*), 64.
[2] First printed in Forman, V, xxxv.
[3] Henry Shelley, of Worminghurst, was the grandson of Edward

Shelley, of Worminghurst. Sir William Shelley, of the Michelgrove Shelleys, had a younger brother named Edward, probably identical with Edward Shelley of Worminghurst. Seventeenth-century ancestors of the poet bore the Michelgrove Shelley arms without apparent protest, and the claim is admitted by Burke and Berry — though it is not advanced in the Shelley ancestry deposited in 1816. The common statement that Shelley was related by descent to Sir Philip Sidney is doubtful, since it rests upon the fact that Elizabeth Michelgrove, of the Michelgrove Shelleys, was of Sidney descent. The descendants of Shelley's grandfather by his second marriage were descendants of Sir Philip Sidney's father through a second son, but the poet was descended from his grandfather's first marriage. The present head of the elder branch of the Shelley family is Sir John Frederick Shelley, 10th baronet, of Sholbrooke Park, Crediton.

4 The inscription that commemorates John Shelley's name in the church at Worth, Sussex, may be quoted as establishing the origin of the poet's second name and for its emphasis upon a virtue highly prized by the poet:

> In a Vault near this Place lieth the body of John Shelley of Fen Place in this Parish Esquire: of the ancient family of the Shelleys of Worminghurst: He was Son and Heir of Timothy Shelley, Gent. By Catherine his Wife, Daughter of Edward Michell of Stammerham, Esq. Was born at Wolf's Hill in West Cheltington in this County, January 27th, 1666. And died February 4th, 1739. He married Hellen Daughter of Roger Bysshe of Fen Place Esq. By whom he had Nine children. He was very remarkable for that exalted Part of Humanity, forgiving Injuries. How great Soever And for many other eminent Virtues A Recital of which this Monument could not contain which is dedicated to the Memory of the Best of Husbands by his most sorrowful Wife who was born April 16th 1667 and died February 10, MDCCXLII.

5 Not "in New England," as English biographers were misled to believe through the association of the Newark settlement with that of Guilford, in Connecticut.

6 Quoted by the discoverer, John Malone, in "A Search for Shelley's American Ancestor," *Century Magazine*, n.s. XXII, 634–6 (August 1892).

7 In addition to Fen Place, John Shelley's will disposes of £2,000 in money, personal property, certain freehold hereditaments, and certain copyholds of undetermined value.

[8] Hogg, op. cit., I, 296.

[9] *Shelley in England*, I, 13. For Medwin's statements, see *Revised Life*, 7–12.

[10] In the churchyard at Horsham is a tombstone erected by his employer to this man, John Groombridge, who died in 1789, which carries the unfinished inscription: " He was ——." The local explanation is that Sir Bysshe had been warned of this man's dishonesty in vain and had discovered his peculations only after his death and only after the inscription had already been carved half-way through some such inscription as " He was an honest man." See W. Hale White: "Notes on Shelley's Birthplace," *Macmillan's Magazine*, XXXIX, 461–5 (March 1879).

[11] Medwin, op. cit., 9–12; Shelley to Elizabeth Hitchener, January 26, 1812 (Julian *Works*, VIII, 254), and *Fraser's Magazine*, XXIII, 702 (June 1841).

[12] Mrs. Matilda C. Houstoun: *A Woman's Memories of World-Known Men* (3rd ed., London, 1883), 68.

[13] Maud Rolleston: *Talks with Lady Shelley* (London, 1925), 95, 138. According to Medwin (op. cit., 105), Timothy Shelley sent his younger son to school with the admonition: " Don't you be like your brother. Take care you don't learn too much," and carried his hatred of books to the extent of opposing education for the poor and of never employing a steward who could read and write.

[14] See Chapter vi, page 125, quoting Hogg.

[15] Mrs. Matilda C. Houstoun, op. cit., 69.

[16] He became Sir Timothy in 1815, on the death of his father.

[17] It is to this fact that we owe the fullness of Mrs. Shelley's Notes to her edition. They were written to supply as far as possible the lack of a biography.

[18] Maud Rolleston, op. cit., 68.

[19] N.s. XXII, 206 (August 1844).

[20] Shelley to Hogg, April 28, 1811, Julian *Works*, VIII, 77.

[21] P. 65.

Chapter II

GENERAL SOURCES

Julian *Works,* as cited for Chapter i.

Thomas Jefferson Hogg: *The Life of Shelley,* ed. Humbert Wolfe. London, 1933.

Thomas Medwin: *Revised Life of Shelley,* ed. H. B. Forman. London, 1913.

Middlesex and Hertfordshire Notes and Queries, Vol. II (1896).

Middlesex, painted by John Fulleylove, R.I., described by A. R. Hope Moncrief. London, 1907.

Sir John Rennie: *Autobiography.* London, 1875 (written 1867).

NOTES AND REFERENCES

[1] Dowden: *Life,* I, 7.

[2] The authenticity of this portrait has been doubted. There seem to be no definite and absolute grounds for either repudiating or accepting it. See "The Portraits and Busts of Shelley," Appendix VI.

[3] Hogg, op. cit., 21–33. Since Hellen was seven years the poet's junior and can hardly have had any recollections of her own prior to Shelley's tenth or eleventh year, it is obvious that some of her testimony depends upon the memory of older members of the family and that what she herself remembered of the poet must begin with his vacations and holidays from Syon House Academy, which he entered in his tenth year. They continue through Shelley's years at Eton. They are not dated or given in chronological order. I have relied upon my own judgment in presenting her recollections in three groups, as applying to Shelley's vacations from Syon House Academy and the earlier and later Eton vacations. The other children in the family besides the poet were: Elizabeth, born May 10, 1794; Hellen, born January 29, 1796, died four months later; Mary,

born June 9, 1797; Hellen, born September 26, 1799; Margaret, born January 20, 1801; John, born March 15, 1806.

[4] Medwin, op. cit., 14.

[5] See Fred Turner: " Memorable Brentford Houses: Percy Bysshe Shelley at Syon House Academy," *Middlesex and Hertfordshire Notes and Queries,* II (1896), 25–7, 88–90.

[6] *Autobiography.* The first two pages deal with Syon House Academy and Shelley. Two years Shelley's junior, Sir John Rennie became later a great engineer, next to Shelley the school's most distinguished alumnus.

[7] W. C. Gellibrand, whose death at ninety-three is recorded in an article by Augustine Birrell in the *Athenæum,* May 3, 1884, p. 567. The article quotes his recollections of Shelley.

[8] Op. cit., 16.

[9] Rennie, op. cit., 2.

[10] *Ealing Gazette,* July 15, 1922, letter of W. H. Woolen.

[11] Medwin, op. cit., 21. Medwin, who seems to consider the incident primarily as a prank rather than as a piece of dishonesty, tells the story as an illustration of Greenlaw's ignorance. The verses were:

> *Me miserum! quanti montes volvuntur aquarum!*
> *Jam, jam tacturas sidera summa putes —*

which the master gustily derided as bad Latin. " ' Jam, jam! ' — Pooh, pooh, boy! raspberry jam! " concluding, with a final box on the ear: " Putes! you may think this very fine, but to me it is all balderdash, hyperbolical stuff."

[12] Hogg, op. cit., II, 154 (letter of Charles Grove to " My dear H.," February 16, 1857). Charles Grove's mother was a Pilfold, sister of Shelley's mother.

[13] Rennie, op. cit., 2.

[14] Medwin (op. cit., 28) says " second or third year," but Shelley was there only two years.

[15] Ibid.

[16] Viz.: (1) General Properties of Matter, (2) Mechanics, (3) Principles of Chemistry, (4, 5) Pneumatics, (6) Hydrostatics, (7, 8) Electricity, (9) Optics, (10, 11, 12) Astronomy.

[17] Walker, op. cit., 85, 86.

[18] Medwin, op. cit., 28.

[19] Walker, op. cit., 55, 29. Professor Carl Grabo (*A Newton among Poets,* 119–20) quotes a passage from Father Giovanni Bat-

tista Beccaria's *Artificial Electricity* which notes scientifically many of the cloud-phenomena Shelley's poem describes. There is no evidence beyond the similarity, however, that Shelley read this treatise. The selection quoted by Professor Grabo contains two phrases similar to phrases in " The Cloud," but one of these also occurs in Adam Walker's *Syllabus,* and both may have occurred in the lecture which Shelley heard — in fact Walker, a purveyor of science, may well have based his lecture on Beccaria's treatise, which had been available in English since 1776, and had attracted the attention of the Royal Society.

Shelley's scientific knowledge of light, which Professor Grabo traces to his reading of Newton's *Optics,* was also anticipated in one of Walker's lectures, and to another lecture he may owe his first interest in carbonic-acid gas and nitrous air, which Professor Grabo finds reflected in *Prometheus Unbound* and supposes to come from scientific authors between whom and Shelley he is not always able to demonstrate a connection.

[20] Charlotte Dacre's *Zofloya* was not published until 1806 and could not have been read by Shelley at Syon House, as Medwin says. This novel, whose influence is easily traceable in Shelley's *Zastrozzi,* was read during the early days at Eton.

[21] Given in the *Harleian Miscellany,* Volume II, and in Edward V. Lucas: *Highways and Byways in Sussex* (London and New York, 1904), 126–9.

[22] Dowden: *Life,* I, 10.

[23] Hogg, op. cit., 24 (letter of Hellen Shelley).

[24] Mentioned by Medwin, op. cit., 72, but not by Hellen. Possibly this was during a later vacation, from Eton.

[25] Medwin, op. cit., 24.

[26] Ibid., 28.

[27] Rennie, loc. cit.

[28] Loc. cit.

[29] Julian *Works,* VIII, 8, dated Monday, July 18, 1803, and addressed to " Miss Kate." The Tom is probably Tom Medwin, who first printed the letter as addressed to an aunt of his.

[30] " An Essay on Friendship " (1822?), Julian *Works,* VII, 143–4.

[31] Sir John Rennie (op. cit., 2) mentions one Syon House contemporary of Shelley's, another peculiar character, named Tredcroft, from the same county, Sussex; " he also had considerable poetical talent, but unfortunately lost his health, and ultimately, I understand, died completely imbecile at an early age." Shelley must

have known both the Horsham and the Syon House Tredcroft, but whether they were identical with each other or with the friend Shelley described is uncertain. The description, but not the history, of the Syon House Tredcroft suggests that he may have been the friend Shelley described. The Tredcrofts were a good Sussex family established at Horsham since the sixteenth century. Nathaniel Tredcroft, Esq., of Horsham, had a son, Henry, who was three or four years Shelley's senior, but the only additional information about him that I have been able to obtain is that he married in 1828. The Horsham Tredcrofts were distantly related to the Shelleys through the Michells and Pilfolds.

Dowden, who has noted Rennie's mention of Tredcroft (but not the family or local connections of Shelleys and Tredcrofts), suggests that Shelley may have been referring to either Halliday or (*Life,* I, 20) Price, whom he knew a year or two later at Eton, but thinks it unlikely.

[32] *Laon and Cythna,* Dedication: To Mary —(1817) stanzas iii–vi, and "Hymn to Intellectual Beauty" (1816), stanzas v and vi. The two passages both refer to a spring day in early boyhood, but one describes Shelley's dedication to a warfare against tyranny and the other his dedication to the pursuit of the spirit of beauty, interests that with Shelley were complementary. If Shelley's recollection was as particular as he asserted, the experience, as Mr. Ingpen has observed (*Shelley in England,* I, 44), must have occurred at Syon House, rather than at Eton, where Shelley would have walked forth upon a brick pavement instead of " glittering grass."

Chapter III

GENERAL SOURCES

Julian *Works,* Medwin, and Hogg, as cited for Chapter ii.

A. Clutton-Brock: *Eton.* London, 1900.

E. S. Creasy: *Memoirs of Eminent Etonians.* London, 1850; 2nd ed., 1876.

Edward Dowden: *The Life of Percy Bysshe Shelley*. 2 vols. London, 1886.

Sir Henry C. Maxwell Lyte: *A History of Eton College*. London, 4th ed., 1911.

[Joseph Gibbons Merle]: "A Newspaper Editor's Reminiscences," in *Fraser's Magazine*, XXXIII, 699–710 (June 1841).

Ralph Nevill: *Floreat Etona*. London, 1911.

H. S. Salt: *Memories of Bygone Eton*. London, n. d.

H. E. C. Stapylton: *The Eton School Lists 1791–1877*. London, 1885 (preface dated 1864).

Francis St. John Thackeray: *Memoir of Edward Craven Hawtrey, D.D., Headmaster and afterwards Provost of Eton*. London, 1896.

(For a number of useful criticisms and suggestions, most of which are specified in the following notes, I am indebted to Mr. C. H. K. Masten, Vice-Provost of Eton, and to Eton's antiquary, Mr. R. A. Austen-Leigh.)

NOTES AND REFERENCES

[1] Dowden says Keate became master a year before Shelley entered Oxford; but Mr. C. H. K. Masten, Vice-Provost of Eton, informs me that the college Minutes state that he was "elected Upper Master and took the oath" on December 28, 1809. Shelley ceased residence at Eton on July 30, 1810. Thus he was subject to Keate as headmaster only seven months, two weeks of which were holidays. But Keate was master of the lower part of the school during the short time Shelley was in the lower school.

[2] Many are the stories of Dr. Keate's floggings. When the names of several candidates for confirmation were sent up to him on a strip of paper resembling that used for flogging-requests he flogged the candidates forthwith, treating their attempted explanations as aggravating the offence. He was the author of several famous wholesale floggings. In 1825 he flogged forty-six boys in succession and in 1832 he suppressed a student rebellion by flogging over eighty boys in succession, working far into the night. One author (*Etoniana*, London, 1865, p. 12) claims rather proudly: "He flogged half the ministers, bishops, generals and dukes of the present century."

[3] Alexander W. Kinglake: *Eothen, or, Traces of Travel Brought Home from the East* (New York, 1850), Chapter xviii.

[4] See note 1 above.

[5] Lyte, op. cit., 425, quoted from *Hawtrey's Sermons and Lectures* (privately printed, 1849), 111–12. Dr. Hawtrey was Shelley's senior at Eton by three years and had himself been bullied and hunted by fellow students. On one occasion he was almost suffocated to death by an older student. Cf. Thackeray, op. cit., 12–14, 95–6.

[6] *Edinburgh Review*, LI (1830), 65–80. I see no reason why this should not have been substantially true of Eton from 1804 to 1810 as in 1830, since the histories indicate only slight changes between the dates, and those in the direction of improvement. Mr. C. H. K. Masten justly reminds me that there were always plenty of boys at Eton from cultured homes who employed much of their leisure in reading, and cites Gladstone, whose serious use of his time there (1821–9) is abundantly established in Moreley's *Life of Gladstone*.

[7] Lyte, op. cit., 318–19.

[8] *Edinburgh Review*, LI (1830), 65–80. See note 6 above.

[9] This seems a little inconsistent with Lyte, who says (op. cit., 311) that the last week before summer and winter holidays respectively was set apart for the study of Greek plays and that the sixth- and upper-fifth-form boys had two extra school hours weekly through the year in which to construe about a hundred lines of a Greek play.

[10] *Edinburgh Review*, XV, 47 (October 1809). My own statement that the exercises were seldom adequately read must go undocumented, but I think it a reasonable inference from general conditions and from the very small number of tutors in proportion to the number of boys.

[11] Lyte, op. cit., 311, quoting an eighteenth-century writer.

[12] Ibid., Chapter xvi.

[13] Ibid., 382–3.

[14] These accounts form the principal basis for our knowledge of the outward and visible facts of Shelley's life at Eton. The basis is not an altogether satisfactory one. Anecdotes shared by a group of alumni and handed down as a part of the tradition of the old school have a habit of not bothering too much about literal accuracy and of fastening a stock story to any conspicuous character. Such stories would still have a general truth if they can be felt to fit the character.

But when the notion of a character that has been a dormant notion for over thirty years is confronted with a more definite notion of that character, recently built up and supported by good authority, the recollections may easily be warped to suit the more definite notion. In the things recollected under these circumstances of Shelley at Eton, there is a somewhat suspicious sameness on the one hand, and variation on the other. The stories of electrifying his tutor and of burning the willow tree have each several variant forms. The incidents of Shelley's fight as described by Captain Gronow are made to cover two distinct fights in the recollection of another Etonian who is merely handing down the story. The characteristic incident of the story — spouting lines from Homer — had already been narrated of a fight previous to Shelley's. And Captain Gronow, on other points not connected with Shelley, is quite inaccurate in his memories of Eton and is so designated by other Etonians. There are also several variants of the story of administering the electric shock to Bethell.

Nearly all the testimony for Shelley at Eton comes either from such sources as Captain Gronow or from letters written to Lady Shelley by old Etonians, courteous old gentlemen who knew what she expected. I can find few traces of these letters since they were used and quoted (incompletely) by Lady Shelley and Professor Dowden. It is quite possible that Lady Shelley destroyed or withheld unfavourable testimony, as some of the English Shelleyans who knew her suspected she might do later. She actually did destroy some letters of Trelawny reflecting on Mary Shelley.

[15] Medwin, op. cit., 32. Mrs. Shelley, as quoted by Hogg (op. cit., I, 33), speaks of Shelley's " systematic and determined resistance " to fagging. Nevertheless Shelley fagged for Henry Matthew, later a judge, and author of *The Diary of an Invalid.* His co-fag, Andrew Amos, mentions Shelley's fagging and says nothing of his opposition to the practice. See letter of Amos in Appendix III.

[16] So Hogg explains the term (op. cit., I, 91–2). Medwin and others were unable to find that the word had any such special meaning at Eton. Perhaps Hogg was softening the actual facts, as he did in quoting Shelley's letters later. Nevertheless Shelley's letters bear evidence that if he ever became a genuine atheist it was not until after he left Eton. Mr. C. H. K. Masten, Vice-Provost of Eton, comments on this passage: " My impression is that boys are inclined to call any one an ' atheist ' whose views are unorthodox, and not too much importance need be attached to the name."

[17] " Although disliked by his masters and hated by his superiors in age, he was adored by his equals " — Mrs. Shelley as quoted by Hogg, op. cit., I, 35.

[18] John Taylor Coleridge, in a footnote to his review of Leigh Hunt's *Foliage,* in the *Quarterly Review,* XVIII, 327 (January 1818).

[19] Nevill, op. cit., 95. For other reasons than his record in school Shelley's name continued unpopular at Eton long after his death. Swinburne as a young Etonian was forbidden to read Shelley (Peck: *Life,* I, 22). About the middle of the nineteenth century the provost refused to allow a bust of Shelley to be placed in the school, because he was " a bad man " (Salt, op. cit., 129). Some years later the feeling was still hostile (Salt, op. cit., 191), and as late as 1880 an upper-form boy was applauded by his fellows when he referred to Shelley in a debate as " a mad fool " (Nevill, op. cit., 169). Eton now possesses manuscripts of five Shelley poems; viz., " Remembrance," " Love's Philosophy," " Good Night," " Time Long Past," and " Autumn — A Dirge."

[20] So spelled in the *Eton School Lists* — not Styles, as in Gronow, Ingpen, and Peck.

[21] *Reminiscences and Recollections of Captain Gronow* (London, 1889), II, 79–80. Cf. note 14 above.

[22] Nevill, op. cit., 95.

[23] The *Eton School Lists,* 51, 58. This is apparently a second edition. Mr. C. H. K. Masten, Vice-Provost of Eton, informs me that the first edition, dated June 1863, omits Shelley's fight with Lyne.

[24] Dowden: *Life,* I, 24.

[25] Ibid.

[26] Thornton Hunt (*Atlantic Monthly,* II, 192, February 1863) says the immediate provocation was a dare, growing out of his resistance to oppression. Peacock (*Memoir,* II, 313) was acquainted with the story (substituting a penknife for the fork), but thought it a product of Shelley's imagination. One of Mary Shelley's letters gives an account of the episode, as told to her by Shelley.

[27] According to John Taylor Coleridge, a senior schoolmate, as quoted in *Notebook of the Shelley Society* (Shelley Society Publications, 1st Series, no. 2, 1888), 14.

[28] Hellen Shelley's reminiscent letters previously cited. For the final incident the sole authority is the Reverend Dr. Sadler, of Horsham, as quoted by Dowden: *Life,* I, 11, note.

[29] Ibid., I, 26, note.

[30] Nevill, op. cit., 123. This story, which occurs elsewhere among Etonians, is unnoted by Shelley's biographers.

[31] Lord Monson: "My Grandfather's Reminiscences of Eton," *Nineteenth Century,* XLIX (April 1906).

[32] See *Gentleman's Magazine,* LXXIV, 1065, 1165 (November 1804).

[33] See the reminiscent letters of Merle and Amos, quoted in full in Appendix III.

[34] Ingpen: *Shelley in England,* I, 67.

[35] Hogg, op. cit., I, 36–7. The account of these supernatural exploits is Shelley's own, as told to Hogg a year or two later and as possibly heightened in the retelling by Hogg.

[36] Op. cit., 58.

[37] "Hymn to Intellectual Beauty," stanza v. Cf. *Alastor,* lines 20–35, where the young poet, largely an autobiographical character, gives an almost identical account of his own youthful search for truth.

[38] Ginotti, the hero of Shelley's *The Rosicrucian,* written at the end of his career at Eton, begins his autobiographical account in Chapter x: "From my earliest youth . . . *curiosity,* and a desire to unveil the latent mysteries of nature, was the passion by which all the other emotions of my mind were intellectually organized." In other respects also Ginotti's youth seems based upon the author's, though there are a number of points in which they do not match.

[39] Hogg, op. cit., I, 38–9.

[40] Amos also speaks of boating with Shelley at Eton. See his letter quoted in Appendix III.

[41] "The Boat on the Serchio" (1821), lines 76–83.

[42] Grandfather of the Hon. Stephen Coleridge, who records the recollection in *Memories* (London and New York, 1913), 2–3, quoted by Ingpen.

[43] Shelley to J. T. T. Tisdall, January 10, 1808, in Julian *Works,* VII, 289. The four short letters from Shelley to Tisdall were first published in the London *Times,* August 30, 1928, by Professor R. Warwick Bond. Timothy Tisdall, Esq., appears to have been a ward of Lord Charleville. He and Shelley exchanged letters and possibly visits in 1808 and 1809. Inviting Tisdall to visit Field Place at Easter 1809, Shelley refers to the "Beaus and Belles of the Horsham Ball" with quite normal youthful gusto. These letters also show Shelley already writing "Novels and Letters," and poetry.

[44] Hogg, op. cit., I, 47. Shelley is somewhat similarly described by

Joseph G. Merle (see *post*), who met him some months before Shelley's meeting with Hogg at Oxford.

[45] The phrase is Dowden's and is vaguely misleading. It means only that Shelley's position in both parades was a regular rank-and-file one. The published Montem Lists show that as a lower-form boy Shelley was one of two attendants marching with an upper-form boy, with the situation reversed when Shelley was an upper-form boy in the 1808 procession.

[46] Henry Mitchell Wagner (quoted by Ingpen: *Shelley in England*, I, 59), a King's Scholar, according to the *Eton School Lists*, in the same forms with Shelley in 1805 and 1808.

[47] *Shelley Memorials*, ed. Lady Jane Shelley (3rd ed., London, 1875), 6.

[48] See his letter quoted in Appendix III.

[49] Dowden and *Shelley Memorials* both quote Packe direct, but neither gives the full name nor the full letter.

[50] The *Eton School Lists* records James Thomas Price as a King's Scholar, in the same forms with Shelley in 1805 and 1808.

[51] Dowden: *Life*, I, 26, note. Checking this information against the *Eton School Lists* and Montem Lists for Shelley's residence at Eton, I find no Edward Leslie, but an Edmund Leslie who was in the remove in 1808 and also in the Montem. There was no Lord Howe, but a Lord Howard, in the fifth form in 1814, and a Henry Howard in the fifth form in 1811. There was no Charles Ball, but a Charles Wall, in the upper fifth in 1811, and an Edward H. Ball in the fourth in 1811.

[52] Hogg, op. cit., I, 41–2.

[53] Possibly the same play as that dealt with in Shelley's letter to Edward Graham dated " Field Place, Sunday," Julian *Works*, VIII, 8.

[54] Hellen Shelley to Lady Shelley, in Hogg's *Life*, I, 25.

[55] Peacock: *Memoirs*, II, 348.

[56] Timothy Shelley to William Whitton, April 18, 1811, quoted in Ingpen: *Shelley in England*, I, 242.

[57] Hogg, op, cit., II, 106.

[58] Ibid., I, 24. When his sister Margaret was about five years old, hence about 1806, during the same year as his father's illness.

[59] Described in Shelley's account of Dr. Lind, p. 48.

[60] This identification, generally accepted and extremely probable from internal evidence, is nowhere avowed by Shelley himself, but it is stated by Medwin (op. cit., 33) for both poems and by Mrs. Shelley for *Laon and Cythna,* in her note on that poem.

[61] Hogg, op. cit., I, 35–6. Both Hogg and Medwin knew of Shelley's esteem for Dr. Lind. Hogg had heard the madhouse story many times, and considered it a part of Shelley's delirium that had been remembered as reality. Possible distortions of fact and mixture of fact with fancy must be guarded against in Shelley's autobiographical statements. Nevertheless, the story may easily be true. There was insanity in the family, and young Shelley had already been thought at least a trifle mad by people in Horsham, Brentford, and Eton. The Horsham doctor might well have suggested confinement. Even well-trained city physicians recommended commitments for insanity that would be regarded today as absurd. Shelley told the same story to Dr. Polidori in Geneva in 1816 (*Diary of Dr. John William Polidori*, ed. W. M. Rossetti, London, 1911, p. 112, dated June 1, 1816).

[62] Shelley to Edward Graham, April 22, 1810, Julian *Works*, VIII, 6.

[63] Shelley to Edward Graham, April 23, 1810, op. cit., VIII, 9. This account of Graham is based on "A Newspaper Editor's Reminiscences," *Fraser's Magazine*, XXIII, 699–710 (June 1841), and R. Ingpen: "Notes on Shelley's Correspondents," Julian *Works*, VIII, xxiii–xxv. After Shelley's elopement with Harriet Westbrook, however, there is no evidence of further contact between the two. Possibly Graham felt compelled to side with Mr. Timothy Shelley against his son.

[64] Previously referred to in Shelleyan biography as "The Newspaper Edition," from his anonymous article "A Newspaper Editor's Reminiscences," cited above. Dowden (*Life*, I, 124) suggested that he might be William Henry Merle, author of *Costanza, A Poem*, and *Odds and Ends of Verse*. This was also H. B. Forman's opinion, as quoted by Ingpen (*Shelley in England*, I, 86, and Julian *Works*, VIII, 8, note). Mr. Ingpen adds that Dr. Richard Garnett asserted that the author was Gibbons Neale [meaning probably Gibbons Merle], editor of the *White Dwarf*. None of these conjectures was apparently supported by more information than is furnished under the name Merle in the Catalogue of the British Museum.

My own efforts to settle the uncertainty developed the surprising coincidence that W. H. Merle was in the upper fifth form at Eton with Shelley in 1808. Therefore he could hardly be the Merle whose acquaintance Shelley speaks of in May 1810 as having been formed quite recently. Nor can I find that he ever edited a newspaper, though he contributed to magazines. He knew Shelley, however, and afterwards wrote a letter about him to the *Athenæum* (see Appendix III).

Considerable searching failed to find a single trace of Gibbons Neale — another evidence of the mischievous power of misprints.

Of Gibbons Merle, however, I eventually found obituary notices first in the *Gentleman's Magazine* (June 1855, n.s. XLIII, 654) and later in *Galignani's Messenger,* Paris (January 25, 1855). The former of these, under the name of Gibbons Merle, records that he had long been one of the editors of *Galignani's Messenger* at the time of his death, January 19, 1855, and that he had formerly been editor of the London *Courier,* and London correspondent of the *Journal des Débats.* The account in *Galignani's Messenger* names him Joseph Gibbon, Baron Merle, speaks of him as formerly editor of the *Courier* and afterwards of the *Globe,* and mentions his descent from an ancient French family and, on his mother's side, from Shakespeare — two statements that were made of himself by the anonymous "Newspaper Editor" in *Fraser's Magazine.* Thus the two seem to be identified. In addition, Joseph Gibbons Merle becomes identifiable with Josh. G. Merle, of Brighton, author of the poem so signed in Ackerman's *Poetical Magazine,* and that poem becomes identifiable with the poem mentioned by the "Newspaper Editor" as published by himself in that magazine and as being the occasion of his acquaintance with Shelley. To Mr. Ernest Male, Librarian of the Brighton Public Library, I am indebted for the information that *Cobby's Brighthelmstone Directory* for 1800 lists "Joseph Merle, Victualler (One Tun Inn) 52 Ship Street," whom I conclude to be probably the father of Joseph Gibbons Merle.

[65] "Lines on the Stage," signed "Josh. G. Merle, Brighton, April 19, 1809," *Poetical Magazine,* (June 1809), 111. Most of the poems in the magazine are anonymous. Among these may be some juvenile verse by Shelley. In a letter to Graham dated simply "Field Place, Sunday," concerning an unfinished tragedy he proposed offering to Covent Garden, Shelley says: "I should be happy to get Mr. Ackerman's notice, but am by no means certain I could get mention in his repository, as though in the title page 'authors are requested to give information as to the works which they have in hand,' yet when in London I spoke to Merle about it and he said the Notice was a favour."

[66] See the letter quoted in the preceding note, Julian *Works,* VIII, 8.

[67] Merle's account is not precise as to dates, but he speaks of Shel-

ley as an Oxford student and an author at the time of their first acquaintance. Shelley had been enrolled at Oxford since April 10, 1810, though he did not take up residence until October. In April *Zastrozzi* was published, and Shelley had also published with his grandfather's help some verses now lost. Shelley's first dated reference to Merle is in a letter of May 20, 1810 in which Merle seems to be spoken of as a recent acquaintance. Merle's poem that was the occasion for the friendship was published in the *Poetical Magazine* for June 1809, but this number may well have appeared late. Some time must have elapsed before Graham saw the poem and after that, before a meeting could be arranged.

68 Shelley to Graham, May 20 and 29, 1810, Julian *Works,* VIII, 11, 13. Merle had bought some crayons for Shelley as a gift for Harriet Grove, which did not seem to Shelley a sufficient basis for the romantic friendship Merle offered in his letters.

69 It is of course possible that Shelley actually broke off the connection as he intended in the letters obviously written soon after it was formed. In that case Merle's undoubtedly authentic information about Shelley must have been derived from Graham, but his attitude toward Shelley would hardly have been the friendly one it was. Moreover, Shelley's letter to Graham dated " Field Place, Sunday," was evidently written after the letters renouncing Merle, though placed before them by the Julian editors. This letter indicates that Shelley was on fairly intimate terms with Merle.

70 Medwin, op. cit., 35, 37; Hogg, op. cit., I, 42; Mrs. Shelley's Note on *Queen Mab.*

71 Medwin, op. cit., 37. Mrs. Shelley (Hogg, op. cit., I, 33) says Shelley translated half of the *Natural History* at Eton.

72 Medwin, op. cit., 33. Medwin's statement seems to be a conclusion from the lines he quotes from " Prince Athanase " showing Prince Athanase and Zonoras reading the *Symposium* together. The journal of Shelley and Mary shows that Shelley read the *Symposium* at the time of writing " Prince Athanase," which accounts for the lines more convincingly than Medwin's supposition.

73 Medwin, op. cit., 34.

74 Francis St. John Thackeray: *Memoir of Edwin C. Hawtrey* (London, 1896), 13, 14. Hawtrey was, like Shelley, a victim of bullying and was often " hunted " (p. 12). It was Hawtrey as headmaster who lectured the boys on the evils of bullying and instanced the effects in two cases, obviously those of Shelley and W. S. Walker (pp. 95–6).

[75] Shelley to Godwin, January 16, 1812, Julian *Works,* VIII, 242–3.

[76] Dowden: *Life,* I, 26, note.

[77] See Peck: *Life,* I, 54–6; also A. H. Koszul: *La Jeunesse de Shelley* (1910), and A. M. D. Hughes: "Shelley's *Zastrozzi* and St. *Irvyne,*" *Modern Language Review,* VII, 54–63 (January 1912).

[78] Professor Dowden (*Life,* I, 28) thinks Shelley read *Political Justice* at Eton, but the evidence seems to indicate that he read it first at Oxford. In his second letter to Godwin, written January 10, 1812 (Julian *Works,* VIII, 239–41), Shelley says it is more than two years since he became acquainted with *Political Justice.* Four days later, in his next letter, he tells Godwin that he had written both *Zastrozzi* and *St. Irvyne* before he had read any of Godwin except *St. Leon. St. Irvyne* was very probably unfinished when Shelley left Eton. On November 19, 1810 he ordered a copy of *Political Justice* from Oxford. This does not preclude an earlier reading, but it is after that date that the effects of the book on Shelley are to be noted. Had he read the book at Eton with the effects he describes, they would have been evident in his two novels, as he himself implies. Between the composition of the two novels he did read *St. Leon,* without noticing its Godwinian reason, he says. He could scarcely have overlooked this side of the book if he had read *Political Justice.* Hence, of Shelley's two conflicting dates, the latter is preferable.

[79] *Revised Life,* 34.

[80] Shelley to Godwin, January 10, 1812, Julian *Works,* VIII, 239.

[81] Shelley to Godwin, June 3, 1812, ibid., VIII, 331.

[82] *Revised Life,* 50.

[83] Op. cit., 44–5. Medwin's memory is slightly at fault as to dates. He mentions the year 1809. *The Curse of Kehama* and *The Lady of the Lake* were both published in 1810. Shelley presented his friend Edward Leslie with copies of *The Lay of the Last Minstrel, Marmion,* and *The Lady of the Lake* (Dowden: *Life,* I, 26).

[84] Medwin, op. cit., 37, 50.

[85] This is a point to be stressed lightly, if at all. Such opinions are not unique in novels of this class. There is definitely more religious orthodoxy than heresy in Shelley's two novels. His letters for some months after *St. Irvyne* was published show that his early orthodox views were not even then entirely dead. See Ellsworth Barnard: *Shelley's Religion* (Minneapolis, 1937), 18–20, and Amiyakumar Sen: *Studies in Shelley* (University of Calcutta Press, 1936), 1–5.

Chapter IV

GENERAL SOURCES

Julian *Works*, Medwin, Hogg, and Joseph Gibbons Merle as
  cited in previous chapters.
Richard Garnett, ed.: *Original Poetry by Victor and Cazire.*
  London and New York, 1898.
Harriet Grove's MS. journal for 1809–10.
Roger Ingpen, ed.: *The Journal of Harriet Grove for the Years
  1809–1810.* Privately printed, 1932, 12 copies only.
Lady Jane Shelley: *Shelley Memorials.* London, 1859.
John James Stockdale: *Stockdale's Budget.* London, 1826–7.

NOTES AND REFERENCES

[1] "A Newspaper Editor's Reminiscences," *Fraser's Magazine,*
XXIII (June 1841), 699–707, particularly 702. These bills must also
have included the small volume of verse, immediately suppressed
by the family, which Shelley brought out for his sister Hellen.

[2] Medwin, op. cit., 39.

[3] Ibid.

[4] Julian *Works*, VIII, 4.

[5] The recently recovered journal of Harriet Grove seems to fix
the date of publication as the last week in March. On March 28
she wrote: "Bysshe has sent C[harlotte] and me Zastrozzi as it is
come out." MacCarthy (*Shelley's Early Life*, 12) erroneously gives
June 5, 1810 as the date of publication. It was listed among publications for the month in the *British Critic* for April 1810. It is also
included among the list of books published in April by the *Monthly
Magazine* for May, and is listed in *La Belle Assemblée, or Bell's
Court and Fashionable Magazine* for 1811 as published the previous
year. It was advertised in *The Times* for June 5 and 12 and was
reviewed in the *Gentleman's Magazine* for September 1810, and in
the *Critical Review* for November 1810.

[6] Shelley to Graham, April 1, 1810, Julian *Works,* VIII, 5.

[7] *Gentleman's Magazine,* LXXX (part 2), 258 (September 1810).

[8] *Critical Review,* XXI, 329–31 (November 1810).

[9] Harriet Grove did, and was even asserted by Medwin to have written some of the chapters. This assertion is not supported by Harriet's recently available journal and seems inconsistent with the personality revealed there, though she did rather resent her brother Charles's criticism of the book.

[10] Packe, quoted in *Shelley Memorials,* 3rd ed., p. 6. Dr. John W. Polidori, in his *Diary* (ed. W. M. Rossetti, London, 1911, p. 107) under the date of May 30, 1816, recorded that Shelley told him he had received £30 for *Zastrozzi* and £100 for *St. Irvyne.* Unfortunately for Polidori's accuracy, Stockdale, the publisher, records that there was a loss of nearly £300 on the latter. If £40 was received, it was more than Shelley received from all the rest of his publications combined, except *The Cenci,* during his whole life. On the basis of a ten-per-cent royalty it would represent an anticipated sale of 1,600 copies.

[11] Shelley to John Joseph Stockdale, September 6, 1810, Julian *Works,* VIII, 14.

[12] See the reprint of *Original Poetry,* ed. Richard Garnett (London and New York, 1898). In 1826 and 1827 Stockdale published a somewhat disreputable journal known as *Stockdale's Budget,* which contained an account of his dealings with Shelley. Otherwise the anonymous authors might never have been identified or the long-lost volume recovered.

[13] Harriet's copy of *Original Poetry by Victor and Cazire* was possibly the one from which the text was ultimately recovered from oblivion. Previous to 1897 no copy was known. In that year Mr. V. E. G. Hussey, grandson of Harriet's brother Charles, brought to the publishing firm of John Lane a copy bound with several Byron publications in a volume bearing the bookplate of Charles Grove. This copy was edited for the publisher by Dr. Garnett and is the source of the text. It is now in the library of the University of Texas. Two other original editions discovered subsequently are in the Ashley Library (British Museum), and the Huntington Library.

[14] *Stockdale's Budget* as quoted in Garnett's reprint of *Original Poetry by Victor and Cazire* (London, 1898). I have read the original files in the British Museum, but am unable to cite pages and numbers.

[15] Peck: *Life,* I, 30. The volume is now owned by Mr. Carl Pforzheimer, of New York.

[16] Peck: *Life,* I, 35. See also Medwin, op. cit., 44, 45, where the stanza is quoted as one of his earliest poems and is said to be " almost taken " from Chatterton.

[17] There is some doubt as to the date of composition. Medwin wrote in 1833 as if it were the latter part of 1807, but in 1847 he gave the time as the winter of 1809–10. Dowden concluded on good evidence (*Life,* I, 44) that the later date is correct.

[18] *The Shelley Papers* (1833), 7, and *Life of Shelley* (1847), repeated in *Revised Life,* 41.

[19] These observations of Medwin fit the published poem rather badly, as pointed out by Bertram Dobell in his edition of the poem, *Shelley Society Publications,* 2nd series, No. 12 (1887), pp. xxiv ff.

[20] See note 14. Stockdale preserved two letters showing that Shelley had sent him a second copy when he learned that the first had failed to arrive from Ballantyne, and that Shelley later asked for the return of one of the copies for correction. Thereafter the poem was entirely lost until two differing versions of it were printed, one in the *Edinburgh Literary Journal* for June 20 and 27 and July 4, 1829, and the other in *Fraser's Magazine* for July 1831. The *Fraser's* version probably represents a revision by Shelley, following Campbell's discouraging criticism, which Medwin thought had killed the poem. This would partly explain the differences between the poem Medwin describes and the poem actually published.

An unpublished note kindly placed at my disposal by the author, Mr. Walter G. Neale, Jr., clears up the history of the *Edinburgh Literary Journal* version. This was the copy sent by Shelley to Ballantyne and Co. in 1810. John Ballantyne, who died in 1821, handled the publishing end of the business and probably wrote the letter of rejection that Shelley received. But the manuscript was not returned, for it came into the hands of James Ballantyne after his brother's death. James, who was probably ignorant of its history, loaned it to Henry Glassford Bell, editor of the *Literary Journal,* to reprint in that journal in 1829. In an address delivered in Glasgow in 1871 Bell claimed credit for first publishing the poem, " which he [Shelley] had left and forgotten in the hands of James Ballantyne of Edinburgh " (*Memoirs and Portraits of One Hundred Glasgow Men,* Anon., Glasgow, 1886, I, 30).

[21] The translation was " a scrap of paper " picked up in Lincoln's Inn Fields by either Shelley or Medwin. It was from *La Belle*

Assemblée, or Bell's Court and Fashionable Magazine, for January 1809, pp. 19–20, and not the *Germanic Museum* for 1801, as Dowden and others have supposed. A close textual comparison of these two translations with Schubart's original shows that the 1809 translation is copied from the 1801 translation. There are several slight verbal variations in the two, and Shelley's version agrees in these with the 1809 version. It has been several times erroneously assumed from the accounts left by Medwin and Mrs. Shelley that the fragment was in German, which Shelley translated.

The history of this wind-blown scrap of soiled paper illustrates the peculiar tenacity of Shelley's mind where his favourite interests were concerned. An inaccurate paraphrase of part of it appears as a foot-note in Shelley's *The Wandering Jew.* Supposing his "scrap" to be a fragment of some longer prose work, Shelley made his first inquiry at the Bodleian Library in an effort to locate this non-existent book. In 1811, when in a state of high excitement, he knew the translation so well that he unconsciously quoted a sentence from it as a part of his own state of mind (see p. 105). Later he gave his friend Hogg a manuscript copy of the translation, of which Hogg preserved and printed the last page, including the final sentence, which Shelley would not print himself because it showed the wrath of the Eternal to have been appeased. Finally, in 1813, Shelley reprinted the whole fragment, with the exception of the last sentence, in the Notes to *Queen Mab.*

Certain well-known phrases in Shelley's later poems show that the actual phraseology of this translation continued to live in his memory after having long since been adopted as his own. Shelley wrote:

"To see his enemies writhe, and burn, and bleed." From *Laon and Cythna,* X, xlv, 4 (1817).

"Thus to be lost, and thus to sink and die." From "To Constantia Singing" (1817).

"I die, I faint, I fail." From "Indian Serenade," iii, 2 (1819).

"I fall upon the thorns of life, I bleed." From "Ode to the West Wind," IV, 12 (1819).

"I pant, I sink, I tremble, I expire." From *Epipsychidion,* 591 (1821).

These highly characteristic expressions are obviously related to each other. The following, from the "scrap of paper" of 1809 or 1810, seems to be their common ancestor: "that I may lie extended, may pant, and writhe, and die."

[22] Shelley to Edward Graham, April 22, 1810, Julian *Works*, VIII, 8.

[23] Medwin, op. cit., 108.

[24] Ibid., 58, 59.

[25] Hogg, op. cit., I, 26.

[26] Shelley to Hogg, July 28, 1811, Julian *Works*, VIII, 134.

[27] Shelley to Edward Graham, dated only " Sunday," ibid., VIII, 8.

[28] Hogg, op. cit., I, 164.

[29] Harriet's mother was Charlotte Pilfold, a sister of Shelley's mother. Her father, Thomas Grove, had an estate, Ferne House, in Wiltshire and also an estate of ten thousand acres at Cwm Elan near Rhayader, in Radnorshire, which Shelley later visited as the guest of Thomas Grove, Jr., and his wife. Shelley was on intimate terms in London in 1811 with two of Harriet's brothers, John and Charles.

[30] Medwin, op. cit., 47.

[31] See note 40 below.

[32] Dowden: *Life*, I, 48, note.

[33] "Melody to a Scene of Former Times," in *Posthumous Fragments of Margaret Nicholson* (1811).

[34] Charles Grove to Hellen Shelley, February 16, 1857, Hogg, op. cit., II, 154. Charles speaks of the visit as taking place in August, but Harriet's journal shows it was April 16–21, 1810.

[35] Charles Grove's second letter, Hogg, op. cit., II, 157.

[36] Ibid.

[37] Shelley to Edward Graham, April 22, 1810, Julian *Works*, VIII, 7. The poem was printed in *St. Irvyne* in 1811, with the omission of these stanzas and two others.

[38] Shelley and Elizabeth to Edward Graham, postmarked April 24, 1810, Julian *Works*, VIII, 9–11.

[39] See notes 34, 35.

[40] *The Journal of Harriet Grove for the Years 1809–1810.* The bracketed passages represent marked-out passages in the MS., whether deciphered or not.

Through the courtesy of Mr. Gabriel Wells, present owner, I have studied the original MS. and have attempted, with expert assistance from the Fogg Art Museum, to discover a means of reading the deleted passages, but I am unable to add significantly to the passages restored by Mr. Ingpen. Dr. Garnett quoted two or three lines from this journal in editing *Original Poetry by Victor and Cazire*, after which the manuscript disappeared from view.

[41] "Song," stanzas 1, 3, 4, 5 (Julian *Works*, I, 10). Dr. Garnett, in

the Preface to his edition of *Original Poetry*, lists eight of the seventeen poems as dealing with Shelley's love for Harriet. Three of the eight Mr. Peck (*Life*, I, 32) seems inclined to doubt. In my opinion only three of the poems seem clearly inspired by this motive, namely "Song," dated April 1810, and the two poems dated August 1810 and entitled "Song: To ——." Even the last of these three is subject to some doubt, since its most love-stricken stanza occurs among some verses that Shelley wrote down for Hogg at Oxford as specimens of his sister's poetry (Hogg, op. cit., I, 126). The three poems on Despair, Sorrow, and Hope are thoroughly general and contain among them only one phrase: "Torn is dear affection's tie," that could be regarded as having an individual rather than a general meaning, though it seems to me to be clearly a general statement. Both Dr. Garnett and Mr. Peck misread the poem "Hope" to refer to Harriet, when a close reading would indicate that it is flowers, not Harriet, whom "God never made to deceive."

[42] Harriet received "a part of B—'s Poem" (through Elizabeth) on February 23, 1810, *Zastrozzi* on March 28, *Original Poetry by Victor and Cazire* on September 17. The art crayons and other books we learn of from Shelley's letters to Graham, May 29 and August 13 (the latter first printed in Appendix III of this work). Perhaps Harriet refers to a similar gift on March 5: "Most agreeably surprised by receiving a Parcel and letter from My Greatest Friend."

[43] *The Shelley Papers* (London, 1833), 5.

[44] Ibid., 6.

[45] Timothy Shelley to William Whitton, April 18, 1811, Ingpen: *Shelley in England*, I, 242.

Chapter V

GENERAL SOURCES

Medwin, Hogg, Joseph Gibbons Merle ("The Newspaper Editor"), Shelley's Letters (Julian *Works*, Vol. VIII) as previously cited. Though I have used the Julian *Works* for the Shelley-Hogg correspondence, I have corrected all quotations and inferences from the galley proofs of Professor George Stuart Gordon's forthcoming *Shelley Letters,* which for the first time print these letters correctly from the original manuscripts. I have not, however, undertaken to restore the original spelling and punctuation. I am greatly indebted to Professor Gordon, and to his publishers, Messrs. Grayson and Grayson, Limited, of London, and Henry Holt and Co., of New York.

William Carr: *A History of University College.* London, 1902.

Alexander Chalmers: *A History of the Colleges, Halls, etc. of the University of Oxford.* 2 vols. London, 1810.

Andrew Clark: *The Colleges of Oxford — Their Histories and Traditions.* London, 1891.

Alfred Denis Godley: *Oxford in the Eighteenth Century.* London and New York, 1908.

J. R. Green and George Roberson: " Oxford during the Eighteenth Century," in *Studies in Oxford History,* ed. C. L. Stainer. Oxford, 1901.

A Historical Register of the University [of Oxford, to the end of Trinity Term, 1888]. Oxford, 1888.

Rowley Lascelles: *The University and City of Oxford, in a Series of Seventy-two Views,* etc. London, 1821.

Letters to and from Charles Kirkpatrick Sharpe, ed. Alexander Allardyce. 2 vols. Edinburgh and London, 1888.

Dennis Florence MacCarthy: *Shelley's Early Life.* London, 1872.

Robert Montgomery: *Oxford, a Poem.* [Third ed., 1833, and subsequent editions contain Henry Slatter's note on Shelley.] London, 3rd ed., 1833.

A New Pocket Companion for Oxford, or Guide through the University, etc. Oxford, 1810.

The Oxford University Calendar. Oxford, 1810, et seqq.

Elizabeth Grant Smith: *Memoirs of a Highland Lady,* ed. Lady Strachey. London, 1898.

J. J. Stockdale, ed.: *Stockdale's Budget.* London, 1827.

James Storer: *The Oxford Visitor,* etc. London, 1822.

W. Wade: *Walks in Oxford.* Oxford, 1818.

John Walker: *Oxoniana.* London, 1809 (?).

N. Whitlock: *Topographical and Historical Description of the University and City of Oxford,* etc. London, 1828.

NOTES AND REFERENCES

[1] Hurdis, whose " Vindication " is summarized in A. D. Godley, op. cit., 58–9.

[2] Quoted by J. R. Green, op. cit., 78.

[3] Probably the most conspicuous exercise of discipline in the century was the expulsion of six students from St. Edmund's Hall on March 11, 1768. This action elicited considerable protest and was defended by Dr. Johnson in his famous remark about the impropriety of a cow in a garden. The young men were charged with low birth, ignorance of the learned languages, attending (and in one case holding) " illicit conventicles," praying extempore, and associating with reputed Methodists, " for which crimes " they were officially deemed " worthy of being expelled." Had Shelley been acquainted with the details of this trial he would no doubt have been interested to know that the principal witness against the accused was a man notorious for deistic utterances, whose apology was accepted on the ground that he was drunk at the time of the utterances that were reported, and who was later given a good living.

[4] *Edinburgh Review,* XI, 283 (January 1808).

[5] Ibid., XV, 45 (October 1809).

[6] Ibid., XVI, 163 (April 1810).

[7] Ibid., XV, 50 (October 1809).

[8] *A Reply to the Calumnies of the Edinburgh Review against Oxford,* and *A Second Reply* . . . , both 1810, Oxford; and *A Third Reply* . . . , Oxford, 1811. The articles in the *Edinburgh Review* were respectively: January 1808 (review of La Place); July 1809 (review of the Oxford edition of Strabo); October 1809 (review of Edgeworth on *Professional Education*); and April 1810 (review of Copleston's *Reply*).

[9] Copleston: *Reply,* etc., 166, 150, 152.

[10] Mrs. Elizabeth Grant Smith, op. cit., 124 ff., quoted by Peck: *Life,* I, 61, 62.

[11] See second poem in Shelley's *Original Poetry by Victor and Cazire.*

[12] Sir Francis was then the rallying-cry for all opponents of the

repressive acts of government. Shelley's interest in him continued for some time. In the autumn of 1810, probably, he sent Sir Francis a copy of *Posthumous Fragments of Margaret Nicholson,* which was found still unopened among the properties of the Baroness Burdett-Coutts sold in 1923. In August 1812 he mailed a number of letters and packages to Sir Francis from Lynmouth. (See the letter of the town clerk of Barnstable, reprinted by W. M. Rossetti in *Fortnightly Review,* XV, 68–9, January 1871.) In 1817 he directed his publisher to send Sir Francis a copy of his *Proposals for Putting Reform to the Vote* (Julian *Works,* IX, 222).

¹³ Medwin: *Revised Life,* 86.

¹⁴ Ibid., 86. D. F. MacCarthy (op. cit., 24) quotes part of a letter answering Medwin's description, which he found in the *Morning Chronicle* of November 15, 1809, which he thinks was written in part by Shelley for his father. MacCarthy also thinks that the *Oxford University and City Herald* was read at Field Place at this time, and cites an early Latin epigram of Shelley's as a translation of an Engglish epigram appearing in the *Oxford Herald* of September 16, 1809.

¹⁵ In 1558 Lord Leicester's bequest provided £20 annually for each of two scholars at University College, to be appointed by his heirs. Bysshe Shelley's marriage into the family no doubt accounts for the nomination of Timothy and Percy Shelley.

¹⁶ It is not definitely stated by Mr. Henry Slatter in his account, in his letter in the third edition of Robert Montgomery's *Oxford* (1833), whether this visit was when Shelley enrolled in April or when he entered residence in October, but the circumstances all indicate the latter.

¹⁷ According to *A History of University College* by William Carr (London, 1902), all government and control seems to have been in the hands of Rowley, who was unpopular and imposed a good many penalties and rustications. Shelley was entered on the books " sub tutamine Magistri Rowley et Domini Davison."

¹⁸ Henry Slatter, as cited in note 16 above.

¹⁹ The term opened October 10, and Shelley's father remained several days afterwards. Hogg says " at the commencement of Michaelmas term, that is, at the end of October."

²⁰ Hogg, op. cit., I, 167–8, 174. The spirited picture of undergraduate Oxford in these very years, painted from experience by John G. Lockhart in *Reginald Dalton* (1823), supports Hogg's account. Miss Grant's account, previously cited, tells of undergradu-

ate uproar at University College in this year, culminating in a mock fox-hunt under the Dean's window, as a protest against his restrictions upon fox-hunting.

21 Hogg's account exhibits both the merits and the defects of the excellent raconteur. His memory, particularly for physical impressions, is extraordinarily good. He is quite given to exaggeration; some of his most colourful passages are exaggerated to the point of being almost libellous; for example, his accounts of Mr. Timothy Shelley, Eliza Westbrook, and Elizabeth Hitchener. He probably exaggerates for effect both the eccentric and the " divine " elements he finds in his friend. He alters letters when printing them, sometimes apparently to render Shelley's expression less extreme, sometimes to disguise his own romantic love for Elizabeth Shelley, and especially in order to cover up his own attempt to seduce Harriet Shelley. His extreme egotism, besides being responsible for a great deal of intrusive matter in his book, also takes rather excellent care to shield the biographer from incidental criticism. While he did not always enjoy Shelley's confidence to the extent he supposed or pretended, even before their estrangement (for example, he never saw Harriet nor heard of Elizabeth Hitchener till after Shelley's marriage), he actually knew Shelley much better than anyone else who wrote about him — not even excluding Mary Shelley. His account is in many respects the best account of Shelley by one who knew him.

The tone of Hogg's biography proved so distasteful to the Shelley family that the materials placed at his disposal were withdrawn upon the publication of the first two volumes (London, 1858). Another volume was later completed and was known to be in existence in 1864 and in the hands of the publisher Moxon, after which it vanished (Sylva Norman: *After Shelley*, London, 1934, p. xxxiii).

22 Hogg, op. cit., I, 55–6. Since all accounts of Shelley at Oxford must be based principally on Hogg's account, I shall make no effort in the following pages to give a reference for every statement of individual fact, but shall give references only for direct quotations except in particular cases where a reference seems desirable. Otherwise Hogg's life of Shelley may be assumed to be the authority.

23 *Edinburgh Annual Register for 1809*, " State of University of Oxford," II, pt. 2, p. 406.

24 First quoted by Peck: *Life*, I, 75. Among Shelley's fellow students who signed the books of University College at about the same time with him were James Maxse, later one of the four masters of

the Quorn foxhounds; R. W. Sibthorpe, who became a widely known evangelical preacher; Thomas Hodgson, whose biography is confined to the hunting-field; John Brewster; W. Yorke; Edmund Fearon Burke; Christopher Dodson; J. Ricketts; D. Bramwell; I. Holliday; R. Potenger; J. T. Moore; J. Hilton; T. H. Biggs. There is no evidence of Shelley's connection with any of these. See " Shelley is Expelled," by Edmund Blunden, in *On Shelley,* by Edmund Blunden, Gavin de Beer, and Sylva Norman (London, 1938), 2, 3.

[25] Hogg, op. cit., I, 192. Hogg is not certain as to Wadham.

[26] *The Registers of Wadham College, Oxford, Part II, 1719–1871,* edited with Biographical Notes by the Rev. Robert Bartlow Gardiner, M.A., F.S.A. (London, 1895), 230.

[27] Thomas Barnes to Leigh Hunt, July 4, 1836, in Edmund Blunden: *Shelley and Keats as They Struck Their Contemporaries* (London, 1925), 10.

[28] *The Registers of Wadham College,* etc., 231.

[29] This incident, as Mr. Ingpen has pointed out, may have occurred only two days before Shelley's expulsion, as a " superfine blue velvet coat " is listed on Shelley's tailor's bill under date of March 23. The bill, quoted by Ingpen (*Shelley in England,* I, 178), covers Shelley's whole residence at Oxford from November 1. It remained unpaid on Shelley's expulsion and was paid by Timothy Shelley's attorney, Whitton, on January 11, 1814.

[30] Hogg, op. cit., I, 147–8.

[31] Ibid., I, 86, 87.

[32] Ibid., II, 82–3.

[33] *Letters to and from Charles Kirkpatrick Sharpe,* 442–3.

[34] Medwin's statement that he was " plain and loud " in avowing his sentiments seems to apply to this period (when Medwin claims to have visited him at Oxford) better than to the actual time of the election, when Shelley was still at Eton. In his very first conversation with Hogg at Oxford Shelley criticized the Oxford curriculum in terms similar to those used by the *Edinburgh Review.* Hogg (op. cit., 155–7) states that Oxford, and particularly University College during the whole period of Shelley's residence there, seethed with rancour over the recent election and that Shelley " was regarded from the beginning with a jealous eye " because he rejoiced openly in the election of Lord Grenville.

[35] " He enumerated with extreme rapidity and in his enthusiastic strain some of the benefits and comforts of college life.

"'Then the *oak* is such a blessing,' he exclaimed with peculiar fervour, clasping his hands and repeating often — 'the oak is such a blessing!' slowly and in a solemn tone. 'The oak alone goes far toward making this place a paradise. In what other spot in the world . . . can you say confidently it is perfectly impossible, physically impossible, that I should be disturbed? Whether a man desires solitary study, or to enjoy the society of a friend or two, he is secure against interruption.'" Hogg, op. cit., I, 67–8.

[36] *Fraser's Magazine,* XXIII, 703 (June 1841).

[37] Hogg, op. cit., I, 189.

[38] Shelley to Edward Graham, undated, Julian *Works,* VIII, 54.

[39] Hogg, op. cit., I, 164.

[40] Ibid., I, 166.

[41] He mentions as under way "a new Romance," probably *St. Irvyne,* in a letter of April 1, 1810, and on April 22 encloses to the same correspondent, Graham, some verses later printed in *St. Irvyne.* The title *St. Irvyne* is probably a reflection of his admiration for Godwin's *St. Leon* and of his recent moonlight walks with Harriet Grove at St. Irving's, the Duke of Norfolk's place at Horsham Strode.

[42] Ingpen: *Shelley in England,* I, 124.

[43] In 1840 it was reprinted, as Shelley's, in No. 60 of the *Romancist.* It was originally published as "By a Gentleman of the University of Oxford."

[44] An excellent summary may be found, however, for such general readers as prefer the lesser evil, in Peck: *Life,* I, 90–2.

[45] Forman: *Prose Works,* I, 269–71. In his *Revised Life* (p. 51) Medwin again quotes the passage, with his characteristic verbal inexactness, but does not explicitly label it as autobiographical. The statements about love and atheism hardly apply to Shelley at the time he wrote.

[46] Shelley to J. J. Stockdale, November 14, 1810, Julian *Works,* VIII, 18.

[47] Dowden and Ingpen mention only the *British Critic* for January 1811, pp. 70–1. It was also noticed in the *Literary Panorama* for February 1811, pp. 252–3, and more extensively in the *Anti-Jacobin Review* for January 1812, pp. 60–72. The last review elicited a letter to the editor, signed "An Oxford Collegian," giving a brief unfavourable account of the anonymous author. Since this letter has previously escaped Shelley's biographers it is here given in full (*Anti-Jacobin Review,* XLI, 221, February 1812):

Salutary attention to morals in the University of Oxford.

To the Editor of the Antijacobin Review

Sir, — I am happy to say that your excellent review now begins to be much more properly appreciated, and particularly at this University, where it is gaining ground rapidly. Of late I attribute this to your very excellent critique on the Oxford University Romance, St. Irvyne, on the subject of which I now trouble you with these few lines. This iniquitous and absurd romance is attributed to the pen of a very young gentleman, who I understand is heir to a title and a landed estate of ten thousand a year, which he will, if he lives, be in possession of very soon. And this reputed author was not long after the publication of this romance, expelled from the University, in consequence of the freedom with which he avowed his singularly wicked sentiments. He had a companion in the college, who was expelled at the same time. These facts appear to have been kept out of all public prints, but I think their promulgation will do good, as they will at once hold out a warning to others, and prove to the world, that a vigilant eye is still kept in this University over improprieties of conduct,

Your well-wisher

An Oxford Collegian.

Oxford University, Feb. 8th, 1812.

Report says that our ex-collegian, on being discountenanced by his friends, ran off with a young lady of no fortune, to Scotland, after a very sudden acquaintance, and has married her. I presume in revenge!

This communication may have some connection with Shelley's Oxford acquaintance Charles Kirkpatrick Sharpe, whose letters show a full acquaintance with Shelley's literary activities at the time and who had become a contributor to the *Anti-Jacobin Review* about ten years before. However, the style suggests another author.

48 *Stockdale's Budget,* January 3, 1827, p. 26.

49 See note 47.

50 *Letters to and from Charles Kirkpatrick Sharpe,* I, 442, 443 (March 15); and I, 445 (March 17).

51 *Posthumous Fragments of Margaret Nicholson* was advertised in the *Oxford Herald* of November 17 as " just published."

52 Hogg, op. cit., I, 158 ff.

53 Ibid., I, 162, and Shelley to Edward Graham, November 30, 1810, Julian *Works,* VIII, 20.

[54] Appendix to R. Montgomery's *Oxford* (3rd ed., 1833).

[55] Shelley to Edward Graham, November 30, 1810, Julian *Works,* VIII, 20.

[56] Hogg, op. cit., I, 162.

[57] Montgomery: *Oxford* (1833). Slatter supposed the book to be Shelley's. But Professor Fred L. Jones, in "Shelley's *Leonora,*" *Modern Philology,* XXXIII, 391–5 (May 1935), shows that it was almost certainly Hogg's. His conclusion is confirmed by Professor George Stuart Gordon's *Shelley Letters* (soon to be published), in which Shelley's references to the novel, garbled by Hogg, are corrected.

[58] December 18, 20, 1810, and May 15, 1811, Julian *Works,* VIII, 22, 23, 85.

[59] *Fraser's Magazine,* XXII (June 1841), "A Newspaper Editor's Reminiscences."

[60] Shelley to Godwin, January 16, 1812, Julian *Works,* VIII, 242–4.

[61] MacCarthy, op. cit., 57–62.

[62] Montgomery: *Oxford* (1833).

[63] He had originally made an offer of assistance to Mr. Strong, a friend of Miss Phillips, who showed him the poems in manuscript; but after his expulsion Mr. Strong would not deal with him and a brief correspondence with the author leaves the inference that she declined his assistance. Dowden: *Life,* I, 107; Ingpen: *Shelley in England,* I, 281–3; MacCarthy, op. cit., 110.

[64] Dowden records that the publishers never doubted Shelley's willingness to pay, but that "his prospects suddenly changed, he never afterwards was wealthy." Sterner critics may still wonder why the debt was not provided for in the financial settlement with his father following the death of Sir Bysshe Shelley in 1815. Ingpen (*Shelley in England,* II, 629–32) prints letters from Henry Slatter endeavouring vainly to collect the amount from Sir Timothy in 1823. On Sir Timothy's death in 1844 the sum with interest amounted to £1,605. Sir Timothy also declined to repay money borrowed of John Slatter by Shelley and Stockdale's bill for *St. Irvyne,* amounting to £300 by 1827.

[65] This note was sold in 1921 by the Anderson Art Galleries, at the George D. Smith Sale. In the *Gentleman's Magazine* index of names from 1811 to 1870 I can find only two Sandham families mentioned. One of these had its seat at Rowdell House, Pullborough, Sussex, some fifteen miles from Horsham. I have found no mention of a William Sandham, but I would suppose him to be of the Rowdell House family.

[66] Hogg, op. cit., I, 84–5.

[67] Medwin: *Revised Life*, 75.

[68] *Letters to and from Charles Kirkpatrick Sharpe*, II, 204.

[69] Hogg, op. cit., I, 89.

[70] The reading of Shelley's lifetime, so far as it could be recovered from statements of his own and of his early biographers, is systematically listed in Adolph Droop's *Die Belesenheit Percy Bysshe Shelleys* . . . (Inaugural Diss. Jena; Weimar, 1906).

[71] Hogg, op. cit., I, 76.

[72] Ibid.

[73] Ibid., I, 138.

[74] Ibid., I, 121–2.

[75] Ibid., I, 127. For Landor's attitude toward Shelley, see Chapter xxii, note 3.

[76] Shelley to J. J. Stockdale, December 2, 1810, Julian *Works*, VIII, 21.

[77] H. B. Forman, *A Shelley Library* (Shelley Society Publications, 4th series, No. 1, 1886), 20.

[78] Shelley to J. J. Stockdale, November 19, 1810, Julian *Works*, VIII, 19. The time at which he first read *Political Justice* is confused by Shelley himself — see Chapter iii, note 78, and Chapter vii, note 96.

[79] Shelley to Hogg, December 20, 1810 and January 16, 1811, Julian *Works*, VIII, 23, 46.

[80] Considering the fact that he also completely ignores Shelley's interest in Peter Finnerty and Leigh Hunt while at Oxford, insulates the political radicalism in *Posthumous Fragments,* and minimizes the religious and social radicalism which he could not ignore because of the circumstances of the expulsion (even garbling Shelley's letters to this end), Hogg stands convicted of softening Shelley's early radicalism, either out of loyalty or to conform to the desires of Mary Shelley, and afterwards Lady Shelley, to make Shelley as " respectable " as possible — or perhaps also to shield himself.

[81] Shelley to Godwin, January 10, 1812, Julian *Works*, VIII, 239.

[82] Hogg, op. cit., I, 74.

[83] Ibid., I, 71.

[84] It will be remembered that witnesses already quoted have mentioned an impression in Horsham, at Syon House, Eton, and Oxford, that Shelley was " mad," or " half-mad "; also that this was the personal impression of a large proportion of those who have left comments on Shelley as they knew him in his early life. In one of his most discerning comments Leigh Hunt took note of the common im-

pression of Shelley's madness. " He was one of those great and rare spirits, who, by a combination of the extremes of intellectual perceptiveness and nervous sensibility, may be said, instead of being the madmen that ordinary judgments would pronounce them, to possess reason itself to excess " (" A Word or Two Respecting the *Shelley Memorials,"* in the *Spectator,* August 13, 1859, pp. 733 ff.). In such a combination, if the nervous sensibility occasionally overbalanced the intellectual perceptiveness, the result might well be for a time the actual madness that it otherwise only seemed to be to the " ordinary judgment."

[85] *Stockdale's Budget,* 1827, quoted by Ingpen: *Shelley in England,* I, 136.

[86] Shelley to Hogg, December 20, 1810, Gordon: *Shelley Letters,* galley proofs.

[87] Shelley to Hogg, December 23, 1810, ibid.

[88] Ingpen: *Shelley in England,* I, 162.

[89] Shelley to Hogg, January 11, 1811, Gordon: *Shelley Letters,* galley proofs.

[90] Shelley to Hogg, December 26, 1810, ibid.

[91] See *ante,* p. 13.

[92] Shelley to Hogg, January 23, 1811, Gordon: *Shelley Letters,* galley proofs.

[93] Shelley to Hogg, January 11, 1811, ibid.

[94] Shelley to Hogg, December 20, 1810, ibid.

[95] See Shelley's second letter to Godwin, previously cited; also Medwin: *Revised Life,* 101, 102, and Hogg, op. cit., I, 156.

[96] Merle, who soon after quarrelled with Shelley on the issue of religion, also believed that Shelley was being badly influenced by a set of evil companions — a belief which may be based on solid information or may be merely a reflection of Stockdale's opinion, reaching Merle later through Timothy Shelley by way of Edward Graham. See his account in *Fraser's Magazine,* June 1841.

[97] Shelley to Hogg, January 11, 1811, Gordon: *Shelley Letters,* galley proofs. Harriet was not married to Mr. William Helyar until the following autumn; Shelley may have intended to write, as Peacock suggested: " She married! " referring to news of her engagement. Mr. Helyar, the " clod of earth," was a gentleman farmer whose family had owned an estate near that of the Groves since 1617 (Ingpen, p. xvii of his introduction to *The Journal of Harriet Grove*) and whose brother, a neighbouring clergyman, is much admired in Harriet's journal for his sermons.

[98] Shelley to Hogg, December 28, 1810, Gordon: *Shelley Letters,* galley proofs.

[99] Shelley to Hogg, January 3, 12, and 2, 1811, ibid.

[100] Hellen Shelley to Lady Jane Shelley, undated, Hogg, op. cit., I, 28. For the tenacity with which Shelley held Harriet Grove in memory, see ibid., II, 154; Medwin: *Revised Life,* 107; Peck: *Life,* I, 93–4.

[101] Shelley to Hogg, December 23, 1810, Gordon: *Shelley Letters,* galley proofs. This and various other references to the Hogg-Elizabeth affair were garbled by Hogg by exchanging personal pronouns in a way to make them refer to Shelley and Harriet.

[102] Shelley to Hogg, January 6, 1811, ibid.

[103] Shelley to Hogg, January 2, 1811, ibid.

[104] Shelley to Hogg, January 3, 1811, ibid.

[105] Shelley to Hogg, January 12, 1811, ibid.

[106] Shelley to Hogg, December 23 and 26, 1810, ibid. This and similar passages Hogg consistently garbled in order to tone down Shelley's violence, by substituting " intolerance " for " Christianity," " avenger " for " Antichrist," etc.

[107] Shelley to Hogg, December 20, 1810, ibid.

[108] Shelley to Hogg, January 3, 1811, ibid.

[109] Charles Grove to " My dear H—," February 16, 1857, Hogg, op. cit., II, 155. It was probably after December 13, when Shelley had copies of the book sent to Medwin, Hogg, and Miss Marshall, and before January 11, when he directed a copy to be sent to Harriet at her home in London.

[110] Shelley to J. J. Stockdale, January 28, 1811, Julian *Works,* VIII, 49.

[111] Hogg, op. cit., I, 141.

[112] Ibid., I, 151–2.

[113] Some of the incidents may belong to the period before the vacation, just as some of those previously treated in this volume may belong to the later period. It is impossible to relate all Hogg's reminiscences to particular times. For example, his famous story of the microscope Shelley pawned in order to relieve an old man's poverty has the ring of general truth, but is placed definitely (ibid., 151) as " On returning to town after the long vacation, at the end of October." If this means 1810 Shelley and Hogg were not acquainted; if it means 1811, they were already expelled.

[114] Ibid., I, 86.

[115] Ibid., I, 86.

[116] Ibid., I, 90.

[117] *Atlantic Monthly*, XI, 193 (February 1863).

[118] Since Thornton Hunt was an admirer of Shelley, he certainly did not report this impression maliciously, and it therefore deserves to be noted in any impartial account. But Hunt's informant is as likely to have been mistaken as Hogg is to have been an elaborate and *unnecessary* liar, even though he has been convicted of lying *for cause*. Mr. Walter E. Peck has obviously felt that the statement called for a closer scrutiny of Shelley's life at Oxford with a view to his relations with women. In this it seems to me that he correctly interpreted the duty of a biographer; but having reached inconclusive results, he has given them undue weight by publishing them without sufficient safeguards against misinterpretation. Thus he quotes Miss Grant's account of Shelley's Oxford career (*Life*, I, 107), the last sentence of which is: "Quiet was restored to our sober walls after the disturber of its peace had been got rid of, *although some suspicious circumstances connected with the welfare of a principal favorite* [131a] *of my aunt's still required to be elucidated, as Mr. Rowley said, and at once checked.*" [132] (My italics, his footnote numbers.)

The second footnote is a quotation of Thornton Hunt's statement that Shelley contracted venereal disease at Oxford. There is no other word in the *Memoirs of a Highland Lady* to suggest the identity or even the sex of her aunt's favourite. Nor is there any suggestion as to why the Dean, the Master, and the Master's wife should be so free-spoken on such a subject as the footnote implies, before a fifteen-year-old girl. Their utter silence when they screened her windows with muslin because they had observed they overlooked a student's windows (p. 128, two paragraphs preceding) would argue for complete reticence. Also what still remained to be "checked," granting the suggested circumstances, is puzzling. These difficulties may be met by regarding the paragraph quoted by Mr. Peck as closely connected with the preceding ones. Miss Grant is discussing the general subject of student disturbances. Shelley, as "ringleader," gets a separate paragraph. The final sentence winds up the whole discussion, not merely Shelley's part in it, and the latter half of the sentence was probably never intended to have any reference to Shelley at all.

Mr. Peck's first footnote refers the reader to Appendix S (*Life*, II, 446), where he says that the reference is probably to a young lady and wonders if it could be the "Miss Burton" referred to in a letter from E. B. Impey to Charles Kirkpatrick Sharpe, dated March 18, 1811. Impey wrote as follows:

> As for the literary meteor who is now performing his perielion [*sic*] in your learned hemisphere, I have nothing to do — but hide my diminished beams — and congratulate myself on being beyond the scope of his fiery tail — which he seems to whisk about with such wonderful volubility that I would have Miss Burton beware of the laws of gravitation and vigilantly guard her centre of attraction.

There seems to be no certainty that Shelley is the "literary meteor," but assuming that he is, one naturally searches for further information about Miss Burton. I find in the *Letters to and from Charles Kirkpatrick Sharpe* thirteen references to Miss Burton, three to Dr. James Burton, and an explanatory footnote (I, 218). Together they make it clear that Miss Burton is Dr. Burton's unmarried sister, who was an Oxford "toast" and a standing joke in Sharpe's circle. Since Dr. Burton was sixty-six years old in 1811 (according to his obituary in the *Gentleman's Magazine* for July 1825), Sharpe twenty-nine, and Shelley nineteen, the age discrepancies render Mr. Peck's suggestion absurd. As a sister of Dr. Burton and a standing jest in Sharpe's circle Miss Burton was almost certainly two or three times Shelley's age. If the reference really does connect Shelley and Miss Rachel Burton, it might more reasonably be connected with supposed literary pretensions or love of notoriety on her part.

Dr. Burton was married and had two daughters, one of whom was unmarried in 1811. But the date of his marriage (1774) suggests that even his daughters were probably too old to fit plausibly into the supposed situation — and the references in the letters are plainly to Rachel Burton, the sister.

Thus Thornton Hunt's statement must stand or fall on its own anonymous authority, and must be regarded (at least by me) as improbable, but possible. Certain obvious elements in both *St. Irvyne* and the "Epithalamium" in *Posthumous Fragments* suggest that Hogg's statement may well be too sweeping and Hunt's not entirely lacking in psychological basis.

[119] Hogg, op. cit., I, 129.

[120] Ibid., I, 133. This same streak of aristocratic prejudice seems indicated by Shelley, Mary, and Jane Clairmont in occasional references in their journals of 1814 to their fellow travellers down the Rhine and again in Shelley's treatment of the "swinish multitude"

in *Swellfoot the Tyrant,* in 1820. Stockdale hints an impression similar to Hogg's. As late as 1820, according to the unpublished journal of Maria Gisborne, the Leigh Hunts and Gisbornes laughed together over certain little aristocratic touches in Shelley's talk and behaviour.

[121] *Letters to and from Charles Kirkpatrick Sharpe,* I, 443.

[122] Most of the information on this subject was discovered by D. F. MacCarthy and printed in his *Shelley's Early Life.* An excellent brief discussion of it is to be found in H. B. Forman's *The Shelley Library* (1886), 20–2. It may be suggested as a further possibility that Sharpe and Slatter were both right in saying that Shelley gave the profits of *Posthumous Fragments of Margaret Nicholson* to Peter Finnerty. The editor of the Dublin *Weekly Messenger* says that Shelley remitted Finnerty nearly £100 as the profits of "a very beautiful poem," but he obviously exaggerates the profits, and he does not specify the poem. Hence it is quite possible that Shelley remitted the profits — if any — from *Posthumous Fragments,* and suppressed "A Poetical Essay." Dowden suggests plausibly (*Life,* I, 110–11) that the poem may have been revised and incorporated in *Queen Mab* as the section dealing with the Present. In that case Medwin's statement that *Queen Mab* was begun at Oxford may refer to this section of *Queen Mab,* as originally the "Poetical Essay."

[123] Julian *Works,* VIII, 55.

[124] For whom Munday and Slatter published the next year a very bad poem entitled *The Widower.* In one section of this poem, quoted by Ingpen in *Shelley in England,* I, 187, "vicious infidels" are most harshly addressed.

[125] Shelley to Timothy Shelley, February 6 and 17, 1811, Julian *Works,* VIII, 50, 54.

[126] Mr. Ingpen thinks (*Shelley in England,* I, 188) that this may have been done during the holidays at Field Place. From its similarity in some points to passages in Shelley's letter of February 6 to his father, it would appear to have been done near the time of the letter.

[127] See the letter of Mr. Barclay Phillips quoted by T. J. Wise and Percy Vaughan in their reprint of *The Necessity of Atheism* for the Rationalist Press Association, London, 1906.

[128] Shelley to Edward Graham, February 13, 1811, Julian *Works,* VIII, 53.

[129] *Ante,* p. 108.

[130] This account is from the recollections of Henry Slatter, printed

in Montgomery's *Oxford* (4th ed., 1835), 168. Roger Ingpen, in his *Shelley in England* (I, 194), adds a letter to the printers from William Whitton, Timothy Shelley's London lawyer, dated April 13, 1811, strongly condemning their conduct and advising them against printing anything more.

131 Henry Slatter, loc. cit.

132 According to Mr. Ridley's account of Shelley's expulsion, the advertisement was generally understood to have been written by Hogg. Ridley's statement is printed by Dowden (*Life*, I, 123).

133 Shelley to Godwin, January 10, 1812, Julian *Works*, VIII, 240–1.

134 Hogg, op. cit., I, 93–4.

135 Ibid., I, 71.

136 *Letters to and from Charles Kirkpatrick Sharpe*, I, 443.

137 Medwin: *Revised Life*, 83.

138 As cited in note 130 above.

139 Shelley to Edward Graham, undated, Julian *Works*, VIII, 54.

140 According to Mr. Previté-Orton of St. John's College, Cambridge, as quoted in a letter from Sir Michael Sadler to Mr. Edmund Blunden, November 16, 1931. From an unpublished MS. loaned me by Mr. Blunden.

141 A. D. Godley: *Oxford in the Eighteenth Century* (London, 1908), 140.

142 Edward Coplestone: *Reply to the Calumnies of the Edinburgh Review*, 166.

143 Shelley to Godwin, January 10, 1812, Julian *Works*, VIII, 241.

144 This letter is quoted in note 88, Chapter vii.

145 Hogg, op. cit., I, 168 ff.

146 There are nine accounts of Shelley's expulsion, presenting a considerable number of minor errors and discrepancies. Hogg's, the most detailed and circumstantial, is certainly mistaken in supposing that the decree was prepared before the interview with Shelley, because the grounds stated were furnished by the interview itself.

Of the two accounts representing the official point of view, C. J. Ridley's (first quoted in Dowden's *Life*, I, 123–4), written down some years after the event, makes an error of one year in the date and mentions no decree of expulsion until after both culprits had testified and left the room; while Miss Elizabeth Grant's (in *Memoirs of a Highland Lady*), written at least thirty-four years after the event, is obviously wrong in speaking of a " private " expulsion and a long consultation with the poet's father before it was executed.

Chapter VI

GENERAL SOURCES

Hogg's *Life of Shelley*, Medwin's *Revised Life, Shelley Memorials*, the Shelley-Whitton papers as quoted in Ingpen's *Shelley in England* (some of which I have been able to examine in MS.) — all as previously cited — and Elizabeth Hitchener's letters to Shelley, reprinted in Peck's *Shelley* (which I have also read in MS. in the British Museum, Add. MSS. 37,496). The principal source is Shelley's letters as found in Volume VIII of the Julian *Works* and the galley proofs of Professor Gordon's forthcoming *Shelley Letters,* as cited previously.

NOTES AND REFERENCES

[1] Medwin: Revised *Life*, 87–8.

[2] Hogg, op. cit., II, 156.

[3] Mr. Ingpen has pointed out in *Shelley in England* (I, 213) that in a lyric in *St. Irvyne* Shelley lifted two lines from Byron's " Lachin-y-Gair," published in *Hours of Idleness* (1807).

[4] Dowden (*Life*, I, 140) assigns these visits to this time.

[5] *Shelley Memorials* (3rd ed., 1875), 21.

[6] Shelley to Timothy Shelley, February 6, 1811, Julian *Works*, VIII, 50.

[7] Later his letters emphasize his son's impiety more and more, but within two months after the expulsion he apparently confided to Captain Pilfold (perhaps disingenuously) that he himself was little more than a sceptic (Julian *Works*, VIII, 86, May 15, 1811).

[8] Ingpen: *Shelley in England*, I, 217.

[9] Julian *Works*, VIII, 60–1.

[10] As a Godwinian, Shelley had little respect for the traditional sense of duty. He scorned it as a motive for Harriet Grove's be-

haviour (April 26, 1811, Julian *Works,* VIII, 75), but treated it respectfully in his letter to Hogg's father [April, 1811], Julian *Works,* VIII, 63.

[11] Ingpen: *Shelley in England,* I, 223, says this Mr. Graham was Edward Graham's father. Hogg names him only as " Mr. Graham, whom I had seen before."

[12] Hogg, op. cit., I, 183–5.

[13] Timothy Shelley to William Whitton, April 18, 1811, quoted by Ingpen, *Shelley in England,* I, 243.

[14] Hogg, op. cit., I, 195–6. Mr. Clarke's report, dated April 6, 1811, regarded the offence rather more lightly than Mr. Shelley did. Clarke thought that the publication was foolish, but contained no striking impiety, and that the trouble mostly proceeded from a desire on the part of the boys to " show off."

[15] Ingpen: *Shelley in England,* I, 226.

[16] Julian *Works,* VIII, 61, dated by the editors April 10, 1811.

[17] Ibid., VIII, 63, undated. Hogg is careful to say (*Life,* I, 195) that he does not believe Mr. Timothy Shelley meant to leave this impression. Elsewhere Hogg seems to be at pains to show Mr. Shelley's goodwill toward him. On this point he may well be suspected of special pleading.

[18] Captain Pilfold, a retired naval officer and Shelley's maternal uncle, if not already Shelley's favourite kinsman, was soon to become so. Mr. Robert Parker, husband of Mr. Timothy Shelley's oldest sister, was sufficiently liked by Shelley to receive the first presentation copy of *St. Irvyne.*

[19] John Grove to Timothy Shelley, April 11, 1811, in Ingpen: *Shelley in England,* I, 230–1.

[20] Robert Parker to Timothy Shelley, April 12, 1811, ibid., I, 229–30.

[21] Julian *Works,* VIII, 67.

[22] Shelley to Hogg, January 12, 1811, ibid., VIII, 45.

[23] Ingpen: *Shelley in England,* I, 228.

[24] Hogg, op. cit., I, 188.

[25] Ingpen: *Shelley in England,* I, 226–7.

[26] Julian *Works,* VIII, 67.

[27] Ibid., VIII, 62.

[28] Ingpen: *Shelley in England,* I, 236–7.

[29] Ibid., I, 237, 238.

[30] William Whitton to P. B. Shelley, undated, quoted ibid., I, 249, and dated conjecturally April 18, 1811.

31 Julian *Works,* VIII, 67–8.
32 Ingpen: *Shelley in England,* I, 237.
33 Ibid., I, 242–3.
34 Ibid., I, 254.
35 Julian *Works,* VIII, 66.
36 Shelley to Hogg, May 8, 1811, ibid., VIII, 81. As printed here, from Hogg's *Life,* Hunt appears only as an anonymous " man of letters," but he is named in Professor Gordon's restored text of the letter in his *Shelley Letters* — thus invalidating the Julian editors' suggestion that the " man of letters " was Rowland Hunter, the radical bookseller of St. Paul's Churchyard. Thornton Hunt stated (in a note to Leigh Hunt's *Autobiography* cited by the Julian editors, VIII, 81) that it was through Rowland Hunter that Shelley met Leigh Hunt.
37 Leigh Hunt's *Autobiography* (London, 1860), 232–3.
38 As reported by John Grove, Hogg, op. cit., I, 197.
39 Medwin: *Revised Life,* 88–91.
40 Shelley to Hogg, May 19, 1811, Julian *Works,* VIII, 94.
41 Ibid., VIII, 69.
42 As Ingpen suspects, *Shelley in England,* I, 266.
43 Hogg, op. cit., I, 275.
44 Dowden: *Life,* I, 142.
45 Hellen Shelley, in Hogg, op. cit., I, 32; Peacock: *Memoirs,* II, 338; and Southey, *passim,* in his letters to and concerning Shelley.
46 Shelley to Hogg, April 24, 1811, Julian *Works,* VIII, 70.
47 Medwin: *Revised Life,* 101, and Hogg, op. cit., II, 156.
48 Shelley to Hogg, April 24, 1811, Julian *Works,* VIII, 70.
49 Shelley to Hogg, April 29, 1811, ibid., VIII, 79.
50 Shelley to Hogg, May 8, 1811, ibid., VIII, 81.
51 Shelley to Hogg, April 26, 1811, ibid., VIII, 74–5.
52 Shelley's letters to Hogg were originally published in Hogg's *Life of Shelley* and have been known to have been considerably garbled. In the latter part of the nineteenth century Mr. W. M. Rossetti was allowed to examine the original MSS. and made numerous notes which he allowed the late Mr. T. J. Wise to transfer to his copy of Hogg's *Life,* now in the British Museum. It was from this copy that the late Mr. Roger Ingpen derived the corrections embodied in the Julian edition.
53 Medwin: *Revised Life,* 91.
54 *Queen Mab,* VII, 12–49.
55 Hogg, op. cit., I, 315.

⁵⁶ Shelley to Janetta Philipps, undated [May 1811], Julian *Works,* VIII, 89.

⁵⁷ Shelley to Hogg, April 28, 1811, ibid., VIII, 77.

⁵⁸ Shelley to Hogg, May 9, 1811, ibid., VIII, 84, misdated "?May 13."

⁵⁹ Shelley to Hogg, undated [April 25, 1811?], ibid., VIII, 72.

⁶⁰ Shelley to Hogg, April 28, 1811, ibid, VIII, 76.

⁶¹ Shelley to Hogg, May 8, 1811, ibid., VIII, 82.

⁶² Shelley to Hogg, May 9, 1811. Cf. note 58.

⁶³ Ingpen: *Shelley in England,* I, 276–7.

⁶⁴ Shelley to Edward Graham, undated, Julian *Works,* X, 416.

⁶⁵ Timothy Shelley to P. B. Shelley, December 19, 1811, in *Shelley in England,* II, 365. Confirmation of Mr. Shelley's statement that Shelley had so agreed is found in Shelley's letter of October 8, 1811, to Elizabeth Hitchener: "When last I saw you I was about to enter into the profession of physic." Julian *Works,* VIII, 152.

⁶⁶ This letter was known to Professor Dowden, who mentions it briefly (*Life,* I, 131, note). Forman (Aldine ed., 1892, I, xix) describes the poem and quotes the first four lines of the postscript, and Mr. Harry B. Smith ("Books and Autograph Letters of Shelley," *Scribner's Magazine,* July 1922, pp. 84, 85) quotes the first eight lines and describes the paper as bearing an 1810 watermark. It was first published in 1927, Julian *Works,* III, 92–4.

⁶⁷ Shelley to Mrs. Elizabeth Shelley, dated by the Julian editors October 22, 1811. In Julian *Works,* VIII, 163–4.

⁶⁸ Shelley to Hogg, June 16, 1811, ibid., VIII, 105.

⁶⁹ Shelley to Hogg, June 21, 1811, ibid., VIII, 112.

⁷⁰ Shelley to Hogg, May 18, 1811, ibid., VIII, 93.

⁷¹ Shelley to Hogg, June 23, 1811, ibid., VIII, 113.

⁷² Shelley to Hogg, August 15, 1811, ibid., VIII, 141.

⁷³ Shelley to Mrs. Elizabeth Shelley [October 22, 1811], ibid., VIII, 163–4.

⁷⁴ Elizabeth Shelley died unmarried, December 17, 1831.

⁷⁵ Shelley to Hogg, April 25, 1811, Julian *Works,* VIII, 72. I believe Mr. Ingpen is mistaken in taking this sentence (*Shelley in England,* I, 272) as referring to Harriet.

⁷⁶ Shelley to Hogg, May 15, 1811, Julian *Works,* VIII, 87.

⁷⁷ Shelley to Hogg from Rhayader, undated except by Shelley's residence at Rhayader in July 1811, ibid., VIII, 127.

⁷⁸ Harriet Shelley to Elizabeth Hitchener, March 14, 1812, ibid., VIII, 295.

[79] Shelley to Hogg, May 19, 1811, ibid., VIII, 94.

[80] Hogg, op. cit., II, 55. Medwin did not know Miss Hitchener or much about her; he remembered her only from Shelley's later ridicule of her (*Revised Life*, 117–18).

[81] Letter of the Earl of Chichester, quoted in MacCarthy: *Early Life*, 313.

[82] Her letters, reprinted in an appendix to Mr. Peck's *Life*, do not indicate to me as they do to Mr. Peck that Elizabeth Hitchener was from the first a schemer, after Shelley's money. She does not mention money for some time and then not for herself, and only after Shelley seems to have suggested something of the kind. The only financial obligation that ever seems to have existed between the two was a loan from Miss Hitchener to Shelley, after his marriage. The exchange of letters is to me fully convincing as the sincere expression of two enthusiastic, eccentric personalities genuinely attracted to each other.

[83] Shelley to Elizabeth Hitchener, June 11, 1811, Julian *Works*, VIII, 101.

[84] Ibid., VIII, 101–2.

[85] Her letters to Shelley were first printed in Peck: *Life*, though Dowden had used them.

[86] Shelley to Elizabeth Hitchener, June 20, 1811, Julian *Works*, VIII, 108–9.

[87] Charles Grove to Hellen Shelley, February 25, 1857, quoted by Hogg, op. cit., II, 158.

[88] Ibid., I, 197.

[89] Timothy Shelley to William Whitton, in Ingpen: *Shelley in England*, I, 242.

[90] Shelley to Hogg, May 14, 1811, Julian *Works*, VIII, 87, misdated May 15.

[91] Hogg is apparently not to be told about Elizabeth Hitchener.

[92] Julian *Works*, VIII, 117, dated by the editors " about June 27, 1811."

[93] Charles Grove to Hellen Shelley, February 16, 1857, in Hogg, op. cit., II, 156.

[94] Shelley to Hogg, June 21, 1811, Julian *Works*, VIII, 110.

[95] Ibid., VIII, 116.

[96] Ibid. Shelley's only observation of the " peasantry " is recorded in a letter to Miss Hitchener written apparently the day after his arrival at Cwm Elan (postmarked July 15, 1811, Julian *Works*, VIII, 125):

My window is over the kitchen, in the morning I threw it up, and had hardly finished dressing when " for Charity's dear sake " met my ear, these words were pronounced with such sweetness that on turning round I was surprised to find them uttered by an old beggar, to whom in a moment the servant brought some meat, I ran down and gave him something: — he appeared extremely grateful. I tried to enter into conversation with him . . . in vain. I followed him a mile asking a thousand questions. At length I quitted him finding by this remarkable observation that perseverance was useless. " I see by your dress that you are a rich man. They have injured me and mine a million times . . . you appear to be well intentioned but I have no security of it while you live in such a house as that, or wear such clothes as those. It would be charity to quit me."

It is surprising that this old beggar, whose normal speech must have been Welsh, spoke pure Shelleyan to Shelley.

[97] Shelley to Hogg, dated by the editors " about June 27, 1811," Julian *Works*, VIII, 118.

[98] The " pressing business " may have been connected with the lost poem on the Carleton House fête. This is the first time Shelley is known to have been in London since that event, and there were now several good reasons why he would have preferred having the printing done in London rather than Sussex. It was also his best opportunity to throw copies into carriages at Carleton House, as related by Charles Grove. Perhaps his letter to Graham, as soon as he reached Cwm Elan, bears on the same business: " I hope you will quickly set to music that heavenly ode " (July 15, 1811).

[99] Shelley to Elizabeth Hitchener, July 15, 1811, Julian *Works*, VIII, 124.

[100] *Coombe Ellen,* 1798.

[101] Shelley to Graham, July 15, 1811, Julian *Works*, VIII, 123.

[102] Shelley to Hogg, July 25, 1811, ibid., VIII, 126.

[103] Shelley to Elizabeth Hitchener, July 26, 1811, ibid., VIII, 133.

[104] *Coombe Ellen* (1798), ll. 290–304. Much of the scenery described by Bowles and Shelley has been under water since 1894. See *The Vale of Nantgwillt: A Submerged Valley,* etc., by R. Eustace Tickell (London, 1894).

[105] Charles Grove to Hellen Shelley, February 16, 1857, in Hogg, op. cit., II, 156.

[106] Shelley to Hogg, dated by the editors " ?July 28, 1811," Julian

Works, VIII, 135. Hogg garbled this letter in printing by exchanging pronouns so that Shelley seemed to be arguing with himself, not Hogg.

[107] Shelley to Hogg, dated by the editors " ?July 30, 1811," ibid., VIII, 136.

[108] Shelley to Hogg, dated by the editors " ?July 25, 1811," ibid., VIII, 126.

[109] Shelley to Elizabeth Hitchener, July 26, 1811, ibid., VIII, 133.

[110] Shelley to Hogg, July 30 and 28 (?), 1811, ibid., VIII, 136, 135. A peculiar hardship for such a letter-writer was the fact that the post arrived only three times a week.

[111] Shelley to Hogg, dated by the editors " ?July 28, 1811," ibid., VIII, 134.

[112] See Carl H. Grabo: *A Newton among Poets* (Chapel Hill, 1930).

[113] Julian *Works,* VIII, 130.

[114] Shelley to Hogg, undated, July, 1811, Julian *Works,* VIII, 128. The postscript to this letter, presented as a part of a novel, is another instance of Hogg's falsification. In the original it is not postscript, and deals openly with Hogg's love for Elizabeth, changed by Hogg to Sophia.

[115] Shelley to Hogg, dated by the editors " ?July 28, 1811," ibid., VIII, 135. See note 106.

[116] Shelley to J. J. Stockdale, August 1, 1811, ibid., VIII, 137. These essays, if ever written, vanished even more completely than Stockdale's hopes of being repaid. In his *Budget* Stockdale testified that the debt then amounted to not less than £300, and that he had never doubted Shelley's earnest desire to pay it.

[117] Shelley to Hogg, June 21 and 23, 1811, Julian *Works,* VIII, 110, 114.

[118] Shelley to Hogg, undated, " July 25? 1811 " suggested by Julian editors, ibid., VIII, 126.

[119] Shelley to Hogg, undated [?July 1811], ibid., VIII, 128.

[120] Shelley to Hogg, undated, July 30, 1811 suggested by Julian editors, ibid., VIII, 136.

[121] Ibid., VIII, 110, 126, 136, 138, 140, 141, 142.

[122] Shelley to Elizabeth Hitchener, dated by the editors " October 27, 1811? " ibid., VIII, 169. The mention of suicide is in accord with Hogg's later testimony that Harriet constantly talked of suicide.

[123] Shelley to Hogg, undated, probably August 3, 1811, ibid., VIII, 138.

[124] There is no record of any action of his in consequence, but it must have increased his suspicious vigilance toward his son.

[125] Mrs. Field, quoted by Dowden: *Life*, I, 149.

[126] Shelley to Hogg, undated, probably August 3, 1811, Julian *Works*, VIII, 138. Except for punctuation, this letter as printed from Hogg's *Life* contains only two slight verbal variations from the text as recently restored by Professor Gordon, and these two I have incorporated.

[127] Shelley to Hogg, undated [July 1811], Julian *Works*, VIII, 127, 129.

[128] In letters to Hogg, August 15, 1811, and to Sir James Henry Lawrence, August 17, 1812, ibid., VIII, 142, and IX, 17.

[129] Hogg's opinion on this point, though biased by his hatred of Eliza, is blunt and sweeping: " Eliza had tended, guided, and ruled Harriet from her earliest infancy; she doubtless had married her, had made the match, had put her up to everything that was to be said or done, as Shelley's letters plainly show" (*Life*, I, 274).

[130] Charles Clairmont to Francis Place, January 12, 1815 [for 1816]. British Museum Add. MSS. 35,152, ff. 191–194. I have reprinted the letter in Appendix III.

[131] Shelley to Elizabeth Hitchener, August 10, 1811, Julian *Works*, VIII, 139.

[132] Charles Grove to Hellen Shelley, February 16, 1857, in Hogg, op. cit., II, 156.

[133] Shelley to Elizabeth Hitchener, dated by the editors " ?October 27, 1811," Julian *Works*, VIII, 169.

[134] Shelley to Hogg, undated. The Julian editors suggest August 14 and 15, 1811, ibid., VIII, 140, 141.

[135] Shelley to Hogg, August 15, 1811, ibid., VIII, 142.

[136] Shelley to Elizabeth Hitchener, undated, ibid., VIII, 169. The editors suggest October 27, 1811.

[137] I cannot find any authority for Dowden's statement (*Life*, I, 170) that this was a visit Shelley had expected to make to Captain Pilford; Shelley himself refers to it as a visit to Field Place, and his business was transacted at Horsham. See note 145.

[138] Shelley to Elizabeth Hitchener [October 8, 1811], Julian *Works*, VIII, 152.

[139] C. G. Harper: *The Great North Road* (London, 1901), I, 56–8.

[140] Shelley to the Duke of Norfolk, October 28, 1811, Julian *Works*, VIII, 171.

[141] Shelley to Hogg, August 15, 1811, ibid., VIII, 142.

[142] Whitton papers, as quoted in Ingpen: *Shelley in England,* I, 301–2.

[143] Shelley expected to be in Field Place on August 11, as shown by his letter of August 10. His first (undated) letter to Hogg on his return preceded one dated August 15, so that his absence could hardly have been of more than four days and may have been less. Shelley says in the letter of October 27 to Elizabeth Hitchener that his return and the consequent elopement were in response to a summons from Harriet, which is scarcely reconcilable with his statement to the Duke of Norfolk that he borrowed money in Horsham for the purpose of eloping.

[144] Shelley to Hogg, August 15, 1811, Julian *Works,* VIII, 142.

[145] Professor Dowden's tact and understanding seem to me to be somewhat at fault in his account of the elopement with Harriet. As much as possible he allows the story to be told by Shelley himself — as he told it to Elizabeth Hitchener. He makes no allowance for psychological factors likely to affect Shelley's accounts to both Miss Hitchener and Hogg. To my mind this makes Shelley more passive and Harriet more aggressive than they actually were after Shelley reached London. My own interpretation is based upon the following considerations:

Shelley must have faced a certain embarrassment in explaining the situation to both Hogg and Elizabeth Hitchener. The former was his close and "eternal" friend, who was showing some alarm over the situation. Unconsciously Shelley must have wished to reassure both Hogg and himself that the new situation would have no effect on their close relationship. Hence Shelley's insistence on Hogg as his primary interest still, at the same time that he admits Harriet's situation is engrossing all his time and thought; hence also the remark that he does not expect to be launched on either free love or matrimony — in the same letter in which he allows himself a glint of sardonic amusement at the astonishment probably awaiting his father. In short, Shelley shrank from allowing Hogg to see that his alarm about the situation was justified. It will be noted that Hogg was never told that a marriage was decided on. He was confronted with a *fait accompli,* like the rest.

The case is similar with Elizabeth Hitchener. Neither in his letters nor in his interview at the time did Shelley so much as mention Harriet to her. The whole thing was explained to her *de novo* after it was a *fait accompli.* Meanwhile she had become the "sister of his soul," a position he himself made clear did not compromise his love for Harriet. He felt that his actions needed explanation to her, and he explained them in the way that would least wound her vanity or arouse her jealousy. Thus he wished her to suppose that his visit to Field Place was something already planned, instead of a trip to get money — which his letter to the Duke of Norfolk, and also Medwin's account, seem to demonstrate it was. If Harriet seemed composed when he went to Field Place, as he wrote Miss Hitchener, there was not the same reason for secrecy as there would otherwise have been, and there was not the same reason for borrowing money *for the purpose of eloping.* Shelley both maintained secrecy and borrowed money, and admitted the latter to the Duke of Norfolk.

I conclude, therefore, (1) that when Shelley left Cwm Elan it was with his mind made up to marry Harriet if she could not otherwise be made happy. His letters to Hogg and to Charles Grove seem to show this clearly. (2) That the period of waiting in London was "embarrassed and melancholy" for several reasons — for example, an effort to convert Mr. Westbrook to Harriet's point of view, an effort to convince himself that Harriet really was desperately in love with him, some worry about money, and some worry about Hogg's attitude. It is quite possible that Shelley persuaded Harriet to wait awhile to see if her father really would insist on her return to school; also that he wished if possible to wait for his quarter's allowance, apparently due on September 1. (3) That the argument with Harriet of which he told Hogg was one in which Shelley urged Hogg's arguments for matrimony against unknown arguments by Harriet — possibly the same as Adeline Mowbray's in the book she had asked him to read.

[146] The last part of this paragraph, except the meeting with Mr. Dunn, is based entirely upon Professor Dowden's account (*Life,* I, 172–3), which must have a specific source unstated by him and undiscovered by me. Charles Grove's letter previously cited from Hogg's *Life of Shelley,* the only source cited by Professor Dowden or known to me, says nothing of the note to Harriet, the wait, or the breakfast. These details are so specific, and Professor Dowden usually so careful, that I think they must have had a definite basis.

[147] Julian *Works,* VIII, 145, note.

[148] *A New and Accurate Description of All the Direct and Principal Cross Roads in England and Wales and Part of the Roads of Scotland,* etc., etc., by Lieut.-Colonel [Daniel] Paterson (15th ed., London, 1811).

[149] Hogg, op. cit., I, 261. Mr. Peck has conjectured with consid-

erable plausibility that the lawyer was the Mr. Hutchinson who is mentioned in the *Letters to and from Charles Kirkpatrick Sharpe* as accompanying Sharpe and Shelley to a dance in Edinburgh. There was a young advocate named Gilbert Hutchinson in Edinburgh at the time. The letter mentioning Shelley is undated, and refers to Shelley's father as *Sir* Timothy over three years before he inherited his title, if we consider that the letter was written in 1811. Partly on this ground Mr. Ingpen omitted the incident in his *Shelley in England,* but it still seems as easy to suppose the note written in 1811 as to make it fit any other particular date. See the *Athenæum,* February 11, 1921, p. 163, and the *Nation and Athenæum,* April 16, 1921, p. 91.

[150] The documents are quoted by Ingpen: *Shelley in England,* I, 308–10. The attached statement of their marriage by the officiating minister is undated, but the date is given as August 29 in the papers connected with Shelley's remarriage in 1814. The Reverend Joseph Robertson, who married the couple, was sentenced in 1818 for similar practices to three months in prison and transportation for life (Edinburgh *Evening Dispatch,* July 7, 1922).

[151] From the Whitton papers, Ingpen: *Shelley in England,* I, 307–8.

Chapter VII

GENERAL SOURCES

Godwin's journal, as quoted in C. K. Paul: *William Godwin, His Friends and Contemporaries,* London, 1876; Elizabeth Hitchener's letters, as quoted in W. E. Peck: *Shelley, His Life and Work,* Boston and New York, 1927 (I have examined the original MSS. in the British Museum — Add. MSS. 37,496); Hogg's *Life of Shelley* as previously cited; D. F. MacCarthy: *Shelley's Early Life,* London, 1872; the Shelley-Whitton papers as quoted in Roger Ingpen: *Shelley in England,* London, 1917; and Shelley's letters as given in the Julian *Works,* Volume VIII, and in the galley proofs of George Stuart Gordon: *Shelley Letters,* to be published in London and New York.

NOTES AND REFERENCES

[1] Peck: *Life,* I, 172.

[2] Ingpen: *Shelley in England,* I, 326, 327.

[3] Peacock: *Memoirs,* II, 320–1. Peacock thought the story probable.

[4] Hogg, op. cit., I, 264–5.

[5] Ibid., I, 265.

[6] Loc. cit.

[7] Ibid., I, 261.

[8] Ibid., I, 269.

[9] Shelley's letter of August 30 to his father (Julian *Works,* VIII, 147) mentions a friend who promised to lionize him. This is probably the young advocate whom he met en route; it is unlikely that he established connections with Sharpe so soon. An undated note of Sharpe's (*Letters to and from C. K. Sharpe,* I, 497–8) asks permission of an Edinburgh hostess to bring Shelley to dance at her house. See two articles by Mr. W. E. Peck as cited in note 149, Chapter vi.

[10] Shelley to Elizabeth Hitchener, October [15?], 1811, Julian *Works,* VIII, 159.

[11] Shelley to Timothy Shelley, August 30, September 15 and 27, Julian *Works,* VIII, 146, 147, 150.

[12] Ingpen: *Shelley in England,* I, 320.

[13] P. B. Shelley to Timothy Shelley, September 27, 1811, Julian *Works,* VIII, 149–50.

[14] Timothy Shelley to John Hogg, September 8, 1811, Ingpen: *Shelley in England,* I, 316.

[15] William Whitton to Timothy Shelley, September 16, 1811, Ingpen: *Shelley in England,* I, 317.

[16] As quoted by Hogg, op. cit., I, 270.

[17] From Shelley's letters to Hogg from Keswick, shortly afterwards, it would appear that they moved to Mrs. Strickland's, in Blake Street. Shelley's letters to Hogg are so addressed, and in one of them he asks Hogg to send Mrs. Strickland's bill, which he had evidently failed to pay before departing. (Gordon: *Shelley Letters,* galley proofs.)

[18] Mr. Shelley recognized both the significance and the inspiration of this and similar passages. Writing to Whitton on October 27, he

said: " He is such a Pupil of Godwin that I can scarcely hope he will be persuaded that he owes any sort of obedience or compliance to the wishes or directions of his Parents " (Ingpen: *Shelley in England,* I, 348).

[19] Shelley to Timothy Shelley, October 12, 1811, Julian *Works,* VIII, 154.

[20] Ibid., VIII, 156.

[21] From Hogg's account (op. cit., I, 273), Shelley left York for London the night after reaching York, but from the dates and post-marks of Shelley's letters it is plain that he remained in York for about ten days.

[22] Elizabeth Hitchener to Shelley, October 11, 1811, as quoted by Peck (*Life,* II, 326) from the MS. in the British Museum.

[23] Shelley to Elizabeth Hitchener, October 15 [?], 1811, Julian *Works,* VIII, 156–9. Miss Hitchener's answer to this letter reached Shelley at York after his return from the flying trip to Sussex, during which he had seen her at the home of the Pilfolds. She professed herself deeply affected at Shelley's offer of unreserved friendship, " a gift the world could not purchase," but she thought Shelley's money, when it came into his control, could be better used by him for the benefit of society than by her. However, there was a Miss Adams, an elderly schoolteacher, to whom she had long been de-voted and to whom she owed most of her own development; perhaps she might later allow Shelley to assist her in helping Miss Adams. (Peck: *Life,* II, 327–30.)

[24] Whitton papers, Ingpen: *Shelley in England,* I, 336–7.

[25] Ibid., I, 347.

[26] Ibid., I, 342.

[27] Timothy Shelley to Whitton, October 27, 1811; Ingpen: *Shelley in England,* I, 349. By courtesy of the owner I have examined this and the other Shelley-Whitton papers of this period in the original MSS., owned in 1936 by Mr. C. A. Stonehill.

[28] Ibid., I, 343.

[29] Shelley to Elizabeth Hitchener and to Charles Grove, October 27 and 29, 1811, Julian *Works,* VIII, 169, 173.

[30] Ingpen: *Shelley in England,* I, 343–4.

[31] Ibid., 347, 349, and a letter of October 29 not quoted by Ingpen, which I quote by permission from the MS., owned in 1936 by Mr. C. A. Stonehill.

[32] Shelley to Timothy Shelley, postmarked October 26, 1811, Julian *Works,* VIII, 166.

[33] The letter is printed in Ingpen: *Shelley in England,* I, 344–5, and Julian *Works,* VIII, 165, note.

[34] Shelley to William Whitton, postmarked November 1, 1811, Julian *Works,* VIII, 165.

[35] Ingpen: *Shelley in England,* I, 346.

[36] Ibid., I, 344.

[37] Shelley to the Duke of Norfolk, October 28, 1811, Julian *Works,* VIII, 171–2.

[38] MacCarthy, op. cit., 119–20.

[39] John Hogg to Timothy Shelley, October 21, 1811, in Ingpen: *Shelley in England,* I, 333–4. Shelley seems to have left York on the night of the 15th and returned on the 25th or 26th. If the Hoggs heard of Shelley's departure at once and wrote to Harriet immediately, Harriet's answer must have been written between October 17 and 19. And if Harriet wrote to Eliza at the same time and Eliza came at once, she should have arrived between October 22 and 24. Since she did arrive a day before Shelley, she must have arrived on the 24th or 25th.

[40] Hogg, op. cit., I, 277. Though it apparently has much fundamental truth, Hogg's picture is obviously exaggerated, as may be seen from Shelley's earlier accounts of Eliza in letters to Hogg, and from Harriet's complaints against the tyranny of her relations, just before her marriage.

[41] Ibid., I, 277. Miss Warne was an elderly friend of Eliza's, Harriet informed Hogg, and really an old frump; but her name was the sceptre with which Eliza ruled Harriet's conduct.

[42] George Stuart Gordon: *Shelley Letters,* galley proofs.

[43] Hogg, op. cit., I, 273. From this it would appear either that Harriet told Hogg nothing of the letter from his mother or that she had not summoned Eliza to come earlier, but had told her of Mrs. Hogg's letter, with the result that Eliza came at once on her own initiative.

[44] Harriet's story was told probably two or three days after Shelley's return to York, which was on October 25 or 26. Hogg's account indicates a brief period of tranquillity after Shelley's return. In itself this would have little weight, but neither Shelley's letter of October 27 to Elizabeth Hitchener nor of the 29th to Charles Grove shows any of the emotional turmoil into which Shelley was thrown by the disclosure. If, as MacCarthy states without authority (*Early Life,* 118), the Shelleys left York on October 29, it would appear that Harriet told her story on the 29th. But Shelley's subsequent letters

indicate that the departure came two or three days after the revelation. Shelley's next letter to Hogg is dated only "Wednesday," but refers to several days of travel since leaving York, which makes Wednesday, November 6, its probable date. Very probably, therefore, Harriet's disclosure was made on October 29 and the party left York on November 1 or 2.

[45] Shelley to Elizabeth Hitchener, undated [November 8, 1811?], Julian *Works*, VIII, 180. Shelley amplifies the account in this letter in a second letter, November 14, ibid., VIII, 187–8, and refers to it in others.

[46] Shelley to Hogg, dated "Wednesday" [November 6?], 1811, Gordon, op. cit.

[47] See note 44 above.

[48] Shelley's first note to Hogg from Keswick is dated conjecturally November 6, Julian *Works*, VIII, 177.

[49] Hogg's letters have been lost, but can be partly reconstructed from Shelley's answers. Shelley's letters to Hogg were preserved, but were so garbled and suppressed by Hogg in his *Life of Shelley* that their whole story was falsified. Hogg's misuse of these materials has long been known, and the attempted seduction of Harriet has for over half a century been accepted as a fact, though it was actually only a plausible hypothesis until Shelley's letters to Hogg were found and prepared for publication by Professor George Stuart Gordon in his *Shelley Letters*. For the first time the whole story now becomes clear and indisputable.

[50] Shelley to Hogg, undated [November 1811], Gordon, op. cit. Like Professor Gordon, I have retained Shelley's distracted punctuation and spelling. In every instance except the second the rows of dots are Shelley's own and do not indicate editorial condensation.

[51] Shelley to Hogg, undated [November 1811], ibid.

[52] Shelley to Hogg, undated [November 1811], ibid.

[53] Shelley to Elizabeth Hitchener, December 26, 1811, Julian *Works*, VIII, 224. The reduction was through the good offices of Southey, whose family thereafter supplied the linen. On November 26 Shelley had written to his uncle Thomas Medwin that the rent was £1 10s. 0d. (ibid., VIII, 207). Dowden's footnote on this detail (*Life*, I, 195) is slightly misleading.

[54] De Quincey's essay on Shelley, De Quincey's *Works*, ed. David Masson (London, 1897), XI, 369. This essay contains one or two other details about the Shelleys at Keswick which, if correct, slightly supplement my account. De Quincey says the Duke of Norfolk in-

fluenced Shelley's move to the Lake region (which seems doubtful) and that the Duke immediately wrote to neighbouring gentlemen to show him friendly attentions.

⁵⁵ Julian *Works,* VIII, 197–8.

⁵⁶ Ibid., VIII, 212. Mr. Peck, in quoting these passages (*Life,* I, 194), has suggested that they are significant as expressions of the keen interest in clouds and mists that is a prominent feature of Shelley's mature poetry. Professor Carl Grabo, in his *Prometheus Unbound* and *The Meaning of The Witch of Atlas* (Chapel Hill, N. C., both 1935), has found Shelley's use of these phenomena for symbolic purposes quite similar to that of the Neo-Platonic writers, with whose ideas Shelley later became acquainted.

⁵⁷ Shelley to Elizabeth Hitchener, January 7, 1812, Julian *Works,* VIII, 235. These impressions of economic and social ills at Keswick are somewhat confirmed by Southey's letters of similar date. Shelley's expression of them happens to come toward the end of the Keswick residence, but they are implied in his letter of November 26 to his uncle Thomas Medwin (ibid., VIII, 207), when he wished to take a house in Sussex, in a picturesque, retired spot, far removed from barracks or from "any *populous manufacturing dissipated* town."

⁵⁸ Harriet Shelley to Elizabeth Hitchener [January 29, 1812], ibid., VIII, 263.

⁵⁹ Shelley to Elizabeth Hitchener, November 14, 1811 and January 2, 1812, ibid., VIII, 189, 231.

⁶⁰ Elizabeth Hitchener to Harriet Shelley, December 17, 1811, quoted by Peck: *Life,* I, 195.

⁶¹ Shelley to Elizabeth Hitchener [November 26, 1811], Julian *Works,* VIII, 203.

⁶² Shelley to Medwin, Senior, November 30, 1811, ibid., VIII, 208.

⁶³ MacCarthy, op. cit., 120, 121.

⁶⁴ Shelley to Mr. Timothy Shelley, Julian *Works,* VIII, 215–16.

⁶⁵ Timothy Shelley to Percy Bysshe Shelley, December 19, 1811, quoted in Ingpen: *Shelley in England,* II, 365.

⁶⁶ Shelley to Timothy Shelley, December 23, 1811, Julian *Works,* VIII, 222.

⁶⁷ Shelley to Elizabeth Hitchener, January 26, 1812, ibid., VIII, 253.

⁶⁸ Shelley to Elizabeth Hitchener, December 15 [1811], ibid., VIII, 216–17. The intention would have been to prevent Shelley's dissipation of the estate, an intention which seems to be the motive

of the fifth codicil of Sir Bysshe's will, which was added at this time
(October 29, 1811). See Ingpen: *Shelley in England,* II, 366–7, 453;
also *ante,* pp. 467 and 718.

⁶⁹ Julian *Works,* VIII, 221, dated by the editors December 16,
1811.

⁷⁰ Shelley to Elizabeth Hitchener, December 11, 1811, ibid., VIII,
211.

⁷¹ Shelley to Elizabeth Hitchener, November 23, 1811, ibid., VIII,
199. Yet Shelley was perfectly capable of passing a shrewd, man-of-
the-world estimate of the Duke's character: " The D[uke] is a deist.
The Duke is far from the best of the English Noblemen: he is not a
moral man, but certainly is not attached to Catholicism. He desires
and votes for Reform, tho' he has not virtue enough to begin it in
his own person. He is in every respect a character of mediocrity. . . ." (to Elizabeth Hitchener, January 29, 1812, ibid., VIII,
262).

⁷² Gordon, op. cit., galley proofs.

⁷³ Shelley to Elizabeth Hitchener, December 15 and 26, 1811,
Julian *Works,* VIII, 217–18, 225.

⁷⁴ Ibid., VIII, 214.

⁷⁵ " The Last of the Calverts," anon., in the *Cornhill Magazine,*
n.s. XIV, 507 (May 1890). Several details of my account of Mr. and
Mrs. William Calvert are also drawn from this article, to which my
attention was first called by Professor Clarence Gohdes. Dowden
had talked or corresponded with Mrs. Stanger, whom he quotes
(*Life,* I, 227) as saying the neighbours doubted the attack made
upon Shelley by robbers.

⁷⁶ Shelley to Elizabeth Hitchener, November 12, 1811, Julian
Works, VIII, 185. The four following references are all to letters to
Miss Hitchener, dated [November 14], 23, [26], and December 15,
ibid., VIII, 189, 199, 206, 218.

⁷⁷ Shelley to Elizabeth Hitchener, December 15, 1811, ibid., VIII,
218–19.

⁷⁸ Shelley to Elizabeth Hitchener, December 26, 1811, ibid., VIII,
224.

⁷⁹ Shelley to Elizabeth Hitchener, December 26, 1811, ibid., VIII,
223.

⁸⁰ Shelley to Elizabeth Hitchener, December 26, 1811, January 2,
and January 7, 1812, ibid., VIII, 225, 227, 229, 235, 236.

⁸¹ To Elizabeth Hitchener, January 2, ibid., VIII, 231.

⁸² Hogg, op. cit., I, 289. Hogg's story of Shelley's falling asleep

as Southey was reading him an epic is rather too exaggerated to be taken seriously.

⁸³ See his letter to Godwin, July 29, 1812 (Julian *Works,* IX, 11), and to Leigh Hunt, September 27, 1819 (ibid., X, 87).

⁸⁴ Harriet to Elizabeth Hitchener, January 26, 1812, ibid., VIII, 256.

⁸⁵ Hogg, op. cit., I, 294.

⁸⁶ Southey to Grosvenor C. Bedford, January 4, 1812, *Life and Correspondence of Robert Southey* (1850), III, 325–6, quoted by Dowden: *Life,* I, 211.

⁸⁷ Dowden: *Life,* I, 213.

⁸⁸ Southey to John Rickman, January 6, 1812. Since this letter has not previously entered into the texture of Shelleyan biography, it may well be quoted entire, in all that relates to Shelley:

> . . . Do you know Shelley the member for Shoreham? (not the Lewes Member). His eldest son is here under curious circumstances. At Eton he wrote poetry and romances, went to University College, and not liking Oxford society amused himself with studying Hebrew, metaphysics, and Godwin's original quartos. What may become of the Hebrew remains to be seen, what came of the metaphysics was the usual result, followed however by consequences not quite so usual, for the youth happened to have an excellent heart, high moral principles, and enthusiasm enough for a martyr. So he prints half a dozen papers which he entitled The Necessity of Atheism, prefixed a short advertisement requesting that any person who felt able would publish a reply to it in the same brief clear and methodical form, folded up one of the pamphlets with this taking title, and directed to Copplestone. Copplestone either tracing the handwriting, or finding out the author thro' the printer (for he printed it at Worthing), sends the argument to the Master of University. He calls for Shelly [*sic*], and asks if the argument be his, which the philosopher of course avows. Dr. Griffiths then offers to pass it over if he will recant his opinion. A Christian might do that, was his reply, but I cannot. Expulsion of course followed instanter. — Away goes Shelley to a graduate (a friend of Hannah More's) whom he had been zealously helping to raise a subscription for some protégée, to settle this business with him, tells him for what he came, and that the reason was that he was about to leave Oxford having just been expelled for atheism, at which terrific word the man absolutely

fainted away!! Poor Shelly a little astonished at finding himself possessed of this sort of basilisk property, used his best endeavours to recover him, lets him out into the garden, and had the farther pleasure of hearing himself addressed, as soon as the Evangelist recovered his speech in these charitable words, I pray God, sir, that I may never set eyes on you again.

Well, the story does not end here. My philosopher, feeling how much better he himself was made by his own philosophy (which in truth he was for he would have been burnt alive for it as willingly as the Evangelical would have burnt him), thought it incumbent upon him to extend the benefits of his saving anti-faith, and after the examples of Mahomet and Taylor the Pagan began with his own family. Of his father and mother there was no hope, but he had a sister at school who was old enough for an example. Accordingly he writes to her upon this pleasant subject. The correspondence is forbidden, but as she loved her brother dearly, means are found of carrying it on thro' a Miss Westbrook, her schoolfellow and esteemed friend. This is discovered at last. Miss W. gets miserably tormented (I believe the school was an Evangelical one) — becomes very unhappy in consequence, — dreads the thoughts of returning to this place of suffering after the holydays, and he to deliver her proposes a journey to Gretna Green, — he 19 she 17. His father has cast him off, — but cannot cut off £6000 a year, tho' he may deprive him of as much more, — her's allow them £200 a year, and here they are. The D. of Norfolk is trying to bring about a reconciliation. I, liking him as you may suppose the better for all this, am in a fair way of convincing him that he may enjoy £6000 a year when it comes to him, with a safe conscience, that tho' things are not as good as they will be at some future time, he has been mistaken as to the way of making them better, and that the difference between my own opinion and his is — that he is 19 and I am 8 and 30. No other harm has been done than the vexation to her from her family, for as for the early marriage I consider that rather a good than an evil, seeing — as far as I have yet seen — that he has chosen well. If you know the father well enough to speak upon such a subject — endeavour to make him understand that a few years will do everything for his son which he ought to wish. He is got to Pantheism already, and in a week more I shall find him a Berkeleyan, for I have put the Minute Philosopher at his hands. He will get rid of his eccentricity, and he will retain his morals, his integrity and his genius, and unless I am greatly deceived there is every reason to believe he will become an honour to his name and his country. No possible chance [could] have thrown him in the way of a better physician, nor of one who would have taken a more sincere interest in the patient. — God bless you,

R. S.

(First published by Orlo Williams: *Life and Letters of John Rick-Man,* Boston and New York, 1912, pp. 158–60.)

[89] Shelley to Elizabeth Hitchener, January 7, 1812, Julian *Works,* VIII, 236. To Godwin, Shelley wrote in cold disillusion: " Southey, the poet, whose principles were pure and elevated once, is now the paid champion of every abuse and absurdity " (January 16, 1812, ibid., VIII, 244).

[90] January 20, 1812, ibid., VIII, 246.

[91] Hogg, op. cit., I, 300. Hogg does not state when and to whom this letter was written, nor where it was to be found. I do not find it in the collections of Coleridge's letters by either E. H. Coleridge or Earl Leslie Griggs, neither of which indexes a single reference to Shelley in Coleridge's letters. Coleridge's opinion of Shelley on June 25, 1820, as recorded in the unpublished journal of Maria Gisborne, was that he had much genius, but was " very wicked " and his treatment of Harriet " barbarous."

[92] Shelley to Hogg, December 20, 1810, Julian *Works,* VIII, 25; and Shelley to Godwin, January 3, 1812, ibid., VIII, 233.

[93] Shelley to Elizabeth Hitchener, January 2, 1812, ibid., VIII, 231.

[94] Shelley to Godwin, January 3, 1812, ibid., VIII, 233.

[95] C. Kegan Paul: *William Godwin: His Friends and Contemporaries* (London, 1876), II, 201.

[96] Shelley to Godwin, January 10, 1812, Julian *Works,* VIII, 239–40. Shelley's autobiographical sketch in this letter is probably as reliable psychologically as it is untrustworthy on several points of factual detail. *Zastrozzi* and *St. Irvyne* he stated as being published respectively more than eight months and more than sixteen months before they were. His first acquaintance with *Political Justice* is dated in terms conflicting with those of his next letter. He states, contrary to all available evidence, that he was twice expelled from Eton. " My father has ever regarded me as a blot, a defilement of his honour," he asserted with obvious exaggeration. " He wished to induce me by poverty to accept of some commission in a distant

regiment, and in the interim of my absence to prosecute the pamphlet, that a process of outlawry might make the estate, on his death, devolve to my younger brother." This statement, like Shelley's assertion a few months earlier that his mother tried to trick him into signing away his heritage, has been generally accepted as pure imagination. Shelley was probably aware that his father had consulted Mr. Whitton with a view to disinheriting him if possible, and he knew that he had been desirous of sending him to Greece in order to separate him from Hogg.

A partial clue to these inaccuracies may lie in Shelley's closing tribute to Godwin as "the regulator and former of my mind." Unconsciously he desired to emphasize as complete a sympathy as possible with William Godwin, a phenomenon which seems to be present in the ardent stage of all of Shelley's friendships. Thus the two novels, which he no longer cared for, should be separated from the influence of the man whom he most cared for, who would probably think them worthless. Likewise Godwin, presumably much persecuted, must get the full flavour of his disciple's persecutions. See Chapter iii, note 78.

[97] C. Kegan Paul, op. cit., II, 203–4.

[98] P. Patrickson, a youthful admirer whom Godwin rescued from an unhappy home life in 1810 and placed as a sizar at Emmanuel College, Cambridge, supported by subscriptions solicited by Godwin. He continued morbid, and committed suicide about ten days after Shelley's elopement with Mary Godwin. C. Kegan Paul, op. cit., II, 192 ff., 218.

[99] Shelley to Godwin, January 16, 1812, Julian *Works*, VIII, 242–4.

[100] Shelley to Elizabeth Hitchener, January 20, 1812, ibid., VIII, 245, 246.

[101] Shelley to Elizabeth Hitchener, December 26, 1811, ibid., VIII, 226.

[102] Shelley to Elizabeth Hitchener, ibid., VIII, 213, 225, 231.

[103] Details in this paragraph are from letters to Miss Hitchener, in the Julian *Works*, VIII, respectively December 11, p. 214; December 26, pp. 225, 226; January 2, p. 231; January 20, p. 249; January 26, p. 254.

[104] The volume was being prepared for publication by the Dublin publisher Stockdale when the Shelleys left Ireland. Probably a part of it had been printed, as the publisher for a while refused either to proceed or to surrender the manuscript without payment. Eventu-

ally it was recovered. Professor Dowden was allowed to inspect it by Shelley's grandson, Mr. Charles E. J. Esdaile, but it has never been incorporated into the body of Shelley's works.

[105] Shelley to J. J. Stockdale, August 1, 1811, Julian *Works*, VIII, 137. The references in letters to Miss Hitchener are, respectively, December 26, 1811, p. 225; January 2 and 20, 1812, pp. 231, 249.

[106] Mentioned in letters to Miss Hitchener, January 2, 7, and 20, 1812, ibid., VIII, 231, 235–6, 249.

[107] Mentioned to Miss Hitchener January 20 and 26, and to Godwin January 28, 1812, ibid., VIII, 246, 253, 258.

[108] Shelley to Elizabeth Hitchener, January 20 and 29, 1812, ibid., VIII, 245, 262.

[109] Based on the account in the *Cumberland Pacquet* for January 28, 1812, as reported by Dowden (*Life*, I, 227), and on comments upon the occurrence by both Shelley and Harriet in their joint letter to Elizabeth Hitchener, January 26, 1812 (Julian *Works*, VIII, 253, 256). Harriet's earlier and longer account to Miss Hitchener has not been preserved.

[110] So Dowden (*Life*, I, 227) was informed by Mr. William Calvert's daughter, Mrs. Stanger. Yet two days before Shelley's adventure Southey had written to Grosvenor C. Bedford (*Life and Correspondence of Robert Southey*, 1850, III, 326–7) that the village was alarmed over the presence of two rough fellows who had been hanging about, and that he had oiled up an old Spanish fowling piece and was looking for a watchdog, a brace of pistols, and a watchman's rattle. That Southey accepted Shelley's story at the time is shown by his letter of January 23, 1812, four days after the event, in which he narrates the incident and gives details about the general state of alarm.

[111] "The cheering beam which gilds this wintry day of life"; Shelley to Elizabeth Hitchener, November 24, 1811, Julian *Works*, VIII, 202. It is interesting to see that Shelley applied the same figure of speech to his last spiritual ideal, Emilia Viviani.

[112] Shelley to Elizabeth Hitchener, November 20, 1811, ibid., VIII, 194.

[113] Shelley to Elizabeth Hitchener, respectively October 27, November 12, 26, 1811, and January 20, 1812, ibid., VIII, 170, 184, 205, 246.

[114] Shelley to Elizabeth Hitchener, December 26, 1811, ibid., VIII, 225.

[115] Shelley to Elizabeth Hitchener, October [15?], November 20, 1811, and January 2, 1812, ibid., VIII, 159, 195–6, 227–8.

[116] Shelley to Elizabeth Hitchener, November 26, 1811, ibid., VIII, 204.

[117] Shelley to Elizabeth Hitchener, November 12, 24, and [26], 1811, ibid., VIII, 184–5, 201, 204.

[118] Shelley to Elizabeth Hitchener, October [15?], 1811, ibid., VIII, 158.

[119] E.g., the following passages in letters to Miss Hitchener, ibid., VIII, 202, 213, 226, 227, 238, 251:

I will say then that all Nature is animated; that microscopic vision, as it has discovered to us millions of animated beings whose pursuits and passions are as eagerly followed as our own; so might it, if extended, find that Nature itself is but a mass of organized animation. *Perhaps* the animative intellect of all this is in a constant rotation of change, perhaps a future state is no other than a different mode of terrestrial existence to which we have fitted ourselves in this mode. [November 24, 1811.]

— are we but bubbles which arise from the filth of a stagnant pool, merely to be again re-absorbed into the mass of its corruption? I think not: I feel not. [Gives some examples of general belief in immortality.] [December 11, 1811.]

I *will* live beyond this life. [December 26, 1811.]

I think reason and analogy seem to countenance the opinion that life is infinite, that, as the soul which now animates this frame was once the vivifying principle of the *infinitely* lowest link in the Chain of existence, so it is ultimately destined to attain the highest . . . that everything is animation . . . and in consequence being infinite one can never arrive at its termination. [January 2, 1812.]

I find you begin to doubt the eternity of the soul: I do not. More of that hereafter. [January 7, 1812.]

You have said no more of the immortality of the soul. Do you not believe it? I do; but I cannot tell you why in a letter — at least, not clearly. You will want some feelings which are to me cogent and resistless arguments. Do not consider it a gloomy subject: do not think me prejudiced. We *will* reason, and abide by the result. I shall get Godwin's opinion of this when I can. [January 20, 1812.]

[120] Shelley to Hogg [June 16, 1811], ibid., VIII, 106.

[121] Shelley to Elizabeth Hitchener, June 20, 1811, ibid., VIII, 107. For the connection with *The Missionary,* see "Some Recent English Shelley Literature," by A. M. D. Hughes, in *Englische Studien,* XLV (1912), 293–9.

[122] Shelley to Elizabeth Hitchener [October 18, 1811], Julian *Works,* VIII, 160.

[123] Shelley to Elizabeth Hitchener [November 20, 1811], ibid., VIII, 194. A later letter to Miss Hitchener (January 26, 1812, ibid., VIII, 252) shows Shelley basing his optimistic view of human nature on a conviction that all evil is traceable "to the sophistications of society," whereas in *Prometheus Unbound* he traces them beyond institutions to the mind of man.

[124] Shelley to Elizabeth Hitchener, October [?15], 1811, Julian *Works,* VIII, 158.

[125] Shelley to Hogg [?November 8, 1811], ibid., VIII, 181.

[126] Shelley to Godwin, January 10, 1812, ibid., VIII, 240.

[127] Shelley to Elizabeth Hitchener, December 11, 1811, ibid., VIII, 212.

[128] Shelley to Elizabeth Hitchener, January 20, 1812, ibid., VIII, 248, and January 26, 1812, ibid., 253.

[129] Shelley to Elizabeth Hitchener, January 20, and to William Godwin, January 28, 1812, ibid., VIII, 240–7, 258.

[130] January 26, 28 (to Godwin), 29, and February 3, from Whitehaven, ibid., VIII, 253, 258, 262, 267.

[131] Shelley to Godwin, January 28, 1812, ibid., VIII, 258.

[132] Shelley to Elizabeth Hitchener, December 11, 1811 and [January 29, 1812], ibid., VIII, 214 and 262.

[133] Shelley to Elizabeth Hitchener, January 26, [29], and February 3, ibid., VIII, 253 and 255, 262 and 264 (by Harriet), 267.

[134] I cannot help suspecting that Shelley may owe to George Ensor much more than can be established by formal proof. In 1817 he directed Ollier to send a copy of *A Proposal for Putting Reform to the Vote* to Ensor. The particular section in Ensor's *National Education* (London, 1811) that he commended to Miss Hitchener is a discussion of the usefulness of poetry developed from the quotation: "Let

me but make the ballads of a nation and I care not who makes the laws " that is quite similar to Shelley's later view of poets as "unacknowledged legislators." "Poetry seems to me," says Ensor (p. 263), "the most powerful means of instructing youth, which, as Plato says of Music, penetrates the recesses of the soul " — after which he shows that to Plato and the ancients both music and philosophy were comprehended in poetry, which they regarded as of primary importance for inculcating virtue. "It was under the impression of the power of song that legislators have used poetry to subdue the savage nature of the people " (p. 283).

The remainder of the book is so completely pleasing to Shelley's known tastes — more so than almost any other volume in which I have followed Shelley's reading — that it seems to me very improbable that he would not secure the same author's *National Government, The Independent Man* (1806), and *Principles of Morality* (1801), all listed on the title page — provided he was not already acquainted with them. There are several passages for which fancied echoes may be found in Shelley's subsequent letters, but unfortunately for purposes of demonstration, the constant attacks upon priestcraft, aristocracy, patronage, monarchy, luxury, and the educational system are too common to radical literature for Shelley's indebtedness to any particular expression of them to be demonstrable merely from general similarity. The same is perhaps true of his encomiums of charity, benevolence, sympathy, simple non-cruel sports, and plain diet.

Ensor's other volumes are all quite similar. *The Principles of Morality* derives all knowledge from the senses, rejects innate ideas and immateriality, finds fear and superstition the basis of religion, scorns prophecy, doubts immortality, and finds religion a foe to real morality. It is strongly idealistic and concludes that selfishness is *not* the universal motive.

The Independent Man is a two-volume effort of 1,007 pages designed as a guide-book for young men of independent means who desire to achieve worthy distinction in literature or government office. It starts with early childhood and offers advice through early manhood. It is anti-Christian and condemns luxury, duelling, the present educational system, etc. It recommends friendship, sympathy with animals, vegetable diet. Ideas in common with Shelley's are quite frequent, as shown by the following running list (page references in parentheses):

Mothers should nurse their own children and avoid wet-nurses

(2, 3, 5), children should not be taught by fear, even of God (20), no cruelty to animals should be permitted (25); nor even rude despoiling of trees — "Some have conjectured" that "vegetables feel like animated beings" (25); *no* lying should be permitted, for any purpose (30), nor corporal punishment (34); study of the classics is valuable, but overemphasized (63); letter-writing is far better for developing writing-ability than themes (85); the present rage for physical science has been overemphasized to the detriment of more valuable moral science (93), but physical sciences should be cultivated in reason (95). The best of all exercises for the Independent Man are walking, rowing, shooting (but not wanton destruction of life), and riding (96, 97, 98). Travel offers better educational advantages than universities. Parents should be respected (125, 126). Vegetable diet should be chosen (190–9), animals should not be slaughtered for food or sport (193–5). Anger and duelling should be avoided (201–2), brute force is abhorrent, but sometimes necessary (203). Wealth may be justified if honestly acquired and used for the general good (208), but moderate individual means are preferable for the good of the state (210). "Monarchs are at once slaves and despots" (211). Economy and charity should be carefully cultivated (216–17), friendship is to be idealized as one of life's greatest values (223), a friend's errors should be reasoned with before he is deserted (236). Genius, especially in literature, must be nourished by ardent study (250). From page 272 to the end he surveys and recommends reading in the principal branches of knowledge and art, displaying a really extensive familiarity with ancient and modern literature, except the north European.

With the exception of respect for parents and for marriage this reads almost like a summary of Shelley's ideas and conduct from 1809 to 1812. Some of these ideas were expressed by Shelley to Hogg on first coming to Oxford. If there were any supporting external evidence, such as a letter to Ensor or to someone else in praise of Ensor, written in 1809 or 1810, one might well suppose that Shelley took Ensor as a guide before he took Godwin. If by any chance he did, he must almost certainly have written Ensor such letters as he later wrote to Godwin and to Lawrence, author of *The Empire of the Nairs*.

Shelley might have become acquainted with Ensor's earlier books through Dr. Lind or through reviews that appeared in the *Monthly Review* (May 1802), the *Eclectic Review* (April and May 1807), the *Quarterly Review* (December 1811), etc.

[135] Shelley to Elizabeth Hitchener [January 29, 1812], Julian *Works*, VIII, 262. Other passages will be found in a letter of October 27 [?] to Miss Hitchener and the letter of January 10, 1812 to Godwin, ibid., VIII, 167 and 240.

[136] Shelley to Elizabeth Hitchener, February 3, 1812, ibid., VIII, 267.

[137] Shelley to Elizabeth Hitchener, February 3, 1812, ibid., VIII, 268.

[138] Shelley to Elizabeth Hitchener, October [?15] and 27, 1811, ibid., VIII, 158, 168; November [14] and 23, ibid., VIII, 188, 197.

[139] Shelley to Elizabeth Hitchener, October [?15] and November 12, 1811, ibid., VIII, 159, 184.

[140] Shelley to Elizabeth Hitchener, December 26, 1811, ibid., VIII, 224.

[141] Shelley to Elizabeth Hitchener, November [?8], 12, and [20], 1811, ibid., VIII, 179, 183, 195.

[142] Shelley to Elizabeth Hitchener [November 20, 1811], ibid., VIII, 195.

[143] E.g., [October 18], November 12, 14, [20], [26], December 11, 1811; January 7, 20, 26, February 3, 1812, ibid., VIII, 160, 185, 188, 195, 203, 212, 235, 247, 253, 268.

[144] E.g., October [?15] and 27, 1811, [January 29, 1812], ibid., VIII, 158, 167, 260.

[145] Shelley to Elizabeth Hitchener, January 26, 1812, ibid., VIII, 253.

[146] Peck: *Life,* I, 183, 258. See note 23 above and Chapter vii, note 82.

[147] Shelley to Elizabeth Hitchener, November 26, 1811, Julian *Works*, VIII, 206.

[148] Shelley to Elizabeth Hitchener, January 2, 26, and [29], 1812, ibid., VIII, 230, 254, 261. In such phases one perceives the germinal idea of the rôle played by Cythna in *Laon and Cythna,* even though Elizabeth Hitchener herself was then no longer in Shelley's thought.

[149] Shelley to Elizabeth Hitchener, December 26, 1811, ibid., VIII, 226.

[150] Shelley to Elizabeth Hitchener, February 3, 1812, ibid., VIII, 268: " We felt regret at leaving Keswick."

[151] Shelley to Elizabeth Hitchener, January 20, 1812, ibid., VIII, 248.

Chapter VIII

GENERAL SOURCES

John Carr: *The Stranger in Ireland, or a Tour in the Southern and Western Part of That Country in the Year 1805.* Philadelphia, 1806.

Nathaniel Jeffereys: *An Englishman's Descriptive Account of Dublin,* etc. London, 1810.

G. Locker Lampson: *A Consideration of the State of Ireland in the Nineteenth Century.* London, 1907.

Dennis Florence MacCarthy: *Shelley's Early Life,* Shelley's letters (Julian *Works,* Vol. VIII), Hogg's *Life,* and Ingpen's *Shelley in England,* all as previously cited.

William O'Connor Morris: *Ireland from 1798 to 1898.* London, 1898.

NOTES AND REFERENCES

[1] Shelley to Elizabeth Hitchener, February 3, 1812, Julian *Works,* VIII, 267.

[2] Shelley to Elizabeth Hitchener, February 13, 1812, and to William Godwin, February 24, 1812, ibid., VIII, 269, 279.

[3] John Carr, op. cit., 31.

[4] Nathaniel Jeffereys, op. cit., 86.

[5] My remarks on the state of Ireland at the time are based mainly on G. Locker Lampson, as cited above.

[6] Shelley may very well have derived moral fervour as well as information from some of Curran's speeches; for example, Curran's account of informers, in his defence of Finnerty:

"But the learned gentleman is further pleased to say that the traverser has charged the government with the encouragement of informers. This, gentlemen, is another small fact that you are to deny at the hazard of your souls, and upon the solemnity of your oaths. You are upon your oaths to say to the sister country that the government of Ireland uses no such abominable instruments of destruction as informers. Let me ask you honestly what you feel when in my hearing, when in the face of this audience, you are called upon to give a verdict that every man of us, and every man of you, knows by the testimony of your own eyes to be utterly and absolutely false? I speak not now of the public proclamation of informers with a promise of secrecy and of extravagant reward; I speak not of the fate of those horrid wretches who have been so often transferred from the table to the dock, and from the dock to the pillory; I speak of what your own eyes have seen day after day during the course of this commission from the box where you are now sitting; the number of horrid miscreants who avowed upon their oaths that they had come from the very seat of government — from the castle, where they had been worked upon by the fear of death and the hopes of compensation to give evidence against their fellows, that the mild and wholesome councils of this government are holden over those catacombs of living death, where the wretch that is buried a man lies till his heart has time to fester and dissolve, and is then dug up a witness. . . . Have you not marked when he entered, how the stormy wave of the multitude retired at his approach? Have you not marked how the human heart bowed to the supremacy of his power, in the undissembled homage of deferential horror? How his glance, like the lightning of heaven, seemed to rive the body of the accused, and mark it for the grave, while his voice warned the devoted wretch of woe and death; a death which no innocence can escape, no art elude, no force resist, no antidote prevent?" (*Speeches of the Right Honourable John Philpot Curran, etc., on the Late Very Interesting State Trials* (2nd ed., J. Stockdale & Sons, Dublin, 1808, pp. 292–3.)

[7] Mr. W. E. Peck quotes a number of parallel passages showing Shelley's indebtedness to Curran's speeches: *Life,* II, 341–3.

[8] Shelley to Elizabeth Hitchener, February 14 and 24, 1812, Julian *Works,* VIII, 275, 277. The Paine extracts were intended to be published as a book, but disappeared with most of Shelley's other Irish papers.

[9] Shelley to Elizabeth Hitchener, February 27, 1812, Julian *Works,* VIII, 285. Mr. Ingpen, loc. cit., suggests that this project may have been the same as the *Biblical Extracts* referred to in Shelley's letter of December 17, 1812, to Hookham.

[10] Shelley to Elizabeth Hitchener, February 14, 1812, Julian *Works,* VIII, 270.

629

¹¹ Shelley to Elizabeth Hitchener, February 14, 1812, ibid., VIII, 274.

¹² Noted first by Dowden and later, more particularly, by the Julian editors, in a footnote to the passage, ibid., VIII, 271.

¹³ Shelley to Godwin, February 24, 1812, ibid., VIII, 279.

¹⁴ Godwin to Shelley, March 4, 1812, Hogg, op. cit., I, 321.

¹⁵ Shelley to Godwin, March 8, 1812, Julian *Works*, VIII, 288.

¹⁶ Godwin to Shelley, March 14, 1812, Hogg, op. cit., I, 329.

¹⁷ MacCarthy, op. cit., 149 ff.

¹⁸ Ingpen: *Shelley in England*, II, 384.

¹⁹ The name of Shelley's Irish servant is often given as Hill because he himself gave it as Hill when arrested at Barnstaple. Mrs. Blackmore, niece and adopted daughter of Shelley's landlady at Lynmouth, remembered it years afterwards as Healey. Dowden (*Life*, I, 295) prefers Healey on the supposition that he gave the authorities a false name. Hogg, who knew him in London in 1813, mentions him only as " Dan " and " Daniel," a " stupid, starved savage," and describes him as " a short, thick set, hard-featured man, of a pure Celtic type. He could not, or would not, speak, or understand, the English language, or comprehend anything whatever " (Hogg, *Life*, I, 390).

²⁰ Shelley and Harriet to Elizabeth Hitchener, February 27, 1812, Julian *Works*, VIII, 283–6.

²¹ Harriet to Elizabeth Hitchener, March 18, 1812, ibid., VIII, 300. The *Address to the Irish People* was a 22-page " stabbed " octavo pamphlet, poorly printed on poor paper, in accordance with Shelley's original intention of cheap publication for the masses. Its price was fivepence, but there is no indication that anyone paid the price. Shelley's instructions to his agents (*North British Review*, November 1847, VIII, 237) were to get what they could for the pamphlets, but at all events to distribute them.

²² Julian *Works*, V, 229–30.

²³ *Proposals for an Association*, Julian *Works*, V, 266.

²⁴ Ibid., V, 266–7.

²⁵ Various histories differ according to the author's bias. Professor Dowden, after an examination of the histories and public documents, seems unable to reach a definite decision on this point (*Life*, I, 236–7).

²⁶ William O'Connor Morris, op. cit., 15.

²⁷ Twenty-two years after Shelley's death the following curious notice of Shelley's *Address* occurs in a letter from H. White, Dub-

lin, September 28, 1844, to Robert Peel: "P. S. As a matter of curiosity I send the title page of a pamphlet of which I believe no other copy exists but mine. It is curious for recommending the very course of peaceable agitation and of political science of which O'Connell boasts himself the originator. It is also curious for the fulfillment of one of its prophecies. Beware the other. Beyond this page the pamphlet is not worth reading. In matter and style it has all the marks of boyhood. The language is often vague and vulgar and the sentences long, intricate, parenthetical and ungrammatical, like the advertisement. Let it be returned. H. W." (Peel Papers, Brit. Mus. Add. MSS. 40,551, fol. 384).

[28] The cutting from a Lewes newspaper declining to notice the address of P. B. S., Esq., which Mr. Ingpen found among the Shelley-Whitton papers (*Shelley in England,* II, 383) seems to apply to the *Address to the Irish People,* rather than to the newspaper accounts of Shelley that Shelley wished Miss Hitchener to insert in the Sussex papers (Julian *Works,* VIII, 292). Shelley says: "Make them insert the account of *me,*" (Shelley's italics) and in the same letter Harriet says: "Send us the Paper in which you *have* inserted the 'Address'" (my italics).

[29] Shelley to Elizabeth Hitchener, February 27, 1812, Julian *Works,* VIII, 283.

[30] Ingpen: *Shelley in England,* II, 382–3.

[31] The *Freeman's Journal,* February 29; repeated by the *Hibernian Journal,* March 2, and *Walker's Hibernian Magazine,* February 1812; also the Dublin *Evening Post,* February 29, and *Saunders News-Letter,* February 29, the latter of which was repeated by the *Patriot,* March 2, 1812. These accounts were all found by Mr. MacCarthy and are presented in his *Shelley's Early Life,* 240–3.

[32] March 14, 1812, Julian *Works,* VIII, 297. Hogg quotes Shelley as saying he was "interrupted by savage yells" and even threatened, when he claimed tolerance for Protestants as well as Catholics (*Life,* I, 337).

[33] MacCarthy, op. cit., 238–9.

[34] As reported in an anonymous review of several books on Shelley in the *North British Review,* VIII, 236 (November 1847). The author is referred to by MacCarthy and Dowden as Dr. Anster. This account of Shelley's oratorical style is somewhat at variance with Medwin's assertion that it "displayed that eloquence for which he was remarkable" (*Revised Life,* 113) and John Grove's account of his eloquent speech in London in 1811.

[35] MacCarthy, op. cit., 253–4.

[36] Ibid., 255.

[37] Both letters are quoted by MacCarthy, op. cit., 250–2 and 256–60.

[38] Ibid.

[39] Ibid., 258.

[40] Shelley to Godwin, March 8, 1812, Julian *Works,* VIII, 289.

[41] Shelley to Elizabeth Hitchener, March 10, 1812, ibid., VIII, 290–1.

[42] Shelley to Godwin, April 25, 1812, ibid., VIII, 313. References for the preceding details, under the dates given, are successively ibid., 274, 280, 285, 289.

[43] Harriet to Catherine Nugent, August 11, 1812, ibid., IX, 16.

[44] Shelley and Harriet to Elizabeth Hitchener, March 10, 1812, ibid., VIII, 292–3.

[45] Shelley to Elizabeth Hitchener, March 14, 1812, ibid., VIII, 297.

[46] *A Compendium of the History of Ireland, from the Earliest Period to the Reign of George I. By John Lawless, Esq., a member of the Catholic Board.* Dublin, 1814.

[47] Hogg, op. cit., I, 334.

[48] MacCarthy, op. cit., 304. MacCarthy also points out that Conway and Lawless " had life-long differences " and that Conway himself had secret relations with the English officials.

[49] Harriet to Catherine Nugent, October 11, [1813], Julian *Works,* IX, 78.

[50] Shelley to Elizabeth Hitchener, March 14, 1812, ibid., VIII, 297.

[51] Harriet to Elizabeth Hitchener, March 18, [1812], ibid., VIII, 298–9.

[52] " Sunday morng " [?March 15, 1812] and " Wednesday," ibid., VIII, 299.

[53] The discovery in 1881 of Harriet Shelley's letters to Catherine Nugent first compelled biographers to listen to Harriet's account of her desertion by Shelley. Though first published in the New York *Nation,* June 6 and 13, 1889, they were used in MS. by Professor Dowden in writing his life of Shelley.

[54] Miss Nugent's recollections, including the account of the beginning of her acquaintance with the Shelleys, were first published in the previously cited article, attributed to Dr. Anster in the *North British Review* (November 1847), VIII, 237.

⁵⁵ Harriet to Elizabeth Hitchener, March 14, 1812, Julian *Works,* VIII, 295–6.

⁵⁶ Harriet to Elizabeth Hitchener, February 27, [1812], ibid., VIII, 286.

⁵⁷ Shelley to Elizabeth Hitchener, March 10, 1812, ibid., VIII, 292.

⁵⁸ Shelley to Elizabeth Hitchener, February 27, [1812], ibid., VIII, 285.

⁵⁹ Shelley to Elizabeth Hitchener, March 14, 1812, ibid., VIII, 297.

⁶⁰ Harriet to Elizabeth Hitchener, February 27, [1812], ibid., VIII, 286.

⁶¹ Shelley to Elizabeth Hitchener, March 10, 1812, ibid., VIII, 291.

⁶² Shelley to Elizabeth Hitchener, [?April 16, 1812], ibid., VIII, 308.

⁶³ The *Declaration of Rights* was printed in Dublin. Dowden (*Life,* I, 292) and W. M. Rossetti (*Fortnightly Review,* January 1871, XLIX, 67 ff.) believe that *The Devil's Walk* was printed later at Barnstaple. Professor Willis M. Pratt, after examining the copy in the University of Texas library, writes me that its typography more nearly resembles the Barnstaple than the Dublin publications.

⁶⁴ Shelley to Godwin, March 18, 1812, Julian *Works,* VIII, 300, 301, 302.

⁶⁵ Harriet to Elizabeth Hitchener, March 18, 1812, ibid., VIII, 300.

⁶⁶ Shelley explained to Miss Hitchener that it was all due to the stupidity of his Irish servant, Daniel Hill or Healey (March 10, 1812, ibid., VIII, 292; cf. VIII, 279, note). Devices of the sort were common at the time, to avoid the high postal rate on letters from Ireland — 1*s.* 1*d.* from Dublin to London.

⁶⁷ MacCarthy, op. cit., 321. Medwin (*Revised Life,* 115) quotes Shelley as saying the departure from Dublin was hastened by a hint from the police. Shelley could not have heard of the incident of the intercepted letter until some time after his return to England, as his letter of [?April 16] shows, nor is the assertion otherwise credible.

⁶⁸ Harriet to Catherine Nugent, April 16, [1812], Julian *Works,* VIII, 310.

⁶⁹ Shelley to Elizabeth Hitchener [?April 16, 1812], ibid., VIII, 308.

Chapter IX

GENERAL SOURCES

John Roberts Chanter: *Sketches of the Literary History of Barnstaple*, 1866.

Daniel Isaac Eaton: *Trial of Daniel Isaac Eaton*, etc. London, 1812.

Godwin's journal and letters (from C. K. Paul: *William Godwin, His Friends and Contemporaries*); Hogg's *Life;* D. F. MacCarthy: *Shelley's Early Life;* the Whitton papers (from Roger Ingpen: *Shelley in England*); the letters of Shelley and Harriet (from Julian *Works,* VIII and IX) — all as previously cited.

W. M. Rossetti: "Shelley in 1812–13," in *Fortnightly Review,* n. s. LXVII, January 1871.

NOTES AND REFERENCES

[1] I can find no authority for Mr. Peck's statement (*Life,* I, 234) that it also contained *The Devil's Walk*, which is not mentioned by either of the zealous officials who reported the contents of the box.

[2] Mr. Ingpen (Julian *Works,* VIII, 298, note, and 308, footnote), citing MacCarthy's account, says: "The letter . . . was never delivered . . . is now in the Public Record Office," and "The box never arrived." Subsequent correspondence of the Shelleys and Miss Hitchener throws no light on the matter. MacCarthy, however, who examined the letter in the Public Record Office and printed it (*Early Life,* 317–20), twice refers to it as a "copy" of Harriet's letter (309, 315). According to the letters of the two local officials, Harriet's letter was "shown," not delivered, to the local postmaster, and the customs surveyor asked if the box and letter "should be . . . transmitted to London, and withheld from the

person to whom they are addressed " (315). Receiving no such instructions, he presumably held the box for a while and then sent it to its destination, with Harriet's original letter.

³ This might indicate that Elizabeth Hitchener must have succeeded in getting " the account of *me* " inserted in the Sussex papers; though Lord Chichester's information may have proceeded indirectly from Field Place or Captain Pilfold.

⁴ All details of this incident are drawn from MacCarthy, op. cit., 308 ff.

⁵ Shelley to Elizabeth Hitchener, and Harriet to Catherine Nugent, both April 16, 1812, Julian *Works,* VIII, 307, 310.

⁶ Shelley to Godwin, April 25, 1812, ibid., VIII, 312. Godwin's novel, *Fleetwood, or the New Man of Feeling* (London, 1805), is mentioned more than once in Shelley's letters. Three months earlier Shelley had written to Godwin (Julian *Works,* VIII, 281): " I had pictured to my fancy that I should first meet you in a spot like that in which Fleetwood met Russigny [Fleetwood's spiritual mentor]." Chapter iv of Volume II of *Fleetwood* opens with a description of the dangers of living entirely to oneself that is notably suggestive of Shelley's *Alastor,* written four years later.

⁷ Shelley to Elizabeth Hitchener, [?April 16] and June 2, 1812, and to Godwin, April 25, 1812, Julian *Works,* VIII, 307–8, 328, 313–14.

⁸ Shelley to Catherine Nugent, May 7, 1812, ibid., VIII, 326.

⁹ Ibid., VIII, 311, footnote.

¹⁰ Shelley to Elizabeth Hitchener, April 25, 1812, ibid., VIII, 316.

¹¹ Shelley to Elizabeth Hitchener, April 29, 1812, ibid., VIII, 317.

¹² Shelley to Elizabeth Hitchener, May 7, 1812, ibid., VIII, 324.

¹³ Shelley to Thomas Hitchener, April 30, 1812, ibid., VIII, 318–19.

¹⁴ Shelley to Thomas Hitchener, May 14, 1812, ibid., VIII, 327.

¹⁵ Shelley to Elizabeth Hitchener, May 7, 1812, ibid., VIII, 322.

¹⁶ Shelley to Elizabeth Hitchener, May 7, 1812, ibid., VIII, 323, and to William Godwin, June 3, 1812, ibid., VIII, 330.

¹⁷ Shelley to Elizabeth Hitchener, June 6, 1812, ibid., VIII, 333–4.

¹⁸ Shelley to Elizabeth Hitchener, June 2, 1812, ibid., VIII, 328.

¹⁹ Harriet to Catherine Nugent, June 7, [1812], ibid., VIII, 333.

²⁰ Shelley to Elizabeth Hitchener, [?April 16], 1812, ibid., VIII, 308.

²¹ Ibid., III, 104–5. Both poems may have been written in Ireland.

²² Shelley to Elizabeth Hitchener, March 10, 1812, ibid., VIII,

290. This indicates that Shelley may have been corresponding with Sir Francis Burdett at the time, as he was in August of the same year, to the extent of " many . . . Packages and Letters," according to the Town Clerk of Barnstaple (Peck: *Life,* I, 271, quoted from the Public Record Office). His interest in Sir Francis in 1810 has been already noted; there are occasional references in his letters showing the continuance of this interest to the end of his residence at Marlow. Like Mr. MacCarthy, I have been unable to locate the correspondence of Sir Francis for this period.

[23] Shelley to Elizabeth Hitchener and to Catherine Nugent, both May 7, 1812, Julian *Works,* VIII, 324, 325–6.

[24] Ingpen: *Shelley in England,* II, 383–4.

[25] Shelley to Godwin, June 11, 1812, Julian *Works,* VIII, 337.

[26] Shelley to Godwin, June 3, 1812, ibid., VIII, 332.

[27] " The Retrospect," etc., III, 103, lines 139–54.

[28] E.g., in the *Examiner,* March 15 and April 5, 1812. Dowden and Peck both give May 8 as the date of the sentence, but Eaton's own account (*Trial of Daniel Isaac Eaton, etc.,* London, 1812), which was on sale by May 26, says that he was tried March 6, brought up for judgment April 30, and received final judgment May 15.

[29] Shelley to Godwin, June 11, 1812, Julian *Works,* VIII, 337.

[30] Shelley to Elizabeth Hitchener, June [18, 1812], ibid., VIII, 339.

[31] Harriet to Catherine Nugent, June 7, [1812], ibid., VIII, 333.

[32] Charles Grove to Hellen Shelley, February 16, 1857, Hogg, op. cit., II, 157.

[33] Dowden: *Life,* I, 269, from the account of his friend Mr. W. J. Craig.

[34] Shelley to Elizabeth Hitchener, June 11, 1812, Julian *Works,* VIII, 335.

[35] Shelley to Elizabeth Hitchener, June [18, 1812], ibid., VIII, 338.

[36] Harriet to Catherine Nugent, June 30, 1812, ibid., IX, 3–4.

[37] Hogg, op. cit., I, 347–8.

[38] Shelley to Godwin, July 5 and 7, 1812, Julian *Works,* IX, 5, 7. Today the quaint little village of Lynmouth looks very much as it did to Shelley and Harriet; even the small, neat cottage, though partially rebuilt after a fire in 1907, must be almost as Shelley left it. (For its partial destruction, see the London *Daily Graphic,* April 30, 1907, and the London *Daily Telegraph,* May 21, 1907.)

³⁹ Shelley to Godwin, July 5, 1812, Julian *Works,* IX, 5.

⁴⁰ Shelley to Godwin, July 5, 1812, ibid., IX, 5, 6.

⁴¹ Harriet to Catherine Nugent, August 4, [1812], ibid., IX, 15.

⁴² Harriet to Catherine Nugent, August 4 and 11, [1812], ibid., IX, 15, 16.

⁴³ Shelley to Thomas Hookham, July 29, 1812, ibid., IX, 10. The books ordered were received on August 17 and were: Milton's *Prose Works,* Sir Humphry Davy's *Elements of Chemical Philosophy, Medical Extracts,* Hartley's *Essay on Man,* and Mary Wollstonecraft's *Rights of Woman.*

⁴⁴ Harriet to Catherine Nugent, August 11, [1812], ibid., IX, 16.

⁴⁵ I suppose this book to be *Patriotic Sketches of Ireland,* by Miss Owenson [Lady Sydney Morgan] (London, 1807; Baltimore, 1809). The preface of the book announces its author's purpose of removing prejudice against the Irish. Its contents — descriptive, anecdotal, and reflective — not only seek to establish Ireland's claim to respect, but comment fearlessly on the religious, social, and economic outrages done by the Anglo-Irish. On August 4 Harriet wrote Miss Nugent that Miss Owenson's *Patriotic Sketches* "have won my heart" and that she regretted not having known her in Dublin. Thus *Patriotic Sketches* was fresh in Shelley's mind when he wrote Hookham, and it answers the description he gives. The tone of Harriet's letter would suggest that it had been received from Dublin, rather than America — which would also have been easier, under the circumstances of the preceding six months.

⁴⁶ Shelley to Thomas Hookham, August 18, 1810 [for 1812], Julian *Works,* IX, 18–20.

⁴⁷ Thomas L. Peacock: *Works* (London, 1875), p. xxxiii. Dowden (*Life,* I, 274) rather doubts if she is correct, but inconsistently assumes on the next page that this meeting led to Shelley's acquaintance with Hookham, Peacock's friend and publisher. Peacock's own statement was (*Memoirs,* II, 323): "I saw Shelley for the first time in 1812, just before he went to Tanyrallt." Shelley went from London to Tanyrallt on November 12. Peacock's latest editors, H. F. Brett-Smith and C. E. Jones, correctly date the meeting two or three months after Shelley's letter to Hookham and attribute it to Hookham's interest in Peacock (*Works of T. L. Peacock,* Halliford Edition, London, 1934–6, I, li). This is supported not only by Peacock's statement, but by the tone of Shelley's letter, which suggests that he was unacquainted with the author to whom his attention

had obviously been invited. Mr. Peck (*Life,* I, 288, 289) says that Shelley met Peacock in London in October or November, but is obviously in error when he says that Peacock probably introduced Shelley to Hookham, with whom Shelley was in correspondence in July.

[48] Peacock: *Memoirs,* II, 323.

[49] Shelley to Sir James Henry Lawrence, April 17, 1812, Julian *Works,* IX, 17.

[50] See Walter Graham: "Shelley and the Empire of the Nairs," *P.M.L.A.,* XL, 881–91 (March 1925).

[51] Shelley to Godwin, July 29, 1812, Julian *Works,* IX, 10–14.

[52] The titles, as phrased and spelled by Shelley (ibid., IX, 34, 35, 36), are: Kant; Spinosa; Gibbons Decline & Fall of the Rom. Emp. (Cheapest poss. Edit.); Hume's Hist. of England (Cheapest poss. Edit.); Humes Essays; Darwins Zoonomia; Vertot (French) Histoire de la Rome; Gillie's History of Greece; Herodotus, Thucidydes, Zenophon, Plutarch, with Latin or English Translations subjoined; Adolphus's continuation of the History of England (Cheapest poss. Edit.); Moor's Indian Pantheon; Rumford on Stoves; Spencers Works Fairy Queen &c. (Cheapest poss. Edit.); Southey's History of the Brazil; Marcus Antoninus; Seneca's Works; Plato (with a translation); Nicholson's Enclopedia [*sic*] (Boards); Æschylus; Epicurus; Celsus; Ptolemaeus; Confusius a translation only; Euripides; Polybius; Tacitus; Procopius; Hippocrates; Diodorus Siculus; Lucius Florus; Justin of Samaria the original only; Pythagoras; Theophrastus; Titus Livius; Josephus; Sappho; Shakespeare's works (cheap edition); Cowley's works; Blackstone's "Commentaries"; Sir W. Jones's works; Lord Monboddo "on the origin and progress of language"; Robertson's "History of Scotland"; do. "History of America"; Robertson's "Historical Disquisition on India"; Bishop Berkeley's works; Garcilaso de la Vega; Spallanzani's works either English or Italian; Les Ouvres de Diderot; do. do. Condorcet; Roscoe's "History of the Houses of Medicis"; Sir W. Drummond's Essay on a Punic Inscription; Darwin's "Temple of Nature"; Trotter on Nervous Temperament; do. "Essay on Drunkenness"; Poems by Clio Rickman; "Metrical Tales" by Southey; Southey's "Thalaba"; Wordsworth's Poems 4 vols.; Coleridge's Poems; Tooke's "Diversions of Purley"; Godwin's "Enquirer"; do. "Caleb Williams"; do. "St. Leon"; do. "Fleetwood."

For the group which begins with Æschylus and ends with Sappho, there was this specification: "original and translation, if possible, united — ."

53 Hogg, op. cit., I, 358–9.

54 Dowden: *Life*, I, 284–5.

55 " To Harriet," and " To Harriet on Her Birthday," Julian *Works*, III, 105–7.

56 In charging the jury Lord Ellenborough dismissed Eaton's defence with contempt, explained the gravity of the offence charged against Eaton, and said: " I am sure no impunity will be given to such an offence by the verdict you return to-day." If, as I suppose, Shelley read Eaton's own published account of his trial (*Trial of Daniel Isaac Eaton for Publishing the third and last Part of Paine's Age of Reason, before Lord Ellenborough, Court of King's Bench, March 6, 1812. Defence and Prince Smith's Speech.* London, 1812), he knew from Eaton's own testimony enough about the man himself to add a personal element to his indignation. Eaton described himself under oath as a man educated by six years of private schooling and some time at a Jesuit college, who was in 1812 sixty years old and in broken health, had suffered since 1792 six prosecutions, a three years' exile, destruction of £2,800 worth of books, and solitary imprisonment for eighteen months. Eaton himself published accounts of four of his trials for libels on either the King or Christianity, from three of which he emerged successful. The repeated prosecutions of Eaton were by no means exceptional, as will be seen from the similar cases of Leigh Hunt and Richard Carlile, in both of which Shelley became interested. Nor do these cases represent the extreme of government severity. George Ensor, in a book which Shelley may well have read (*Defects of the English Laws*, London, 1812, p. 348), points out that Mr. Brougham stated in Parliament on July 17, 1811, that " Mr. Muir, a learned and accomplished barrister, was transported for fourteen years to New South Wales because he informed an acquaintance who wished to borrow Paine's *Rights of Man* that he would find the book in his great-coat pocket."

Shelley's own *Queen Mab* was twice adjudged blasphemous by English courts, in 1821 and 1840, and was in 1840–2 made an instrument by the radicals in mitigating the operation of the law of blasphemous libel. See Newman I. White: " Literature and the Law of Libel: Shelley and the Radicals of 1840–42," in *Studies in Philology*, XXII, 34–47 (January 1925).

57 *Letter to Lord Ellenborough*, Julian *Works*, V, 290.

58 Shelley to Hookham, July 29, 1812, ibid., IX, 9.

59 Harriet to Catherine Nugent, August 4, [1812], ibid., IX, 15.

Dowden (*Life*, I, 291) states that copies were also sent to Lord Sidmouth and some private friends, but omits to state his authority, which I am unable to discover.

[60] John Roberts Chanter, op. cit., 56. This account of Shelley at Barnstaple and Lynmouth was first quoted, with some additional matter, by MacCarthy, op. cit., 345 ff.

[61] Now in the Bodleian Library, where it was deposited by Sir Percy Florence and Lady Shelley. Lady Shelley seems to have secured it from Leigh Hunt, who, according to Chanter, had it from a Mr. Barry, apparently of Barnstaple.

[62] " Shelley was of the opinion, that for some time after he had left Ireland, he was under the surveillance of the police, and that his life was in danger from its emissaries; doubtless a most erroneous notion. . . . He was many years afterwards under a similar delusion in Italy — and told me that on quitting Naples he was afraid of being arrested" (Medwin: *Revised Life*, 116). Cf. Chapter viii, note 67.

[63] *The Declaration of Rights* had been printed in Dublin and brought to England. It was a roughly printed single sheet, setting forth thirty-one propositions in short, pithy paragraphs, such as: " xi — A man has a right to think as his reason directs; it is a duty he owes to himself to think with freedom, that he may act from conviction." They are related to similar declarations by the National Assembly of France during the Revolution, also to the eighteenth-century French philosophers, but they contain very little not already implied by Shelley's two Irish pamphlets. They are discussed in detail by W. M. Rossetti in the *Fortnightly Review* for January 1871, and by Peck: *Life*, I, 236 ff.

The Devil's Walk was begun in Keswick and is partly modelled on *The Devil's Thoughts*, by Coleridge and Southey. It was printed as a broadside ballad (either in Dublin or at Barnstaple; cf. Chapter viii, note 63) in three columns of ten stanzas each. It is rough, crude verse, appealing directly to the people with its attacks on priests and kings, the privileged classes generally, and on British misdeeds in Ireland and Spain. It is discussed more fully by Rossetti and Peck, as cited above. Both broadsides are definitely propaganda for the common people. Only three copies of the former and one of the latter have been recorded as extant.

[64] " On Launching Some Bottles Filled with Knowledge into the Bristol Channel " and " To a Balloon Laden with Knowledge," *Juilan Works*, III, 108.

[65] Dowden: *Life*, I, 292.

[66] Published as an article entitled "Shelley in 1812–13: An Unpublished Poem and Other Particulars," *Fortnightly Review*, n.s. LXVII, 67–85 (January 1871). The documents were subsequently examined by MacCarthy, who corrected some slight errors, and by Peck, who reprinted (*Life*, I, 270) the town clerk's first letter corrected. Further details of the episode were added by MacCarthy from Chanter's *Sketches of the Literary History of Barnstaple*, and by Dowden from statements secured by Miss Mathilde Blind from Mrs. Mary Blackmore, adopted daughter of Shelley's landlady. The last is authority for Shelley's attempt to succour Daniel Hill (*Life*, I, 297). The municipal records of Barnstaple, rich as they are for earlier periods, are rather thin for the opening years of the nineteenth century, and I have searched their index in vain for the case of Daniel Hill or Healey.

The official correspondence is responsible for the preservation of the only known copies of *The Devil's Walk* and *Declaration of Rights*.

[67] *Reminiscences and Recollections of Captain Gronow* (ed. 1900), I, 155. Captain Gronow relates the incident as occurring "soon after leaving school and about the year 1810." I follow Dowden (*Life*, I, 300) and Peck (*Life*, I, 273) in supposing him to have been mistaken in the date. Such a visit scarcely fits the known facts of Shelley's activities in 1810. There is no reason for supposing that Shelley visited Swansea from Cwm Elan in 1811, a distance of about fifty miles, even though he was entering upon an *affaire de cœur* at that time. For 1812, however, the circumstances are more favourable.

[68] Godwin's journal, and letter to Mrs. Godwin, in C. Kegan Paul, op. cit., II, 210–12.

[69] In a note dated December [for November?] 19, 1812, from London, Shelley sent £20 and promised to send the remaining £10 "as soon as I can"; Julian *Works*, IX, 26. The fact that Shelley gave Mrs. Hooper a probably worthless draft upon Mr. John Lawless suggests that "Honest Jack" was under financial obligations to Shelley, whether or not Shelley succeeded in borrowing the £500 he wished to obtain for their publication venture.

Chapter X

GENERAL SOURCES

Letters of Shelley and Harriet (Julian *Works,* IX), Dowden's *Life* (mainly for Godwin's journal and Mrs. John Williams's recollections), C. Kegan Paul's *William Godwin, His Friends and Contemporaries* (mainly for Godwin's journal), Ingpen's *Shelley in England* (Whitton papers), Hogg's *Life,* and Peacock's *Memoirs,* all as previously cited.

Also Margaret L. Crofts: " Strange Adventure of Shelley's and Its Belated Explanation," the *Century Magazine,* October 1905, XLVIII, 905–9; Margaret L. Woods: " Shelley at Tan-yr-all-t," the *Nineteenth Century,* November 1911, LXX, 890–903; unpublished letters of W. A. Madocks to John Williams, and other documents in the papers of the Madocks estate (through the courtesy of Mr. Adrian Stokes, and with the assistance of Mr. W. M. Richards, both of Portmadoc); unpublished letters and papers of Griffith John Williams, Esq., of Bangor (obligingly placed at my disposal by Professor H. Wright, of the University College of North Wales, through the good offices of his colleague, Mr. R. W. King).

NOTES AND REFERENCES

[1] Harriet to Miss Nugent, undated, Julian *Works,* IX, 24.

[2] *The Cambrian Tourist, or Post-Chaise Companion through Wales,* etc. Anon. (5th ed., London, 1825), pp. 203, 223. On visiting Tremadoc in 1936 I found the church still in use, and the handsome market-house sheltering the grain business of John Williams and Son. Mr. Madocks's theatre was later converted into a dissenting chapel. For the best account of the neighbourhood since 1813 see " Shelley at Tan-yr-all-t," by Margaret L. Woods, in the *Nineteenth Century,* as cited above.

³ *The Cambrian Tourist,* etc., as above.

⁴ Thomas Love Peacock: *Headlong Hall,* 1816, Halliford edition
(1934), I, 74.

⁵ The fifth edition of *The Cambrian Tourist,* etc., (1825), 204,
speaks of the gap as still a hundred yards wide and urges the feasi-
bility of closing it with sunken hulks. Peacock, however, stated correctly in *Headlong Hall,* 1816 (Halliford edition, I, 73), that the
embankment "has . . . been completed."

⁶ S. Girdlestone to John Williams, September 17, 1812, quoted in
full in Appendix III.

⁷ Medwin (*Revised Life,* 119) says £500, and *Y Gestiana* (Tremadoc, 1892, p. 174) says £50, but Mr. Williams, as later reported
by his widow, recollected the sum as £100. I have one of the two
copies of a resolution of thanks drawn up on May 2, 1812, at the
London home of Lord Bulkeley, to which was added a list of subscriptions, among them Shelley's subscription of £100. This resolution was printed in the *North Wales Gazette,* Bangor, October 1,
1812. Even the £100 was probably not cash, but a promise to pay
on reaching his majority in the following August.

⁸ Shelley to John Williams, November 7, 1812, Julian *Works,*
IX, 23.

⁹ Dr. William Roberts's two letters, one to Sir Timothy Shelley,
dated February 7, 1824, and one to Thomas Love Peacock (an executor of Shelley's will), dated June 12, 1844, are reprinted from the
Whitton papers by Ingpen: *Shelley in England,* II, 633–4.

From the town clerk of Carnarvon and from Mr. W. G. Roberts, a
descendant of Dr. William Roberts's brother, I learned that Shelley's
friend was a prominent citizen of the town and a surgeon of some
distinction. He was, about 1832, the first elected Mayor of Carnarvon, and for some time previously was deputy mayor for the
Lord Lieutenant of Wales, Lord Bulkeley.

¹⁰ From an unpublished manuscript in the Library of the University College of North Wales, by permission of Mr. Thomas Richard,
Librarian. I have omitted the first paragraph of the letter, which
relates to other business between Bedwell and Evans. The Mr.
Rumsey Williams who represented the plaintiff was a prominent
solicitor in Carnarvon who is mentioned several times in the unpublished letters of Mr. Madocks to John Williams, as handling matters
both for and against Mr. Madocks.

The letter of Dr. Roberts previously cited states explicitly that
Shelley paid the sum for which he was arrested. It is unlikely that

any former creditor of Shelley's except possibly Mrs. Hooper, his Lynmouth landlady, could have learned his new address so soon, nor could she have been the suitor in this case, for her bill was only £30, of which Shelley sent her £20 on November or December 19, 1812.

[11] See the letter from S. Girdlestone to John Williams, in Appendix III.

[12] From the Madocks estate papers, by the permission of Mr. Adrian Stokes, of the firm of Breese, Jones, Casson, and Stokes, trustees of the estate. I also owe thanks to Mr. W. M. Richards, of the Portmadoc school, for his very intelligent and obliging assistance in examining the papers of the estate. Cf. J. Girdlestone to John Williams, September 28, 1813, in Appendix III.

[13] Quoted by Dowden: *Life*, I, 356. Harriet gives him a much worse character in her letters to Hookham, March 12, [1813], Julian *Works*, IX, 55. He is mentioned, without prejudice, as a tenant, in Mr. Madocks's letters to John Williams.

[14] C. Kegan Paul, op. cit., II, 212.

[15] According to Dowden (*Life*, I, 304), £2,000 or £3,000 had been collected in Wales. The list of contributions made public at the Beaumaris meeting totals £1,235. The Chester *Courant* of October 20, 1812 reports that " upwards of £1200 " had been subscribed. Hogg (op. cit., I, 368) is responsible for the statement that £20,000 was needed.

[16] Shelley to John Williams, November 7, 1812, Julian *Works*, IX, 23; also Hogg, op. cit., I, 368.

[17] Paraphrased from Hogg's description of Godwin in 1813, op. cit., II, 98–102.

[18] Dowden: *Life*, I, 304–5. Some of the dates and details of the Shelleys' visit to London occur in Paul's life of Godwin, where a short section of Godwin's journal is printed; others depend upon Dowden's use of the complete journal in manuscript.

[19] Mrs. Godwin's two children by her former husband, Mr. Clairmont, were members of the household, but Charles Clairmont was employed in Edinburgh at the time, and Jane Clairmont (or Claire, as she later named herself for romantic reasons), who was several years older than Fanny, was at home during only two days of the Shelleys' stay in London.

[20] From Lewis's Hotel, St. James's Street, undated, Julian *Works*, IX, 24.

[21] Dowden: *Life*, I, 304. Godwin's journal is known only in the

excerpts printed by Dowden, Mrs. Marshall, and C. Kegan Paul, in their biographies, authorized by the Shelley family.

²² According to information furnished Professor Dowden by Madame Gatayes, one of the Newtons' daughters, Shelley visited the Newtons first on Guy Fawkes Day, November 5, for which God- win's journal merely records that the Shelleys and Miss Hitchener dined with the Godwins. On November 7 Godwin records dining with the Shelleys and adds: " W. and P. B. S. to Newton's " (Dow- den: *Life*, I, 307). Both accounts may be correct, as there is nothing to show that the November 7 visit was the first one.

²³ Ibid.

²⁴ Hogg, op. cit., I, 364–5.

²⁵ Ibid., II, 56–7.

²⁶ Harriet to Catherine Nugent, November 14, [1812], Julian *Works*, IX, 25.

²⁷ Shelley to Hogg, December 3, 1812, ibid., IX, 27.

²⁸ Dowden: *Life*, I, 312.

²⁹ " A Newspaper Editor's Reminiscences," *Fraser's Magazine*, XXIII, 709–10 (June 1841).

³⁰ Captain Pilfold to John Williams, January 6, 1814, Julian *Works*, IX, 60.

³¹ Shelley to John Williams, March 30, 1813, ibid., IX, 59.

³² " A Newspaper Editor's Reminiscences," as cited in note 29.

³³ The lines are quoted in Medwin: *Revised Life*, 118, note. After failing to re-establish her school at Hurstpierpoint, Miss Hitchener went to the Continent as governess in an English family, leaving her Shelley letters in the hands of Mr. Henry J. Slack and never subse- quently reclaiming them. She married an Austrian officer, but soon parted from him, resumed her maiden name, and returned to Eng- land. With her sister she set up a school at Edmonton, where she was admired and respected by her students, one of whom told Professor Dowden (*Life*, I, 315): " I consider her to have been a high-prin- cipled, clever woman, with a remarkable capacity for teaching." She died shortly before March 8, 1822. The originals of some of Shelley's letters to her and her transcripts of some of her letters to Shelley are now in the British Museum. When her estate was being settled in 1822, the lawyer who wrote to Sir Timothy Shelley was in possession of other letters that have never been published.

None of Shelley's extant cheques has to do with payments to Miss Hitchener, nor have I found any other record of any payment. Peck's statement (*Life*, I, 281) that a first payment was made seems to be without support. In the desperately involved state of Shelley's finances it is hard to see how any payment could have been made for some time after her departure from London. On August 6, 1822 H. Holste, 22 Bush Lane, London, wrote to Sir Timothy Shelley in an attempt to collect £100 due to her estate from Shelley. This could only have been a loan from Elizabeth Hitchener to Shelley, and not a payment of her allowance, since the transaction preceded the separation by five months, and the money is plainly stated to have been a loan in June 1812. "The documents relating thereto are in my possession, and also many letters from him and his family" (Ingpen: *Shelley in England,* II, 552).

[34] Medwin: *Revised Life,* 118.

[35] Shelley to his mother and to John Williams, both on November 7, 1812, Julian *Works,* IX, 21 and 22.

[36] Shelley to Fanny Imlay, December 10, 1812, ibid., IX, 31.

[37] Harriet to Catherine Nugent, January 16, [1813], ibid., IX, 41.

[38] According to a statement of Dr. Richard Garnett quoted by the editor of the *Century Magazine,* October 1905 (XLVIII, 909). I find no basis for the account of the loaded ship. Harriet's letter to Miss Nugent, January 16, 1813, says: "We have been the means of saving the bank from utter destruction" (Julian *Works,* IX, 41). Cf. note 5, above.

[39] December 3, 1812 and "Friday Ev.," ibid., IX, 29, 30.

[40] Shelley's *Queen Mab,* footnote to Note on Vegetarianism.

[41] Medwin: *Revised Life,* 119.

[42] Dowden: *Life,* I, 319. Mrs. Williams's recollections are of her husband's talk about the events and people dealt with. She did not become the wife of Mr. Williams until 1820.

[43] Shelley to Hogg, February 7, 1813, Julian *Works,* IX, 43.

[44] Harriet to Catherine Nugent, January 16, [1813], ibid., 41.

[45] Shelley to Hogg, February 7, 1813, ibid., IX, 45.

[46] Shelley to Thomas Hookham, December 3, 1812, ibid., IX, 29. The lady quoted is supposed by the editors to have been Mrs. Madocks. On the same day Shelley expressed more briefly to Hogg the same opinion of Welsh society: "The society in Wales is very stupid. They are all aristocrats and saints" (ibid., IX, 28).

[47] Robert Leeson to Shelley, March 5, 1813, ibid., IX, 51. Leeson had previously made a similar oral statement to Shelley, but had apologized in Williams's presence and admitted that Miss Hitchener was his informant. His note was written later and convinced Shelley that Williams was guilty as charged.

⁴⁸ Shelley to John Williams, ["After March 5, 1813"], ["After March 9], 1813," and March 21, 1813, ibid., IX, 51, 54, 57.

⁴⁹ Shelley to his mother, November 7, 1812, ibid., IX, 21.

⁵⁰ Shelley to Hogg, February 7, 1813, ibid., IX, 43.

⁵¹ Shelley to Fanny Imlay, December 10, 1812, ibid., IX, 31.

⁵² No letters from Shelley to Godwin are extant between July 29, 1812 and January 7, 1816, but Godwin's journal records writing seven letters to Shelley at Tanyrallt (Dowden: *Life*, I, 326, note).

⁵³ Shelley to Hogg, December 3, 1812, Julian *Works*, IX, 27.

⁵⁴ Byron's speech in the House of Lords, February 27, 1812, R. E. Prothero: *Letters and Journals of Lord Byron* (London, 1898), II, 430.

⁵⁵ Julian *Works*, IX, 43.

⁵⁶ The *Examiner*, March 22, 1812, No. 221, p. 179.

⁵⁷ Shelley to Hogg, December 27, 1812, Julian *Works*, IX, 37–8.

⁵⁸ Shelley to Hookham, February 19, 1813, ibid., IX, 46–7. Leigh Hunt commented in his autobiography on the fact that the real purpose of the article, "The Prince on Saint Patrick's Day," had been to show the contempt in which the Regent was held by describing the repeated hisses every time his name was mentioned at the St. Patrick's Day dinner. This was a fact outside the realm of opinion. Shelley's analysis of the conviction is interesting in this respect, for had the prosecution been pressed on this ground, a defence of truth could easily have been maintained.

⁵⁹ *Leigh Hunt's Autobiography*, ed. Roger Ingpen (Westminster, 1903), II, 13.

⁶⁰ Ibid.

⁶¹ Julian *Works*, IX, 26, note.

⁶² Shelley to Hookham, February 19, 1813, ibid., IX, 47.

⁶³ D. E. Varney to John Williams, May 20, [1815], quoted in Appendix III. Also Ingpen: *Shelley in England*, II, 635, and Julian *Works*, IX, 57. The £100 from Owen Williams was to be repaid in the sum of £200 on the deaths of Shelley's father and grandfather, and was presumably paid by Peacock after Sir Timothy Shelley's death. Shelley's financial affairs at this time were partly handled by a Mr. Bedwell, of 6 Tooley Street, Canterbury Square, Southwark, and a Mr. Caldecott, who are referred to in his letters of December 24, 1812, March 21, and March 30, 1813. Caldecott was evidently a money-lender, and Bedwell seems to have been something of a general agent and possibly a money-lender also. Hookham seems to have rendered Shelley some financial serv-

ices of an unknown nature, possibly inquiries only, for which he received Shelley's thanks on January 2.

[64] Hogg, op. cit., I, 347.

[65] Shelley to Hogg, December 3, 1812, Julian *Works*, IX, 26.

[66] Shelley to Hogg, December 27, 1812, ibid., IX, 38.

[67] Timothy Shelley to P. B. Shelley, dated "Jan. 1814" apparently for 1813, ibid., IX, 39.

[68] *Shelley Memorials* (London, 1875), 45–8.

[69] That they were mostly read is of course an assumption, based upon Shelley's obviously serious and thorough reading habits and upon acquaintance with many of them which he demonstrated later. Some of them were books he had previously read. He could hardly have read Spallanzani in the Italian, however, as his list implied. He also fails to distinguish between Celsus the Greek Platonist and Celsus the Roman author of *De Medicina;* and the two Garcilasco de la Vegas — the Spanish poet or the historian of Peru. The latter alternative in each case would seem to be indicated by the general nature of the list. Is "Marcus Antonius" an editorial slip for Marcus Aurelius? Dowden read it as Marcus Aurelius (*Life*, I, 334). While most of the books in this list were probably chosen as a result of Godwin's letters of advice, three of them were favourites with Shelley's new acquaintance Thomas Love Peacock and are thought by Carl Van Doren (*Life of Thomas Love Peacock*, 1911, p. 56) to have been suggested by Peacock — namely, the titles by Monboddo, Sir William Drummond, and Horne Tooke.

[70] Shelley to Hookham, December 17, 1812, Julian *Works*, IX, 33.

[71] Preface to *Shelley's Essays, Letters from Abroad,* etc. (London, 1840), I, xvi–xvii.

[72] Ibid., xii.

[73] Shelley to Hookham, January 26, [1813], Julian *Works*, IX, 42.

[74] Shelley to Hogg, February 7, 1813, ibid., IX, 44, 45.

[75] Shelley to Hookham, February 19, 1813, and undated [March?], ibid., IX, 47, 56.

[76] Shelley to Hookham, December 17, 1812, January 2 and 26, 1813, ibid., IX, 33, 40, 42.

[77] Namely, the poem dedicating *Queen Mab* to Harriet, the dialogue between Falsehood and Vice, both in the *Queen Mab* volume, and the poem beginning: "The pale, the cold and the moony smile," published in revised form in the *Alastor* volume. The Julian editors were allowed to publish the same poems, newly collated with the manuscripts.

[78] Professor Dowden, who examined the manuscripts, says that, according to Shelley's count as there indicated, the number of lines is 2,822 (*Life*, I, 345).

[79] Godwin, in the letter previously quoted, had praised the writers he was recommending to Shelley because " Every line is pregnant with sense."

[80] Harriet to Miss Nugent, undated, from London, also November 14, [1812], and January 16, [1813], Julian *Works*, IX, 24, 25, 41.

[81] Shelley to Elizabeth Hitchener, February 27, [1812], ibid., VIII, 285; and to Hookham, December 17, January 2 and 31, ibid., IX, 33, 40, 43.

[82] Two of the three references to this work in the Shelleys' extant letters are mutilated and one is undated, which makes any comment upon it partly guess-work. In his letter of December 3 to Hookham, Shelley asks: " When does God save [. . .] I am anxious for th . . ." In an undated fragment he concludes, " Oh! and is God Save the King done. My loyal soul pants for its arrival." On March 30 Harriet instructed John Williams to forward a certain box to London rather than Dublin, because " If it came to us the Custom house men would take it, as it contains G . . ."

[83] Harriet to Miss Nugent, November 14, [1812]; and to Hookham, January 31, [1813], Julian *Works*, IX, 25, 43.

[84] Harriet to Hookham, March 12, [1813], ibid., IX, 55. Hogg claimed to have received the same account from Harriet immediately after the event, in a letter subsequently lost.

[85] Substantially the same as that given later to Medwin by Mr. Madocks. Both Mr. Madocks and Medwin considered it a delusion. Medwin's statement (*Revised Life*, 117) that Shelley made a deposition of the circumstances to Mr. Madocks is generally discredited, on Mrs. Williams's testimony that Mr. Madocks was not in Tremadoc while the Shelleys were there.

[86] Statement by Mrs. Williams in 1860, from recollection of her husband's conversation in 1820 and later, quoted by Dowden: *Life*, I, 354–5.

[87] A sketch from this copy was printed with Miss Margaret L. Croft's article in the *Century Magazine*, XLVIII, 905–9 (October 1905). Mrs. Williams-Ellis, the owner of Tanyrallt in 1936, told me then that she had often seen this sketch, but did not know its present whereabouts, though she believed it was still in her family.

[88] Dowden: *Life*, I, 354. But Dowden was inclined to believe that some actual attack was the basis of Shelley's narrative (ibid., 356).

[89] Margaret L. Croft's article as cited in note 87.

[90] Ingpen: *Shelley in England,* II, 399, and Peck: *Life,* I, 291–2. Ingpen states categorically that Shelley's account is "now proved to have been correct."

[91] One of these daughters, now Mrs. Williams-Ellis, of Tany-rallt, told me in the spring of 1936 that she distinctly remembered listening to Robin Pant Ifan when she was a girl of ten. "He was a lively old man — not so old, either. I wouldn't believe a word he said." On August 4, 1931 she wrote to Mr. Griffith John Williams of Bangor: "As a child I remember Robin Pant Ifan well, and as a man of about forty or fifty — and always full of story! But he was a very young child — if indeed alive — at the date Shelley was here and could have taken no part in the attack. My sister was strong on this point!" (Papers of Griffith John Williams, Esq., MS.)

[92] "Robin Pant Ifan," whose name was Robert Williams, was the son of William Williams, postmaster of Tremadoc, and Laura Jones, daughter of Robert Jones, owner of Pant Ifan. Robert Jones left him the Pant Ifan farm on his death in 1832 (May 24, aged 89). According to his death certificate (No. 272, Registration District of Festiniog, sub-district of Tremadoc), he died at Pant Ifan on June 3, 1878, aged 68. (Papers of Griffith John Williams, Esq., and Penmorfa church register.)

[93] Harriet's account places the first episode at about 11.00 p.m. and the second at 4.00 a.m. According to a calculation made in 1918 by Mr. Phillip Lake, of the Sedgwick Museum, Cambridge (for Mr. G. J. Williams), loaned to me by Professor H. Wright, of University College, Bangor, North Wales, the moon rose at a quarter to four at Tremadoc on February 26, 1813. From another basis of calculation Mr. Hugh S. Rice, Associate in Astronomy at the Hayden Planetarium, New York, informs me that on that day the moon rose "roughly speaking — about 5.50 a.m." When I called his attention to the descrepancy Mr. Rice was willing for me to quote him as saying that the moon rose "about 5.00 a.m." In neither case, however, could the moon have furnished any appreciable visibility.

[94] Mrs. Godwin to Lady Mountcashell (Mrs. Mason), February 15, 1815, as summarized by Dowden: *Life,* I, 355, note.

[95] *Shelley Memorials,* 56.

[96] Mrs. Godwin to Lady Mountcashell, as in note 94 above.

[97] Peacock: *Memoirs,* II, 322–3.

[98] Hogg, op. cit., I, 389–91.

[99] Shelley to Hookham, March 6, 1813, Julian *Works,* IX, 52.

[100] Shelley to Hookham, undated. Quoted by Dowden (*Life*, I, 350) as written the day after the attack; but dated conjecturally in the Julian edition (IX, 49) " [Tanyrallt, Tremadoc, March 3, 1813]." It could hardly have been written from Tanyrallt, for the Shelleys left it at once, but the date March 3 seems preferable to February 27, the intervening days being accounted for by Shelley's illness. The £20 mentioned was the money recently sent for Leigh Hunt.

[101] Thornton Hunt: " Shelley, by One Who Knew Him," *Atlantic Monthly*, XI, 185–6 (February 1863).

[102] So he and Harriet asserted immediately after the assault, and so Shelley believed when his obsession revived in 1815. It is curious, therefore, that a note from Shelley to John Williams soon after the event, expressing surprise that nothing had been done to apprehend his assailant, does not mention Leeson; and a later note to Williams, for which Leeson was the actual occasion, does not suggest any suspicion of him as the assailant (Julian *Works*, IX, 50, 51).

[103] Shelley to John Williams, undated, ibid., IX, 50, and [? after March 9], IX, 54.

[104] Shelley to Hookham, March 6, 1813, ibid., IX, 53.

[105] Shelley to John Williams [? after March 9], 1813, ibid., IX, 54.

[106] Shelley to Hookham, undated, ibid., IX, 56–7.

[107] Hogg, op. cit., I, 392.

[108] Harriet to Catherine Nugent, August 4, [1812], Julian *Works*, IX, 15. Lady Morgan's *Memoirs* (London, 1862, 2 vols.) shows several opportunities of later contact with Shelley, none of which resulted in a meeting. She was acquainted with Prince Mavrocordato in Geneva just before he left for Italy, where he knew the Shelleys, and she called on Miss Amelia Curran in Rome early in February 1820, when she probably had Shelley's uncompleted portrait in her lodgings. She was in Florence in early October 1819, and thereafter in Naples, Rome, and Venice. She talked with Godwin about Shelley in 1835, met Mary Shelley, and was a friend of Shelley's friend, Horace Smith.

[109] Shelley to Hogg, March 31, 1813, Julian *Works*, IX, 61.

[110] April 20, 1818, ibid., IX, 297.

[111] Hogg, op. cit., II, 2. Eliza Westbrook's letter from Dublin to John Williams, quoted in Appendix III, shows that Shelley's books at Tanyrallt were not sent to Ireland.

[112] Hogg, op. cit., II, 2.

Chapter XI

GENERAL SOURCES

Shelley's poems as published in Julian *Works;* the letters of Shelley and Harriet in Julian *Works,* VIII and IX, and the letters of Timothy Shelley in the same and in Ingpen's *Shelley in England;* the journal of William Godwin and the letters of Mrs. Godwin as published in Dowden's *Life;* Hogg's *Life of Shelley;* Peacock's *Memoirs of Shelley;* and Medwin's *Revised Life* — all as previously cited.

The Elopement of Shelley and Mary as Related by William Godwin, privately printed by the Bibliophile Society for W. K. Bixby, and edited by H. B. Forman, 1911.

NOTES AND REFERENCES

[1] Shelley to Timothy Shelley, marked " Rec'd 4 o'ck 18th May, 1813," mistakenly dated by Dowden May 4. Julian *Works,* IX, 66.

[2] Harriet to Catherine Nugent, May 21, 1813, ibid., IX, 67.

[3] John Lawless to Hogg, May 3, 1813, ibid., IX, 65.

[4] Hogg, op. cit., II, 3.

[5] Shelley to Timothy Shelley, received May 18, 1813, Julian *Works,* IX, 66.

[6] Timothy Shelley to P. B. Shelley, May 26, 1813, ibid., IX, 69. His previous letter and Shelley's answer are lost, but their nature is inferable from this letter and from Harriet's letter of June 22.

[7] Only once thereafter is Shelley known to have written directly to his father and then it was about financial matters. The impossibility of a genuine reconciliation was apparently taken for granted on both sides.

[8] Shelley to the Duke of Norfolk [May 28, 1813], Julian *Works,* IX, 68.

[9] Shelley to Thomas Hookham, August 18, 1812, ibid., IX, 19.

[10] Richard Carlile offered for sale in his *The Republican* (December 27, 1822, p. 979) 180 copies of the original edition of 250.

[11] The only known recipients were Harriet, Hogg, Mary Godwin, Fanny Imlay, Mrs. Boinville, Byron, Baptista Pereira (unless he used only a borrowed copy), Thomas Moore, and a Mr. Waller. Godwin, Newton, Peacock, Ollier, and Hookham may of course be guessed with practical certainty. It was originally intended to send copies to America, and it was later asserted that copies were sent to Germany. No copies have been discovered in America. The German story is also dubious; see my *The Unextinguished Hearth* (1939), p. 45.

[12] It has been suggested that the dedication was originally to Harriet Grove, whose name corresponds with the number of asterisks. If so, it would support Medwin's statement that *Queen Mab* was begun at Oxford. But the dedication as published could not apply to anyone except Harriet Shelley.

[13] Shelley's acknowledged source for his vegetarian ideas was John Frank Newton's *The Return to Nature*. But see note 44.

[14] Ahasuerus had first appealed to Shelley primarily because of his eternal life and intense experience, as his poem *The Wandering Jew* clearly testifies. A later poem, "The Wandering Jew's Soliloquy," written probably about the time Shelley began *Queen Mab*, infuses the orthodox horrors of Schubart's poem with a definitely Shelleyan hatred of the Author of his hero's sufferings. In *The Assassins* (1814) the Wandering Jew becomes benevolent.

There is brief mention of the Wandering Jew in *Alastor* (1816). In his last appearance, in *Hellas* (1822), Ahasuerus loses his original symbolic force, which had been absorbed by the character of Prometheus (1819), and becomes a type of patient wisdom. His evolution is paralleled by that of Shelley's Christ. In *Prometheus Unbound* (1819) Christ's sufferings are treated with sympathy; He is viewed as the victim of the perversion of Christianity rather than its cause. In *Hellas* (1822) the attitude toward Christ is sympathetic rather than antagonistic. If the *Essay on Christianity* was written, as W. M. Rossetti believed, in 1815, the change toward a sympathetic attitude was accomplished by that time.

The vegetarian theory, which is incongruously important in *Queen Mab*, appears thereafter in Shelley's works only in two or three slight allusions. The doctrine of Necessity persists in Shelley's later poetry, but is absorbed about 1816 in Shelley's doctrine of Love, or

Universal Sympathy. The history of this change is in fact the history of the growing influence on Shelley's mind of idealistic philosophy and his partial realization of the inconsistency of Necessity with freedom of the will and sympathy.

[15] See my article: "Shelley and the Active Radicals of the Early Nineteenth Century," *South Atlantic Quarterly*, XXIX, 248–61 (July 1930).

[16] See my "Literature and the Law of Libel: Shelley and the Radicals of 1840–42," *Studies in Philology*, XXII, 34–47 (January 1925).

[17] Professor David Lee Clark has shown in his "The Date and Source of Shelley's *A Vindication of Natural Diet*" (*Studies in Philology*, XXXVI, 70–6, January 1939) that the essay was composed before the note, probably in November 1812.

[18] Ruth S. Granniss: *A Descriptive Catalogue of the First Editions of the Writings of Percy Bysshe Shelley* (New York, 1923), 36, 37.

[19] Hogg, op. cit., II, 3.

[20] Hogg is the only authority for Shelley's changes of residence before he removed to Bracknell, and his testimony is confusing. Shelley's extant letters until July 27 are all dated from Cooke's Hotel. Hogg says that the Shelleys resided for a few days at a hotel in Dover Street after leaving the house of Mr. Westbrook (op. cit., II, 1 and 68). Though he mentions the Dover Street hotel more than once, this may mean that the Shelleys used Cooke's Hotel only as an accommodation address. He speaks of the lodgings in Half-Moon Street much too precisely to permit of supposing him mistaken about their existence, and he says the Shelleys lived there " some weeks or months " (ibid., II, 26) and then went to Pimlico, where Harriet's baby was born (ibid., II, 68). Since Ianthe was born near the end of June, it seems unlikely that Shelley spent much more than a month in either Cooke's Hotel or the Half-Moon Street lodgings. Dowden believed (*Life*, I, 366–7, note) that the Shelleys remained at Cooke's Hotel until near the end of May. Whenever he left the hotel, it is evident from his own letters that he continued to use it in his correspondence as a convenient address, even after his removal to Pimlico.

[21] Hogg, op. cit., II, 5.

[22] Hogg mentions Shelley's dining with the Duke of Norfolk after the removal to Half-Moon Street (op. cit., II, 5).

[23] Shelley to Thomas Charles Medwin, November 30, 1811, Julian *Works,* VIII, 208.

[24] Shelley to Thomas Charles Medwin, postmarked June 16, 1813, ibid., IX, 70.

[25] *The Elopement of Shelley and Mary as Related by William Godwin,* 10, 13, 14. Two letters in Francis Place's unpublished autobiography (Brit. Mus. Add. MSS. 35,145, Vol. IV, folios 37 and 49) seem to confirm this statement. In August 1813 Godwin was about ready to " firmly call on my young friend to assist me," and on September 5, 1813 Shelley's assistance was already promised, and Godwin refers to "the money to be raised on Shelley's security." In a letter of December 16, 1824 to Francis Place, John Taylor of Norwich mentioned his understanding that in 1813 or 1814 Shelley signed a bond to guarantee Godwin's debt to Taylor (ibid., folios 67–69). A letter from Francis Place to Edward Wakefield (Brit. Mus. Add. MSS. 35,152, folio 33) gives a brief picture of Godwin's state of mind and purse on January 18, 1814: ". . . he fears he shall not succeed in obtaining the loan which has for its object to repay the advances of his friends amounting in bills and cash to about £2700, some of whom will be ruined if he fail — and this distracts him, a more miserable creature than he seems to be hardly exists. . . ."

[26] Shelley to Thomas Charles Medwin, June 28, 1813, Julian *Works,* IX, 73.

[27] Shelley to Thomas Charles Medwin, July 6, 1813, and to Hogg, [July 9], ibid., IX, 74, 75.

[28] Harriet Shelley to Catherine Nugent, August 8 and September 10, 1812, ibid., IX, 76, 77.

[29] Hogg, op. cit., II, 51. From Hogg's account the adventure evidently occurred at the home of the Newtons.

[30] Ibid., I, 390; and Harriet to Catherine Nugent, June 22, October 11, November 23, 1813, Julian *Works,* IX, 71, 78, 80. According to Dowden (*Life,* I, 392), Harriet was unable to pay Dan his wages. This is a reasonable inference from the letters, but appears to be inference only.

[31] Hogg, op. cit., II, 30.

[32] Ibid., II, 82. Elsewhere, however, Hogg speaks of Shelley as being moderately fond of his negus at Oxford.

[33] Ibid., II, 31–3.

[34] Harriet to Catherine Nugent, May 21, [1813], Julian *Works,* IX, 67.

[35] Only a few at most, as Peacock was in Wales a good part of this time. Hogg did not meet Peacock until the next winter or spring.

[36] Harriet to Catherine Nugent, May 21 and June 22, Julian *Works,* IX, 67, 71.

[37] Shelley to John Williams, June 27, 1813; also to Hogg, June 27; ibid., 72, 73.

[38] Dowden: *Life,* I, 364, note: "There is no entry respecting Shelley in Godwin's journal from March 30 . . . to June 8" [1813].

[39] See *ante,* p. 266.

[40] Hogg, op. cit., II, 105, 79. Hogg tells that the Earl of Oxford delighted Shelley by inquiring at the Duke of Norfolk's dinner: "Who is that very strange old man at the top of the table, sitting next to his Grace, who talks so much, so loudly, and in so extraordinary a manner, and all about himself?" To which Shelley had replied: "He is my father, and he is a very strange old man indeed." But would Shelley have been seated so near the Earl of Oxford at such a dinner?

[41] Ibid., II, 3, 6.

[42] Ibid., II, 11, 13, 44.

[43] The date seems to be fixed by the fact that his endorsement on the letter of John Lawless (Julian *Works,* IX, 65) indicates that Hogg then knew the Newtons.

[44] John Frank Newton: *The Return to Nature; or, A Defence of the Vegetable Regimen; With Some Account of an Experiment Made During the Last Three or Four Years in the Author's Family* (1st edition, London, 1811). As reprinted in the *Pamphleteer,* the essay is to be found in the volumes for 1821 and 1822, XIX, 497–530, and XX, 97–118, 411–28. The passage quoted in the text is at XX, 116. The reference to distilled water in the passage quoted is fortified by a footnote of half a page showing the dire effects of common water. Even when using distilled water, Newton explains elsewhere, one should throw away the first three gallons distilled and the last three or four gallons remaining in the container.

Newton was born in St. Christopher's, East Indies, in 1767. He came to England shortly after his seventh birthday and entered Christ Church, Oxford, July 8, 1786, at the age of nineteen, leaving without a degree. From 1786 to 1804 he suffered severely and frequently from asthma. In 1804 he adopted Dr. William Lambe's distilled-water treatment, which he supplemented, on Dr. Lambe's advice, with vegetarianism, beginning in 1807. In 1808 he testified in Dr. Lambe's book to his complete cure, and to the beneficial effects of Dr. Lambe's regimen in his family. His own book was written largely out of gratitude to Dr. Lambe. (Joseph Foster: *Alumni Oxonienses 1715–1886*, Oxford, 1888, III, 1019, and William Lambe: *Reports on the Effects of a Peculiar Regimen*, etc., London, 1809, pp. 180–4.) In 1814, according to Dowden (*Life*, I, 467, note), the Newtons moved into Hampshire, where Mrs. Newton died shortly afterwards. Mr. Newton died at Weymouth on May 1, 1837, at the age of seventy, according to the *Gentleman's Magazine* (n.s. VII, 668, June 1837).

Shelley's note on vegetarianism in *Queen Mab*, and his *A Vindication of Natural Diet*, lean heavily on Newton's book, with an additional stress on the social and political benefits of vegetarianism. Newton, in turn, makes no pretence to originality; his purpose is to offer personal testimony and general philosophic support to the system laid down by his friend Dr. William Lambe, principally in *Reports on the Effects of a Peculiar Regimen on Schirrhous Tumors and Cancerous Ulcers* (London, 1809).

It has recently been shown that Joseph Ritson's *Essay on the Abstinence from Animal Food* was an important source of Shelley's ideas, probably more so than Newton's essay (David Lee Clark: "The Date and Source of Shelley's *A Vindication of Natural Diet*," in *Studies in Philology*, XXXVI, 70–6 (January 1939). A writer in the *London Magazine and Theatrical Inquisitor* for July 1821 who was evidently well acquainted with Shelley seems to link Shelley's vegetarianism definitely with Newton, Lambe, and Ritson. (See my *The Unextinguished Hearth*, 1938, pp. 263–9.)

⁴⁵ Hogg, op. cit., II, 84.

⁴⁶ Ibid., II, 87, 88.

⁴⁷ Peacock: *Memoirs*, II, 324–5. One sees that Shelley was familiar with this theory of Newton's from *Alastor*, lines 116–19, where the wandering poet surveys "the Zodiac's brazen mysteries" in a ruined ancient temple.

⁴⁸ Hogg, op. cit., II, 92–3.

⁴⁹ Madame Gatayes (one of the Newton children), as quoted by Dowden: *Life*, I, 363.

⁵⁰ Hogg, op. cit., II, 28 and 116.

⁵¹ Ibid., II, 71. Hogg does not mention Mrs. Newton by name, but Shelley's letter dated Friday [July 1813] which immediately precedes Hogg's account (ibid., II, 69) appears both to identify the hostess and to fix the date.

⁵² Ibid., II, 8. Hogg was acquainted with the Countess and may

have been responsible for her interest in Shelley. Hogg's memory of the details of this period is not to be trusted implicitly. Thus he tells (ibid., II, 94) of a projected meeting between Shelley and Horne Tooke and of his own meeting with Tooke in Newton's company. Since Horne Tooke died March 18, 1812, while Shelley was still on his first visit to Ireland and before either Shelley or Hogg had met Newton, there seems to be no way of accounting for Hogg's story except deliberate fabrication or confusion of Horne Tooke with some other person of whom the narration was true.

[53] Ibid., II, 10–11. In 1796 the name of John Frank Newton appears with that of James Boswell, Samuel Parr, and eighteen others as having endorsed the Ireland Shakespeare forgeries (William Ireland's *Vindication of his Conduct,* etc., London, 1796, pp. 21–2). This could have been Shelley's friend, but was more probably the Reverend John Frank Newton, son of the Bishop of Salisbury. He was probably the uncle of Shelley's friend, whose father was named William. Samuel Parr was a friend of Fanny Burney's and a former friend of Godwin's, both of whom visited in the Newton home. Thus the Newtons might have had reasonable hopes, through their friends, of making Shelley acquainted with Dr. Parr. The plan could also have originated with the Boinvilles, since Dr. Parr was a good friend of Dr. Lambe, and Dr. Lambe's daughter married Mrs. Boinville's son Alfred. Or the idea may have been that of Dr. Lambe, with whom Hogg was acquainted, and probably Shelley.

[54] Hogg, op. cit., II, 75.

[55] Ibid., II, 76–7. A recently published letter from Shelley to Hogg, written February 14, 1817, remonstrates with Hogg's ill humour over Shelley's failure to keep appointments (Gordon, op. cit.).

[56] Hogg, op. cit., II, 106. The date cannot be fixed precisely. Hogg states that Ianthe was born here and that the residence in Pimlico was for only a month. Harriet's confinement was expected from about the middle of June; Ianthe was born shortly before June 28, and the first extant letter written from Bracknell was dated July 27. From these facts one would suppose the Pimlico residence to have been between the middle of June and the middle of July.

[57] Shelley to Peacock, April 6 or 16, 1819, Julian *Works,* X, 45, 46.

[58] Professor Dowden, through Mr. Thomas Constable, inquired of members of the Boinville and Turner families for letters from Shelley, but none were known to be in existence (Dowden: *Life,* I, 382, note).

⁵⁹ Hogg, op. cit., II, 107–8. " I generally found there," Hogg con-
continues,

> two or three sentimental young butchers, an eminently philo-
> sophical tinker, and several very unsophisticated medical practi-
> tioners, or medical students, all of low origin, and vulgar and of-
> fensive manners. They sighed and turned up their eyes, retailed
> philosophy, such as it was, and swore by William Godwin and
> *Political Justice;* acting, moreover, and very clumsily, the parts
> of Petrarchs, Werters, St. Leons, and Fleetwoods. This strange
> selection was made, this queer medley was brought together,
> partly from a certain French love of presiding over, ruling,
> forming, and managing, and it was imagined — a great mistake —
> that low people would prove the most tractable and submissive;
> and partly through the love of equality, of levelling, and frater-
> nizing.

Peacock's briefer and more tolerantly phrased account of the same
group (*Memoirs*, II, 323–4) is not radically different from Hogg's.

⁶⁰ Hogg., op. cit., II, 108.

⁶¹ Ibid., II, 129.

⁶² Ibid., II, 8.

⁶³ Ibid., II, 19–21.

⁶⁴ Ibid., II, 34–5.

⁶⁵ Ibid., II, 25. This lady, unnamed by Hogg, speaks of having
lived in Spain with her mother and sister. As the Newton family,
according to Newton's *Return to Nature,* had lived in Spain, she
may have been Mrs. Newton's sister, Miss Collins.

⁶⁶ Mr. Humbert Wolfe, in the Introduction to the edition of Hogg
here used, states that Hogg, principally in the incidents just related,
" deliberately created the impression that Shelley was a reckless and
light-headed amorist." Mr. Wolfe contends that Shelley was in fact
"one of those rare men who could love a woman's mind without
desiring her body." With the latter I heartily agree. It is a phenomenon which it seems clear to me Hogg observed without understanding. I can see no evidence that Hogg wished to make Shelley appear
an amorist, unless we suppose his whole book to be an elaborate
sarcasm at the expense of a man he professed to love but secretly
hated. This is in fact practically what Mr. Wolfe does suggest as
Hogg's purpose. I find it inconsistent with Hogg's attitude to Shelley as revealed in letters written between Shelley's death and Hogg's

first articles on Shelley, inconsistent with Hogg's friendship with Peacock, Hunt, and Trelawny, all of whom would have detected and resented such an attitude, and inconsistent with Hogg's book itself. Hogg's repeated assertions of the purity of Shelley's thoughts and conduct are certainly not sarcastic. I cannot find in Hogg's narration of the incidents themselves any suggestion that the ladies were deceived in their estimate of Shelley; Hogg seems to be accepting, in a rather ill-bred smoking-room manner, an unusual and amusing phenomenon.

[67] Hogg, op. cit., II, 21.

[68] Ibid., II, 29.

[69] Ibid., II, 104, 23, and I, xiv. That Harriet also was occasionally annoyed by Hogg's scoffing may be seen from his rude comments on Robert Emmet previously cited. In May or June 1813 he seems to have offended Harriet seriously enough for Shelley to think it necessary to write him a note of explanation (Julian *Works,* IX, 69).

[70] Hogg, op. cit., II, 68.

[71] Ibid., II, 26–8.

[72] Ibid., II, 3.

[73] Ibid., II, 60.

[74] Ibid., II, 61.

[75] Ibid., II, 63–6.

[76] Ibid., II, 61; also cf. II, 12, 26.

[77] While the Shelleys were at Cooke's Hotel and in Half-Moon Street, Hogg saw them constantly in their rooms. During the month in the Pimlico house and the later period spent at Bracknell, Hogg never entered their house, but he saw Shelley constantly in the company of other members of the Newton and Boinville circles, on Shelley's frequent trips to town after moving to Bracknell, and on the long walks they took together. There is a gap of four or five months in the association caused by Hogg's departure for his vacation in the north in August 1813, and the Shelleys' absence in Edinburgh; yet for nearly two years Hogg had an unrivalled opportunity of observing Shelley. What he later recorded is subject to various discounts, such as egotism, ignorance, lack of complete sympathy, and the influence of an intervening tradition upon natural lapses of memory. By all these factors it must have been warped in some respects from the absolute truth, but it is supported by the more meagre account of the same period left by Peacock, and must still be accepted, with due allowances, as a valuable, though distorted, record of Shelley's thoughts and habits at the time.

[78] Captain Kennedy's account, in Hogg, op. cit., II, 152–4. Dowden quotes a briefer, similar description furnished him by Madame Gatayes (one of the Newton children) and also quotes Henry Reveley, who knew Shelley in Italy, as characterizing Kennedy's description as "the best and most truthful I have ever seen" (*Life*, I, 390, note).

[79] Hogg, op. cit., II, 83.

[80] Ibid., II, 38.

[81] Peacock: *Memoirs*, II, 330.

[82] Hogg, op. cit., II, 47.

[83] Ibid., II, 48–9.

[84] Quoted by Dowden from Madame Gatayes (*Life*, I, 373).

[85] Hogg, op. cit., II, 38–40. Peacock's more condensed account of the same delusion agrees completely with Hogg's. He dates the occurrence as "about the end of 1813" (*Memoir*, II, 326). Later delusions are described by Peacock: *Memoirs*, II, 341–3, 354.

[86] Hogg, op. cit., II, 73.

[87] Ibid., II, 88.

[88] Ibid., II, 77.

[89] Ibid., II, 43.

[90] Ibid., II, 23.

[91] Ibid., II, 80–1. Hogg's insistence on the wildness of Shelley's laughter receives some support from a recently published letter of Mary Shelley's to Hogg. Describing a performance of *Der Freischütz*, Mary says: ". . . and the incantation scene would have made Shelley scream with delight . . ." (October 3, 1824, Gordon, op. cit.).

[92] Peacock: *Memoirs*, II, 348–9. Peacock is here speaking of Shelley in 1817.

[93] Hogg's free method in handling humorous material is illustrated by his story of the old woman whom Shelley frightened from the stagecoach (*Life*, II, 23–4), compared with the account of the same incident furnished by Hunt, an eyewitness. See Chapter xvii, note 52.

[94] My own opinion is that Hogg and Peacock both recognized this fact, as shown by their treatment of Shelley's delusions, but that they did not regard Shelley's abnormality as serious; otherwise Hogg in particular would hardly have acted as he did at the time or written so farcically of Shelley's peculiarities in retrospect. Peacock may have taken the matter a shade more seriously than Hogg, and this may account in part for his steady refusal to write a biog-

raphy of Shelley. In addition to his dislike for Mary Shelley he was unwilling, as he said, to deal with Shelley's fits of anger (a subject discussed by Gibbons Merle, 'the " Newspaper Editor "), on which Hogg and every other writer who knew Shelley are silent, except for one or two schoolboy episodes. Ordinary outbursts of temper would not trouble a biographer who did not hesitate to report delusions, but such outbursts as those reported to Whitton by Shelley's father (see pp. 166, 167) were certainly not ordinary.

[95] E.g., " His flight was to escape from, not to pursue, to get away from some object for which he had conceived a sudden dislike" (Hogg, op. cit., II, 29).

[96] Peacock: *Memoirs*, II, 341. See also ibid., 314, where Peacock says Shelley thought his father was continuously seeking a pretext for locking him up. This fear, according to Peacock, haunted Shelley through life and was closely related to his frequent changes of residence, which were often preceded by mysterious warnings of his father's designs. See Chapter v, note 84.

[97] The *Athenæum*, August 25, 1832, p. 555.

[98] Harriet to Hogg, " Sunday morning," and to Catherine Nugent, August 8, [1813]; also Shelley to Hogg, [July 9?]; Julian *Works*, IX, 66, 76, 75.

[99] Hogg, op. cit., II, 106–7.

[100] Peacock: *Memoirs*, II, 323.

[101] Hogg, op. cit., I, 136.

[102] Quoted by Dowden: *Life*, I, 376, from the Esdaile MSS.

[103] Hogg, op. cit., II, 128. Hogg is said to have spoken privately of Harriet's intemperance, and Richard Garnett thought in 1905 that her intemperance caused the alienation of Shelley (*Letters about Shelley*, 248, and cf. 126). Shelley would undoubtedly have been disturbed by this condition, if it were a fact. But a sneer and a rumoured remark in conversation hardly establish it as such.

[104] Shelley's last extant letter from London is dated by the Julian editors July 9(?); the first extant letter from Bracknell, July 27, 1813. Harriet's condition would probably require remaining in the Pimlico lodgings until near the middle of July.

[105] Mrs. J. F. Newton to Hogg, October 21, 1813, Hogg, op. cit., II, 115–16.

[106] Ibid., II, 116–17. This passage reads very much as if Hogg thought Peacock responsible for the journey. Hogg seems never to have questioned Peacock on the cause of the journey, and Peacock offers no cause in his own brief account (*Memoirs*, II, 334–5).

Professor Dowden, in pointing out the fallacy of W. M. Rossetti's belief that the journey was to remarry Harriet in Edinburgh, surmised that Shelley's motive was to escape creditors and to render a service to Peacock, whom "for reasons of his own it suited to be absent from London at this time" (*Life,* II, 392, and 393, note). Shelley's London friends, according to Hogg, knew of no financial or any other necessity for the journey and would have succoured him in such a case (op. cit., II, 117).

Peacock's biographers mention no necessity for his leaving London at this time. It seems to me that Peacock can be implicated only by supposing that Shelley's desperate financial condition was not sufficiently desperate to make such an expensive move necessary and that Peacock, for selfish reasons, encouraged Shelley to make the move. This is possible, but is unsupported by evidence, nor is Peacock's influence necessary to account for Shelley's actions. The financial situation (no doubt partly concealed from his friends) was sufficient motive. Harriet had foreseen the possibility when they first moved to Bracknell and had written to Mrs. Nugent on August 8: "I fear our necessities will oblige us to remove to a greater distance" (Julian *Works,* IX, 76).

[107] Peacock: *Memoirs,* II, 329.

[108] Harriet to Catherine Nugent, August 8, 1813, Julian *Works,* IX, 76; and September 10, [1813], ibid., IX, 77. The first shows that Harriet anticipated being forced by "necessity" to go further from London than Bracknell; the second shows that Shelley feared arrest and wished his northern address kept secret.

[109] William Godwin to John Taylor, *The Elopement of Shelley and Mary,* 10.

[110] Harriet to Catherine Nugent, October 11, [1813], Julian *Works,* IX, 78.

[111] Harriet to Catherine Nugent, August 8, September 10, October 11, [1813], ibid., IX, 76, 77, 78.

[112] Shelley to Hookham [endorsed October 6, 1813], ibid., IX, 78.

[113] Dowden: *Life,* I, 393.

[114] Harriet to Catherine Nugent, October 11 and 20, [1813], Julian *Works,* IX, 78, 79. Their lodgings at 36 Frederic Street were quite near their former lodgings at 60 George Street.

[115] Shelley to Hogg, November 26, 1813, Julian *Works,* IX, 81. It is evident from the comment on Peacock that Peacock and Hogg were not yet acquainted. Peacock had been absent in Wales during much of the time Shelley was seeing Hogg in London and had seen

Shelley only once or twice before the Shelleys moved to Bracknell. His intimacy began almost exactly where Hogg's was interrupted by his northern vacation.

116 On September 14, 1815 Shelley addressed a letter to an " A. B. Pereira," who the Julian editors suggest in a footnote (IX, 118) may be the Baptista of Peacock's account (*Memoirs,* II, 334). The guess is a reasonable one simply on internal evidence. It seems to me to be definitely confirmed by *Nomina Eorum Qui Gradum Medicinæ Doctoris in Academia Jacobi Sexti Scotorum Regis Quæ Edinburgi est Adepti Sunt,* etc. (Edinburgh, 1846). Here, on p. 240, we find: " Pereira, Joach. B. Brazil. De Erysipelate, 1815," and on p. 50: " Joach. Ber. Pereira, Braziliensis, De Erysipelate." The only other Pereira between 1800 and 1820 in this list or in the *Catalogue of Graduates in the Faculties of Arts, Divinity, and Law of the University of Edinburgh,* etc. (Edinburgh, 1858), is that of Ignazio Joseph A. Pereira, M.A., May 18, 1814 (*Catalogue of Graduates,* p. 218). Thus, in spite of inconsistencies in initials, Shelley's Brazilian medical student and his correspondent " A. B. Pereira " could have been no other than the Joach. B. Pereira who received his degree in 1815 and was later in London (as mentioned by Peacock) when Shelley addressed him as A. B. Pereira in 1815.

117 Peacock: *Memoirs,* II, 334–5.

118 Fourteen such poems, published and republished before 1823, are quoted in my *The Unextinguished Hearth* (1938).

119 Shelley to Hogg, November 26, 1813, Julian *Works,* IX, 81. This was probably for the interview he had expected to have with his father in November. But the interview was abandoned on account of Mr. Timothy Shelley's illness, and Shelley seems to have remained in Edinburgh.

120 Julian *Works,* IX, 82. The date is in another hand. The unidentified correspondent would appear to be a man with whom Shelley had already corresponded on financial matters, whose acquaintance was on a formal business basis, and who was associated with a " Mr. S." Possibly the letter was addressed to Hookham, who was in some way concerned in Shelley's recent sale of a post-obit to Mr. Starling.

121 Ingpen: *Shelley in England,* II, 636–7, quotes the coachmaker's account from the Shelley-Whitton papers. It was still unpaid in July 1823, when it amounted, with interest, to £20.

122 According to Godwin's journal, as quoted by Dowden (*Life,* I, 395), he had breakfast with Godwin on December 10th.

[123] Peacock: *Memoirs,* II, 335; Hogg, op. cit., II, 133. On March 16 Shelley had " been staying with Mrs. B[oinville] for the last month " (Shelley to Hogg, March 16, 1814, Julian *Works,* IX, 85).

[124] Dowden: *Life,* I, 391, note. Whatever letter Professor Dowden used as his authority appears to be no longer extant. See the letters of Girdlestone and Varney printed in Appendix III.

[125] Harriet to Catherine Nugent, October 11, [1813], Julian *Works,* IX, 78.

[126] Godwin's journal as quoted by Dowden: *Life,* I, 395; also Julian *Works,* IX, 83. See also note 25 above.

[127] Doubtful as any reader must feel about the precise time of most of the occurrences recollected by Hogg after so many years, the changes he noticed in Harriet can only have been noted between December 10 and about December 30. Hogg's order of narration places them after the return from Edinburgh. It could not have been before that time, because the removal to Bracknell occurred soon after Ianthe's birth and Hogg never called on the Shelleys at Bracknell before his own departure for Yorkshire, where he remained until shortly before the return of the Shelleys from Edinburgh. The Shelleys moved to Windsor about the beginning of the year, and Hogg was so busy during the spring that he saw little of Shelley. The narrative itself plainly indicates London. Hence it must refer to the last three weeks of December 1813.

[128] Hogg, op. cit., II, 128–9. Hogg evidently intended this account as a partial background for the account of Shelley's desertion of Harriet which he was not to be permitted to publish. His third volume, completed but not published, should have begun with Shelley's elopement with Mary. See Chapter v, note 21.

[129] See J. Mitford's memorandum of conversations with Thomas Hookham, Brit. Mus. Add. MSS. 32,574, folios 19–21, quoted in Peck: *Life,* II, 409–11.

[130] Hogg, op. cit., II, 132–3. Hogg does not endorse or condemn the surgeon's opinion.

[131] *The Elopement of Shelley and Mary,* etc., 11–14.

[132] Ingpen: *Shelley in England,* II, 412.

[133] Shelley to Timothy Shelley, March 13, 1814, Julian *Works,* IX, 84.

[134] Ingpen: *Shelley in England,* II, 412.

[135] Medwin: *Revised Life,* 121.

[136] Ingpen: *Shelley in England,* II, 413.

[137] Shelley to John Williams, [April 14] and May 14, 1814, Julian

Works, IX, 88, 89. See the letters of D. E. Varney in Appendix III.

¹³⁸ Mr. Ingpen (*Shelley in England*, II, 407) speaks of Mrs. Boin-ville's daughter as unmarried when Shelley met the Boinvilles, stat-ing she "afterwards became Mrs. Turner." I can find no date for the marriage. Professor Dowden speaks of her throughout as Mrs. Turner. She was Mrs. Turner in the letters written by Mrs. Godwin in the autumn of 1814, and according to a statement there quoted from Harriet (Dowden: *Life*, II, 543) she was Mrs. Turner during the course of Shelley's acquaintance with her.

¹³⁹ Hogg speaks of this young man both as "a youth . . . who had been educated abroad, in France" and as a "young French-man" (op. cit., II, 142). He might be Mrs. Boinville's son, Alfred, whose father was French and who may have been educated abroad. Alfred was acquainted with Shelley at this time.

¹⁴⁰ Hogg, ibid., II, 141–5. Hogg dates this visit (ibid., II, 138) as during the spring circuit. It occurred between March 11, when a letter of Mrs. Boinville to Hogg (ibid., II, 135) speaks of Mrs. Newton as in London, and April 18, when her second letter to Hogg (ibid., II, 145) refers to his visit as in the past. The first of these letters partly corroborates and considerably tones down the impres-sion Hogg gives of principles set forth in Mrs. Boinville's conversa-tion. One sentence: "A loving soul bears about within itself a living spring of affections, which keeps it fresh in spite of blights from evil things and evil men," etc., is a curious anticipation of the Italian sentence from Emilia Viviani's essay on True Love used by Shelley as a motto to *Epipsychidion* (1821): "L'anima amante si slancia fuori del creato, e si crea nel infinito un Mondo tutto per essa, diverso assai da questo oscuro e pauroso baratro." Shelley was with Mrs. Boinville when her letter was written.

¹⁴¹ Peacock: *Memoirs*, II, 324.

¹⁴² *A View of the Nervous Temperament*, etc., by Thomas Trotter, M.D. (London, 1806), 18, 92, 93, 175, 240–1 in the American ed. (Troy, N. Y., 1808). Shelley ordered this book December 24, 1812, and quoted from it in the notes to *Queen Mab*.

¹⁴³ Entry in Brooke's diary for March 27, 1899, in Lawrence Pearsall Jacks: *Life and Letters of Stopford Brooke* (New York, 1917), II, 506. Brooke heard the story from Lady Shelley, who had it from Peacock, and believed it.

¹⁴⁴ Shelley to Hogg, March 16, 1814, Julian *Works*, IX, 87.

¹⁴⁵ Ibid., IX, 85–6.

¹⁴⁶ Dowden (*Life*, I, 373), on the authority of Alfred Turner, her

son. It is uncertain whether this applies to Shelley's period of residence at Bracknell or at Windsor.

¹⁴⁷ Ingpen (*Shelley in England*, II, 422–3) prints from the Vicar General's records the "Allegations" of March 22 and 23, sworn to by Shelley and Mr. John Westbrook, also the record of the marriage (p. 424) from the register of Saint George, Hanover Square. Although this second marriage was prompted by the knowledge that the Scotch marriage was open to question because it was based on a false certification, the same question might have been raised about the English marriage, since Shelley swore that he was of age more than four months before his twenty-first birthday.

¹⁴⁸ In March Shelley was seeking a house in Bracknell (Hogg, op. cit., II, 134). Jane Clairmont speaks of Bracknell as the home of Harriet and Shelley when Shelley left the home of Mrs. Boinville (Dowden: *Life*, II, 549). Godwin speaks of Shelley's family in Bracknell in June (*The Elopement of Shelley and Mary*, 11).

¹⁴⁹ Mrs. Boinville to Hogg, April 18, 1814, Hogg, op. cit., II, 145.

¹⁵⁰ "Stanzas — April, 1814" — first published by Dowden from the Esdaile MSS.

¹⁵¹ See Mark Twain: "In Defense of Harriet Shelley," in *How to Tell a Story, and Other Essays* (New York, 1897). On the other hand, a letter from Hogg to Newton, seen by Richard Garnett in March 1905, seemed to suggest to him that Hogg did not believe Shelley's attachment to Cornelia serious (*Letters about Shelley*, 248–9).

¹⁵² Letters from Mrs. Godwin to Lady Mountcashell, August 7, 1814–April 7, 1815, given from inaccurate copies by Jane Clairmont, in an Appendix by Dowden: *Life*, II, 541–51. Mark Twain ("In Defense of Harriet Shelley") accused Dowden of suppression in not using these materials in his account of the elopement with Mary. Dowden's reasons were that Mrs. Godwin was an inaccurate and mendacious witness, which he proved by confronting various statements of hers with Godwin's journal and facts known from other sources. He takes no stock in Mrs. Godwin's testimony as to Shelley's love for Cornelia, because it is alleged of two different times, one of which was possible and the other contradictory. Nevertheless, an assertion may be quite false as to date and yet true in its essence. Dowden also observes that if Mr. Turner took his wife away, he let her return and receive Shelley's attentions in March and April — thus accepting for purposes of refutation the earlier date for the affair, which he had already shown to be unacceptable. He

does not consider that it may have been in May when Mr. Turner's alleged action took place. He does point out, however, that Mr. Turner was an early and friendly visitor after Shelley returned to London with Mary, which seems inconsistent with his alleged resentment. Dowden also shows that Mrs. Boinville nursed Shelley in London within about two months of the time she broke off his acquaintance, according to Jane Clairmont.

153 "To —— (Oh! There are spirits of the air)," Julian *Works*, I, 201. Mrs. Shelley states that this poem "was addressed in idea to Coleridge," but Dowden wonders whether it was not rather addressed in a despondent mood by Shelley to his own spirit.

154 Julian *Works*, III, 115.

155 The quotation is from Dowden (*Life*, I, 414), who repeats (*Life*, I, 415): "it seems certain that . . . she maintained an appearance of hardness." Though Shelley does urge Harriet, in the poem written to her in May, not to be unforgiving, she cannot on that basis be pronounced unforgiving except at the moment, and in Shelley's mind. There is no other evidence.

As for her alleged desertion of Shelley, Dowden (*Life*, I, 414) quotes Thornton Hunt's statement that Harriet left Shelley of her own accord and adds that she is next heard of in Bath in July, two months later, while Shelley remained in London, except for a brief interval of ten days, between the latter part of May and July. Professor Dowden does not refer to Peacock's ringing denial, from Harriet herself, that she "left Shelley of her own accord," though he quotes it in another connection, nor does he refer to Jane Clairmont's statement that Harriet remained for some time at Bracknell, which he gives only in an appendix (II, 549). He was probably unaware of Godwin's letter to John Taylor, which shows that Shelley's family was at Bracknell as late as the third week in June and that Shelley was anxious to join them there. Mr. Ingpen and Mr. Peck both follow Dowden in overlooking this evidence from Godwin's letter.

156 This is a plain inference from Godwin's statements in *The Elopement of Shelley and Mary*. It is corroborated by Mrs. Godwin's statement that "Mrs. Shelley remained greatly at home" and that shortly after Shelley declared his love for Mary (i.e., the last week in July 1814), Harriet came up "from Bracknell" to see the Godwins (Dowden: *Life*, II, 542, 543).

157 He called or dined at Godwin's on May 5, 6, 13, 23 [1814], and was not once there in April (Dowden: *Life*, II, 543). He dated letters from London on May 6 and 14. Again he seems to have been

in London from the latter part of May until June 8, except for an absence of ten days (Dowden: *Life*, I, 414, based presumably on Godwin's journal). When he went to London again on June 18, he would seem to have arrived from Bracknell (*The Elopement of Shelley and Mary*, p. 11). Shelley's last visit to Field Place, " in the early summer of 1814," can hardly have taken place at any time other than his ten days' absence from London ending on June 8.

[158] Harriet to Catherine Nugent, September 10, 1813, Julian *Works*, IX, 77.

[159] William Godwin to John Taylor, in *The Elopement of Shelley and Mary*, 10, 11.

[160] Mrs. Boinville to Hogg, March 14, 1814, Hogg, op. cit., II, 134.

[161] Shelley to Hogg, March 16, 1814, Julian *Works*, IX, 85 and 86.

[162] The charges made against Harriet may be briefly stated and answered:

1. She neglected her study and reading. The *responsibility* for this might be fixed on Shelley as easily as upon Harriet, but the *effect* probably did render the marriage less satisfactory than formerly.

2. She laughed at some of the absurdities of Bracknell with Peacock. This is not the same as to say that she consistently made fun of Shelley's friends. Both Peacock and Hogg laughed, too, without incurring resentment, and Shelley on one occasion laughed with Hogg.

3. She forced Shelley to buy a carriage and plate when he could not afford it. It is not shown that Shelley did this against his will. If he did, Harriet's extravagance was not unnatural and it was less than his own in other ways. Moreover, the carriage would appear to have been bought in anticipation of the Edinburgh journey — Shelley's extravagance, if anyone's.

4. She declined to suckle her own infant. True, and Shelley vehemently disapproved. But she can hardly be condemned without hearing her reasons, which are not forthcoming.

5. She obtruded on Shelley a sister that he hated. Eliza withdrew after the hatred became violent.

6. She displayed a keen interest in shops, hats, and new clothes. True; most women after recovery from childbirth need new hats and new clothes, and there is no evidence that Shelley objected. Also, most women like to visit shops in the two weeks preceding Christmas, as Harriet did.

7. She is supposed to have become an intemperate drinker. This

669

is based upon a sneer of Hogg's, equivocal in itself, but supported
by Hogg's supposed conversation with unnamed persons. It can
hardly be regarded as established, on such a basis.

8. She was unfaithful to Shelley. This charge will be discussed
later. Shelley could never have entertained it while he was seeking
a reconciliation. Most of the foregoing charges are discussed and
scornfully dismissed in Mark Twain's " In Defense of Harriet Shelley."

[163] See note 156.

[164] Captain Kennedy's recollections, as quoted by Hogg, op. cit.,
II, 152–4.

Chapter XII

GENERAL SOURCES

Shelley's letters as in Julian *Works*, IX, Gordon's *Shelley Letters* (both previously cited) and Leslie Hotson's " Shelley's Lost
Letters to Harriet," first published in the *Atlantic Monthly* for
January and February 1930; the journal of Shelley and Mary
as privately printed in *Shelley and Mary* (see note 44 below);
the MS. journal of Claire Clairmont; the letters of Mrs. William
Godwin as published in Dowden's life of Shelley; William God-
win's letter to John Taylor as published in H. B. Forman's *The
Elopement of Shelley and Mary* (privately printed for W. K.
Bixby in 1911); C. K. Paul's *William Godwin, His Friends and
Contemporaries*, 2 vols., London, 1876; Mrs. Julian Marshall's
Life and Letters of Mary Wollstonecraft Shelley, 2 vols., Lon-
don, 1889; and Peacock's *Memoirs* as previously cited.

In the collection of Mr. Carl Pforzheimer is a variant version
of a part of Claire Clairmont's journal, in sixteen manuscript
pages covering the dates August 14–22, 1814. It is marked
" Copy " and is supposedly in the hand of Paola Clairmont,
Claire's niece. From internal evidence I conclude that it was
amplified from the original journal a few years after 1814 and
copied years later. This variant makes no material addition to

the earlier journal and offers no inconsistencies with it; but it is in many of the incidents (particularly of conversation) livelier and more detailed. It was used by Professor Peck in his biography (I, 384), but was subsequently mislaid and was rediscovered too late for its use in the present work.

NOTES AND REFERENCES

[1] Mary Wollstonecraft Godwin was born August 30, 1797, four days before the death of her mother. Godwin's second marriage, to Mrs. Clairmont, in 1801, was primarily to provide a mother for Mary and her half-sister, Fanny Imlay. In their early childhood the second Mrs. Godwin seemed a satisfactory stepmother, but as the girls approached maturity her characteristic failings made home often uncomfortable. In June 1812 Mary was sent to Scotland for the improvement of her health, as a visitor in the home of Godwin's friend William Baxter, of Dundee. One of Mr. Baxter's daughters, Isabel, was for years her closest friend; another, Christian, accompanied her on her return to London. It was on November 11, 1812, the day after her return, that Mary met Shelley and Harriet at her father's dinner table. On June 3, 1813 Mary returned to Dundee for a ten months' visit. When Hogg first saw her, on June 8, 1814, she still wore a tartan smock, though she had been in London since March 30.

A rather full account of the Baxter family, quoting the journal of "Christie" Baxter, may be found in the Dundee *Advertiser* for July 8, 1922.

[2] C. Kegan Paul, op. cit., II, 214.

[3] James Stuart: *Reminiscences* (privately printed, London, 1911), 10.

[4] Mrs. Julian Marshall, op. cit., I, 29.

[5] This is Mrs. Godwin's statement to Lady Mountcashell (Dowden: *L* II, 542–3), which Dowden shows to be very inaccurate in details of time and place. I have therefore accepted the important facts of Mrs. Godwin's impressions, which Dowden does not challenge, and have fitted them to establish details of time and place.

[6] Shelley to Hogg, October 5, 1814, Gordon: *Shelley Letters*, galley proofs. The "speedily" and "so long" of the first and last sentences seem to contradict each other, but the suddenness of

Shelley's passion as described by Godwin in the letter next quoted seems to establish the "speedily" and suggest that the "so long" refers to the comparative length of time during which Shelley was in love with Mary without realizing it.

[7] Julian *Works*, III, 117.

[8] William Godwin to John Taylor, August 27, 1814, reprinted with a commentary by H. Buxton Forman as *The Elopement of Shelley and Mary*, 11.

[9] Ingpen: *Shelley in England*, II, 434–5.

[10] Julian, *Works*, IX, 91, dated by the editors July 6 or 7, 1814. This letter demands an interpretative comment that should have been obvious from its first printing. No estranged couple corresponds so frequently that a hiatus of four days causes serious alarm. No wife who has deserted her husband or regards him coldly is so upset in such conditions as Harriet was. In addition, the letter confirms Godwin's statements as to the time and the suddenness of Shelley's infatuation for Mary, and also Godwin's evidence of the devotion of Shelley to his wife and child up to the week beginning June 26. It seems unfortunate that Professor Dowden (*Life*, I, 424) regards this letter only as evidence that Harriet "would now gladly have retraced her steps" — the "steps" themselves being purely a matter of inference.

[11] Harriet to Catherine Nugent, November 20, [1814], Julian *Works*, X, 420. The phrase "desperately in love" is Mrs. Godwin's quotation from Harriet (Dowden: *Life*, II, 543). Other details are plain inferences from Shelley's letter to Harriet after the interview. Harriet's view remained traditional in her family. "You know, in this family we don't think much of Mary," Shelley's grandson, Mr. Esdaile, informed Elinor Wylie ("Shelley's Grandson and Some Others," *Bookman*, New York, LVII, 611–12, August 1923). It will be noted that Harriet's imputation of the original responsibility to Mary is supported by Shelley's letter to Hogg on October 5, 1814, previously quoted, and possibly by Shelley's poem to Mary.

[12] Leslie Hotson: "Shelley's Lost Letters to Harriet," *Atlantic Monthly*, CXLV, 129 (January 1930), undated. But since "tomorrow at 12" probably refers to the joint interview with the Godwins on the 15th, and since Harriet arrived on the 14th and saw Shelley at once, this letter should obviously be dated July 14, 1814.

This letter corroborates Harriet's statement to Catherine Nugent that Mary appealed to Shelley's sympathies and threatened suicide. It completely confounds Shelley's statement to Mary within the next ten days that Harriet had already been guilty of adultery, and it shows that at a time Shelley has been supposed to have been estranged from Harriet he " derided . . . short-sighted prophecies " that such a thing could ever happen.

[13] Godwin's journal, as quoted by Kegan Paul, op. cit., II, 216. Godwin's previously cited letter to John Taylor (*Elopement of Shelley and Mary*, 15) shows that he wrote at least two letters to Shelley, at uncertain dates between July 15 and July 28.

[14] Dowden: *Life*, II, 543–4. Professor Dowden relegated to an appendix (without referring the reader to it in the course of his chapter) all the letters of Mrs. Godwin to Lady Mountcashell and all of Jane Clairmont's comments on them, except for one passage on Harriet's alleged affair with Major Ryan — the only damaging allegation about Harriet — which he quotes in the chapter on the elopement (I, 424), without reference to the full context printed in the appendix (II, 541 ff.). This seems inconsistent with his general distrust of Mrs. Godwin. Neither Mrs. Godwin nor Jane is an unimpeachable witness. But in the passage I have just quoted they support each other at different times. The account of Harriet's unaccompanied visit to the Godwins is far too circumstantial to be dismissed by proving from Godwin's journal that Shelley and Harriet visited the Godwins together. The two statements are not mutually exclusive. Godwin's journal shows that he visited the Shelleys both individually and together. Mrs. Godwin's story, in this episode at least, seems convincing in itself and has external support.

[15] Harriet Shelley to Catherine Nugent, November 20, [1814], Julian *Works*, X, 420. By this time Harriet was convinced that the original corrupter of Shelley's character was William Godwin: " Mr. Shelley has become profligate and sensual, owing entirely to Godwin's *Political Justice*."

[16] Mrs. Godwin is probably wrong in calling it a week. See note 23, below.

[17] Kegan Paul, op. cit., II, 216.

[18] Mrs. Godwin to Lady Mountcashell, Dowden: *Life*, II, 544.

[19] Again Mrs. Godwin is obviously wrong in speaking of it as a week; see note 23, below.

[20] C. Kegan Paul (op. cit., II, 215) remarks meaningly: " Jane Clairmont's influence was neither then, nor at any other time, used, or likely to be used, judiciously." Whether he bases this statement on impressions from Godwin's journal or on Lady Shelley's later opinion (known to be quite unfavourable to Jane) is not clear.

Jane told her mother that she did not know the plans to elope on July 28.

[21] Peacock: *Memoirs*, II, 336. Peacock does not date the episode, which cannot have happened after the 28th of July or hardly before the 14th. It seems to come most naturally before Shelley's attempted suicide.

Peacock's account of Shelley's health and state of mind at this time is supported by Thomas Hookham. A letter from Robert Browning to Professor Dowden (printed in T. J. Wise: *A Shelley Library*, 1924, p. 7) quotes Hookham as saying about 1858 that just before the elopement Shelley was suffering from an intense bodily pain, from which he "would roll himself suddenly on the ground, pulling the sofa-cushions upon him," and that he constantly went about with a bottle of laudanum in his hand. Elsewhere (*Letters about Shelley*, ed. R. S. Garnett, London, 1917, p. 28) Hookham is said to have told Browning that Shelley was practically insane at this time.

[22] Shelley to Elizabeth Hitchener, October [15?], 1811, Julian *Works*, VIII, 157.

[23] Dowden: *Life*, II, 545. Again I see no reason for doubting the substantial verity of Mrs. Godwin's account, though her chronology is shown to be wrong. She records that Godwin visited Shelley on July 27, three weeks after Shelley took the laudanum, upon which Professor Dowden remarks that this would date the poisoning on July 6, and that Godwin's journal shows Shelley dining with the Godwins on July 6 and busy about London until the 18th. This merely shows the inaccuracy of one detail of Mrs. Godwin's narrative, which is consistent and convincing for the rest of this episode. It is obvious, however, that Mrs. Godwin is wrong in speaking of a week as elapsing between Harriet's call and Shelley's proposal of suicide to Mary, and another week after that before Shelley's attempted suicide. Harriet's call is definitely fixed by Godwin's journal as July 15. Two weeks thereafter would be the 29th. This would place Shelley's attempted suicide, with an ensuing convalescence of more than a week, just one day after he eloped with Mary. Trelawny, in his old age, more than once spoke to W. M. Rossetti about Shelley's attempted suicide (Rossetti to Garnett, February 25, 1872, in *Letters about Shelley*, 51).

[24] Mrs. Godwin's statement, Dowden: *Life*, II, 545–6.

[25] Jane Clairmont's note on Mrs. Godwin's letters to Lady Mountcashell, ibid., I, 424–5.

[26] The Major Ryan of Shelley's charges against Harriet can be

practically identified with Brevet-Major Matthew Ryan, of the 30th Foot Regiment. It is first necessary, however, to validate the fact of Shelley's charges, since they occur in a body of testimony that Professor Dowden has treated as generally dubious, though he accepts and uses this particular story. That Shelley actually made the charge as related by Jane Clairmont is established by four facts: (1) Jane could not have invented the name, for she says it was unknown in her family, and thus indicates her own doubt of Shelley's truth; (2) unknown to Jane, Harriet's correspondence of the previous year does mention a Mr. Ryan as an Irishman on fairly intimate terms with the Shelleys; (3) a "Ryan" is mentioned in Mary Shelley's journal of January 4 and 6, 1815, as having some unspecified dealings with Shelley; and (4) Charles Clairmont's letter of January 12, 1816 (quoted in Appendix III) mentions Harriet as associating ("I do not at all mean what the world calls criminally") with an "Irish adventurer whom she commissioned to take all possible legal advantage of Shelley," at a time when she knew him to be in severe financial difficulties. Since the Ryan of Mary's journal called at a time of financial difficulty, as Charles Clairmont's "Irish adventurer" did, they are probably the same; and since the "Irish adventurer" is Harriet's friend and her letters of May 21 and June 22 mention an Irish friend named Ryan, the two Ryans are probably identical with each other and with the "Major Ryan" of Shelley's false charges against Harriet in July 1814.

There are only two Ryans in the British *Army Lists* from 1813 to 1817. Both were brevet-majors. Richard Ryan, brevet-major since January 1, 1812, was in 1813 by regimental rank a captain in the 93rd Foot. Since he was presumably in active service at that time, Harriet should have used his military title when referring to him. In any case, however, he could not have been the Ryan mentioned in January 1815, for he was severely wounded at New Orleans on January 8, 1815, two days after "Ryan" is mentioned by Mary as in London.

Matthew Ryan, on the other hand, seems not to have been in active service in 1813, and the first mention of his army rank as major seems to be on June 4, 1813. Thus Harriet may have known him at first only as "Mr.," while Shelley in July 1814 could properly refer to him as "Major," though his regimental rank at that time was that of captain in the 30th Foot. There is no proof that he was Irish, but his name later occurs in both English and Irish half-pay lists. The date of his appointment to the 30th Foot, with a regimental rank

of captain, was June 4, 1813, though he seems not to have joined
his regiment until May 26, 1814. The *Army List* for 1814 mentions
him as on half-pay from the 85th Foot. If we now turn to the " Mr.
Ryan " of Harriet's letters we find that he was a friend of the
Shelleys' friends John Lawless and Catherine Nugent, both Irish,
that he had come to London from Dublin about the middle of May
1813, and that in June, soon after the Major Ryan of the *Army Lists*
received his appointment to regimental duty, Harriet's Mr. Ryan
was momentarily expecting to quit London.

In 1814 and probably earlier the 85th Foot contained a Captain
Henry Shelley, which may possibly explain the first acquaintance
of the Shelleys with Ryan.

Thus Harriet's " Mr. Ryan," Shelley's and Jane's " Major Ryan,"
Mary's " Ryan," and Charles Clairmont's unnamed " Irish adven-
turer " seem to coalesce in the person of Brevet-Major Matthew
Ryan, of the 30th Foot Regiment.

[27] See his letter to Francis Place, quoted in Appendix III.

[28] But he later believed a similar story communicated to him by
Godwin in January 1817. " I learnt just now from Godwin that he
has evidence that Harriet was unfaithful to me *four months* before
I left England with you," Shelley wrote Mary on January 11 (Julian
Works, IX, 216). He indicated a desire to establish the fact in his
chancery case. Godwin's evidence may or may not have been received by Shelley; on May 12 Godwin wrote Mr. William T. Baxter
only that he had been convinced of Harriet's guilt " from an unquestionable authority " — which proves only that Godwin was convinced
of what he wished to believe. Again, on August 17, 1820 (ibid., X,
204) Shelley wrote to Southey: " If you were my friend I could tell
you a history that would make you open your eyes," etc. — but
neither Shelley nor Godwin nor Godwin's " unquestionable authority " ever told any such story where it could be subjected to examination. Under these conditions it might have been better for a biographer not to mention the story.

Dr. Richard Garnett, who later believed that Shelley's supposed
alienation from Harriet was due to intemperance on Harriet's part,
advised Professor Dowden against saying anything about either infidelity or intemperance (*Letters about Shelley*, 125). But Professor Dowden used the story of infidelity, not to endorse it, but to
show that Shelley's belief in it justified Shelley's conduct to himself. Shelley's genuine belief in it in 1814 is highly doubtful, but
there is no uncertainty about the beliefs of all who knew Harriet.

Trelawny, who resented Lady Shelley's statements derogatory to Harriet's reputation (*Letters of Edward John Trelawny*, ed. H. B. Forman, London and New York, 1910, p. 251), questioned Hookham, Hogg, Peacock, and " one of the Godwins " and was assured by all that " Harriet was perfectly innocent of all offence." His letter cited above was to Jane Clairmont and assumes her concurrence in the same belief. Thornton Hunt wrote in the *Atlantic Monthly* for February 1863 (XI, 197): " There is not a trace of evidence or a whisper of scandal against her before her voluntary departure from Shelley." If Mary Shelley believed the story later she was careful to say nothing to support it; in fact, she later claimed that Shelley's conduct was to be justified on other grounds. Hookham and Peacock have also recorded their opinions elsewhere than in Trelawny's report; see Peck: *Life*, II, 411, and Peacock: *Memoirs*, as quoted in this chapter. No biographer since Dowden has credited the idea.

Mary Shelley told Lady Shelley, who later told Richard Garnett, that Hogg alone knew the reason for the " separation " (*Letters about Shelley*, 125). Lady Shelley believed, as shown by an appendix she added to several copies of *Shelley and Mary*, that the real causes for the " separation " were to be found in the Edinburgh visit and that Peacock was at the bottom of them. Dr. Garnett, in the letter cited, advised Dowden against taking this view in his biography and Dowden accepted his advice. Garnett wrote Dowden in 1884 (*Letters about Shelley*, 104) that he often thought the " separation " may have been due to ill-advised efforts on Harriet's part to pique Shelley into a reconciliation — which rather puts the cart before the horse. Dowden's letters at the time show that he was determined to accept no dictated opinions and that he anticipated more trouble than he actually encountered from Sir Percy and Lady Shelley over his treatment of Harriet and of Godwin (ibid., 113–19). I was informed by Mr. T. J. Wise, however, who had a number of Professor Dowden's letters, that Professor Dowden was at one time tempted to discontinue his biography as a result of the interference of the Shelley family.

[29] Shelley to Harriet, [July 14], 1814, *Atlantic Monthly*, CXLV, 129 (January 1930).

[30] How much money Shelley had at this time, and what became of it, are a mystery apparently incapable of solution. According to Godwin, Shelley had received half the income from the post-obit sale of July 6, something over £1,100. If this is true, Shelley must

have intended at the time to invest most of it in the acquisition of a place in Wales (probably his former scheme of acquiring Nant-gwillt). He did not do so, however. Shelley's debts at the time were probably sufficient to absorb most of the sum, if applied to that purpose, but there is every indication that it was not so applied. Less than two months later, when Shelley returned from France, he was hounded by creditors and forced to go into hiding. Shelley carried so little money with him to France that on August 4 he was forced to sell his watch and chain, and on his return he found that the bank balance had already been exhausted by Harriet. Obviously he had deposited only a moderate sum after the post-obit sale of July 6. What, then, became of the £1,100?

One answer is that Godwin really received all the proceeds of the post-obit and lied to his correspondent. According to Francis Place's opinion of his business dealings, this would have been quite characteristic. Harriet Shelley's letter of November 20, 1814 to Catherine Nugent speaks of the post-obit as if it were entirely for Godwin's benefit. In that case, however, Shelley appears to have had *too much* money on hand. Moreover, it was usual with Shelley when raising money for Godwin's benefit to use some of it for his own needs. And if Godwin lied, it was a lie already uttered long in advance, for he refers to the divison of the sum as something previously understood by Taylor. If Shelley did not expect to use some of the money, how could he have planned to acquire a place in Wales? My belief is that Godwin did not lie, and that Shelley must have used a large part of his £1,100 for a purpose of which no trace now remains. The £1,200 which Shelley was soon afterwards trying to raise for Godwin (see Chapter xiii, note 60) may very well have been the other half of the post-obit sale that Godwin failed to receive in 1814.

[31] Shelley's journal, July 28, *Shelley and Mary*, I, 1. According to Jane Clairmont's account (Dowden: *Life*, II, 547) Mary waked her at four for an early walk. They met Shelley with the chaise at the corner of Hatton Gardens and Jane was urged to go with them to France. She wished to return home, but Mary entreated her and Shelley pushed her into the coach — after which they said not a word to her.

[32] Godwin's journal (Marshall, op. cit., I, 70 and 71) and his letter (*Elopement of Shelley and Mary*, 12). It was after one o'clock, according to Mrs. Godwin (Dowden: *Life*, II, 545), that the destination of the fugitives was ascertained.

³³ *Shelley and Mary,* I, 2. The preceding paragraphs of my text, except where noted, are paraphrased from Shelley's account in *Shelley and Mary.* Dowden (*Life,* I, 442–3) quotes entire the entries for July 29 and 30, noting two slight variations in Shelley's and Mary's *History of a Six Weeks' Tour* (1817), which is based on this journal.

³⁴ *The Elopement of Shelley and Mary,* 12–13. This indicates Godwin's agreement with Mr. Timothy Shelley's opinion that Shelley was actually dangerous when violently aroused.

³⁵ Peacock: *Memoirs,* II, 335–6. In her novel *Lodore* (1835), Mary Shelley accepted, at least for fictional purposes, the theory that Eliza was responsible for the ruin of Shelley's first marriage. Lady Santerre, obviously based mainly on Eliza, insists on preserving her dominion over the mind of her daughter after she has married Lodore. By various devices, all of which have been charged against Eliza Westbrook, she produces an alienation of affections followed by desertion. The correspondence is much too sustained and exact to be unintentional. The same novel closely parallels both Shelley's distress in London after his return from the Continent and the story of Emilia Viviani. For a convenient summary, see Dowden: *Life,* I, 436–8.

³⁶ Peacock: *Memoirs,* II, 337.

³⁷ When Shelley and Mary returned from France, Mrs. Boinville's son, Alfred, expressed the opinion that Shelley had been " playing a German tragedy," to which Shelley replied: " Very severe, but very true." Dowden (*Life,* I, 467, note) considered this an allusion to Goethe's *Stella.* But since the anecdote was not recorded till 1872, and Shelley was probably unacquainted with Goethe's *Stella,* it may possibly refer to *Agathon,* with " tragedy " where " novel " was meant originally.

³⁸ Peacock: *Memoirs,* II, 336. Peacock adds that Shelley told another friend [Hogg? Hookham?] that he thought this nobility of Harriet's would induce her to consent to his union with Mary.

³⁹ Ibid., II, 338.

⁴⁰ Shelley to Harriet, October 3 [?], 1814, *Atlantic Monthly,* CXLV, 169 (February 1930).

⁴¹ " Your thoughts alone can awaken mine to energy. . . . My understanding becomes undisciplined without you. I believe I must become in Mary's hands what Harriet was in mine." Shelley to Mary [October 28, 1814], Julian *Works,* IX, 103. See also IX, 102.

⁴² Probably Shelley should have said 26 June. It was on Sunday,

June 26, according to Godwin (as previously quoted), that Shelley first realized his love for Mary. Godwin was evidently repeating what Shelley had told him on July 6. Sunday fell on the 26th, not the 27th. Thus, within a margin of one day, the accuracy of Godwin's account of the elopement seems to be confirmed by Shelley.

[43] "Mary looked over with me the papers contained in her box. . . . She promised that I should be permitted to read and study these productions of her mind that preceded our intercourse. I shall claim this promise at Uri" (Journal for August 2, 1814, in *Shelley and Mary*, I, 3).

[44] This journal was begun by Shelley and was continued, with several breaks, until after Shelley's death, but after the first few days most of the entries were made by Mary. It was from this journal that Mary gathered the materials of *A History of a Six Weeks' Tour through a Part of France, Switzerland, Germany and Holland* (1817). She used it as an *aide-mémoire* in the biographical notes she attached to the 1839 edition of Shelley's poems. Except for Shelley's letters, it is the most important source of information about Shelley. Professor Dowden and Mrs. Marshall had the use of it in writing their biographies of Shelley and Mary respectively, working mainly from copies printed in *Shelley and Mary* in 1882 by Lady Shelley. Thereafter it was not available to scholars until 1922. Until the present no detailed biography of Shelley since Dowden's has been based upon it except indirectly. The present volume draws its quotations from Professor Dowden's copy, long owned by Mr. T. J. Wise, and now in the British Museum.

In 1882, Lady Jane Shelley printed twelve copies of a four-volume book which she called *Shelley and Mary* and which included, besides the journal, numerous letters to, from, and about Shelley. The original manuscripts of many of the letters are in the Bodleian Library, but the manuscript of the journal disappeared while still in Lady Shelley's possession. It has recently been located, and though not generally available, it was used by Miss R. Glynn Grylls in her life of Mary Shelley (London, 1938). It is impossible for me to say whether various gaps in the printed journal are due to Lady Shelley or to the original MS. A limited examination kindly made for me by Miss Grylls suggests that though Lady Shelley handled the MS. with considerable freedom or carelessness, the principal omissions occur also in the MS. When Professor Dowden received his copy of *Shelley and Mary* the original MS. of the journal was still with Lady Shelley. On a visit to Boscombe Manor he made the discovery "that

Shelley and Mary, wherever I looked, is a far from accurate rendering of the MSS. and that a careful collation will be necessary" (*Letters about Shelley*, 145). The printed *Shelley and Mary* is fully described by Mr. T. J. Wise in his *A Shelley Library* (privately printed,
London, 1924), and the manuscript journal by Miss Grylls (*Mary
Shelley*, 1938, pp. 269–75).

Mary Shelley's anonymous *History of a Six Weeks' Tour* was altered from the original account by the omission of some of the purely
personal matter and the addition of descriptive details, but in other
matters its occasional variations are insignificant. For a few slight
details I have drawn on this rather than the earlier account.

Jane Clairmont also kept detailed journals at different periods of
her life. Her journal for the period of the "Six Weeks' Tour" begins
(in Mr. Wise's MS.) August 14 and ends November 9, 1814. Jane's
journals have never been printed. They were used in MS. by Professor Dowden only and until recently (except for a portion owned
by Mr. Carl Pforzheimer) were in the possession of the late Mr. T. J.
Wise, who generously allowed me to use both *Shelley and Mary*
and Jane's journals in preparing this biography. Both are now in the
British Museum.

⁴⁵ *Shelley and Mary* has a hiatus for August 15 and 16, which is
supplied from Jane's journal. The hiatus does not occur in *A History
of a Six Weeks' Tour*. With the place-names in this chapter I have
followed the contemporary spellings of my sources.

⁴⁶ *The Fortunes of Perkin Warbeck* (1830), II, 300–2. The passage is quoted, condensed, in Peck: *Life*, I, 381, with a mistaken
reference to Vol. III.

⁴⁷ Mary described a valley in the foothills near Noe with a feeling
that was evidently so near to Shelley's own that a fine descriptive
passage in *Prometheus Unbound*, five years later, seems to be a
definite memory of Mary's account:

"From the summit of one of the hills we see the whole expanse
of the valley filled with a white undulating mist over which the
piny hills pierced like islands. The sun had just risen, and a ray
of the red light lay on the waves of this fluctuating vapour. To the
west, opposite the sun, it seemed driven by the light against the
rock in immense masses of foaming cloud until it becomes lost in
the distance, mixing its tints with the fleecy sky." (Quoted from
the journal, August 18, 1814, from which it was reprinted with
slight verbal alterations in *A History of a Six Weeks' Tour*.)

Cf. *Prometheus Unbound*, II, iii, 17–27 and 43–50. The parallel was first pointed out by Charles I. Elton: *An Account of Shelley's Visit to France, Switzerland and Savoy, 1814–1816* (London, 1894), pp. 30–1. Peck (*Life*, I, 382–4) reprints the passages in parallel columns.

[48] *Shelley and Mary*, I, 13, Friday, August 19. Reprinted with slight changes in *A History of a Six Weeks' Tour*.

[49] Shelley to Harriet, August 13, 1814, Julian *Works*, IX, 95.

[50] The Assassins are presented as a Christian sect who fled from Jerusalem as it was being invested by the Romans and established a community of their own in a secluded " happy valley " of Mount Lebanon. Here for four centuries they developed an ideal Shelleyan religion, free from the contaminations of Rome. Indifferent to the world's opinion, they believed in the pure joy of existence; " to love, to be beloved, suddenly became an insatiable famine " to them. The benignant Spirit they had formerly worshipped they now identified with " the delight that is bred among the solitary rocks and has its dwelling alike in the changing colours of the clouds and the inmost recesses of the caverns." An Assassin would certainly be misunderstood by the rest of the world, Shelley explained:

> . . . No Assassin would submissively temporize with vice. . . . His path through the wilderness of civilised society would be marked with the blood of the oppressor and the ruiner.

Together with the preceding sentences, this passage reads very much like Shelley's view of himself.

Into the happy valley of the Assassins is introduced a stranger. Desperately wounded, he is found by a young man as a serpent and vulture are waiting for his death. Somewhat like the old alchemist in Godwin's *St. Leon*, the stranger accompanies the young man home, where he observes his children playing happily with a pet snake. Here the narrative ends, having lasted just long enough to show the germinal materials of one of Shelley's most significant images, the eternal conflict of good and evil as a struggle between a snake and a vulture. (See *Laon and Cythna*, I, 280–306.) The Wandering Jew, who reappears in *The Assassins*, has undergone a partial change from his earlier character as a symbol of celestial tyranny and vengeance and is half-way metamorphosed into a benevolent Promethean champion.

Joseph von Hammer's *Geschichte der Assassinen* was not translated into English until 1835, and Shelley's historical knowledge con-

cerning them was limited to a few scraps in Tacitus and Gibbon —
hence their very faint connection, in Shelley's account, with historical
truth. His fragment shows the influence of Tacitus, whose account of
the fall of Jerusalem he was reading the day before he began the
novel. The happy valley seems to owe its physical traits to the Alpine valley before Shelley's eyes, and its other traits to the ideal city-
state of Tarentum, as described in Wieland's *Agathon,* which Shelley
had read a few months before. Possibly it also owes something to
the happy valley in Dr. Johnson's *Rasselas.*

51 *A History of a Six Weeks' Tour,* August 25, 1814.

52 Ibid. Mary's published account gives both the inconvenience
of the stove and the lack of funds as reasons for departure.

53 Ibid., August 29, 1814.

54 Ibid., August 28, 1814. It may be noted as odd that neither
contemporary account mentions this, the most exciting incident of
the journey. Either it seemed at the moment imprudent to record
such an event, or it never occurred.

55 *Shelley and Mary,* I, 16, August 30, 1814.

56 Thursday, August 18, in Claire's later revision of her journal, as
quoted by Dowden (*Life,* I, 453). The passage does not occur in
her original journal.

57 Dowden: *Life,* II, 545. Mrs. Godwin gives this as Shelley's
statement to Mr. Marshall at Calais. Mr. Marshall did not follow
Shelley to Calais, and Shelley did not speak to Mrs. Godwin there;
still I cannot dismiss the utterance as pure invention, as Dowden
does. The opinion attributed to him by Mrs. Godwin is precisely the
one Shelley held. I suggest the statement was made by Shelley to
Jane and repeated by her to Mrs. Godwin at Calais.

58 Dowden: *Life,* II, 547.

59 The distractions of the ensuing months offered Shelley no
further opportunity to continue it, but a note in the journal for
April 8, 1815 seems to show that even then he did not regard it as
permanently abandoned.

60 Preface to *A History of a Six Weeks' Tour* (1817) .

Chapter XIII

GENERAL SOURCES

Journal of Mary and Shelley in *Shelley and Mary*; MS. journal of Jane (Claire) Clairmont; letters of Shelley in *Julian Works*, Vol. IX, in the *Atlantic Monthly* for January and February 1930, and in George Stuart Gordon's *Shelley Letters*; and letters of Mrs. Godwin in Dowden's *Life*, Vol. II — all as previously cited.

NOTES AND REFERENCES

[1] Apparently friends of the Godwins and Shelleys, about whom I have no information. Mentioned only in Jane's account.

[2] Dowden (*Life*, I, 464) gives Jane as authority for the statement that Harriet gave Shelley £20 and added the reproaches of an injured wife. He appears to be referring to Jane's journal, yet I do not find the statement there or elsewhere.

[3] Probably his own clothes, left at Hookham's. In J. Mitford's memorandum of a conversation with Hookham about the Shelleys, Hookham is quoted as saying that Shelley often stayed at his house in Bond Street when coming in from the country. The document is quoted by Peck (*Life*, II, 409-11). But Harriet also had some of Shelley's clothes and books and may have supplied him on this occasion.

[4] Most of the entries are by Mary. Wherever quoted in this book, entries are to be presumed to be by her unless designated as by Shelley.

[5] I quote Jane's journal rather than Mary's because it is fuller and more detailed, and because Professor Dowden has already quoted large sections of Mary's. Sections in parentheses are my additions by collation with Mary's journal.

[6] A friend of the Godwins to whom Jane had written on the 14th.

[7] From *The Excursion,* Book I.

[8] The bond-broker through whom Shelley expected to auction a post-obit.

[9] Shelley's solicitor, to whom Harriet had appealed. See Shelley's letter to her dated September 26, 1814, *Atlantic Monthly*, CXLV, 166 (February 1930).

[10] A lawyer with whom Shelley dealt.

[11] First printed by Professor Leslie Hotson: "Shelley's Lost Letters to Harriet," *Atlantic Monthly*, CXLV, 133 (January 1930).

[12] According to Robert Browning, who apparently was so informed by Thomas Hookham; quoted in *Letters about Shelley*, 28.

[13] Shelley to Harriet, October 12, 1814, *Atlantic Monthly*, CXLV, 171 (February 1930).

[14] This statement may be hazarded on the basis of Mrs. Newton's letter to Hogg referring to Harriet as "the lady whose welfare must be so important in your estimation" (Hogg: *Life*, II, 115).

[15] Shelley described this interview to both Hogg and Peacock. The former recorded only the direct quotation (*Life*, I, 246). The latter (*Life*, II, 337) — assuming the two interviews to be the same — added the detail of Mary Wollstonecraft's portrait. I accept Peacock's assumption. See Chapter xiv, note 30.

[16] Shelley to Hogg, October 5, 1814 (referred to in Mary's journal under October 4), Gordon, op. cit.

[17] According to Dowden (*Life*, I, 467, note), the Newtons appear to have moved away from London in 1814. There is no evidence that they exchanged any letters with Shelley, but Harriet appears to have maintained her acquaintance with them. A letter of hers to John Frank Newton on his wife's illness, dated June 5, 1816, is printed in Julian *Works*, X, 422.

[18] Shelley described Peacock to Hogg, in his letter of November 26, 1813, in somewhat tepid terms. To Harriet, in his letter from Troyes, he had called Peacock "cold." On October 14 Shelley wrote in his journal: "I take some interest in this man, but no possible conduct of his could disturb my tranquillity." Mrs. Newton distrusted him as an associate of Shelley (Hogg, op. cit., II, 115–16); Hogg was for many years his friend, but in the end also appears to have distrusted him; Trelawny and Thornton Hunt both spoke of him as a selfish exploiter of Shelley's friendship.

[19] At this point Mrs. Boinville passes out of Shelley's life, except to act once as his messenger to Eliza Westbrook in December 1816. Shelley expressed passing kindly reminiscences of her in letters

from Italy (Julian *Works,* X, 45, 65, 73, 160, 249). He is said to have written to her when he thought he might return to England from Italy. This letter Professor Dowden (*Life,* I, 379) says Mrs. Boinville answered by saying that on account of some of his opinions she could not entertain him at her house. Shelley's opinions were never more radical than in *Queen Mab,* of which Mrs. Boinville cherished a copy (Dowden: *Life,* II, 550), so it is more likely to have been Shelley's conduct than his opinions that she objected to. According to Dowden (*Life,* I, 379) Mrs. Boinville was living at Sidmouth shortly before Shelley's death. She appears briefly in the last chapters of Thomas Constable's *Memoir of the Reverend Charles Chastel de Boinville* (London, 1880), upon whose first chapter Dowden's sketch of her is based. Both she and her daughter Cornelia are described in her grandson's journal and letters as truly noble souls. Mrs. Boinville lived in Paris from 1833 (and possibly before) until her death on March 1, 1847. Cornelia was apparently living with her. Cornelia died October 25, 1874 at the age of seventy-nine. Constable's *Memoir* contains two letters from Mrs. Boinville to her grandson.

[20] Peacock: *Memoir,* II, 339.

[21] William Whitton to Mr. Amory, January 6, 1815, Ingpen: *Shelley in England,* II, 449.

[22] Peacock was an enthusiastic paper-boat sailor before he met Shelley. But Shelley could hardly have learned the habit from Peacock, since Medwin (*Revised Life,* 91) had seen Shelley sail paper boats on the Serpentine in 1811.

[23] Shelley still enjoyed such reading. See the reading list for 1814 in Appendix VII.

[24] As printed and punctuated in Shelley's account it is difficult to be certain whether it was Jane or Shelley who was accused of looking horrible, but from the later context it seems to be Shelley. Shelley seldom wrote in the journal, but this was a matter he could hardly delegate to Mary. It is one of the longest entries in the whole journal. Jane's account, which agrees with and supplements Shelley's, is likewise an unusually long entry. Dowden (*Life,* I, 480–2) quotes most of both accounts.

[25] Eight of these, with one letter written before the elopement, were discovered by Professor Leslie Hotson and printed in the *Atlantic Monthly* for January and February 1930 (CXLV, 122–33 and 166–77). Their dates are September 15, 16, 26, 27, and October 3(?), 5, 12, and 25(?). The journal shows that Shelley wrote

also on October 10 and 23, and Jane on October 23; and that Shelley received letters from Harriet on September 22 and October 5, 10, 11, 23. Harriet's letters to Shelley have been lost, but their nature can sometimes be inferred from Shelley's answers.

²⁶ As late as the early part of November Harriet visited the Godwins and told them cheerfully that " every one " still expected Shelley to return to her (Mrs. Godwin to Lady Mountcashell, November 15, 1814, Dowden: *Life*, II, 546).

²⁷ Jane's journal for October 23, 1814. Jane speaks of the sum as £50; Shelley in his letter of October 25 as £30.

²⁸ Judging from the two daily records, Shelley's statements to Harriet about his health and about his destitution are both wildly exaggerated. He had previously written Harriet, on October 10, about a complaint of his lungs, and Harriet had responded with some health suggestions. On October 6 Mary recorded: " Shelley very unwell," and on October 29: " Shelley is not well," but Shelley was active on both days, and there is no other mention of illness.

²⁹ See note 38, below.

³⁰ September 26, 27, *Atlantic Monthly*, CXLV, 167, 168 (February 1930).

³¹ Mrs. Godwin to Lady Mountcashell, November 15, 1814, Dowden: *Life*, II, 546.

³² November 20, [1814], Julian *Works*, X, 420.

³³ Shelley to Harriet, September 26, 1814, *Atlantic Monthly*, CXLV, 167 (February 1930).

³⁴ October 5, 1814, ibid., CXLV, 170.

³⁵ Both phrases from Shelley's letter of September 27, ibid., 168.

³⁶ The attitude of the Godwins a little later shows that this letter must have urged either that she enter a family as governess or that she return home, but neither journal makes it clear what he urged in this particular letter. A little earlier they had talked of placing Jane in a convent.

³⁷ See notes 27 and 38.

³⁸ " I must hide myself till the 6th," he wrote to Harriet on or about October 25, *Atlantic Monthly*, CXLV, 172 (February 1930). For some reason Shelley seemed to know that he would either obtain money on the 6th or else know definitely then that none was obtainable. The predetermined date seems to bear no relation to his creditors. Of these the most pressing was Charters, on account of the carriage bought in 1813, and a Mrs. Stewart. It has been alleged that the debts for which Shelley was " persecuted " were

Harriet's, which is probably not the whole truth. Shelley paid off
Harriet's debts in June 1815. At that time, after nearly two years
of separation during which she had borne a child, the amount was
only £200. Compared with Shelley's debts for any similar period,
this should not encourage charges of extravagance against Harriet.

The Charters bill is rather perplexing. Harriet undertook on October 23 to raise money for Charters. The amount needed was then
£50 or £30. Yet an undated letter from Shelley to G. B. Ballachey,
written apparently about the first week in November, instructs
Ballachey to send Charters a bill for £100 (Julian *Works,* IX,
109). Charters again presented his bill on February 2, 1815 (journal,
February 2). A letter from Thomas Charters to Peacock, as Shelley's
executor, dated August 31, 1844, shows that Charters had in his
possession an unredeemed bill at four years, covering work done
up to November 1815, amounting to £532 11s. 6d. (Ingpen: *Shelley in England,* II, 638). From this it might be inferred that Harriet
kept and used the coach after her desertion by Shelley and continued to have its upkeep charged against Shelley.

Shelley's letters to Mary dated by the Julian editors November
2, 4, and "uncertain" (Julian *Works,* IX, 105, 109, 110) show that
the real danger was more from Mrs. Stewart than from Charters,
and that the danger from Mrs. Stewart was past when the last of
the three letters was written. Hookham dealt for Shelley with both
creditors. This last fact, together with Harriet's prompt promise to
co-operate in the matter of Charters, would seem to indicate the
good faith of both Harriet and Hookham.

[39] "About half-past eight," with Peacock, according to Jane's
journal.

[40] Mary to Shelley, November 3, 1814, Julian *Works,* IX, 107.

[41] Shelley believed that Godwin might be arrested for debt on
Thursday, November 10, apparently on account of a debt of £150
due Lambert.

[42] Shelley to Harriet, October 12, 1814, *Atlantic Monthly,* CXLV,
171 (February 1930).

[43] Mary to Shelley, October 28, 1814, Julian *Works,* IX, 104.

[44] Ibid., IX, 97, 98, 100, 101, 105.

[45] Ibid., IX, 97.

[46] Ibid., IX, 100.

[47] Ibid., IX, 102.

[48] Ibid., IX, 103.

[49] Ibid., IX, 110.

[50] Ibid., IX, 107.

[51] Ibid., IX, 109.

[52] Shelley to John Williams, Julian *Works,* IX, 112.

[53] Jane's journal is abruptly discontinued on the day of his return, November 9. Her next extant journal begins January 1, 1818.

[54] At about this time Jane arbitrarily changed her name to Clara, or Claire, and was generally so called thereafter. Hereafter in this biography she will be called Claire.

[55] Mrs. Godwin to Lady Mountcashell, November 15, 1814, Dowden: *Life,* II, 547. This delusion may have been suggested by *Caleb Williams,* with which Shelley was already familiar, and which Claire was reading at about this time and probably discussing with Shelley. Caleb was not only a victim of society, as Shelley saw himself, but was dogged for years by a personal avenger.

[56] Mrs. Godwin to Lady Mountcashell, November 15, 1814, Dowden: *Life,* II, 546.

[57] These gaps occur following pages 61 and 62, Volume I, and include the six days following January 7 and the ten days following January 13.

[58] Long after Shelley's death, when Mary was a sedate Victorian lady whose trials were mainly in the past, she told her daughter-in-law that Claire had been the plague of her whole life. Maude Rolleston: *Talks with Lady Shelley* (London, 1925), 41.

[59] There is no specific mention of this transaction in the journal of Shelley and Mary. It is a part of Mrs. Godwin's letter of February 7, 1815 to Lady Mountcashell, printed by Dowden (*Life,* II, 547).

[60] Francis Place had been interested in Godwin's debts for some time previously and had already met Shelley in this connection. He met Shelley only once, and disliked him. He denied ever attempting to raise money for Godwin on Shelley's post-obit, though he had accepted Shelley's post-obit as security for a debt owed him by Godwin and had informed Shelley that it could be redeemed at any time with simple interest. This, he said, was Godwin's device to shift the responsibility to Shelley's shoulders. Place represents Godwin as perfectly heartless in his financial impositions, and gives some interesting remarks on the state of his indebtedness. From Godwin's own accounts Place shows that for ten years ending with 1814 Godwin had received from friends an average of £400 a year. Peck (*Life,* II, 412–20) quotes extensively from Place's papers in the British Museum. The debt of £1,200 here mentioned was probably the same as that for which Shelley entered a charge of £1,200

in settling with his father in April 1815. Perhaps this was the £1,200 which Godwin claimed he did not receive from the post-obit sale of July 1814. See Chapter xii, note 30.

[61] This could hardly have been Shelley's half-uncle, Sir John Shelley-Sidney, though the Julian editors print the name, in Shelley's letter of November 4, as "Sir John [Shelley-Sidney]." Mr. John Shelley-Sidney was not made a baronet until 1818. It must therefore have been Sir John Shelley of the Michelgrove Shelleys, M.P. for Lewes, fairly well known at the time in betting circles.

[62] William Whitton to Shelley, December 10, 1814, in Ingpen: *Shelley in England*, II, 448–9.

[63] Ibid.

[64] On October 5 Mary had entered in the journal: "£400 for £2400." On October 31 Ballachey had made a "rascally proposition" of £300 a year until Mr. Timothy Shelley's death for £15,000 in post-obits, and on November 4 Pike had proposed £12,000 in ready money for the reversion of Castle Goring, which had cost more than £80,000.

[65] October 6: "Shelley very unwell; he reads one canto of 'Queen Mab' to me"; October 29: "Shelley is not well"; December 9: "Shelley unwell"; December 27 (when Mary was ill): "Shelley is very unwell." The second of these is probably an echo from Shelley's letter of October 28 to Mary: "My head aches, I am not well."

[66] October 25, *Atlantic Monthly*, as cited, p. 172. This exaggeration seems to have misled Professor Leslie Hotson, in editing his newly discovered letters to Harriet, into stating (loc. cit., 170) "that Shelley suffered an attack of lung trouble" at this time and that his health was undermined.

[67] Claire's fits of sullenness or horrors were usually preceded or followed by brief illnesses. On November 24 she was apparently quite ill with an inflammation of the liver for which bleeding was necessary. When her mother saw her shortly afterwards she looked like a person who had been through a fairly serious illness (Dowden: *Life*, II, 547). During November and December Mary was ill November 14–23, December 3–6, 17–23, and 27. These illnesses may have been connected with her pregnancy and were not considered serious enough, except once, to require medical attention. Though they forced her for brief periods (November 22–4 and December 19, 21–3, and 26) to resign the keeping of the journal to Shelley, they did not stop her reading and study nor her interest in the daily occurrences of the household.

⁶⁸ Viz., November 14 and 15, December 15, 24, 31.

⁶⁹ One of Shelley's lost letters to Mary during his period of concealment was so full of his vindication of love against Peacock's argument that Mary protested (November 3, 1814) that she stood much more in need of news as to their present situation than of a demonstration of theories she had never thought of questioning.

⁷⁰ Journal for January 12 (presumably). The passage is an undated fragment following a hiatus of six days and is immediately followed by the entry for January 13. A hiatus of ten days beginning on January 14 successfully obscures the conclusion of Peacock's adventure.

⁷¹ Journal for November 14, 1814.

⁷² On November 14, 16, 20, 24, 27, and 29, December 4, 8, 11, 14, 16, 18, 20, 22, 24, 25, 27, 30, continuing into 1815.

⁷³ Journal for December 14, 1814.

⁷⁴ Hogg's novel had been published in November 1813, by Shelley's publisher, Hookham, possibly through Shelley's good offices. Shelley praised it extravagantly in his letter to Hogg from Edinburgh, on November 26, 1813. Both Mary and Claire read the novel with interest and admiration at about the time Shelley was writing his review. While Shelley's review praises the novel as a work of great genius, it condemns Hogg's somewhat materialistic treatment of love. It was published anonymously in the *Critical Review* for December 1814. Mary's journal mentions Hookham's sending copies of the review to Shelley and Mary on January 3.

⁷⁵ Shelley to Harriet, *Atlantic Monthly,* CXLV, 171, 167, 169, 170.

⁷⁶ Harriet to Catherine Nugent, December 11, [1814], Julian *Works,* X, 421.

⁷⁷ Journal, Tuesday, December 6, 1814.

⁷⁸ Harriet to Catherine Nugent, as in note 76 above.

⁷⁹ Journal of Shelley and Mary, Tuesday, December 20, 1814.

⁸⁰ Harriet to Catherine Nugent, January 24, [1815], Julian *Works,* X, 421–2.

⁸¹ Mary to Hogg, dated only January 1815 (evidently written before January 4), Gordon, op. cit. In this and the following letters I have slightly clarified Shelley's punctuation.

⁸² Ibid.

⁸³ Ibid.

⁸⁴ Mrs. Shelley's note to *Alastor*. Mrs. Shelley adds that the signs of consumption disappeared almost miraculously soon thereafter, never to return, and that Shelley's health improved greatly.

⁸⁵ On March 10 Mary wrote in her journal: "Hogg now remains with us." Thereafter until April 17 he is no longer mentioned as coming at a certain hour, but always as going, and the context indicates his continuous presence. On April 17 Mary states: "Hogg goes to the Courts," and within a few days thereafter it is a clear inference from the journal that he is again living in his old quarters. Professor Dowden seems to have overlooked Hogg's residence with the Shelleys.

⁸⁶ Ingpen: *Shelley in England,* II, 449.

⁸⁷ Journal of Shelley and Mary, Friday, January 13, 1815; also Whitton's journal, quoted in Ingpen: *Shelley in England,* II, 450, note.

⁸⁸ Shelley to Elizabeth Hitchener, January 26, 1812, Julian *Works,* VIII, 254.

⁸⁹ Ingpen: *Shelley in England,* II, 453–4.

⁹⁰ Ibid., II, 451–4.

⁹¹ Dowden: *Life,* I, 508.

⁹² Shelley clearly explained these matters to Godwin, in his letter of February 26, 1816 (Julian *Works* IX, 142–3).

⁹³ Dowden: *Life,* I, 508.

⁹⁴ Journal, February 5, 1815. Mary adds: " all this is very odd and inconsistent, but I never quarrel with inconsistency; folks must change their minds."

⁹⁵ Shelley to Godwin, February 26 and January 7, 1816, Julian *Works,* IX, 142 and 123–4.

⁹⁶ Abstracts of the three deeds by which these transactions were completed were printed by Ingpen: *Shelley in England,* II, 643–6. The documents printed by Mr. Ingpen were a part of the Whitton papers originally sold by Sotheby, Wilkerson and Hodge on July 24, 1918. Many of these papers were resold in the Harry B. Smith sale of 1936, and those purchased by Mr. C. A. Stonehill were examined by me in May 1936. The indenture of 1791, one of the complications of the Shelley estate, is explained in a MS. in the Bodleian Library entitled: "Observations on Shelley's Settlement," 107 pages, MS. Shelley Adds. c. 3. Other documents and letters concerning the estate were offered for sale by Maggs Brothers in 1931.

⁹⁷ Mary Shelley to Hogg, April 26, 1814, Gordon, op. cit.

⁹⁸ The missing section of the journal, from May 13, 1815 to July 21, 1816, may of course have contained references to Harriet, who is mentioned twice in 1816 in letters of Fanny Imlay and Peacock, respectively October 3 and June 24. Peacock's letter is not to be found,

but its contents are referred to by Dowden who dates it June 24 (*Life*, I, 511, note).

⁹⁹ Printed by permission of Mr. C. A. Stonehill, owner of the document in May 1936. The first post-obit mentioned was probably the agreement made on December 21, 1814 to receive £3,000 for £10,000. Evidently the money had not changed hands by May 13. I can throw no light on the North, Viner, and Laing items; but the post-obit to Starling is obviously the one on which Shelley gave £2,000 for £500 in early October of 1813. I cannot reconcile this memorandum with Shelley's statement to the Court of Chancery in 1817 that his debts at the time of this settlement were £5,000.

¹⁰⁰ Shelley to Godwin, January 21, 1816, Julian *Works*, IX, 129.

¹⁰¹ Shelley to Godwin, January 28, 1816, ibid., IX, 134–5.

¹⁰² *Shelley and Mary*, I, 74. Shelley's letter of June 22 to John Williams (Julian *Works*, IX, 112) shows that he had then paid a bond of £100 presumably to John.

¹⁰³ Shelley to Godwin, January 18, 21, and 23, 1816, ibid., IX, 127–31.

¹⁰⁴ Shelley to Godwin, February 18 and March 21 and 29, 1816, ibid., IX, 138, 151, 152. This opinion seemed to require further elucidating and explaining, as it was not until April 23 that Whitton informed Sir Timothy of the issue. See Ingpen: *Shelley in England*, II, 462.

¹⁰⁵ Shelley to Godwin, February 26, 1816, Julian *Works*, IX, 142.

¹⁰⁶ Mary Shelley's journal, January 7, 1815.

¹⁰⁷ Ibid., March 2, 1815.

¹⁰⁸ There is a gap of nine days in the journal following March 29.

¹⁰⁹ Gordon, op. cit.

¹¹⁰ Mary to Leigh Hunt, March 18, 1817, in Harper: *Letters of Mary W. Shelley* (1918), 41. For a similar, more detailed opinion in April 1819, see ibid., 63–4.

¹¹¹ *Diary of John William Polidori*, ed. W. M. Rossetti (London, 1911), 128.

¹¹² Shelley to Hogg, January (no day) 1818, Gordon, op. cit.

¹¹³ Shelley's payment of £1,000 to Godwin seems to be dated by a letter of Claire Clairmont to Fanny Imlay as occurring shortly after May 13. On that day Claire left Shelley's household and Shelley concluded his financial arrangement with his father. On May 28 Claire wrote to Fanny: " I was quite delighted to hear that Papa had at last got £1000." The letter is quoted in Dowden (*Life*, I, 519–21) from *Shelley and Mary*, I, 79–81.

[114] Mrs. Godwin to Lady Mountcashell, July 28, 1815, Dowden: *Life*, II, 549.

[115] So Claire told her mother earlier, quoting Shelley as concurring. Later, at the time Claire left, she told her mother that she refused to remain because Mary was jealous (ibid., II, 549).

In an article entitled "Shelley and Claire Clairmont" (*P.M.L.A.*, LIV, 785–814, September 1939) Professor John H. Smith has argued that the relations between Shelley, Claire, and Mary which have been detailed in this chapter indicate a love-affair between Shelley and Claire. Obviously his conclusion is possible, but it can be made plausible only when the case is prejudged so that all the circumstances are considered only on one hypothesis. If the same circumstances fit another and more natural hypothesis equally well or better, the more natural hypothesis should be preferred. I have carefully studied the facts on the basis of Professor Smith's hypothesis; and though I reject most of his conclusions I am glad that he has saved me the labour of stating the case as he sees it.

The deleted passages in Claire's journal at this time were once an object of suspicion to me, as they are to Professor Smith. Since his article leaves them so, I will state that with the aid of infra-red photography and enlargements I have deciphered some of these passages completely and all of them sufficiently to be able to show that some have no reference to Shelley and that none has any real bearing upon the hypothesis of guilty relationship with Shelley. Miss R. Glynn Grylls has very obligingly collated for me, with the original MS. of Mary's journal, a list of missing passages in *Shelley and Mary*. Her collation shows that practically all excisions were by Mary Shelley in the original MS. Whether or not they referred to Shelley and Claire, or to Mary's peculiar affair with Hogg, or to totally unrelated matters, is pure guess-work, with two exceptions noted in this chapter, both of them quite unrelated to Claire.

[116] Mary's journal for March 20, 1815 contains the following, which would appear to refer to an advertisement: "Return, and find more letters for 'A. Z.' — one from a 'Disconsolate Widow.'" I have been able to search only *The Times* for the twenty days before March 20, and there I find nine advertisements so signed, one of which, on March 17, might refer to Claire:

Young lady now in France wants governess position. Speaks French, a little Italian, plays piano. A-Z. Mrs. Palmers, 222 Piccadilly.

¹¹⁷ From Mrs. Godwin's account to Lady Mountcashell (Dowden: *Life*, II, 549) it would appear to have been on Mrs. Godwin's advice. But from the opening sentences of Claire's letter to Fanny, written after she had been two weeks in Lynmouth, it would appear that Fanny did not know where she was going, which suggests that the decision was influenced by Shelley rather than by Mrs. Godwin.

¹¹⁸ Claire Clairmont to Fanny Imlay, May 28, 1815, *Shelley and Mary*, I, 80. Quoted in part in Chapter xiv, p. 413. Dowden quotes this letter entire: *Life*, I, 519–21.

¹¹⁹ Under these circumstances it seems inadequate to apply Mary's word "regeneration" merely to the relief of Claire's departure, as Lady Shelley does in *Shelley and Mary*, and as M. Koszul does (*La Jeunesse de Shelley*, Paris, 1910, p. 239).

¹²⁰ Mary's journal, March 23, 1815.

¹²¹ November 16, 1814, *Shelley and Mary*, I, 48; Julian *Works*, VI, 359.

¹²² Quoted in note 26, Chapter xiv.

¹²³ Peacock: *Memoirs*, II, 339.

¹²⁴ Shelley to Hogg, August 26, 1815, Gordon, op. cit.

¹²⁵ Note on *Alastor*, Julian *Works*, I, 198.

¹²⁶ Mrs. Godwin to Lady Mountcashell, August 20, 1814, in Dowden: *Life*, II, 545.

¹²⁷ Mrs. Godwin to Lady Mountcashell, February 7, 1815, ibid., II, 545. Mrs. Godwin does not mention the Greek, but Jane's journal does. The French seems a bit odd, for Claire had at least a better speaking knowledge of French than Shelley. Her journal, however, shows considerable reading in French at this time.

¹²⁸ Shelley to Mary, [?November 1, 1814], Julian *Works*, IX, 104.

¹²⁹ Shelley to Mary, October 28, 1814, ibid.

¹³⁰ Claire's journal, October 28, 1814. Both Mary and Claire also attempted writing. Mary, after reading Louvet's *Memoirs* started a biography of Louvet on November 12. Claire, on November 5, wrote what she called "a scene in 'Gertrude' — very shocking." Nothing more is known of either work.

¹³¹ Mary's reading lists quoted in Appendix VII.

¹³² See the reading list for 1815, quoted in Appendix VII. Of the 84 days for which the journal contains entries in 1815, there are 10 in which no reading is mentioned, 74 in which Mary is reading something, and 42 in which Shelley is mentioned as reading.

¹³³ Shelley gave up possession of his house at Bishopsgate on

August 3, 1816, presumably on the expiration of a year's lease. Dowden: *Life,* I, 525, note.

[134] Shelley to John Williams, June 22, 1815, Julian *Works,* IX, 112. Cf. D. E. Varney to John Williams, Appendix III.

[135] Mary Shelley to Shelley, July 27, 1815, in *Shelley and Mary,* I, 82–4; also Dowden: *Life,* I, 524–5.

[136] This fact and this suspicion were first noted by Bertram Dobell in the *Athenæum* for March 7, 1885, p. 313.

[137] Thanks largely to information recently placed in my hands by Professor Louise S. Boas, of Wheaton College, I am able to supply more definite facts about the *Theological Inquirer* and its writers than appear in my note in *The Unextinguished Hearth.*

The *Theological Inquirer* was the organ of a radical group of Unitarians centred in the chapel of the Reverend Mr. Robert Wedderburn, in Soho. Wedderburn's pamphlet *High Heeled Shoes for Dwarfs in Holiness* contains a quotation from *Queen Mab.* The account of his trial was edited in 1820 by Erasmus Perkins, who is referred to by a reviewer in the *Monthly Repository* as "a man of straw."

Some copies of the so-called "first American" edition of *Queen Mab,* now known to have been printed by William Benbow, contain in small Greek letters at the foot of the title page the initials E. P., which suggests that Erasmus Perkins was the editor who signs himself "A Pantheist." This would explain why the editorial matter in that edition was so largely reprinted from the *Theological Inquirer* and why Shelley's reviewer, who signed himself F. in the *Inquirer,* should be so confidently quoted as "my friend," R. C. F.

On the basis of the initials R. C. F. and the fact that Shelley had ordered a copy of his *Proposal for Putting Reform to the Vote* sent to General Sir Ronald Crawfurd Ferguson, I suggested in *The Unextinguished Hearth* that this liberal general and M.P. may have been Shelley's reviewer. I now believe that Mr. Bertram Dobell's guess (in the *Athenæum* as cited in note 136) was correct. Mr. Dobell stated his belief that F. was Fare, or Fair. Though he does not say so, his belief was evidently based on the following lines in a poem published in the *Theological Inquirer* and addressed to F.:

> From bitter reflection some moments to spare
> I take up my pen to address my friend ——.

An "Ode to Major Cartright" in Volume II (1818) of the *Black Dwarf* is signed R. Fare. A series of four articles in Arliss's *Pocket*

Magazine is signed F. for the first two and R. F. for the other two. Two articles with these signatures appeared in the *Monthly Repository*. Though these articles and poems are all of a style and character similar to those signed F. in the *Theological Inquirer,* it is of course impossible to prove that they were all by the same man. These data do prove, however, that there was an R. Fare who wrote verse of a similar nature to the poem to Shelley in the *Theological Inquirer*. Since this poem was signed F. and was written by a man whose name rhymed with " spare," and since this F. is also the R. C. F. quoted in the " American edition" of *Queen Mab,* I conclude that Shelley's reviewer and poetical eulogist was a radical Unitarian named R. C. Fare.

Beyond this both Fare and Erasmus Perkins remain mysteries. Either or both names may have been aliases for William Benbow, about whom almost nothing is known except that he was a shrewd, unscrupulous radical publisher. Erasmus Perkins was almost certainly a pseudonym, but what slight evidence exists suggests that Fare was a real name. At all events he knew Shelley well enough to obtain one of the rather closely guarded copies of *Queen Mab*. His statement in his first review that he obtained several copies in Berlin, after hearing the poem praised by Kotzebue, is obviously false; but it suggests that he was acquainted with Shelley in 1815 and that the story may have come from Shelley himself, for one of the books read by Shelley at that time was Kotzebue's *Travels*.

[138] " Ode to the Author of ' Queen Mab,' " by F., stanza 3. From the *Theological Inquirer, or Polemical Magazine,* July 1815, pp. 380–1. For the complete poem and other items on Shelley in the *Inquirer,* see my *The Unextinguished Hearth*.

Chapter XIV

GENERAL SOURCES

Shelley's letters and works, Mary Shelley's notes, Peacock's *Memoirs,* and Medwin's *Revised Life* — all as previously cited. Also letters of Charles and Claire Clairmont as given in *Shelley and Mary,* and the Francis Place papers in the British Museum.

NOTES AND REFERENCES

[1] As described in the London *Evening Standard* for July 10, 1922, from the account furnished Miss Alice Helen Lock, of Bishopsgate, the owner, by Dr. F. J. Furnivall, whose father attended Mary there as her physician. In 1922 the house was said to have been only slightly changed from its appearance in Shelley's day. A picture of the cottage, owned by the late Roger Ingpen, was published in the *Review of Reviews*, LXVI, 46 (July 1922).

[2] The second part of the description, following the quotation, is from Mrs. Shelley's *The Last Man*, I, 74–6, as quoted by Peck: *Life*, I, 415–16.

[3] Claire Clairmont to Fanny Imlay, May 28, 1815, in *Shelley and Mary*, I, 79–81, quoted entire by Dowden: *Life*, I, 519–21.

[4] Mrs. Shelley's Note on the Early Poems.

[5] Shelley to Hogg, August 26, 1815, Julian *Works*, IX, 116 (dated and corrected from the Gordon text).

[6] Charles Clairmont to Claire Clairmont, September 16, 1815, in *Shelley and Mary*, I, 84–6, quoted by Dowden: *Life*, I, 528–30. The letter is incomplete. It appears to have been written about three weeks after the beginning of his visit, and indicates that the project of Claire's accompanying him to Ireland had developed while Claire and Charles were together in Skinner Street, early in October.

[7] Julian *Works*, IX, 120.

[8] The excursion is described in some detail by Charles Clairmont in the letter already quoted, and by Peacock: *Memoirs*, II, 340–1. Mrs. Shelley, in her Note on the Early Poems, mentions it briefly and erroneously as taking place in July.

[9] Charles Clairmont, as cited in note 6 above. Shelley's room is now part of the Junior Common Room.

[10] Peacock: *Memoirs*, II, 340.

[11] Ibid.

[12] Charles Clairmont, as above.

[13] Shelley to Hogg, September 1815, Julian *Works*, IX, 118–19 (slightly corrected by Gordon, op. cit.). In August, before the Thames expedition, Shelley had written to Hogg commenting on his improved health and his reading.

[14] Charles Clairmont to Francis Place, January 12, 1815 (for

1816). Since Shelley's extant letters and journals are entirely silent upon the episode, we owe our knowledge of it to this interesting and partly unpublished letter, quoted more fully in Appendix III.

¹⁵ British Museum, Add. MSS. 35,152, fol. 194.

¹⁶ William Whitton to Sir Timothy Shelley, November 30, 1815, quoted in full in Ingpen: *Shelley in England*, II, 457–8. The last paragraph of Whitton's letter reports a rumour that Shelley was acting in Shakespeare's plays on the Windsor stage, under the name of Cooks, and offers to investigate, since he knew something of the manager, named Penley. His journal, as referred to by Mr. Ingpen (II, 459), records a conversation with Shelley's solicitor on the subject, but does not establish the report. Shelley's boyish fondness for acting at Field Place and Eton makes the truth of the report seem possible. It is difficult, however, to see how Hogg and Peacock, both frequent visitors at Shelley's home — and Peacock probably at the local theatre as well — could have been ignorant of such activity, if it existed, or could have refrained from mentioning it in their accounts, had they known. Peacock states (*Memoirs*, II, 330): "He had a prejudice against theatres which I took some pains to overcome." A few months later Claire Clairmont informed Byron that Shelley almost never attended the theatre. The journal of Shelley and Mary is missing for the time involved, and Whitton seems to have dropped the subject within two days of broaching it. In such circumstances the most reasonable tentative conclusion would seem to be that some acquaintance of Hogg or Peacock may have told Whitton (what Mary's book-list actually records) that Shelley read part of Shakespeare's plays aloud — and that Whitton misunderstood.

¹⁷ To Lackington, Allen and Co., London, September 10, November 9, and December 17, 1815; and to William Laing, Edinburgh, September 27, 1815, Julian *Works*, IX, 117, 122, and 120, respectively.

¹⁸ Note on *Alastor*, 1839.

¹⁹ The Greek word Alastor, meaning an evil genius or, more rarely, the victim of an evil genius, was suggested by Peacock when Shelley asked him for a proper title for the poem (Peacock: *Memoirs*, II, 341). Peacock evidently had in mind only the more common meaning, but the poem seems to fit the secondary meaning, thus leading many readers into the error, as Peacock called it, of considering Alastor to be the name of the hero.

²⁰ It has been suggested (Paul Mueschke and Earl Leslie Griggs: "Wordsworth as The Prototype of The Poet in Shelley's *Alastor*," *P.M.L.A.*, XLIX, 229–45, March 1934) that Shelley's pathetic poet

is Wordsworth rather than himself. While there is a certain plausibility in the suggestion that Shelley had Wordsworth partly in mind, I cannot doubt that the character is mainly autobiographical.

Recently Professor John H. Smith ("Shelley and Claire Clairmont," *P.M.L.A.*, LIV, 785–815, September 1939) has argued that *Alastor* is based mainly on the emotional situation between Shelley, Claire, and Mary during 1815. Until definite facts and conclusions are available to establish the situation which Professor Smith believes existed, this argument can be no more than surmise — and in my opinion probably erroneous.

Something of the germ idea of *Alastor* may be found in Shelley's letter of June 20, 1811 to Elizabeth Hitchener (Julian *Works*, VIII, 107) before he knew either Claire or Mary. Here he cautions Miss Hitchener against too much introspection, which leads to the pursuit of virtue, but induces gloom and dispels happiness. "This is the tree [of] which it is dangerous to eat, but which I have fed upon to satiety. . . . We look around us . . . we find ourselves reasoning upon the mystery which involves our being . . . we see virtue and vice . . . each is separate, distinct . . . yet how racking it is to the soul . . . to find that perfect virtue is very far from attainable, to find reason tainted by feeling, to see the mind when analysed exhibit a picture of irreconcileable inconsistencies, even when perhaps a moment before, it imagined that it had grasped the fleeting Phantom of virtue." On May 8 of the same year, in a letter to Hogg (as pointed out by Mr. Peck: *Life*, I, 426), Shelley expressed his strong feeling of "the horror, the evil, which comes to *self* in solitude."

At the same period at which these letters were written Shelley was reading with especial enthusiasm and admiration *The Missionary*, by Miss Sydney Owenson [Lady Morgan], and William Godwin's *Fleetwood*. Both novels have definite points in common with *Alastor*. The former, like *Alastor*, is the story of a priest who tries to lead a life of isolated high idealism, who forsakes this way of life to follow Ideal Beauty in the form of a beautiful priestess ("the divine Luxima," as Shelley called her), and thereby comes to ruin. Like *Alastor*, it contains journeys, impressive scenery, and also a Tartar horse. The meeting of Hilarion and Luxima in the sacred glen (pp. 57–9) suggests the closing episode of *Alastor*. Godwin's *Fleetwood* devotes a whole chapter (New York, 1805, Vol. II, Chapter 4) to a philosophic exposure of the disastrous effects of selfish isolation. "I hear people talk of the raptures of solitude," Macneil tells Fleetwood in the opening paragraph,

— and with what tenderness of affection they can love a tree, a rivulet, or a mountain. Believe me, they are pretenders; they deceive themselves, or they seek, with their eyes open, to impose upon others. In addition to their trees and their mountains, I will give them the whole brute creation; still it will not do. There is a principle in the heart of man, which demands the society of his like. He that has no such society, is in a state but one degree removed from insanity. He pines for an ear into which he might pour the story of his thoughts, for an eye that shall flash upon him with responsive intelligence, for a face, the lines of which shall talk to him in dumb, but eloquent discourse, for a heart that shall beat in unison with his own. . . . I venerate the grand and beautiful exhibitions and shapes of nature, no man more; I delight in solitude; I could shut myself up in it for successive days. But I know, that Christ did not with more alacrity come out of the wilderness . . . than every man, at the end of a course of this sort, will seek for the interchange of sentiments and language.

It will be noted that the sentence beginning: "He pines . . ." is strikingly similar to a part of Shelley's essay "On Love" quoted in this chapter.

Finally, C. M. Wieland's *Agathon,* which Shelley read with such enthusiasm with the Boinvilles and which, according to Mary Shelley's reading list, he seems to have re-read with Mary later in 1814, contains some similarities to *Alastor* that are of possible significance. Agathon, like the young poet, is an intense idealist who has suffered persecution. His idealism does not lead him to his death, but in the end he concludes that it went beyond the bounds of true wisdom, though still preferable to materialism — which is Shelley's conclusion in his Preface. Psyche, Alastor's spiritual love, is a person rather than a spirit, but is obviously a personification of Platonic love. In a graphic vision Agathon sees her and follows her in vain, somewhat as Shelley's young poet follows his vision. The same book shows Agathon and his two former lovers living together in the end in purely Platonic love (which may have suggested Shelley's proposal to Harriet after eloping with Mary) and contains passages on ideal beauty quite suggestive of Shelley's Intellectual Beauty. In the French translation read by Shelley the phrase "*Beauté Intellectuelle*" occurs twice.

[21] Shelley to John Gisborne, June 18, 1822, Julian *Works,* X, 401.
[22] Note on *Alastor,* 1839.

[23] See B. P. Kurtz: *The Pursuit of Death, A Study of Shelley's Poetry* (New York, 1933).

[24] Hogg, op. cit., I, 36, represents Shelley as planning to spend a night in the vaults of Warnham Church.

[25] Peacock (*Memoirs*, II, 328) comments upon Shelley's great admiration for the poetry of Wordsworth, Coleridge, and Milton, and in a less degree Southey. The Wordsworthian echoes are most fully pointed out by Paul Mueschke and Earl Leslie Griggs, in the article cited in note 20. Echoes from Wordsworth and other poets are listed in C. D. Locock's edition of Shelley's poems, Peck's *Life* (I, 422–31), and Richard Ackerman, in *Quellen, Vorbilden, Stoffe zu Shelleys Poetischen Werke*. For studies of the meaning of the poem see Harold L. Hoffman: *An Odyssey of the Soul, Shelley's " Alastor "* (New York, 1933); R. D. Havens: " Shelley's ' Alastor,' " *P.M.L.A.*, XLV, 1098–1115 (December 1930); and Marion C. Weir: " Shelley's ' Alastor ' Again," *P.M.L.A.*, XLVI, 947–50 (March 1931), with Professor Havens's reply, ibid., 950–1.

[26] Shelley's only known blank verse between *Queen Mab* and *Alastor* is a fragment of fifty-one lines, entitled " The Sunset " (1816), and some lines in his handwriting on the blank pages in the back of Claire Clairmont's journal for August–November 1814. When the latter was written is uncertain. The same blank pages contain in Shelley's handwriting several scraps of Latin and Italian — chiefly the Latin motto of *Alastor*, about a dozen lines from the Francesca and Paolo episode in Dante's *Inferno*, and some half-obliterated erotic lines in Latin which I am totally unable to place. From the fact that all of these scraps centre on the subject of love and one is definitely connected with *Alastor*, it might possibly be supposed that while the idea of *Alastor* was germinating in Shelley's mind he used the blank pages in the back of Claire's journal for notes in connection with it. In that case the notes and the English verses were probably written in the spring of 1815, before Claire's departure from the Shelley household.

The English verses, hitherto unpublished, are as follows:

> How beautiful it sails
> Along the silent and serene expanse
> Blending its solemn and aerial tints
> With the pale sky — now an extinguished moon
> The frail dim specter of some quenched orb
> Beamless and broad on the still air upheld

It hangs in Heaven's deep azure — like a flame
Sphered by the hand of some belated gnome
That chides for its delay the pausing blast
Where the red light of evening's solemn smile
Hangs on the skirts of the exhausted [sea?]
As when the embattled clouds of orient day
Allow short respite to the waning stars
Now the aeolian chords within your bowers
Most like a [poet?] that mocks the [wandering?]
When . . . . ray —
In . . . . [beam? dream?]

And on the next page:

Now the dark bows of the æolian pine
Swing to the sweeping wind, and the light clouds
And the blue sky beyond, so deep and still
Commingles like a sympathy of sight
With the sweet music.

The thoughts of my past life
Rise like the ghosts of an unquiet dream
Blackening the cheerful morn

27 It is described in H. B. Forman's *The Shelley Library* (London, 1886), 35–46.

28 Shelley to John Murray, January 16, 1816; and to Carpenter and Son, February 6, 1816, Julian *Works*, IX, 125 and 135. The poem was listed as in press in the April 1816 issues of the *Monthly Magazine or British Register* (which curiously repeated the notice in February 1818), the *New Monthly Magazine,* and the *Eclectic Review;* also in the May issue of the *British Review and London Critical Journal.*

29 Ingpen: *Shelley in England*, II, 463.

30 Shelley to Southey, March 7, 1816, Julian *Works*, IX, 146–7. This letter, which has the tone of a first communication since his Irish experience, suggests that Hogg and Peacock may have been wrong as to either the facts or the date of the meeting between Shelley and Southey following Shelley's return from the Continent in 1814. See Chapter xiii, note 15.

31 Reviews appeared in the *Monthly Review*, April 1816, (LXXIX, 433); the *British Critic*, May 1816 (n.s. V, 545–6); and the *Eclectic Review*, October 1816 (n.s. V, 391–3). The *Liter-*

ary Panorama for May (n.s. IV, 297) quoted the two translations from the volume (a sonnet by Dante and a fragment of Moschus), ascribing them to Shelley, but without comment or mention of the volume. Four years later Christopher North, in *Blackwood's Edinburgh Magazine,* November 1819 (VI, 148–54), which had not come into existence in 1816, gave *Alastor* a review really worthy of its quality.

[32] See Chapter vii, pp. 191–2. The dating of Shelley's prose fragments is extremely difficult and uncertain. Rossetti (*Shelley's Poetical Works,* London, 1870) assigns to 1815 " On Love," " Speculations on Morals," " On the Punishment of Death," " On Christianity." He says of " On Life " (p. clxvii): " I should presume it to be probably between 1815 and 1818, rather of the earlier than the later limit of dates." Dowden (*Life,* I, 534–5) dissents only in the case of " On Life," which he thinks was written in 1819. H. B. Forman (*Shelley's Prose Works,* London, 1880) accepts Rossetti's dates and Mrs. Shelley's date of 1815 for " Speculations on Metaphysics." See also A. H. Koszul: *Shelley's Prose in the Bodleian Manuscripts,* and notes to the Julian edition, Vol. VII. It would appear certain at least that the " Speculations on Metaphysics " and the " Speculations on Morals " were begun in 1815 (if not resumed at that time from 1811) and resumed in 1819 and later. None of these essays was ever completed or published by Shelley. Thus it is impossible to prove that every passage I quote from these fragments belongs to the year 1815. The passage quoted from " On Life," however, is so closely akin to *Alastor* that if it was written in 1819 it was probably rewritten from an earlier similar draft. The same might also apply to " On Love." Only the Bodleian fragments, which I have not quoted, occur in an Italian notebook; the others are either upon paper watermarked 1815 or unwatermarked. Hence I conclude that " Speculations on Morals " and " Speculations on Metaphysics," as I have quoted them, fairly represent Shelley in 1815.

[33] " On Love," Julian *Works,* VI, 201.

[34] See *ante,* Chapter vii, p. 184.

[35] Julian *Works,* VI, 194. Mrs. Shelley's note (*Essays, Letters from Abroad,* 1840) says: " Shelley was a disciple of the Immaterial Philosophy of Berkeley."

[36] " Speculations on Metaphysics," Julian *Works,* VII, 67.

[37] Mrs. Shelley's note on this occurrence (Julian *Works,* VII, 67, note) is an interesting comment on Shelley's extremely sensitive nervous organization:

This remark closes this fragment, which was written in 1815. I remember well his coming to me from writing it, pale and agitated, to seek refuge in conversation from the fearful emotions it excited. No man, as these fragments prove, had such keen sensations as Shelley. His nervous temperament was wound up by the delicacy of his health to an intense degree of sensibility, and while his active mind pondered for ever upon, and drew conclusions from his sensations, his reveries increased their vivacity, till they mingled with, and made one with thought, and both became absorbing and tumultuous, even to physical pain.

[38] "Speculations on Metaphysics," Julian *Works,* VII, 65.

[39] Ibid., VII, 62, 65.

[40] "On Life," ibid., VI, 197.

[41] "Speculations on Metaphysics," ibid., VII, 64.

[42] Ibid., VII, 75.

[43] Mary Shelley: *The Fortunes of Perkin Warbeck,* I, 91. Quoted by Peck: *Life,* I, 435–6.

[44] Shelley to Godwin, January 25, 1816, Julian *Works,* IX, 134.

[45] Many passages in Hogg's *Two Hundred and Nine Days; or The Journal of a Traveller on the Continent* (London, 1827) show that even then he was a pronounced liberal in matters of government and violently opposed to the clergy.

[46] Peacock: *Memoirs,* II, 341.

[47] In *Nightmare Abbey,* written in 1817, Peacock never affirmed or denied that Scythrop was intended for Shelley, but Shelley accepted the character. Scythrop's dilemma is that of Shelley between Harriet and Mary, with the character of Claire Clairmont substituted for Mary. Obviously none of the characters is intended as a complete or literal portrait.

[48] Peacock: *Memoirs,* II, 339, 341.

[49] Ibid., II, 348.

[50] Shelley to Godwin, January 7, 1815 [for 1816], Julian *Works,* IX, 125.

[51] Shelley to Mr. Hayward, October 19, 1815, Julian *Works,* IX, 121. A note of Shelley's dated December 24, 1815, directing his bankers to pay Joseph Hume £200 (Julian *Works,* IX, 123), was probably for Godwin's benefit. Though Godwin is known to have been in Hume's debt for £40 in May 1811 (see Peck: *Life,* I, 433, note 90), Shelley's cheque was not to pay Hume. It seems to me to be Shelley's answer to an undated letter of Godwin's from which

Dowden quotes (*Life,* I, 538): "I return your cheque because no consideration can induce me to utter a cheque drawn by you and containing my name. . . . You may make it payable to Joseph Hume or James Martin or any other name in the whole directory. I should prefer its being payable to Mr. Hume."

⁵² Eighteen letters, between January 7 and May 3, 1816, Julian *Works,* IX, 123–61. Of all Shelley's twenty-seven extant letters between these two dates, including five to William Bryant, only three, which deal with *Alastor,* are not occasioned by financial complications.

⁵³ Most of Place's comments on Godwin and Shelley have been reprinted from his voluminous papers in the British Museum by Mr. Peck (*Life,* II, 412–20). He has, however, overlooked the correspondence between Place and Charles Clairmont and the following extract from a letter of Place to Edward Wakefield, dated January 23, 1814 (Brit. Mus. Add. MSS. 35,152, folio 33): "— he is in some respects a poor creature, — he fears poverty, not I think much on his own account, but for his family — this I think very silly — he fears shame this I think quite as silly in a man who does nothing in itself shameful — he fears he shall not succeed in obtaining the loan which has for its object to repay the advances of his friends amounting in bills and cash to about £2700, some of whom will be ruined if he fail — and this distracts him, a more miserable creature than he seems to be hardly exists, he is not a man of the world in the sense he ought to be to obtain a living by business, — or to make his grown-up girls maintain themselves, but luckily for him should he obtain the loan, he will be freed from the trouble of business by the return of his son-in-law who has been about three years with Constable at Edinburgh — who gives him a most extraordinary character and under whose management the business will flourish." (See Chapter xiii, note 60.)

⁵⁴ Even in his extremity Godwin refused to see Shelley personally. The Mr. Turner was the husband of Shelley's friend of Bracknell days, Cornelia Boinville Turner, and still lived at Bracknell at this time.

⁵⁵ Shelley to Godwin, April 8, 1816, Julian *Works,* IX, 152–3.

⁵⁶ Shelley to William Bryant, April 14, 1815 [?1816], ibid., IX, 153.

⁵⁷ Josiah Wedgwood to Francis Place, August 29, 1815, and Place's reply, September 2, 1815, Brit. Mus. Add. MSS. 35,145, folio 60.

⁵⁸ Shelley to Godwin, May 3, 1816, Julian *Works,* IX, 159–60. The actual amount that Sir Timothy was to lend Shelley is not mentioned

by Shelley, but Mr. Ingpen (*Shelley in England,* II, 468), evidently on Whitton's authority, states that it was £2,000.

⁵⁹ Shelley to Godwin, March 29, 1816, Julian *Works,* IX, 151.

⁶⁰ Shelley to Godwin, January 18, 1816, ibid., IX, 127.

⁶¹ Shelley to Godwin, January 25 and February 16, 1816, ibid., IX, 133–4, 137.

⁶² Godwin's journal, as quoted by Dowden (*Life,* I, 553), records that on March 24, 1816 Shelley called three times, Charles Clairmont twice; and that Claire Clairmont slept at the house in Skinner Street.

⁶³ Shelley to Godwin, March 7, 1816, Julian *Works,* IX, 147. Godwin expressed a conviction, the more irritating because of its substantial truth, that Shelley did not desire his kindness without his approbation, adding that no torture could extract his approbation of Shelley's elopement. It was for this reason, no doubt, that he resolutely refused to cash a cheque of Shelley's to his order, lest it should seem to others to be an act of approval. "As long as understanding and sentiment shall exist in this frame I shall never cease from my disapprobation of that act of yours which I regard as the great calamity of my life." What he considered a betrayal of trust was perhaps as bitter to Godwin as what Shelley considered Godwin's betrayal of principle was to Shelley. (Godwin's letters of this period expressing his sentiments toward Shelley are unavailable, except for a few brief extracts and summaries in Dowden's *Life,* I, 538, 551–2.)

⁶⁴ Shelley to Godwin, February 26, 1816, Julian *Works,* IX, 144. Almost every recorded instance of Shelley's illness was preceded by some unusual nervous excitement. This fact, which suggests that Shelley's illnesses were partly due to and sometimes magnified by his hypersensitiveness, seems not to have been taken into sufficient account by the "eminent physicians" who were so patently and consistently mistaken in their diagnoses.

⁶⁵ Shelley to Godwin, March 6, 1816, ibid., IX, 145.

⁶⁶ Shelley to Godwin, May 3, 1816, ibid., IX, 161. See also ibid., 147.

⁶⁷ The order, dated March 2, 1816, is printed from the Shelley-Whitton papers by Ingpen: *Shelley in England,* II, 461.

⁶⁸ Shelley to Godwin, February 16 and 21, 1816, Julian *Works,* IX, 136, 140.

⁶⁹ Shelley to Godwin, February 26, March 6 and 7, 1816, ibid., IX, 144, 145, 147.

⁷⁰ Shelley to Godwin, May 3, 1816, ibid., IX, 160.

[71] Peacock: *Memoirs,* II, 341–2, 343. Shelley's dealings with his father over the settlement, as told by Shelley to Godwin, do not suggest any such fear, nor does such a fear seem probable at this time. In 1818, however, as Shelley was on the verge of his third departure for the Continent, Captain Pilfold and Sir Timothy were in communication over Shelley's debt to the former, and the Captain actually did have Shelley arrested. Shelley knew his danger at this time, and so, very likely, did Peacock. After nearly fifty years Peacock may have attributed to Shelley's second departure for the Continent what was really true only of the third. At the same time I credit Peacock's account of Shelley's "delusion" as being too detailed and circumstantial to reject, except that any warning Shelley imagined himself receiving from Williams of Tremadoc would be much more likely to concern his old "persecutor," Leeson, than Shelley's own family. Dowden, without accepting Shelley's story, suggests (*Life,* II, 3) that it might still be true, even to the extent of the diamond necklace, which Harriet may have left in Tremadoc as a pledge for Shelley's debts.

[72] Peacock, op. cit., II, 341–3. Peacock calls this a semi-delusion, rather than a delusion, because it was based upon a real and firm belief that his father and uncle had designs on him. He mentions similar semi-delusions, without giving any account of them.

[73] Godwin's journal, as quoted by Dowden (*Life,* II, 5), indicates that she was with the Shelleys on New Year's Day and with the Godwins for three days immediately following. Shelley's letter of February 16, 1816 to Godwin shows that Claire was with the Godwins on that date. Her undated letters to Byron indicate that she was in London during a good part of the spring, but the addresses given may be accommodation addresses only.

[74] Peck (*Life,* II, 436) published the cheques. There are no later extant cheques of Shelley to Claire until after she was discarded by Byron.

[75] R. E. Prothero: *Letters and Journals of Lord Byron,* III, 437. Claire's extant letters to Byron, with an editorial note, occupy pages 427–37. Part of an additional letter is printed in *Shelley and Mary,* I, 90. All these letters have recently been printed more fully from the John Murray papers by Miss R. Glynn Grylls, in her *Claire Clairmont* (London, 1939), 59–62. For still more material from and about these letters, see George Paston and Peter Quennel: *To Lord Byron* (London, 1939), 203–59.

[76] The time is indicated by a reference in an earlier letter to a

copy of *Alastor* sent Byron by Claire. *Alastor* could hardly have been published before about the middle of February. But a set of sheets such as Shelley sent Murray might have been given to Byron by Claire shortly after the middle of January. Byron's daughter Ada was born on January 5. It was on January 15 that Lady Byron left London, never to see her husband again. It would thus appear fairly certain, as Lord Ernle argues, that Claire Clairmont did not become Byron's mistress until after Lady Byron had left him.

⁷⁷ An undated letter of Claire's to Byron, which from the last sentence would seem to have been written immediately before Byron's departure, informed Byron that Mary would accompany Claire to meet him and begged him not to betray to Mary the secret of their connection (*Shelley and Mary*, I, 90). Only five short sentences of this letter are printed. They were copied by Lady Shelley from the Byron collection of Lady Dorchester, but the letter of which they form a part does not occur in Mr. Murray's *Lord Byron's Correspondence* (1922), in which the letters in Lady Dorchester's collection were published. The last sentence of the extract is: "I shall stay a few minutes after her departure, to receive your last instructions."

⁷⁸ Shelley to Hogg, May [2?] 1815 [for 1816] and July 18, 1816, Gordon, op. cit.

⁷⁹ Claire Clairmont to Lord Byron, May 6, 1816, in *Shelley and Mary*, I, 91–2. Quoted there from the Lady Dorchester Papers; not included in Murray's *Lord Byron's Correspondence* (1922). A MS. note of Dowden's suggests that the letter should have been dated May 8. This seems to be established by Mary Shelley's letter to Peacock (Julian *Works*, VI, 117) in which she states that they reached Paris May 8. Allowing three days in which to reach Paris (their previous journey from Calais to Paris required two days and a night), this would date their departure from Dover as on May 3 according to Claire, or May 5 according to Mary. May 5 would seem to be the preferable date, since Shelley, writing to Peacock on May 15 (Julian *Works*, IX, 161) speaks of "a journey of ten days," which he probably meant to include the two days' wait in Paris mentioned in Mary's letter to Peacock.

⁸⁰ Medwin (*Revised Life*, 204–7) tells this story with much detail, quoting parts of a very novelistic conversation with the disciple as reported to him by Shelley. Mary, according to Medwin, never heard the story or suspected the woman's existence. The only incident that can be connected with facts otherwise known is the spy-

glass incident; the Shelley-Byron party at Geneva are known to have been observed with spy-glasses by curious English tourists. This story is curiously connected with the "mystery at Naples" in 1818, as discussed in Chapter xx.

The story contains a typically Medwinian confusion of time. Medwin says the first meeting occurred in 1814 and that the lady learned that Shelley was going to Geneva. He thus confused Shelley's first and second trips to the Continent. From the rest of the story it is evident that he should have written 1816 for 1814.

Chapter XV

GENERAL SOURCES

Letters of Shelley (Julian *Works*, IX), letters of Mary Shelley (as first published with *A History of a Six Weeks' Tour*, etc.), Mary Shelley's Note on the Poems of 1816, Mary Shelley's journal, letters of Charles and Claire Clairmont (*Shelley and Mary*) — all as previously cited.

W. M. Rossetti, ed.: *Diary of Dr. John William Polidori*. London, 1911. Thomas Moore: *Letters and Journals of Lord Byron*, etc., London, 1830. R. E. Prothero: *Letters and Journals of Lord Byron*, etc., London, 1899.

NOTES AND REFERENCES

[1] *The Last Man*, III, 145, quoted by Peck: *Life*, I, 446.

[2] Fanny Imlay to Mary Shelley, July 29, 1816, in *Shelley and Mary*, I, 110.

[3] For a picture of the shocking behaviour of all foreign troops except English in France after Waterloo, see a letter of John Murray to his wife, July 22, 1815, in S. Smiles: *A Publisher and His Friends* (London, 1891), I, 274–5. "The Prussians," he writes, "have been particularly outrageous in their demands; pillaging, devastating and destroying in the provinces . . . even to burning the houses and inhabitants upon whom they had lived. This is truly horrible, etc."

Murray gives a contrasting account of the behaviour of the English. In the same year Murray published a book by Helen Maria Williams, whom Shelley and Mary had sought to find on their previous visit to Paris, entitled *The State of France in 1815.*

⁴ Mary Shelley to T. L. Peacock, May 17, 1815, in *A History of a Six Weeks' Tour* (1817), Julian *Works,* VI, 120. This letter, with a succeeding one to Peacock dated June 1 (ibid., 121) and Shelley's letter of May 15 to Peacock, is the basis for all that is known of Shelley and Mary between May 5 and June 23, 1816.

⁵ Shelley to Peacock, May 15, 1816, Julian *Works,* IX, 162.

⁶ *A History of a Six Weeks' Tour* (London, 1817), Julian *Works,* VI, 87–143.

⁷ The first record of their meeting is to be found in Polidori's journal (*The Diary of Dr. John William Polidori,* ed. W. M. Rossetti, 1911). On the 27th he describes (p. 101) Shelley as he appeared at dinner with Byron as " bashful, shy, consumptive " — also as " twenty six," though Shelley was not yet twenty-four. The same entry shows that Polidori knew the situation between Byron and Claire. A note in Prothero's *Letters and Journals of Lord Byron* (III, 333, note 2) states that Byron stopped at Dejean's Hôtel d'Angleterre. This supports Dowden's statement that the two parties lodged in the same hotel. Polidori's diary is noncommittal on this point, and I find no contemporary evidence to establish it. Shelley's letter of May 15, 1816 to Peacock has always been printed with the heading: " Hôtel de Sécheron, Geneva." But the original MS. of this letter, in the Widener Library at Harvard, is headed only " Geneva," with the date. This letter, as inaccurately printed, is, I believe, the only reason why Shelley's residence has commonly been given as the Hôtel de Sécheron.

⁸ See note 11, Chapter xi, and note 76, Chapter xiv.

⁹ Mary Shelley to Peacock, May 17, 1816, in *A History of a Six Weeks' Tour,* Julian *Works,* VI, 120.

¹⁰ *Childe Harold's Pilgrimage* (1816), III, stanzas 86, 87. See following note.

¹¹ Mary Shelley to Peacock, June 1, 1816, in *A History of a Six Weeks' Tour,* Julian *Works,* VI, 121. This is perhaps the same storm as the one made memorable by Byron in *Childe Harold's Pilgrimage,* III, stanzas 102–4. But whether or not Byron's stanzas on Lake Leman were aided by Mary's observations is uncertain, since Mary's two letters, though written before Byron's stanzas, were not published until afterwards, and may have been amended in publication.

¹² Thomas Moore, op. cit., II, 27.

¹³ Ibid., II, 24.

¹⁴ Ibid., II, 30. The episode is not mentioned in Polidori's *Diary* unless he referred to it when he wrote that he had " threatened to shoot Shelley one day on the water."

¹⁵ Polidori's *Diary*, as cited in note 7 above, pp. 116 and 127. Mary was in fact two years younger than Polidori.

¹⁶ Thomas Moore, op. cit., II, 27–8. Polidori did commit suicide in August 1821.

¹⁷ Polidori's *Diary*, 125–8. Corroborated in general by Byron's letter to Murray, May 15, 1819 (*Letters and Journals of Lord Byron,* IV, 296–8).

¹⁸ Moore, op. cit., II, 21. Moore's informant was Mary Shelley. Byron's letter of May 15, 1819 to Murray (*Letters and Journals of Lord Byron,* IV, 296–8) omits this detail.

¹⁹ Mrs. Shelley's Preface to *Frankenstein* (revised ed.). Mary testifies here that her efforts were constantly stimulated by Shelley, but that he furnished none of the incidents and wrote no part of it except the original Preface. The *Quarterly* reviewer, as Mary knew from Peacock, had supposed the novel was written by Shelley.

²⁰ On July 24, in the midst of the Chamouni expedition, Mary entered in her journal: " I read ' Nouvelle Heloise ' and write my story." *Shelley and Mary,* I, 100.

²¹ These dates are not quite certain. Polidori's diary dates the departure June 22, but Shelley dated a letter: " Geneva, June 24." However, another letter of Shelley's dated June 23 speaks of the voyage as already begun. Shelley wrote Peacock that the return journey from Ouchy began " Saturday, the 29th June " and lasted two days.

²² Shelley to Peacock, July 12, [1816], Julian *Works,* IX, 167–77.

²³ Shelley's letter cited above omits the final detail, which is supplied from Moore, op. cit., II, 32. Byron's letter cited in notes 17 and 18 above corroborates Moore's account.

²⁴ *Childe Harold's Pilgrimage,* III, stanza 101. This passage in its entirety (stanzas 99–104) shows Byron going far beyond the love described by Rousseau. Professor Peck remarks (*Life,* I, 461) that Byron is here reflecting Shelley's doctrine of Love. At this stage of Shelley's development I should prefer calling it Intellectual Beauty, but the two are so much the same that the difference is hardly worth a quibble.

²⁵ Shelley to Peacock, July 12, 1816, Julian *Works,* IX, 173.

[26] *Childe Harold's Pilgrimage,* III, stanza 107.

[27] Shelley to Peacock, July 12, [1816], Julian *Works,* IX, 176.

[28] Ibid., IX, 174.

[29] Ibid., IX, 170, 175.

[30] Mrs. Shelley says (Notes on Poems of 1816) that the boat excursion was the "inspiration" for "Hymn to Intellectual Beauty." Shelley wrote Leigh Hunt (December 8, 1816, Julian *Works,* IX, 208) that it was "composed under the influence of feelings which agitated me even to tears."

[31] Shelley obtained a detailed view of these distresses in Fanny Imlay's letter of July 29, 1816 (*Shelley and Mary,* I, 104–13), printed with omissions by Dowden (*Life,* II, 39–42).

[32] Godwin to Shelley, May 29, 1816, in *Shelley and Mary,* I, 93.

[33] Shelley to Godwin, June 23, 1816, Julian *Works,* IX, 165–6.

[34] Shelley to Godwin, July 17, 1816, ibid., IX, 177–8.

[35] Shelley to R. Hayward, June 24, 1816, ibid., IX, 166–7.

[36] Shelley-Whitton papers as quoted in part by Ingpen: *Shelley in England,* II, 467–9.

[37] Shelley to Peacock, July 17, 1816, Julian *Works,* IX, 178–81.

[38] Shelley to Peacock, August 2, 1816, ibid., IX, 190. The same letter mentions four unpaid accounts.

[39] Ibid., IX, 181.

[40] Another side of Wordsworth, however, appeared still as odious to Shelley as when he had written his sonnet on Wordsworth's desertion of liberalism. At some time during his Swiss sojourn, inspired apparently by the receipt of a celandine in a letter from Peacock, Shelley wrote the poem "To a Celandine," first printed by Mr. Peck (Boston *Herald,* December 21, 1925, and *Life,* I, 477–9). The poem is considerably below the quality Shelley's verse had now attained, but is interesting as showing Shelley's divided attitude toward Wordsworth. During the year Wordsworth had published several odes and sonnets glorifying Waterloo. Shelley expresses the sad conviction that a deathless poet has sold his soul to infamy when he can be bought to glorify bloodshed.

[41] *Childe Harold's Pilgrimage,* III, stanza 75.

[42] *Shelley and Mary,* III, 894, October 19, 1822, quoted by Dowden (*Life,* II, 25) and Mrs. Marshall (*Mary Shelley,* II, 43).

[43] Shelley to Peacock, July 22, 1816, Julian *Works,* IX, 183–4. Parallel accounts in Shelley's letters and in *Shelley and Mary* show the usual variations in spelling. Thus Servox and Cerveau, Clusis and Cluses, etc.

⁴⁴ *Shelley and Mary,* I, 98.

⁴⁵ Mrs. Shelley (Notes on the Poems of 1816) says that the poem was inspired by a view of Mont Blanc as Shelley lingered " on the Bridge of Arve on his way through the valley of Chamouni." This would seem to date the inception of the poem July 22, the day before Shelley's visit to the glaciers. Shelley dated the poem July 23, which, in view of his experience with glaciers on that day and his letter to Peacock, seems conclusive as to when the poem was written. The idea for it may still have occurred as Mrs. Shelley relates. The viewpoint from which the scenery is described is consistently that of the Bridge, though it is not mentioned. The poem has phrases in common with the journal entry for July 22 and also with the part of Shelley's letter to Peacock, written on the next day.

⁴⁶ This doubt may be due to a feeling that the glaciers were a fit symbol of the destructive spirit, Ahriman, as Shelley had written to Peacock on July 24 (Julian *Works,* IX, 186–7), and suggested Buffon's " sublime but gloomy theory " that the whole earth would eventually become " a mass of frost." Probably Byron's use of Arimanes in *Manfred,* in a general setting identical with what Shelley described in his letter to Peacock, arose from conversation with Shelley inspired by Peacock's letter and Shelley's answer.

⁴⁷ Shelley to Peacock, July 25, 1816, Julian *Works,* IX, 188.

⁴⁸ See the essay " The Atheist: An Incident at Chamonix," by Gavin de Beer, in *On Shelley* (London, 1938), from which my account is largely drawn. The inscription defaced by Byron cannot have been either the Hôtel de Londres or the Montanvert inscription, since both were obviously legible and undefaced after Byron's visit. And as Sallenches was the only other point at which the Byron and Shelley parties had been in the same inn, it must have been an otherwise unreported inscription there which Byron saw and defaced. The October 1824 correspondent of the *Christian Observer* (*On Shelley,* 43) mentions similar inscriptions by Shelley " in several of the albums or registers of the hotels." The page from the Hôtel de Londres register is owned by Lord Crewe and is described in his *Among My Books* (London, 1898), 71.

⁴⁹ From August 13 to 29 Byron called at Mont Alègre on August 18, 20, 21, 24, 25, and 28; Shelley was with Byron on the lake without Mary or Claire on August 19 (with Monk Lewis), 23, and 27 (with Hobhouse and Scrope Davies, apparently); Shelley was at Diodati without the ladies on August 14, 17, 18, 19, 20, 23, 24, 26, and 27, and with Claire (following Byron's calls at Mont Alègre) on August

21 and 25. Claire was at Diodati, copying, on August 14 (*Shelley and Mary*, I, 114–34). This confirms the last statement of Hobhouse in note 56, below.

⁵⁰ *Shelley and Mary*, I, 113 and 114, August 10 and 12 respectively. Polidori, op. cit., 136.

⁵¹ Fanny Imlay to Mary Shelley, July 29, 1816, *Shelley and Mary*, I, 104–13. Printed in part by Dowden (*Life*, II, 39–42) and in full by Mrs. Marshall (*Mary Shelley*, I, 147–55).

⁵² Charles Clairmont to Shelley and Mary, August 8, 1816, *Shelley and Mary*, I, 114–27.

⁵³ Shelley to J. J. Paschoud (fragment), November 9, 1816, Julian *Works*, IX, 203.

⁵⁴ Mary Shelley to Peacock, June 1, 1816, ibid., VI, 121–3.

⁵⁵ In a letter to Jane Williams in 1827 (otherwise undated, *Shelley and Mary*, IV, 1086) Claire commented at some length on the difference between happy and unhappy passions, and speaks from her own experience: "I am unhappily the victim of a *happy passion*. I had one; like all things perfect in its kind, it was fleeting, and mine only lasted ten minutes, but these ten minutes have discomposed the rest of my life."

⁵⁶ R. E. Prothero, op. cit., III, 347–8. Hobhouse, Byron's visitor, further reassured Augusta in a letter written September 9, the day after Byron's letter. "Your excellent relative is living with the strictest attention to decorum, and free from all offence either to God, or man, or woman. The mischief-making telescopes of some inquisitive moralists . . . were said to have discerned certain robes and flounces on his Lordship's balcony, but I can assure you that the petticoats are in the imagination of the spectator [rather] than in the actual company of your belied brother, and that he has given no cause for scandal. . . . There was, indeed, until a fortnight ago, a neighbouring gentleman who had two ladies living in his house under the Château Diodati, and as you may suppose, both and each of these . . . were most liberally assigned to the person who was thought accustomed to consider the care of such kind of appurtenances. . . . However this may have been . . . this respectable château was witness to no sort of disorder, and . . . neither Mr. Davies or myself ever caught a glimpse of anything more suspicious than a second Mrs. Muhle (if she so spells her name) who is the Dame Jacinthe of this residence" (ibid., III, 347). Hobhouse and Davies arrived on August 26.

⁵⁷ In December Byron wrote Augusta: "I forgot to tell you — that

the *Demoiselle* — who returned to England from Geneva — went there to produce a new baby B. who is now about to make his appearance." Lord Lovelace: *Astarte* (London, 1921), 280.

⁵⁸ *Shelley and Mary,* I, 102, 103 (July 28 and August 2).

⁵⁹ In Iris Origo's *Allegra* (London, 1935), 71–4, is quoted a letter from Claire to Byron, written apparently in May 1821, in which Claire reminds Byron of his promise that the child should always live with one of its parents. A passage in her notebook, quoted by Ethel C. Mayne (*Byron,* second ed., 1924, p. 278), states Byron's promise to leave the child with Claire for at least its first seven years.

⁶⁰ *Shelley and Mary,* I, 128–32; first published by Mary Shelley in 1840 in *Essays, Letters from Abroad,* etc.

⁶¹ *Conversations of Lord Byron with Lady Blessington* (1834), 42.

⁶² Journal for August 18, *Shelley and Mary,* I, 128; quoted in Julian *Works,* VI, 147.

⁶³ *Life and Correspondence of M. G. Lewis* (London, 1839), II, 158–63.

⁶⁴ Journal for August 26, 27, 28, in *Shelley and Mary,* I, 133, 134; also Shelley to Byron, September 8, 1816, Julian *Works,* IX, 196. I take it that the anecdote to which Shelley's letter refers was told by Polidori rather than Hobhouse, since only the former seems to have been seen by Shelley on the evening in question.

⁶⁵ Shelley to Byron, September 8, 1816, Julian *Works,* IX, 195.

⁶⁶ *Shelley and Mary,* I, 136; and *Laon and Cythna,* V, stanza xxii.

⁶⁷ Shelley to Byron, September 29, 1816, Julian *Works,* IX, 199; see also Shelley's letter of September 8 to Byron, ibid., IX, 195.

⁶⁸ Shelley to Peacock, July 17, 1816, ibid., IX, 180.

⁶⁹ Journal for May 28, 1817, *Shelley and Mary,* I, 202.

⁷⁰ Southey copied the inscription at Montanvert and talked of it on his return; he did not repeat the incest scandal, which was later supposed to have been spread by Henry Brougham. Byron held Southey guilty of both offences and charged him with his guilt in the Appendix to *The Two Foscari* (1821). Southey's answer may be found in the *Courier* for January 6, 1822, reprinted in the *Examiner* for January 13, 1822. An earlier, somewhat veiled contradiction of the tales of immorality may be found in the *New Monthly Magazine* for April 1819 (XI, 193–5), under Original Communications, entitled "Extract of a Letter from Geneva." The letter describes Byron's life in Geneva, with some account of the Shelleys, including the " atheos " inscription in the inn album.

⁷¹ Journal of Lady Blessington, for October 8, 1822, as quoted in

both the *Observer* and *The Times* (London), July 9, 1922. Lady Blessington adds: "This was, in language somewhat different, the sentiment of our boatman's account of Byron and Shelley, two of the most remarkable spirits of our age. He seemed to admire the first, but it is evident he loved the second."

Chapter XVI

GENERAL SOURCES

Shelley's letters (Julian *Works* IX, and *Atlantic Monthly*, January, February, and March 1930); *Shelley and Mary*, including Mary Shelley's journal; the Shelley-Whitton papers as quoted in Ingpen's *Shelley in England;* the letters of William Godwin as quoted in C. Kegan Paul's *William Godwin, His Friends and Contemporaries* — all as previously cited.

Also the Chancery papers in the case of the Westbrooks versus Shelley, as quoted in H. B. Forman's edition of Medwin's *Revised Life of Shelley* and in the *Atlantic Monthly* for January, February, and March 1930.

NOTES AND REFERENCES

[1] So Shelley understood, as shown by the letters cited in the following note. But Murray's letter of September 20, 1816 to Byron (S. Smiles: *A Publisher and His Friends,* London, 1891, I, 367) speaks only of Kinnaird as standing out for the higher price.

[2] Shelley to Byron, September 11, 29, and November 20, 1816, and to John Murray, October 2 and 30, Julian *Works,* IX, 196, 197, 205, 201, 202, respectively. William Gifford, editor of the *Quarterly Review,* which Murray published, usually read Byron's proofs for Murray. There is no extant letter directing that he read the proofs of *Childe Harold,* Canto iii; on the contrary, Byron had suggested Moore, and, in his absence, Shelley (Prothero: *Lord Byron's Letters and Journals,* III, 344). It is clear, however (contrary to Dowden: *Life,* II, 58), that Shelley did not read the proofs.

³ As quoted by Mr. Peck: *Life,* I, 496, 497. I have been unable to locate the full text of the letters. Murray's changed attitude may have been entirely due to the Chancery proceedings.

⁴ Shelley to Byron, September 11, 1816, Julian *Works* IX, 196.

⁵ Claire Clairmont to Mary Shelley, " Friday, September," 1816, in *Shelley and Mary,* I, 138–9. Shelley, as Hogg had observed before, hated greatcoats.

⁶ Shelley to Godwin, October 2, 1816, Julian *Works,* IX, 200. On September 24 Shelley transferred to Richard Whitton (son of the attorney, acting as trustee for Sir Timothy) his reversionary interests in the estates comprised in the settlements of 1782 and 1791 and received in return £3,500 in Consolidated Bank Annuities. As Shelley needed money immediately, Whitton advanced him £1,700 pending the sale of the securities. The fact that Shelley did not receive cash immediately may account for his delay in notifying Godwin. Since most of Shelley's debts were paid in 1815 at the time of the former settlement and since after paying his subsequent debts there was left only £248, it is evident that in little more than a year Shelley had spent nearly £1,452 beyond his income of £800. This amount coincides rather closely with the cost of his lease and house furnishings at Marlow shortly after this date (the lease alone cost £1,200) and may have been held in reserve by Shelley for this purpose, to which he was already committed. All that is known of the settlement with Whitton is from Shelley's letter of October 2, the Shelley-Whitton papers (Ingpen: *Shelley in England,* II, 470), and from two letters of Fanny Imlay to Mary dated September 26 and October 3, 1816 (*Shelley and Mary,* I, 140–2 and 143–6). The journal mentions no settlement with Sir Timothy at all, and no communication with Longdill either immediately before or immediately after September 24, on which date Shelley is said simply to have gone to London. Fanny's letter and the Shelley-Whitton papers supply the details of this visit.

⁷ Ingpen: *Shelley in England,* II, 470–2. After Harriet's death a new will, dated February 18, 1817, omitted Harriet's legacy, increased that of her children by £1,000 each, added £6,000 for William Shelley, and in other respects repeated the former will. Shortly before his death Shelley intended changing his will to include a bequest of £2,000 to Leigh Hunt and to reduce the legacy to Claire Clairmont, which through his lawyer's mistake (by omitting the word " these " before £6,000) was construed to mean £12,000 (Mrs. Julian Marshall: *Life and Letters of Mary Wollstone-*

craft Shelley, II, 302–3). After the death of Sir Timothy Shelley in 1844 Shelley's will of 1817 was put into effect. Claire received £12,-000 and Leigh Hunt a life-annuity of £120.

⁸ This is partly a matter of inference. On December 6 Mary wrote Shelley: " I shall write to Mrs. Godwin to-morrow, but let me know what you hear from Hayward and Papa, as I am greatly interested in these affairs." And on the same date she wrote in her journal: " Letter from Mrs. Godwin and £100 " (*Shelley and Mary,* I, 168–9).

⁹ Shelley to Byron, September 29, 1816, Julian *Works,* IX, 197.

¹⁰ Kegan Paul, op. cit., II, 241–2, quoted the two items from the *Cambrian,* October 12 and 19.

¹¹ *Shelley and Mary,* I, 81, quoted by Dowden: *Life,* I, 521.

¹² *Shelley and Mary,* I, 94, quoted by Dowden: *Life,* II, 24.

¹³ *Shelley and Mary,* I, 110, 104, quoted by Mrs. Marshall: *Life and Letters of Mary Shelley,* I, 152, 148.

¹⁴ They left on September 24, according to Fanny's letter of September 26 to Mary (*Shelley and Mary,* I, 140).

¹⁵ Kegan Paul, op. cit., II, 243–4.

¹⁶ Shelley to Claire Clairmont, December 30, 1816, Julian *Works,* IX, 214.

¹⁷ Dowden: *Life,* II, 50–1. This mere opinion is rather stressed by Dowden, who ignores Kegan Paul's statement (op. cit., II, 241) that the aunts had arranged for Fanny to visit them in Dublin and had then departed for Wales, where possibly Fanny started to meet them.

¹⁸ Mary to Shelley, December 17, 1816, Mrs. Marshall, op. cit., I, 177.

¹⁹ Maria Gisborne's unpublished journal, under date of July 9, 1820, quotes Godwin as saying " that the three girls were all equally in love with —— [Shelley], and that the eldest put an end to her existence owing to the preference given to her younger sister." In a note (*Life,* II, 50) Dowden discusses this statement and Claire Clairmont's later endorsement of it, and demonstrates its unreliability. Both Mrs. Marshall and Kegan Paul reject the idea of Fanny's love being other than sisterly. Their attitude seems amply supported by the tone of Fanny's letters and by the fact that, after Shelley's elopement with Mary, Fanny saw him probably less than half a dozen times. For Fanny's possible attachment to Shelley before the elopement, see Chapter xii.

²⁰ Shelley to Byron, January 17, 1817, Julian *Works,* IX, 219. At

the W. van R. Whitall sale (Anderson Art Galleries, February 14, 15, 16, 1927) an unpublished undated letter of Shelley's to Godwin was sold to Dr. A. S. W. Rosenbach, which from the excerpts in the sales catalogue seems to refer to Fanny's suicide.

[21] Godwin to Mary, October 13, 1816, *Shelley and Mary*, I, 148. Quoted by Dowden: *Life*, II, 58.

[22] Charles Clairmont to Shelley and Mary, August 8, 1817, *Shelley and Mary*, I, 216.

[23] Godwin to W. T. Baxter, May 12, 1817. This unpublished letter, from which extensive quotations were printed in the Catalogue [Sotheby's?] of the sale of "The Property of a Gentleman living at Leamington," December 8, 1911, was known to Dowden, who quoted (*Life*, I, 425) Godwin's assertion of Harriet's infidelity to Shelley, but who ignores the account it gives of Mary's marriage and of Fanny's death. The latter is important as indicating Godwin's belief at the time that Fanny's depression was due to the elopement, but not to a hopeless love for Shelley. The sentence preceding the passage quoted in the text is: "It grieves me to add that Fanny did not live to witness this favourable revolution in our family" (i.e., Mary's marriage).

[24] Claire Clairmont to Byron, October 27, 1816, *Shelley and Mary*, I, 150.

[25] *The Last Man*, 1826, I, 280 ff. Noted by Peck: *Life*, I, 493, note.

[26] On the basis of Claire's statement alone, ignoring the evidence of the journal, Mrs. Marshall (op. cit., I, 168) says: "Shelley's health was shattered"; and Dowden (*Life*, II, 58): "The shock of excitement and grief caused by so terrible an event was for a time disastrous to Shelley's health. . . . This we learn from a letter of Miss Clairmont." The journal does not prove that Shelley was not deeply affected in spirits, but it quite precludes a shattered state of health, even if we suppose without evidence that Shelley drove himself to the activities there listed.

[27] Claire had separate lodgings at 12 New Bond Street, but spent much of her time at 5 Abbey Churchyard. Shelley wrote several letters from Claire's lodgings. The evidence is not conclusive, but it seems easier (considering Mary's objections to living with Claire) to suppose separate lodgings for Claire than for Shelley.

[28] Shelley to Byron, November 20, 1816, Julian *Works*, IX, 204.

[29] Charles Clairmont to Shelley and Mary, November 18, 1816, *Shelley and Mary*, I, 153–64, incomplete. Shelley wrote to Charles

on December 30, enclosing £20 (referred to in Julian *Works,* IX, 214).

³⁰ Shelley to Godwin, November 24, 1816, Julian *Works,* IX, 206. The money was otherwise secured by December 5.

³¹ Shelley to Leigh Hunt, December 8, 1816, ibid., IX, 207–10. This letter shows that Shelley sent Leigh Hunt his " Hymn to Intellectual Beauty " before he saw the notice in the *Examiner.* Its receipt was acknowledged by Hunt in the *Examiner* for October 6, 1816, but it was not published until January 19, 1817. An entry in Mary's journal shows that Shelley received a letter from Hunt on December 1, which probably informed him that a notice would appear. On December 6 Mary wrote a letter to Shelley (Dowden: *Life,* II, 63, from *Shelley and Mary,* I, 167) in which she mentions that a considerable sum of money had been sent by Shelley to Hunt, whose acknowledgment of its receipt was overdue. Perhaps Hunt's " vexation " at Shelley's " precipitancy " was due to Shelley's writing him a letter to ask if it had been received; perhaps, on the other hand, it was due to the original gift. Professor Dowden thinks this sum may have been either a personal gift or a subscription to a relief fund sponsored by Hunt. The last paragraph of Shelley's letter to Hunt certainly indicates that it was a personal gift from a " friend " of Shelley's, that Hunt refused to accept it other than as a loan and sent Shelley £5 to pay the " interest," and that Shelley gracefully consented to its nominal status as a loan while at the same time he persuaded Hunt to accept the interest as a personal gift. The partial list of Shelley's cheques printed by Peck (*Life,* II, 437) shows a check of £5 to Leigh Hunt or bearer endorsed December 9, 1816, and another for £50, endorsed nine days later.

³² December 6, 1816, *Shelley and Mary,* I, 167, quoted in Marshall, op. cit., I, 172–3; also Dowden: *Life,* II, 61–3. Shelley's choice of a house was probably delayed by his occasional curious desire to duplicate in his own life some situation from a favourite book. He was an admirer of Charles Brockden Brown's *Wieland.* A summer house in that novel so won his admiration, according to Peacock (*Memoirs,* II, 327–8), that " in looking for a country house he always examined if he could find such a summer house, or a place to erect one."

³³ Arthur H. Beavan: *James and Horace Smith* (London, 1899), 136–8.

³⁴ Dowden: *Life,* I, 511, note.

[35] Shelley to Byron, January 17, 1817, Julian *Works*, IX, 219. In this letter Shelley speaks of his two recent sorrows as " overwhelming " and speaks of having been beaten down by grief, but makes no reference to his health.

[36] Thomas Hookham, Jr., to Shelley, December 13, 1816. Quoted in Dowden: *Life*, II, 67–8, and Ingpen: *Shelley in England*, II, 474–5.

[37] Once before Charles's birth and once to visit Bracknell (*Shelley and Mary*, I, 28 and 144).

[38] Shelley dated a letter from 41 Hans Place on January 17, 1815 (Julian *Works*, IX, 111). A deed among the Shelley-Whitton papers dated May 1, 1815 gives his residence as Hans Place, Chelsea (Ingpen: *Shelley in England*, II, 477). Mary's journal shows that Shelley and Mary moved to lodgings in Hans Place on February 8, 1815 and to other unnamed lodgings on March 2. Thus Shelley lived in more than one house in the neighbourhood between January and May 1815.

[39] Hogg first noticed Harriet's interest in suicide while they were seeing the sights of York together, and commented upon it thus (*Life*, I, 280):

> She spoke of self-murder serenely before strangers; and at a dinner party I have heard her describe her feelings, opinions, and intentions with respect to suicide with prolix earnestness; and she looked so calm, so tranquil, so blooming, and so handsome that the astonished guests smiled." (Hogg continues to relate how she once dismayed a vegetarian dinner party by suddenly asking the guests " whether they did not feel sometimes strongly inclined to kill themselves.")

[40] First published by W. Courthope Forman in *Cornhill Magazine* LII, 31–2 (January 1922), reprinted by Peck: *Life*, I, 501–3.

[41] Davis: *Memorials of Knightsbridge* (London), 112–13. On that account, states the same authority, as quoted by Peck (*Life*, I, 504), Harriet's body was spared a suicide's burial. This could only be true if the landlord's daughter, Mary Ann Phillips, suppressed evidence of suicide. Harriet was not legally a suicide till so pronounced by the coroner's jury, which declined to do so.

[42] Ingpen: *Shelley in England*, II, 481.

[43] Shelley's letter to Medwin, October 21, 1811, insisted that Harriet's name should be spelled with a double *t*, and it is so spelled in the documents submitted in the Chancery proceedings by both Shelley and the Westbrooks.

[44] Ingpen: *Shelley in England,* II, 481–2. Burial from her father's home would have revealed Harriet's identity.

[45] Shelley to Mary, December 16, 1816, Julian *Works,* IX, 211. The genuineness of this letter has been challenged and defended in a series of notes in the London *Times Literary Supplement,* March 20, 27, April 3, 10, 17, and 24, 1937. Both Miss Sylva Norman and Mr. Graham Pollard, who suspect the letter, agree with Mr. Seymour de Ricci, its defender, that forged versions of the same letter exist and that these forgeries are based upon a genuine original. No specific reason is advanced why the letter in question may not be this original (as Lady Shelley evidently supposed), but Mr. Pollard has tried to show that its handling when it allegedly went through the mails again in 1859 was not according to postal regulations — which, if established, leaves only a choice between forgery and an all too possible postal irregularity in 1859. I agree with Mr. de Ricci that the handwriting and general appearance of the letter seem convincing, and I am unable to agree with Miss Sylva Norman's suggestion that the style and psychology are un-Shelleyan.

It seems to have occurred to no one that if this letter, dated either December 15 or 16, is a forgery, it could hardly have been answered by Mary Shelley on December 17. Yet Mary Shelley's letter of that date clashes in no detail with the alleged forgery, and the Chancery references in both letters dovetail perfectly. This letter, first published in 1886, could hardly have been used in 1859 or earlier in fabricating a forged letter to which it would be the authenticating "reply."

[46] The complete record of the coroner's investigation is printed in Ingpen's *Shelley in England,* II, 647–51.

[47] Shelley to Southey, August 17, 1820, Julian *Works,* X, 204. For fuller testimony on this point see Chapter xii, note 28, and Charles Clairmont's letter, Appendix III.

[48] Peacock: *Memoirs,* II, 348. Medwin (*Revised Life,* 237) states that in his last years Shelley fell into a mood of distressing melancholy if the conversation turned on suicide.

[49] Mary to Shelley, December 17, 1816, *Shelley and Mary,* I, 172. Printed in Marshall, op. cit., I, 176–8 and Dowden: *Life,* II, 70–1.

[50] Shelley to Eliza Westbrook, December 18, 1816. First printed by Professor Leslie Hotson in the *Atlantic Monthly,* CXLV, 174–5 (February 1930).

[51] Leslie Hotson: "A Footnote to Shelley," *Atlantic Monthly,* CXLV, 353–4 (March 1930).

[52] Claire Clairmont to Edward Trelawny, undated, but evidently written many years after Shelley's death. Claire is paraphrasing a letter from her mother to Lady Mountcashell. Dowden (*Life*, II, 71) evidently used this letter as a basis for his statement that Sir Lumley Skeffington was consulted, but ignored Mrs. Godwin's story of how Mary was summoned to London by Godwin, how Shelley resisted Godwin's insistence upon immediate marriage, and how Mary compelled his assent by a threat of suicide. This story is discredited by Shelley's expressed desire to marry Mary, in his letter written immediately after Harriet's suicide. Claire's letter is to be found in R. Glynn Grylls: *Claire Clairmont* (London, 1939), 272–5.

[53] Shelley to Claire Clairmont, December 30, 1816, Julian *Works*, IX, 214.

[54] Dowden: *Life*, II, 72; also C. Kegan Paul, op. cit., II, 245.

[55] Godwin to W. T. Baxter, May 12, 1817, as quoted in the sales catalogue of " The Property of a Gentleman living at Leamington," December 8, 1911, item 299.

[56] Godwin to Hull Godwin, February 21, 1817, Kegan Paul, op. cit., II, 246.

[57] The Chancery papers relating to the case usually known as "*Westbrooks* vs. *Shelley*" have been published by H. Buxton Forman in an appendix to his edition of Medwin's *Revised Life of Shelley* (London, 1913), 463–86 and by Leslie Hotson in the *Atlantic Monthly* for January, February, and March 1930, CXLV, 122–33, 166–77, and 350–8. The former were fully used by Dowden; the latter have not been used by any biographer of Shelley. See notes 64 and 66, below.

[58] Shelley to Mary, January 11, 1817, Julian *Works*, IX, 215–16.

[59] Ibid. Shelley failed to make use of Godwin's information in his defence. Since he stated a desire to do so, and considered that everything hinged on the issue, it is certain that he must have made every effort to find support for Godwin's statement, and failed.

[60] Shelley to Byron, January 17, 1817, Julian *Works*, IX, 218–19.

[61] Medwin, op. cit., 470, quoted by Dowden: *Life*, II, 78. Mary Shelley has contradicted this statement. Writing to Leigh Hunt (December 28, 1825), correcting certain errors in an article on Shelley that Hunt had submitted to the *Westminster Review*, she says: " They did not part by mutual consent, and Shelley's justification, to me obvious, rests on other grounds." The whole letter is quoted in T. J. Wise: *A Shelley Library* (privately printed, London,

1924), 6. Peacock, to whom Hunt's article had been submitted by the editors, recommended its rejection on account of this and other misstatements. Very probably he also considered that its publication might irritate Sir Timothy Shelley against Mary.

62 Shelley-Whitton papers, quoted by Ingpen: *Shelley in England,* II, 492. He had previously attempted to persuade Shelley of this danger, he added, through Longdill.

63 William Hazlitt: "Lord Eldon — Mr. Wilberforce," in *The Spirit of the Age* (1825), Everyman's Library ed., 311, 310.

64 Wetherell's brief, formerly in the possession of Mr. H. B. Forman, is summarized more fully by Dowden (*Life,* II, 81–3). It was not printed by Forman with the other Chancery papers, but is reproduced in the present work, Appendix IV. Reporters were excluded from the hearing, but the case was briefly reported in the *Globe* and the *Morning Chronicle,* both of January 25, 1817. The *Examiner* for January 26 quotes the *Chronicle* account and comments editorially on the case as one in which a wrong decision might sweep aside gains already achieved by the progress of liberalism.

65 Shelley to Godwin, December 11, 1817, Julian *Works,* IX, 267.

66 Dowden (*Life,* II, 86–8) quotes extensively from Shelley's rough draft of this document, which seems subsequently to have disappeared. It is not printed by H. B. Forman with the other Chancery papers.

67 Peacock: *Memoirs,* II, 346. Shelley could appeal to Parliament.

68 Ibid.

69 Leslie Hotson: "A Footnote to Shelley," *Atlantic Monthly,* CXLV, 350–8 (March 1930).

70 Wetherell's brief states that Shelley had never seen one of his children, and Shelley makes the same statement in his letter of September 20, 1817 to Lord Eldon (Julian *Works,* IX, 241). Yet Shelley had called upon Harriet soon after Charles's birth and had produced him in court (possibly by deputy) during the Chancery proceedings following the death of Sir Bysshe Shelley. As Shelley's children by Harriet appear only once hereafter, when there was a brief stoppage in their allowance in 1821, it is as well to conclude their stories here. The children appeared again in Chancery in 1823, after Shelley's allowance for their maintenance was terminated by his death. Until the middle of 1823 Sir Timothy continued the allowance, but declined to do so indefinitely, since it would be unnecessary if Shelley's legacies to them were executed. On July 21,

1823 the court appointed Sir Timothy guardian to Charles, and Mr. Westbrook and Eliza (Mrs. Farthing Beauchamp) guardians of Ianthe.

Charles was placed in Syon House Academy, his father's first school. He was a delicate child and suffered much from colds. In June 1826 he was seriously ill at Field Place, apparently of consumption. On September 16, 1826 he died, and was buried in Warnham Church. His death made Shelley's second son, Percy Florence, heir to the estates after Sir Timothy's death.

Eliza (Mrs. Beauchamp) took Ianthe into her home in Somersetshire. Ianthe married (September 27, 1837) Edward Jeffries Esdaile, a Somersetshire country gentleman of a well-known Lombard Street banking family, with an income of possibly £4,000. Ianthe died in 1876. She had two children, the second of whom, William, gave Professor Dowden a description of Mrs. Beauchamp as an old lady, along with an eloquent testimony of her kindness to Ianthe. Ianthe visited Field Place with her husband shortly after her marriage and was agreeably entertained by her grandparents. After the death of Sir Timothy she occasionally visited Sir Percy Florence and Lady Shelley. Lady Shelley, who was a Shelley enthusiast, found that Ianthe had been brought up to regard her father's views with disapproval. (See *Talks with Lady Shelley*, 1925, pp. 68 ff.) Lady Shelley wrote of Ianthe on first meeting her: " Ianthe with her husband and children are with us — the first time I have seen her — She does not go along with us in our feelings on this subject, but certainly takes more interest than she will allow to herself in my sanctum where every little object connected with his memory is held sacred." (To Leigh Hunt, June 19, 1858, Brit. Mus., Add. MSS., 38,524, fol. 97.)

Ianthe's second son, the Reverend William Esdaile, died in 1915. A slight sketch of him has been left by the late Elinor Wylie, who knew him in the early 1920's (see Chapter xii, note 11). Her older son, Charles Edward Jeffries Esdaile, became a country gentleman. On October 21, 1922, at the age of seventy-seven, he died as the result of an accident in the hunting-field. Ianthe's grandson, William Esdaile, of Cothelstone House, near Taunton, Somerset, the present head of the family, still preserves the Shelley manuscripts and relics that were first examined by Professor Dowden.

Some time after the Chancery proceedings Eliza Westbrook married Mr. Robert Farthing Beauchamp, who had been associated with the Westbrooks in the trial. He had added the name Beauchamp as the condition of receiving a fortune left him by a lady of that name. Eliza inherited a considerable sum of money from her father in 1835. Ianthe was the intended heiress of both Eliza and her husband.

Chapter XVII

GENERAL SOURCES

Shelley's letters (Julian *Works,* IX); Mary Shelley's letters as quoted in H. H. Harper's *Letters of Mary W. Shelley* (printed only for members of the Bibliophile Society, Boston, 1918); Godwin's letters as quoted in C. Kegan Paul's *William Godwin, His Friends and Contemporaries; The Correspondence of Leigh Hunt;* Mary Shelley's journal; Peacock's *Memoirs* — all as previously cited.

A. H. Beavan: *James and Horace Smith.* London, 1899.

Charles and Mary Cowden Clarke: *Recollections of Writers.* London, 1878.

The Autobiography of Leigh Hunt. New York, 1850.

Thornton Hunt: " Shelley, by One Who Knew Him," *Atlantic Monthly,* February 1863.

NOTES AND REFERENCES

[1] Elizabeth Kent, Hunt's sister-in-law, whose *Flora Domestica or the Portable Flower Garden,* anon., 1823, presents a sketch of Shelley (Preface, p. xix) praising his strong intellect and gentle, sympathetic manners.

[2] Shelley to Mary, undated, Julian *Works,* IX, 218.

[3] Shelley to Claire Clairmont, January 30, 1817, Julian *Works,* IX, 220.

[4] Leigh Hunt's *Autobiography,* II, 28.

[5] Thornton Hunt: " Shelley, by One Who Knew Him," loc. cit., XI, 185–6.

[6] Respectively January 28 and February 16; January 30 and

February 9; February 15, 5, and 12; February 8, 10, and 16.

[7] Godwin's manner is so described by Charles and Mary Cowden Clarke, op. cit., 36–7.

[8] Ibid., 16.

[9] Ibid., 26. Clarke states that three of the circle once plotted to trap Coulson with three questions on widely different subjects. The questions, which he answered correctly, were (1) the value of gold coin in India relative to sterling, (2) the mode of measuring footage in standing timber, (3) a textual puzzle in an ancient classic poet. Coulson visited the Shelleys at Marlow, October 24–6 (Mary Shelley's journal for November 3).

Coulson was apparently one of the few whom Shelley later thought might appreciate *Prometheus Unbound*. A first edition of that poem, inscribed in Shelley's hand: "Coulson Esq. from the Author" was sold by the Anderson Galleries on February 16, 1927 for $1,700.

[10] Charles Cowden Clarke, op. cit., 19. Perhaps this assertion is open to some doubt in that Mary's journal for March 1, 1818 uses the phrase: "meet Mr. Novello" (at Hunt's) and Shelley's one extant letter to Novello (Julian *Works*, X, 231) addresses him formally as "Dear Sir."

[11] Charles Cowden Clarke, op. cit., 25–6.

[12] In a letter of July 25, 1822 apprising Horace Smith of Shelley's death (A. H. Beavan, op. cit., 167, 168) Hunt calls Shelley "divine minded" and says: "I cannot help thinking of him as if he were still alive, so unearthly he always appeared to me and so seraphical a thing of the elements; and this is what all his friends say."

[13] *Autobiography of Leigh Hunt* (New York, 1850), II, 23.

[14] Clarke, op. cit., 26; Shelley to Hunt, August 3, 1817, Julian *Works*, IX, 236.

[15] Hunt's *Autobiography* as cited in note 13, I, 220–1.

[16] "When I gazed upon his beaming countenance . . . when I recalled his exquisite genius, his intellectual illumination, his exuberant philanthropy, his total renunciation of self, the courage and grandeur of his soul, combined with a feminine delicacy and purity, and an almost angelic amenity and sweetness, I could almost imagine that I had been listening to a spirit from some higher sphere . . ." (Beavan, op. cit., 174–5). Horace Smith was also probably the author of the obituary tribute to Shelley that appeared in the Paris *Monthly Review*, 2: 392 (August 1822) under the title of a review of *Hellas*.

17 One of Shelley's numerous gifts to Hunt was for £1,400 (Hunt's *Autobiography,* cited in note 13, II, 31). In 1822 Smith did decline to lend Shelley money for Godwin, on grounds that Shelley promptly approved (Shelley to Horace Smith, June 29, 1822, Julian *Works,* X, 409).

18 Godwin to Mrs. Godwin, May 14, 1817, C. Kegan Paul, op. cit., II, 249. Godwin to Shelley, May 12, 1817 (*Shelley and Mary,* I, 201 A–B) evidently refers to this same matter. "Knowing that you occasionally resemble a blood horse, and start away in furious mood," he wrote, he was uneasy as to how Shelley would receive his request for an explanation.

19 Journal of Maria Gisborne, July 4, 1820. Unpublished MS. in the Ashley Library, British Museum.

20 Shelley to Leigh Hunt, September 27, 1819, Julian *Works,* X, 87.

21 Hazlitt's essay on "Paradox and Commonplace," in *Table Talk,* 1821. Leigh Hunt remonstrated with and even threatened Hazlitt on account of this and similar utterances. In July 1824, reviewing Shelley's *Posthumous Poems* for the *Edinburgh Review,* Hazlitt wrote more appreciatively, but not enthusiastically.

22 Leigh Hunt to the Shelleys, July 11, 1821, *Correspondence of Leigh Hunt* (London, 1862), I, 166.

23 *Diary,* etc. *of Henry Crabb Robinson* (Boston, 1870), I, 369 (November 6, 1817).

24 Medwin: *Revised Life* (London, 1913), 178–9.

25 *Autobiography of Leigh Hunt,* II, 36–7.

26 Keats to Shelley, August 1820, Julian *Works,* X, 195, note. The MS. of this letter, as printed in R. Glynn Grylls: *Mary Shelley* (1938), 136, is dated August 10.

27 John Dix: *Pen and Ink Sketches of Poets, Preachers, and Politicians* (London, 1846), 144. Dix quotes Charles Richards, a printer in St. Martin's Lane, as saying Shelley came to him about the printing of Keats's first volume. Quoted by Dowden: *Life,* II, 132, note.

28 Keats to Benjamin Bailey, October 8, 1817, M. B. Forman: *Letters of John Keats* (London, 1935), 53. When Keats again declined to visit Shelley in 1820 he told Charles Cowden Clarke that his sole motive was his desire to remain a free agent. Charles and Mary Cowden Clarke: *Recollections of Writers* (London, 1879), 151.

29 Mr. Peck (*Life,* I, 519) has commented upon this indebtedness of Keats to Shelley. A much fuller comment is to be found in *More Magic Dethroned,* by L. C. Thompson (London [1935]). It is Mr. Thompson's theory that Keats was extensively influenced by Shel-

ley's poetry; in fact, plagiarized Shelley in many of his best passages and sought to conceal his indebtedness. While I am entirely unconvinced by the theory, and while I regard some of the supporting parallel passages as of doubtful significance, I do find in the parallels, and in a number of unprinted parallels which Mr. Thompson was kind enough to send me, evidence that Keats was influenced by Shelley's poetry somewhat more fully than has been realized.

[30] Marlow consisted of two villages close together, known as Great and Little Marlow. The more prosperous inhabitants lived in Great Marlow. Shelley lived in Great Marlow, but headed his letters simply Marlow.

[31] The furniture was expected to arrive on Saturday, March 8. On March 18 they slept in the house for the first time. From March 2 to 18 they stayed with Peacock and his mother, where Hogg, during the last few days, was also a visitor. During this time Claire and her baby remained in London. The date of their arrival in Marlow is not mentioned in the journal, but the child (and presumably its mother) was there when Shelley wrote to Byron on April 23. These details are from Mary's letters of March 2, 5, and 18 to the Hunts in Henry H. Harper, op. cit., 29–43.

[32] Details of Albion House are taken from Dowden (*Life*, II, 110–11), Thornton Hunt ("Shelley, by One Who Knew Him," loc. cit., XI, 187), Peck (*Life*, I, 519–20), Leigh Hunt's *Autobiography* (II, Chapter xv), and Shelley's letter to Byron (April 23, 1817, Julian *Works*, IX, 227). Shelley leased from a Mr. Tylecote, at £63 annually. In the 1840's the house was divided into three tenements, one of which became a beer-shop. In May 1922 it was described in a London periodical (*Great Thoughts*) as humble, uncomfortable, and rather neglected, with a memorial tablet set in the roof, where it was nearly invisible.

[33] Mary Shelley to the Hunts, March 2 and 18, in Henry H. Harper: *Letters of Mary W. Shelley*, 31, 42. These letters do not mention the manservant, for whom Thornton Hunt is authority. Peacock (*Memoirs*, II, 364) speaks of a previous gardener who was in charge of the grounds during late December, and describes Shelley's discharging him in a fit of passion for mutilating a holly tree.

[34] A letter from Leigh Hunt to Vincent Novello, from Marlow, April 17, 1817, instructs Novello to purchase from Mr. Kirkman for Shelley a cabinet grand piano as quickly as possible, at from fifty to seventy guineas, and agrees to "the security requested" (Charles and Mary Cowden Clarke, op. cit., 196). Shelley's letter to Novello

from Pisa, January 20, 1821 (Julian *Works,* X, 231), shows that the
piano was still unpaid for. He apologizes for the delay and "apparent neglect" in answering Novello's letter, thanks Mr. Kirkman for
his forbearance, and asks to be allowed "a year from this date for
the payment of the remainder."

[35] Shelley to Godwin, March 9, 1817, Julian *Works,* IX, 221.

[36] *Shelley and Mary,* I, 194, journal entry for February 23. Under
this date Mary covers briefly the period February 23–April 10. Godwin's arrival is dated by a MS. note of Dowden's "April 2," presumably from Godwin's journal.

[37] Ibid. The guest is called C., possibly for Walter Coulson or
Charles Cowden Clarke.

[38] Mary Shelley to Leigh Hunt, March 5, 1817, *Shelley and Mary,*
I, 195, and March 2, 1817, Harper, op. cit., 33.

[39] A tablet placed upon the parapet at Albion House in 1867 an-
nounced erroneously that Byron had visited Shelley there. Accord-
ing to the local upholsterer who prepared the house for occupancy,
Shelley had one room draped in black, for an anticipated visit by
Byron (David Booth to Isabel Booth, January 9, 1818, as quoted by
Dowden: *Life,* II, 181, note).

[40] Mary Shelley to Leigh Hunt, March 2, 1817, Harper, op. cit.,
32. The Suspension Act was the suspension of habeas corpus in
1817.

[41] Thornton Hunt: "Shelley, by One Who Knew Him," loc. cit.,
XI, 189; Mary to Marianne Hunt, March 5 and 18, 1817, pp. 38 and
41 in H. H. Harper, op. cit.; Mary to Shelley, September 25, 1817, in
Shelley and Mary, I, 222; Robert Buchanan in *New Quarterly Magazine,* April 1875, p. 249.

[42] Dowden: *Life,* II, 111.

[43] Fragment: "To One Singing"; A Fragment: "On Music"; Another fragment: "On Music"; "To Constantia Singing"; and "To
Constantia." The first of these fragments seems somewhat to anticipate Shelley's famous lyric in *Prometheus Unbound,* "My Soul is an
Enchanted Boat." So far as I know, there is no definite proof that
Constantia was Claire Clairmont, but I concur in the general assumption of Claire's identity with Constantia, on the following
grounds: (1) She was the only woman in the Marlow party who
sang. (2) Claire's journal for January 19, 1818 mentions copying
"part of verses to Constantia" — the only verses of Shelley's she mentions copying during this time. (3) William Graham, in his *Last
Links with Shelley, Byron, and Keats,* 1898 (first published as

" Chats with Jane Clairmont," the *Nineteenth Century,* 1893, 1894),
quotes several conversations with Claire in 1878 in which the identity was taken for granted by both parties. (By itself I should consider this evidence almost worthless.) (4) The stone marking
Claire's grave in the Camposanto della Misericordia di Santa Maria
at Antella (a village about three miles southeast of Florence) bears
the inscription: "Clara Mary Constantia Jane Clairmont, Born
April 27, 1798, died March 19, 1879," etc. This establishes a possibility that Constantia was actually one of Claire's names, and it
shows at the very least that Claire adopted the name from the
poem — which would be enough to show her conviction that it was
written to her.

Had Mary Shelley known that the poem was written to Claire, as
presumably she did, she would have been no more willing to record
the fact than she was to record similar facts about poems written to
Jane Williams later.

Professor John Harrington Smith, in "Shelley and Claire Clairmont," *P.M.L.A.,* LIV, 803 (September 1939), quotes "To Constantia" as evidence of Shelley's having been in love with Claire.
I do not see that it necessarily means more than Shelley's reproach
at having lost a disciple.

⁴⁴ David Booth to Isabel Booth, January 9, 1818, as quoted by
Dowden: *Life,* II, 181, note.

⁴⁵ Peacock: *Memoirs,* II, 345.

⁴⁶ Only the second of these is mentioned in any document by
Shelley or Mary. For the Tyler brothers, see Dowden: *Life,* II, 112,
note. Pilcher is mentioned twice in Mary's journal (April 13 and 18)
as walking with Shelley and Mary. I assume that he was a local
resident, since the journal does not mention his arrival or departure
as a guest, but I am unable to identify him; he may even have been
the Shelleys' manservant, Harry. Mr. Brooks is known simply as the
recipient of a copy of *Queen Mab;* see H. B. Forman: *The Shelley
Library* (London, 1886), 42.

⁴⁷ H. F. B. Brett-Smith: *Works of Thomas Love Peacock, Biographical Introduction* (London, 1934), I, lxxv–lxxvi.

⁴⁸ Dowden: *Life,* II, 120.

⁴⁹ Mary Shelley, Note on the poems of 1817.

⁵⁰ Peacock: *Memoirs,* II, 348.

⁵¹ Mary Shelley, Note on the Poems of 1817.

⁵² Leigh Hunt's *Autobiography,* II, 32. The same story, altered

and heightened, is told by Hogg as occurring en route from London to Field Place, shortly before the elopement with Mary. Since Hunt was present, I take his version as the more authentic one.

[53] Thornton Hunt: "Shelley, by One Who Knew Him," loc. cit., XI, 184–204. Thornton was a remarkably sensitive and precocious child whose memories, though obviously subject to some discount, are entitled to serious consideration.

[54] Leigh Hunt: *Autobiography*, II, 32.

[55] Had Hogg been a little more observant or scrupulous, or had Hunt instead of Hogg been the narrator, perhaps a similar overtone would have survived in the story of Shelley's interviewing the Oxford babe-in-arms on the subject of the soul's pre-existence.

[56] Leigh Hunt to Shelley, April 24, 1818, *Correspondence of Leigh Hunt*, I, 118.

[57] Charles Cowden Clarke, op. cit., 152.

[58] Polly Rose is not mentioned in Mary's journal or in any extant letter. The sole authority for her story is a number of letters written by her to Lady Shelley, nearly fifty years later, which appear to have been lost after they were used by Dowden (*Life*, II, 120, 123, 124).

[59] Mary Shelley, Note on the Poems of 1817. Peacock asserts vigorously and convincingly that there was no ground for such a fear. "No one could be interested in taking them from him; no reason could be alleged for taking them from their mother; the chancellor would not have entertained the question, unless a provision had been secured for the children; and who was to do this?" *Memoirs*, II, 350.

[60] Clara Everina (for Mary Shelley's aunt), born September 2, 1817.

[61] Shelley to Lord Eldon, September 20, 1817, Julian *Works*, IX, 241.

[62] Mary Shelley, Note on the Poems of 1817.

[63] "To the Lord Chancellor," stanza 3.

[64] *Beppo*, xlvii.

[65] Mary to Shelley, September 30, 1817, Dowden: *Life*, II, 147.

[66] Probably the later date. In the *Examiner* for March 2 occurs a brief notice of the pamphlet, with an extract, but Hunt was probably giving the work an advance notice from proof-sheets he is known to have possessed. See Julian *Works*, VI, 351.

[67] Shelley to Charles Ollier before March 14, 1817, Julian *Works*, IX, 222; also February 22, 1817, ibid., IX, 221. For comments on

most of the persons listed, see William H. Davenport: " Footnote for a Political Letter of Shelley," in *Notes and Queries*, April 8, 1939, pp. 236–7.

⁶⁸ It is a nice problem as to whether Shelley and Robert Owen were actually acquainted. Owen was an occasional visitor at Godwin's home in 1816 and possibly later, and Fanny Imlay's letters to the Shelleys in Switzerland speak of him so warmly that Shelley's interests were bound to be excited, even if he had no curiosity about Owen's model mill village of New Lanark, which attracted the notice even of the Czar of Russia. It is well known that after Shelley's death the followers of Owen adopted *Queen Mab* almost as a Bible. But no reference of Owen to Shelley or vice versa is recorded while both were alive, though long after Shelley's death Robert Owen, in one of his spiritualistic séances, greeted " my old friend, Shelley." Leigh Hunt, writing to Shelley on August 27, 1817, says: "What think you of your new counsellor, Robert Owen? He has made a great sensation in town and will unlock myriads of lips" (*Correspondence of Leigh Hunt*, I, 114–15).

⁶⁹ Mary Shelley to Leigh Hunt, March 2, 1817, Harper, op. cit., 31–2.

⁷⁰ Leigh Hunt's *Autobiography*, II, 33–5; also Thornton Hunt, op. cit., XI, 186. Dowden notes (*Life*, II, 107–8, note) that this story was first told in the *Literary Examiner*, August 23, 1823, and later in John Dix's *Pen and Ink Sketches of Poets, Preachers, and Politicians*, Chapter viii. The time might be either 1816 or 1817 in Leigh Hunt's account, but Thornton Hunt states that it was during the early stages of the Chancery trial, hence 1817.

⁷¹ Details of Shelley's relations with the poor of Marlow are missing in Mary's journal, but are here supplied from Mary's Note on *The Revolt of Islam*, Peacock's *Memoirs* (II, 349), Medwin (*Revised Life*, 192), Charles and Mary Cowden Clarke (op. cit., 151), Thornton Hunt (op. cit., 187), Leigh Hunt (*Autobiography*, II, 28), and the recollections of Mr. and Mrs. Madocks as quoted by Dowden (*Life*, II, 120–2). Mr. Peck (*Life*, I, 524) quotes two passages from Mary Shelley's *The Last Man* (1826, II, 188, 233–4) evidently describing these ministrations.

⁷² Horace Smith's recollections of his visit to Marlow in December 1817, in A. H. Beavan, op. cit., 171–4; and Miss Rose's reminiscences of Shelley, as quoted by Dowden: *Life*, II, 123.

⁷³ William Howitt: *Homes and Haunts of the British Poets* (London, 1894), 313–15. The " bad joke " on Shelley's boat was adding

to its name, in chalk, to convert it from *Vaga* to *Vagabond,* at which Shelley only laughed. The forgotten bill was one that the shop-keeper forgot to submit; he testified that when Shelley left Marlow he paid all other bills " honourably, certainly, most honourably." In fact, there were other forgotten bills in Marlow.

74 The *Examiner,* October 10, 1819, p. 653. Hunt makes the same statements more briefly in his *Autobiography,* Chapter xv.

75 Peacock: *Memoirs,* II, 345; Medwin: *Revised Life,* 193.

76 Peacock, op. cit.

77 Thornton Hunt, op. cit., 189.

78 Shelley to Byron, April 23, 1817, Julian *Works,* IX, 227.

79 Peacock: *Memoirs,* II, 344.

80 *Frankenstein* was declined by Murray on June 18 and was sent to Godwin. It was submitted to Ollier on August 3, who also de-clined it before August 16. Before August 22 it was submitted to Lackington, Allen & Co., by whom it was accepted. A month later Shelley was in town, hoping for proofs. Shelley submitted some alterations on October 28 and a dedication on December 3. On December 23 the book was printed but not bound; on January 2, 1818 it was ready for circulation. On the same day Shelley sent a copy of *Frankenstein* to Sir Walter Scott, according to an unpublished letter of that date from Shelley to Scott which was sold at Sotheby's on April 11, 1921. I have seen only Sotheby's descrip-tion of the letter. *Frankenstein* was published in 1818 by Lacking-ton, Hughes, Harding, Mavor and Jones. Shelley handled all corre-spondence and kept the publishers ignorant of the author's identity. See his letters, Julian *Works,* IX, 234, 240, 242, 252, 256, 272, 278.

81 *Autobiography of Leigh Hunt,* II, 31, 32, and 29.

82 Ibid., II, 32–3.

83 Peacock: *Memoirs,* II, 350, 330–31, 349.

Chapter XVIII

GENERAL SOURCES

Shelley's letters and works; Mary Shelley's journal and Notes on the Poems of 1817, on *Rosalind and Helen,* on *The Revolt of*

Islam, and on " Prince Athanase "; the Shelley-Whitton papers
as quoted in Ingpen's *Shelley in England; Peacock's Memoirs;*
and Leigh Hunt's *Autobiography* — all as previously cited.
A. H. Beavan: *James and Horace Smith.* London, 1899.
Charles Cowden and Mary Cowden Clarke: *Recollections of
    Writers.* London, 1878.
[Thornton Hunt:] " Shelley, by One Who Knew Him," in the
    Atlantic Monthly, February 1863.

NOTES AND REFERENCES

¹ " I can well remember, that, when other persons urged upon
him cumulative reasons for any course of action, whether in politics,
or morality, or trifling personal matters of the day, he indignantly
cast aside all such makeweights, and insisted upon the one sufficient
motive. I mention this the more explicitly because the opposite
course is the most common, and some who did not sympathize with
his concentration of purpose afterwards imputed the suppression of
all but one, out of several apparent motives, to reserve, or even to a
want of candor " (Thornton Hunt, op. cit., XI, 188).

² Mary finished *Frankenstein* and wrote to Shelley in London to
obtain from Godwin the outline of a book he had suggested to her.
Claire finished a novel that has been lost. Shelley offered it unsuccessfully both to Lackington and to Taylor and Hessey before October 6, 1817 (Julian *Works,* IX, 248).

³ Mary's journal (November 3, 1817) does not specify the work,
but it was probably the *Tractatus theologico-politicus,* where the
opinions of miracles, prophets, divine law, natural and civil rights
were quite similar to Shelley's own.

⁴ Mary Shelley, Note on the Poems of 1817.

⁵ Ibid.

⁶ " I have arrived at the 380th stanza of my Poem," Shelley wrote
Hunt on August 3 (Julian *Works,* IX, 237).

⁷ Peacock: *Memoirs,* II, 345.

⁸ Shelley to Godwin, December 11, 1817, Julian *Works,* IX,
266–7.

⁹ Ibid., IX, 266. With this letter before her, Mary Shelley wrote
in her Note on the Poems of 1817: " The very illness that oppressed
and the aspect of death which had approached so near Shelley, ap-

pear to have kindled to yet keener life the Spirit of Poetry in his heart. The restless thoughts kept awake by pain clothed themselves in verse." And in her Note on *The Revolt of Islam* she speaks of his clinging to and expressing his opinions with bold ardour " in adversity and through the valley of the shadow of death." But Shelley was in splendid health and spirits when he wrote the first part of the poem, and though his illness is mentioned several times before the poem is finished, it did not interfere except very briefly with any of his regular activities nor did it cause any serious alarm, apparently, until about the time the poem was completed.

[10] An able detailed summary is to be found in Peck: *Life,* II, 10–44. Other summaries and critical discussions are H. S. Salt: *A Shelley Primer* (London: Shelley Society Publications; 1880), 54–7; John Todhunter: *A Study of Shelley* (London, 1880), 54–89. I have seen in manuscript an article by Professor K. N. Cameron, of Indiana University, which demonstrates a considerable and previously unnoted indebtedness of *The Revolt of Islam* to Volney's *Ruins of Empire*.

[11] Preface to *The Revolt of Islam.*

[12] Shelley to Godwin, December 11, 1817, Julian *Works,* IX, 266.

[13] Byron to Murray, November 24, 1818, R. E. Prothero: *Letters and Journals of Lord Byron,* IV, 273.

[14] The *Examiner* (No. 526, January 25) printed 65 lines without comment. The review proper occurs in the issues of February 1, 22, and March 1, 1818 (527: 75–6; 530: 121–2; and 531: 139–41). A large part of the review is given to Hunt's justification of Shelley's optimism and benevolent principles. The passage quoted in my text is from the issue of March 1. Hunt's summary of the action is as follows (I omit his quotations from the poem):

> The two strangers are the hero and heroine of the poem: and here the more human part of the story commences. *Laon,* the hero, relates it. He was an ardent and speculative youth, born in modern Greece; and grew up with great admiration of the beauties and kindnesses of external nature, and a great horror of the superstitions and other oppressions with which his country and mankind in general were afflicted. A beautiful female orphan under the care of his parents shared these feelings with him; and a mutual love was the consequence. She even speculated upon taking some extraordinary though gentle step to deliver the world from its thraldom; when she was torn away from him by some

slaves of the Grand Turk's Seraglio; and he himself, for endeavouring to rescue her, and for taking that opportunity of proclaiming freedom, was shut up in a prison in a rock, where his senses
forsook him. The effect of the circumstance however is not lost.
He is delivered from his dungeon by an old man, and after a
second but milder insanity, is informed by his preserver that the
people had been awakened to new ideas, and that there was a
maiden who went about exciting them to a bloodless freedom. It
was his love *Cythna*, after having been made a victim of the tyrant's lust, and having been likewise imprisoned, and robbed of
her senses. A considerable interval elapses while *Laon* recovers
his reason, but on so doing, and hearing of the exploits of her
whom he justly supposed to be his lovely friend, he takes leave
of the old man, and journeys for Constantinople, or the Golden
City, where he finds the people risen, the tyrant fallen, and
Cythna the predominant spirit of the change. He goes with others
to the palace, and sees the " sceptred wretch " sitting silent and
sullen on the footstool of his throne [quoted lines omitted]. She
clasps the tyrant's feet, and then stands up when the strangers
come nigh [quoted lines omitted]. *Laon* saves his life from the
fury of the crowd; a festival is held at which *Cythna* presides like
a visible angel, and every thing seems happiness and security. The
Revolters however are suddenly assailed by the allies of the tyrant; and the fortune of the contest is changed. *Cythna* reaches
Laon through the lost battle on a huge black Tartarian horse
" whose path makes a solitude; " and they fly to a distance through
a desolate village, in the dwellings of which the flames and human
beings were now dead [quoted lines omitted]. The only survivor
is a female, who has gone mad, and fancies herself the Plague.
The description of her desperate laughter and actions is appalling,
though not without a tendency, we think, to something overwrought and artificial. When the travellers arrive at a place of
rest, *Cythna* tells *Laon* her adventures. They have been briefly
alluded to, and include a finely-fancied and pathetic account of
a child she had in her dungeon, and which was taken from her.
Laon goes out from the retreat occasionally to get food and intelligence, and finds that Revenge, and subsequently Pestilence
and Famine, have been making terrible havoc in the city. The
tyrant and his slaves, in their terror, make frightened addresses
to heaven, and a priest advises them to expiate its " vengeance "
by sacrificing *Laon* and *Cythna*. He accordingly dispatches mem-

bers to hunt them out; upon which *Laon* comes forward disguised and offers to give up the man provided the woman be spared. They take an oath to do so, and he declares himself; but it is then declared impious to have made the oath; and at last, *Cythna* comes voluntarily forward, and shares the funeral pyre with her beloved friend, from which they find themselves suddenly sailing on a beautiful sea to the Paradise in which the Spirit of Good resides, where Cythna meets with her child who had died of the plague; and the poem concludes.

[15] Preface to *The Revolt of Islam*. Compare with Demogorgon's final speech in *Prometheus Unbound*.

[16] Shelley never explained this principle, but it is evident from various references that he believed it to be a force superior to human will, which in due course of time accomplished all sorts of revolutions more or less independent of men's efforts. Thus, in the poem "To the Lord Chancellor," written about the time he began *Laon and Cythna,* he depends on the "high commands" of Mutability, executed by a "slow sure Angel," eventually to overthrow the injustice typified by the Lord Chancellor. One thinks of Demogorgon.

[17] This argument for the probable priority of *Rosalind and Helen* is advanced by Raymond D. Havens in "'Rosalind and Helen,'" *Journal of English and Germanic Philology*, XXX, 218–22 (April 1931).

[18] Mary to Shelley, September 26, 1817, *Shelley and Mary*, I, 224. Lady Shelley (*Shelley Memorials,* 87) says that a "large part" of it was written at Marlow, but there is nothing in *Shelley and Mary* to support the statement. Mary's letter only assumed that Shelley would cast the poem aside in accordance with the doctor's orders; he may not have done so, since he wrote "Prince Athanase" later.

[19] Shelley to Peacock, August 16, 1818, Julian *Works,* IX, 320.

[20] Ibid., and Mrs. Shelley's Note on *Rosalind and Helen*. At this time Shelley must have added the Italian setting (lines 1–218 and 1240–1318) and may have added the whole story of Rosalind and her husband, which is apparently based on the married life of Isabel Baxter Booth, thus making the poem a study of two kinds of love — married and unmarried. If the Rosalind story (without the Italian touches) was written in England, it was probably done at some time after the last week in September 1817, when Mary learned for the first time that Isabel was not entirely happy in her marriage and spoke of her as "another victim of that ceremony." (Mary to Shel-

ley, September 25, 1817; Mrs. Marshall: *Life and Letters of Mary Shelley,* I, 200–1, from *Shelley and Mary.*)

By December the Shelleys knew from the conduct of both Mr. Baxter and Mr. Booth that there was no chance of renewing the friendship with Isabel. Thus all of the poem except the Italian background and a few touches of homesickness for England could have been written before Shelley left England, between December 1817 and March 1818. Why the poem was not published in its earlier state, since it seems to have been sent to a publisher, remains unexplained, but as the time elapsing before the completion of the poem in Italy was only a few months, possibly no explanation is needed.

21 Mrs. Shelley's Note to "Prince Athanase." She adds that it was "a good deal modelled on *Alastor*." In a note on one of the fragments Shelley states that he abandoned the development of Athanase's character because he feared that in aiming at extreme refinement and analysis he might be betrayed into morbidity.

22 Notes on *The Revolt of Islam.*

23 *Revolt of Islam,* II, stanzas 14, 15.

24 Mrs. Shelley, in her Note on the *Revolt of Islam,* states definitely that Laon's adviser was intended to represent Dr. Lind.

25 *The Revolt of Islam,* II, stanza 18, and V, stanza 5. Shelley had several friends in his early years who in his opinion turned false. Hogg, as Mr. Peck has suggested, would seem the most likely candidate. But if the two passages are really intended for Hogg the second shows that in 1817 Shelley believed Hogg innocent of the charges he himself brought in York in 1811, and the first that he believed him guilty. Meanwhile there is no real evidence that Shelley is referring to a false friend in his own life.

26 Mary Shelley to Marianne Hunt, August 16, 1817, Julian *Works,* IX, 238.

27 Hookham published shortly afterwards the *Journal of a Six Weeks' Tour,* entered in the Stationer's Register December 10, 1817.

28 Mary's journal for August 29, 1817.

29 Mary to Shelley, September 26, 1817, in *Shelley and Mary,* I, 225.

30 William Baxter to Isabel Baxter Booth, October 3, 1817, as quoted by Dowden: *Life,* II, 174. I have been unable to locate the original letter.

31 Mary to Shelley, September 28, 1817, in *Shelley and Mary,* I, 228. The letter is reprinted (in part) in Marshall, op. cit., I, 201 ff.

32 Shelley to Byron, September 24, 1817, Julian *Works,* IX, 245.

[33] Mary to Shelley, September 25, 1817, *Shelley and Mary*, I, 222. The letter has been reprinted (in part) by Mrs. Marshall, op. cit., I, 200.

[34] Mary to Shelley, October, 7, 1817, in R. H. Hill: *The Shelley Correspondence in the Bodleian Library* (1926), 18–20; Shelley to Mary, October 6 and 8, Julian *Works*, IX, 247–8 and 249; Shelley to Godwin, December 1 and 7, ibid., IX, 255 and 258. Also Mary to Shelley, October 5, 16, and 18, in *Shelley and Mary*, I, 234, 240, 242.

[35] Mary to Shelley, October 18, 1817, in *Shelley and Mary*, I, 240.

[36] Shelley to Godwin, December 7, 1817, Julian *Works*, IX, 258.

[37] Shelley consulted his old physician, Lawrence, in the latter part of September (Mary to Shelley, September 25, 1817, in *Shelley and Mary*, I, 222). Mary's next letter, September 26 (ibid., 224), says: "It is well that your Poem was finished before this edict was issued against the imagination."

[38] Mary to Shelley, October 18, 1817, *Shelley and Mary*, I, 241–2, printed in Marshall, op. cit., I, 206. See also her letter of September 28, Marshall, op. cit., 202.

[39] Mary to Shelley, September 25, 26, 28, 1817, in *Shelley and Mary*, I, 222–9 (also Marshall, op. cit., I, 200 ff.), and September 30, 1817, in R. H. Hill, op. cit., 16.

[40] Shelley to Mary, October 6, 1817, Julian *Works*, IX, 247.

[41] Shelley to Mary, October 8, 1817, Julian *Works*, IX, 249.

[42] Mary to Shelley, September 26, 1817, *Shelley and Mary*, I, 224. The letter is printed (in part) in Marshall, op. cit., I, 201 ff.

[43] Mary to Shelley, October 7, 1817, R. H. Hill, op. cit., 19. It would appear that even after this there were Marlow debts of which Shelley remained unaware until April 1819. Writing to Peacock on April 6, 1819, he says: "Your communications from Marlow astonish me and give me great pain. I was only aware of one bill unpaid — that of Robbs £19. It pains me very much to hear that Madocks is unpaid," etc. (Julian *Works*, X, 49). Cf. Chapter xvii, notes 34 and 73.

[44] Mary to Shelley, in R. H. Hill, op. cit., p. 17. The letter is dated simply "Thursday," but since the first paragraph refers to Shelley's answer to a point made in Mary's letter of September 26, it must have been written within a day or two of September 30, 1817.

[45] A letter from Charles to Mary dated August 8, 1817 (*Shelley and Mary*, I, 211 ff.) acknowledges receipt of £10 "some days ago." A cheque of Shelley's to Mr. Clairmont, dated January 30, 1818, is

extant (Peck: *Life,* II, 439). But Shelley did not agree to finance Charles's marriage and he remained single.

⁴⁶ Hunt's *Autobiography* (1850), II, 31. Professor H. F. B. Brett-Smith, in his Biographical Introduction to *The Works of Thomas Love Peacock* (London, 1934), I, lxxvii, calculates that Shelley's total payments to Peacock for all purposes for which there is any evidence amounted to £125.

⁴⁷ Shelley greatly admired it and wrote a review which was published in the *Examiner* for December 28, 1817 (No. 522, pp. 826–7). See his letters of December 7 and 11 to Godwin, Julian *Works,* IX, 259–60 and 265–6.

⁴⁸ H. Chorley, ed., *Letters of Mary Russell Mitford* (2nd Series, London, 1872), I, 51. Cited by H. F. B. Brett-Smith, *Works of Thomas Love Peacock,* Biographical Introduction, I, lxxvi, note.

⁴⁹ Thirty-three of these cheques are listed in Peck: *Life,* II, 437–8; another, dated October 24, 1817, to Godwin for £36 10*s.* 10*d.* was in the possession of the Brick Row Book Shop, New York, in 1936. The catalogue of the sale of Shelley papers at Hodgson's on December 15, 1916 lists 19 notes and 130 cheques all together.

⁵⁰ A. H. Beavan, op. cit., 169. Shelley makes substantially the same statement in a letter to Godwin, dated August 7, 1820 (Julian *Works,* X, 198). See also Leigh Hunt: *Autobiography,* II, 31.

⁵¹ *Recollections of the Table Talk of Samuel Rogers* (London, 1903), 184. The occurrence is dated by Shelley's reference to it in his letter to Byron of July 9, 1817.

⁵² See the documents quoted from the Shelley-Brookes correspondence, in Peck: *Life,* II, 381 ff.

⁵³ Between these dates he was in Marlow October 3–4, October 10–12, October 24–November 2. Mary was with him in London November 8–19.

⁵⁴ According to Longdill's statement to William Whitton, who believed them to be much greater. William Whitton to Sir Timothy Shelley, October 22, 1817, quoted by Ingpen: *Shelley in England,* II, 525.

⁵⁵ Mary to Shelley, October 16, 1817, in *Shelley and Mary,* I, 239, printed in Marshall, op. cit., I, 205 ff.

⁵⁶ Whitton's minute-book for October 22 and his letter of the same date to Sir Timothy make it quite clear that Shelley was arrested and held for two days at Captain Pilfold's instance. Unless Whitton is speaking of two separate arrests in the letter, it would appear that Captain Pilfold had accepted one of Shelley's bills for a friend and

that Shelley defaulted payment. See Ingpen, op. cit., II, 523–6.

⁵⁷ Mary to Shelley, October 18, 1817, in *Shelley and Mary*, I, 241. Both Dowden and Mrs. Marshall print Mary's letters of October 16 and 18 mentioning the actual arrest and the threatened one. Mrs. Marshall (like Shelley) says nothing of the "late arrest." Both say only that Mary's fears of an arrest at Marlow were not realized. It is extremely interesting, therefore, to find that in his biography Professor Dowden footnotes the reference to the recent arrest: "Perhaps an arrest of Godwin" (*Life*, II, 153) while in his copy of *Shelley and Mary* (p. 239) he footnotes the same phrase correctly: "At instance of Capt. Pilfold" — showing that he was well acquainted with the facts presumably before he wrote his misleading note.

⁵⁸ Mary's journal, which is somewhat sporadic at this period, dates Shelley's arrival Sunday, October 12, and his departure Wednesday, October 15. Godwin's journal, a much more regular and systematic account, dates the same events October 19 and 22, which is probably accurate, since Godwin's entries were made at the time and Mary's were later.

⁵⁹ Mary to Shelley, October 16, *Shelley and Mary*, I, 239; "Thursday" (October 21), R. H. Hill, op. cit., 18; October 7, ibid., 20, and, again, October 16. Dowden prints the letter of October 16, but not the one dated "Thursday," which is not in *Shelley and Mary*. The letter of October 7 is printed incorrectly in both Dowden and *Shelley and Mary*, with numerous omissions, including the present quotation.

⁶⁰ Shelley to Byron, December 17, 1817, Julian *Works*, IX, 270.

⁶¹ Shelley to William Willats, January 31, 1818, Julian *Works*, IX, 284. This letter acknowledges a loan from Willats and is witnessed by George Adams, William Richardson, and his clerk, of Clement's Inn. Mention of Richardson in connection with finances in letters to Godwin dated December 7 and 11 (op. cit., 258, 265) indicate that Richardson was the broker and Willats the zanker in the transaction as completed and shows that the matter was in train early in December. The Brick Row Bookshop, 42 East Fiftieth Street, New York, owned in 1936 a copy of Shelley's indenture to William Willats and a Warrant of Attorney to Willats, both dated January 31, 1818. The former is a "charge of £4500 on estates toll in remainder." The latter states that in consideration of a loan of £2,000 Shelley holds himself responsible under certain conditions for the sum of £9,000. Dowden, Ingpen, and Peck (II, 181, note; II, 528;

and II, 57 respectively) represent Shelley's liability as £4,500; according to Ingpen, it was to be paid within three months after the death of Shelley's father. Shelley's letter to Willats shows that Willats had insured Shelley's life, so he did not lose money by Shelley's death before receiving his inheritance.

[62] Shelley to Godwin, December 11, 1817, Julian *Works*, IX, 267.

[63] Mary to Shelley, October 16, 1817, *Shelley and Mary* I, 240, reprinted in Mrs. Marshall, op. cit., I, 205.

[64] Mary to Shelley, October 5, 1817, *Shelley and Mary*, I, 234.

[65] Peacock: *Memoirs*, II, 344, 349.

[66] Shelley to Hogg, November 28, 1817, Julian *Works*, IX, 254. Hogg had written to Mary, inviting himself. It is suggestive of Mary's dislike for Hogg that the answer to his letter came from Shelley and not Mary, and that when he did arrive Mary chronicled the fact as briefly as possible (journal, December 6) and thereafter failed to mention either his presence or his departure.

[67] Mary's journal, under the dates mentioned.

[68] Mary's journal, under the dates mentioned. It would appear from the fact that they received calls from both the Hunts and Godwin that they were in lodgings of their own, probably at 19 Mabledon Place, Euston Road, whence Shelley addressed a letter to Ollier on November 12. The Hunts had moved from Hampstead and were now living at 13 Lisson Grove North.

[69] Mary's journal for November 10, 11, 12, and Shelley to Ollier, November 12, 1817, Julian *Works*, IX, 252. Shelley called on Ollier the same day, possibly leaving the note. Although Mary wrote on the 12th: " Shelley finishes his Pamphlet," Shelley's letter shows that he intended sending a final instalment " before evening," by which time he expected a proof of the first instalment.

[70] The text of the sixteen-page pamphlet is based upon the undated edition of Thomas Rodd, published in or about 1843 as a facsimile reprint of an original edition of twenty copies. No specimen of the original edition has been discovered, and Mr. T. J. Wise (*A Shelley Library*, 1924, p. 46) is of the opinion none was printed and that Rodd's text was based upon a manuscript left by Shelley in his box of papers that was later lost at Marlow. He is certain that Shelley would never have ordered an edition limited to twenty copies.

[71] November 13 and 14 respectively.

[72] On December 27 Mr. Baxter wrote Shelley: " This cold weather, however, has obliged me. to have recourse to a little animal food

again, bread and water I found too cold on the stomach " (*Shelley and Mary*, I, 254).

⁷³ Shelley to W. T. Baxter, December 30, 1817, Julian *Works*, IX, 275–6.

⁷⁴ David Booth to Shelley, January 2, 1819 (for 1818?), Julian *Works*, IX, 274, note.

⁷⁵ Shelley to Byron, September 24, 1817, Julian *Works*, IX, 246. This letter was written from Leigh Hunt's house, 13 Lisson Grove North, the day after Shelley finished the poem and went up to London.

⁷⁶ Shelley "to a Publisher," October 13, 1817, Julian *Works*, IX, 250. The letter is incomplete, but from the fact that it assumes that the poem will be referred to Thomas Moore one supposes that the publisher was Longman and Co., who had just published Moore's *Lalla Rookh*. Shelley preferred to sell the copyright, but was willing to publish it on his own account.

⁷⁷ Shelley to Charles Ollier, November 25, 1817, Julian *Works*, IX, 253.

⁷⁸ Shelley to Charles Ollier, December 3, 1817, Julian *Works*, IX, 256. Shelley enclosed notices to be sent to two newspapers, and stipulated that the *Alastor* volume be advertised along with *Laon and Cythna*.

⁷⁹ December 11, 1817, Julian *Works*, IX, 262–5.

⁸⁰ Shelley to Charles Ollier, December 13, 1817, Julian *Works*, IX, 268. Also *Shelley and Mary*, I, 251.

⁸¹ Peacock was certainly in error in stating that only three copies had gone forth. Shelley's letters show that Godwin and Thomas Moore had already received copies. The *Quarterly Review* also had a copy, which it subsequently reviewed. At least two copies were reclaimed by Shelley from Eber's (a circulating library), and Ollier was endeavouring to reclaim a copy or copies sold to another purchaser (Julian *Works*, IX, 273).

⁸² Peacock: *Memoirs*, II, 345, 365.

⁸³ Shelley to Thomas Moore, December 16, 1817, Julian *Works*, IX, 269. After the publisher to whom Shelley sent the first four sheets of the poem had presumably referred them to Moore, Shelley sent Moore a copy of the first edition, which, in *Notes and Queries*, April 12, 1862, was described by Denis Florence MacCarthy as in the Moore Library, Royal Irish Academy, Dublin. In acknowledging the gift Moore guessed that the *History of a Six Weeks' Tour*, etc., was by Mary Shelley. This was the beginning of Shel-

ley's acquaintance with Moore, which was slight. The two appear never to have met.

⁸⁴ For a fuller discussion of Shelley's attitude toward the revision of *Laon and Cythna* see Fred L. Jones: " The Revision of *Laon and Cythna,*" *Journal of English and Germanic Philology,* XXXII, 366–72 (July 1933) and a letter by Marcel Kessel in the *Times Literary Supplement* for September 1933, p. 592, which was answered by Professor H. F. B. Brett-Smith, September 21, p. 631. While I agree with Messrs. Jones and Kessel that Peacock's account is misleading, I think it may well have been true of Shelley's *first* reaction, which was replaced by a very reasonable attitude as soon as Shelley saw the truth of Ollier's point against incest and the ease with which the change could be effected.

⁸⁵ Julian *Works,* IX, 272, 273, 277, 279, 280, 281, 282, 283 — nine letters between [December 22] and January 25, 1818.

⁸⁶ Robert Waithman, an alderman of London, was treasurer of the fund. The subscription list as published in the *Champion* for January 11, 1818 lists Shelley for five guineas. Shelley wrote a cheque of five pounds to Robert Waithman on January 5. On the preceding day he had sent Waithman a check for three pounds. Leigh and John Hunt subscribed five pounds between them (Julian *Works,* IX, 278).

⁸⁷ Dowden: *Life,* II, 123.

⁸⁸ Horace Smith to Sir Timothy Shelley, April 13, 1821, in *Shelley and Mary,* III, 613.

⁸⁹ A. H. Beavan, op. cit., 172, 171. This visit is not dated by Smith, but his last visit to Marlow, according to Mary's journal, was December 26–8, 1817. Even though Smith's recollection may have been aided by his later reading of Shelley, these views are worth quoting as what he recalled as Shelley's opinions in 1817: " However absurd and untenable may be the theory of atheism, he held it to be preferable to that nominal theism, which in fact is real demonism, being a deification of man's worst passions, and the transfer to an imagined fiend of that worship which belongs to an all-loving God. He quoted Plutarch's averment, that even atheism is more reverent than superstition, inasmuch as it was better to deny the existence of Saturn as king of heaven, than to admit that fact, maintaining at the same time that he was such a monster of unnatural cruelty as to devour his own children as soon as they were born; and in confirmation of the same view he quoted a passage from Lord Bacon, asserting the superiority of reason and natural religion. Any attempt

at an impersonation of the Deity, or any conception of Him otherwise than as the pervading spirit of the whole illimitable universe,
he held to be presumptuous; for the finite cannot grasp the infinite.
Perhaps he might have objected to Coleridge's grand definition of
the Creator, as a circle whose centre is nowhere, and whose circumference is everywhere. Without asserting the absolute perfectibility of human nature, he had a confident belief in its almost limit-
less improvability; especially as he was persuaded that evil, an
accident, and not an inherent part of our system, might be so materially diminished as to give an incalculable increase to the sum of
human happiness. All the present evils of mankind he attributed
to those erroneous views of religion in which had originated the
countless wars, the national hatreds, the innumerable public and
private miseries that make history a revolting record of suffering and
crime. Every national creed and form of worship since the world
began had successively died away and had been superseded; experience of the past justifies the same anticipation for the future;
the feuds and schisms and separations in our own established faith
are the rents and cracks that predict the approaching downfall
of the temple. Now, if mankind, abandoning all those evanescent
symptoms, could be brought universally to adopt that religion of
Nature which, finding its heavenly revelation in man's own heart,
teaches him that the best way to testify his love of the Creator is
to love all that he has created; that religion, whose three-leaved
Bible is the earth, and sea, and sky — eternal and immutable Scrip-
tures, written by God himself, which all may read and none can
interpolate, there would be a total cessation of the *odium theo-
logicum* which has been such a fire brand to the world; the human
race, unchecked in its progress of improvement, would be gradually uplifted into a higher state, and all created beings, living together in harmony as one family, would worship their common
Father in the undivided faith of brotherly love and the gratitude of
peaceful happiness " (*ibid.*, 172–4).

⁹⁰ When I talked with Mr. J. Wheeler Williams, grandson of
Edward and Jane Williams, whose children were reared by Hogg
and Jane, I found that the strongest impression of Hogg that he
had received from his father's talk was that within his domestic
circle Hogg was an exacting teacher of the classics.

⁹¹ Hogg's visit was January 3–7, Shelley's illness January 3–5,
Godwin's visit January 20–2, according to Mary's journal, under the
dates given. Godwin's letter to Shelley, January 31, 1818 (*Shelley*

and Mary, II, 258), refers to the financial conversations, which are not mentioned in the journal.

⁹² Godwin to Shelley, January 31, 1818, in *Shelley and Mary,* II, 258–9. The letter is evidently incomplete.

⁹³ Claire Clairmont's journal, January 29, 1818.

⁹⁴ Wednesday, February 4, 1818, according to Lord Houghton: *Life of Keats* (London, 1848), I, 99.

⁹⁵ Mary's journal, February 5–11; Claire's journal, February 9, 10.

⁹⁶ A part of Shelley's bill for lodgings was discovered by Dr. F. J. Furnivall (whose father was Mary's physician at Marlow and Bishopsgate) and was first printed in the *Academy* for October 12, 1889, No. 910. It has been reprinted in the Julian *Works,* IX, 283. Several items are for small sums advanced to Shelley or paid in his behalf, showing that he continued his Marlow habit of delegating small cash payments to others.

⁹⁷ The journals of Mary and Claire, February 12–29.

⁹⁸ Shelley's letter to Hogg on November 28 speaks of " Rhododaphne " as recently completed. Mary's journal for December 4–10 records copying the poem each day, and for February 21 and 23 records copying Shelley's criticism of it. The criticism was first published in H. B. Forman's *Prose Works of Shelley* in 1880, although it was privately printed in his *Notes on Sculpture,* etc. (1879). The poem contains distinct echoes from Shelley's *Alastor,* and in turn is echoed in a passage (lines 11–19) of Shelley's " Fiordispina " (*c.* 1820), as had been pointed out by Professor Peck (*Life,* I, 29 and 426, note). The " Fiordispina " parallel is not inevitable, for Shakespeare's *A Midsummer Night's Dream* contains a similar passage (Act III, Scene ii, lines 203–16) with which Shelley was presumably familiar.

⁹⁹ *Shelley and Mary,* II, 260, quoted by Dowden: *Life,* II, 184.

¹⁰⁰ Peacock: *Memoirs,* II, 349.

¹⁰¹ Shelley to Hunt, March 22, 1818, Julian *Works,* IX, 291.

¹⁰² Claire's journal, March 11 and 12, 1818.

¹⁰³ Charles and Mary Cowden Clarke, op. cit., 26, 152; A. H. Beavan, op. cit., 137; Thornton Hunt, op. cit., XI, 189; Peacock: *Memoirs,* II, 315, 349; Hogg: *Life,* I, 32; Dowden: *Life,* II, 120, 132, note.